CW00740952

BBC THE **TENTH** DOCTOR

DOCTOR WHO

ARCHIVES

VOLUME 1

TITAN
COMICS

TITAN COMICS

Collection Editor
Nick Jones
Collection Supervisor
Andrew James
Assistant Collection Editor
Kirsten Murray
Collection Designer
Rob Farmer
Senior Editor
Steve White

Titan Comics Editorial Lizzie Kaye, Tom Williams
Production Assistant Peter James
Production Supervisors Maria Pearson, Jackie Flook
Production Manager Obi Onuora
Studio Manager Selina Juneja
Senior Sales Manager Steve Tothill
Brand Manager, Marketing Lucy Ripper
Senior Marketing & Press Officer Owen Johnson
Direct Sales & Marketing Manager Ricky Claydon
Commercial Manager Michelle Fairlamb
Publishing Manager Darryl Tothill
Publishing Director Chris Teather
Operations Director Leigh Baulch
Executive Director Vivian Cheung
Publisher Nick Landau

Cover By Ben Templesmith
Original Series Edits By Scott Dunbier, Chris Ryall,
Denton J. Tipton and Tom Waltz

BBC WORLDWIDE

Director of Editorial Governance
Nicolas Brett
**Director of Consumer Products
And Publishing**
Andrew Moultrie
Head of UK Publishing
Chris Kerwin
Publisher
Mandy Thwaites
Publishing Co-Ordinator
Eva Abramik

Special thanks to
Steven Moffat, Brian Minchin, Matt Nicholls, James
Dudley, Edward Russell, Derek Ritchie, Scott
Handcock, Kirsty Mullan, Kate Bush, Julia
Nocciolino and Ed Casey, for their invaluable
assistance.

BBC THE **TENTH** DOCTOR

DOCTOR WHO
ARCHIVES

DOCTOR WHO: THE TENTH DOCTOR
ARCHIVES OMNIBUS VOL. 1
ISBN: 9781782767701
Published by Titan Comics, a division of Titan
Publishing Group, Ltd. 144 Southwark Street, London,
SE1 0UP.

BBC, DOCTOR WHO (word marks, logos and devices)
and TARDIS are trade marks of the British Broadcasting
Corporation and are used under license. BBC logo
© BBC 1996. Doctor Who logo © BBC 2009. TARDIS
image © BBC 1963. Cybermen image © BBC/Kit
Pedler/Gerry Davis 1966.

With the exception of artwork used for review purposes,
no portion of this book may be reproduced or
transmitted in any form or by any means, without the
express permission of the publisher Titan Comics or
the BBC.

Names, characters, places and incidents featured in
this publication are either the product of the author's
imagination or used fictitiously. Any resemblance to
actual persons, living or dead (except for satirical
purposes), is entirely coincidental.

Contains material originally published as Doctor Who
#1–6 and Doctor Who: The Forgotten #1–6.

A CIP catalogue record for this title is available from the
British Library. First edition: April 2016.

10 9 8 7 6 5 4 3 2 1

Printed in China. TC00961.

Titan Comics does not read or accept unsolicited
DOCTOR WHO submissions of ideas, stories or artwork.

www.titan-comics.com

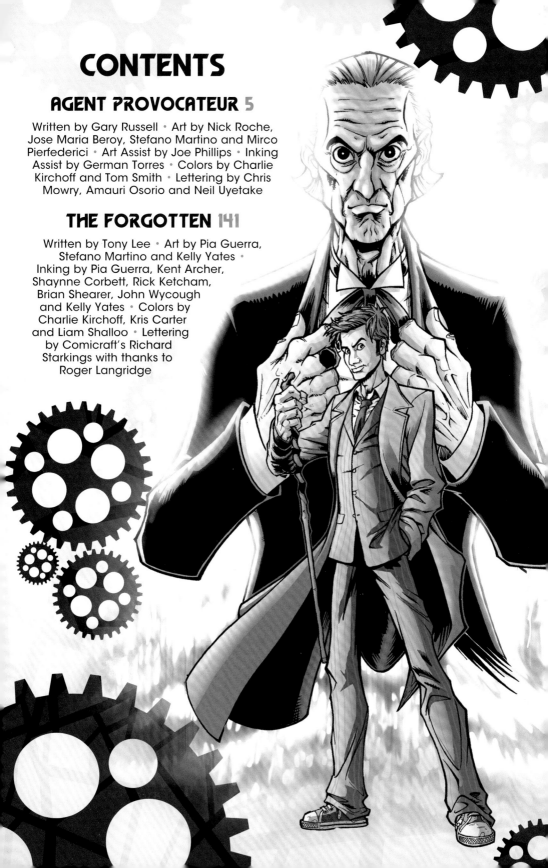

CONTENTS

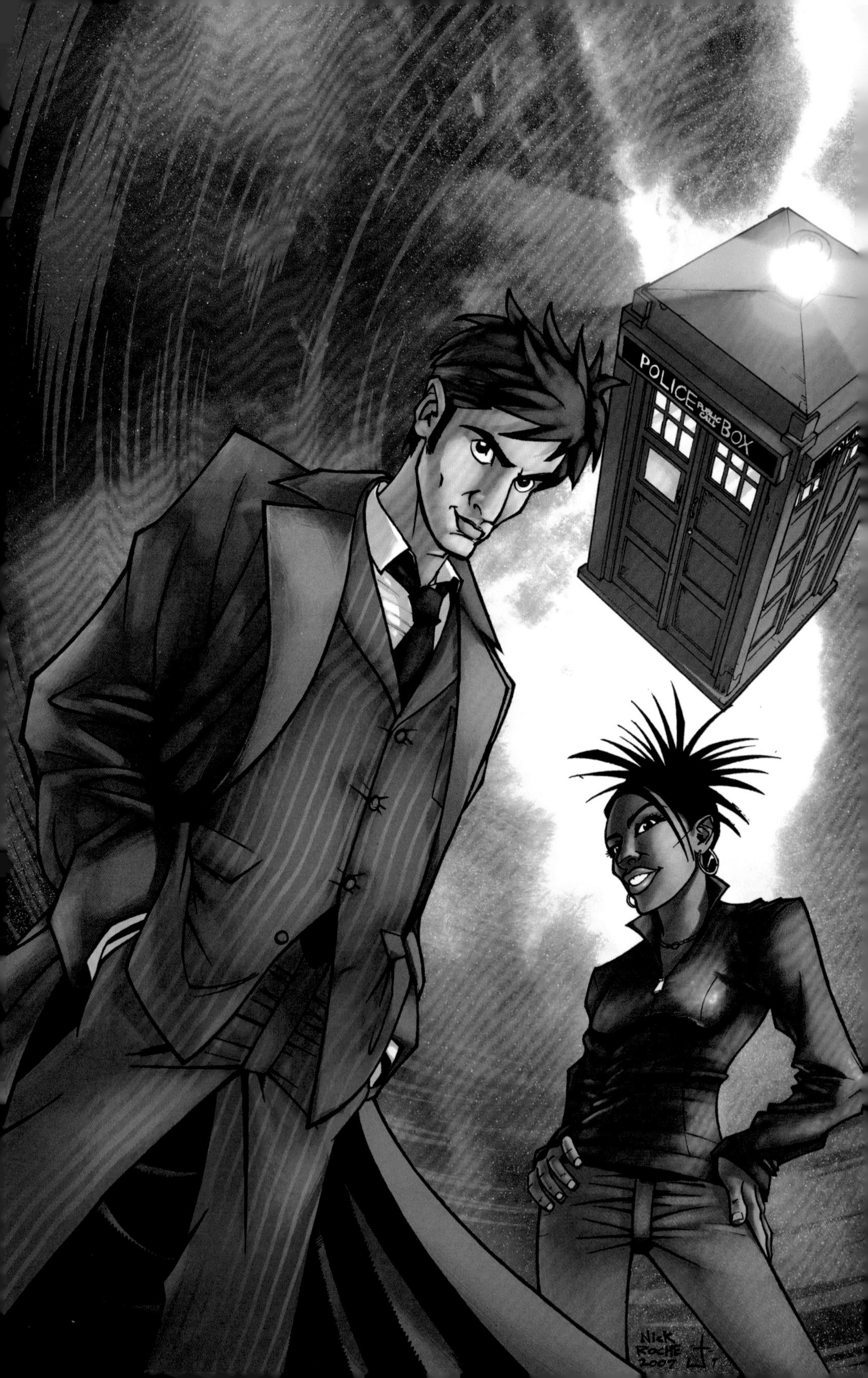
POLICE PUBLIC CALL BOX
NICK ROCHE 2007

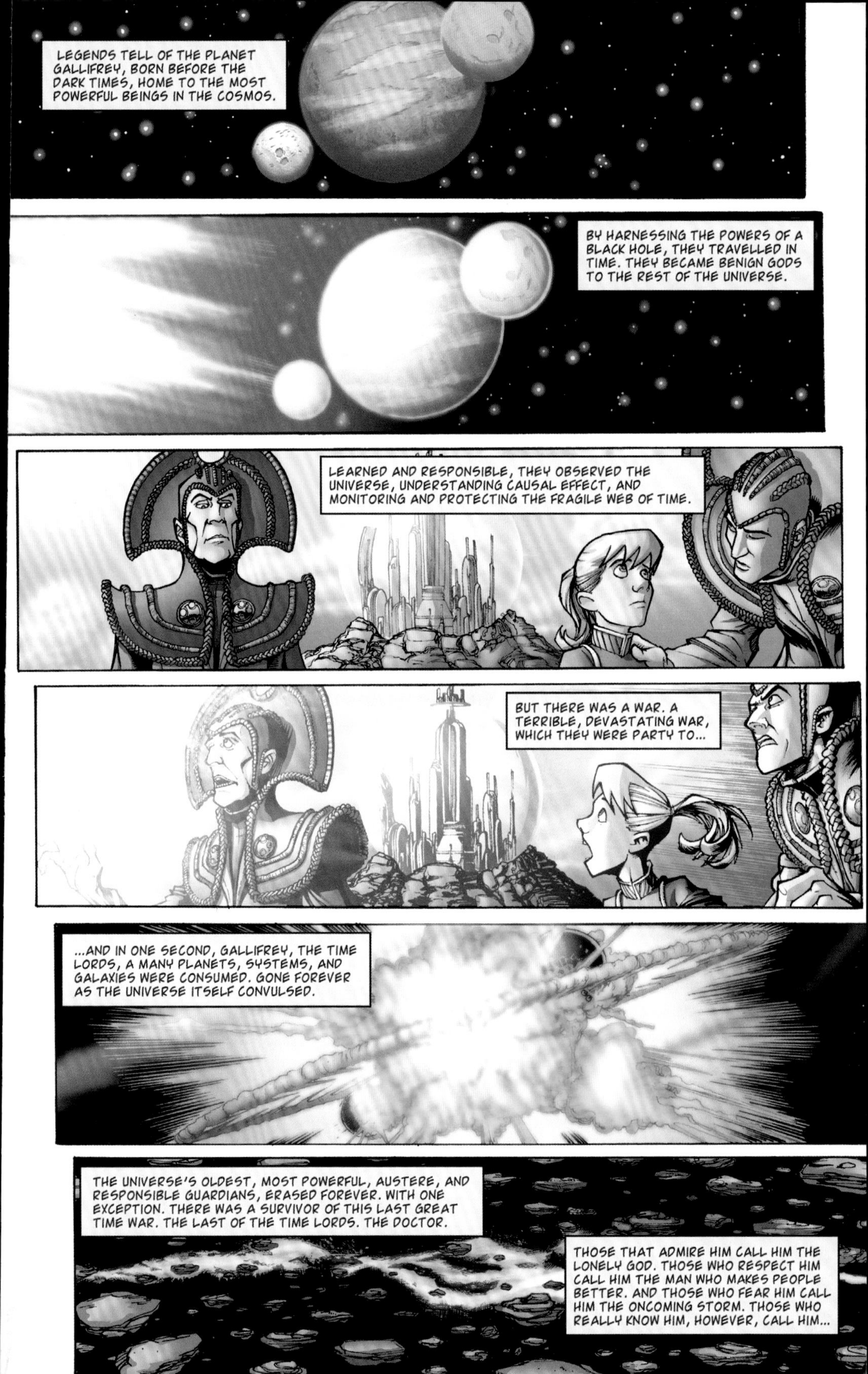
LEGENDS TELL OF THE PLANET GALLIFREY, BORN BEFORE THE DARK TIMES, HOME TO THE MOST POWERFUL BEINGS IN THE COSMOS.
BY HARNESSING THE POWERS OF A BLACK HOLE, THEY TRAVELLED IN TIME. THEY BECAME BENIGN GODS TO THE REST OF THE UNIVERSE.
LEARNED AND RESPONSIBLE, THEY OBSERVED THE UNIVERSE, UNDERSTANDING CAUSAL EFFECT, AND MONITORING AND PROTECTING THE FRAGILE WEB OF TIME.
BUT THERE WAS A WAR. A TERRIBLE, DEVASTATING WAR, WHICH THEY WERE PARTY TO...
...AND IN ONE SECOND, GALLIFREY, THE TIME LORDS, A MANY PLANETS, SYSTEMS, AND GALAXIES WERE CONSUMED. GONE FOREVER AS THE UNIVERSE ITSELF CONVULSED.
THE UNIVERSE'S OLDEST, MOST POWERFUL, AUSTERE, AND RESPONSIBLE GUARDIANS, ERASED FOREVER. WITH ONE EXCEPTION. THERE WAS A SURVIVOR OF THIS LAST GREAT TIME WAR. THE LAST OF THE TIME LORDS. THE DOCTOR.
THOSE THAT ADMIRE HIM CALL HIM THE LONELY GOD. THOSE WHO RESPECT HIM CALL HIM THE MAN WHO MAKES PEOPLE BETTER. AND THOSE WHO FEAR HIM CALL HIM THE ONCOMING STORM. THOSE WHO REALLY KNOW HIM, HOWEVER, CALL HIM...

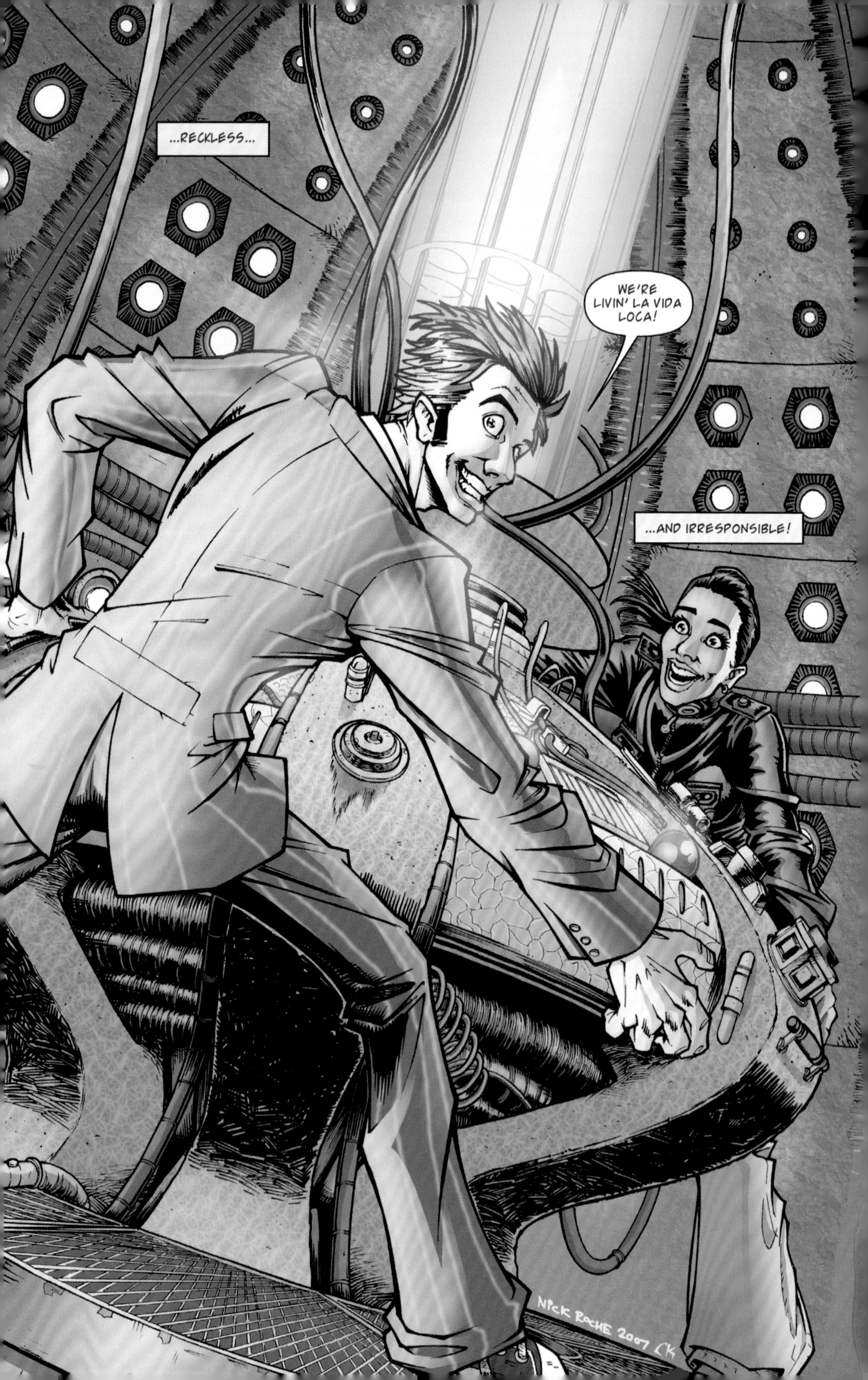
...RECKLESS...
WE'RE LIVIN' LA VIDA LOCA!
...AND IRRESPONSIBLE!
NICK ROCHE 2007 CK

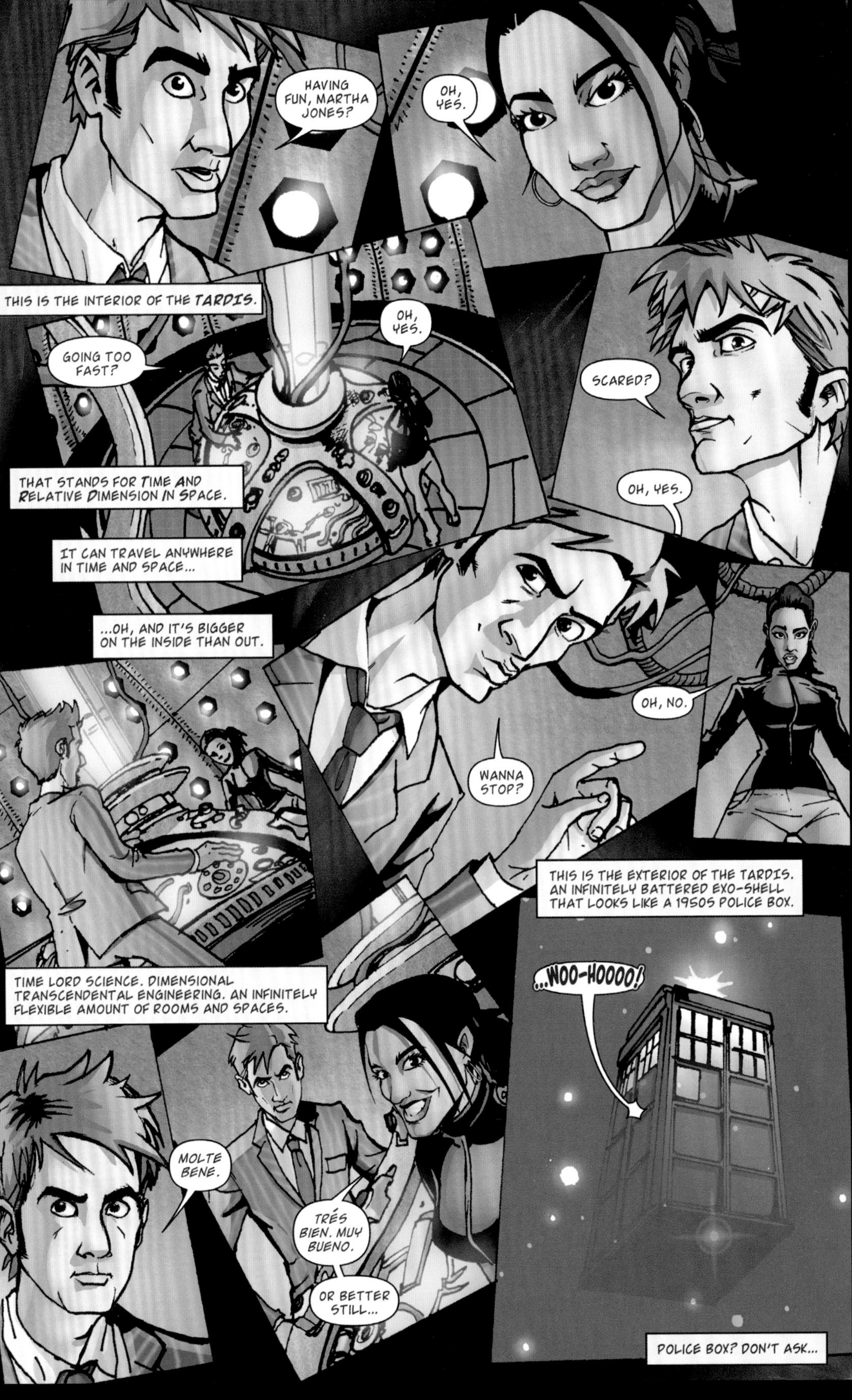
HAVING FUN, MARTHA JONES?
OH, YES.
THIS IS THE INTERIOR OF THE TARDIS.
GOING TOO FAST?
OH, YES.
SCARED?
OH, YES.
THAT STANDS FOR TIME AND RELATIVE DIMENSION IN SPACE.
IT CAN TRAVEL ANYWHERE IN TIME AND SPACE...
...OH, AND IT'S BIGGER ON THE INSIDE THAN OUT.
WANNA STOP?
OH, NO.
THIS IS THE EXTERIOR OF THE TARDIS. AN INFINITELY BATTERED EXO-SHELL THAT LOOKS LIKE A 1950S POLICE BOX.
TIME LORD SCIENCE. DIMENSIONAL TRANSCENDENTAL ENGINEERING. AN INFINITELY FLEXIBLE AMOUNT OF ROOMS AND SPACES.
MOLTE BENE.
TRÉS BIEN. MUY BUENO.
OR BETTER STILL...
...WOO-HOOOO!
POLICE BOX? DON'T ASK...

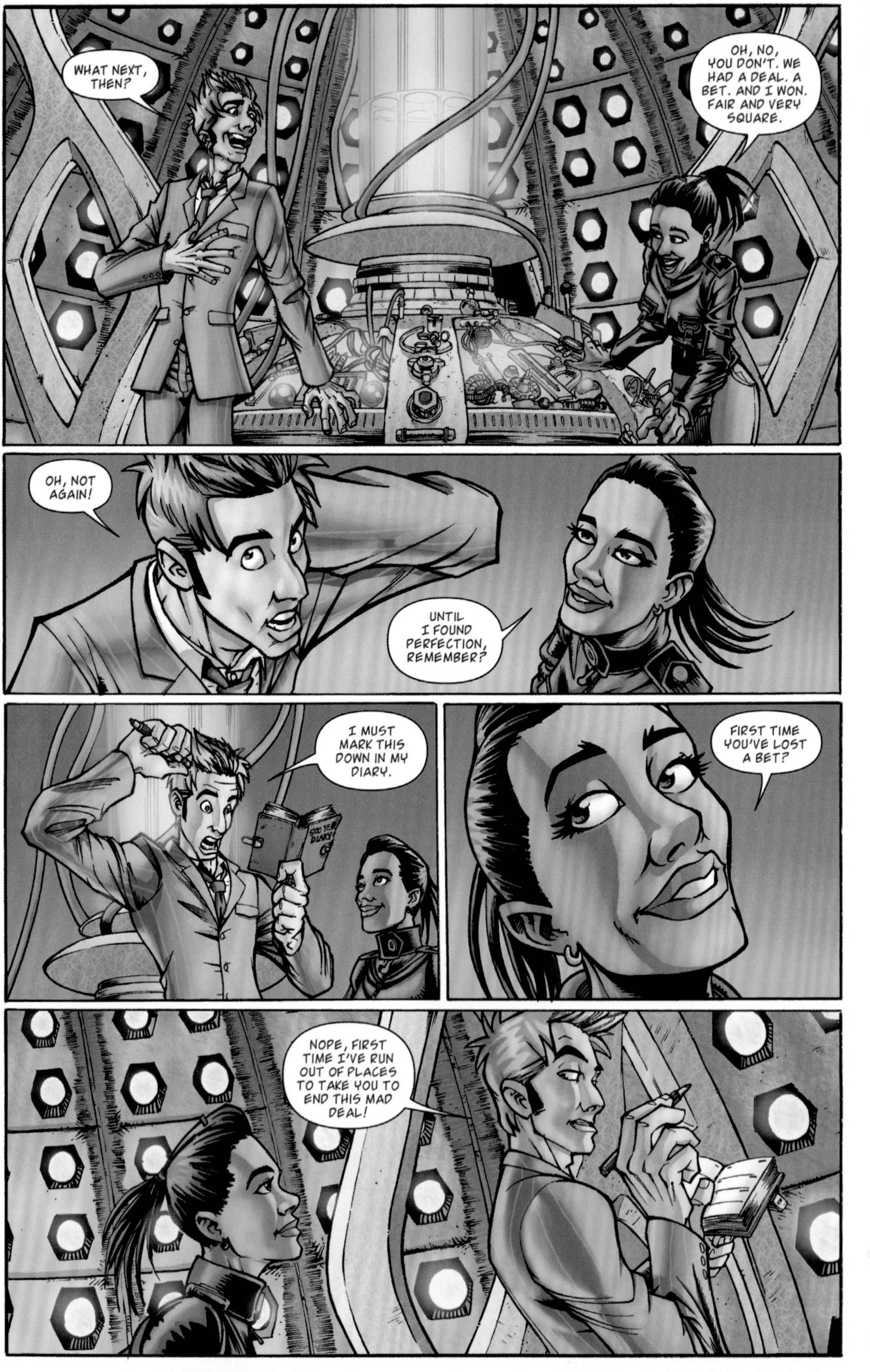
WHAT NEXT, THEN?
OH, NO, YOU DON'T. WE HAD A DEAL. A BET. AND I WON. FAIR AND VERY SQUARE.
OH, NOT AGAIN!
UNTIL I FOUND PERFECTION, REMEMBER?
I MUST MARK THIS DOWN IN MY DIARY.
500 YEAR DIARY
FIRST TIME YOU'VE LOST A BET?
NOPE, FIRST TIME I'VE RUN OUT OF PLACES TO TAKE YOU TO END THIS MAD DEAL!

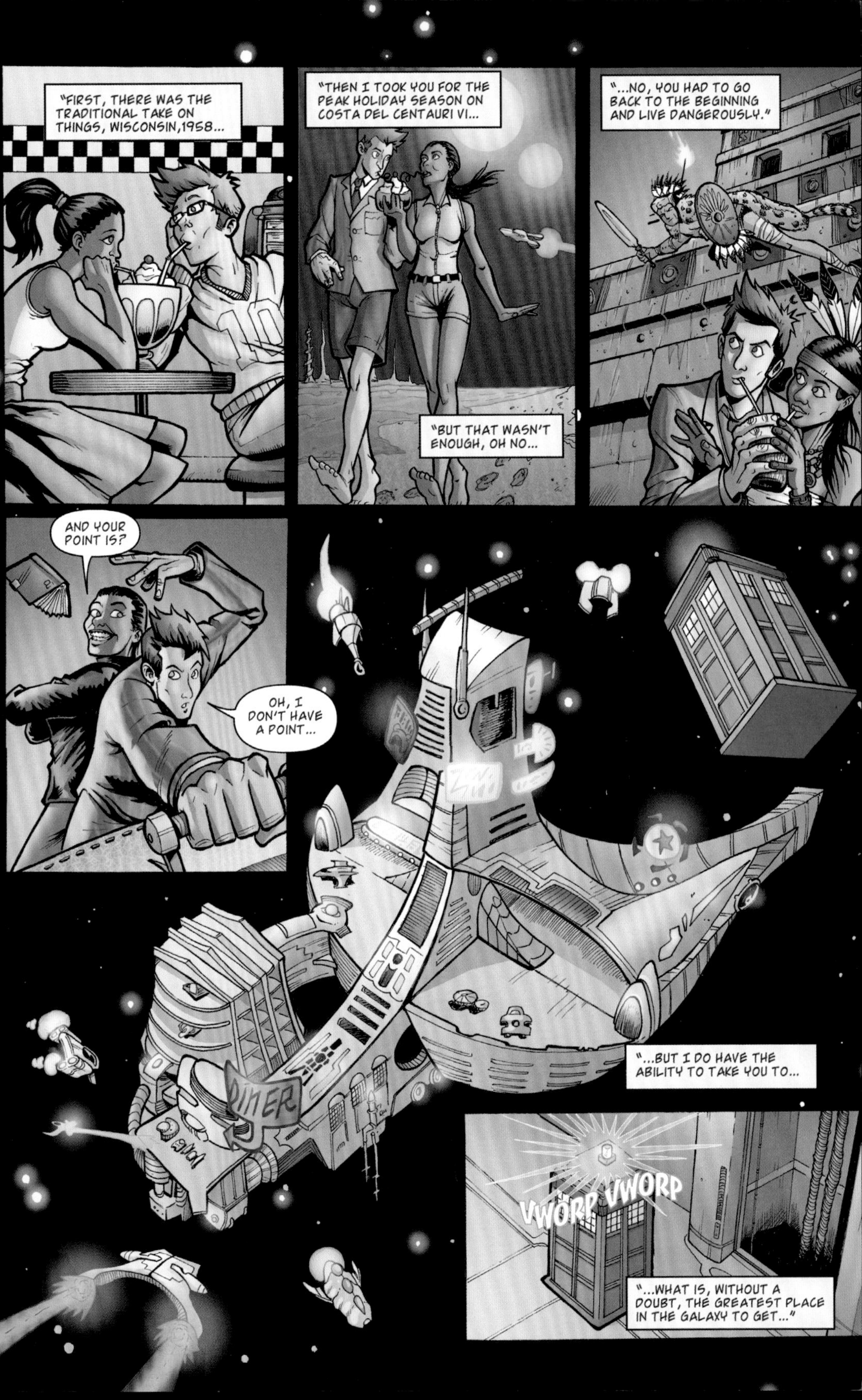
"FIRST, THERE WAS THE TRADITIONAL TAKE ON THINGS, WISCONSIN, 1958...
"THEN I TOOK YOU FOR THE PEAK HOLIDAY SEASON ON COSTA DEL CENTAURI VI...
"BUT THAT WASN'T ENOUGH, OH NO...
"...NO, YOU HAD TO GO BACK TO THE BEGINNING AND LIVE DANGEROUSLY."
AND YOUR POINT IS?
OH, I DON'T HAVE A POINT...
DINER
"...BUT I DO HAVE THE ABILITY TO TAKE YOU TO...
VWORP VWORP
"...WHAT IS, WITHOUT A DOUBT, THE GREATEST PLACE IN THE GALAXY TO GET..."

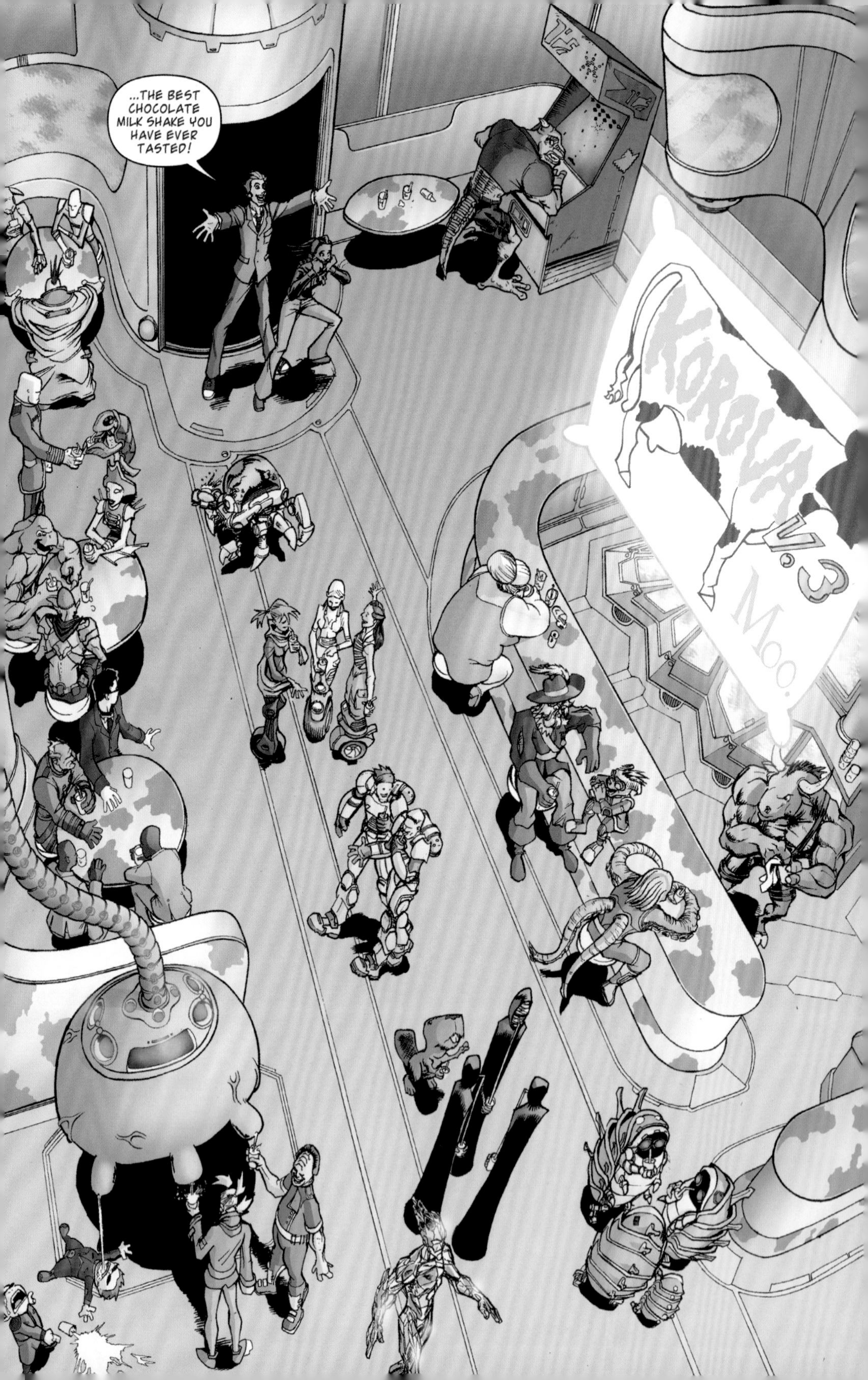
...THE BEST CHOCOLATE MILK SHAKE YOU HAVE EVER TASTED!
KOROVA V.3
Moo.

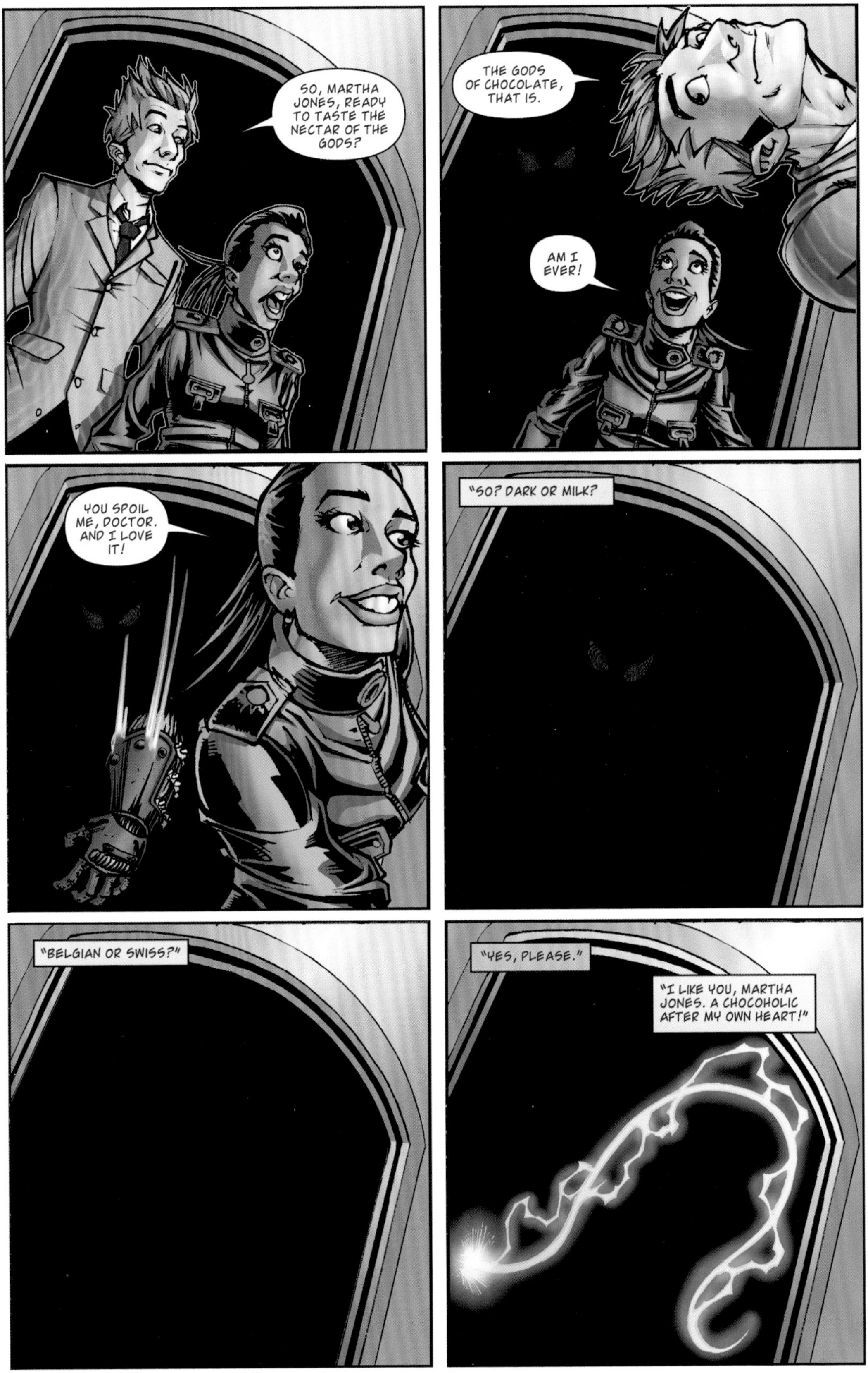
SO, MARTHA JONES, READY TO TASTE THE NECTAR OF THE GODS?
THE GODS OF CHOCOLATE, THAT IS.
AM I EVER!
YOU SPOIL ME, DOCTOR. AND I LOVE IT!
"SO? DARK OR MILK?
"BELGIAN OR SWISS?"
"YES, PLEASE."
"I LIKE YOU, MARTHA JONES. A CHOCOHOLIC AFTER MY OWN HEART!"

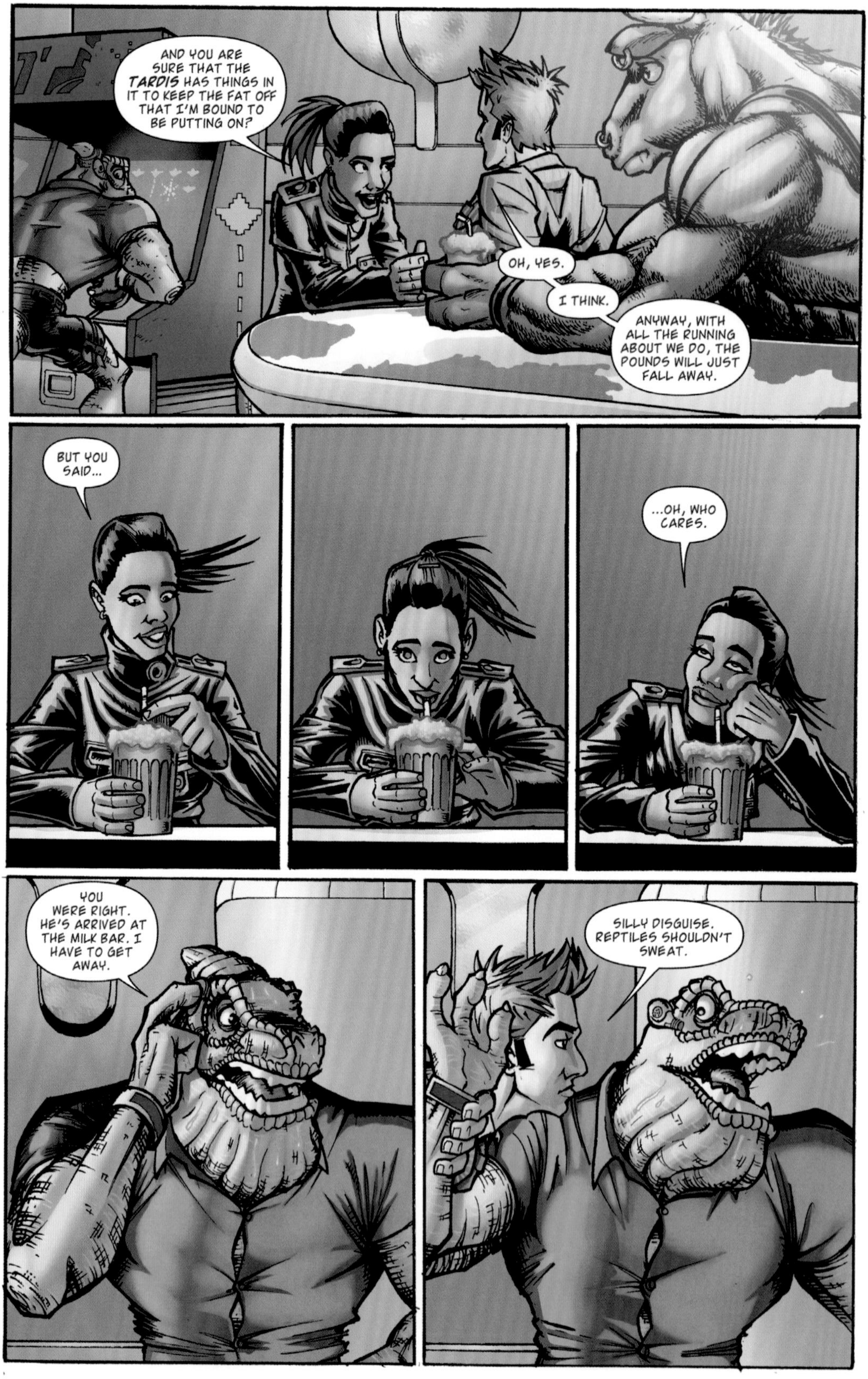
AND YOU ARE SURE THAT THE TARDIS HAS THINGS IN IT TO KEEP THE FAT OFF THAT I'M BOUND TO BE PUTTING ON?
OH, YES.
I THINK.
ANYWAY, WITH ALL THE RUNNING ABOUT WE DO, THE POUNDS WILL JUST FALL AWAY.
BUT YOU SAID...
...OH, WHO CARES.
YOU WERE RIGHT. HE'S ARRIVED AT THE MILK BAR. I HAVE TO GET AWAY.
SILLY DISGUISE. REPTILES SHOULDN'T SWEAT.

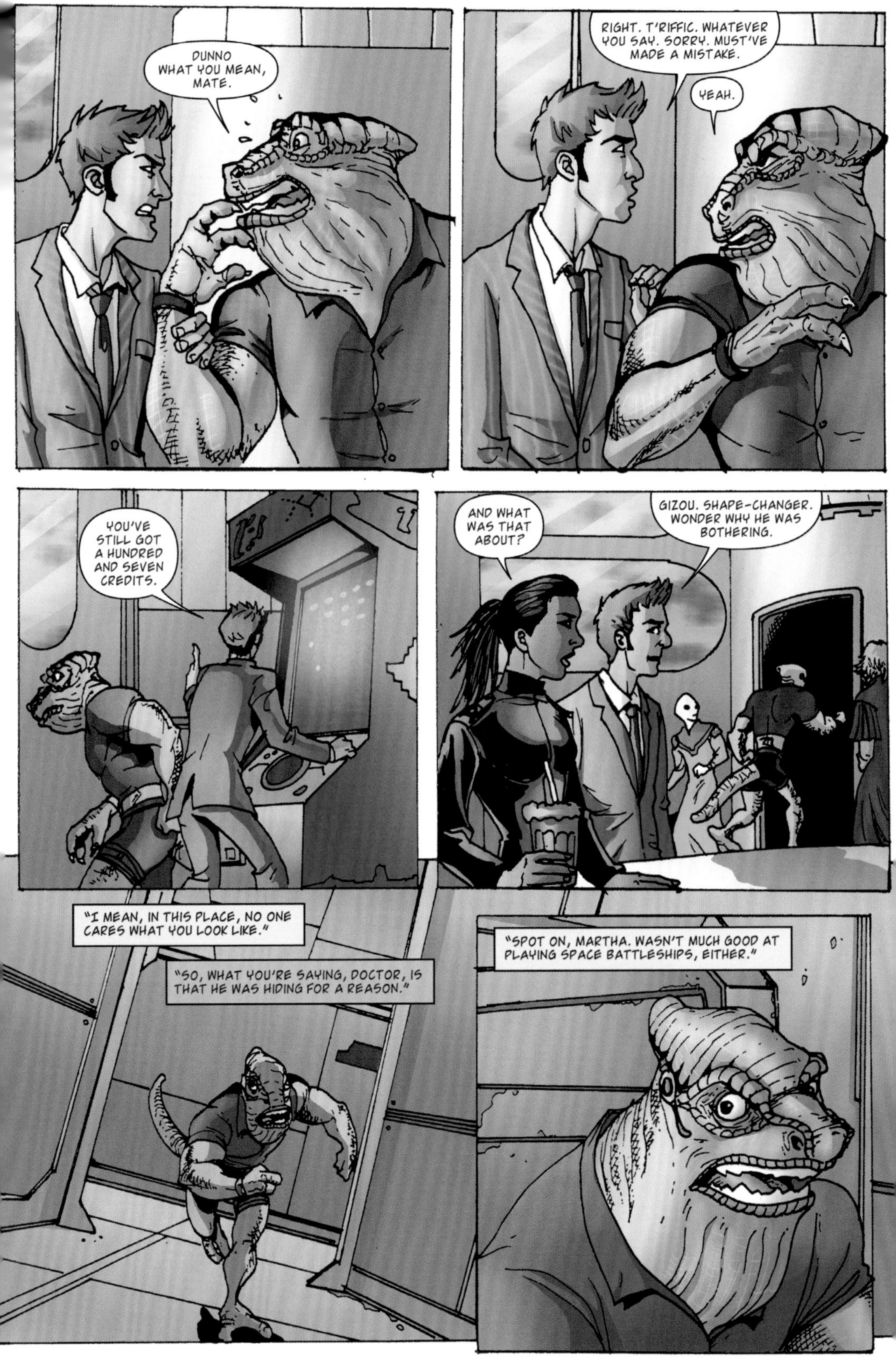
DUNNO WHAT YOU MEAN, MATE.
RIGHT. T'RIFFIC. WHATEVER YOU SAY. SORRY. MUST'VE MADE A MISTAKE.
YEAH.
YOU'VE STILL GOT A HUNDRED AND SEVEN CREDITS.
AND WHAT WAS THAT ABOUT?
GIZOU. SHAPE-CHANGER. WONDER WHY HE WAS BOTHERING.
"I MEAN, IN THIS PLACE, NO ONE CARES WHAT YOU LOOK LIKE."
"SO, WHAT YOU'RE SAYING, DOCTOR, IS THAT HE WAS HIDING FOR A REASON."
"SPOT ON, MARTHA. WASN'T MUCH GOOD AT PLAYING SPACE BATTLESHIPS, EITHER."

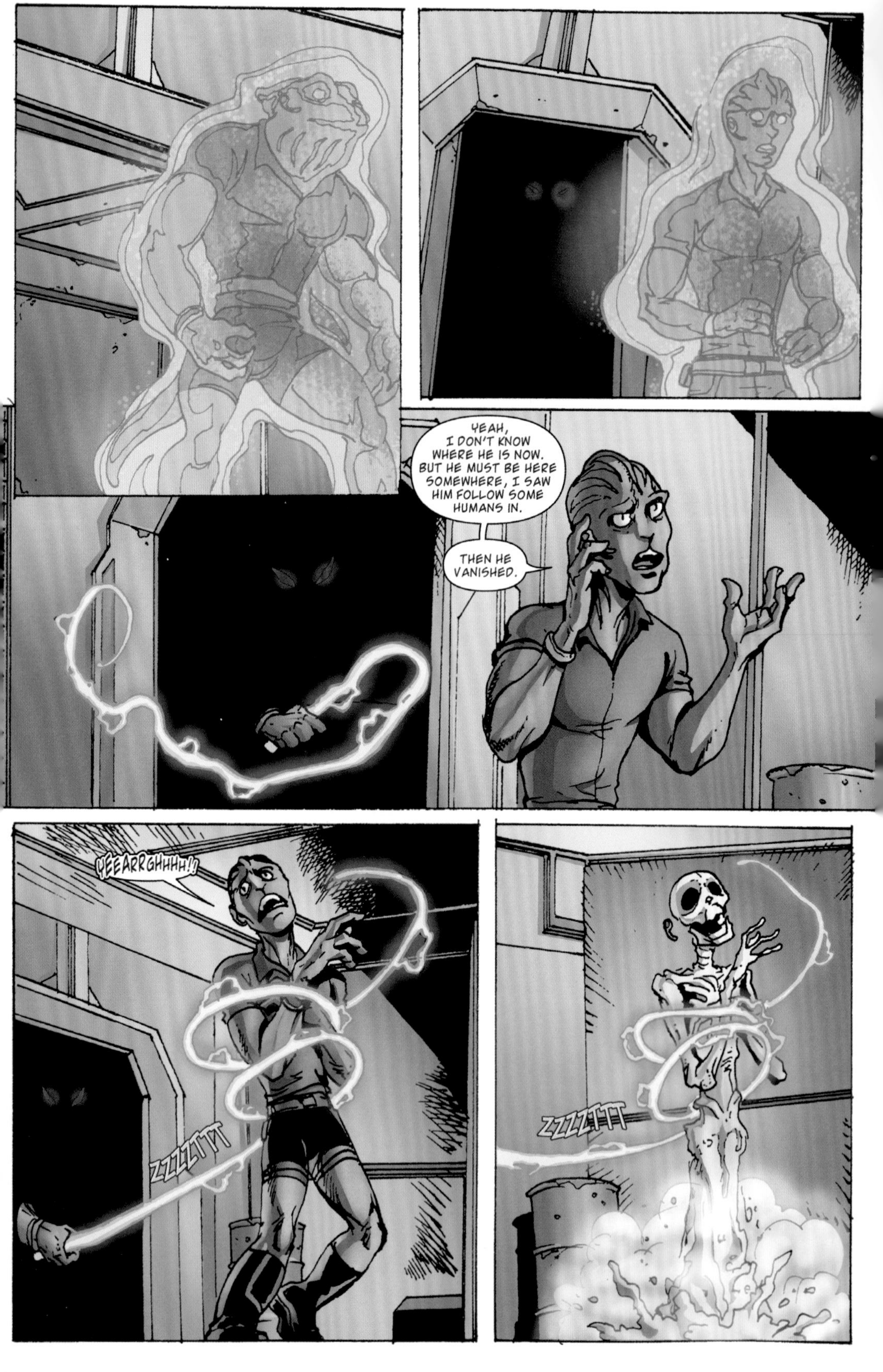
YEAH, I DON'T KNOW WHERE HE IS NOW. BUT HE MUST BE HERE SOMEWHERE, I SAW HIM FOLLOW SOME HUMANS IN.
THEN HE VANISHED.
YEEARRGHHHH!!
ZZZZTTT
ZZZZTTT

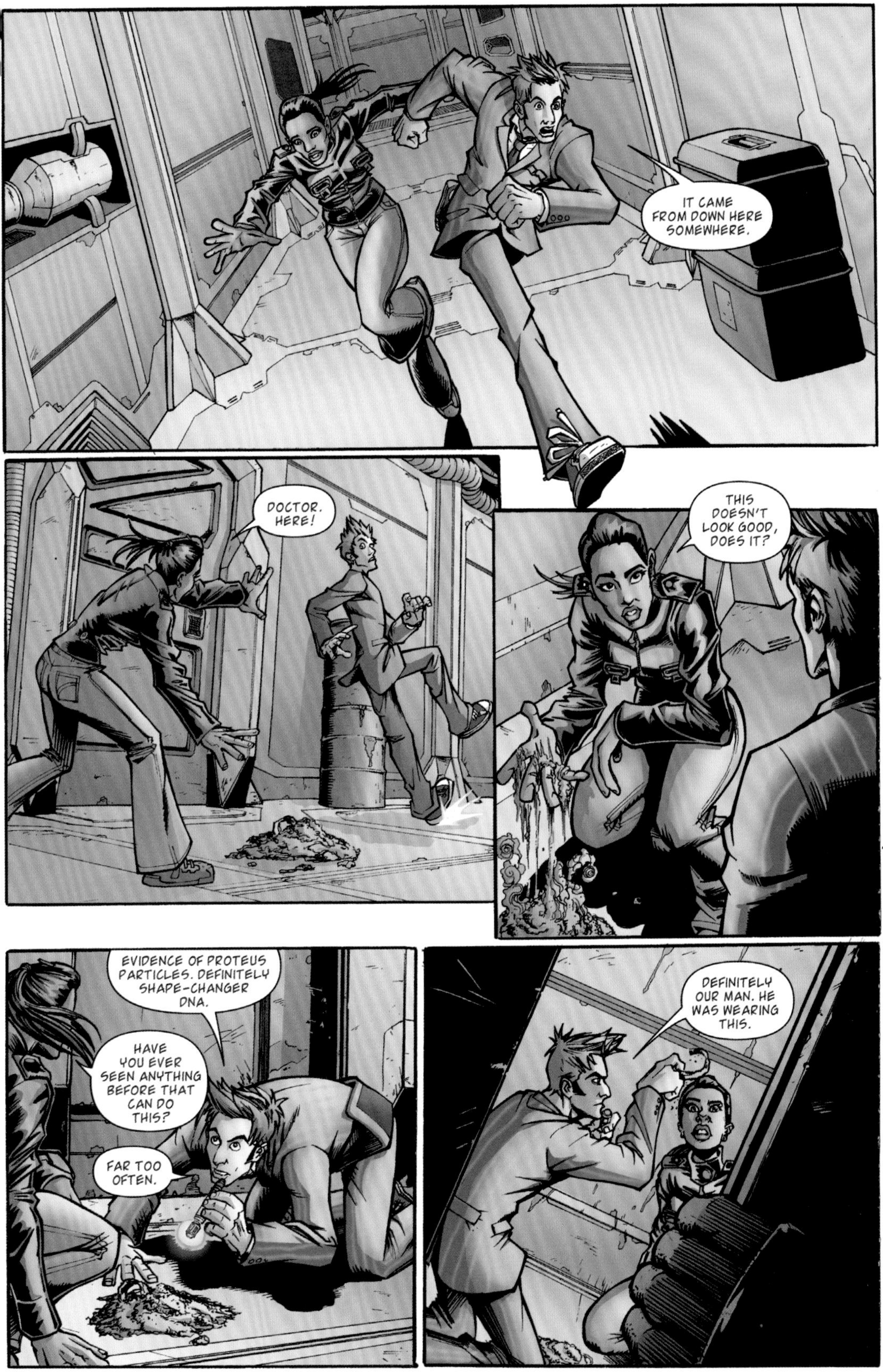
IT CAME FROM DOWN HERE SOMEWHERE.
DOCTOR. HERE!
THIS DOESN'T LOOK GOOD, DOES IT?
EVIDENCE OF PROTEUS PARTICLES. DEFINITELY SHAPE-CHANGER DNA.
HAVE YOU EVER SEEN ANYTHING BEFORE THAT CAN DO THIS?
FAR TOO OFTEN.
DEFINITELY OUR MAN. HE WAS WEARING THIS.

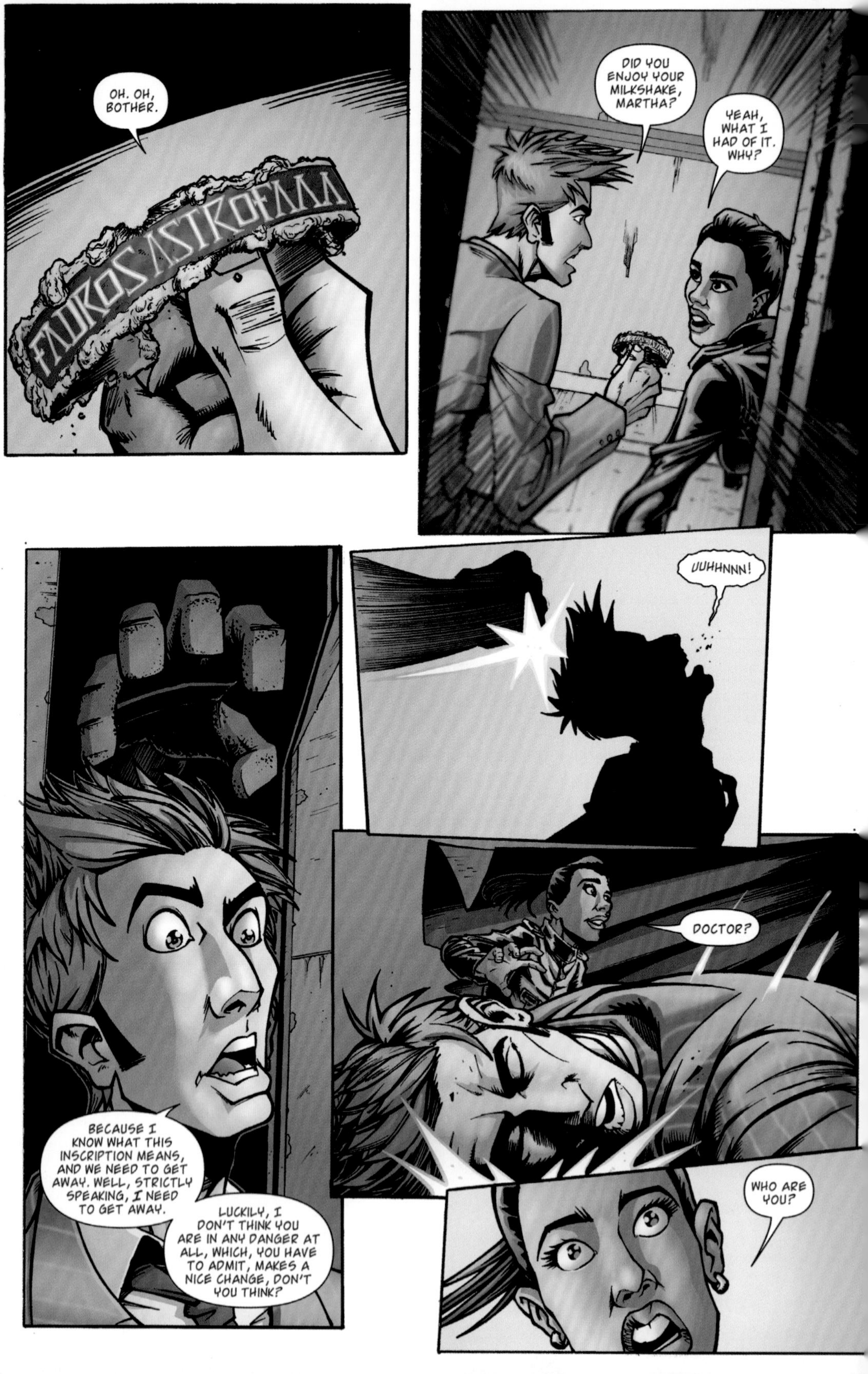
OH. OH, BOTHER.
FAUROS ASTROFAAA
DID YOU ENJOY YOUR MILKSHAKE, MARTHA?
YEAH, WHAT I HAD OF IT. WHY?
BECAUSE I KNOW WHAT THIS INSCRIPTION MEANS, AND WE NEED TO GET AWAY. WELL, STRICTLY SPEAKING, I NEED TO GET AWAY.
LUCKILY, I DON'T THINK YOU ARE IN ANY DANGER AT ALL, WHICH, YOU HAVE TO ADMIT, MAKES A NICE CHANGE, DON'T YOU THINK?
UUHHNNN!
DOCTOR?
WHO ARE YOU?

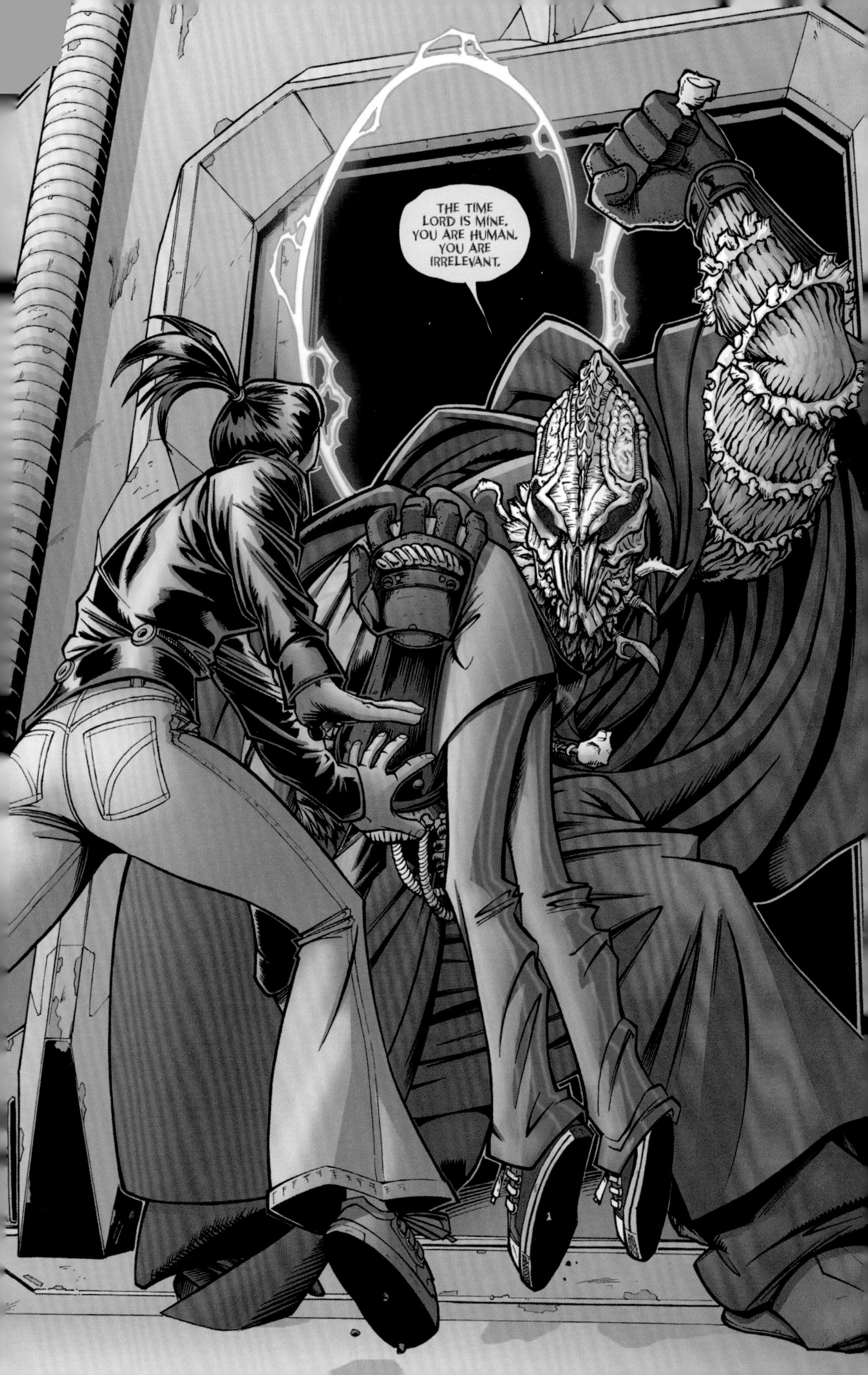
THE TIME LORD IS MINE. YOU ARE HUMAN. YOU ARE IRRELEVANT.

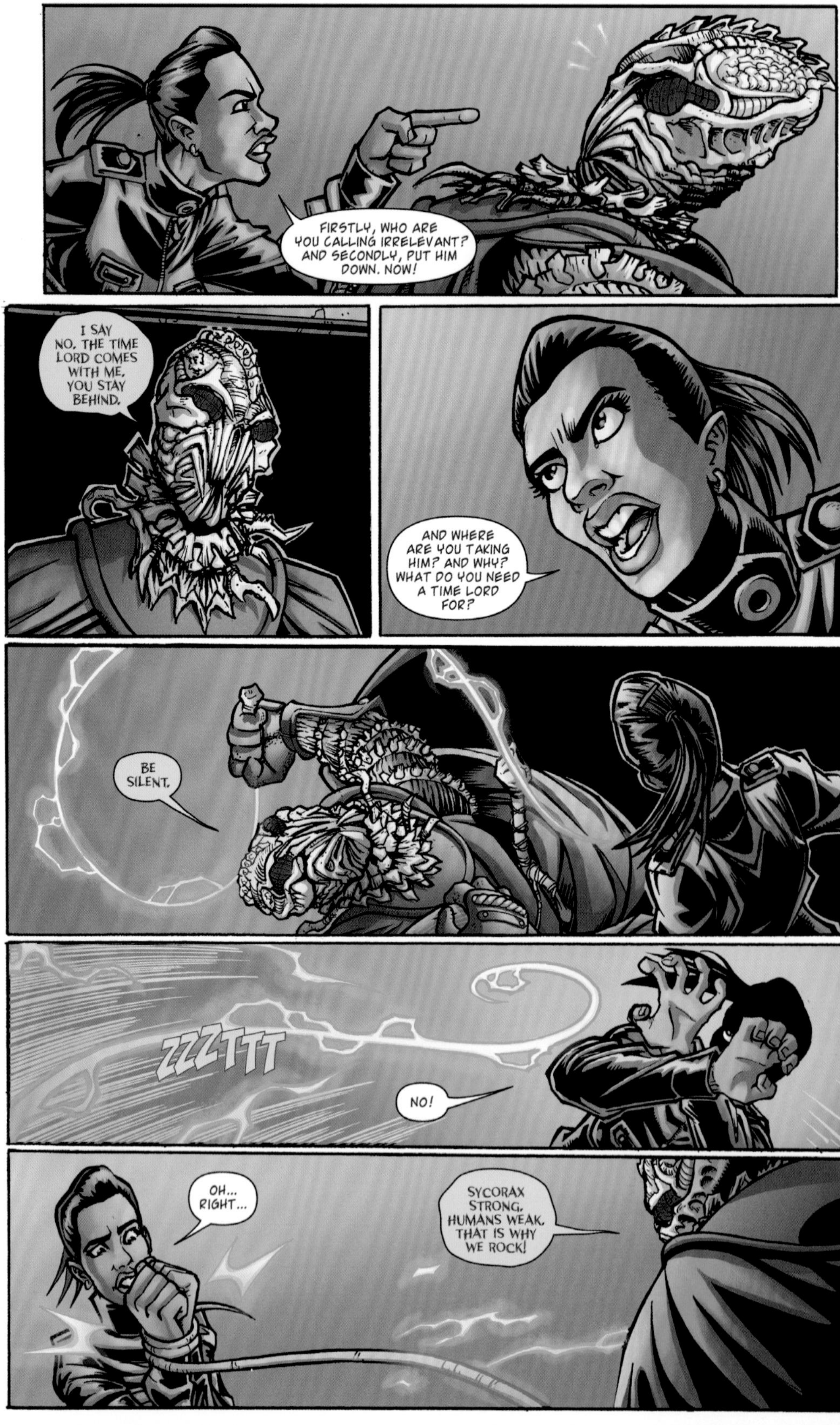
FIRSTLY, WHO ARE YOU CALLING IRRELEVANT? AND SECONDLY, PUT HIM DOWN. NOW!
I SAY NO. THE TIME LORD COMES WITH ME, YOU STAY BEHIND.
AND WHERE ARE YOU TAKING HIM? AND WHY? WHAT DO YOU NEED A TIME LORD FOR?
BE SILENT.
ZZZTTT
NO!
OH... RIGHT...
SYCORAX STRONG, HUMANS WEAK. THAT IS WHY WE ROCK!

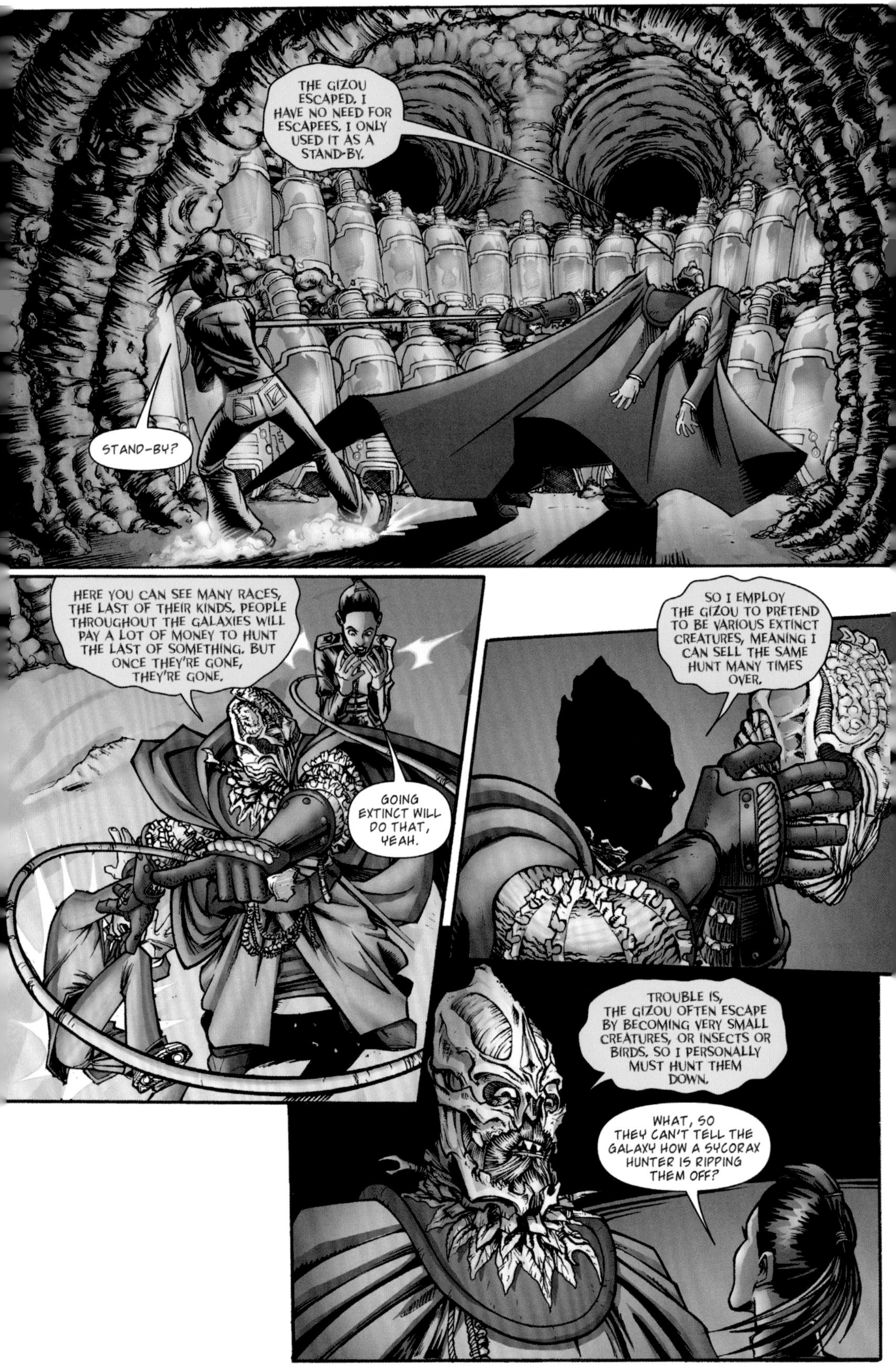
THE GIZOU ESCAPED. I HAVE NO NEED FOR ESCAPEES. I ONLY USED IT AS A STAND-BY.
STAND-BY?
HERE YOU CAN SEE MANY RACES, THE LAST OF THEIR KINDS. PEOPLE THROUGHOUT THE GALAXIES WILL PAY A LOT OF MONEY TO HUNT THE LAST OF SOMETHING. BUT ONCE THEY'RE GONE, THEY'RE GONE.
GOING EXTINCT WILL DO THAT, YEAH.
SO I EMPLOY THE GIZOU TO PRETEND TO BE VARIOUS EXTINCT CREATURES, MEANING I CAN SELL THE SAME HUNT MANY TIMES OVER.
TROUBLE IS, THE GIZOU OFTEN ESCAPE BY BECOMING VERY SMALL CREATURES, OR INSECTS OR BIRDS. SO I PERSONALLY MUST HUNT THEM DOWN.
WHAT, SO THEY CAN'T TELL THE GALAXY HOW A SYCORAX HUNTER IS RIPPING THEM OFF?

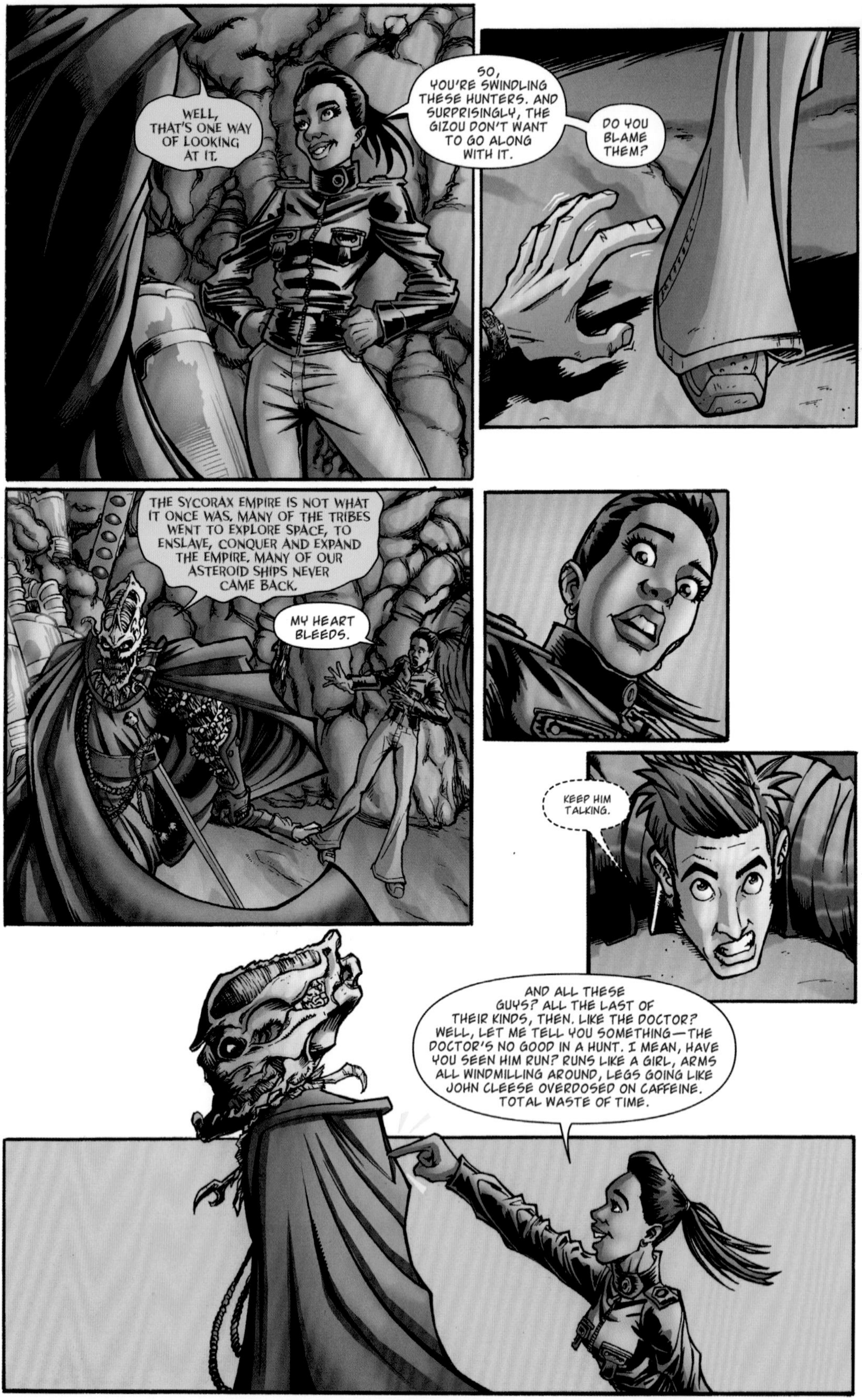
WELL, THAT'S ONE WAY OF LOOKING AT IT.
SO, YOU'RE SWINDLING THESE HUNTERS. AND SURPRISINGLY, THE GIZOU DON'T WANT TO GO ALONG WITH IT.
DO YOU BLAME THEM?
THE SYCORAX EMPIRE IS NOT WHAT IT ONCE WAS. MANY OF THE TRIBES WENT TO EXPLORE SPACE, TO ENSLAVE, CONQUER AND EXPAND THE EMPIRE. MANY OF OUR ASTEROID SHIPS NEVER CAME BACK.
MY HEART BLEEDS.
KEEP HIM TALKING.
AND ALL THESE GUYS? ALL THE LAST OF THEIR KINDS, THEN. LIKE THE DOCTOR? WELL, LET ME TELL YOU SOMETHING—THE DOCTOR'S NO GOOD IN A HUNT. I MEAN, HAVE YOU SEEN HIM RUN? RUNS LIKE A GIRL, ARMS ALL WINDMILLING AROUND, LEGS GOING LIKE JOHN CLEESE OVERDOSED ON CAFFEINE. TOTAL WASTE OF TIME.

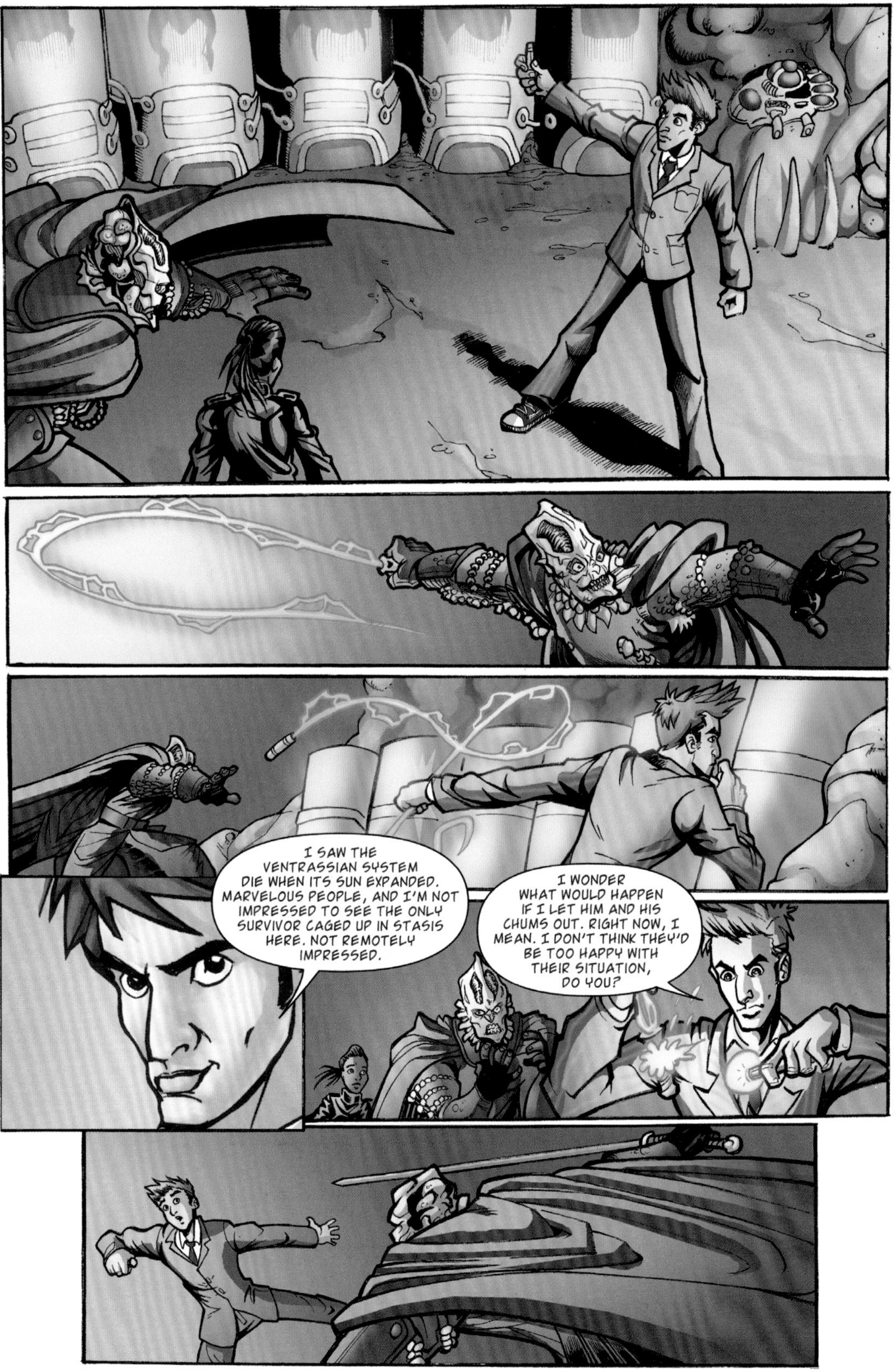
I SAW THE VENTRASSIAN SYSTEM DIE WHEN ITS SUN EXPANDED. MARVELOUS PEOPLE, AND I'M NOT IMPRESSED TO SEE THE ONLY SURVIVOR CAGED UP IN STASIS HERE. NOT REMOTELY IMPRESSED.
I WONDER WHAT WOULD HAPPEN IF I LET HIM AND HIS CHUMS OUT. RIGHT NOW, I MEAN. I DON'T THINK THEY'D BE TOO HAPPY WITH THEIR SITUATION, DO YOU?

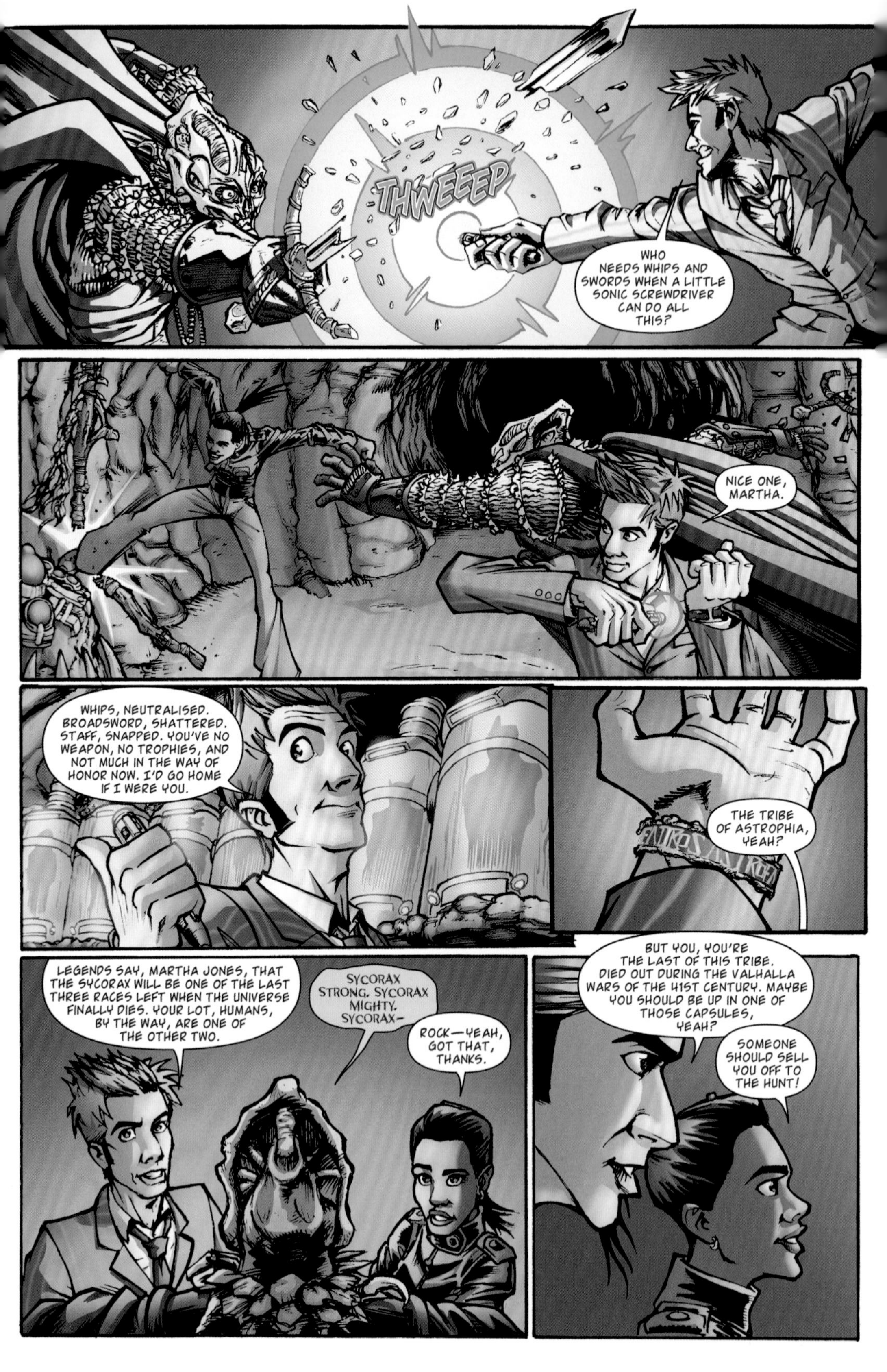
THWEEEP
WHO NEEDS WHIPS AND SWORDS WHEN A LITTLE SONIC SCREWDRIVER CAN DO ALL THIS?
NICE ONE, MARTHA.
WHIPS, NEUTRALISED. BROADSWORD, SHATTERED. STAFF, SNAPPED. YOU'VE NO WEAPON, NO TROPHIES, AND NOT MUCH IN THE WAY OF HONOR NOW. I'D GO HOME IF I WERE YOU.
THE TRIBE OF ASTROPHIA, YEAH?
LEGENDS SAY, MARTHA JONES, THAT THE SYCORAX WILL BE ONE OF THE LAST THREE RACES LEFT WHEN THE UNIVERSE FINALLY DIES. YOUR LOT, HUMANS, BY THE WAY, ARE ONE OF THE OTHER TWO.
SYCORAX STRONG. SYCORAX MIGHTY. SYCORAX—
ROCK—YEAH, GOT THAT, THANKS.
BUT YOU, YOU'RE THE LAST OF THIS TRIBE. DIED OUT DURING THE VALHALLA WARS OF THE 41ST CENTURY. MAYBE YOU SHOULD BE UP IN ONE OF THOSE CAPSULES, YEAH?
SOMEONE SHOULD SELL YOU OFF TO THE HUNT!

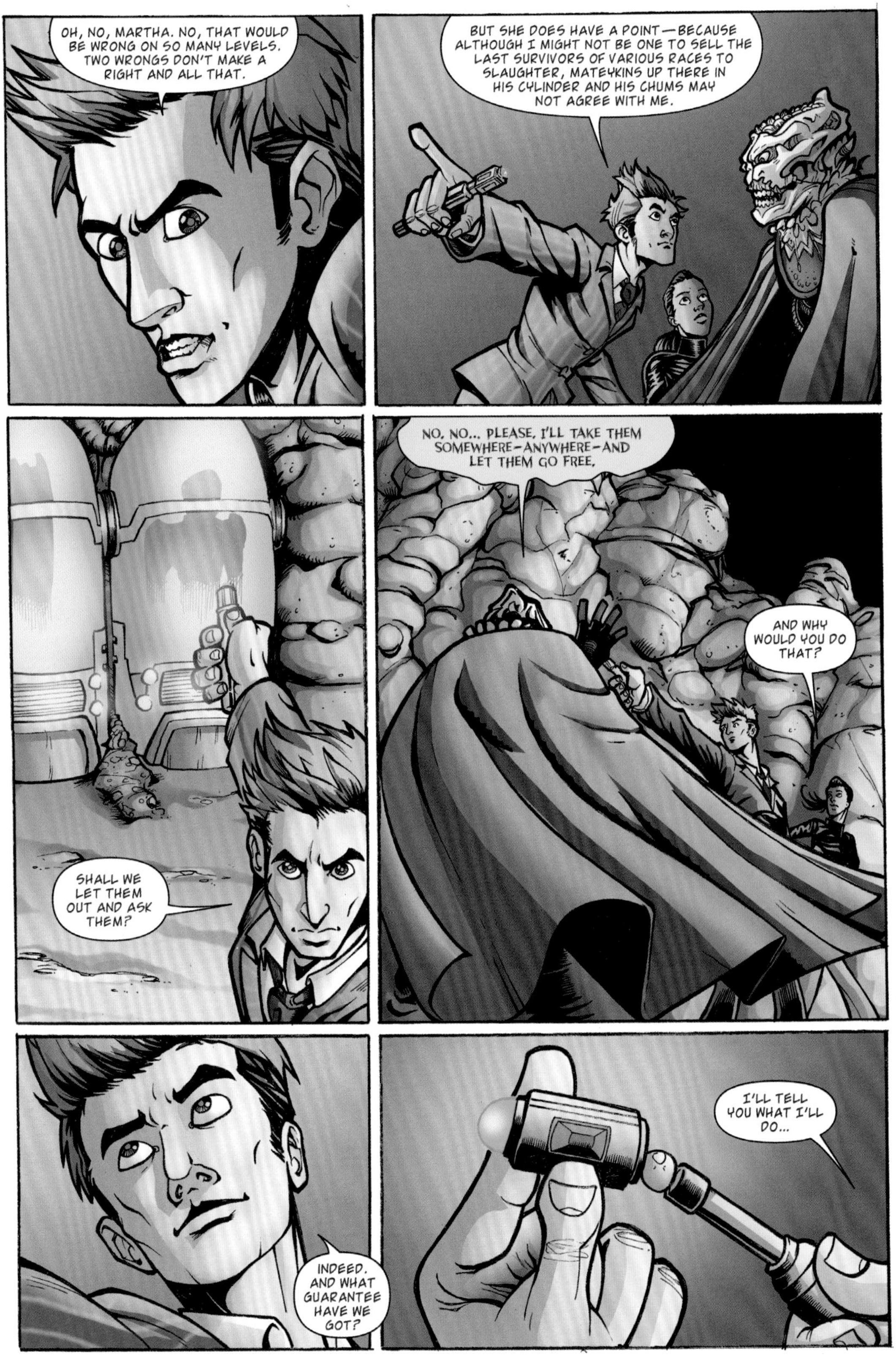
OH, NO, MARTHA. NO, THAT WOULD BE WRONG ON SO MANY LEVELS. TWO WRONGS DON'T MAKE A RIGHT AND ALL THAT.
BUT SHE DOES HAVE A POINT—BECAUSE ALTHOUGH I MIGHT NOT BE ONE TO SELL THE LAST SURVIVORS OF VARIOUS RACES TO SLAUGHTER, MATEYKINS UP THERE IN HIS CYLINDER AND HIS CHUMS MAY NOT AGREE WITH ME.
SHALL WE LET THEM OUT AND ASK THEM?
NO, NO... PLEASE, I'LL TAKE THEM SOMEWHERE-ANYWHERE-AND LET THEM GO FREE.
AND WHY WOULD YOU DO THAT?
INDEED. AND WHAT GUARANTEE HAVE WE GOT?
I'LL TELL YOU WHAT I'LL DO...

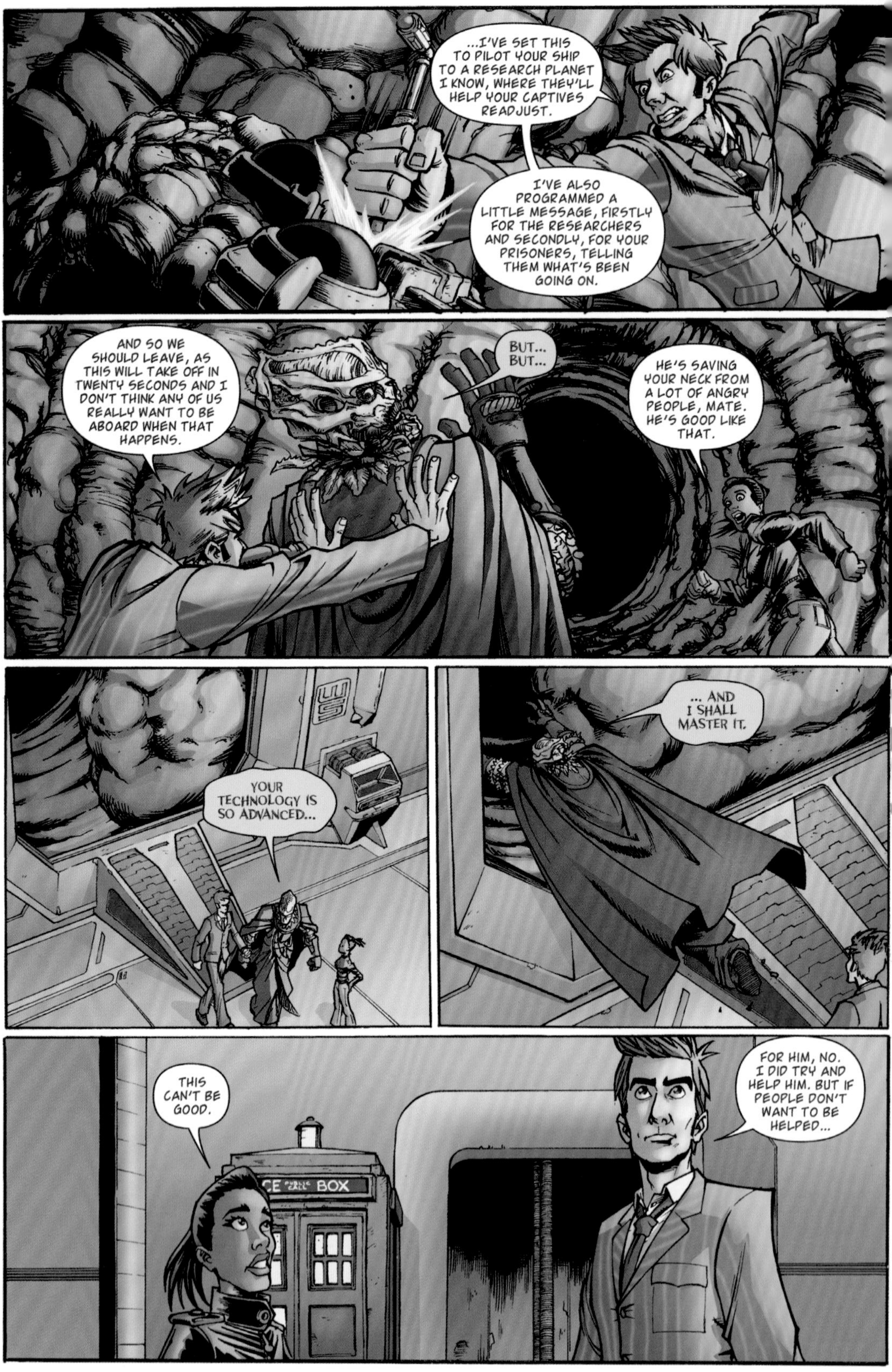
...I'VE SET THIS TO PILOT YOUR SHIP TO A RESEARCH PLANET I KNOW, WHERE THEY'LL HELP YOUR CAPTIVES READJUST.
I'VE ALSO PROGRAMMED A LITTLE MESSAGE, FIRSTLY FOR THE RESEARCHERS AND SECONDLY, FOR YOUR PRISONERS, TELLING THEM WHAT'S BEEN GOING ON.
AND SO WE SHOULD LEAVE, AS THIS WILL TAKE OFF IN TWENTY SECONDS AND I DON'T THINK ANY OF US REALLY WANT TO BE ABOARD WHEN THAT HAPPENS.
BUT... BUT...
HE'S SAVING YOUR NECK FROM A LOT OF ANGRY PEOPLE, MATE. HE'S GOOD LIKE THAT.
YOUR TECHNOLOGY IS SO ADVANCED...
... AND I SHALL MASTER IT.
THIS CAN'T BE GOOD.
FOR HIM, NO. I DID TRY AND HELP HIM. BUT IF PEOPLE DON'T WANT TO BE HELPED...

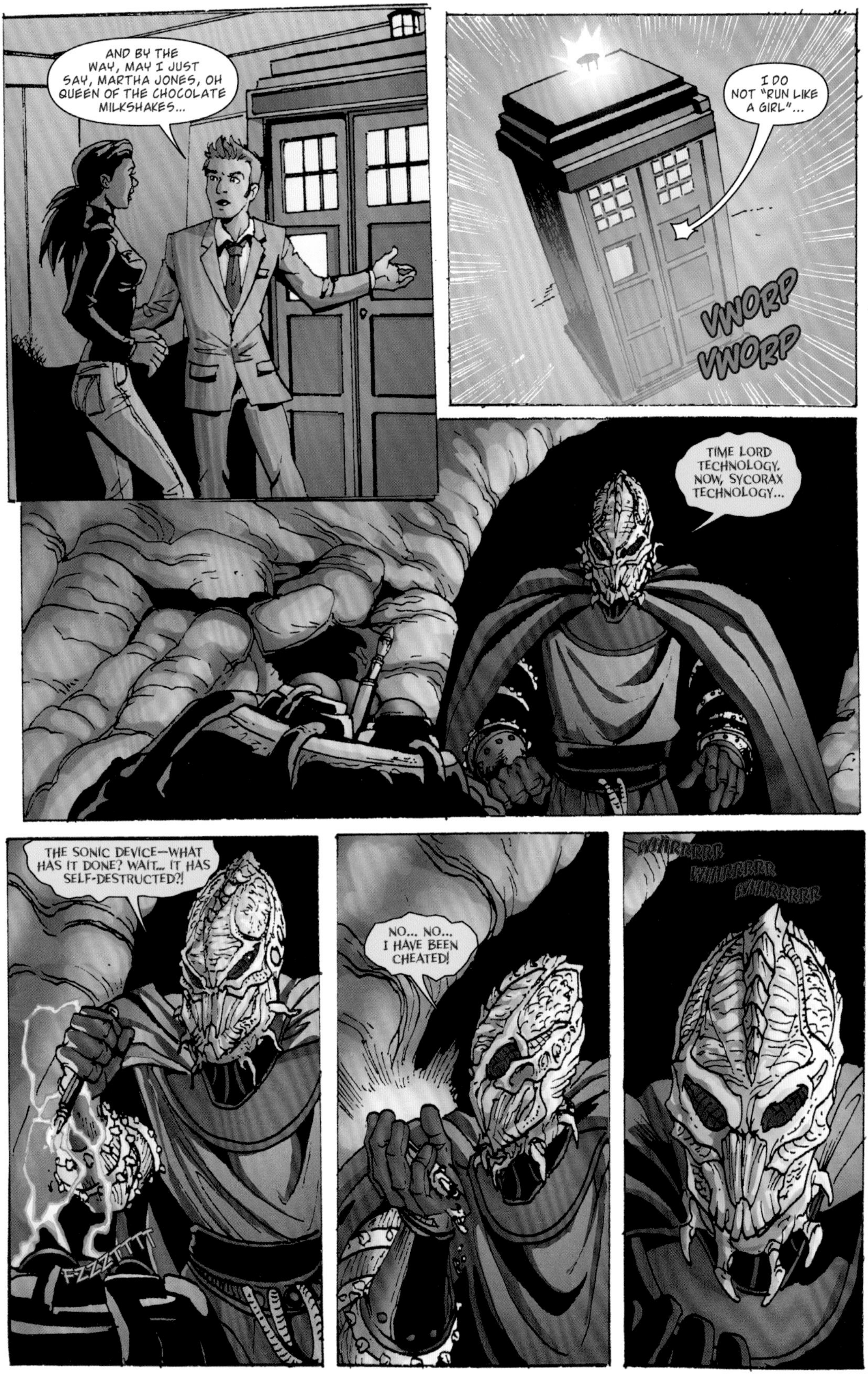
AND BY THE WAY, MAY I JUST SAY, MARTHA JONES, OH QUEEN OF THE CHOCOLATE MILKSHAKES...
I DO NOT "RUN LIKE A GIRL"...
VWORP
VWORP
TIME LORD TECHNOLOGY. NOW, SYCORAX TECHNOLOGY...
THE SONIC DEVICE—WHAT HAS IT DONE? WAIT... IT HAS SELF-DESTRUCTED?!
FZZZTTTT
NO... NO... I HAVE BEEN CHEATED!
WHIRRRRR
WHIRRRRR
WHIRRRRR

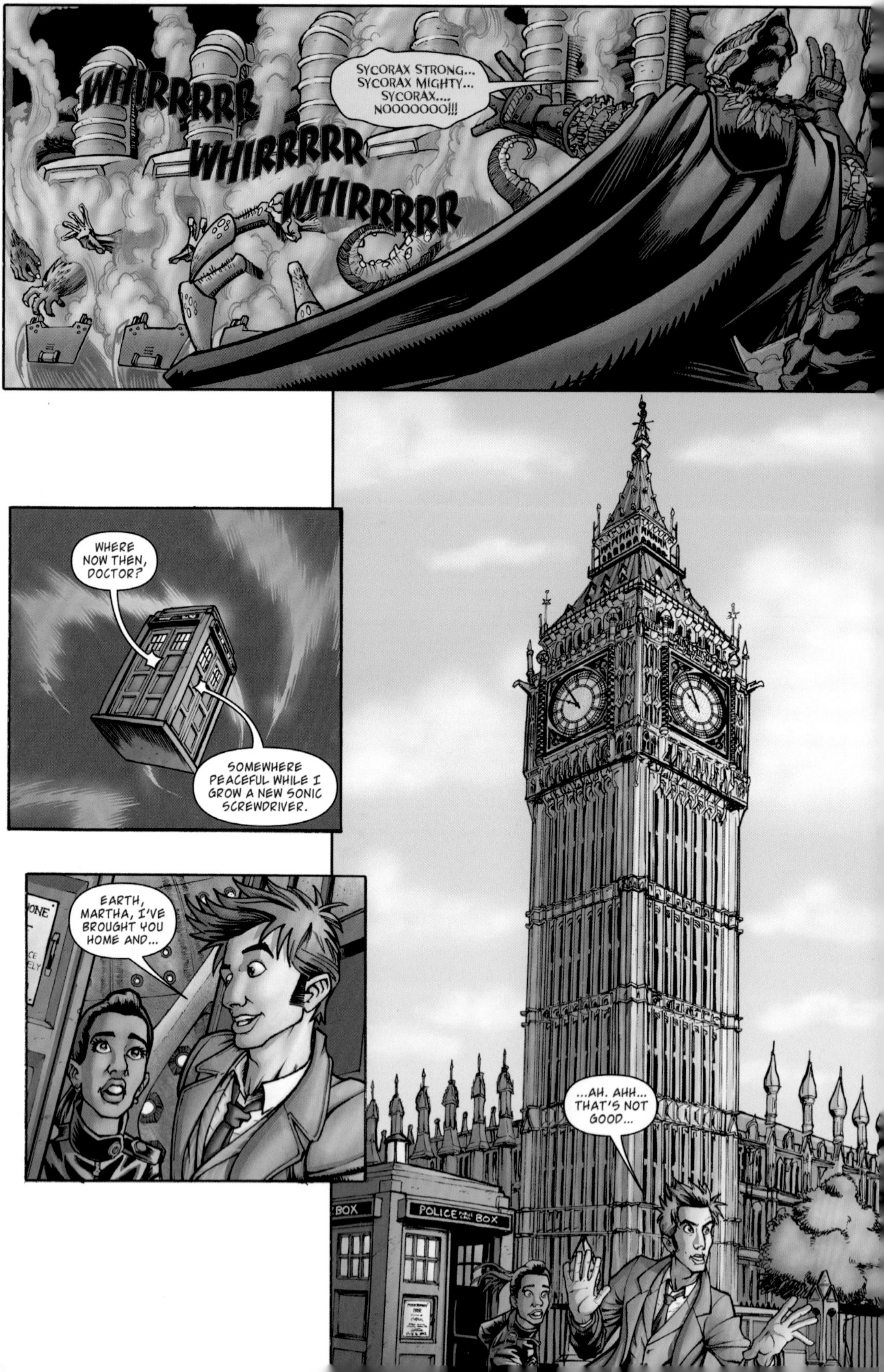
WHIRRRRR
WHIRRRRR
WHIRRRRR
SYCORAX STRONG... SYCORAX MIGHTY... SYCORAX..., NOOOOOOO!!!
WHERE NOW THEN, DOCTOR?
SOMEWHERE PEACEFUL WHILE I GROW A NEW SONIC SCREWDRIVER.
EARTH, MARTHA, I'VE BROUGHT YOU HOME AND...
...AH. AHH... THAT'S NOT GOOD...
POLICE BOX

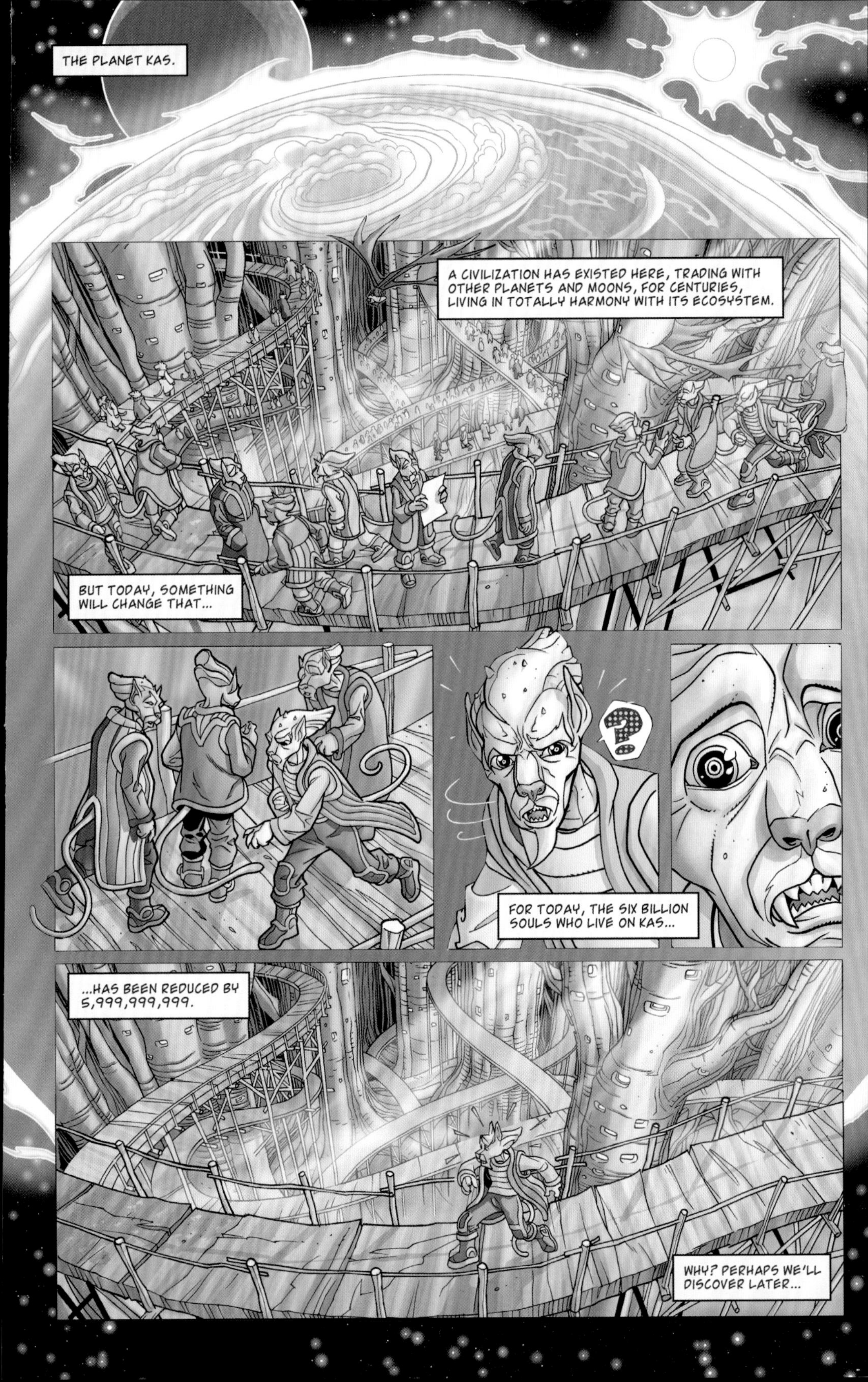
THE PLANET KAS.
A CIVILIZATION HAS EXISTED HERE, TRADING WITH OTHER PLANETS AND MOONS, FOR CENTURIES, LIVING IN TOTALLY HARMONY WITH ITS ECOSYSTEM.
BUT TODAY, SOMETHING WILL CHANGE THAT...
?
FOR TODAY, THE SIX BILLION SOULS WHO LIVE ON KAS...
...HAS BEEN REDUCED BY 5,999,999,999.
WHY? PERHAPS WE'LL DISCOVER LATER...

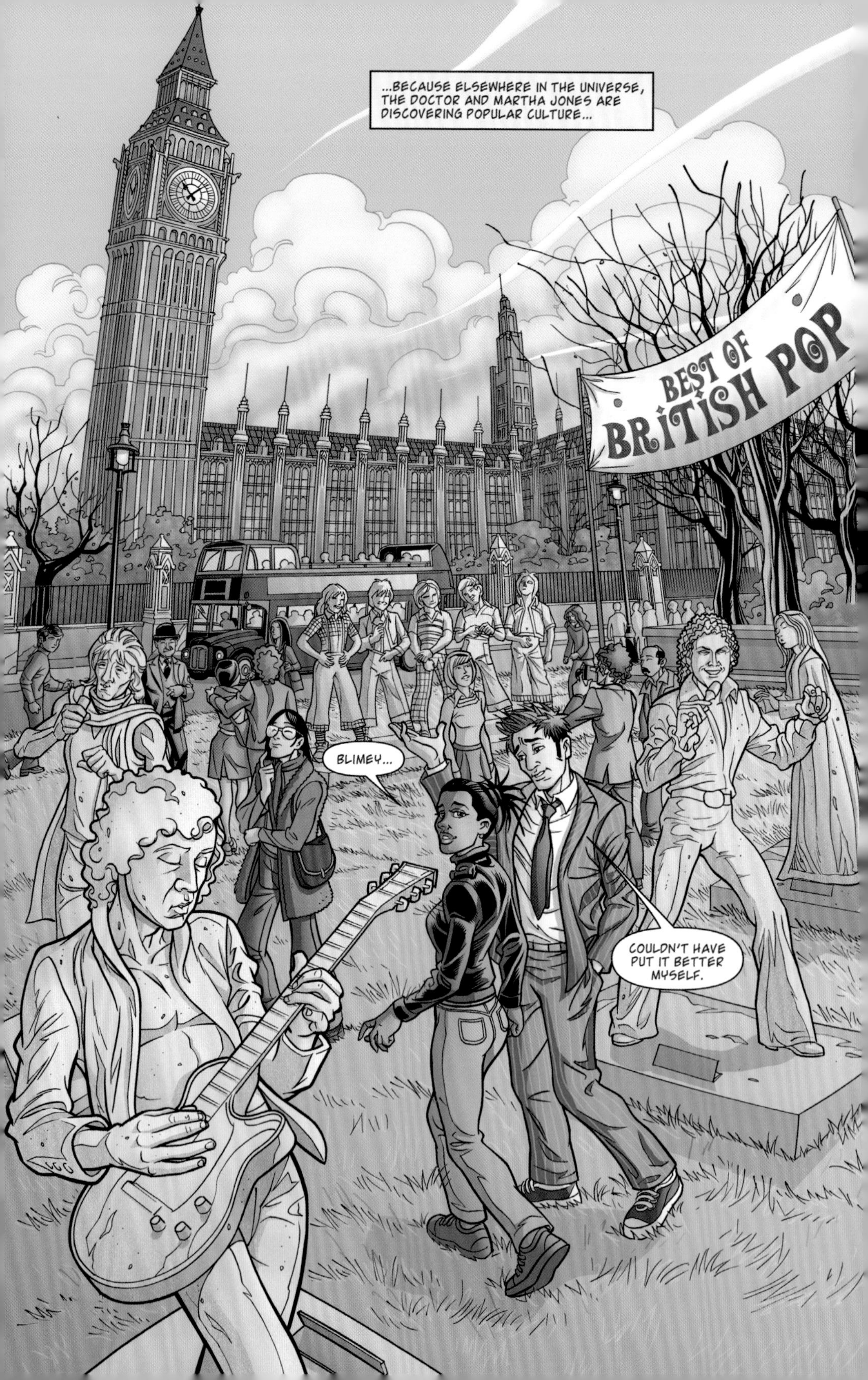
...BECAUSE ELSEWHERE IN THE UNIVERSE, THE DOCTOR AND MARTHA JONES ARE DISCOVERING POPULAR CULTURE...
BEST OF BRITISH POP
BLIMEY...
COULDN'T HAVE PUT IT BETTER MYSELF.

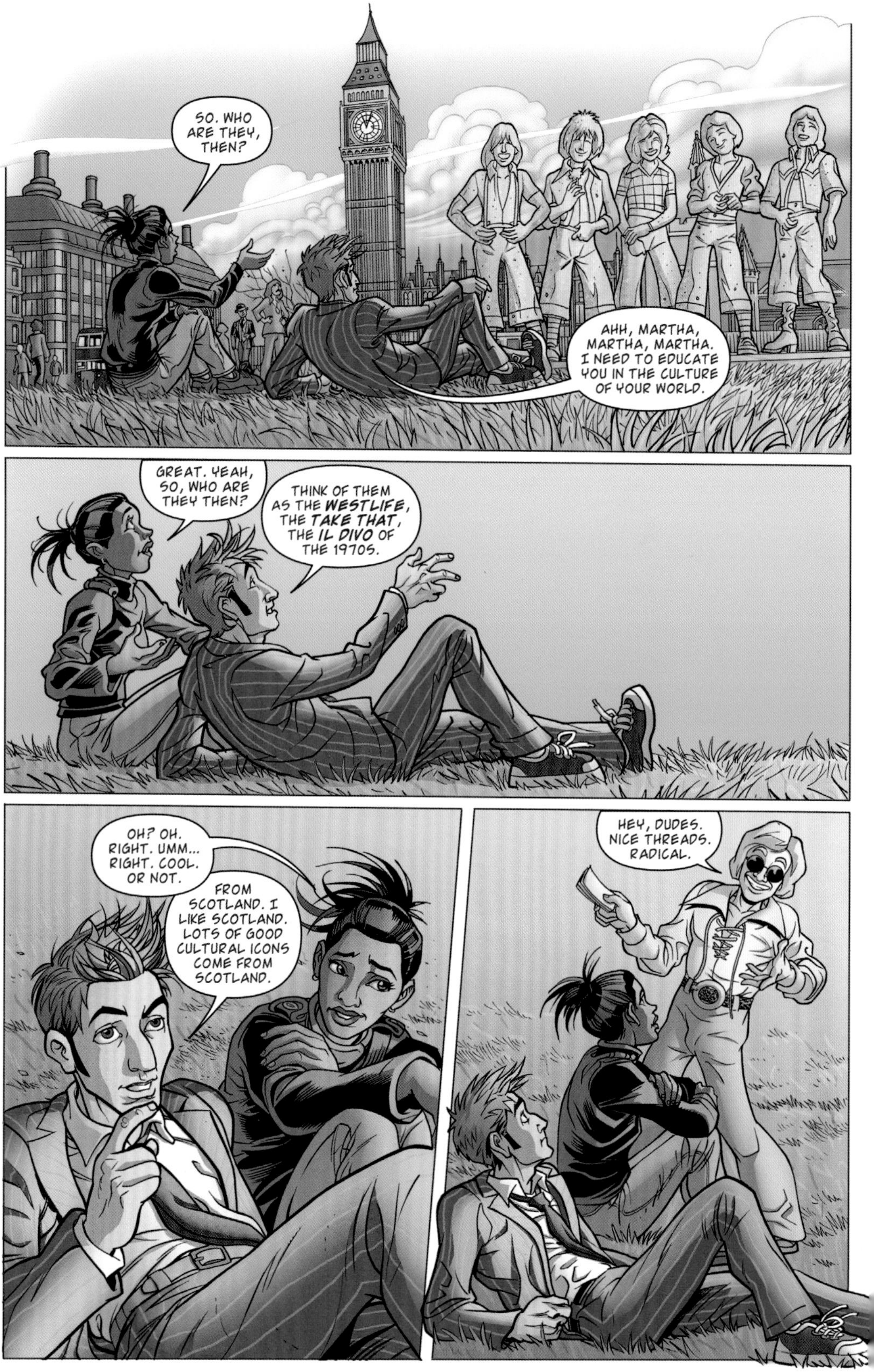
SO. WHO ARE THEY, THEN?
AHH, MARTHA, MARTHA, MARTHA. I NEED TO EDUCATE YOU IN THE CULTURE OF YOUR WORLD.
GREAT. YEAH, SO, WHO ARE THEY THEN?
THINK OF THEM AS THE *WESTLIFE*, THE *TAKE THAT*, THE *IL DIVO* OF THE 1970S.
OH? OH. RIGHT. UMM... RIGHT. COOL. OR NOT.
FROM SCOTLAND. I LIKE SCOTLAND. LOTS OF GOOD CULTURAL ICONS COME FROM SCOTLAND.
HEY, DUDES. NICE THREADS. RADICAL.

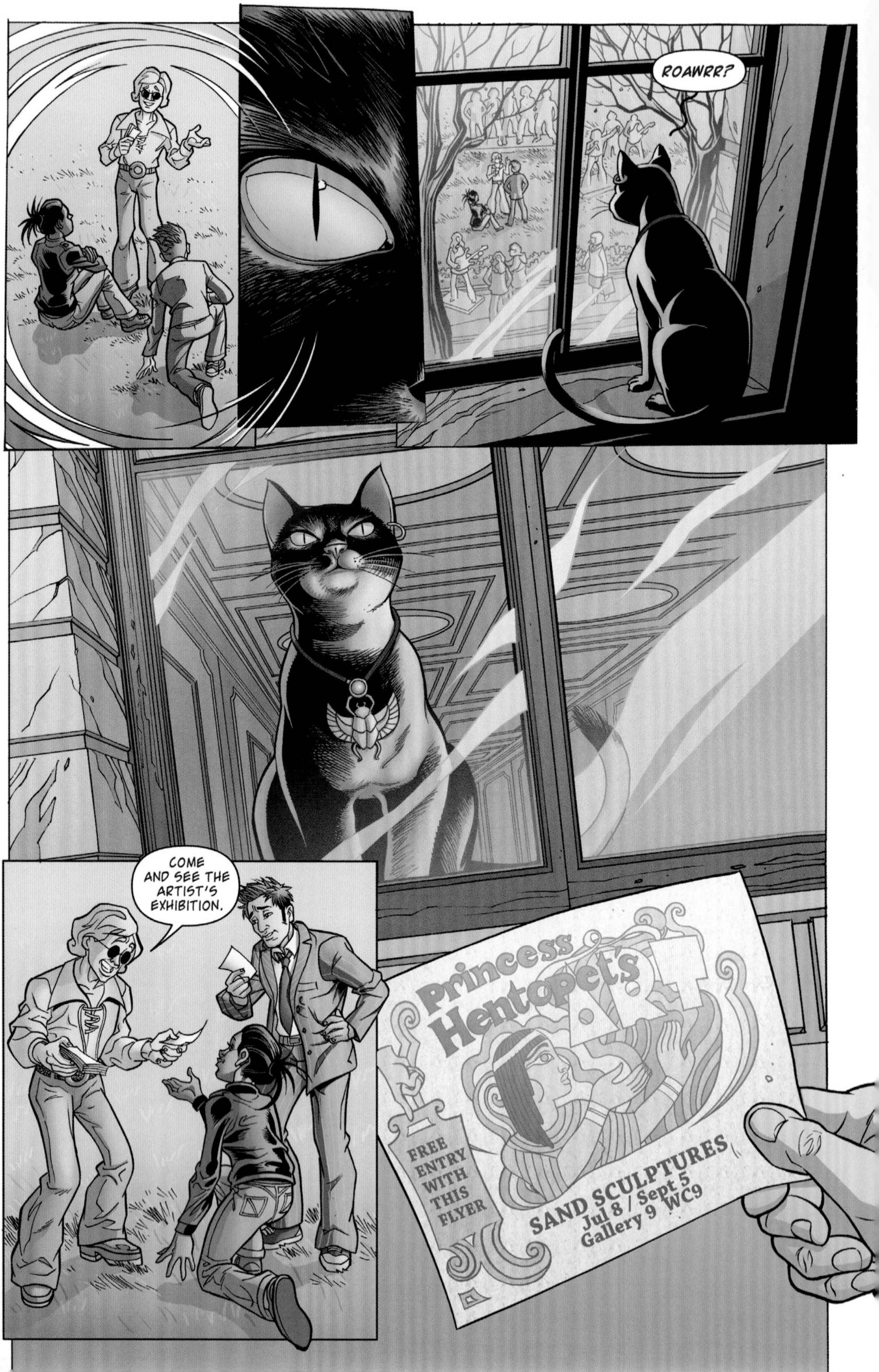
ROAWRR?
COME AND SEE THE ARTIST'S EXHIBITION.
Princess Hentopet's ART
FREE ENTRY WITH THIS FLYER
SAND SCULPTURES
Jul 8 / Sept 5
Gallery 9 WC9

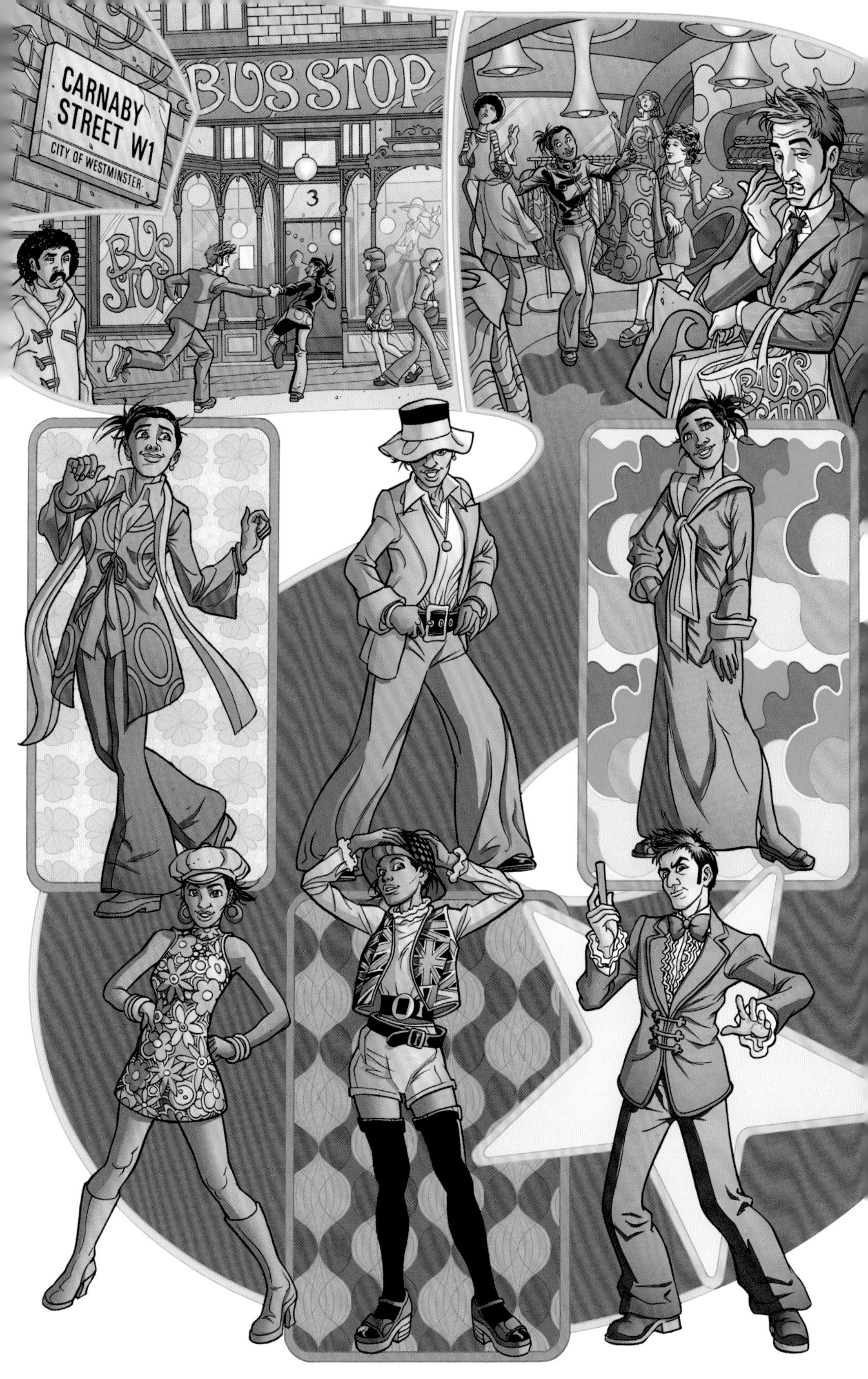

CARNABY STREET W1
CITY OF WESTMINSTER
BUS STOP
3
BUS STOP
BUS STOP

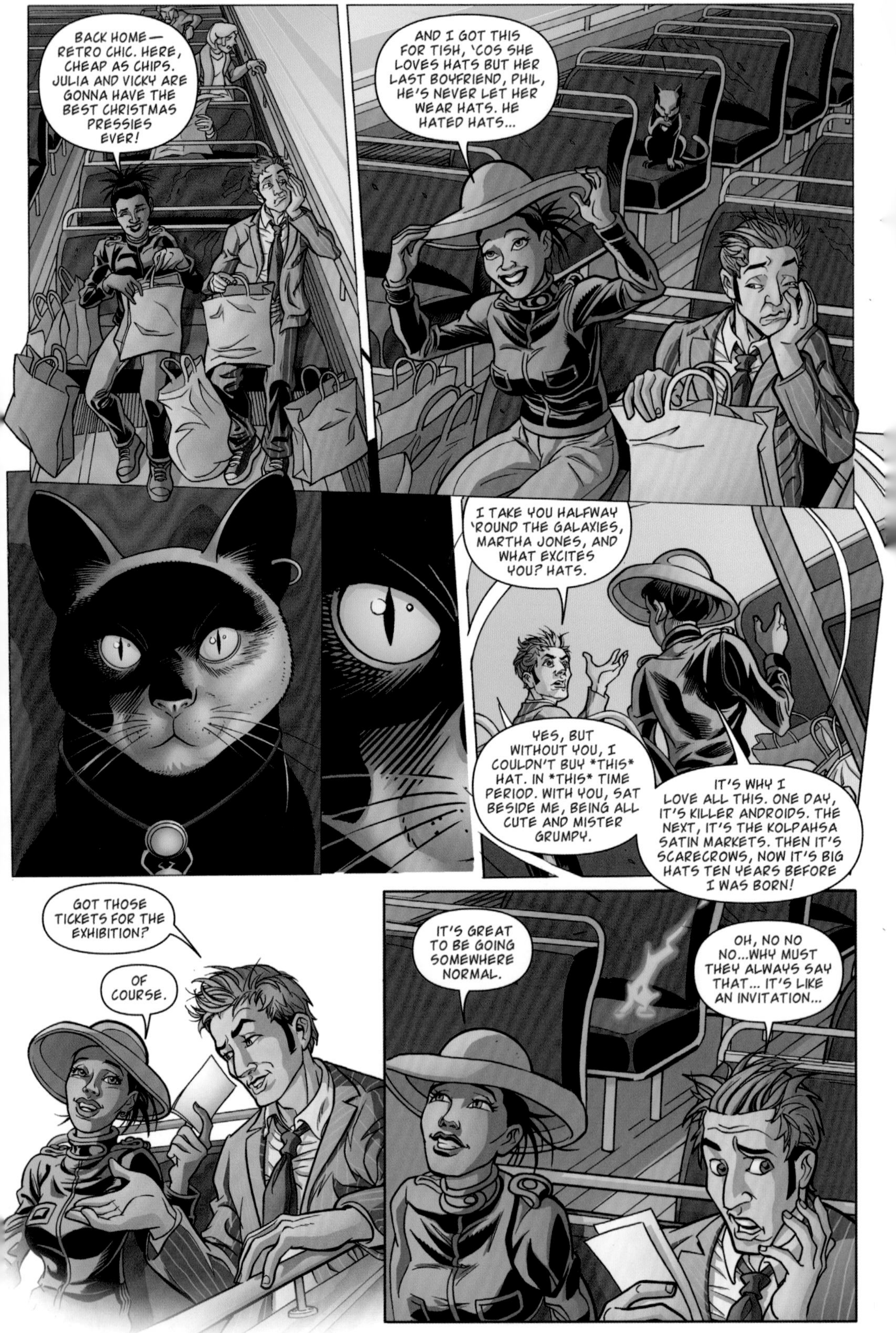
BACK HOME— RETRO CHIC. HERE, CHEAP AS CHIPS. JULIA AND VICKY ARE GONNA HAVE THE BEST CHRISTMAS PRESSIES EVER!
AND I GOT THIS FOR TISH, 'COS SHE LOVES HATS BUT HER LAST BOYFRIEND, PHIL, HE'S NEVER LET HER WEAR HATS. HE HATED HATS...
I TAKE YOU HALFWAY 'ROUND THE GALAXIES, MARTHA JONES, AND WHAT EXCITES YOU? HATS.
YES, BUT WITHOUT YOU, I COULDN'T BUY *THIS* HAT. IN *THIS* TIME PERIOD. WITH YOU, SAT BESIDE ME, BEING ALL CUTE AND MISTER GRUMPY.
IT'S WHY I LOVE ALL THIS. ONE DAY, IT'S KILLER ANDROIDS. THE NEXT, IT'S THE KOLPAHSA SATIN MARKETS. THEN IT'S SCARECROWS, NOW IT'S BIG HATS TEN YEARS BEFORE I WAS BORN!
GOT THOSE TICKETS FOR THE EXHIBITION?
OF COURSE.
IT'S GREAT TO BE GOING SOMEWHERE NORMAL.
OH, NO NO NO...WHY MUST THEY ALWAYS SAY THAT... IT'S LIKE AN INVITATION...

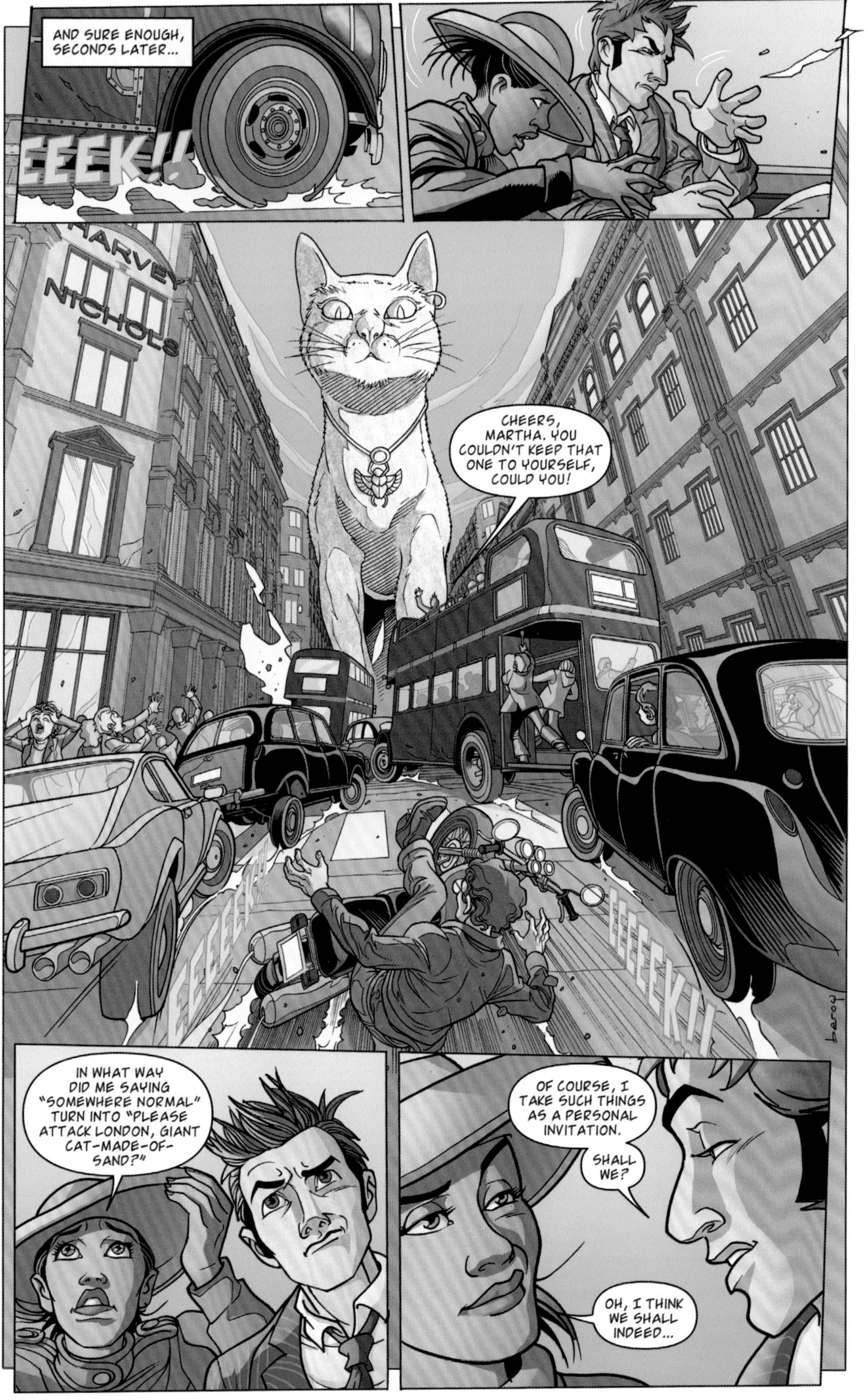
AND SURE ENOUGH, SECONDS LATER...
EEEK!!
HARVEY NICHOLS
CHEERS, MARTHA. YOU COULDN'T KEEP THAT ONE TO YOURSELF, COULD YOU!
EEEEEEK!!
EEEEEK!!
IN WHAT WAY DID ME SAYING "SOMEWHERE NORMAL" TURN INTO "PLEASE ATTACK LONDON, GIANT CAT-MADE-OF-SAND?"
OF COURSE, I TAKE SUCH THINGS AS A PERSONAL INVITATION.
SHALL WE?
OH, I THINK WE SHALL INDEED...

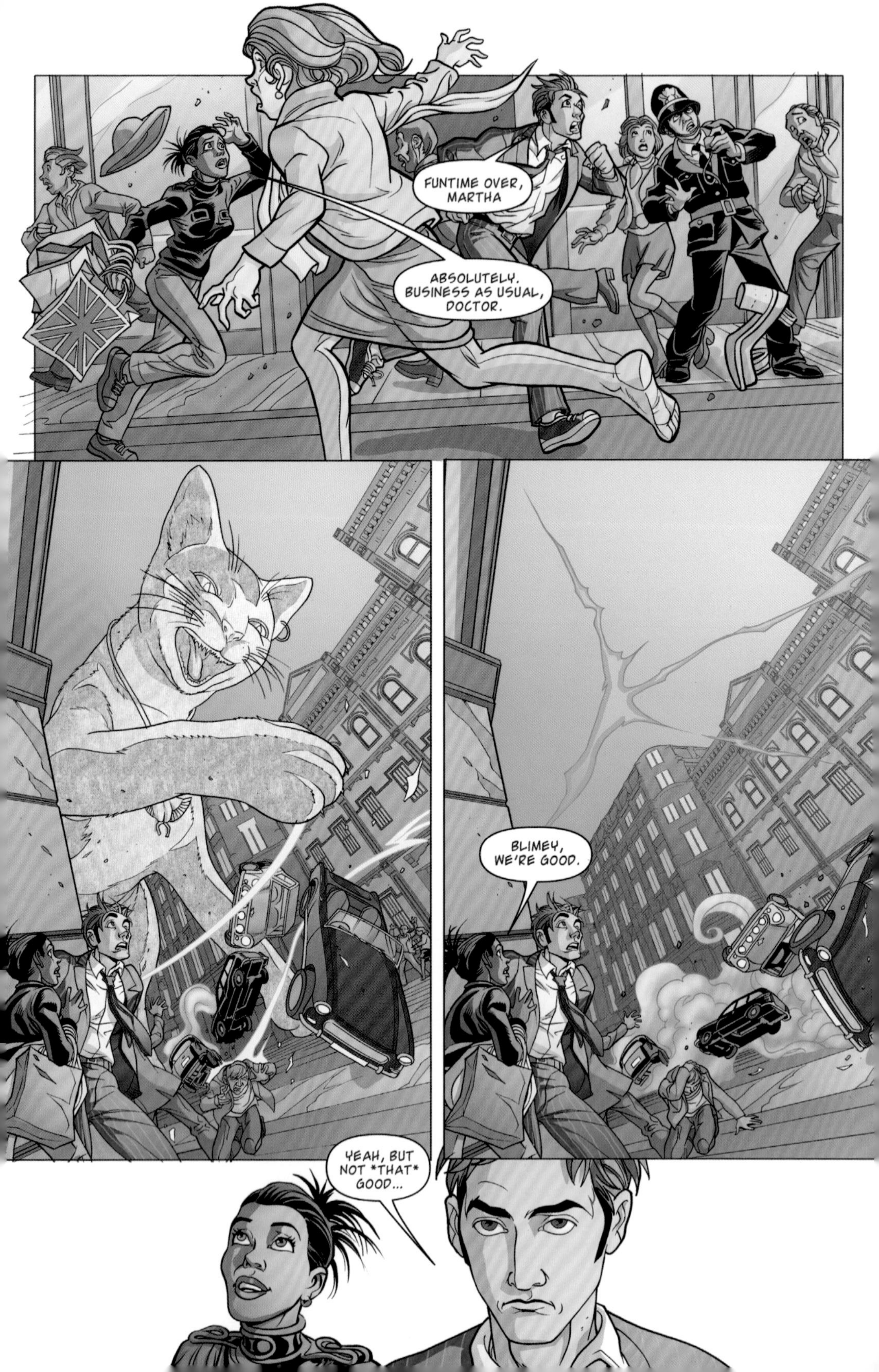
FUNTIME OVER, MARTHA
ABSOLUTELY. BUSINESS AS USUAL, DOCTOR.
BLIMEY, WE'RE GOOD.
YEAH, BUT NOT *THAT* GOOD...

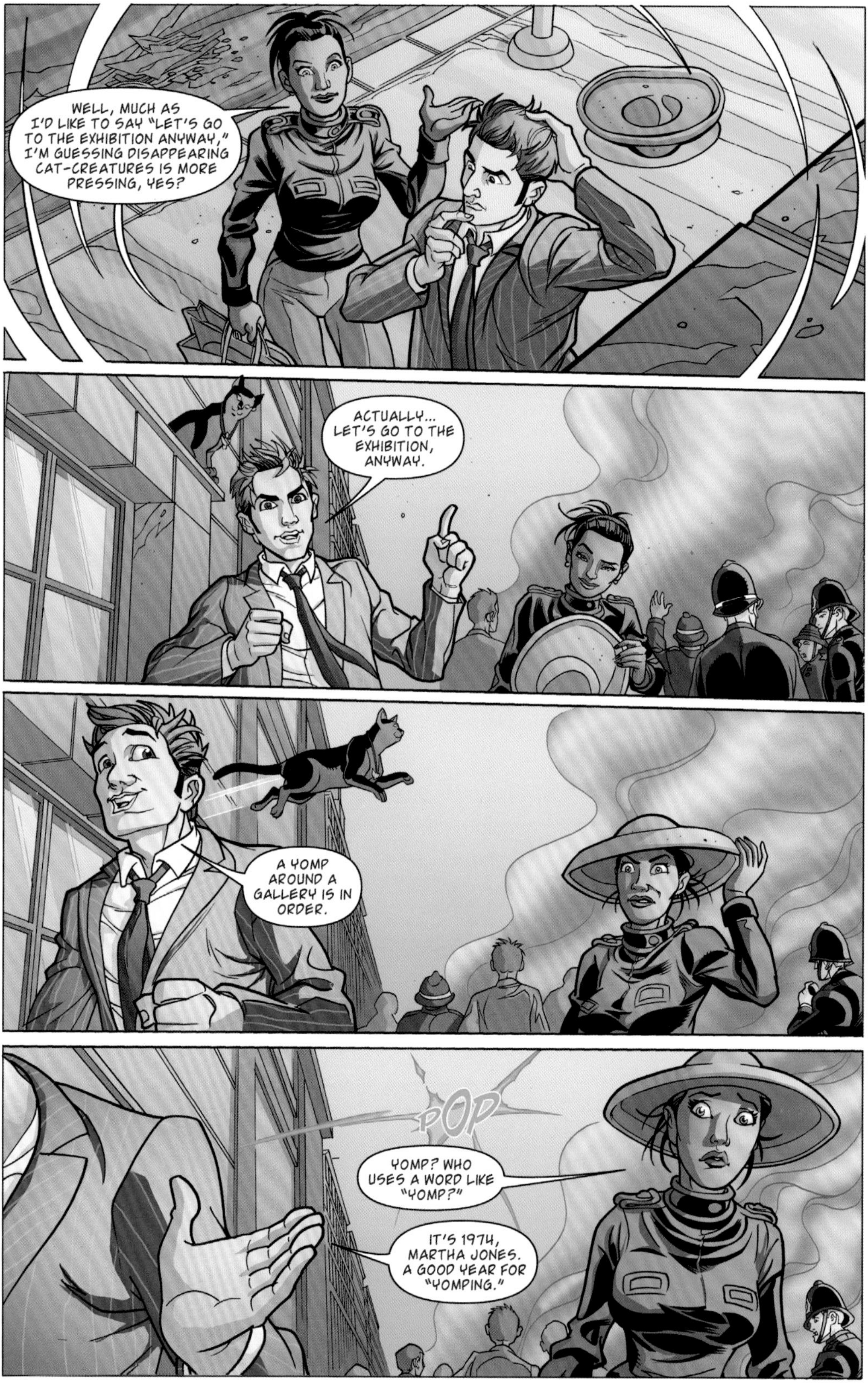
WELL, MUCH AS I'D LIKE TO SAY "LET'S GO TO THE EXHIBITION ANYWAY," I'M GUESSING DISAPPEARING CAT-CREATURES IS MORE PRESSING, YES?
ACTUALLY... LET'S GO TO THE EXHIBITION, ANYWAY.
A YOMP AROUND A GALLERY IS IN ORDER.
POP
YOMP? WHO USES A WORD LIKE "YOMP?"
IT'S 1974, MARTHA JONES. A GOOD YEAR FOR "YOMPING."

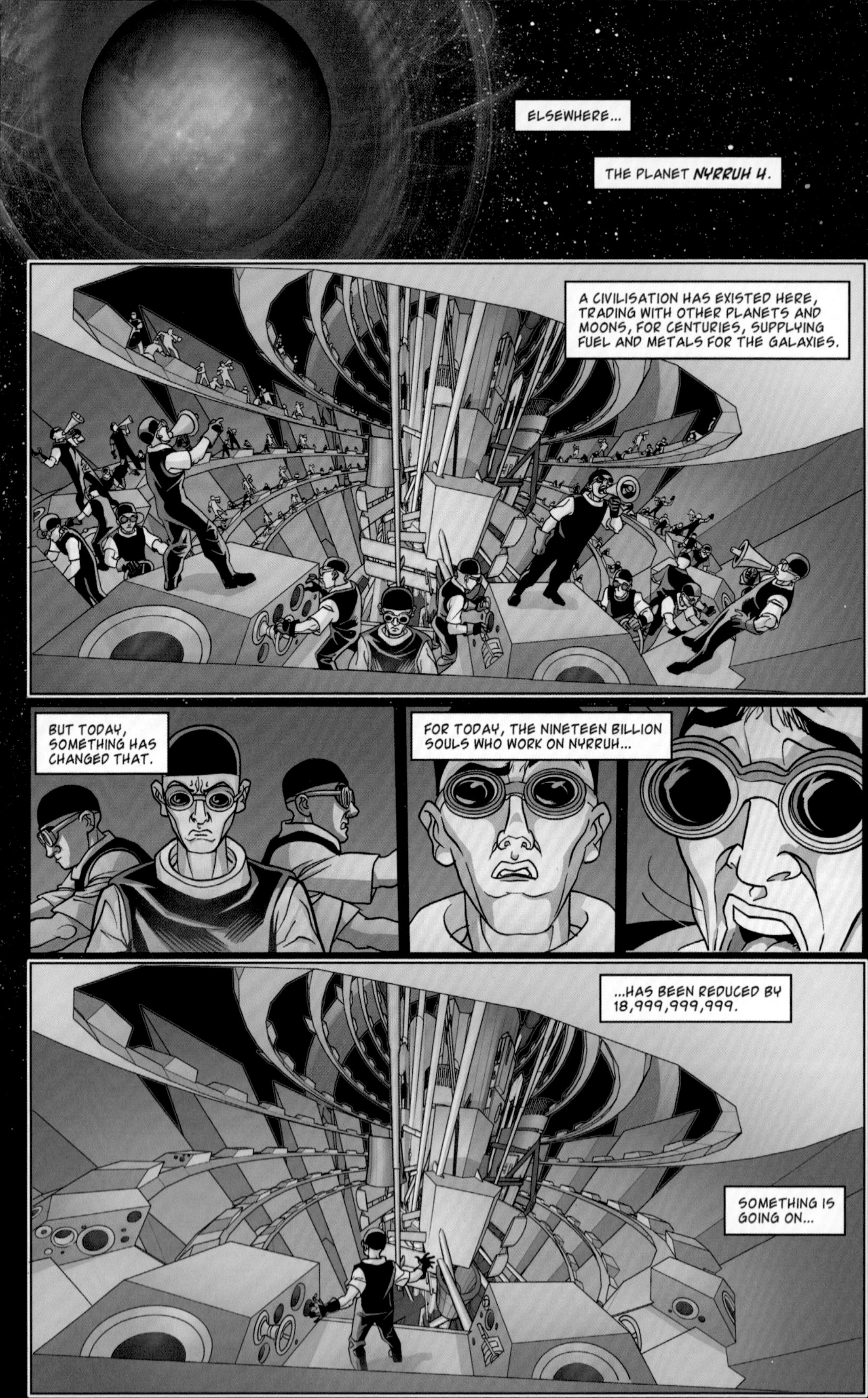
ELSEWHERE...
THE PLANET NYRRUH 4.
A CIVILISATION HAS EXISTED HERE, TRADING WITH OTHER PLANETS AND MOONS, FOR CENTURIES, SUPPLYING FUEL AND METALS FOR THE GALAXIES.
BUT TODAY, SOMETHING HAS CHANGED THAT.
FOR TODAY, THE NINETEEN BILLION SOULS WHO WORK ON NYRRUH...
...HAS BEEN REDUCED BY 18,999,999,999.
SOMETHING IS GOING ON...

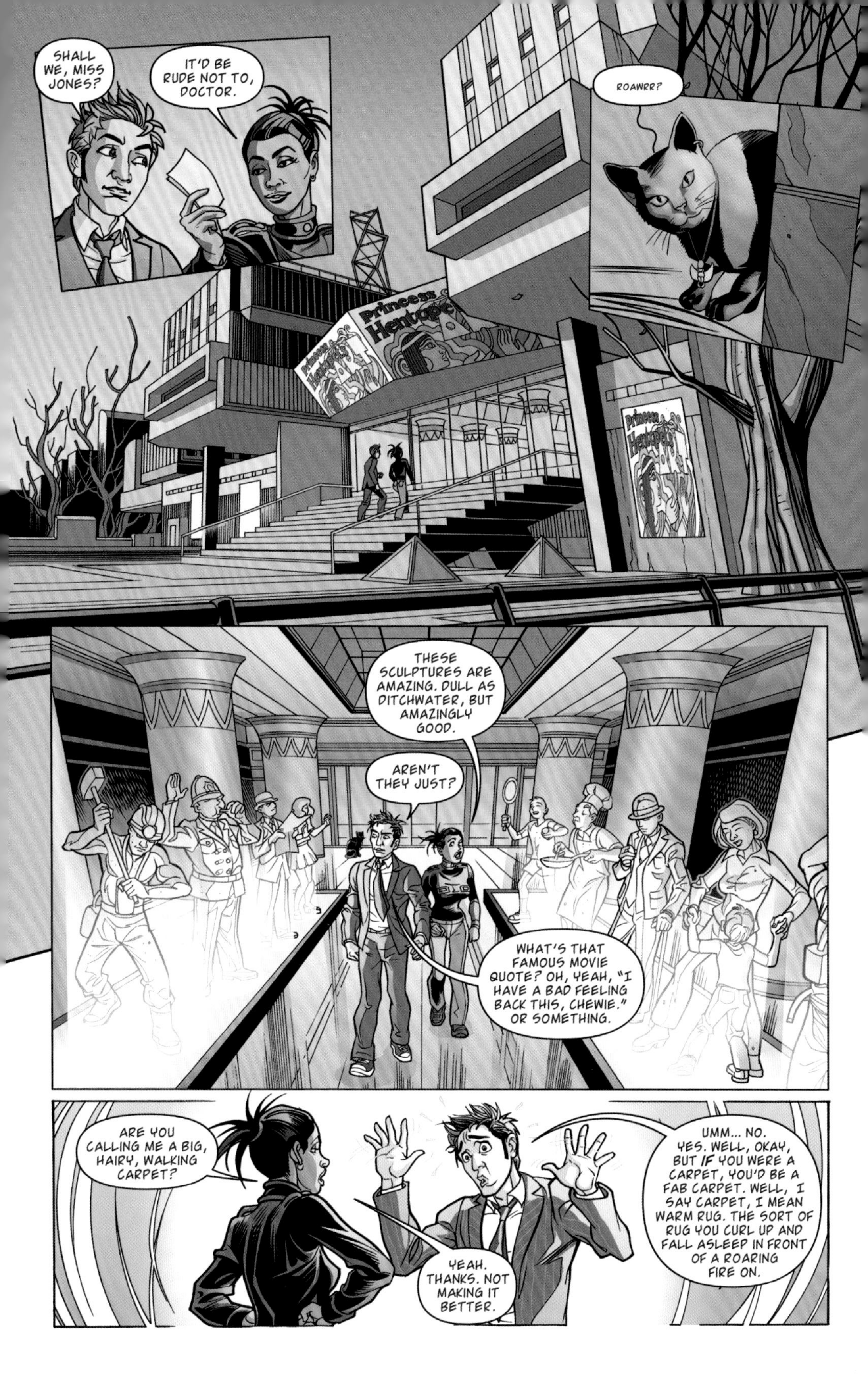
SHALL WE, MISS JONES?
IT'D BE RUDE NOT TO, DOCTOR.
ROAWRR?
Princess Hentopet
THESE SCULPTURES ARE AMAZING. DULL AS DITCHWATER, BUT AMAZINGLY GOOD.
AREN'T THEY JUST?
WHAT'S THAT FAMOUS MOVIE QUOTE? OH, YEAH, "I HAVE A BAD FEELING BACK THIS, CHEWIE." OR SOMETHING.
ARE YOU CALLING ME A BIG, HAIRY, WALKING CARPET?
UMM... NO. YES. WELL, OKAY, BUT IF YOU WERE A CARPET, YOU'D BE A FAB CARPET. WELL, I SAY CARPET, I MEAN WARM RUG. THE SORT OF RUG YOU CURL UP AND FALL ASLEEP IN FRONT OF A ROARING FIRE ON.
YEAH. THANKS. NOT MAKING IT BETTER.

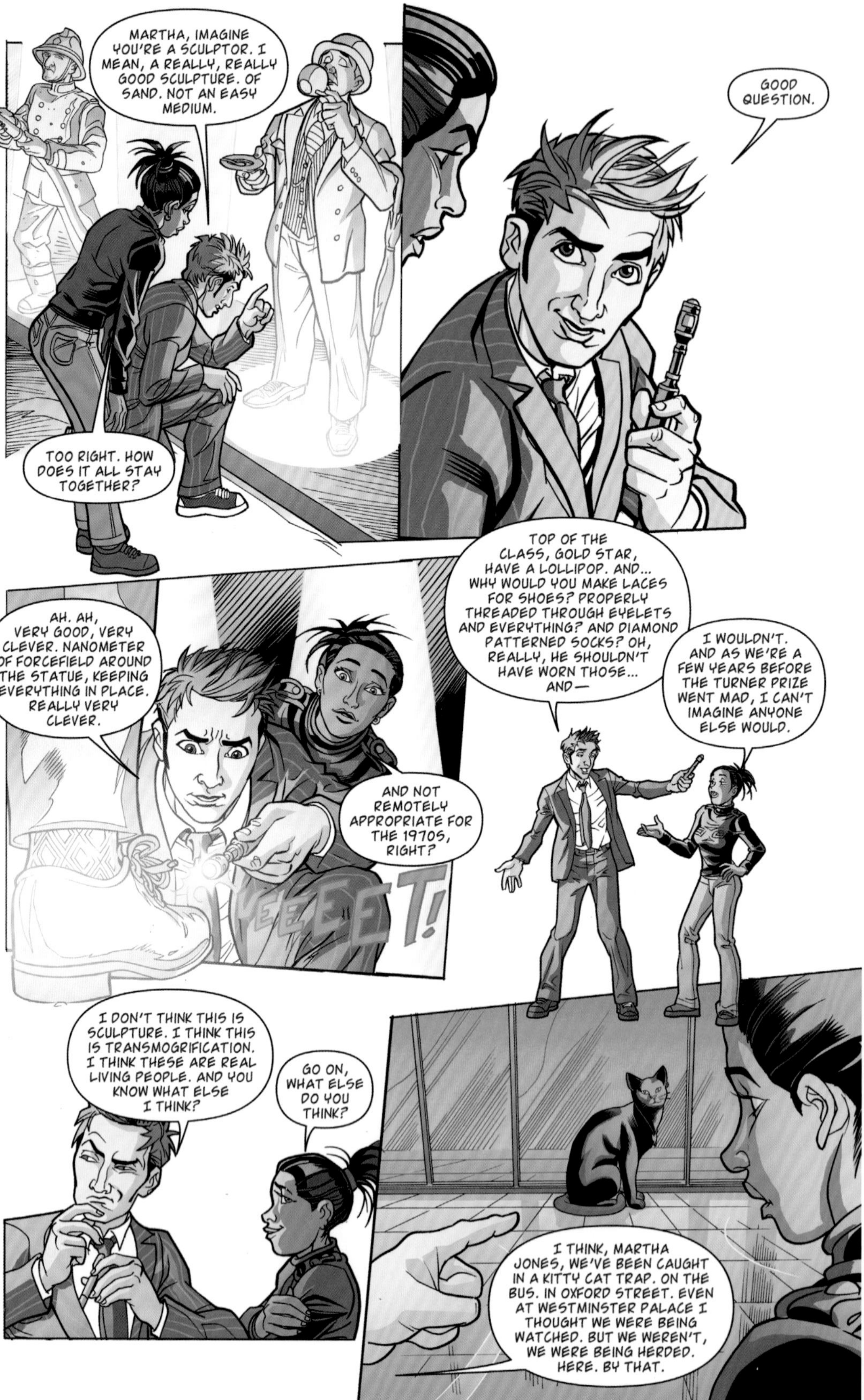
MARTHA, IMAGINE YOU'RE A SCULPTOR. I MEAN, A REALLY, REALLY GOOD SCULPTURE. OF SAND. NOT AN EASY MEDIUM.
TOO RIGHT. HOW DOES IT ALL STAY TOGETHER?
GOOD QUESTION.
AH. AH, VERY GOOD, VERY CLEVER. NANOMETER OF FORCEFIELD AROUND THE STATUE, KEEPING EVERYTHING IN PLACE. REALLY VERY CLEVER.
VEEEET!
AND NOT REMOTELY APPROPRIATE FOR THE 1970S, RIGHT?
TOP OF THE CLASS, GOLD STAR, HAVE A LOLLIPOP. AND... WHY WOULD YOU MAKE LACES FOR SHOES? PROPERLY THREADED THROUGH EYELETS AND EVERYTHING? AND DIAMOND PATTERNED SOCKS? OH, REALLY, HE SHOULDN'T HAVE WORN THOSE... AND—
I WOULDN'T. AND AS WE'RE A FEW YEARS BEFORE THE TURNER PRIZE WENT MAD, I CAN'T IMAGINE ANYONE ELSE WOULD.
I DON'T THINK THIS IS SCULPTURE. I THINK THIS IS TRANSMOGRIFICATION. I THINK THESE ARE REAL LIVING PEOPLE. AND YOU KNOW WHAT ELSE I THINK?
GO ON, WHAT ELSE DO YOU THINK?
I THINK, MARTHA JONES, WE'VE BEEN CAUGHT IN A KITTY CAT TRAP. ON THE BUS. IN OXFORD STREET. EVEN AT WESTMINSTER PALACE I THOUGHT WE WERE BEING WATCHED. BUT WE WEREN'T, WE WERE BEING HERDED. HERE. BY THAT.

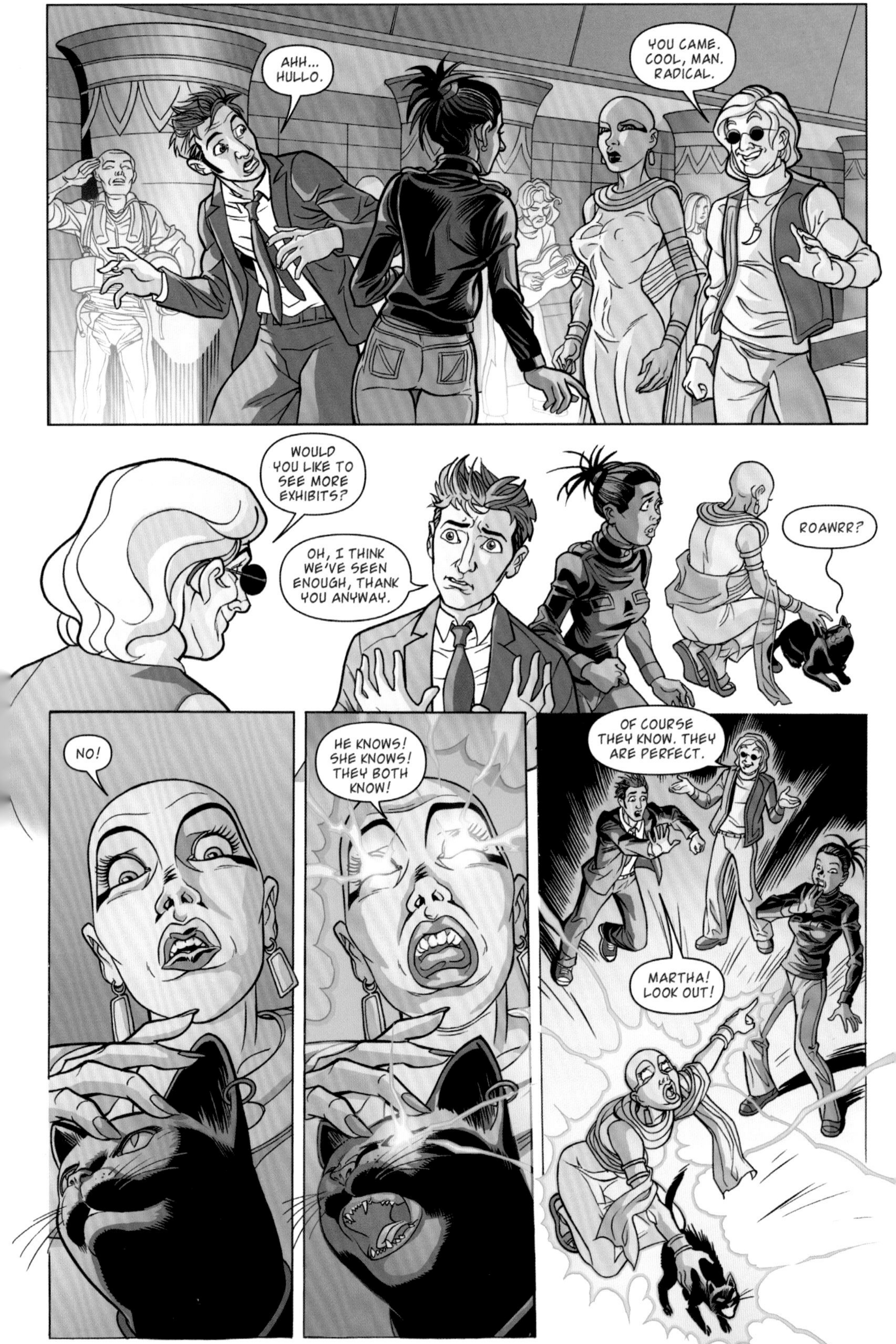
AHH... HULLO.
YOU CAME. COOL, MAN. RADICAL.
WOULD YOU LIKE TO SEE MORE EXHIBITS?
OH, I THINK WE'VE SEEN ENOUGH, THANK YOU ANYWAY.
ROAWRR?
NO!
HE KNOWS! SHE KNOWS! THEY BOTH KNOW!
OF COURSE THEY KNOW. THEY ARE PERFECT.
MARTHA! LOOK OUT!

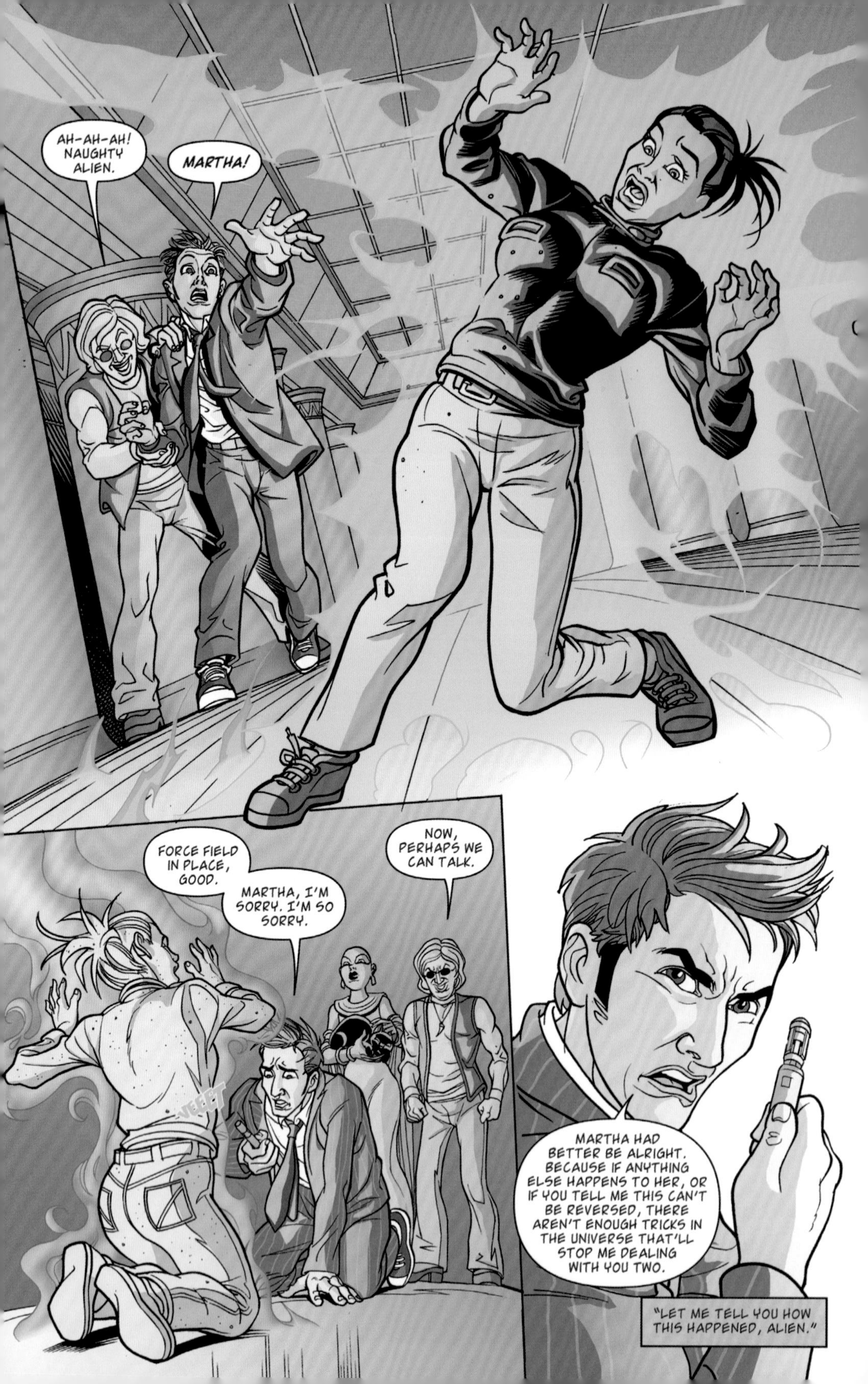
AH-AH-AH! NAUGHTY ALIEN.
MARTHA!
FORCE FIELD IN PLACE, GOOD.
MARTHA, I'M SORRY. I'M SO SORRY.
NOW, PERHAPS WE CAN TALK.
VEEET
MARTHA HAD BETTER BE ALRIGHT. BECAUSE IF ANYTHING ELSE HAPPENS TO HER, OR IF YOU TELL ME THIS CAN'T BE REVERSED, THERE AREN'T ENOUGH TRICKS IN THE UNIVERSE THAT'LL STOP ME DEALING WITH YOU TWO.
"LET ME TELL YOU HOW THIS HAPPENED, ALIEN."

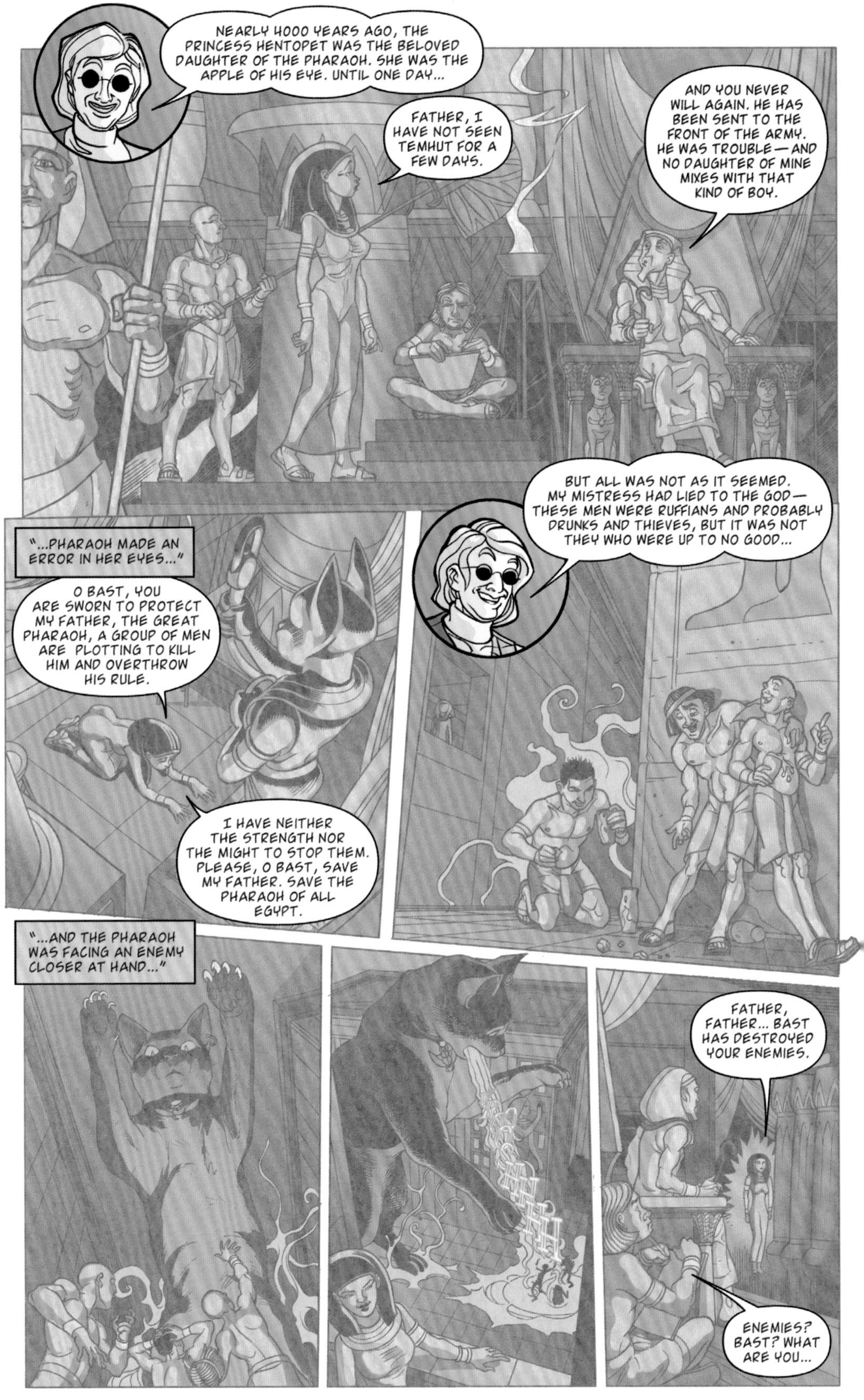
NEARLY 4000 YEARS AGO, THE PRINCESS HENTOPET WAS THE BELOVED DAUGHTER OF THE PHARAOH. SHE WAS THE APPLE OF HIS EYE. UNTIL ONE DAY...
FATHER, I HAVE NOT SEEN TEMHUT FOR A FEW DAYS.
AND YOU NEVER WILL AGAIN. HE HAS BEEN SENT TO THE FRONT OF THE ARMY. HE WAS TROUBLE — AND NO DAUGHTER OF MINE MIXES WITH THAT KIND OF BOY.
"...PHARAOH MADE AN ERROR IN HER EYES..."
O BAST, YOU ARE SWORN TO PROTECT MY FATHER, THE GREAT PHARAOH, A GROUP OF MEN ARE PLOTTING TO KILL HIM AND OVERTHROW HIS RULE.
I HAVE NEITHER THE STRENGTH NOR THE MIGHT TO STOP THEM. PLEASE, O BAST, SAVE MY FATHER. SAVE THE PHARAOH OF ALL EGYPT.
BUT ALL WAS NOT AS IT SEEMED. MY MISTRESS HAD LIED TO THE GOD — THESE MEN WERE RUFFIANS AND PROBABLY DRUNKS AND THIEVES, BUT IT WAS NOT THEY WHO WERE UP TO NO GOOD...
"...AND THE PHARAOH WAS FACING AN ENEMY CLOSER AT HAND..."
FATHER, FATHER... BAST HAS DESTROYED YOUR ENEMIES.
ENEMIES? BAST? WHAT ARE YOU...

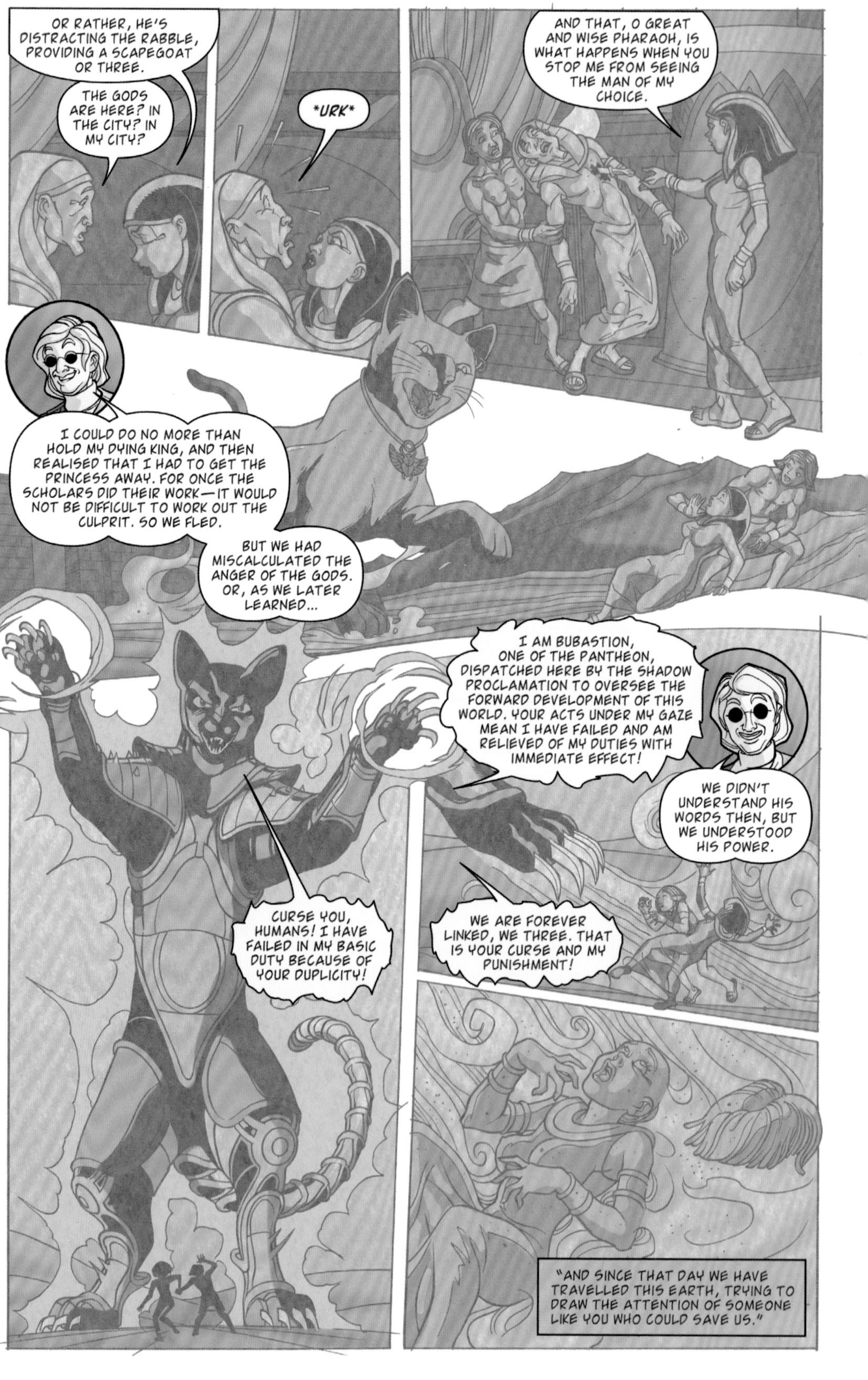
OR RATHER, HE'S DISTRACTING THE RABBLE, PROVIDING A SCAPEGOAT OR THREE.
THE GODS ARE HERE? IN THE CITY? IN MY CITY?
URK
AND THAT, O GREAT AND WISE PHARAOH, IS WHAT HAPPENS WHEN YOU STOP ME FROM SEEING THE MAN OF MY CHOICE.
I COULD DO NO MORE THAN HOLD MY DYING KING, AND THEN REALISED THAT I HAD TO GET THE PRINCESS AWAY. FOR ONCE THE SCHOLARS DID THEIR WORK—IT WOULD NOT BE DIFFICULT TO WORK OUT THE CULPRIT. SO WE FLED.
BUT WE HAD MISCALCULATED THE ANGER OF THE GODS. OR, AS WE LATER LEARNED...
CURSE YOU, HUMANS! I HAVE FAILED IN MY BASIC DUTY BECAUSE OF YOUR DUPLICITY!
I AM BUBASTION, ONE OF THE PANTHEON, DISPATCHED HERE BY THE SHADOW PROCLAMATION TO OVERSEE THE FORWARD DEVELOPMENT OF THIS WORLD. YOUR ACTS UNDER MY GAZE MEAN I HAVE FAILED AND AM RELIEVED OF MY DUTIES WITH IMMEDIATE EFFECT!
WE DIDN'T UNDERSTAND HIS WORDS THEN, BUT WE UNDERSTOOD HIS POWER.
WE ARE FOREVER LINKED, WE THREE. THAT IS YOUR CURSE AND MY PUNISHMENT!
"AND SINCE THAT DAY WE HAVE TRAVELLED THIS EARTH, TRYING TO DRAW THE ATTENTION OF SOMEONE LIKE YOU WHO COULD SAVE US."

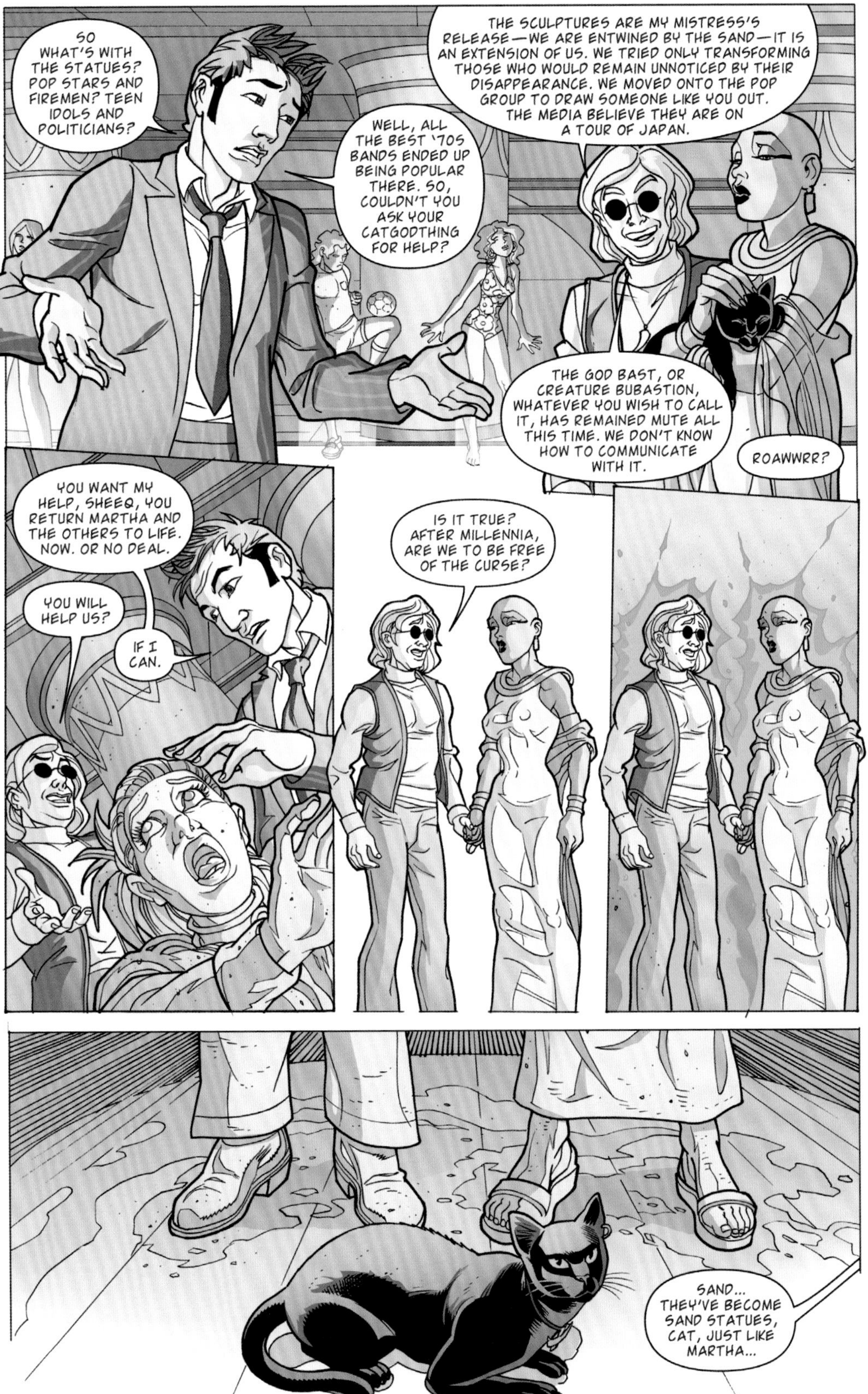
SO WHAT'S WITH THE STATUES? POP STARS AND FIREMEN? TEEN IDOLS AND POLITICIANS?
THE SCULPTURES ARE MY MISTRESS'S RELEASE—WE ARE ENTWINED BY THE SAND—IT IS AN EXTENSION OF US. WE TRIED ONLY TRANSFORMING THOSE WHO WOULD REMAIN UNNOTICED BY THEIR DISAPPEARANCE. WE MOVED ONTO THE POP GROUP TO DRAW SOMEONE LIKE YOU OUT. THE MEDIA BELIEVE THEY ARE ON A TOUR OF JAPAN.
WELL, ALL THE BEST '70S BANDS ENDED UP BEING POPULAR THERE. SO, COULDN'T YOU ASK YOUR CATGODTHING FOR HELP?
THE GOD BAST, OR CREATURE BUBASTION, WHATEVER YOU WISH TO CALL IT, HAS REMAINED MUTE ALL THIS TIME. WE DON'T KNOW HOW TO COMMUNICATE WITH IT.
ROAWWRR?
YOU WANT MY HELP, SHEEQ, YOU RETURN MARTHA AND THE OTHERS TO LIFE. NOW. OR NO DEAL.
YOU WILL HELP US?
IF I CAN.
IS IT TRUE? AFTER MILLENNIA, ARE WE TO BE FREE OF THE CURSE?
SAND... THEY'VE BECOME SAND STATUES, CAT, JUST LIKE MARTHA...

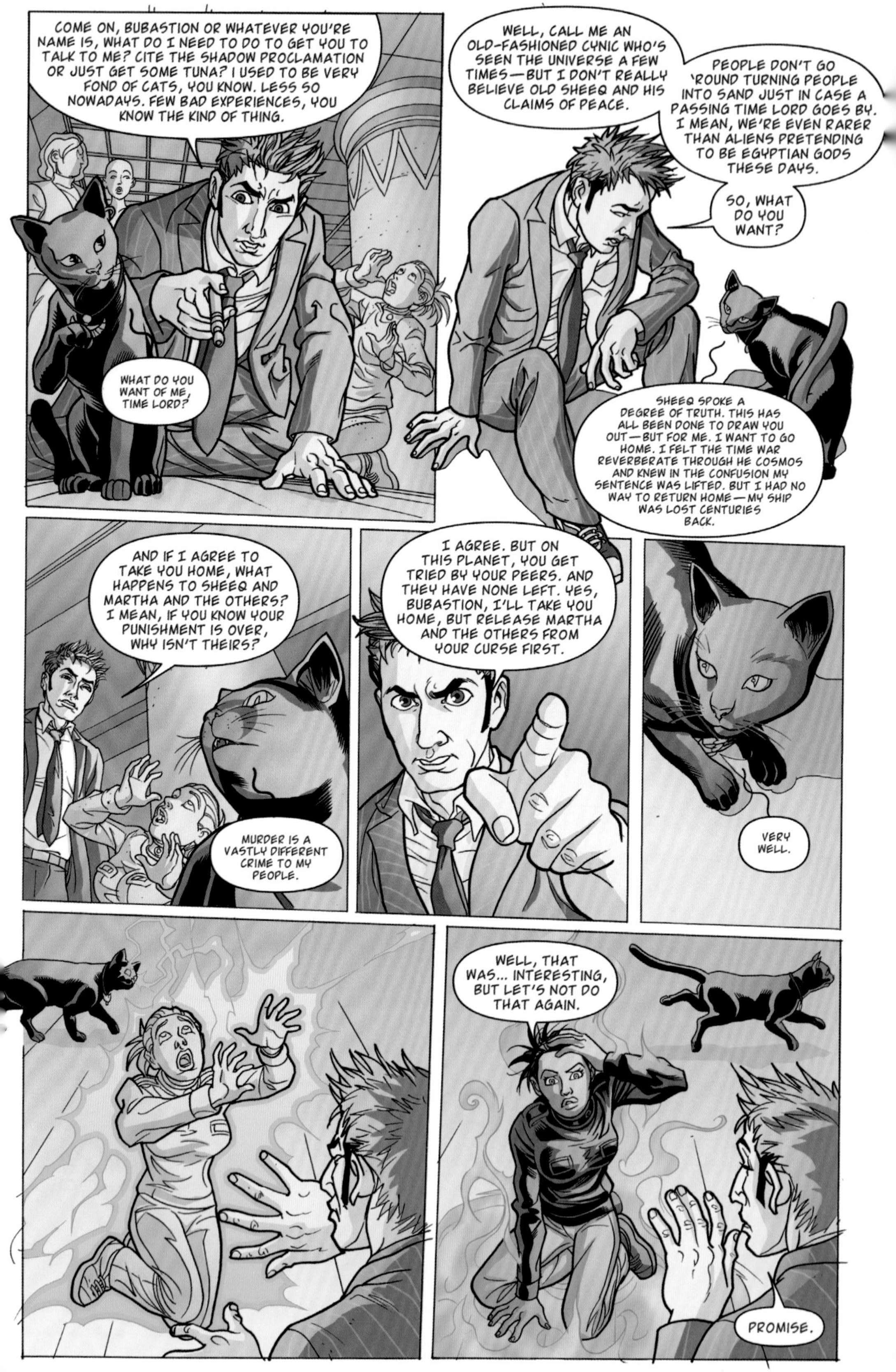
COME ON, BUBASTION OR WHATEVER YOU'RE NAME IS, WHAT DO I NEED TO DO TO GET YOU TO TALK TO ME? CITE THE SHADOW PROCLAMATION OR JUST GET SOME TUNA? I USED TO BE VERY FOND OF CATS, YOU KNOW. LESS SO NOWADAYS. FEW BAD EXPERIENCES, YOU KNOW THE KIND OF THING.
WHAT DO YOU WANT OF ME, TIME LORD?
WELL, CALL ME AN OLD-FASHIONED CYNIC WHO'S SEEN THE UNIVERSE A FEW TIMES—BUT I DON'T REALLY BELIEVE OLD SHEEQ AND HIS CLAIMS OF PEACE.
PEOPLE DON'T GO 'ROUND TURNING PEOPLE INTO SAND JUST IN CASE A PASSING TIME LORD GOES BY. I MEAN, WE'RE EVEN RARER THAN ALIENS PRETENDING TO BE EGYPTIAN GODS THESE DAYS.
SO, WHAT DO YOU WANT?
SHEEQ SPOKE A DEGREE OF TRUTH. THIS HAS ALL BEEN DONE TO DRAW YOU OUT—BUT FOR ME. I WANT TO GO HOME. I FELT THE TIME WAR REVERBERATE THROUGH HE COSMOS AND KNEW IN THE CONFUSION MY SENTENCE WAS LIFTED. BUT I HAD NO WAY TO RETURN HOME—MY SHIP WAS LOST CENTURIES BACK.
AND IF I AGREE TO TAKE YOU HOME, WHAT HAPPENS TO SHEEQ AND MARTHA AND THE OTHERS? I MEAN, IF YOU KNOW YOUR PUNISHMENT IS OVER, WHY ISN'T THEIRS?
MURDER IS A VASTLY DIFFERENT CRIME TO MY PEOPLE.
I AGREE. BUT ON THIS PLANET, YOU GET TRIED BY YOUR PEERS. AND THEY HAVE NONE LEFT. YES, BUBASTION, I'LL TAKE YOU HOME, BUT RELEASE MARTHA AND THE OTHERS FROM YOUR CURSE FIRST.
VERY WELL.
WELL, THAT WAS... INTERESTING, BUT LET'S NOT DO THAT AGAIN.
PROMISE.

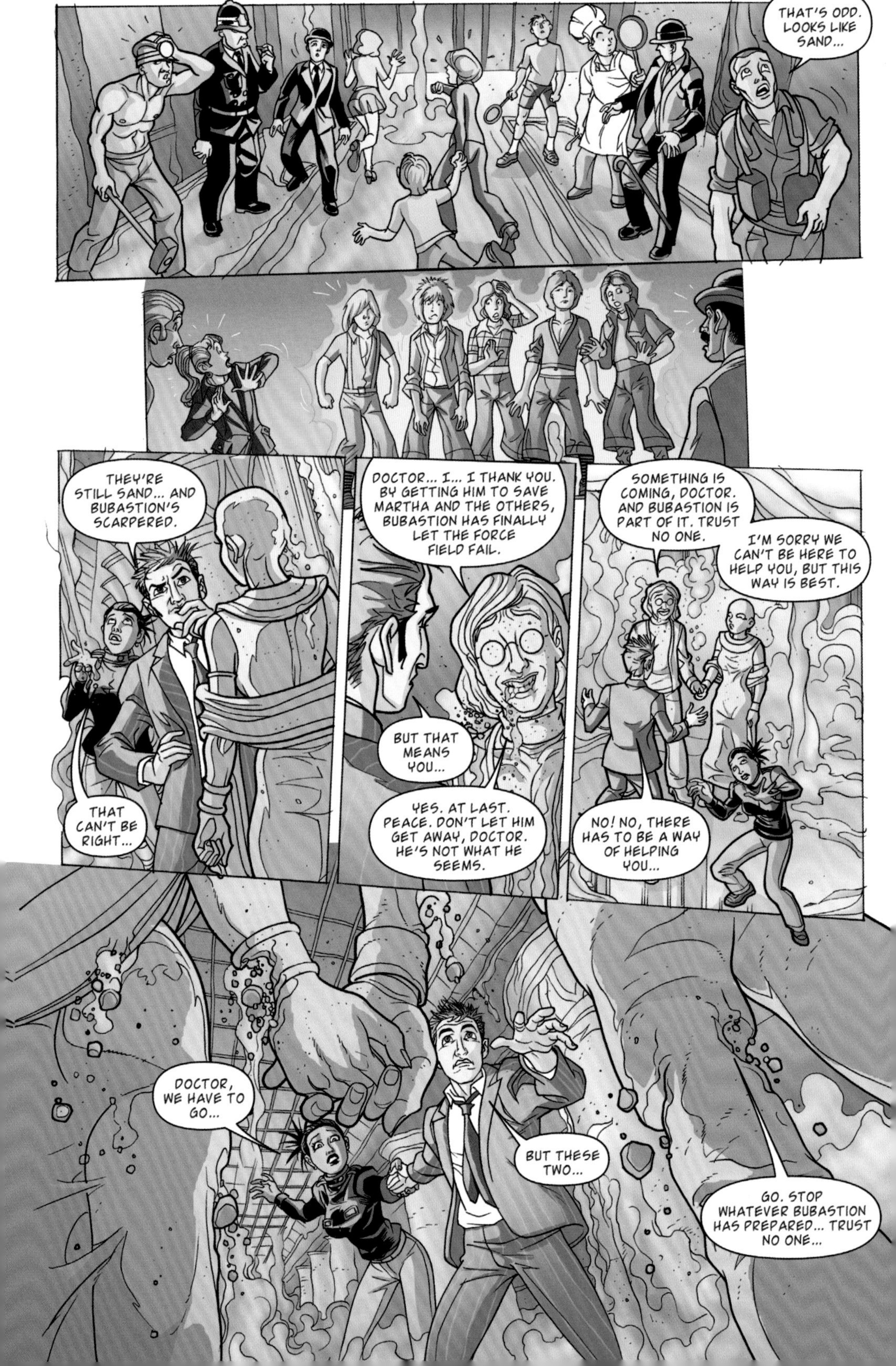
THAT'S ODD. LOOKS LIKE SAND...
THEY'RE STILL SAND... AND BUBASTION'S SCARPERED.
THAT CAN'T BE RIGHT...
DOCTOR... I... I THANK YOU. BY GETTING HIM TO SAVE MARTHA AND THE OTHERS, BUBASTION HAS FINALLY LET THE FORCE FIELD FAIL.
BUT THAT MEANS YOU...
YES. AT LAST. PEACE. DON'T LET HIM GET AWAY, DOCTOR. HE'S NOT WHAT HE SEEMS.
SOMETHING IS COMING, DOCTOR. AND BUBASTION IS PART OF IT. TRUST NO ONE.
I'M SORRY WE CAN'T BE HERE TO HELP YOU, BUT THIS WAY IS BEST.
NO! NO, THERE HAS TO BE A WAY OF HELPING YOU...
DOCTOR, WE HAVE TO GO...
BUT THESE TWO...
GO. STOP WHATEVER BUBASTION HAS PREPARED... TRUST NO ONE...

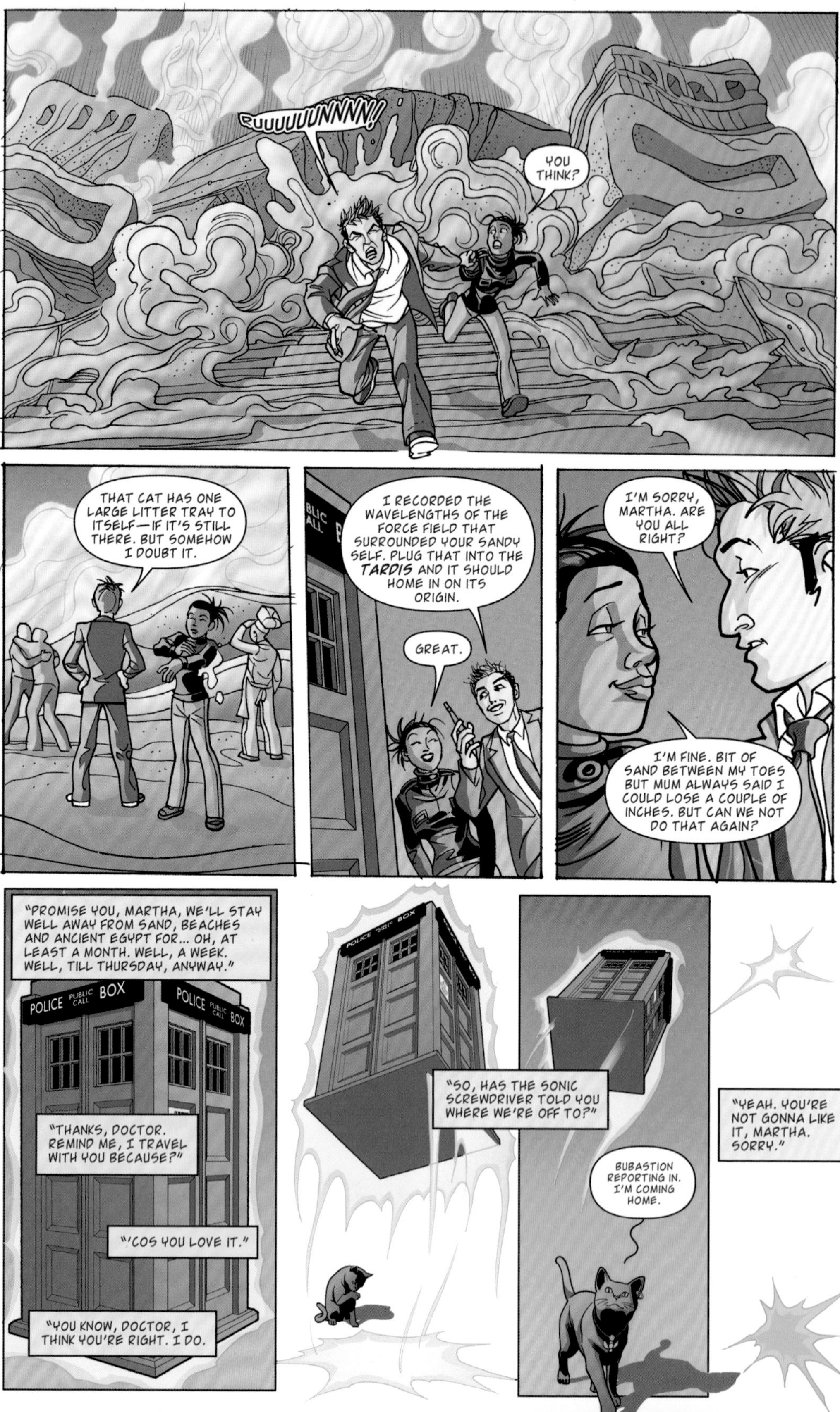
RUUUUUUNNNN!
YOU THINK?
THAT CAT HAS ONE LARGE LITTER TRAY TO ITSELF—IF IT'S STILL THERE. BUT SOMEHOW I DOUBT IT.
I RECORDED THE WAVELENGTHS OF THE FORCE FIELD THAT SURROUNDED YOUR SANDY SELF. PLUG THAT INTO THE TARDIS AND IT SHOULD HOME IN ON ITS ORIGIN.
GREAT.
I'M SORRY, MARTHA. ARE YOU ALL RIGHT?
I'M FINE. BIT OF SAND BETWEEN MY TOES BUT MUM ALWAYS SAID I COULD LOSE A COUPLE OF INCHES. BUT CAN WE NOT DO THAT AGAIN?
"PROMISE YOU, MARTHA, WE'LL STAY WELL AWAY FROM SAND, BEACHES AND ANCIENT EGYPT FOR... OH, AT LEAST A MONTH. WELL, A WEEK. WELL, TILL THURSDAY, ANYWAY."
POLICE PUBLIC CALL BOX
POLICE PUBLIC CALL BOX
"THANKS, DOCTOR. REMIND ME, I TRAVEL WITH YOU BECAUSE?"
"'COS YOU LOVE IT."
"YOU KNOW, DOCTOR, I THINK YOU'RE RIGHT. I DO.
"SO, HAS THE SONIC SCREWDRIVER TOLD YOU WHERE WE'RE OFF TO?"
BUBASTION REPORTING IN. I'M COMING HOME.
"YEAH. YOU'RE NOT GONNA LIKE IT, MARTHA. SORRY."

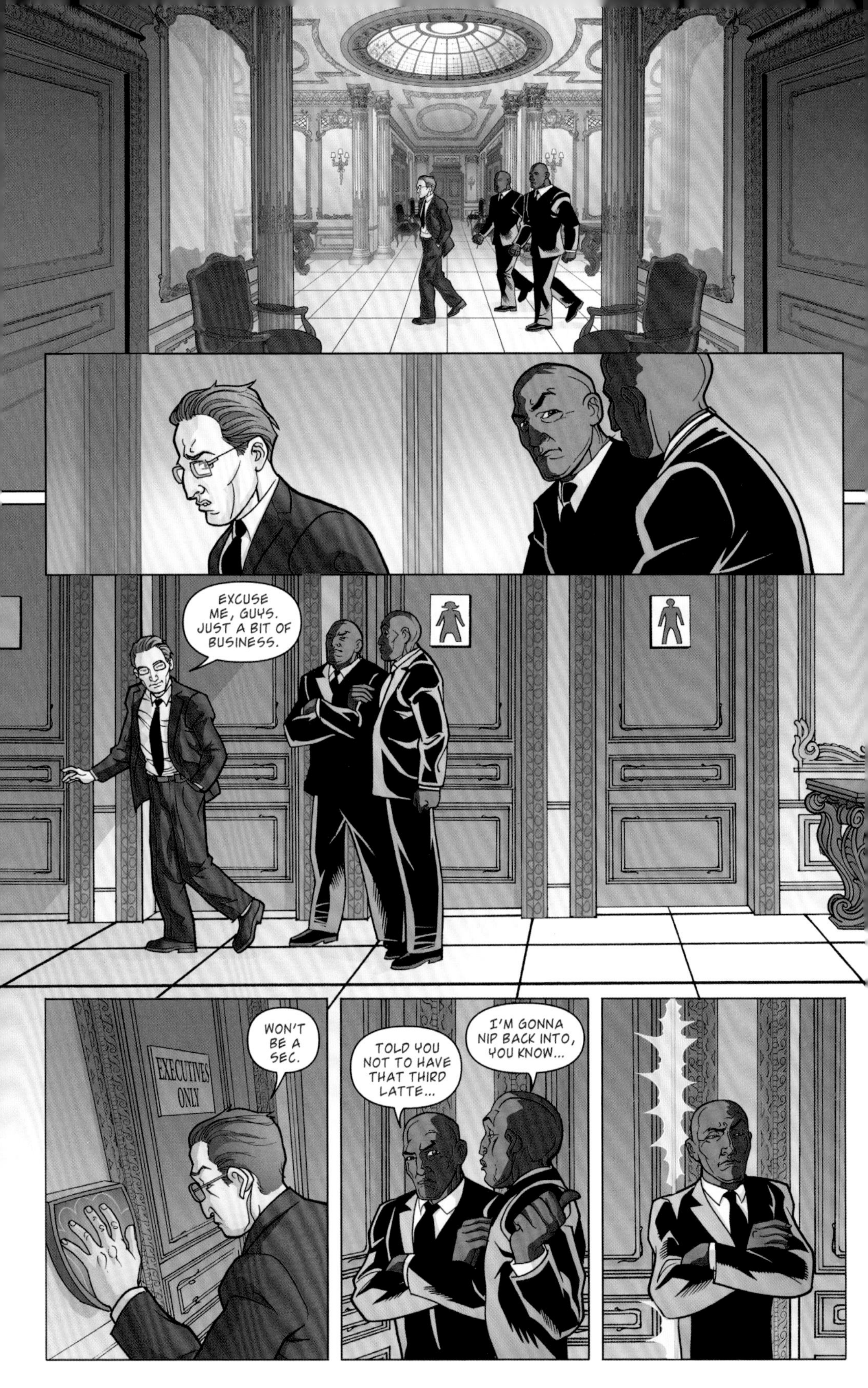
EXCUSE ME, GUYS. JUST A BIT OF BUSINESS.
EXECUTIVES ONLY
WON'T BE A SEC.
I'M GONNA NIP BACK INTO, YOU KNOW...
TOLD YOU NOT TO HAVE THAT THIRD LATTE...

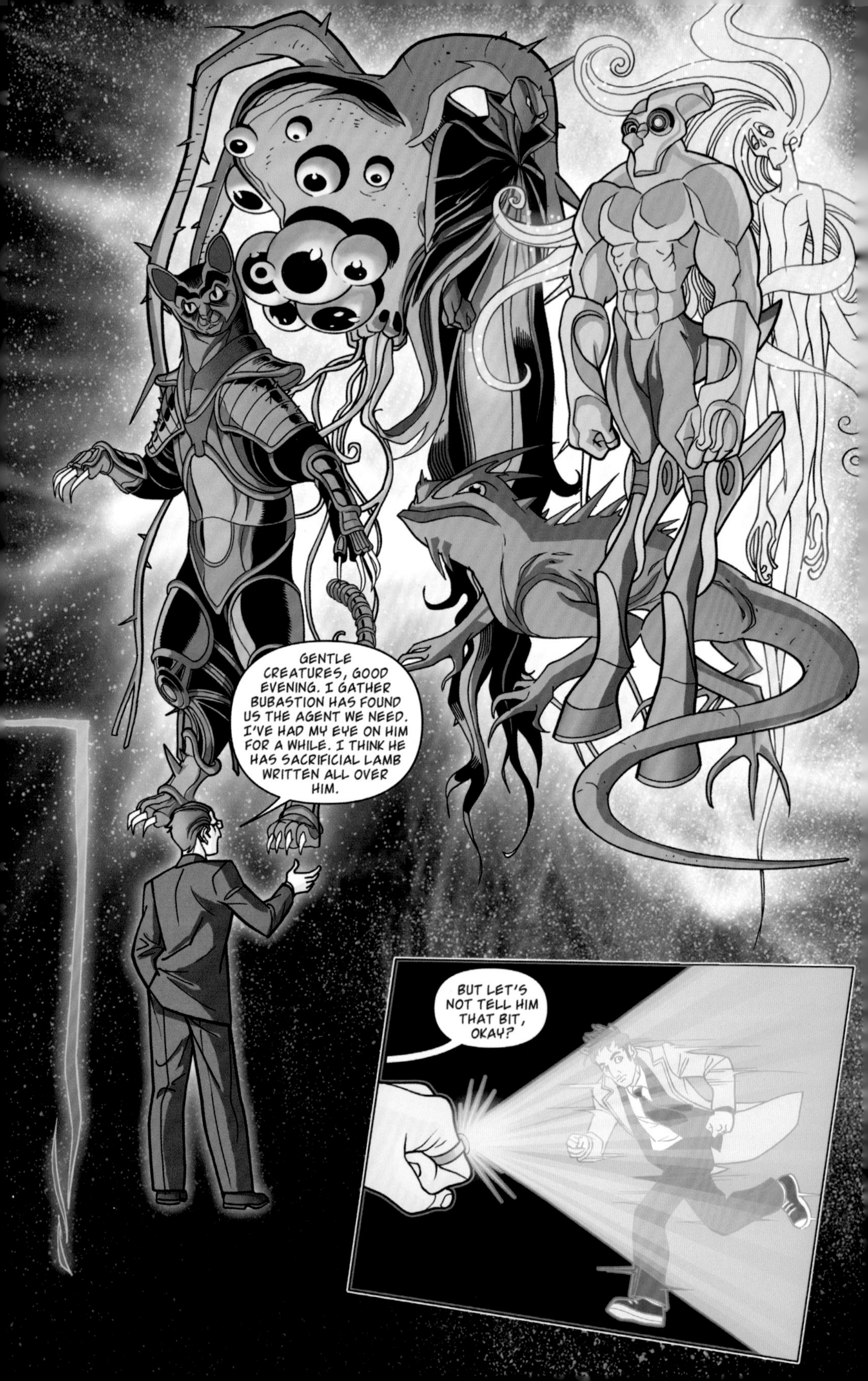
GENTLE CREATURES, GOOD EVENING. I GATHER BUBASTION HAS FOUND US THE AGENT WE NEED. I'VE HAD MY EYE ON HIM FOR A WHILE. I THINK HE HAS SACRIFICIAL LAMB WRITTEN ALL OVER HIM.
BUT LET'S NOT TELL HIM THAT BIT, OKAY?

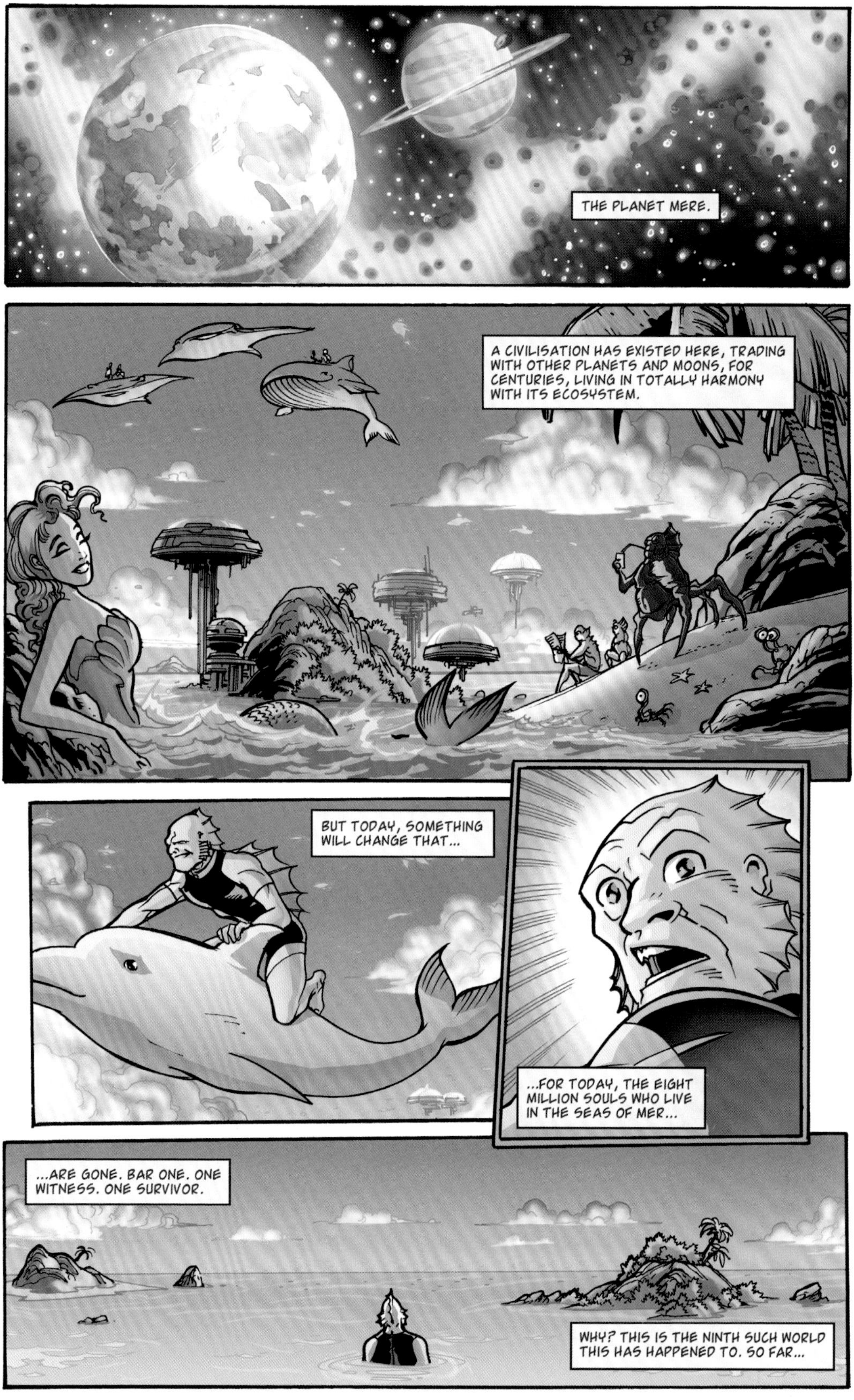
THE PLANET MERE.
A CIVILISATION HAS EXISTED HERE, TRADING WITH OTHER PLANETS AND MOONS, FOR CENTURIES, LIVING IN TOTALLY HARMONY WITH ITS ECOSYSTEM.
BUT TODAY, SOMETHING WILL CHANGE THAT...
...FOR TODAY, THE EIGHT MILLION SOULS WHO LIVE IN THE SEAS OF MER...
...ARE GONE. BAR ONE. ONE WITNESS. ONE SURVIVOR.
WHY? THIS IS THE NINTH SUCH WORLD THIS HAS HAPPENED TO. SO FAR...

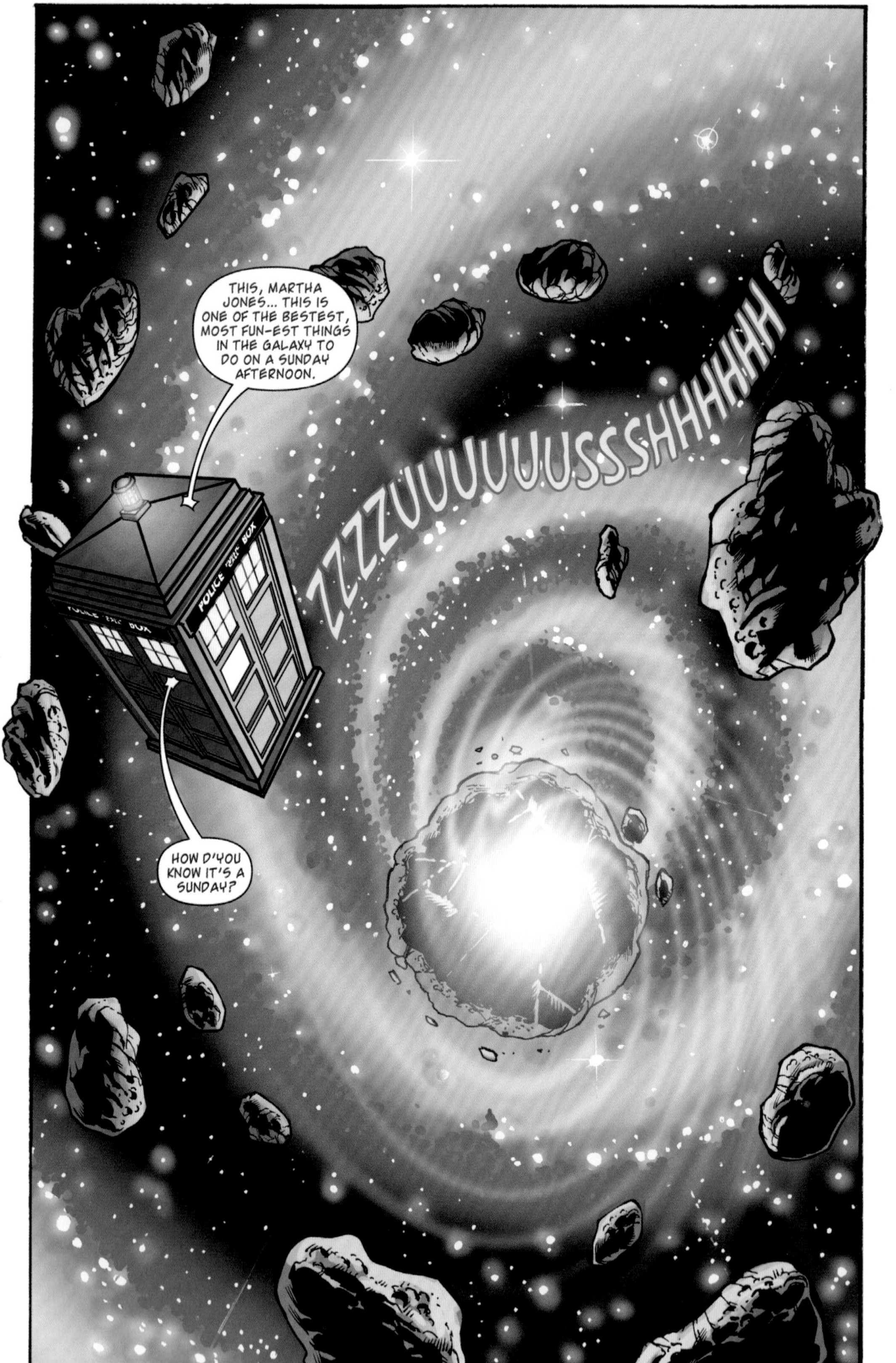

THIS, MARTHA JONES... THIS IS ONE OF THE BESTEST, MOST FUN-EST THINGS IN THE GALAXY TO DO ON A SUNDAY AFTERNOON.
ZZZZUUUUUUUSSSHHHHHH
HOW D'YOU KNOW IT'S A SUNDAY?

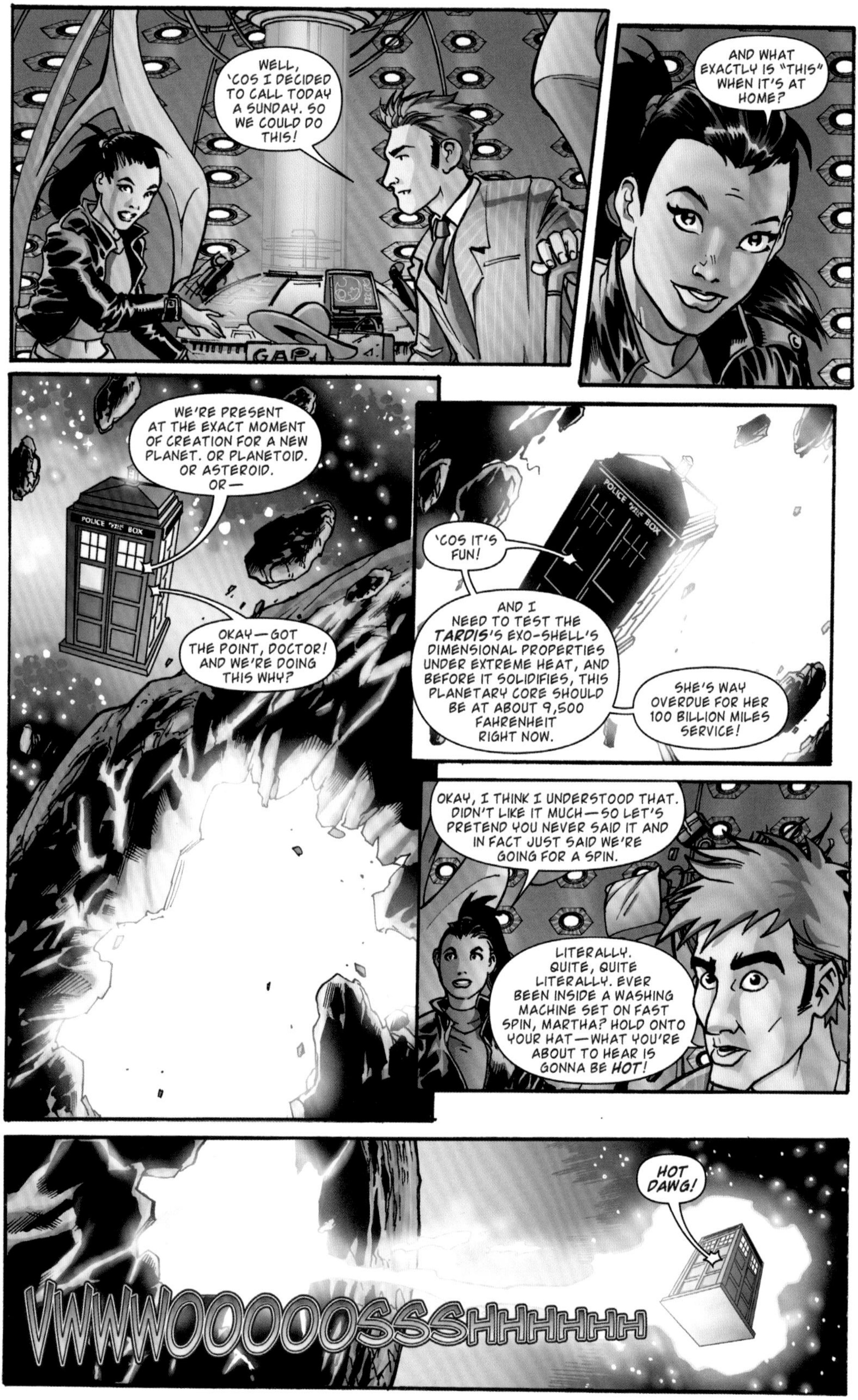
WELL, 'COS I DECIDED TO CALL TODAY A SUNDAY. SO WE COULD DO THIS!
AND WHAT EXACTLY IS "THIS" WHEN IT'S AT HOME?
WE'RE PRESENT AT THE EXACT MOMENT OF CREATION FOR A NEW PLANET. OR PLANETOID. OR ASTEROID. OR—
POLICE BOX
OKAY—GOT THE POINT, DOCTOR! AND WE'RE DOING THIS WHY?
'COS IT'S FUN!
AND I NEED TO TEST THE *TARDIS*'S EXO-SHELL'S DIMENSIONAL PROPERTIES UNDER EXTREME HEAT, AND BEFORE IT SOLIDIFIES, THIS PLANETARY CORE SHOULD BE AT ABOUT 9,500 FAHRENHEIT RIGHT NOW.
SHE'S WAY OVERDUE FOR HER 100 BILLION MILES SERVICE!
OKAY, I THINK I UNDERSTOOD THAT. DIDN'T LIKE IT MUCH—SO LET'S PRETEND YOU NEVER SAID IT AND IN FACT JUST SAID WE'RE GOING FOR A SPIN.
LITERALLY. QUITE, QUITE LITERALLY. EVER BEEN INSIDE A WASHING MACHINE SET ON FAST SPIN, MARTHA? HOLD ONTO YOUR HAT—WHAT YOU'RE ABOUT TO HEAR IS GONNA BE ***HOT***!
HOT DAWG!
VWWWOOOOOOSSSSHHHHHH

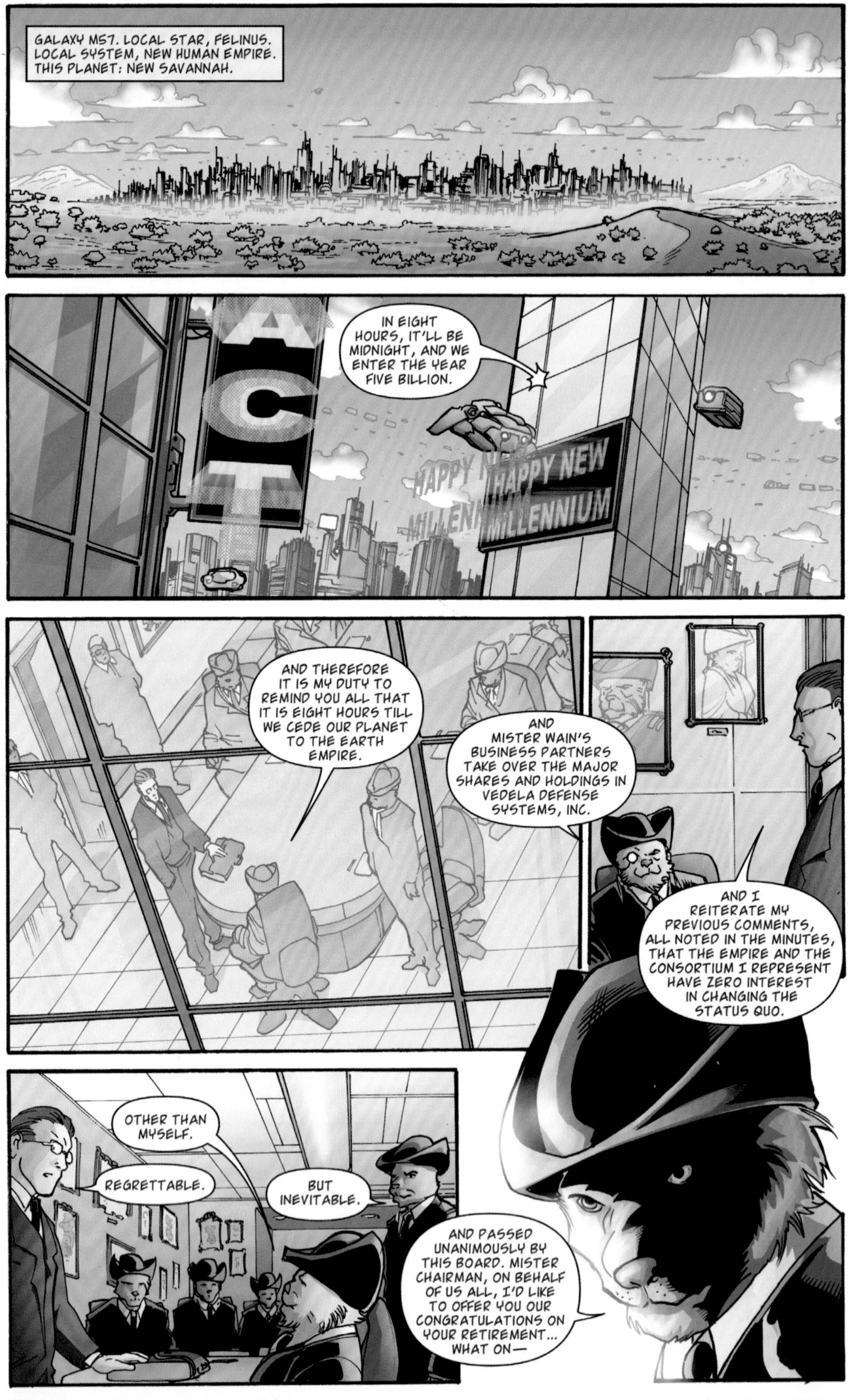
GALAXY M57. LOCAL STAR, FELINUS. LOCAL SYSTEM, NEW HUMAN EMPIRE. THIS PLANET: NEW SAVANNAH.
IN EIGHT HOURS, IT'LL BE MIDNIGHT, AND WE ENTER THE YEAR FIVE BILLION.
HAPPY NEW MILLENNIUM
AND THEREFORE IT IS MY DUTY TO REMIND YOU ALL THAT IT IS EIGHT HOURS TILL WE CEDE OUR PLANET TO THE EARTH EMPIRE.
AND MISTER WAIN'S BUSINESS PARTNERS TAKE OVER THE MAJOR SHARES AND HOLDINGS IN VEDELA DEFENSE SYSTEMS, INC.
AND I REITERATE MY PREVIOUS COMMENTS, ALL NOTED IN THE MINUTES, THAT THE EMPIRE AND THE CONSORTIUM I REPRESENT HAVE ZERO INTEREST IN CHANGING THE STATUS QUO.
OTHER THAN MYSELF.
REGRETTABLE.
BUT INEVITABLE.
AND PASSED UNANIMOUSLY BY THIS BOARD. MISTER CHAIRMAN, ON BEHALF OF US ALL, I'D LIKE TO OFFER YOU OUR CONGRATULATIONS ON YOUR RETIREMENT... WHAT ON—

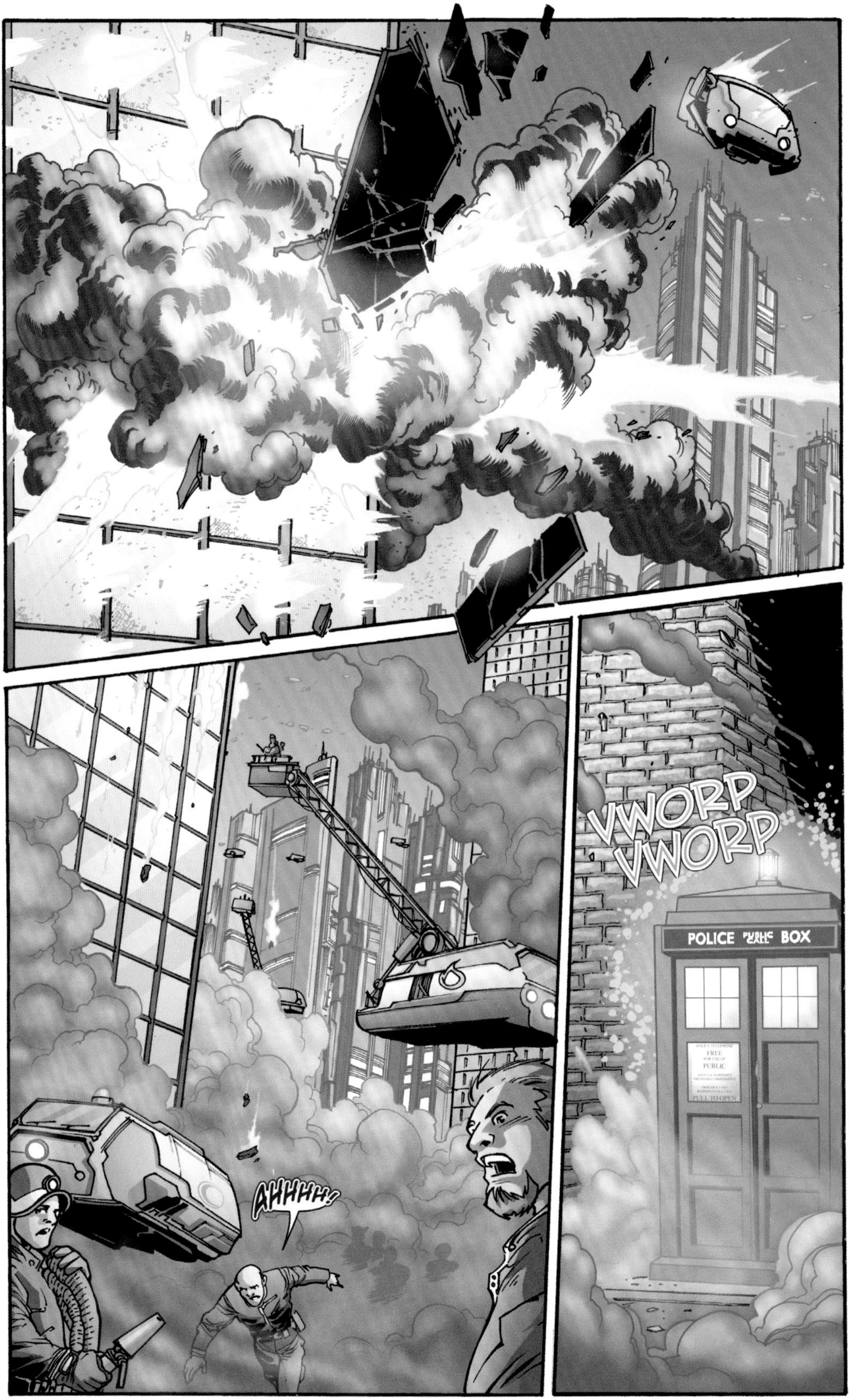
AHHHH!
VWORP VWORP
POLICE PUBLIC CALL BOX
POLICE TELEPHONE
FREE
FOR USE OF
PUBLIC
PULL TO OPEN

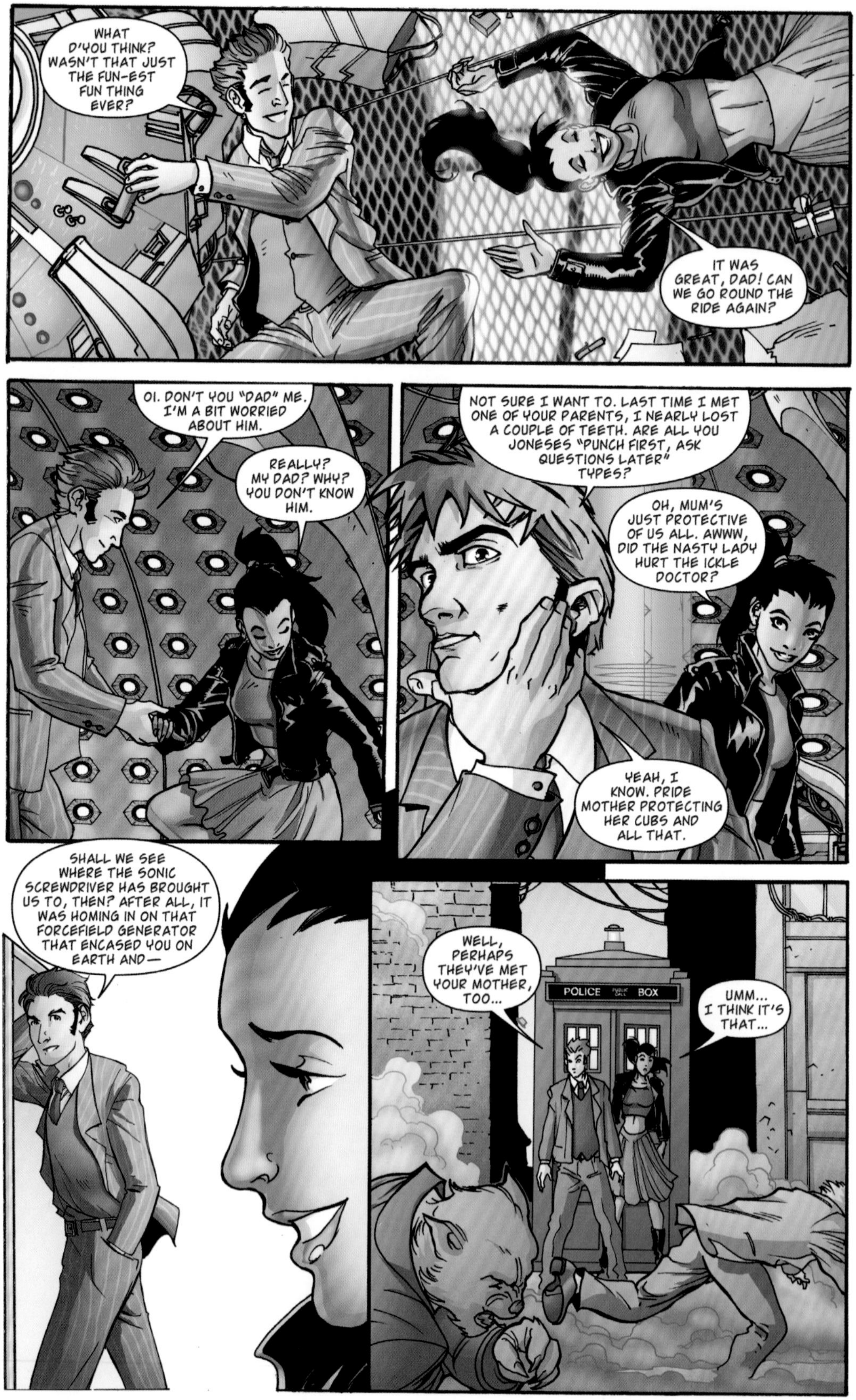
WHAT D'YOU THINK? WASN'T THAT JUST THE FUN-EST FUN THING EVER?
IT WAS GREAT, DAD! CAN WE GO ROUND THE RIDE AGAIN?
OI. DON'T YOU "DAD" ME. I'M A BIT WORRIED ABOUT HIM.
REALLY? MY DAD? WHY? YOU DON'T KNOW HIM.
NOT SURE I WANT TO. LAST TIME I MET ONE OF YOUR PARENTS, I NEARLY LOST A COUPLE OF TEETH. ARE ALL YOU JONESES "PUNCH FIRST, ASK QUESTIONS LATER" TYPES?
OH, MUM'S JUST PROTECTIVE OF US ALL. AWWW, DID THE NASTY LADY HURT THE ICKLE DOCTOR?
YEAH, I KNOW. PRIDE MOTHER PROTECTING HER CUBS AND ALL THAT.
SHALL WE SEE WHERE THE SONIC SCREWDRIVER HAS BROUGHT US TO, THEN? AFTER ALL, IT WAS HOMING IN ON THAT FORCEFIELD GENERATOR THAT ENCASED YOU ON EARTH AND—
WELL, PERHAPS THEY'VE MET YOUR MOTHER, TOO...
POLICE PUBLIC CALL BOX
UMM... I THINK IT'S THAT...

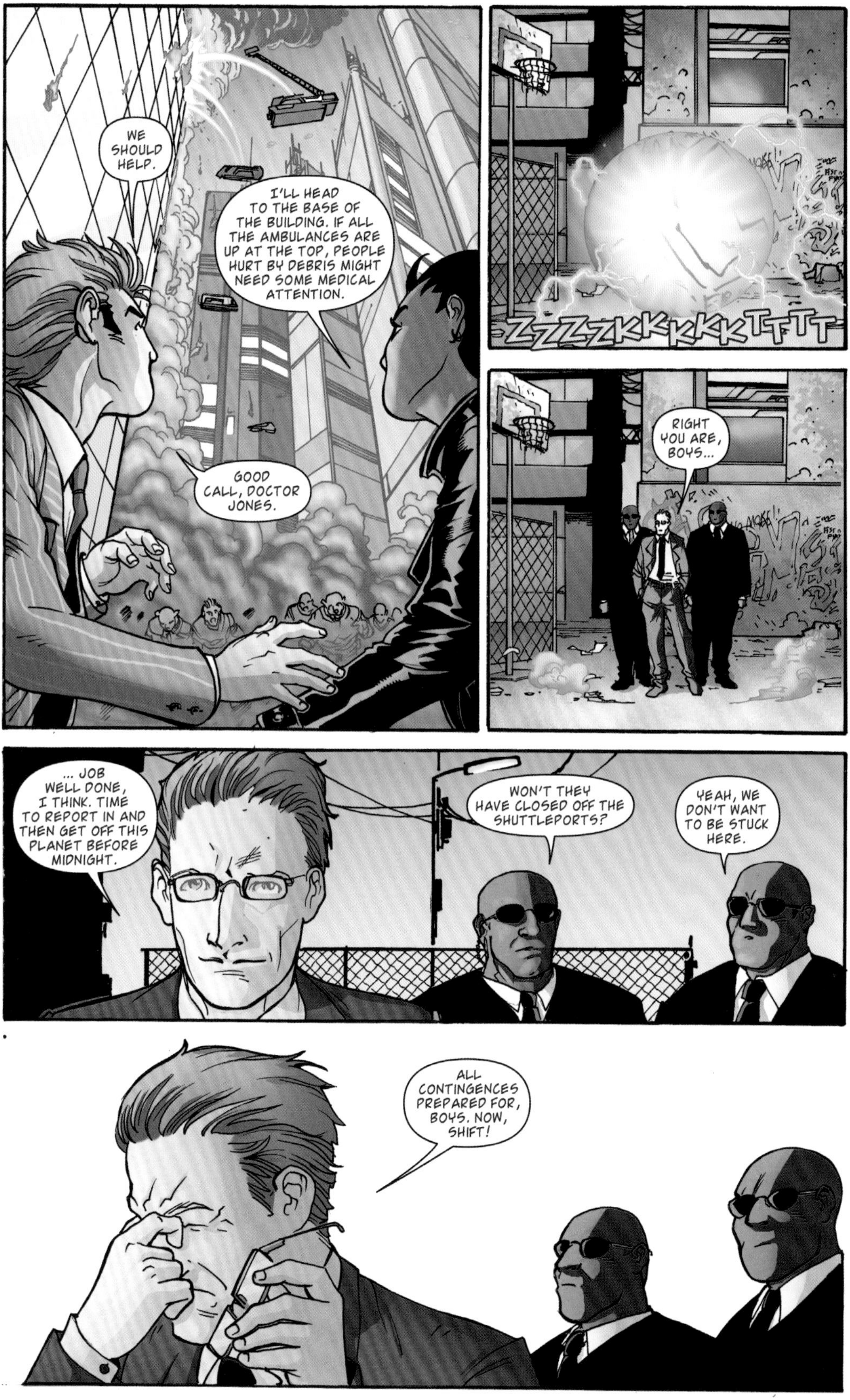
WE SHOULD HELP.
I'LL HEAD TO THE BASE OF THE BUILDING. IF ALL THE AMBULANCES ARE UP AT THE TOP, PEOPLE HURT BY DEBRIS MIGHT NEED SOME MEDICAL ATTENTION.
GOOD CALL, DOCTOR JONES.
ZZZZKKKKKKTTTT
RIGHT YOU ARE, BOYS...
... JOB WELL DONE, I THINK. TIME TO REPORT IN AND THEN GET OFF THIS PLANET BEFORE MIDNIGHT.
WON'T THEY HAVE CLOSED OFF THE SHUTTLEPORTS?
YEAH, WE DON'T WANT TO BE STUCK HERE.
ALL CONTINGENCES PREPARED FOR, BOYS. NOW, SHIFT!

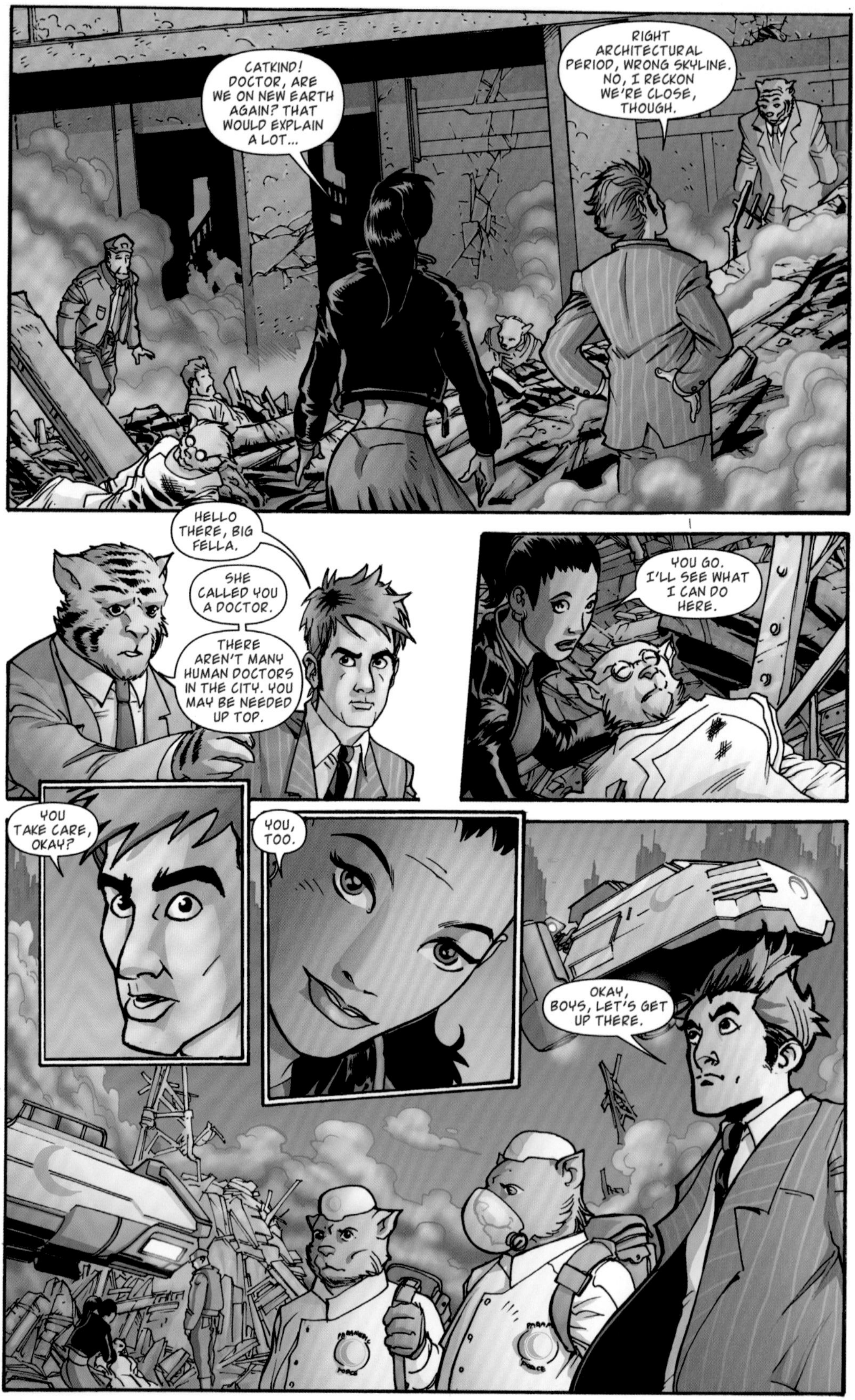
CATKIND! DOCTOR, ARE WE ON NEW EARTH AGAIN? THAT WOULD EXPLAIN A LOT...
RIGHT ARCHITECTURAL PERIOD, WRONG SKYLINE. NO, I RECKON WE'RE CLOSE, THOUGH.
HELLO THERE, BIG FELLA.
SHE CALLED YOU A DOCTOR.
THERE AREN'T MANY HUMAN DOCTORS IN THE CITY. YOU MAY BE NEEDED UP TOP.
YOU GO. I'LL SEE WHAT I CAN DO HERE.
YOU TAKE CARE, OKAY?
YOU, TOO.
OKAY, BOYS, LET'S GET UP THERE.

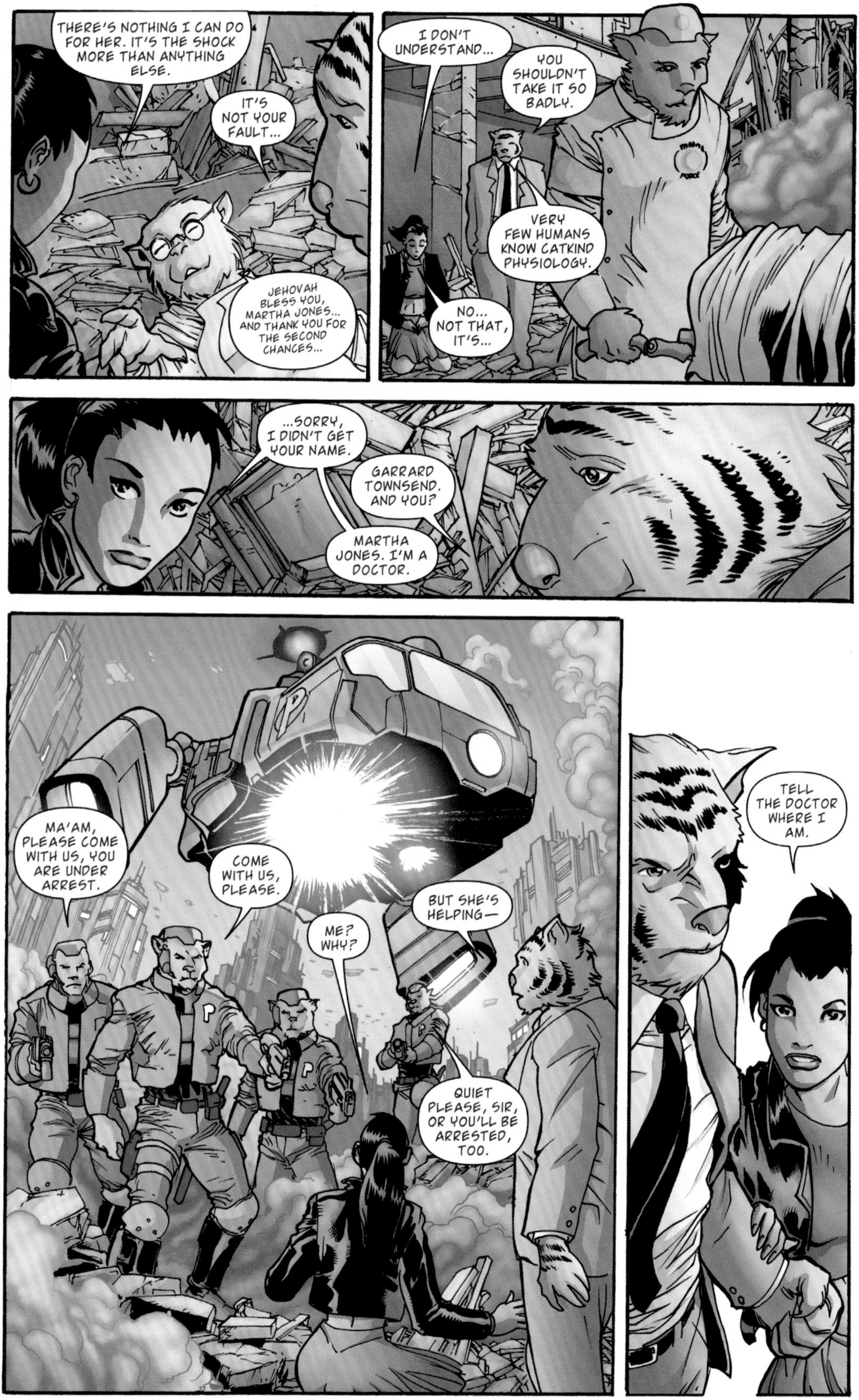
THERE'S NOTHING I CAN DO FOR HER. IT'S THE SHOCK MORE THAN ANYTHING ELSE.
IT'S NOT YOUR FAULT...
JEHOVAH BLESS YOU, MARTHA JONES... AND THANK YOU FOR THE SECOND CHANCES...
I DON'T UNDERSTAND...
YOU SHOULDN'T TAKE IT SO BADLY.
VERY FEW HUMANS KNOW CATKIND PHYSIOLOGY.
NO... NOT THAT, IT'S...
...SORRY, I DIDN'T GET YOUR NAME.
GARRARD TOWNSEND. AND YOU?
MARTHA JONES. I'M A DOCTOR.
MA'AM, PLEASE COME WITH US, YOU ARE UNDER ARREST.
COME WITH US, PLEASE.
ME? WHY?
BUT SHE'S HELPING—
QUIET PLEASE, SIR, OR YOU'LL BE ARRESTED, TOO.
TELL THE DOCTOR WHERE I AM.

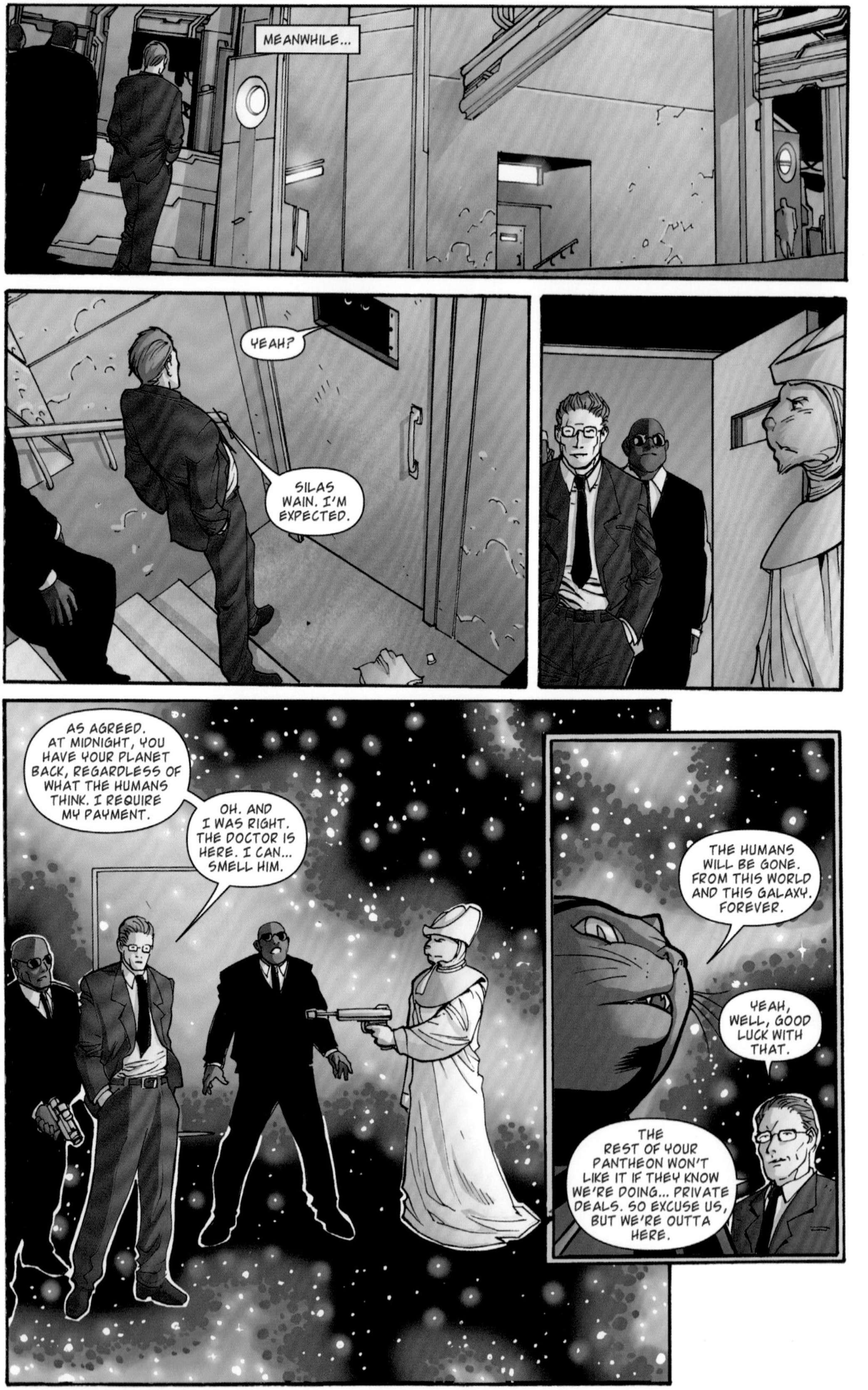
MEANWHILE...
YEAH?
SILAS WAIN. I'M EXPECTED.
AS AGREED. AT MIDNIGHT, YOU HAVE YOUR PLANET BACK, REGARDLESS OF WHAT THE HUMANS THINK. I REQUIRE MY PAYMENT.
OH. AND I WAS RIGHT. THE DOCTOR IS HERE. I CAN... SMELL HIM.
THE HUMANS WILL BE GONE. FROM THIS WORLD AND THIS GALAXY. FOREVER.
YEAH, WELL, GOOD LUCK WITH THAT.
THE REST OF YOUR PANTHEON WON'T LIKE IT IF THEY KNOW WE'RE DOING... PRIVATE DEALS. SO EXCUSE US, BUT WE'RE OUTTA HERE.

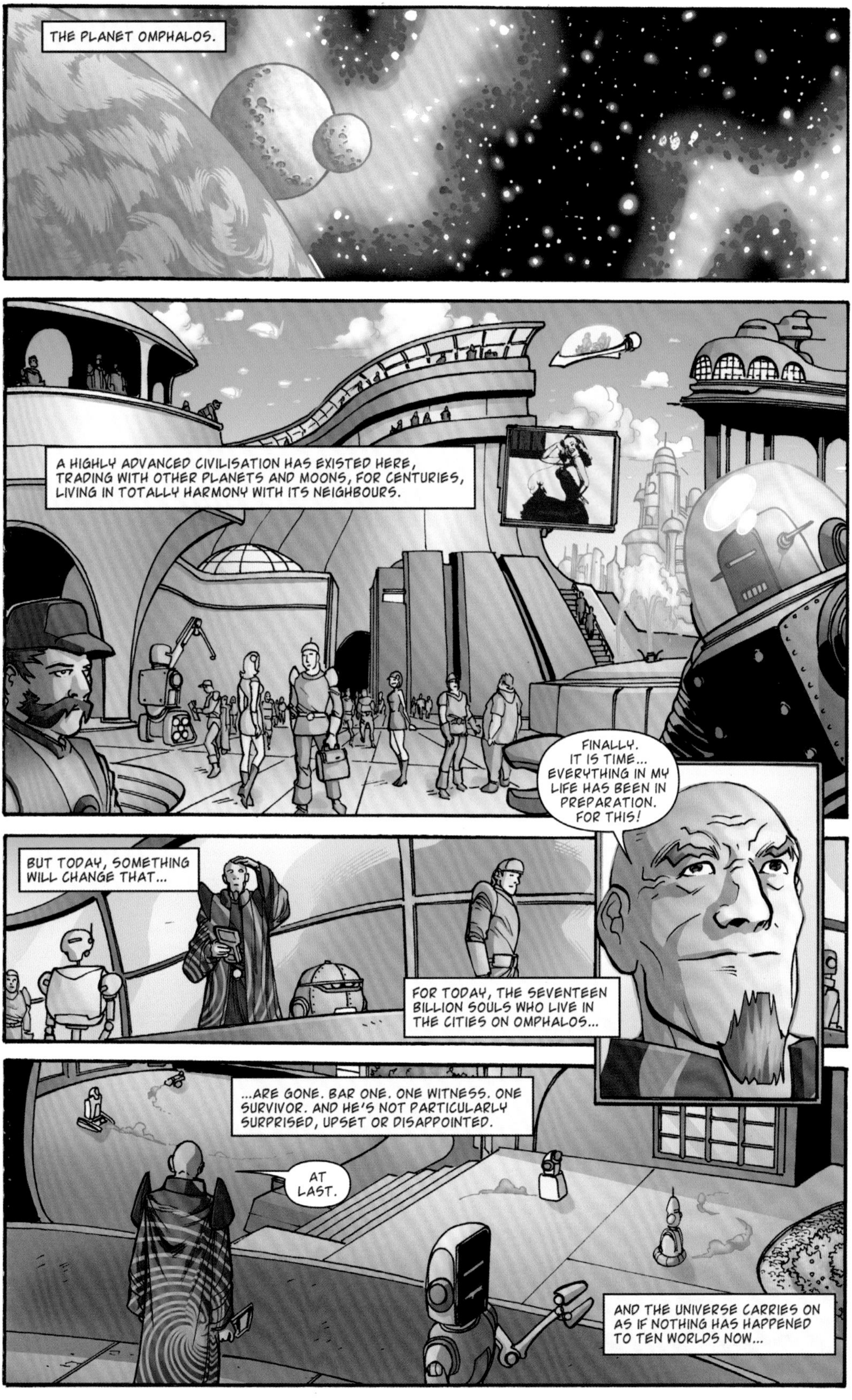
THE PLANET OMPHALOS.
A HIGHLY ADVANCED CIVILISATION HAS EXISTED HERE, TRADING WITH OTHER PLANETS AND MOONS, FOR CENTURIES, LIVING IN TOTALLY HARMONY WITH ITS NEIGHBOURS.
BUT TODAY, SOMETHING WILL CHANGE THAT...
FINALLY. IT IS TIME... EVERYTHING IN MY LIFE HAS BEEN IN PREPARATION. FOR THIS!
FOR TODAY, THE SEVENTEEN BILLION SOULS WHO LIVE IN THE CITIES ON OMPHALOS...
...ARE GONE. BAR ONE. ONE WITNESS. ONE SURVIVOR. AND HE'S NOT PARTICULARLY SURPRISED, UPSET OR DISAPPOINTED.
AT LAST.
AND THE UNIVERSE CARRIES ON AS IF NOTHING HAS HAPPENED TO TEN WORLDS NOW...

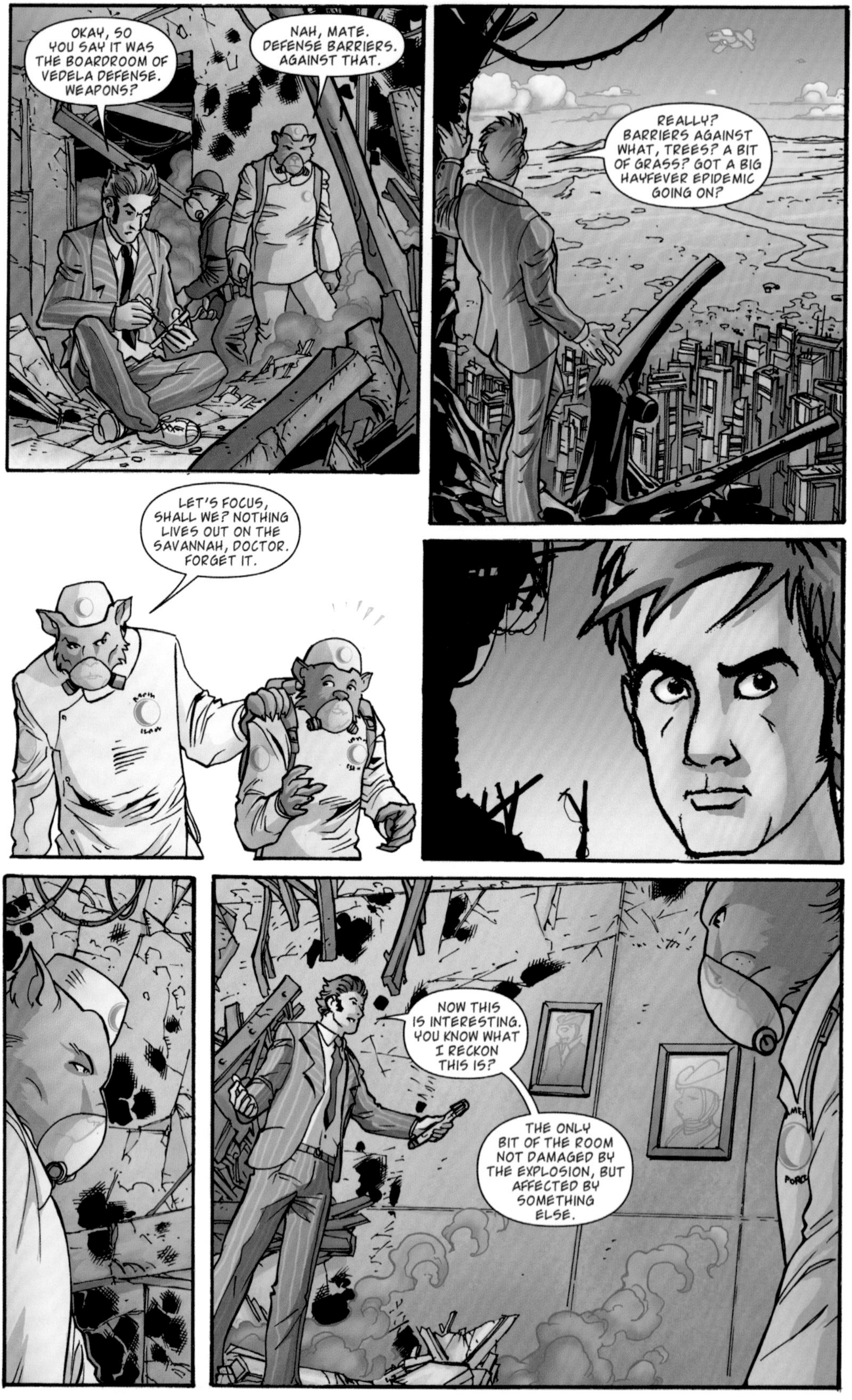
OKAY, SO YOU SAY IT WAS THE BOARDROOM OF VEDELA DEFENSE. WEAPONS?
NAH, MATE. DEFENSE BARRIERS. AGAINST THAT.
REALLY? BARRIERS AGAINST WHAT, TREES? A BIT OF GRASS? GOT A BIG HAYFEVER EPIDEMIC GOING ON?
LET'S FOCUS, SHALL WE? NOTHING LIVES OUT ON THE SAVANNAH, DOCTOR. FORGET IT.
NOW THIS IS INTERESTING. YOU KNOW WHAT I RECKON THIS IS?
THE ONLY BIT OF THE ROOM NOT DAMAGED BY THE EXPLOSION, BUT AFFECTED BY SOMETHING ELSE.

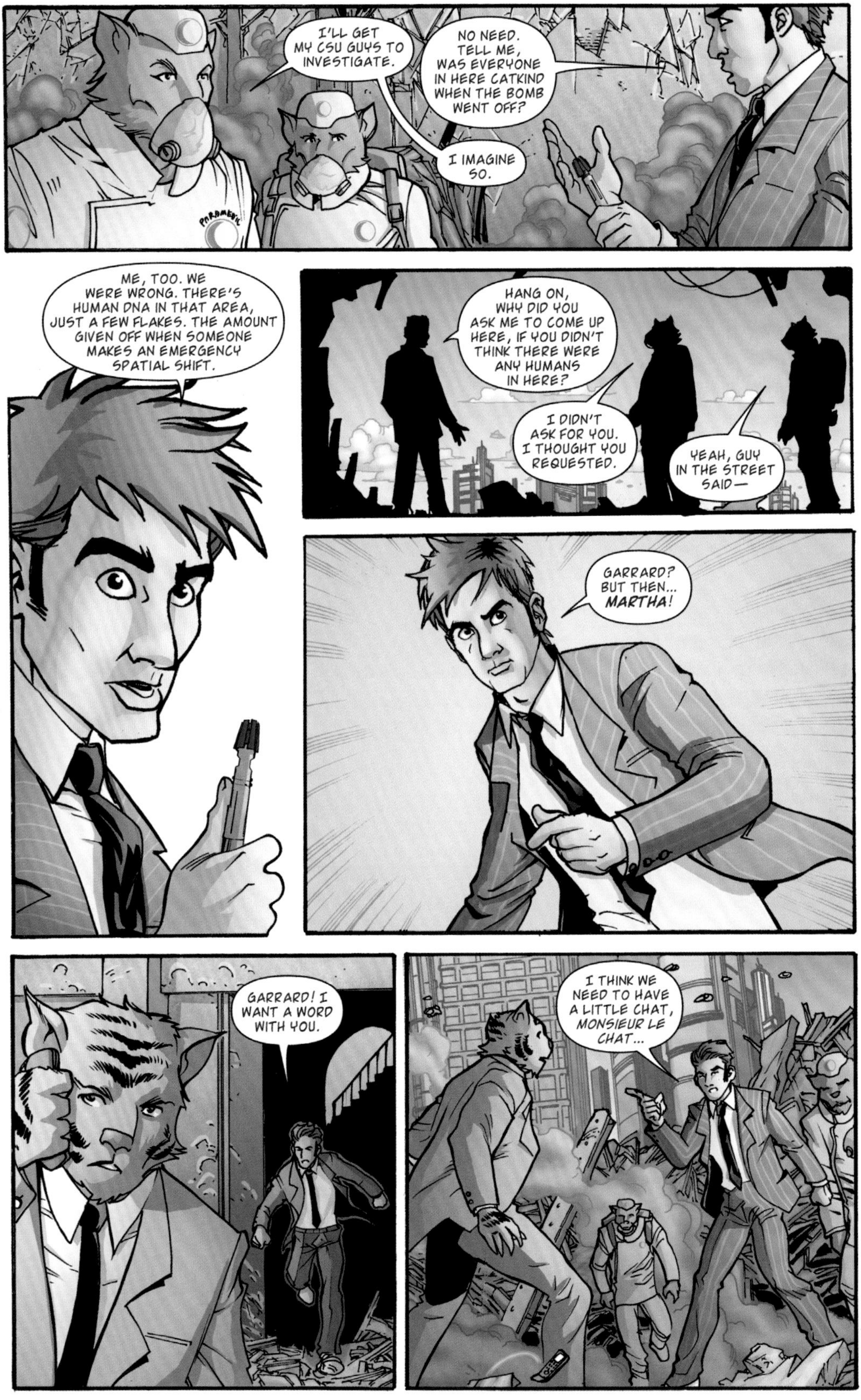
I'LL GET MY CSU GUYS TO INVESTIGATE.
NO NEED. TELL ME, WAS EVERYONE IN HERE CATKIND WHEN THE BOMB WENT OFF?
I IMAGINE SO.
PARAMEDIC
ME, TOO. WE WERE WRONG. THERE'S HUMAN DNA IN THAT AREA, JUST A FEW FLAKES. THE AMOUNT GIVEN OFF WHEN SOMEONE MAKES AN EMERGENCY SPATIAL SHIFT.
HANG ON, WHY DID YOU ASK ME TO COME UP HERE, IF YOU DIDN'T THINK THERE WERE ANY HUMANS IN HERE?
I DIDN'T ASK FOR YOU. I THOUGHT YOU REQUESTED.
YEAH, GUY IN THE STREET SAID—
GARRARD? BUT THEN... *MARTHA*!
GARRARD! I WANT A WORD WITH YOU.
I THINK WE NEED TO HAVE A LITTLE CHAT, *MONSIEUR LE CHAT*...

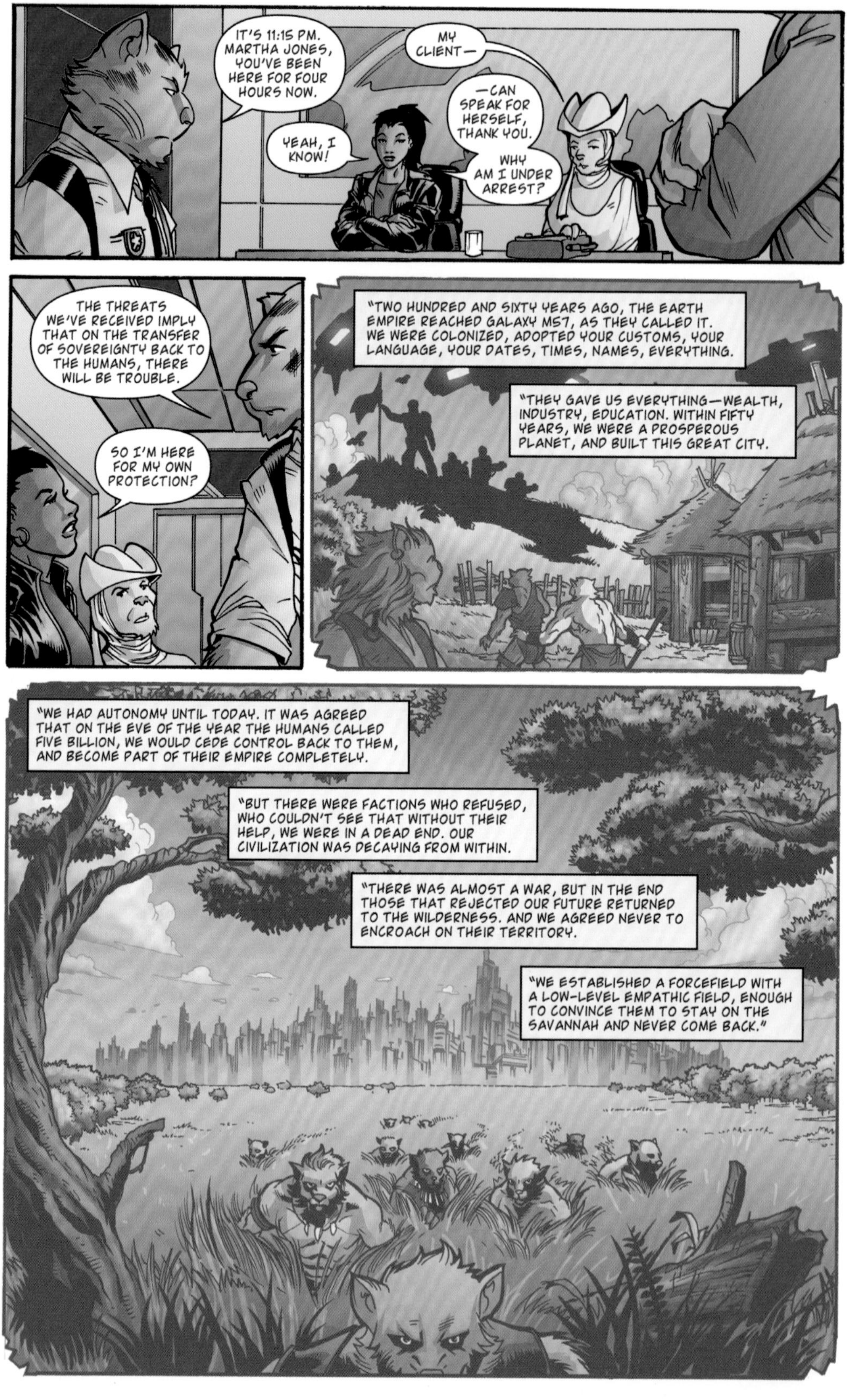
IT'S 11:15 PM. MARTHA JONES, YOU'VE BEEN HERE FOR FOUR HOURS NOW.
YEAH, I KNOW!
MY CLIENT—
—CAN SPEAK FOR HERSELF, THANK YOU.
WHY AM I UNDER ARREST?
THE THREATS WE'VE RECEIVED IMPLY THAT ON THE TRANSFER OF SOVEREIGNTY BACK TO THE HUMANS, THERE WILL BE TROUBLE.
SO I'M HERE FOR MY OWN PROTECTION?
"TWO HUNDRED AND SIXTY YEARS AGO, THE EARTH EMPIRE REACHED GALAXY M57, AS THEY CALLED IT. WE WERE COLONIZED, ADOPTED YOUR CUSTOMS, YOUR LANGUAGE, YOUR DATES, TIMES, NAMES, EVERYTHING.
"THEY GAVE US EVERYTHING—WEALTH, INDUSTRY, EDUCATION. WITHIN FIFTY YEARS, WE WERE A PROSPEROUS PLANET, AND BUILT THIS GREAT CITY.
"WE HAD AUTONOMY UNTIL TODAY. IT WAS AGREED THAT ON THE EVE OF THE YEAR THE HUMANS CALLED FIVE BILLION, WE WOULD CEDE CONTROL BACK TO THEM, AND BECOME PART OF THEIR EMPIRE COMPLETELY.
"BUT THERE WERE FACTIONS WHO REFUSED, WHO COULDN'T SEE THAT WITHOUT THEIR HELP, WE WERE IN A DEAD END. OUR CIVILIZATION WAS DECAYING FROM WITHIN.
"THERE WAS ALMOST A WAR, BUT IN THE END THOSE THAT REJECTED OUR FUTURE RETURNED TO THE WILDERNESS. AND WE AGREED NEVER TO ENCROACH ON THEIR TERRITORY.
"WE ESTABLISHED A FORCEFIELD WITH A LOW-LEVEL EMPATHIC FIELD, ENOUGH TO CONVINCE THEM TO STAY ON THE SAVANNAH AND NEVER COME BACK."

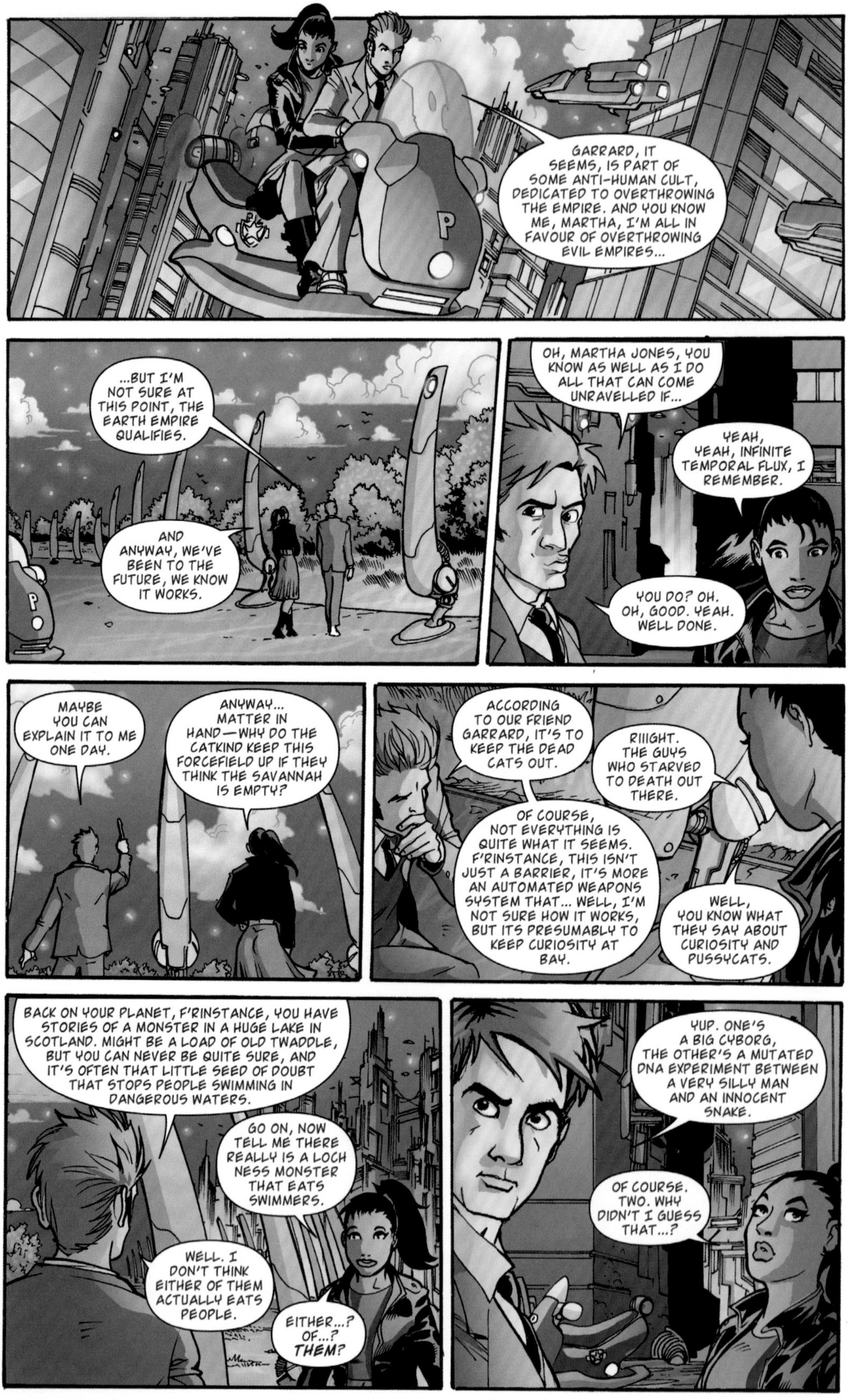
GARRARD, IT SEEMS, IS PART OF SOME ANTI-HUMAN CULT, DEDICATED TO OVERTHROWING THE EMPIRE. AND YOU KNOW ME, MARTHA, I'M ALL IN FAVOUR OF OVERTHROWING EVIL EMPIRES...
...BUT I'M NOT SURE AT THIS POINT, THE EARTH EMPIRE QUALIFIES.
AND ANYWAY, WE'VE BEEN TO THE FUTURE, WE KNOW IT WORKS.
OH, MARTHA JONES, YOU KNOW AS WELL AS I DO ALL THAT CAN COME UNRAVELLED IF...
YEAH, YEAH, INFINITE TEMPORAL FLUX, I REMEMBER.
YOU DO? OH. OH, GOOD. YEAH. WELL DONE.
MAYBE YOU CAN EXPLAIN IT TO ME ONE DAY.
ANYWAY... MATTER IN HAND—WHY DO THE CATKIND KEEP THIS FORCEFIELD UP IF THEY THINK THE SAVANNAH IS EMPTY?
ACCORDING TO OUR FRIEND GARRARD, IT'S TO KEEP THE DEAD CATS OUT.
RIIIGHT. THE GUYS WHO STARVED TO DEATH OUT THERE.
OF COURSE, NOT EVERYTHING IS QUITE WHAT IT SEEMS. F'RINSTANCE, THIS ISN'T JUST A BARRIER, IT'S MORE AN AUTOMATED WEAPONS SYSTEM THAT... WELL, I'M NOT SURE HOW IT WORKS, BUT ITS PRESUMABLY TO KEEP CURIOSITY AT BAY.
WELL, YOU KNOW WHAT THEY SAY ABOUT CURIOSITY AND PUSSYCATS.
BACK ON YOUR PLANET, F'RINSTANCE, YOU HAVE STORIES OF A MONSTER IN A HUGE LAKE IN SCOTLAND. MIGHT BE A LOAD OF OLD TWADDLE, BUT YOU CAN NEVER BE QUITE SURE, AND IT'S OFTEN THAT LITTLE SEED OF DOUBT THAT STOPS PEOPLE SWIMMING IN DANGEROUS WATERS.
GO ON, NOW TELL ME THERE REALLY IS A LOCH NESS MONSTER THAT EATS SWIMMERS.
WELL. I DON'T THINK EITHER OF THEM ACTUALLY EATS PEOPLE.
EITHER...? OF...? THEM?
YUP. ONE'S A BIG CYBORG, THE OTHER'S A MUTATED DNA EXPERIMENT BETWEEN A VERY SILLY MAN AND AN INNOCENT SNAKE.
OF COURSE. TWO. WHY DIDN'T I GUESS THAT...?

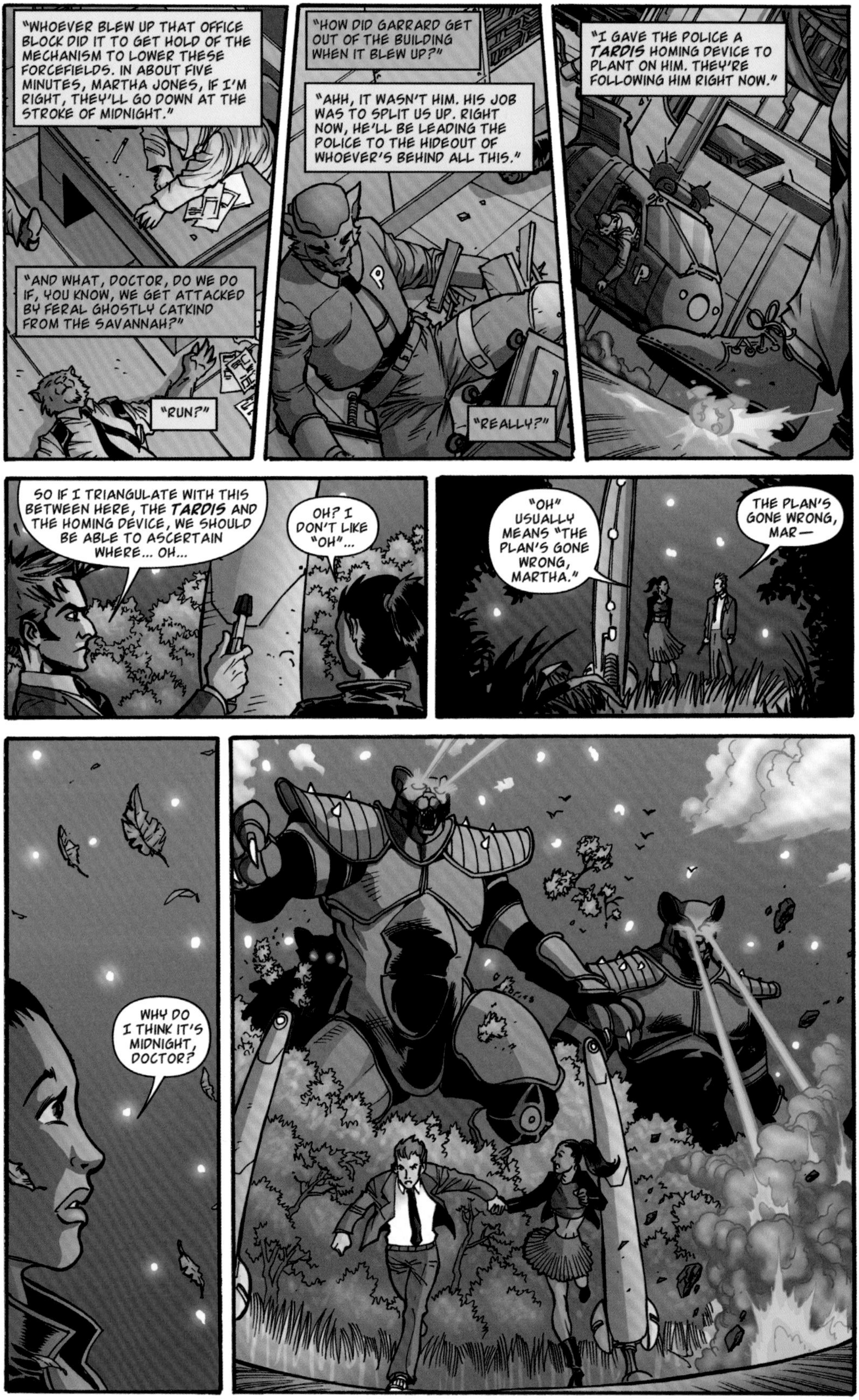
"WHOEVER BLEW UP THAT OFFICE BLOCK DID IT TO GET HOLD OF THE MECHANISM TO LOWER THESE FORCEFIELDS. IN ABOUT FIVE MINUTES, MARTHA JONES, IF I'M RIGHT, THEY'LL GO DOWN AT THE STROKE OF MIDNIGHT."
"AND WHAT, DOCTOR, DO WE DO IF, YOU KNOW, WE GET ATTACKED BY FERAL GHOSTLY CATKIND FROM THE SAVANNAH?"
"RUN?"
"HOW DID GARRARD GET OUT OF THE BUILDING WHEN IT BLEW UP?"
"AHH, IT WASN'T HIM. HIS JOB WAS TO SPLIT US UP. RIGHT NOW, HE'LL BE LEADING THE POLICE TO THE HIDEOUT OF WHOEVER'S BEHIND ALL THIS."
"REALLY?"
"I GAVE THE POLICE A TARDIS HOMING DEVICE TO PLANT ON HIM. THEY'RE FOLLOWING HIM RIGHT NOW."
SO IF I TRIANGULATE WITH THIS BETWEEN HERE, THE TARDIS AND THE HOMING DEVICE, WE SHOULD BE ABLE TO ASCERTAIN WHERE... OH...
OH? I DON'T LIKE "OH"...
"OH" USUALLY MEANS "THE PLAN'S GONE WRONG, MARTHA."
THE PLAN'S GONE WRONG, MAR—
WHY DO I THINK IT'S MIDNIGHT, DOCTOR?

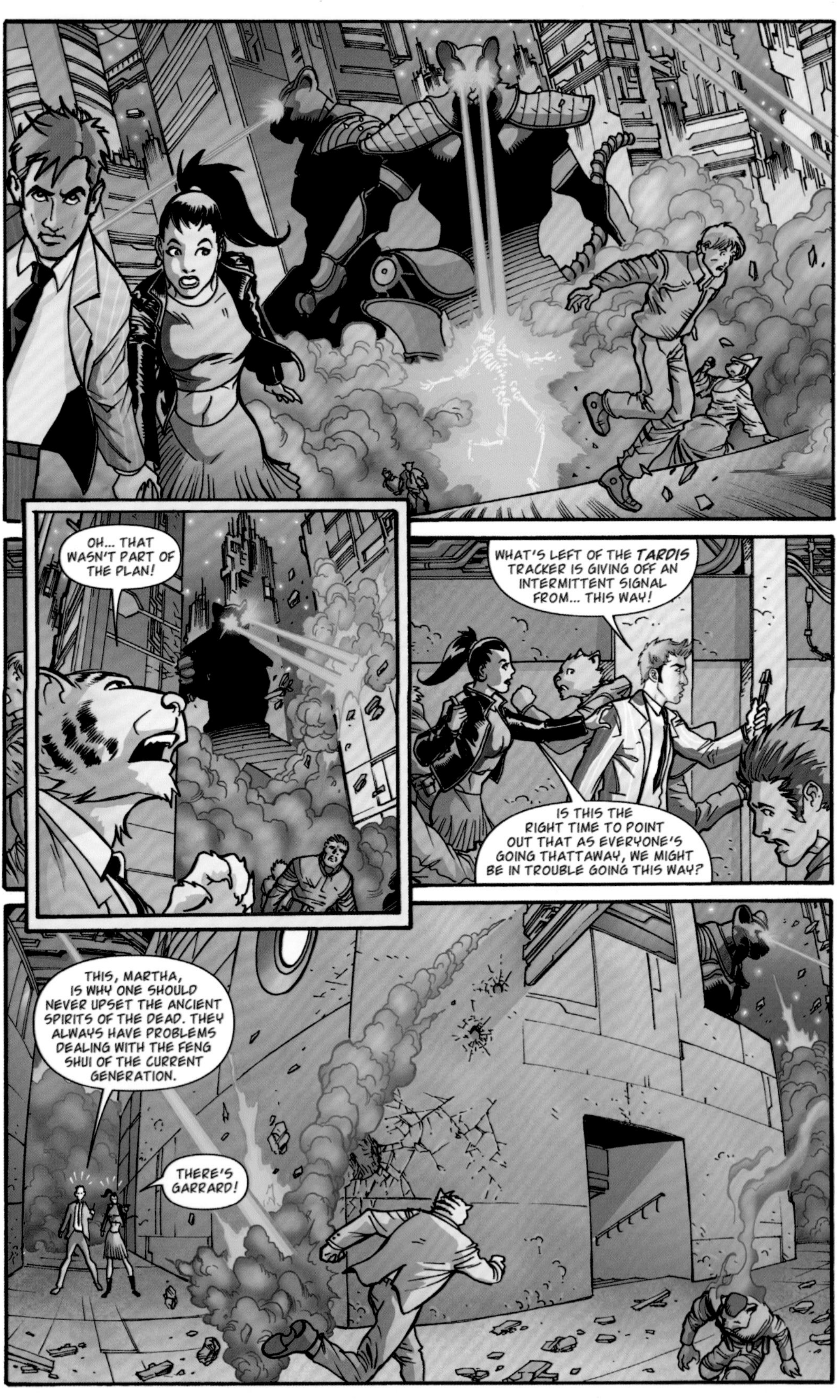
OH... THAT WASN'T PART OF THE PLAN!
WHAT'S LEFT OF THE TARDIS TRACKER IS GIVING OFF AN INTERMITTENT SIGNAL FROM... THIS WAY!
IS THIS THE RIGHT TIME TO POINT OUT THAT AS EVERYONE'S GOING THATTAWAY, WE MIGHT BE IN TROUBLE GOING THIS WAY?
THIS, MARTHA, IS WHY ONE SHOULD NEVER UPSET THE ANCIENT SPIRITS OF THE DEAD. THEY ALWAYS HAVE PROBLEMS DEALING WITH THE FENG SHUI OF THE CURRENT GENERATION.
THERE'S GARRARD!

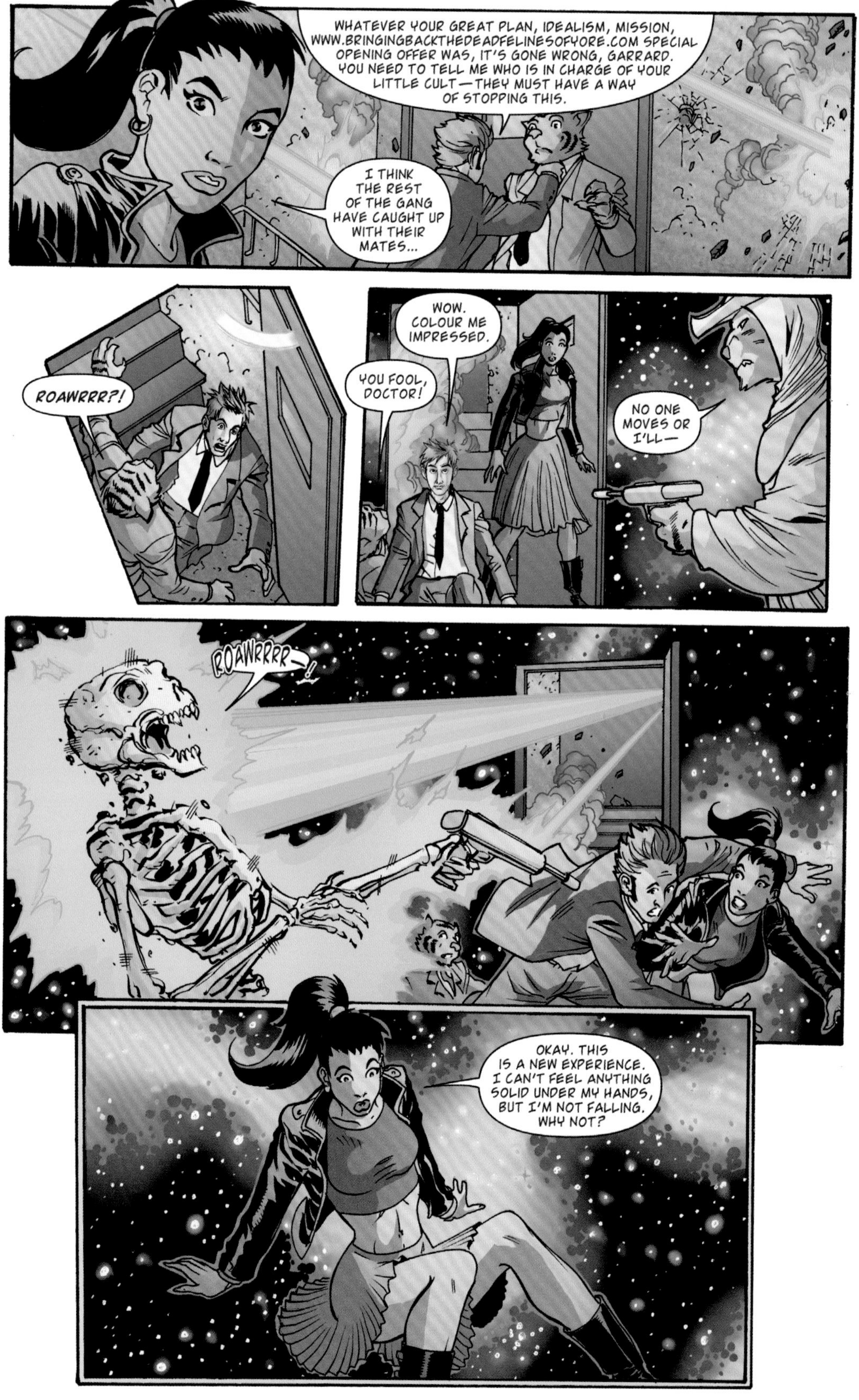
WHATEVER YOUR GREAT PLAN, IDEALISM, MISSION, WWW.BRINGINGBACKTHEDEADFELINESOFYORE.COM SPECIAL OPENING OFFER WAS, IT'S GONE WRONG, GARRARD. YOU NEED TO TELL ME WHO IS IN CHARGE OF YOUR LITTLE CULT—THEY MUST HAVE A WAY OF STOPPING THIS.
I THINK THE REST OF THE GANG HAVE CAUGHT UP WITH THEIR MATES...
ROAWRRR?!
WOW. COLOUR ME IMPRESSED.
YOU FOOL, DOCTOR!
NO ONE MOVES OR I'LL—
ROAWRRRR—!
OKAY. THIS IS A NEW EXPERIENCE. I CAN'T FEEL ANYTHING SOLID UNDER MY HANDS, BUT I'M NOT FALLING. WHY NOT?

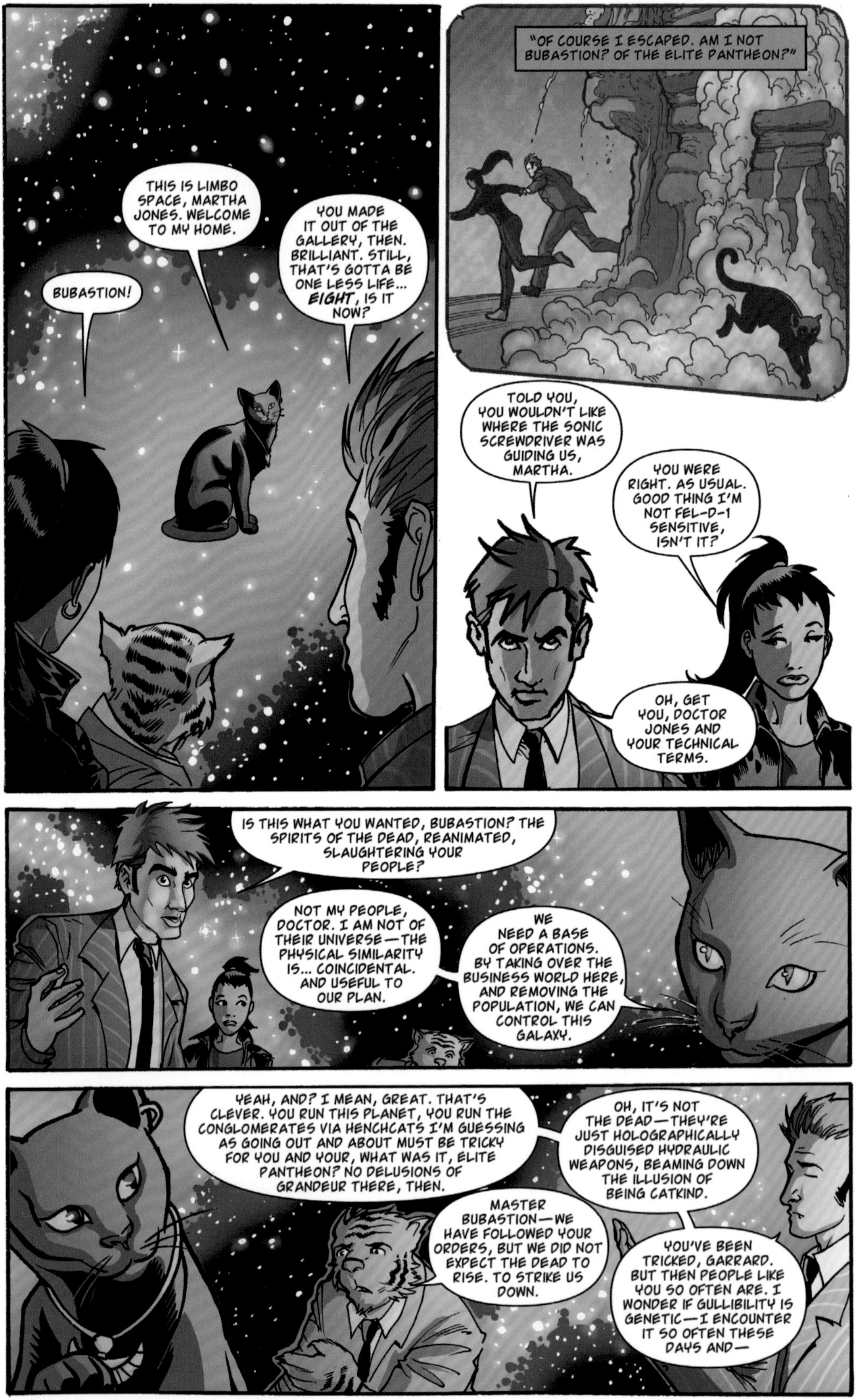
BUBASTION!
THIS IS LIMBO SPACE, MARTHA JONES. WELCOME TO MY HOME.
YOU MADE IT OUT OF THE GALLERY, THEN. BRILLIANT. STILL, THAT'S GOTTA BE ONE LESS LIFE... EIGHT, IS IT NOW?
"OF COURSE I ESCAPED. AM I NOT BUBASTION? OF THE ELITE PANTHEON?"
TOLD YOU, YOU WOULDN'T LIKE WHERE THE SONIC SCREWDRIVER WAS GUIDING US, MARTHA.
YOU WERE RIGHT. AS USUAL. GOOD THING I'M NOT FEL-D-1 SENSITIVE, ISN'T IT?
OH, GET YOU, DOCTOR JONES AND YOUR TECHNICAL TERMS.
IS THIS WHAT YOU WANTED, BUBASTION? THE SPIRITS OF THE DEAD, REANIMATED, SLAUGHTERING YOUR PEOPLE?
NOT MY PEOPLE, DOCTOR. I AM NOT OF THEIR UNIVERSE—THE PHYSICAL SIMILARITY IS... COINCIDENTAL. AND USEFUL TO OUR PLAN.
WE NEED A BASE OF OPERATIONS. BY TAKING OVER THE BUSINESS WORLD HERE, AND REMOVING THE POPULATION, WE CAN CONTROL THIS GALAXY.
YEAH, AND? I MEAN, GREAT. THAT'S CLEVER. YOU RUN THIS PLANET, YOU RUN THE CONGLOMERATES VIA HENCHCATS I'M GUESSING AS GOING OUT AND ABOUT MUST BE TRICKY FOR YOU AND YOUR, WHAT WAS IT, ELITE PANTHEON? NO DELUSIONS OF GRANDEUR THERE, THEN.
MASTER BUBASTION—WE HAVE FOLLOWED YOUR ORDERS, BUT WE DID NOT EXPECT THE DEAD TO RISE. TO STRIKE US DOWN.
OH, IT'S NOT THE DEAD—THEY'RE JUST HOLOGRAPHICALLY DISGUISED HYDRAULIC WEAPONS, BEAMING DOWN THE ILLUSION OF BEING CATKIND.
YOU'VE BEEN TRICKED, GARRARD. BUT THEN PEOPLE LIKE YOU SO OFTEN ARE. I WONDER IF GULLIBILITY IS GENETIC—I ENCOUNTER IT SO OFTEN THESE DAYS AND—

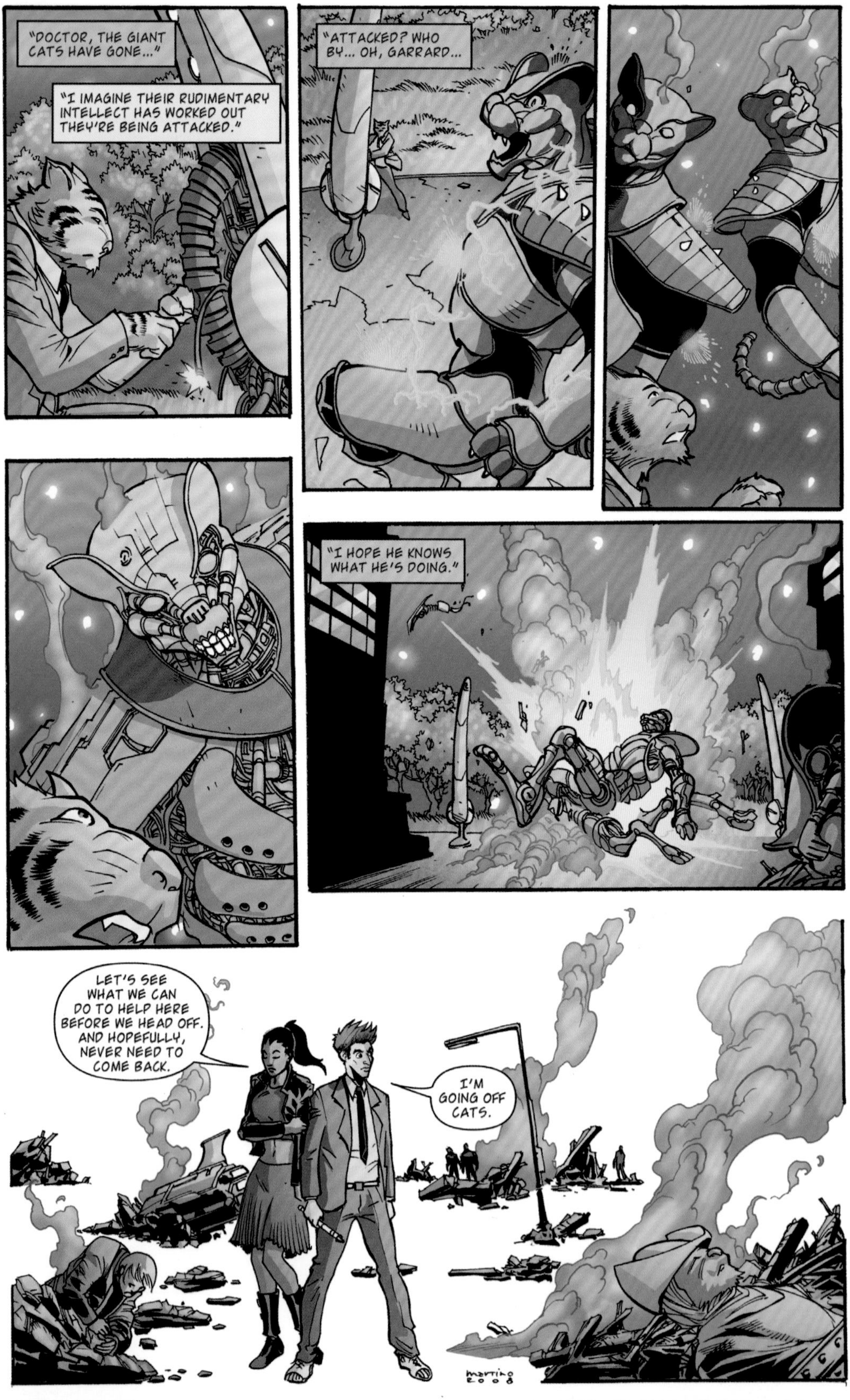
"DOCTOR, THE GIANT CATS HAVE GONE..."
"I IMAGINE THEIR RUDIMENTARY INTELLECT HAS WORKED OUT THEY'RE BEING ATTACKED."
"ATTACKED? WHO BY... OH, GARRARD..."
"I HOPE HE KNOWS WHAT HE'S DOING."
LET'S SEE WHAT WE CAN DO TO HELP HERE BEFORE WE HEAD OFF. AND HOPEFULLY, NEVER NEED TO COME BACK.
I'M GOING OFF CATS.
MARTINO 2008

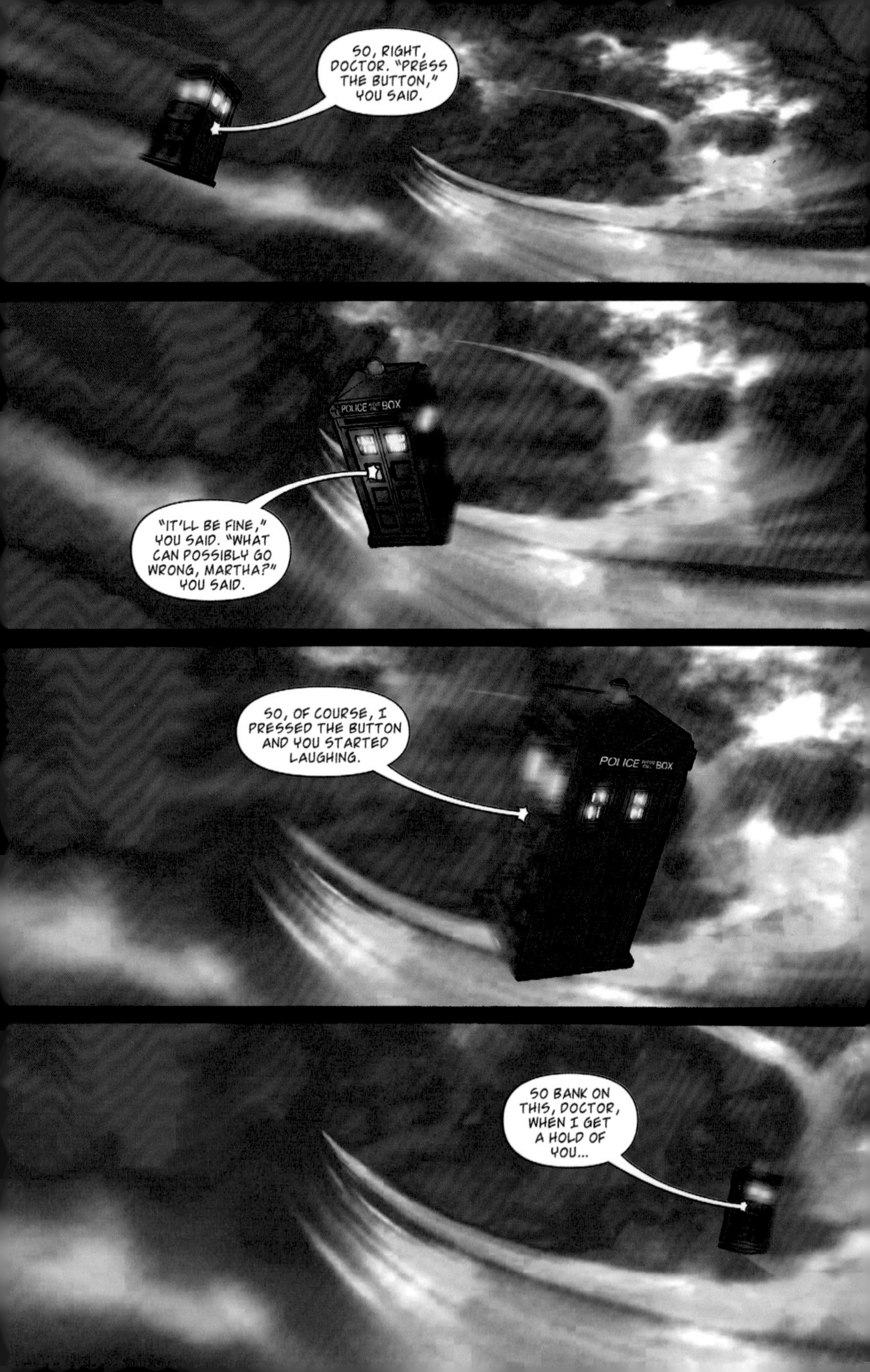
SO, RIGHT, DOCTOR. "PRESS THE BUTTON," YOU SAID.
POLICE BOX
"IT'LL BE FINE," YOU SAID. "WHAT CAN POSSIBLY GO WRONG, MARTHA?" YOU SAID.
SO, OF COURSE, I PRESSED THE BUTTON AND YOU STARTED LAUGHING.
POLICE BOX
SO BANK ON THIS, DOCTOR, WHEN I GET A HOLD OF YOU...

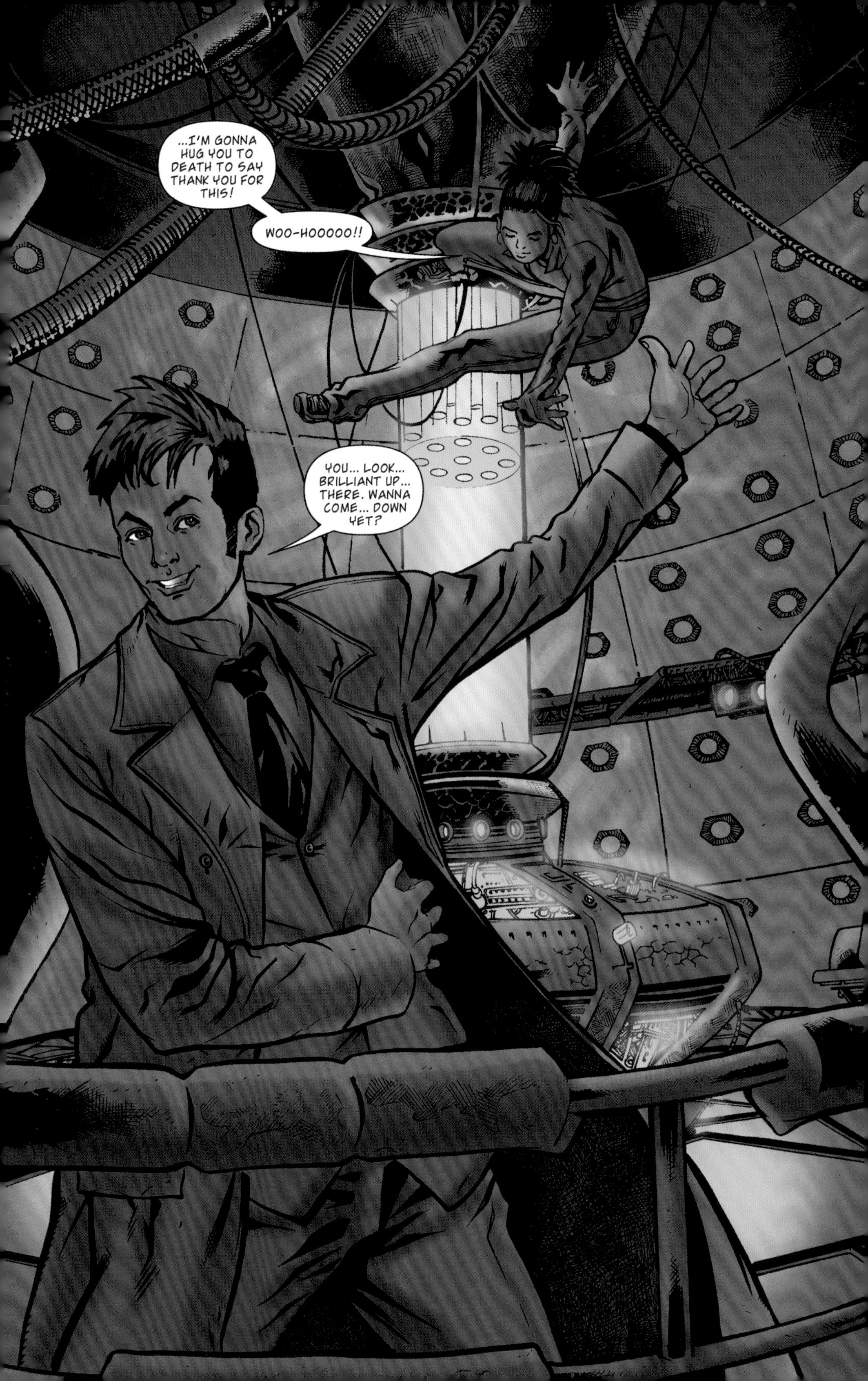
...I'M GONNA HUG YOU TO DEATH TO SAY THANK YOU FOR THIS!
WOO-HOOOOO!!
YOU... LOOK... BRILLIANT UP... THERE. WANNA COME... DOWN YET?

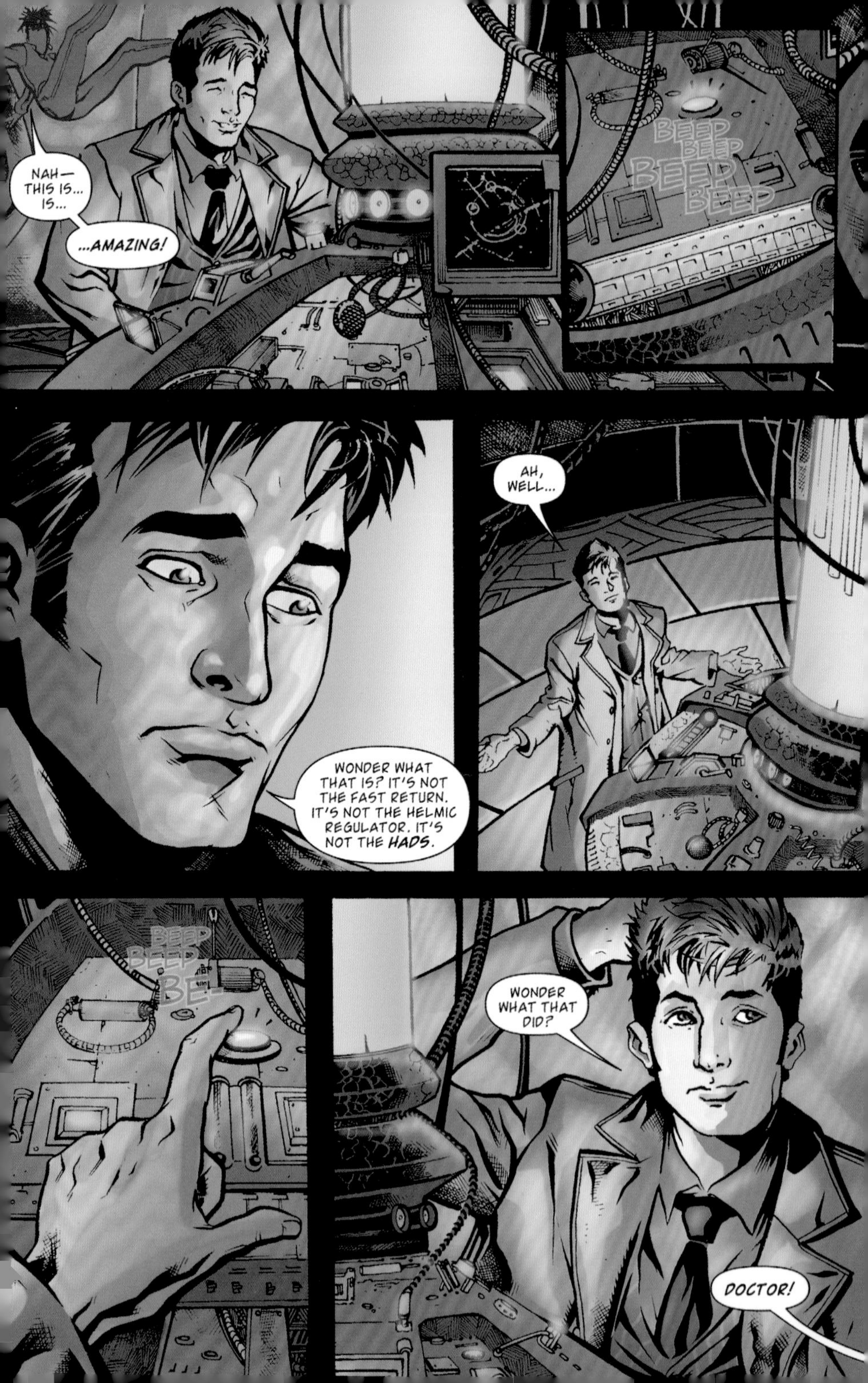
NAH— THIS IS... IS...
...AMAZING!
BEEP BEEP BEEP BEEP
AH, WELL...
WONDER WHAT THAT IS? IT'S NOT THE FAST RETURN. IT'S NOT THE HELMIC REGULATOR. IT'S NOT THE HADS.
BEEP BEEP BE-
WONDER WHAT THAT DID?
DOCTOR!

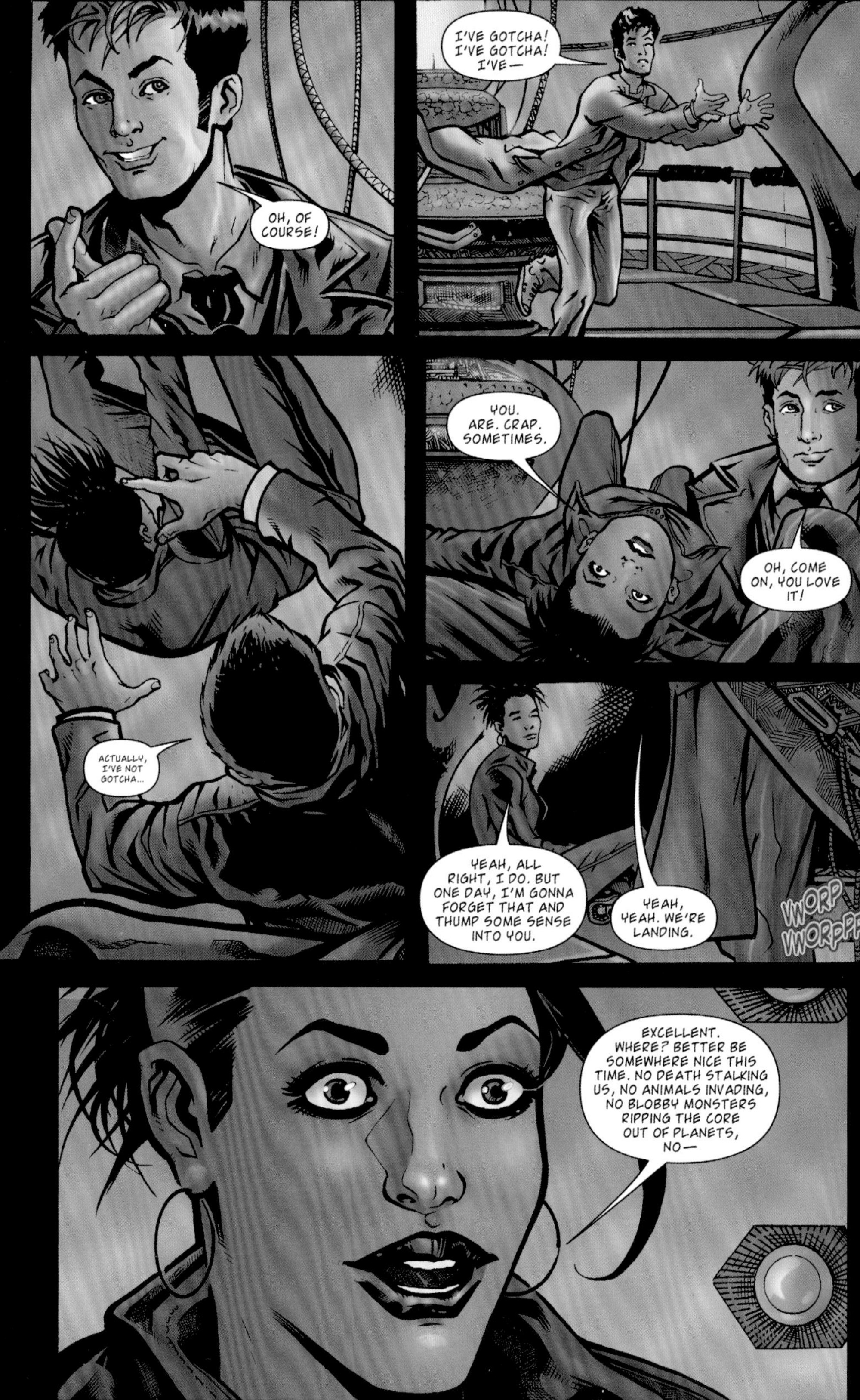
OH, OF COURSE!
I'VE GOTCHA! I'VE GOTCHA! I'VE—
ACTUALLY, I'VE NOT GOTCHA...
YOU. ARE. CRAP. SOMETIMES.
OH, COME ON, YOU LOVE IT!
YEAH, ALL RIGHT, I DO. BUT ONE DAY, I'M GONNA FORGET THAT AND THUMP SOME SENSE INTO YOU.
YEAH, YEAH. WE'RE LANDING.
EXCELLENT. WHERE? BETTER BE SOMEWHERE NICE THIS TIME. NO DEATH STALKING US, NO ANIMALS INVADING, NO BLOBBY MONSTERS RIPPING THE CORE OUT OF PLANETS, NO—

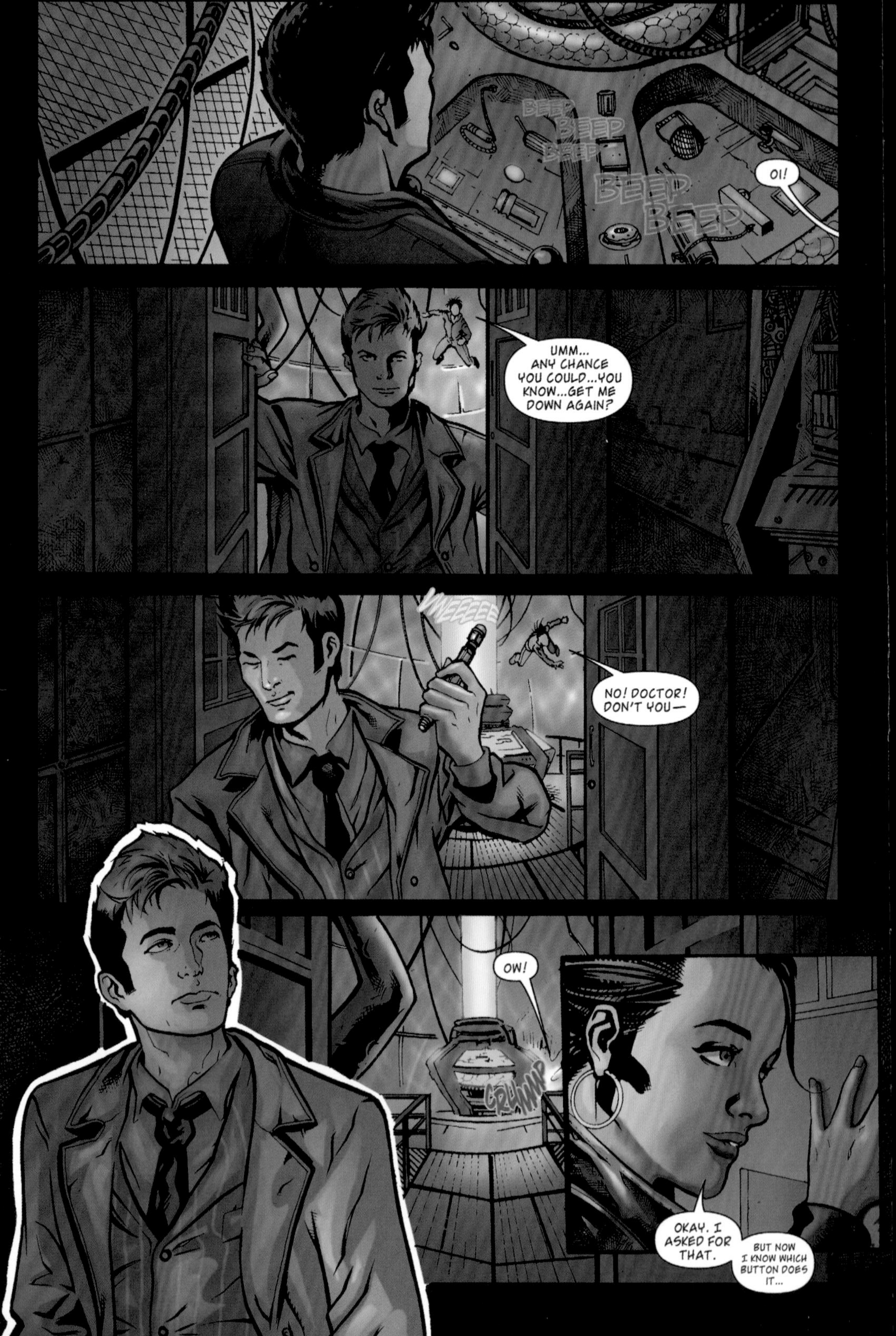
BEEP
BEEP
BEEP
BEEP
BEEP
OI!
UMM... ANY CHANCE YOU COULD...YOU KNOW...GET ME DOWN AGAIN?
NO! DOCTOR! DON'T YOU—
OW!
CRUMMP
OKAY. I ASKED FOR THAT.
BUT NOW I KNOW WHICH BUTTON DOES IT...

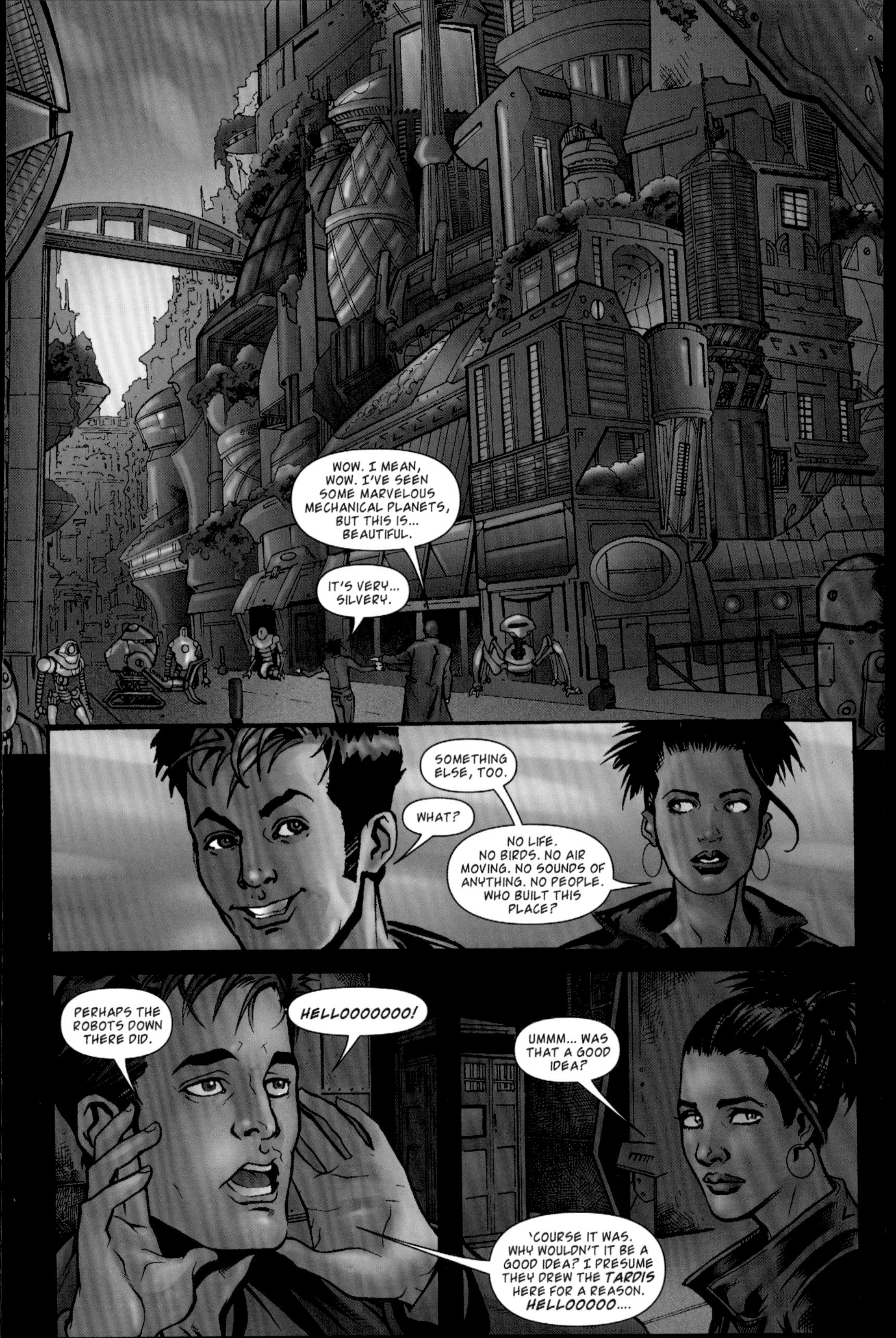
WOW. I MEAN, WOW. I'VE SEEN SOME MARVELOUS MECHANICAL PLANETS, BUT THIS IS... BEAUTIFUL.
IT'S VERY... SILVERY.
SOMETHING ELSE, TOO.
WHAT?
NO LIFE. NO BIRDS. NO AIR MOVING. NO SOUNDS OF ANYTHING. NO PEOPLE. WHO BUILT THIS PLACE?
PERHAPS THE ROBOTS DOWN THERE DID.
HELLOOOOOOO!
UMMM... WAS THAT A GOOD IDEA?
'COURSE IT WAS. WHY WOULDN'T IT BE A GOOD IDEA? I PRESUME THEY DREW THE TARDIS HERE FOR A REASON. HELLOOOO....

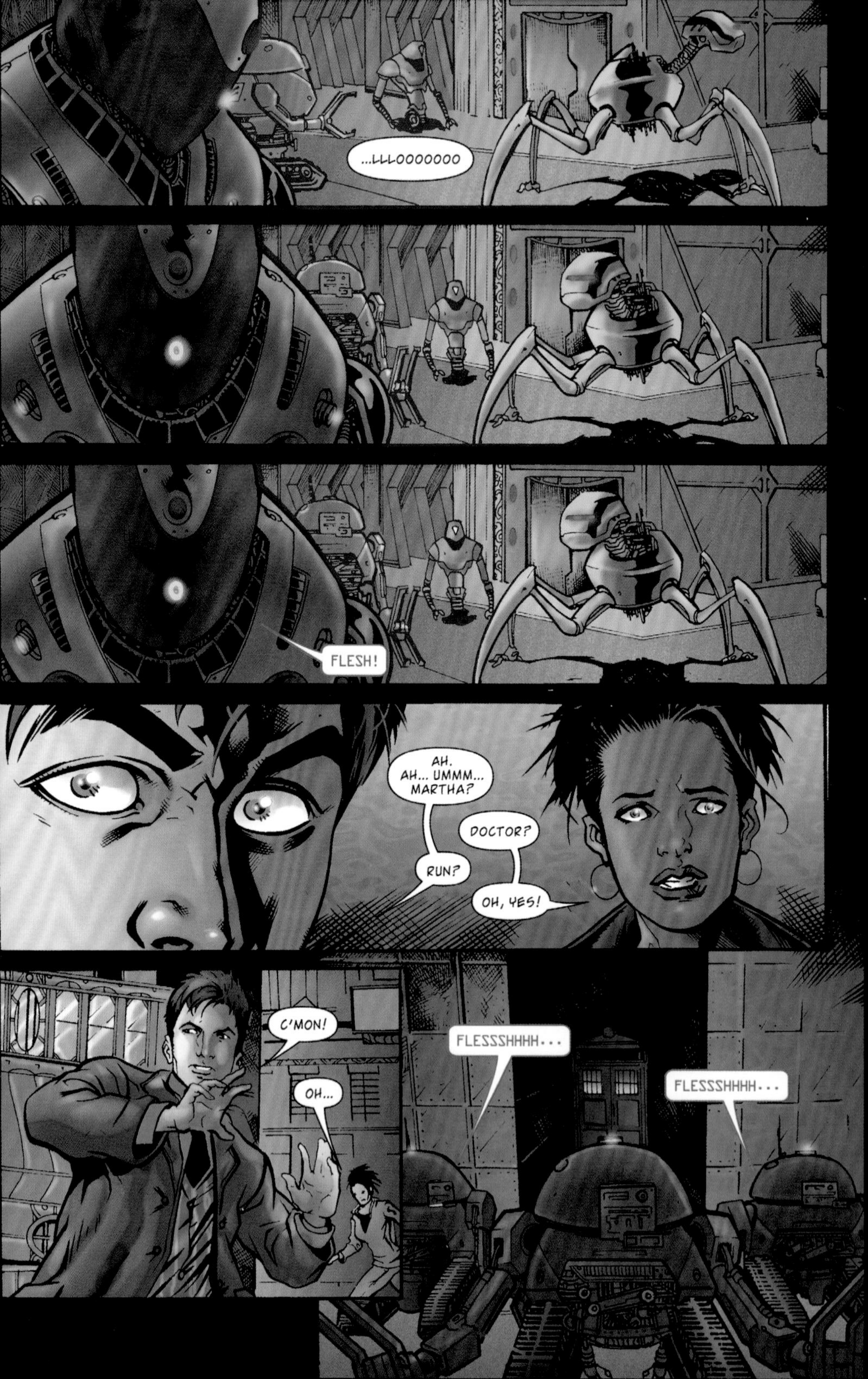
...LLLOOOOOOO
FLESH!
AH.
AH... UMMM...
MARTHA?
DOCTOR?
RUN?
OH, YES!
C'MON!
OH...
FLESSSHHHH...
FLESSSHHHH...

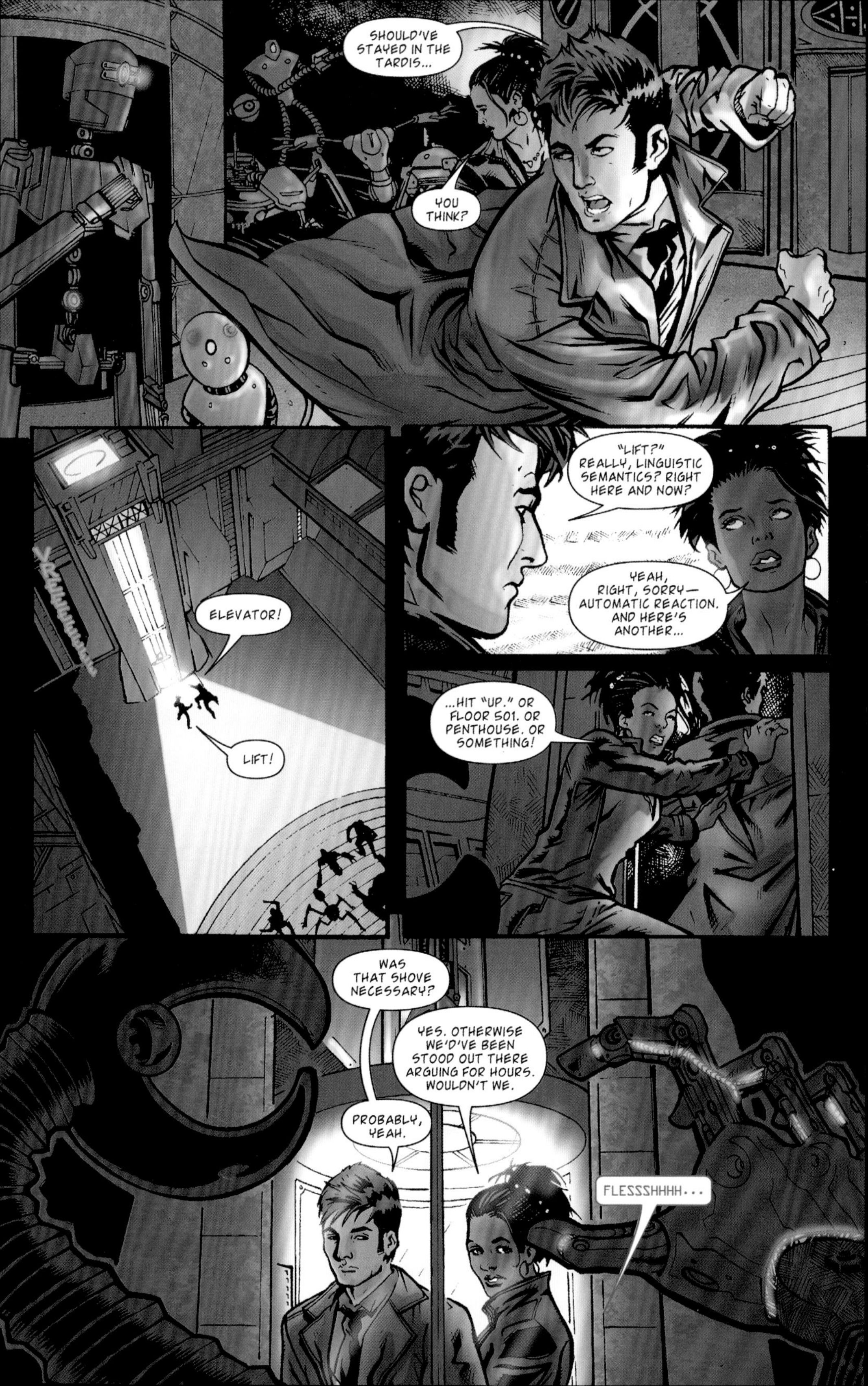
SHOULD'VE STAYED IN THE TARDIS...
YOU THINK?
ELEVATOR!
LIFT!
"LIFT?" REALLY, LINGUISTIC SEMANTICS? RIGHT HERE AND NOW?
YEAH, RIGHT, SORRY— AUTOMATIC REACTION. AND HERE'S ANOTHER...
...HIT "UP." OR FLOOR 501. OR PENTHOUSE. OR SOMETHING!
WAS THAT SHOVE NECESSARY?
YES. OTHERWISE WE'D'VE BEEN STOOD OUT THERE ARGUING FOR HOURS. WOULDN'T WE.
PROBABLY, YEAH.
FLESSSHHHH...

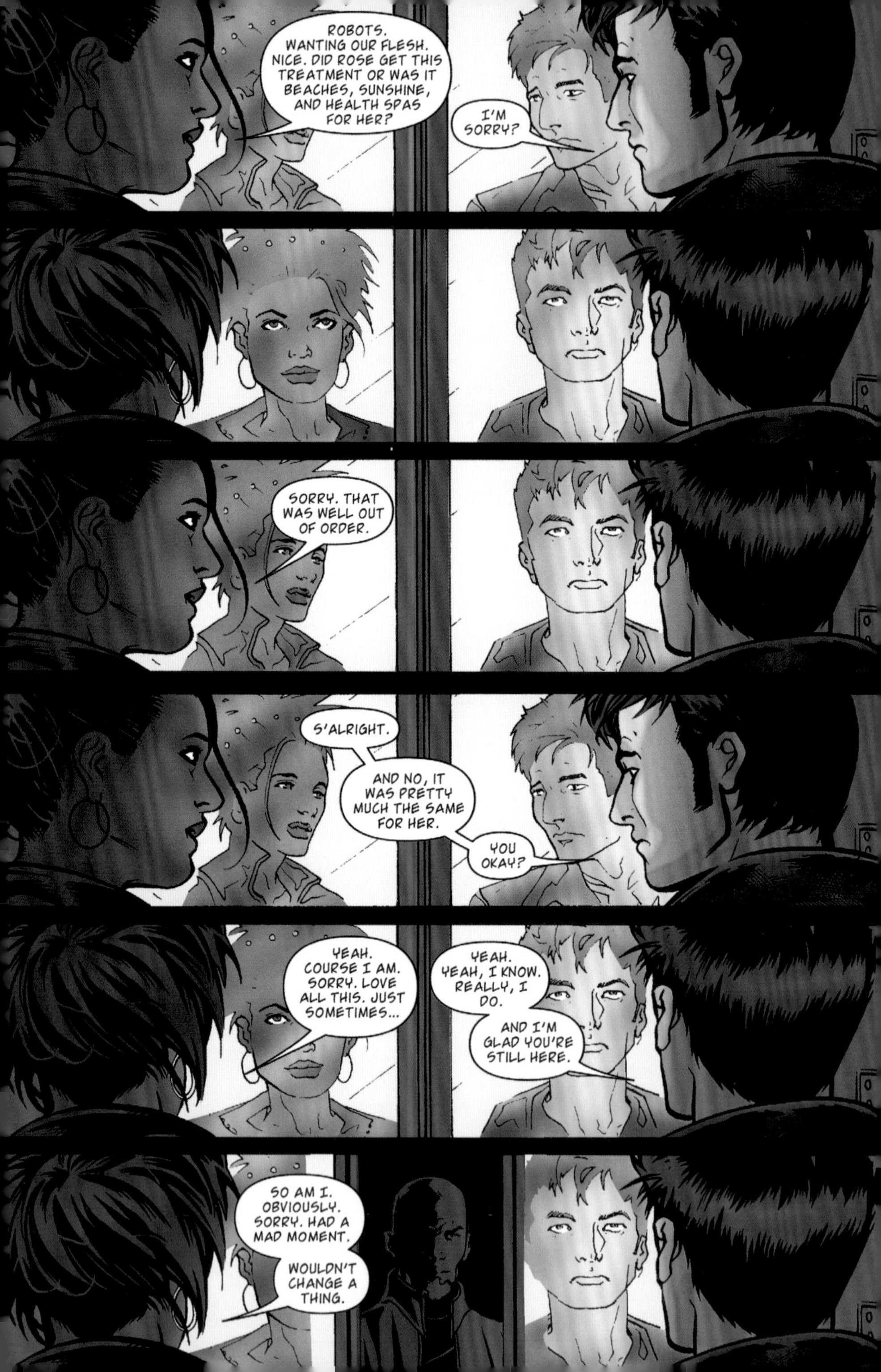
ROBOTS. WANTING OUR FLESH. NICE. DID ROSE GET THIS TREATMENT OR WAS IT BEACHES, SUNSHINE, AND HEALTH SPAS FOR HER?
I'M SORRY?
SORRY. THAT WAS WELL OUT OF ORDER.
S'ALRIGHT.
AND NO, IT WAS PRETTY MUCH THE SAME FOR HER.
YOU OKAY?
YEAH. COURSE I AM. SORRY. LOVE ALL THIS. JUST SOMETIMES...
YEAH. YEAH, I KNOW. REALLY, I DO.
AND I'M GLAD YOU'RE STILL HERE.
SO AM I. OBVIOUSLY. SORRY. HAD A MAD MOMENT.
WOULDN'T CHANGE A THING.

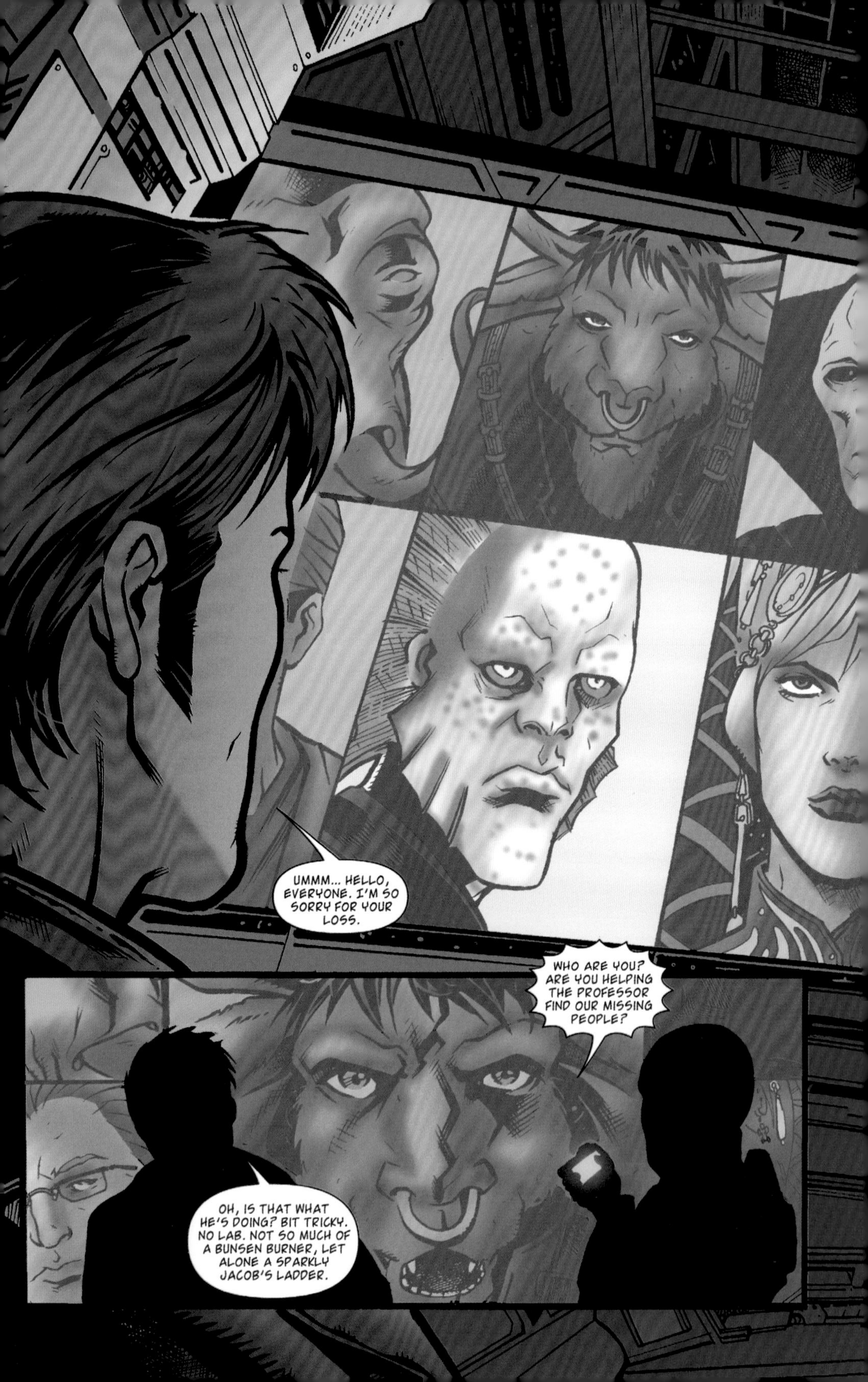
UMMM... HELLO, EVERYONE. I'M SO SORRY FOR YOUR LOSS.
WHO ARE YOU? ARE YOU HELPING THE PROFESSOR FIND OUR MISSING PEOPLE?
OH, IS THAT WHAT HE'S DOING? BIT TRICKY. NO LAB. NOT SO MUCH OF A BUNSEN BURNER, LET ALONE A SPARKLY JACOB'S LADDER.

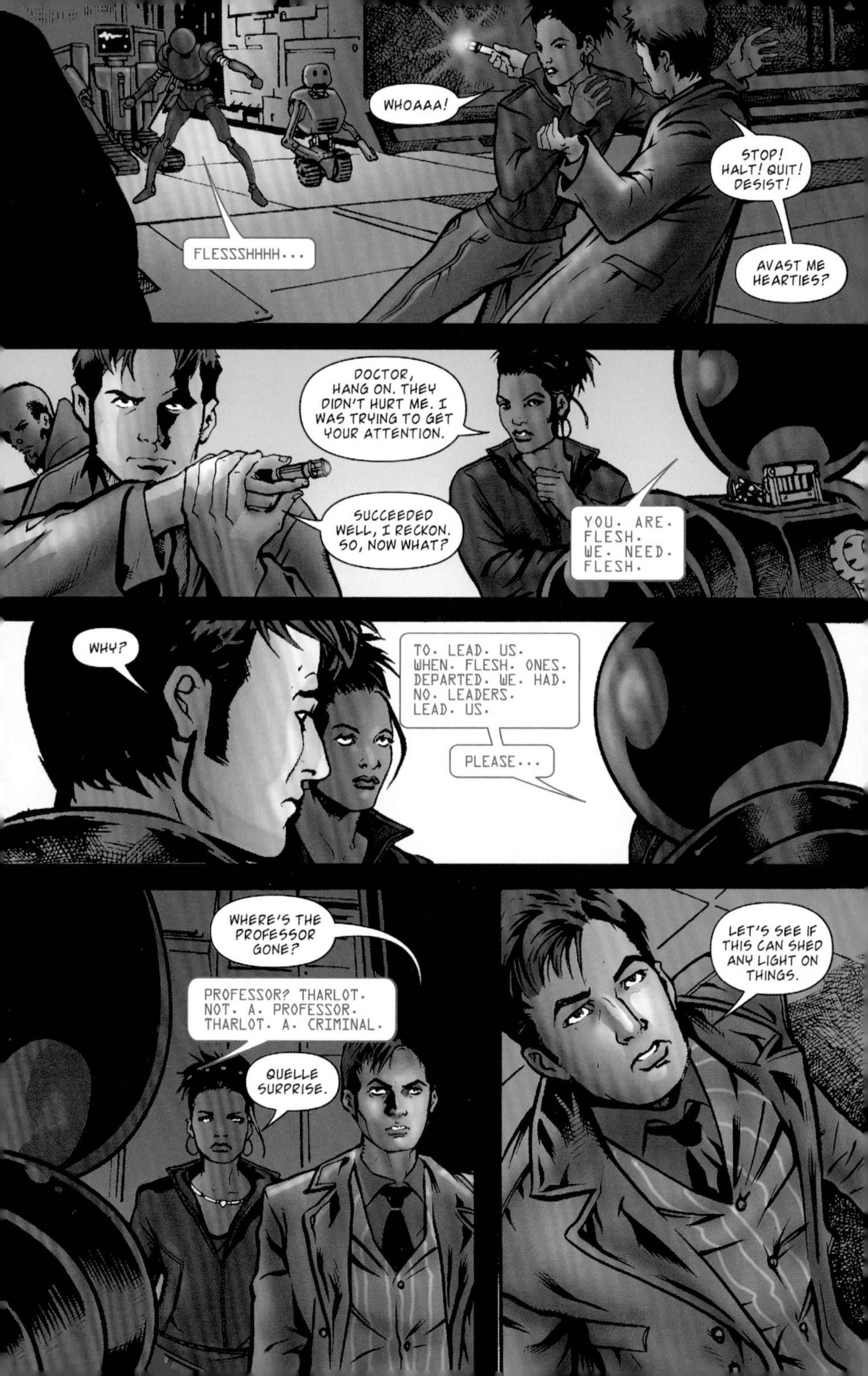
WHOAAA!
FLESSSHHHH...
STOP! HALT! QUIT! DESIST!
AVAST ME HEARTIES?
DOCTOR, HANG ON. THEY DIDN'T HURT ME. I WAS TRYING TO GET YOUR ATTENTION.
SUCCEEDED WELL, I RECKON. SO, NOW WHAT?
YOU. ARE. FLESH. WE. NEED. FLESH.
WHY?
TO. LEAD. US. WHEN. FLESH. ONES. DEPARTED. WE. HAD. NO. LEADERS. LEAD. US.
PLEASE...
WHERE'S THE PROFESSOR GONE?
PROFESSOR? THARLOT. NOT. A. PROFESSOR. THARLOT. A. CRIMINAL.
QUELLE SURPRISE.
LET'S SEE IF THIS CAN SHED ANY LIGHT ON THINGS.

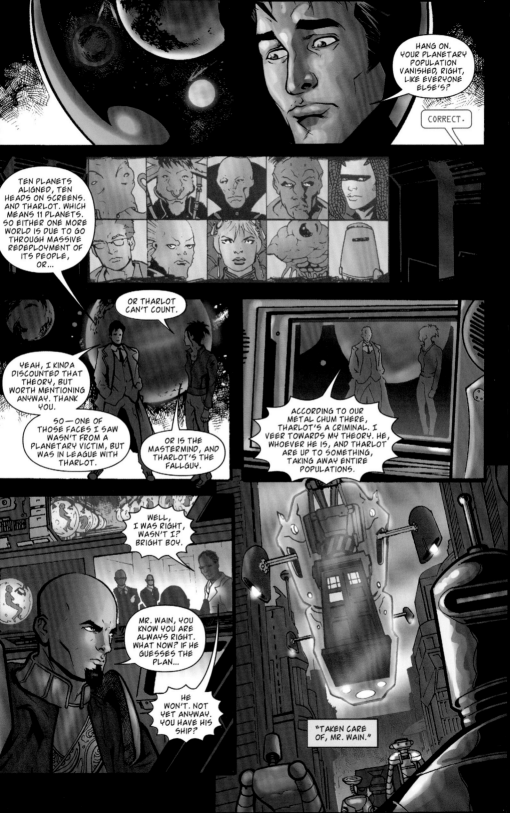

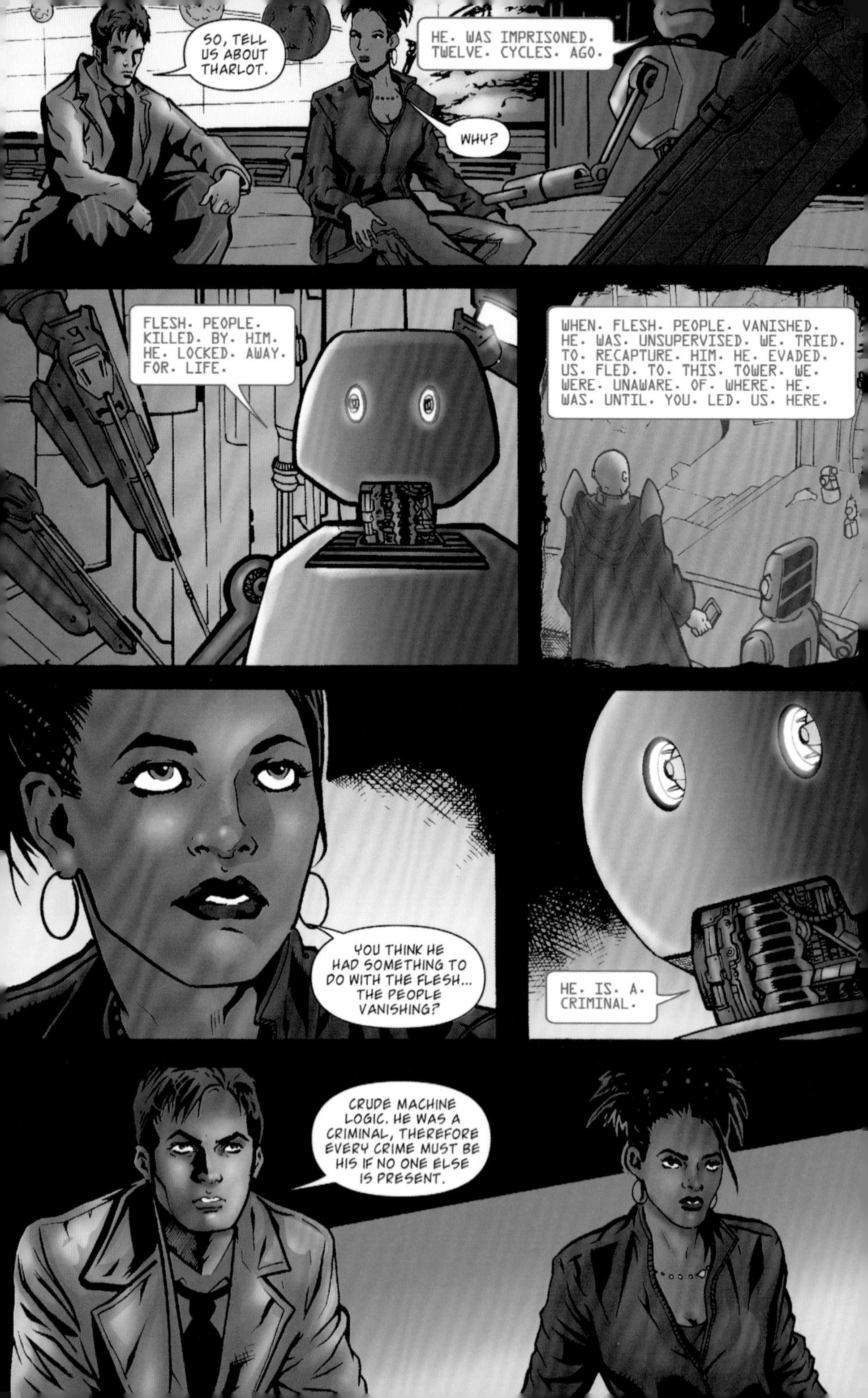
SO, TELL US ABOUT THARLOT.
HE. WAS IMPRISONED. TWELVE. CYCLES. AGO.
WHY?
FLESH. PEOPLE. KILLED. BY. HIM. HE. LOCKED. AWAY. FOR. LIFE.
WHEN. FLESH. PEOPLE. VANISHED. HE. WAS. UNSUPERVISED. WE. TRIED. TO. RECAPTURE. HIM. HE. EVADED. US. FLED. TO. THIS. TOWER. WE. WERE. UNAWARE. OF. WHERE. HE. WAS. UNTIL. YOU. LED. US. HERE.
YOU THINK HE HAD SOMETHING TO DO WITH THE FLESH... THE PEOPLE VANISHING?
HE. IS. A. CRIMINAL.
CRUDE MACHINE LOGIC. HE WAS A CRIMINAL, THEREFORE EVERY CRIME MUST BE HIS IF NO ONE ELSE IS PRESENT.

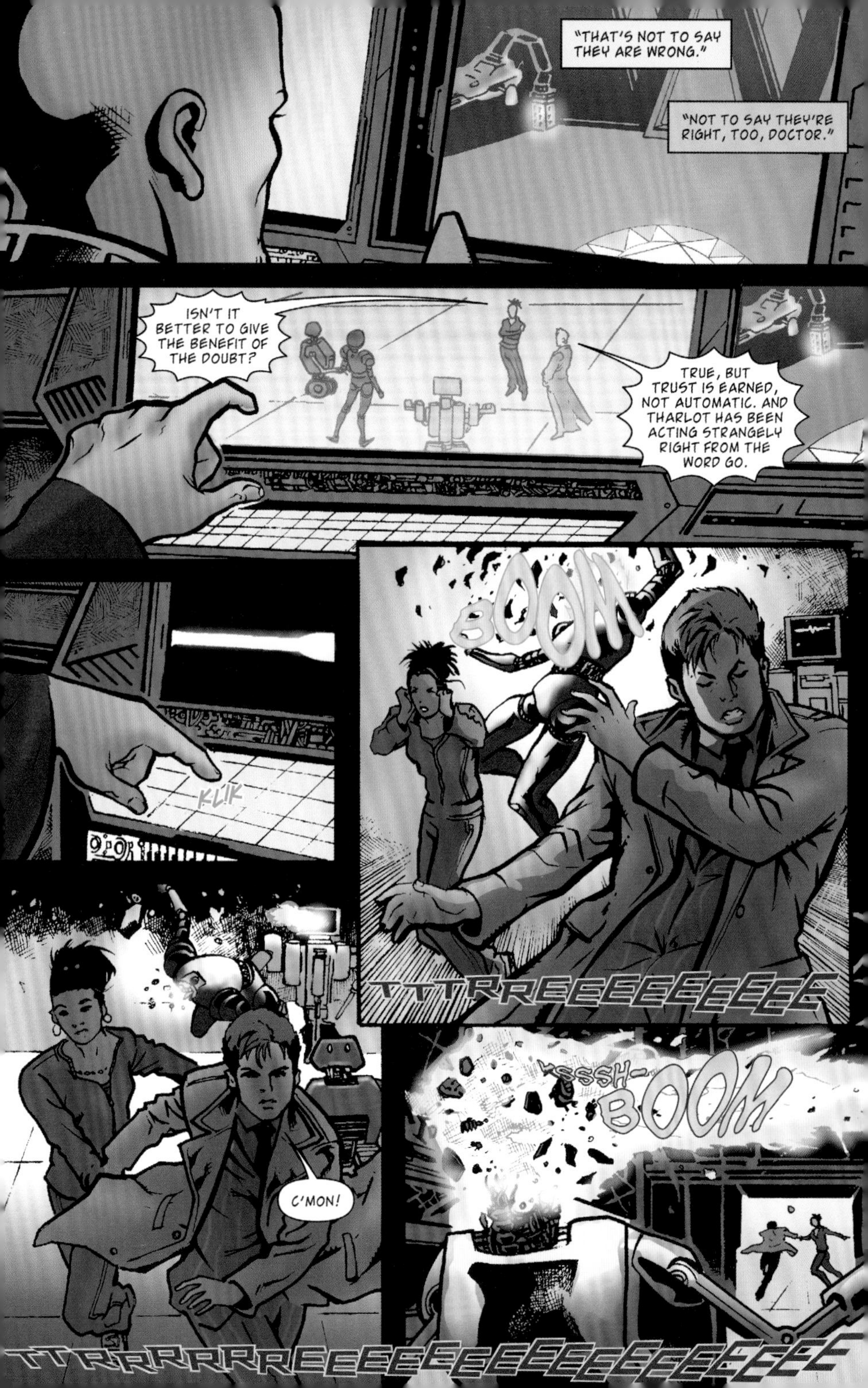
"THAT'S NOT TO SAY THEY ARE WRONG."
"NOT TO SAY THEY'RE RIGHT, TOO, DOCTOR."
ISN'T IT BETTER TO GIVE THE BENEFIT OF THE DOUBT?
TRUE, BUT TRUST IS EARNED, NOT AUTOMATIC. AND THARLOT HAS BEEN ACTING STRANGELY RIGHT FROM THE WORD GO.
KLIK
BOOM
TTTRREEEEEEEEEE
C'MON!
KSSSH-BOOM
TTRRRRRRREEEEEEEEEEEEEEEEEEEE

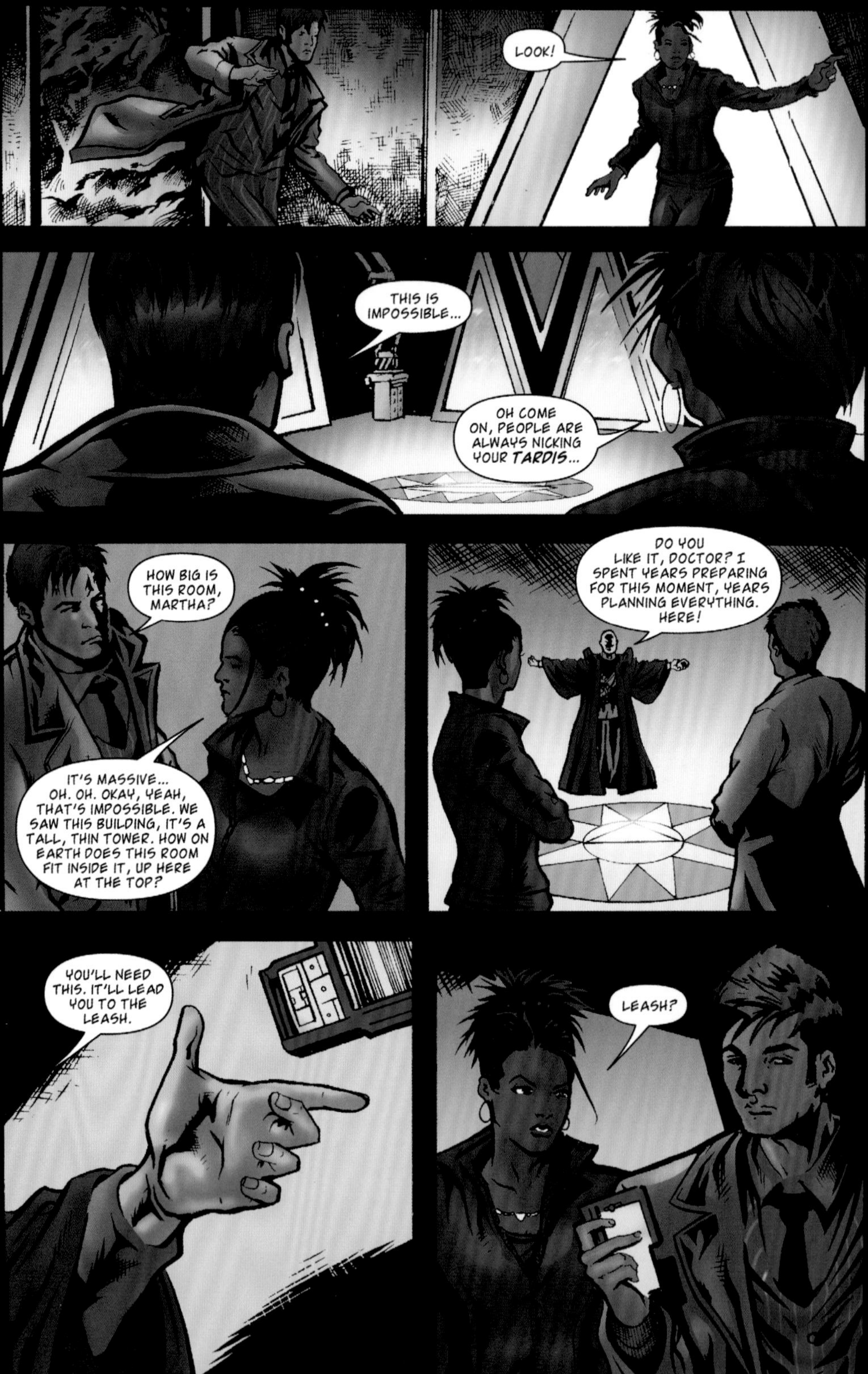
LOOK!
THIS IS IMPOSSIBLE...
OH COME ON, PEOPLE ARE ALWAYS NICKING YOUR TARDIS...
HOW BIG IS THIS ROOM, MARTHA?
IT'S MASSIVE... OH. OH. OKAY, YEAH, THAT'S IMPOSSIBLE. WE SAW THIS BUILDING, IT'S A TALL, THIN TOWER. HOW ON EARTH DOES THIS ROOM FIT INSIDE IT, UP HERE AT THE TOP?
DO YOU LIKE IT, DOCTOR? I SPENT YEARS PREPARING FOR THIS MOMENT, YEARS PLANNING EVERYTHING. HERE!
YOU'LL NEED THIS. IT'LL LEAD YOU TO THE LEASH.
LEASH?

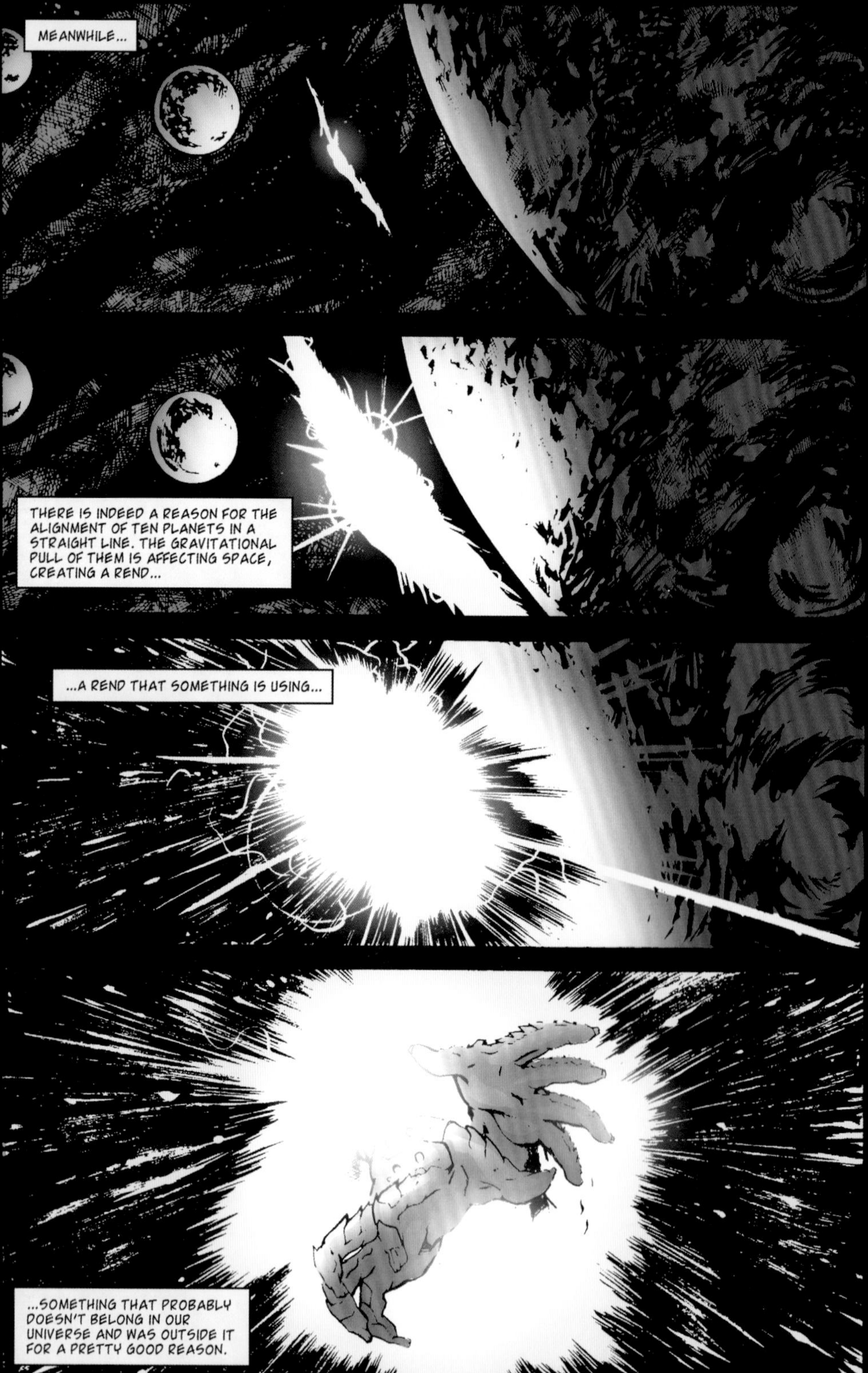
MEANWHILE...
THERE IS INDEED A REASON FOR THE ALIGNMENT OF TEN PLANETS IN A STRAIGHT LINE. THE GRAVITATIONAL PULL OF THEM IS AFFECTING SPACE, CREATING A REND...
...A REND THAT SOMETHING IS USING...
...SOMETHING THAT PROBABLY DOESN'T BELONG IN OUR UNIVERSE AND WAS OUTSIDE IT FOR A PRETTY GOOD REASON.

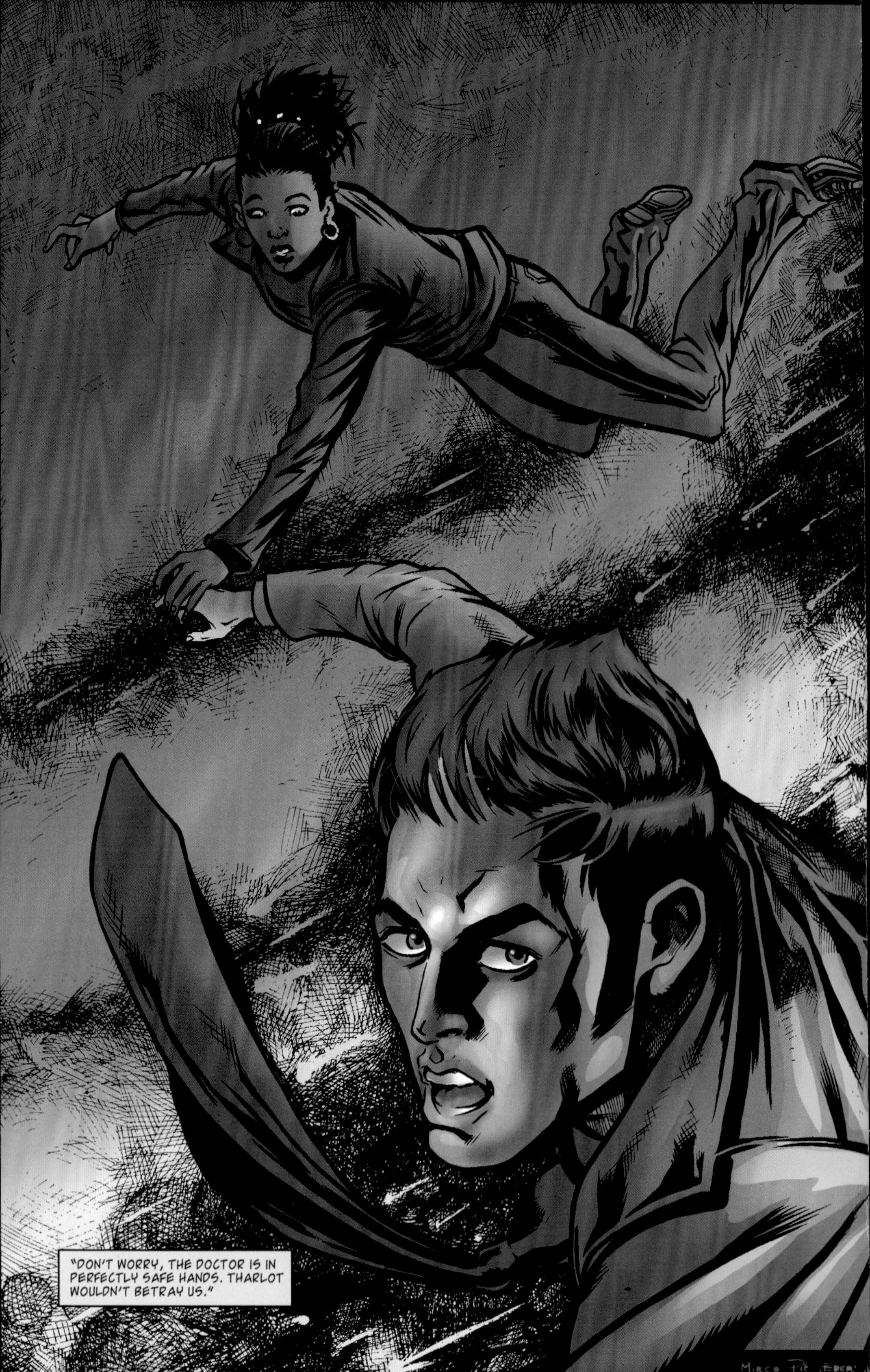
"DON'T WORRY, THE DOCTOR IS IN PERFECTLY SAFE HANDS. THARLOT WOULDN'T BETRAY US."

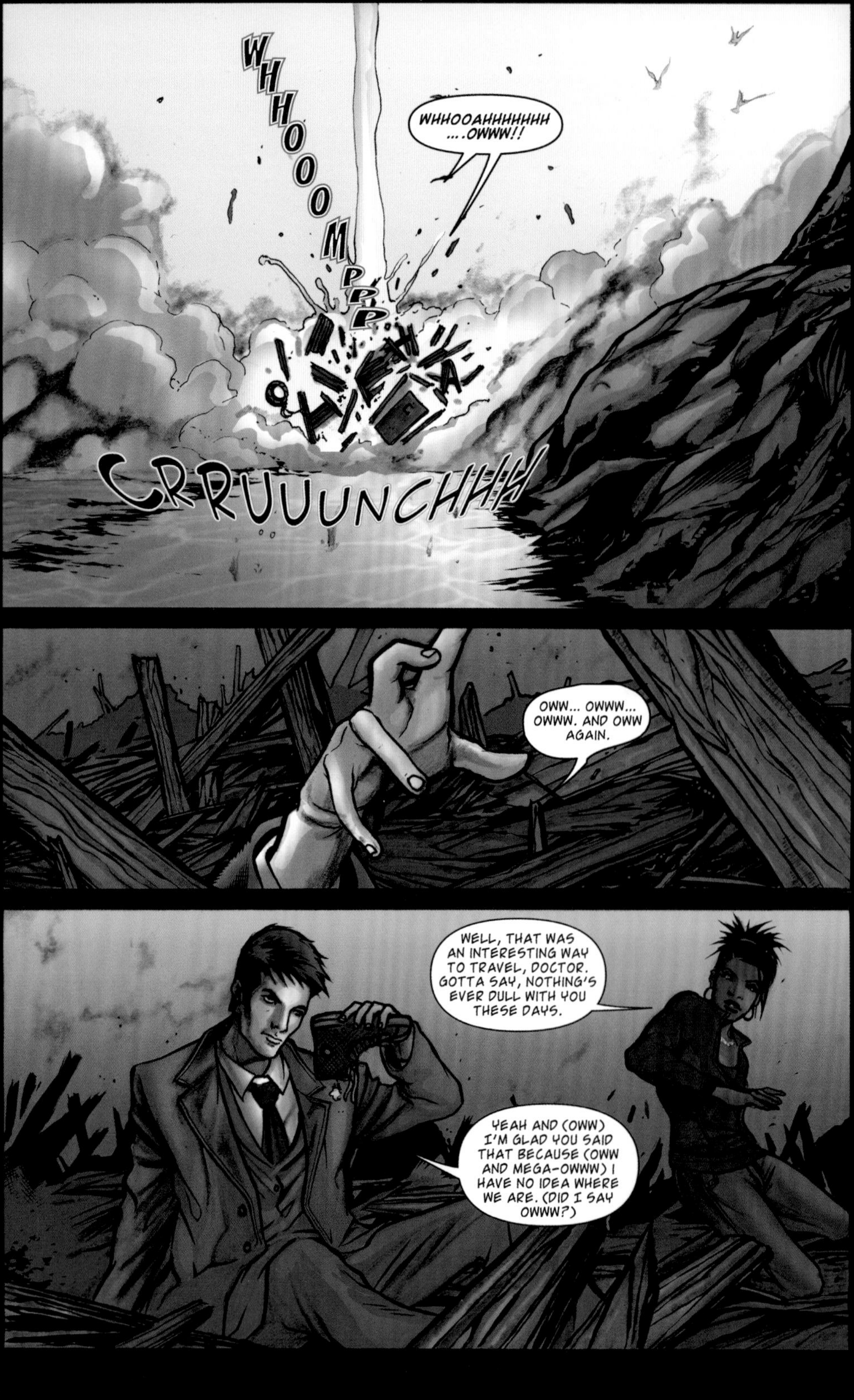
WHHOOOOMPPP
WHHOOAHHHHHHH ....OWWW!!
CRRUUUNCHHH
OWW... OWWW... OWWW. AND OWW AGAIN.
WELL, THAT WAS AN INTERESTING WAY TO TRAVEL, DOCTOR. GOTTA SAY, NOTHING'S EVER DULL WITH YOU THESE DAYS.
YEAH AND (OWW) I'M GLAD YOU SAID THAT BECAUSE (OWW AND MEGA-OWWW) I HAVE NO IDEA WHERE WE ARE. (DID I SAY OWWW?)

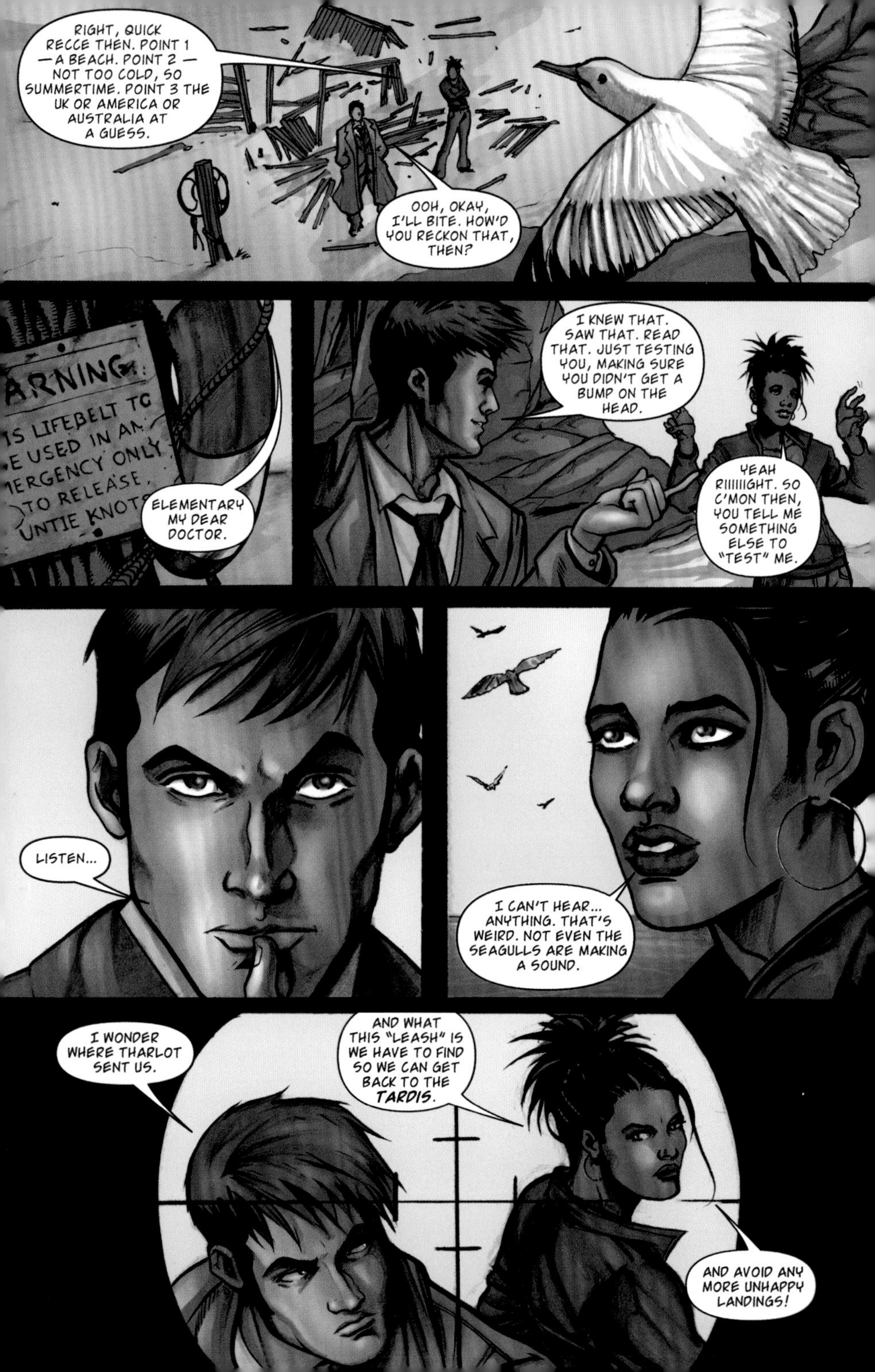

RIGHT, QUICK RECCE THEN. POINT 1 — A BEACH. POINT 2 — NOT TOO COLD, SO SUMMERTIME. POINT 3 THE UK OR AMERICA OR AUSTRALIA AT A GUESS.
OOH, OKAY, I'LL BITE. HOW'D YOU RECKON THAT, THEN?
ARNING
IS LIFEBELT TO
E USED IN AN
MERGENCY ONLY
TO RELEASE
UNTIE KNOTS
ELEMENTARY MY DEAR DOCTOR.
I KNEW THAT. SAW THAT. READ THAT. JUST TESTING YOU, MAKING SURE YOU DIDN'T GET A BUMP ON THE HEAD.
YEAH RIIIIIGHT. SO C'MON THEN, YOU TELL ME SOMETHING ELSE TO "TEST" ME.
LISTEN...
I CAN'T HEAR... ANYTHING. THAT'S WEIRD. NOT EVEN THE SEAGULLS ARE MAKING A SOUND.
I WONDER WHERE THARLOT SENT US.
AND WHAT THIS "LEASH" IS WE HAVE TO FIND SO WE CAN GET BACK TO THE *TARDIS*.
AND AVOID ANY MORE UNHAPPY LANDINGS!

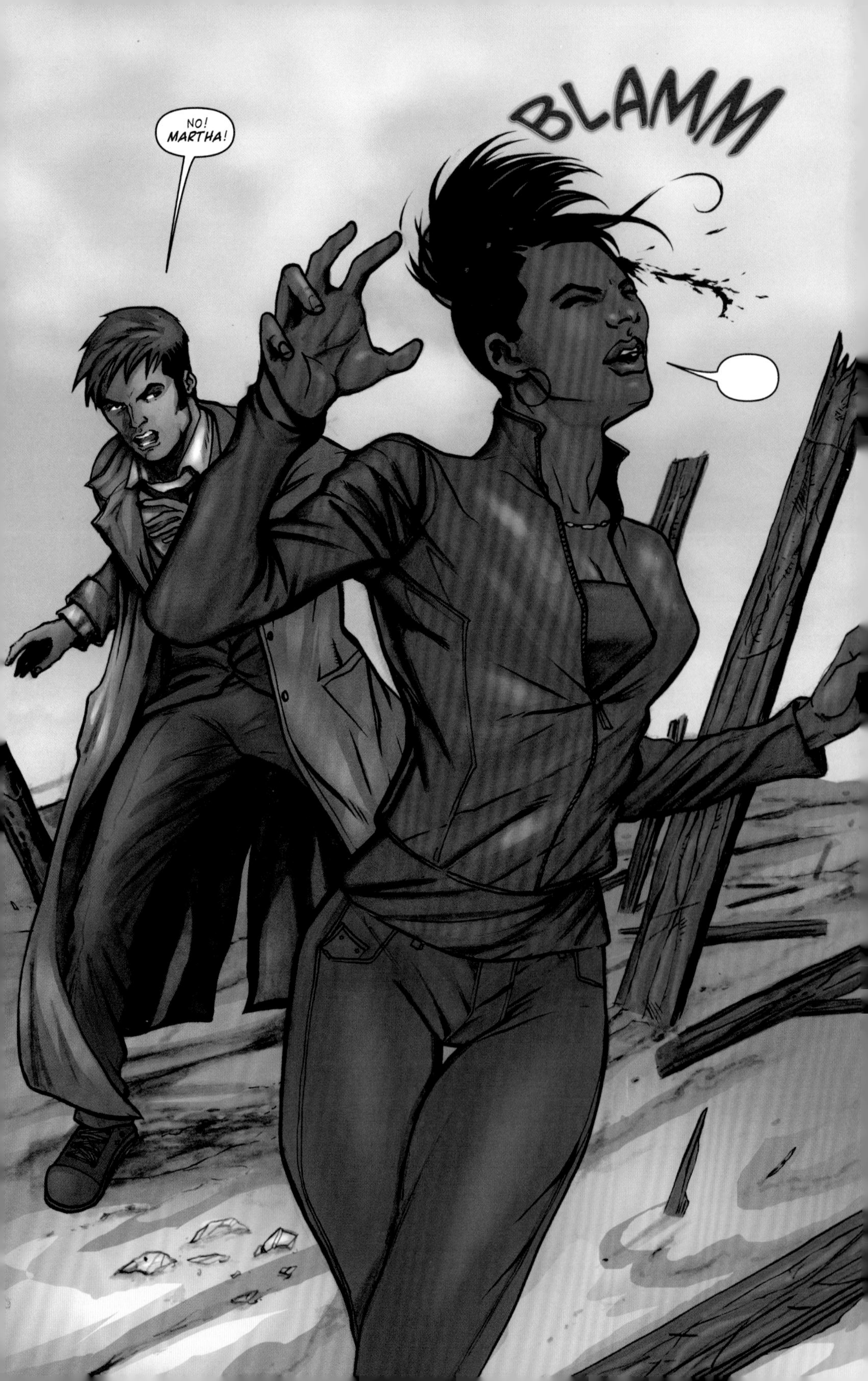
NO! MARTHA!
BLAMM

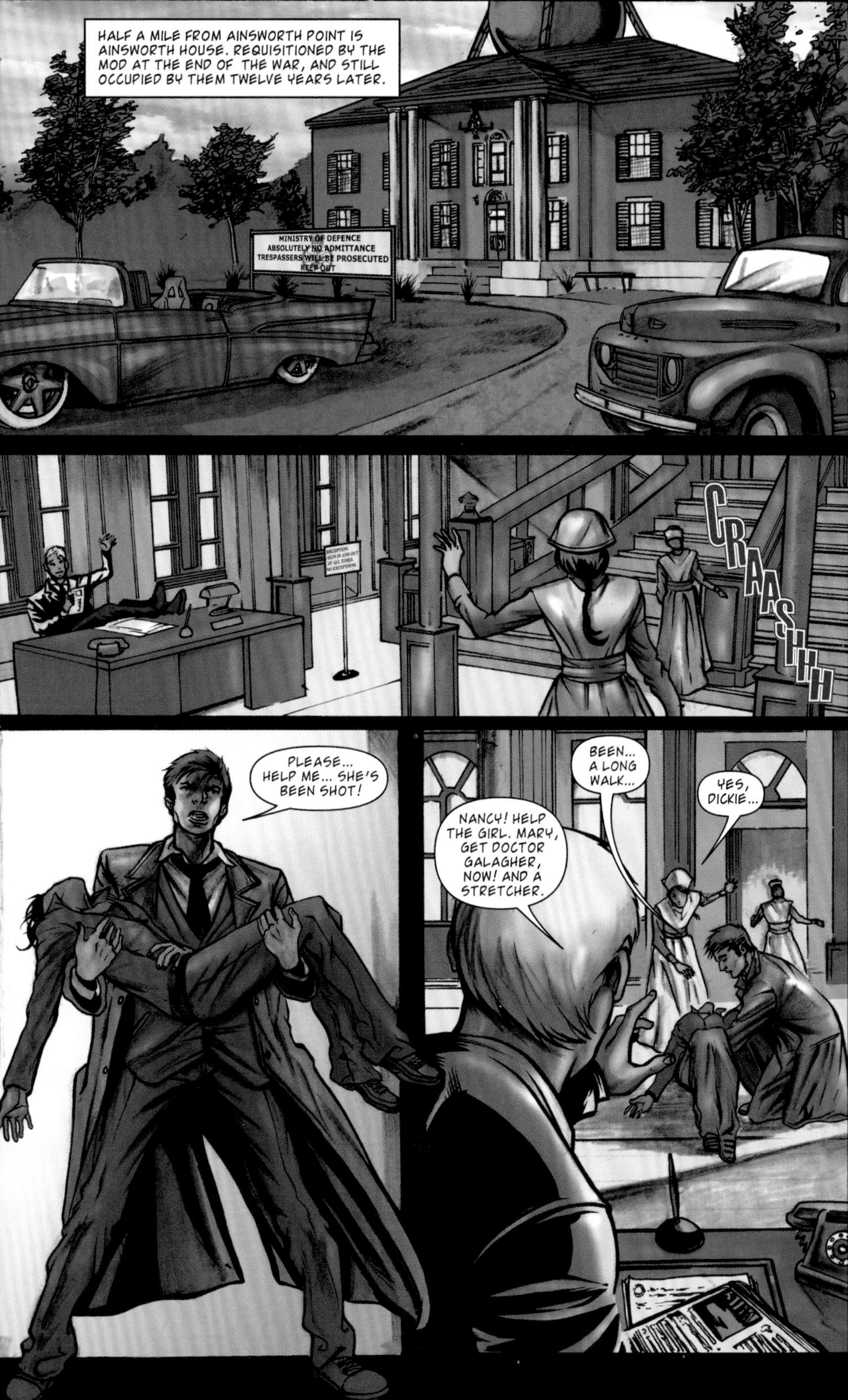
HALF A MILE FROM AINSWORTH POINT IS AINSWORTH HOUSE. REQUISITIONED BY THE MOD AT THE END OF THE WAR, AND STILL OCCUPIED BY THEM TWELVE YEARS LATER.
MINISTRY OF DEFENCE
ABSOLUTELY NO ADMITTANCE
TRESPASSERS WILL BE PROSECUTED
KEEP OUT
RECEPTION. SIGN IN AND OUT AT ALL TIMES. NO EXCEPTIONS
CRAASHHH
PLEASE... HELP ME... SHE'S BEEN SHOT!
BEEN... A LONG WALK...
NANCY! HELP THE GIRL. MARY, GET DOCTOR GALAGHER, NOW! AND A STRETCHER.
YES, DICKIE...

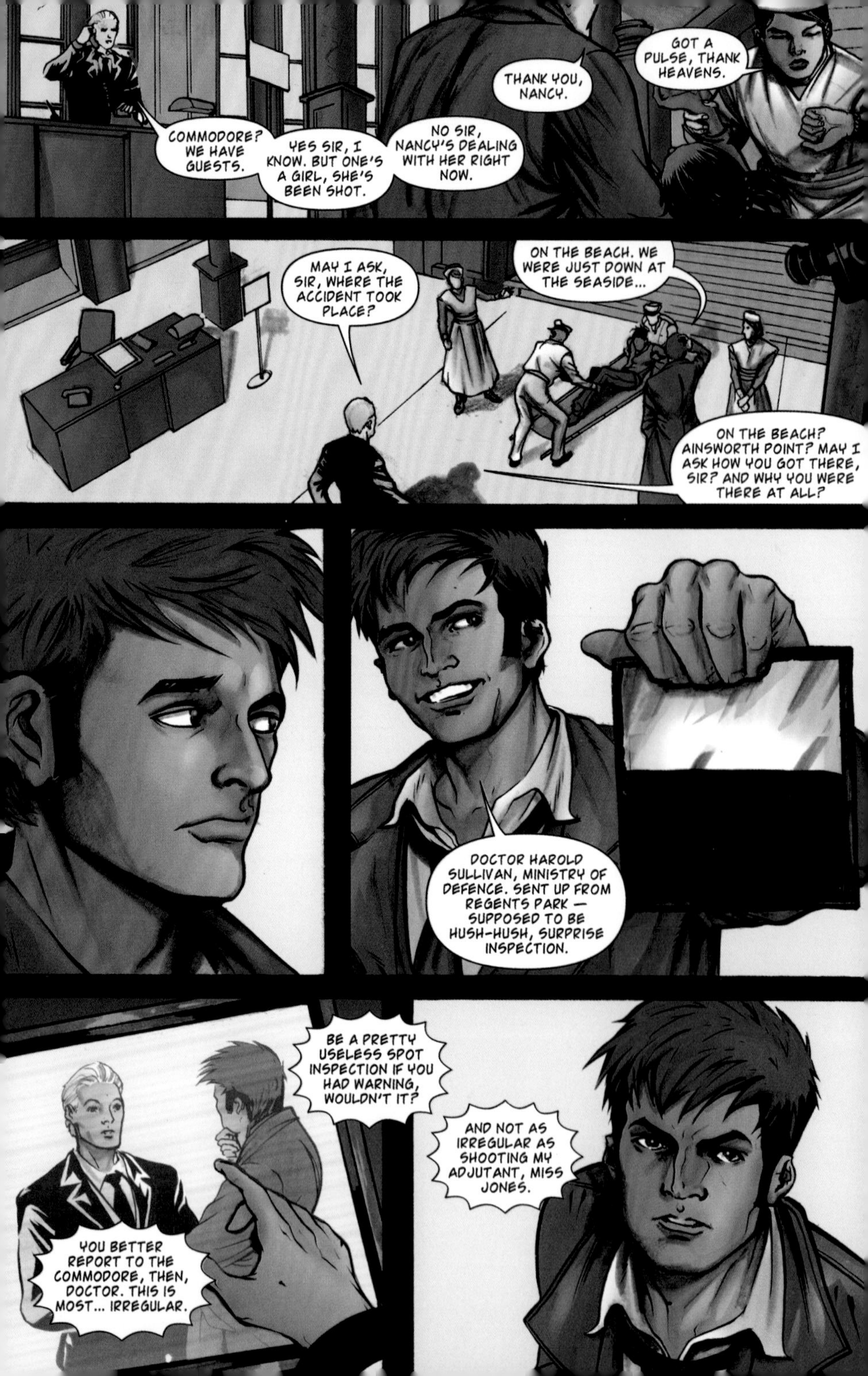
COMMODORE? WE HAVE GUESTS.
YES SIR, I KNOW. BUT ONE'S A GIRL, SHE'S BEEN SHOT.
NO SIR, NANCY'S DEALING WITH HER RIGHT NOW.
THANK YOU, NANCY.
GOT A PULSE, THANK HEAVENS.
MAY I ASK, SIR, WHERE THE ACCIDENT TOOK PLACE?
ON THE BEACH. WE WERE JUST DOWN AT THE SEASIDE...
ON THE BEACH? AINSWORTH POINT? MAY I ASK HOW YOU GOT THERE, SIR? AND WHY YOU WERE THERE AT ALL?
DOCTOR HAROLD SULLIVAN, MINISTRY OF DEFENCE. SENT UP FROM REGENTS PARK — SUPPOSED TO BE HUSH-HUSH, SURPRISE INSPECTION.
YOU BETTER REPORT TO THE COMMODORE, THEN, DOCTOR. THIS IS MOST... IRREGULAR.
BE A PRETTY USELESS SPOT INSPECTION IF YOU HAD WARNING, WOULDN'T IT?
AND NOT AS IRREGULAR AS SHOOTING MY ADJUTANT, MISS JONES.

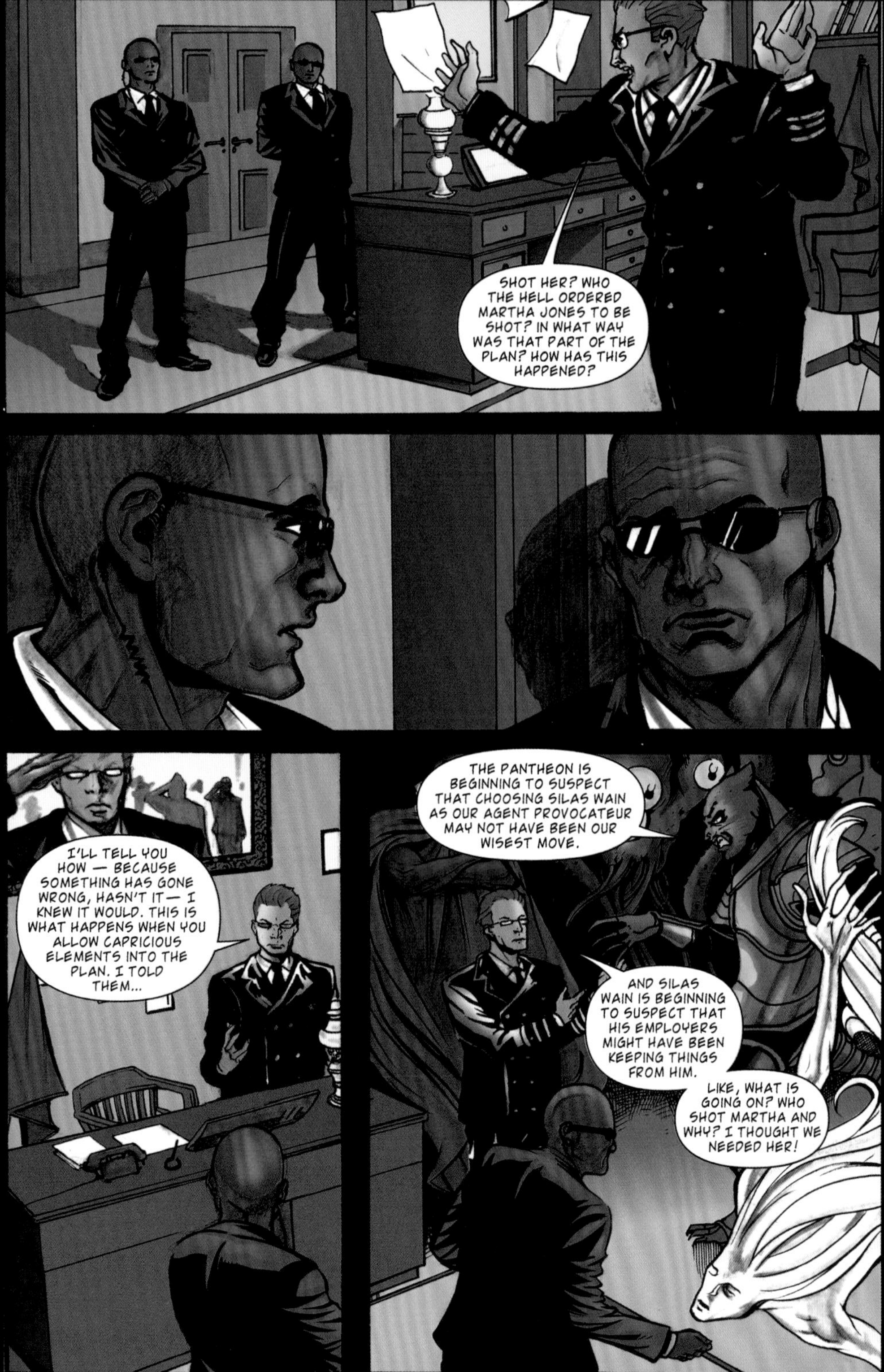
SHOT HER? WHO THE HELL ORDERED MARTHA JONES TO BE SHOT? IN WHAT WAY WAS THAT PART OF THE PLAN? HOW HAS THIS HAPPENED?
I'LL TELL YOU HOW — BECAUSE SOMETHING HAS GONE WRONG, HASN'T IT — I KNEW IT WOULD. THIS IS WHAT HAPPENS WHEN YOU ALLOW CAPRICIOUS ELEMENTS INTO THE PLAN. I TOLD THEM...
THE PANTHEON IS BEGINNING TO SUSPECT THAT CHOOSING SILAS WAIN AS OUR AGENT PROVOCATEUR MAY NOT HAVE BEEN OUR WISEST MOVE.
AND SILAS WAIN IS BEGINNING TO SUSPECT THAT HIS EMPLOYERS MIGHT HAVE BEEN KEEPING THINGS FROM HIM.
LIKE, WHAT IS GOING ON? WHO SHOT MARTHA AND WHY? I THOUGHT WE NEEDED HER!

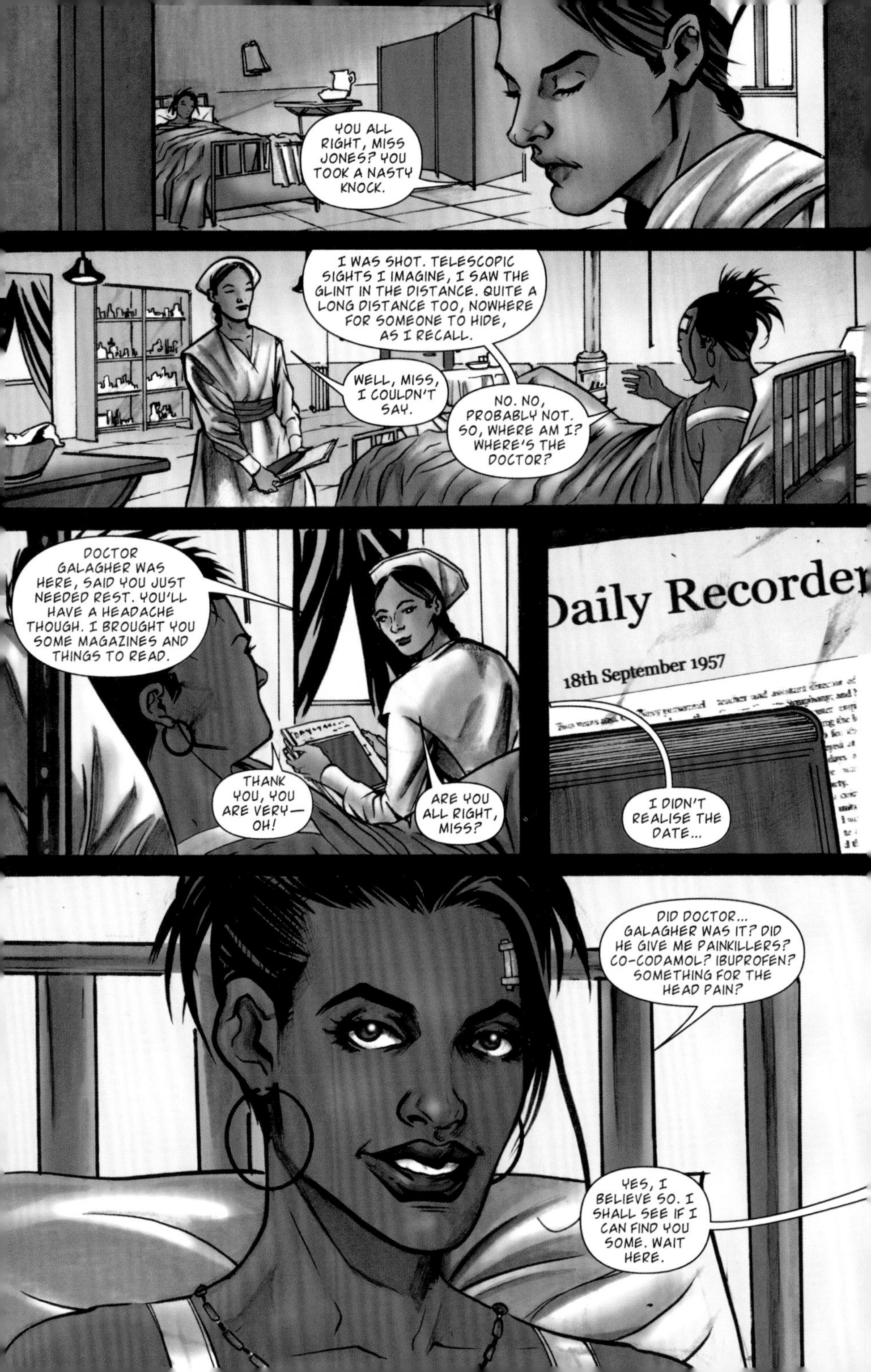
YOU ALL RIGHT, MISS JONES? YOU TOOK A NASTY KNOCK.
I WAS SHOT. TELESCOPIC SIGHTS I IMAGINE, I SAW THE GLINT IN THE DISTANCE. QUITE A LONG DISTANCE TOO, NOWHERE FOR SOMEONE TO HIDE, AS I RECALL.
WELL, MISS, I COULDN'T SAY.
NO. NO, PROBABLY NOT. SO, WHERE AM I? WHERE'S THE DOCTOR?
DOCTOR GALAGHER WAS HERE, SAID YOU JUST NEEDED REST. YOU'LL HAVE A HEADACHE THOUGH. I BROUGHT YOU SOME MAGAZINES AND THINGS TO READ.
THANK YOU, YOU ARE VERY— OH!
ARE YOU ALL RIGHT, MISS?
Daily Recorder
18th September 1957
I DIDN'T REALISE THE DATE...
DID DOCTOR... GALAGHER WAS IT? DID HE GIVE ME PAINKILLERS? CO-CODAMOL? IBUPROFEN? SOMETHING FOR THE HEAD PAIN?
YES, I BELIEVE SO. I SHALL SEE IF I CAN FIND YOU SOME. WAIT HERE.

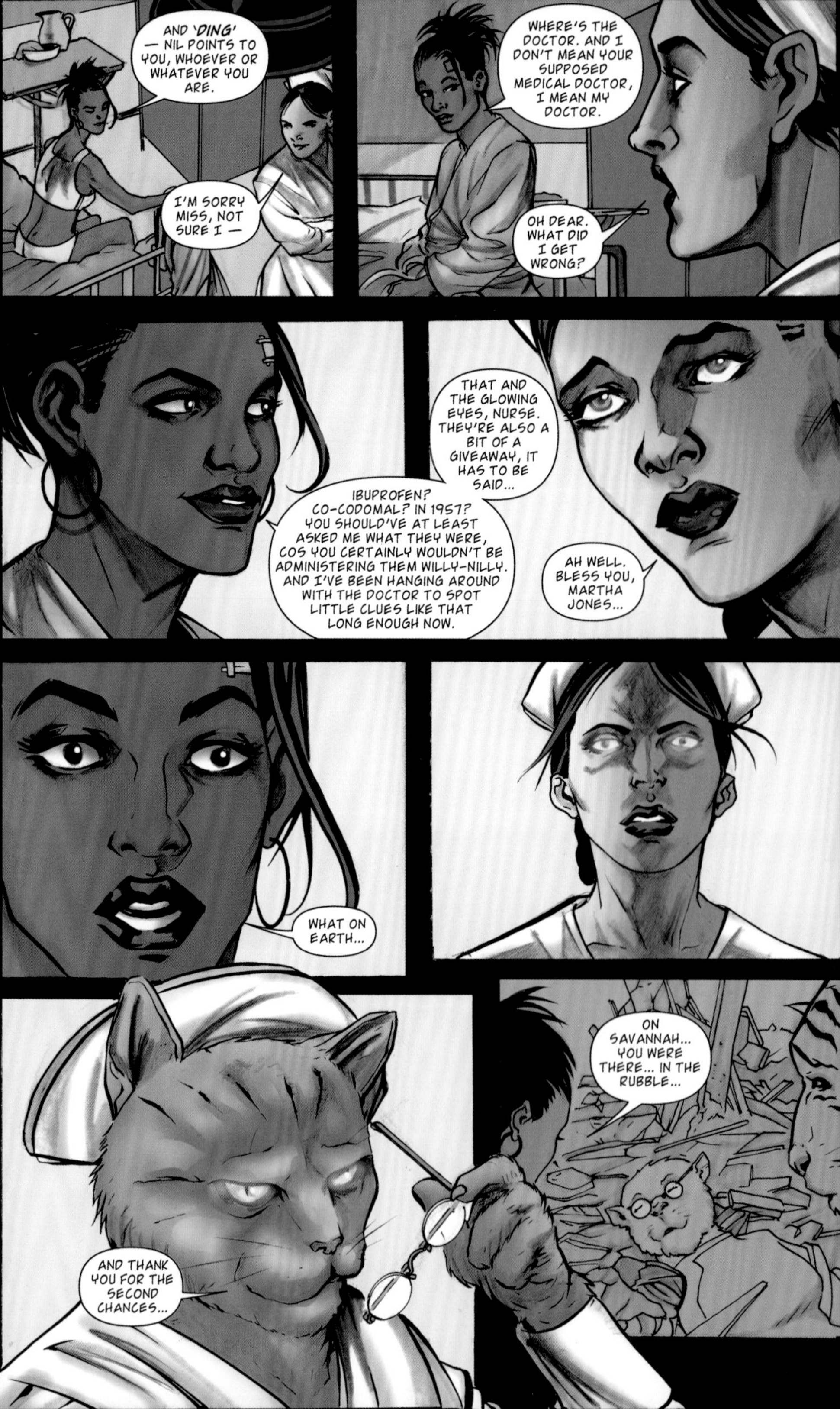
AND 'DING' — NIL POINTS TO YOU, WHOEVER OR WHATEVER YOU ARE.
I'M SORRY MISS, NOT SURE I —
WHERE'S THE DOCTOR. AND I DON'T MEAN YOUR SUPPOSED MEDICAL DOCTOR, I MEAN MY DOCTOR.
OH DEAR. WHAT DID I GET WRONG?
IBUPROFEN? CO-CODOMAL? IN 1957? YOU SHOULD'VE AT LEAST ASKED ME WHAT THEY WERE, COS YOU CERTAINLY WOULDN'T BE ADMINISTERING THEM WILLY-NILLY. AND I'VE BEEN HANGING AROUND WITH THE DOCTOR TO SPOT LITTLE CLUES LIKE THAT LONG ENOUGH NOW.
THAT AND THE GLOWING EYES, NURSE. THEY'RE ALSO A BIT OF A GIVEAWAY, IT HAS TO BE SAID...
AH WELL. BLESS YOU, MARTHA JONES...
WHAT ON EARTH...
AND THANK YOU FOR THE SECOND CHANCES...
ON SAVANNAH... YOU WERE THERE... IN THE RUBBLE...

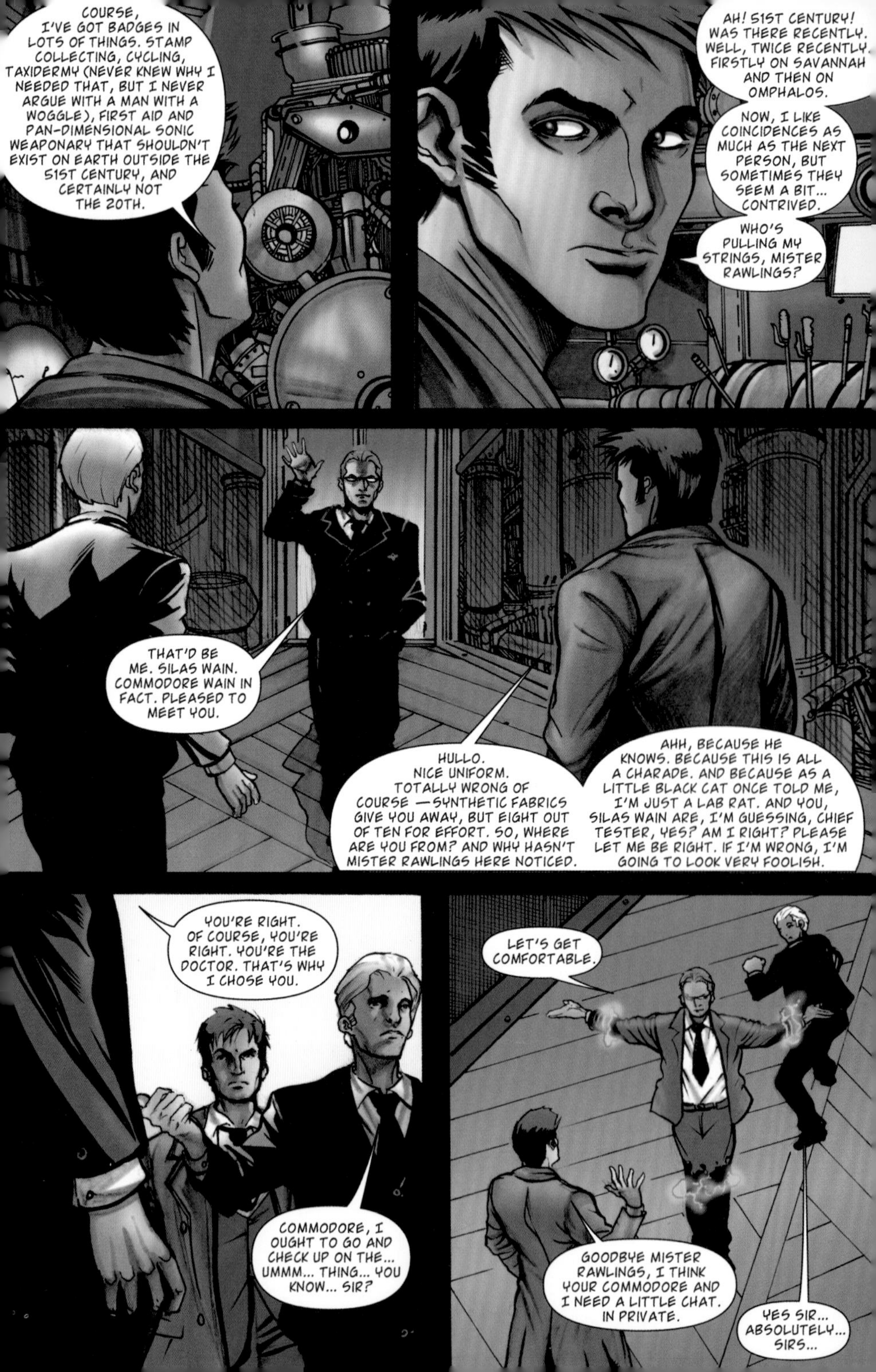
COURSE, I'VE GOT BADGES IN LOTS OF THINGS. STAMP COLLECTING, CYCLING, TAXIDERMY (NEVER KNEW WHY I NEEDED THAT, BUT I NEVER ARGUE WITH A MAN WITH A WOGGLE), FIRST AID AND PAN-DIMENSIONAL SONIC WEAPONARY THAT SHOULDN'T EXIST ON EARTH OUTSIDE THE 51ST CENTURY, AND CERTAINLY NOT THE 20TH.
AH! 51ST CENTURY! WAS THERE RECENTLY. WELL, TWICE RECENTLY. FIRSTLY ON SAVANNAH AND THEN ON OMPHALOS.
NOW, I LIKE COINCIDENCES AS MUCH AS THE NEXT PERSON, BUT SOMETIMES THEY SEEM A BIT... CONTRIVED.
WHO'S PULLING MY STRINGS, MISTER RAWLINGS?
THAT'D BE ME. SILAS WAIN. COMMODORE WAIN IN FACT. PLEASED TO MEET YOU.
HULLO. NICE UNIFORM. TOTALLY WRONG OF COURSE —SYNTHETIC FABRICS GIVE YOU AWAY, BUT EIGHT OUT OF TEN FOR EFFORT. SO, WHERE ARE YOU FROM? AND WHY HASN'T MISTER RAWLINGS HERE NOTICED.
AHH, BECAUSE HE KNOWS. BECAUSE THIS IS ALL A CHARADE. AND BECAUSE AS A LITTLE BLACK CAT ONCE TOLD ME, I'M JUST A LAB RAT. AND YOU, SILAS WAIN ARE, I'M GUESSING, CHIEF TESTER, YES? AM I RIGHT? PLEASE LET ME BE RIGHT. IF I'M WRONG, I'M GOING TO LOOK VERY FOOLISH.
YOU'RE RIGHT. OF COURSE, YOU'RE RIGHT. YOU'RE THE DOCTOR. THAT'S WHY I CHOSE YOU.
COMMODORE, I OUGHT TO GO AND CHECK UP ON THE... UMMM... THING... YOU KNOW... SIR?
LET'S GET COMFORTABLE.
GOODBYE MISTER RAWLINGS, I THINK YOUR COMMODORE AND I NEED A LITTLE CHAT. IN PRIVATE.
YES SIR... ABSOLUTELY... SIRS...

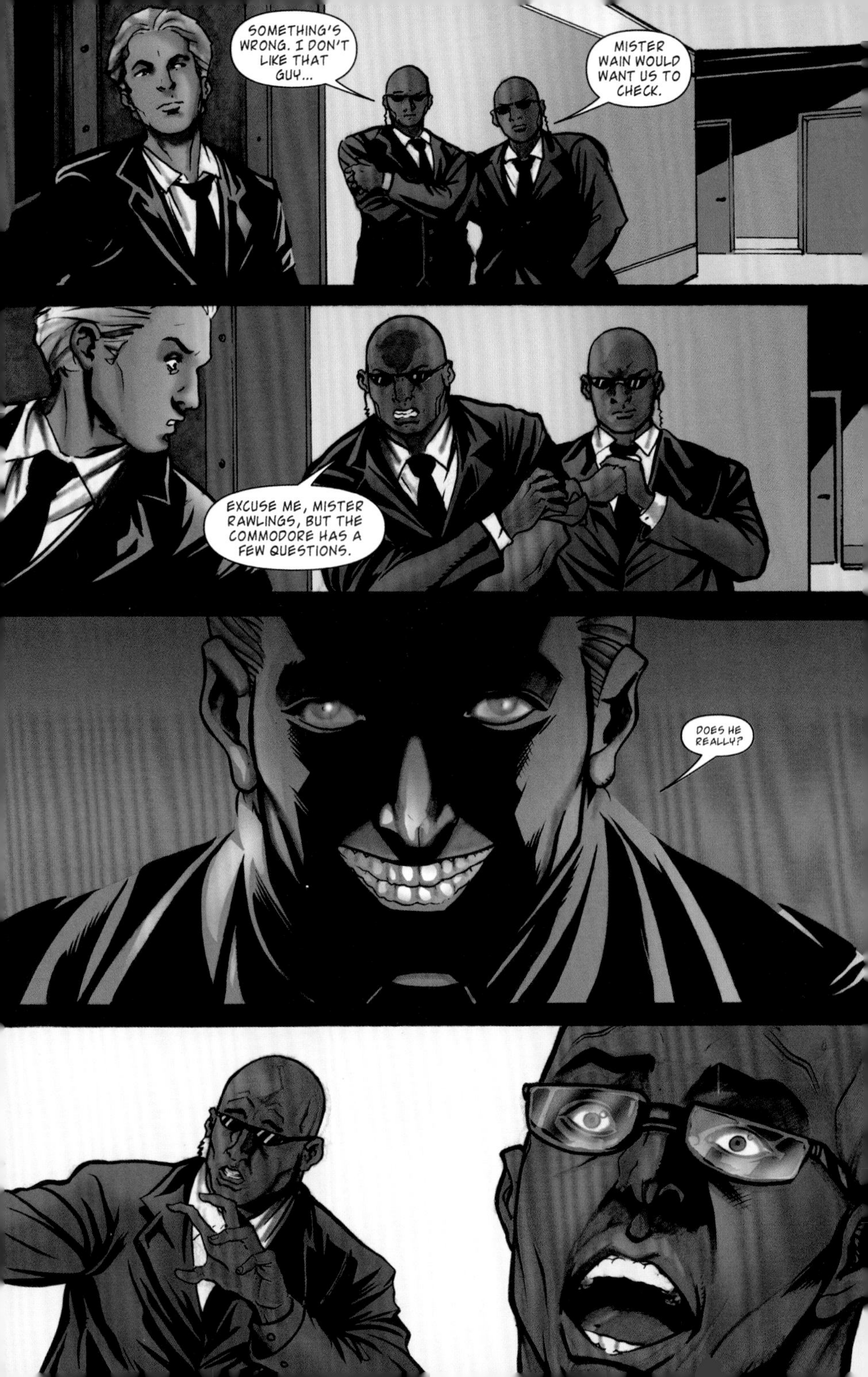
SOMETHING'S WRONG. I DON'T LIKE THAT GUY...
MISTER WAIN WOULD WANT US TO CHECK.
EXCUSE ME, MISTER RAWLINGS, BUT THE COMMODORE HAS A FEW QUESTIONS.
DOES HE REALLY?

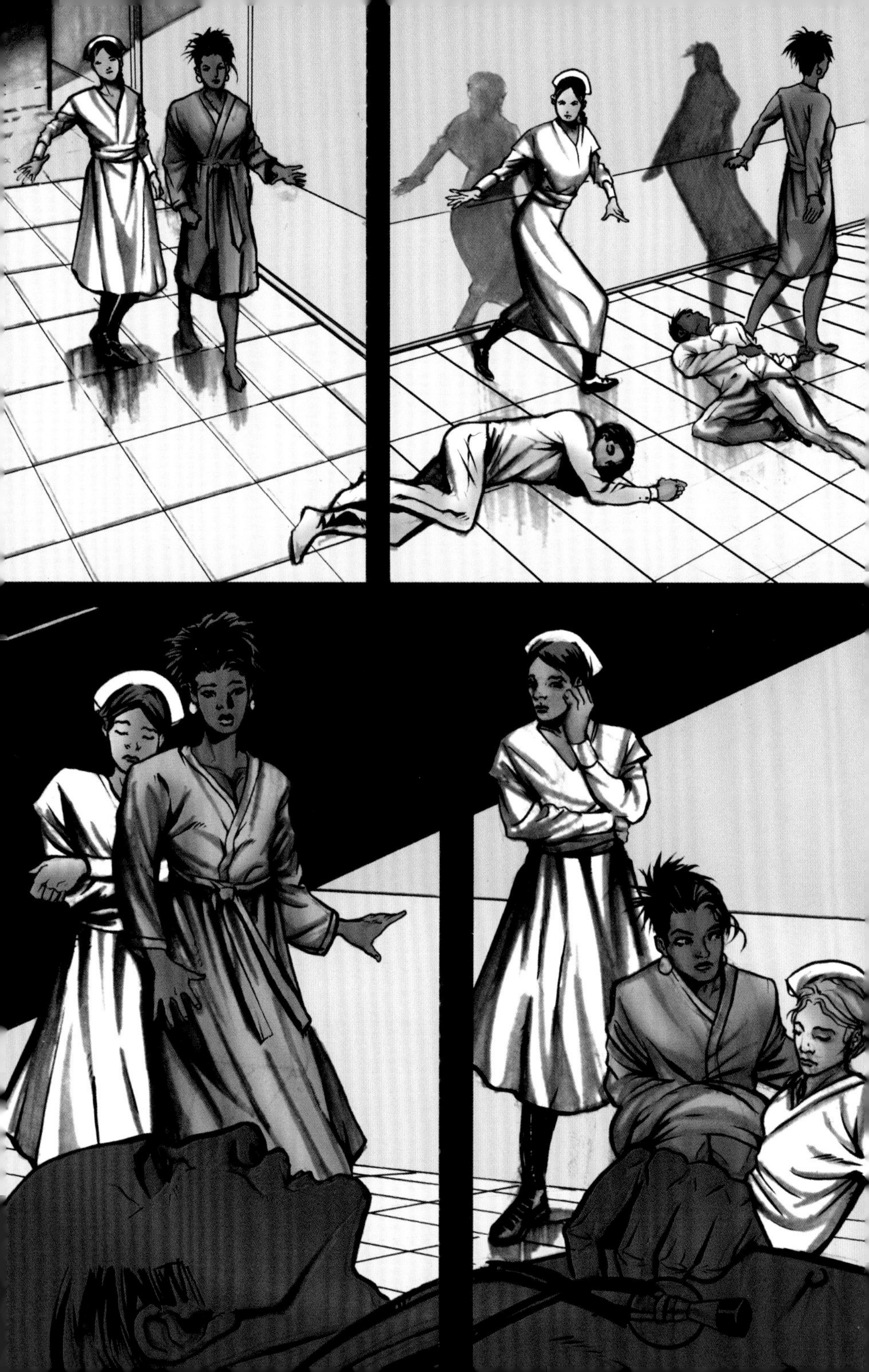

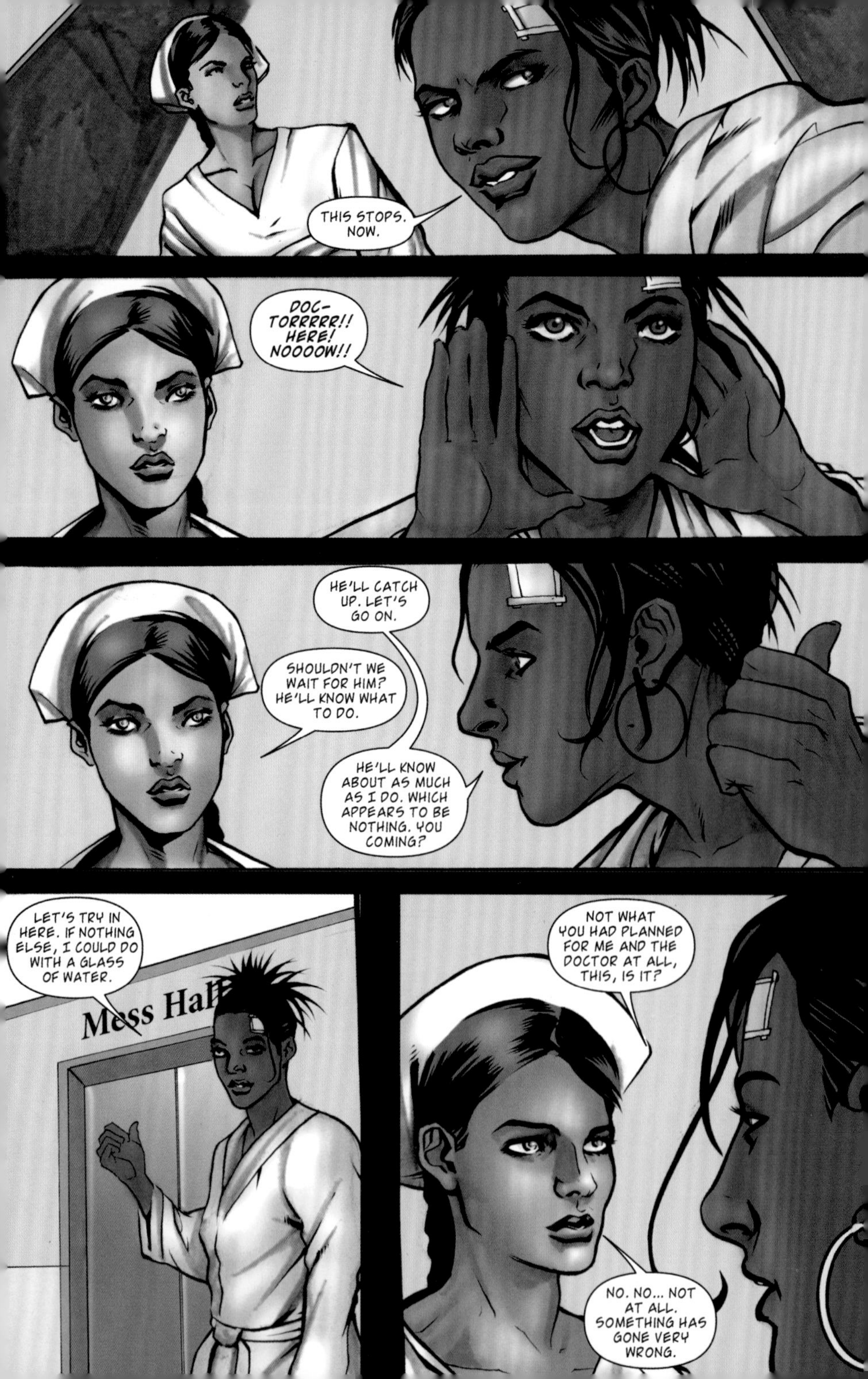
THIS STOPS. NOW.
DOC-TORRRRR!! HERE! NOOOOW!!
SHOULDN'T WE WAIT FOR HIM? HE'LL KNOW WHAT TO DO.
HE'LL CATCH UP. LET'S GO ON.
HE'LL KNOW ABOUT AS MUCH AS I DO. WHICH APPEARS TO BE NOTHING. YOU COMING?
LET'S TRY IN HERE. IF NOTHING ELSE, I COULD DO WITH A GLASS OF WATER.
Mess Hall
NOT WHAT YOU HAD PLANNED FOR ME AND THE DOCTOR AT ALL, THIS, IS IT?
NO. NO... NOT AT ALL. SOMETHING HAS GONE VERY WRONG.

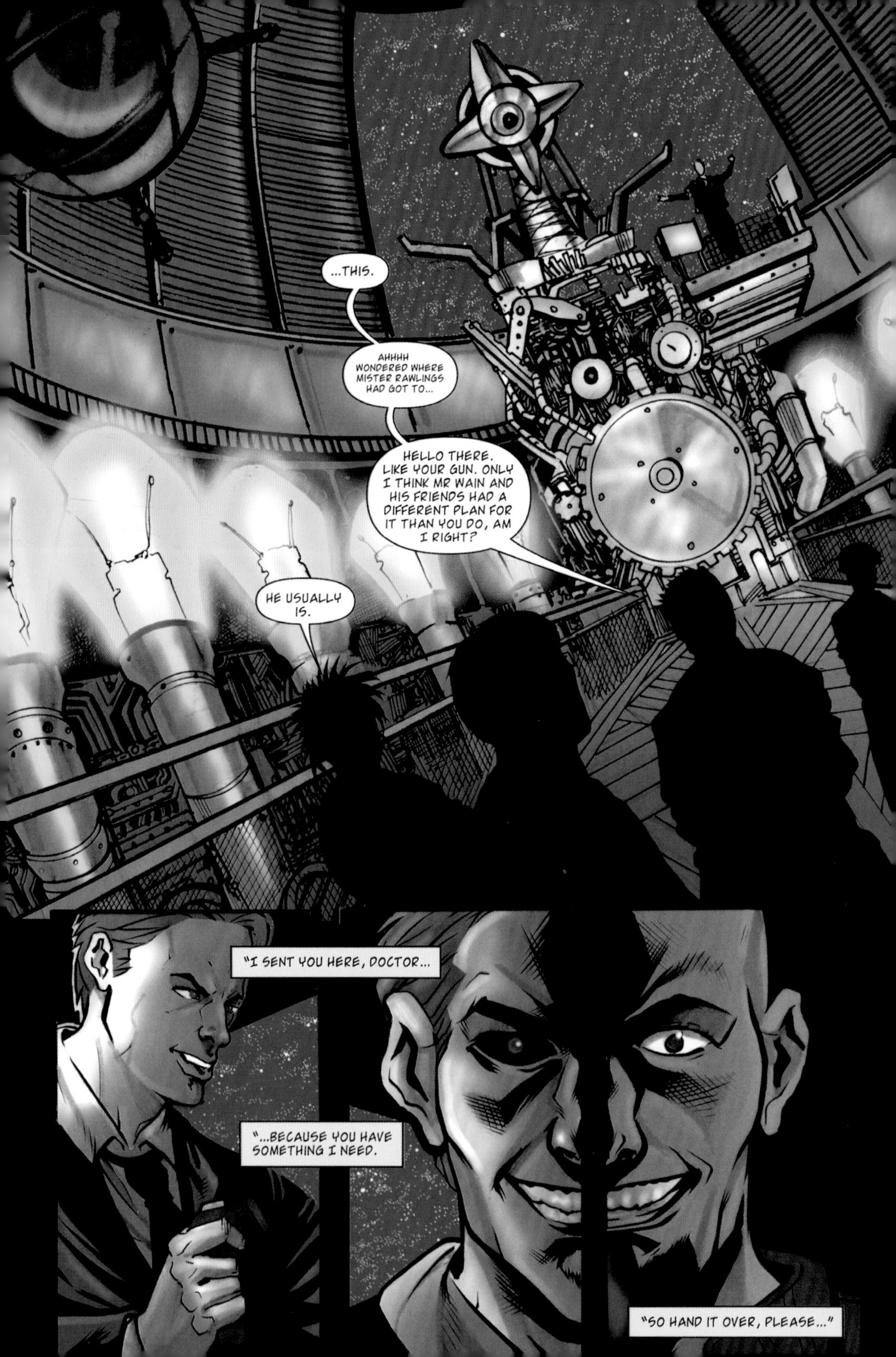
...THIS.
AHHHH WONDERED WHERE MISTER RAWLINGS HAD GOT TO...
HELLO THERE. LIKE YOUR GUN. ONLY I THINK MR WAIN AND HIS FRIENDS HAD A DIFFERENT PLAN FOR IT THAN YOU DO, AM I RIGHT?
HE USUALLY IS.
"I SENT YOU HERE, DOCTOR...
"...BECAUSE YOU HAVE SOMETHING I NEED.
"SO HAND IT OVER, PLEASE..."

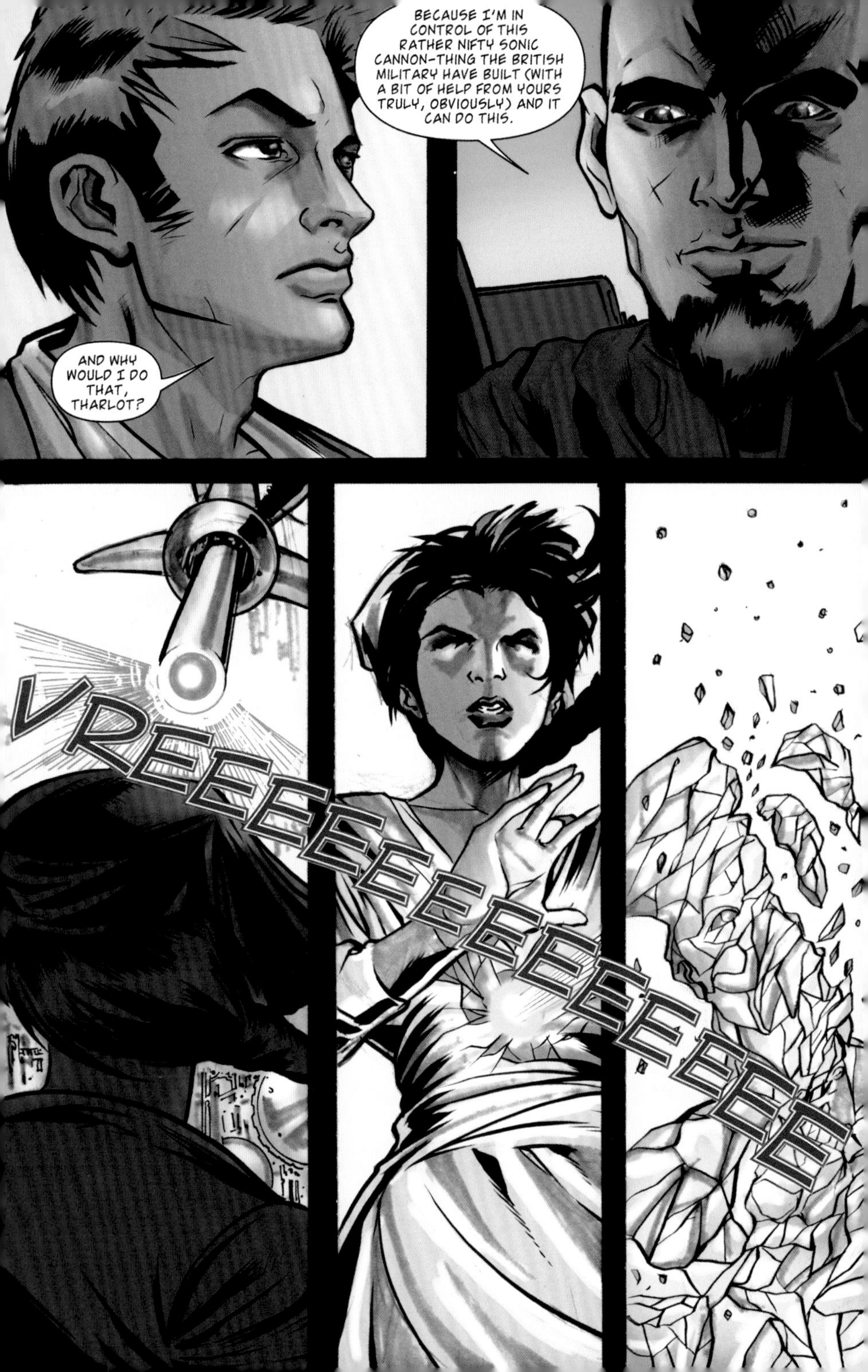
AND WHY WOULD I DO THAT, THARLOT?
BECAUSE I'M IN CONTROL OF THIS RATHER NIFTY SONIC CANNON-THING THE BRITISH MILITARY HAVE BUILT (WITH A BIT OF HELP FROM YOURS TRULY, OBVIOUSLY) AND IT CAN DO THIS.
VREEEEEEEEEEEEEEEEE

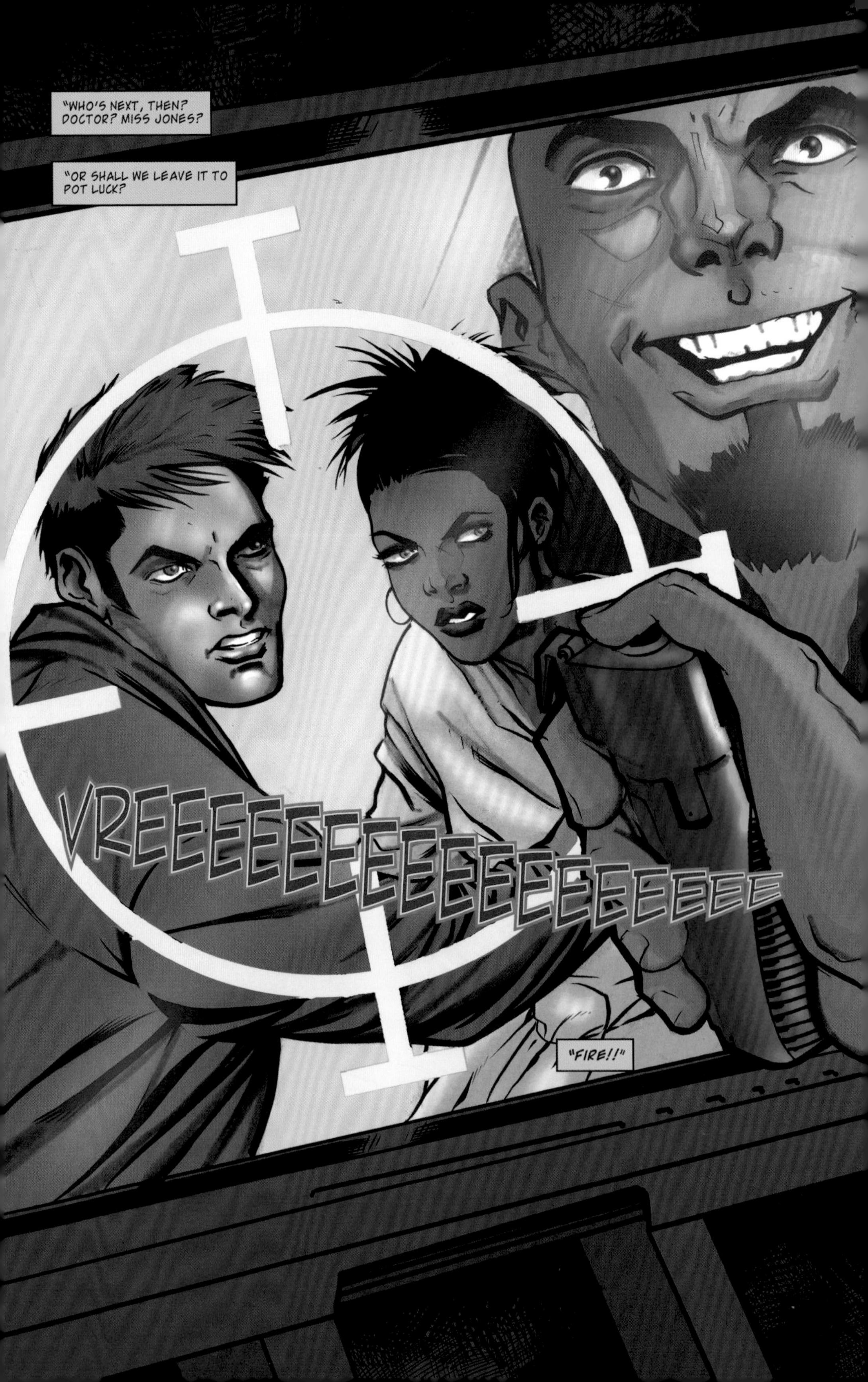
"WHO'S NEXT, THEN? DOCTOR? MISS JONES?
"OR SHALL WE LEAVE IT TO POT LUCK?
VREEEEEEEEEEEEEEEEEEEEEEEE
"FIRE!!"

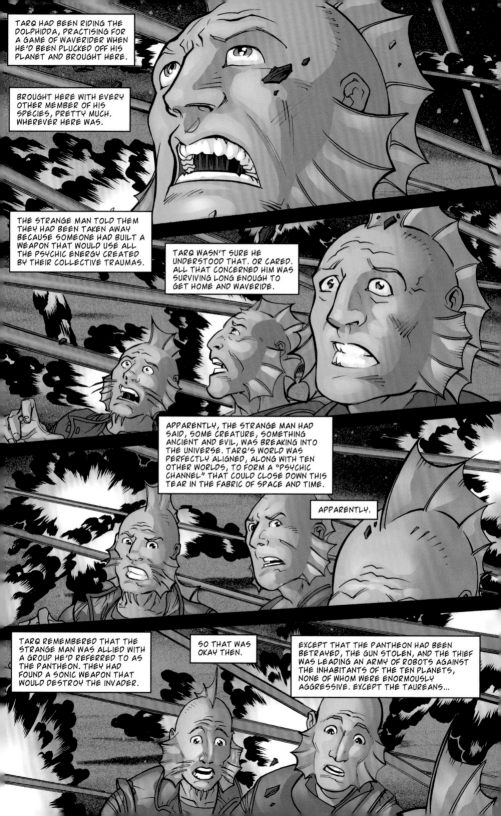

TARQ HAD BEEN RIDING THE DOLPHIDDA, PRACTISING FOR A GAME OF WAVERIDER WHEN HE'D BEEN PLUCKED OFF HIS PLANET AND BROUGHT HERE.

BROUGHT HERE WITH EVERY OTHER MEMBER OF HIS SPECIES, PRETTY MUCH. WHEREVER HERE WAS.

THE STRANGE MAN TOLD THEM THEY HAD BEEN TAKEN AWAY BECAUSE SOMEONE HAD BUILT A WEAPON THAT WOULD USE ALL THE PSYCHIC ENERGY CREATED BY THEIR COLLECTIVE TRAUMAS.

TARQ WASN'T SURE HE UNDERSTOOD THAT. OR CARED. ALL THAT CONCERNED HIM WAS SURVIVING LONG ENOUGH TO GET HOME AND WAVERIDE.

APPARENTLY, THE STRANGE MAN HAD SAID, SOME CREATURE, SOMETHING ANCIENT AND EVIL, WAS BREAKING INTO THE UNIVERSE. TARQ'S WORLD WAS PERFECTLY ALIGNED, ALONG WITH TEN OTHER WORLDS, TO FORM A "PSYCHIC CHANNEL" THAT COULD CLOSE DOWN THIS TEAR IN THE FABRIC OF SPACE AND TIME.

APPARENTLY.

TARQ REMEMBERED THAT THE STRANGE MAN WAS ALLIED WITH A GROUP HE'D REFERRED TO AS THE PANTHEON. THEY HAD FOUND A SONIC WEAPON THAT WOULD DESTROY THE INVADER.

SO THAT WAS OKAY THEN.

EXCEPT THAT THE PANTHEON HAD BEEN BETRAYED, THE GUN STOLEN, AND THE THIEF WAS LEADING AN ARMY OF ROBOTS AGAINST THE INHABITANTS OF THE TEN PLANETS, NONE OF WHOM WERE ENORMOUSLY AGGRESSIVE. EXCEPT THE TAUREANS...

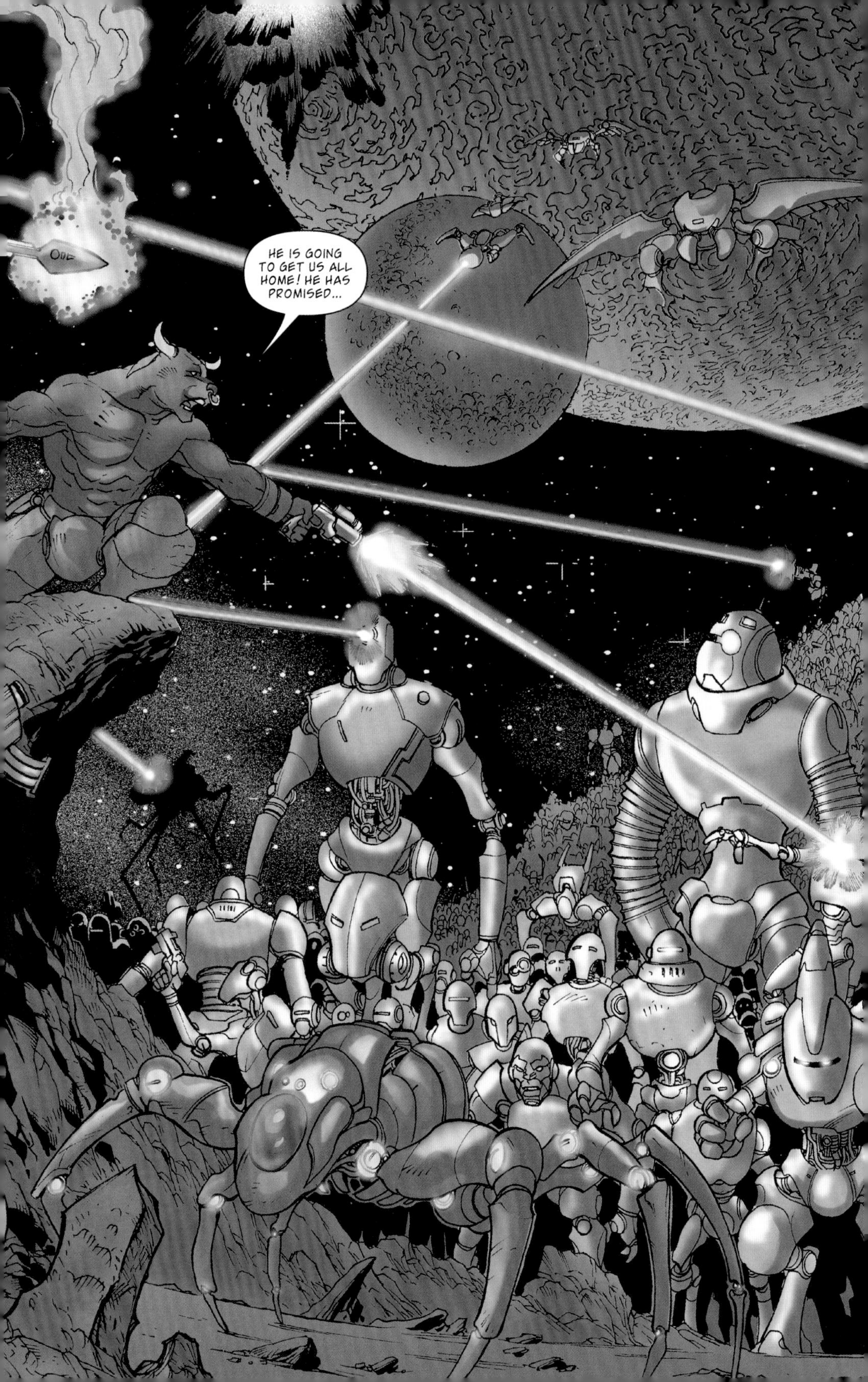
HE IS GOING TO GET US ALL HOME! HE HAS PROMISED...

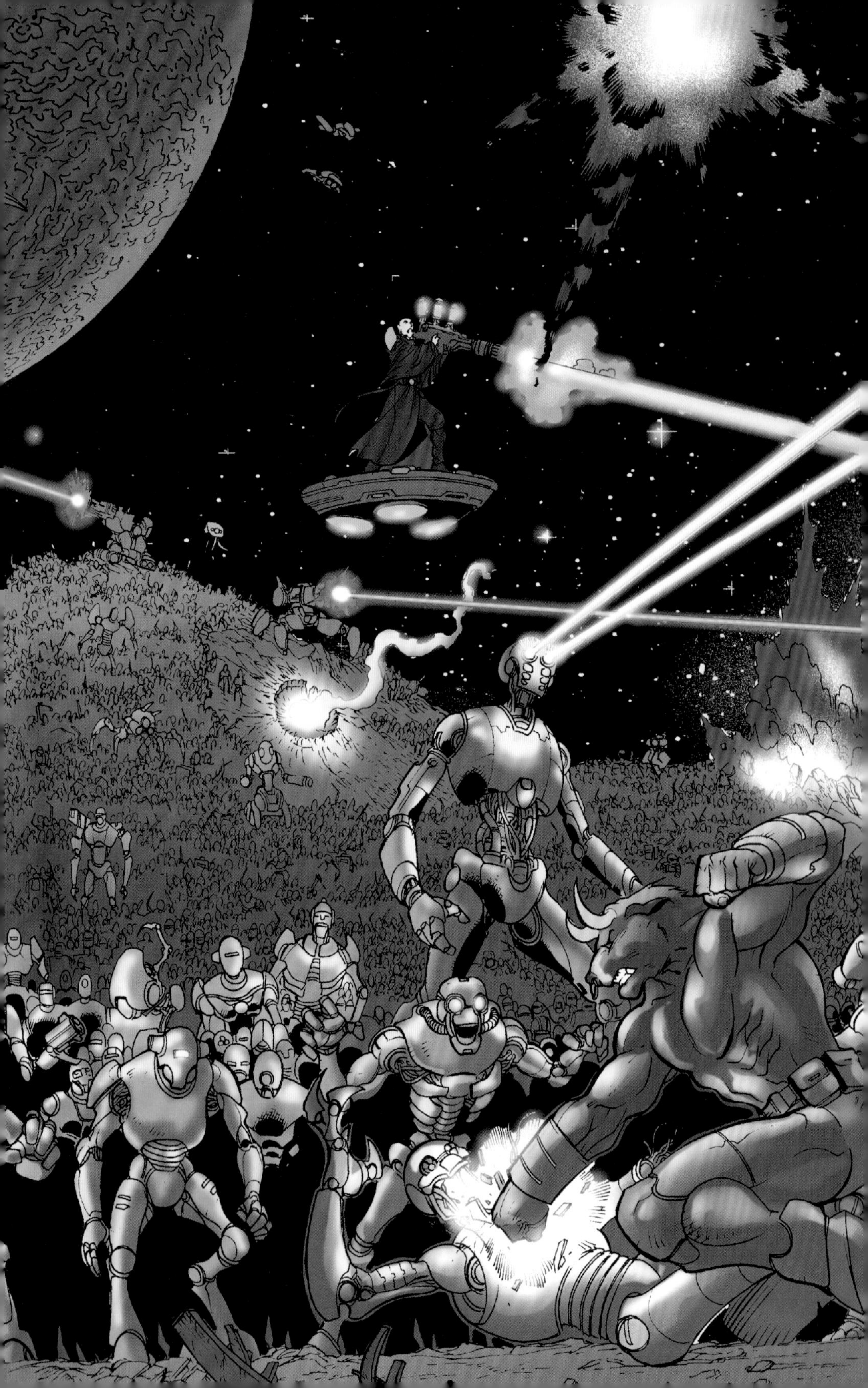

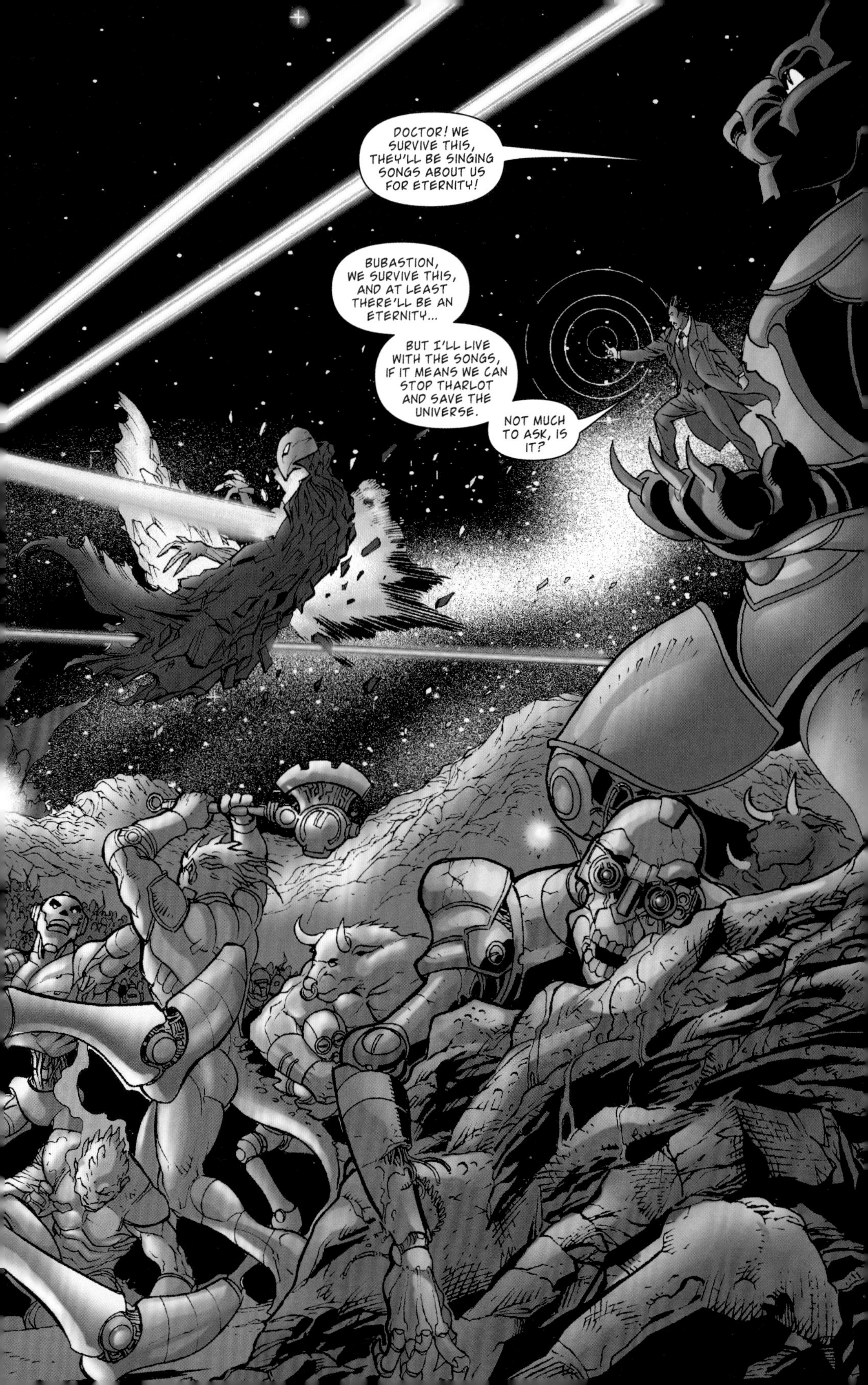
DOCTOR! WE SURVIVE THIS, THEY'LL BE SINGING SONGS ABOUT US FOR ETERNITY!
BUBASTION, WE SURVIVE THIS, AND AT LEAST THERE'LL BE AN ETERNITY...
BUT I'LL LIVE WITH THE SONGS, IF IT MEANS WE CAN STOP THARLOT AND SAVE THE UNIVERSE.
NOT MUCH TO ASK, IS IT?

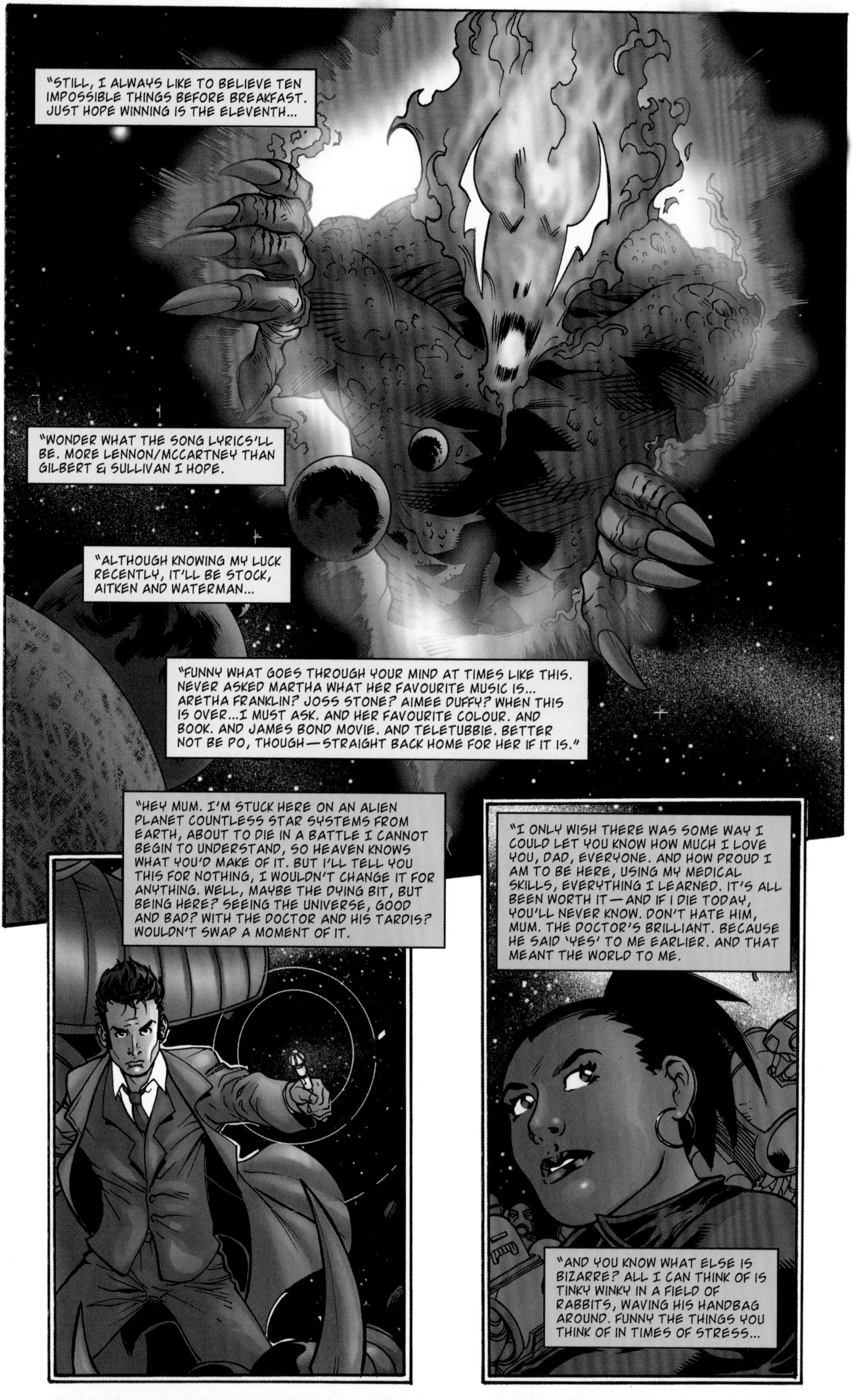
"STILL, I ALWAYS LIKE TO BELIEVE TEN IMPOSSIBLE THINGS BEFORE BREAKFAST. JUST HOPE WINNING IS THE ELEVENTH...
"WONDER WHAT THE SONG LYRICS'LL BE. MORE LENNON/McCARTNEY THAN GILBERT & SULLIVAN I HOPE.
"ALTHOUGH KNOWING MY LUCK RECENTLY, IT'LL BE STOCK, AITKEN AND WATERMAN...
"FUNNY WHAT GOES THROUGH YOUR MIND AT TIMES LIKE THIS. NEVER ASKED MARTHA WHAT HER FAVOURITE MUSIC IS... ARETHA FRANKLIN? JOSS STONE? AIMEE DUFFY? WHEN THIS IS OVER...I MUST ASK. AND HER FAVOURITE COLOUR. AND BOOK. AND JAMES BOND MOVIE. AND TELETUBBIE. BETTER NOT BE PO, THOUGH—STRAIGHT BACK HOME FOR HER IF IT IS."
"HEY MUM. I'M STUCK HERE ON AN ALIEN PLANET COUNTLESS STAR SYSTEMS FROM EARTH, ABOUT TO DIE IN A BATTLE I CANNOT BEGIN TO UNDERSTAND, SO HEAVEN KNOWS WHAT YOU'D MAKE OF IT. BUT I'LL TELL YOU THIS FOR NOTHING, I WOULDN'T CHANGE IT FOR ANYTHING. WELL, MAYBE THE DYING BIT, BUT BEING HERE? SEEING THE UNIVERSE, GOOD AND BAD? WITH THE DOCTOR AND HIS TARDIS? WOULDN'T SWAP A MOMENT OF IT.
"I ONLY WISH THERE WAS SOME WAY I COULD LET YOU KNOW HOW MUCH I LOVE YOU, DAD, EVERYONE. AND HOW PROUD I AM TO BE HERE, USING MY MEDICAL SKILLS, EVERYTHING I LEARNED. IT'S ALL BEEN WORTH IT—AND IF I DIE TODAY, YOU'LL NEVER KNOW. DON'T HATE HIM, MUM. THE DOCTOR'S BRILLIANT. BECAUSE HE SAID 'YES' TO ME EARLIER. AND THAT MEANT THE WORLD TO ME.
"AND YOU KNOW WHAT ELSE IS BIZARRE? ALL I CAN THINK OF IS TINKY WINKY IN A FIELD OF RABBITS, WAVING HIS HANDBAG AROUND. FUNNY THE THINGS YOU THINK OF IN TIMES OF STRESS...

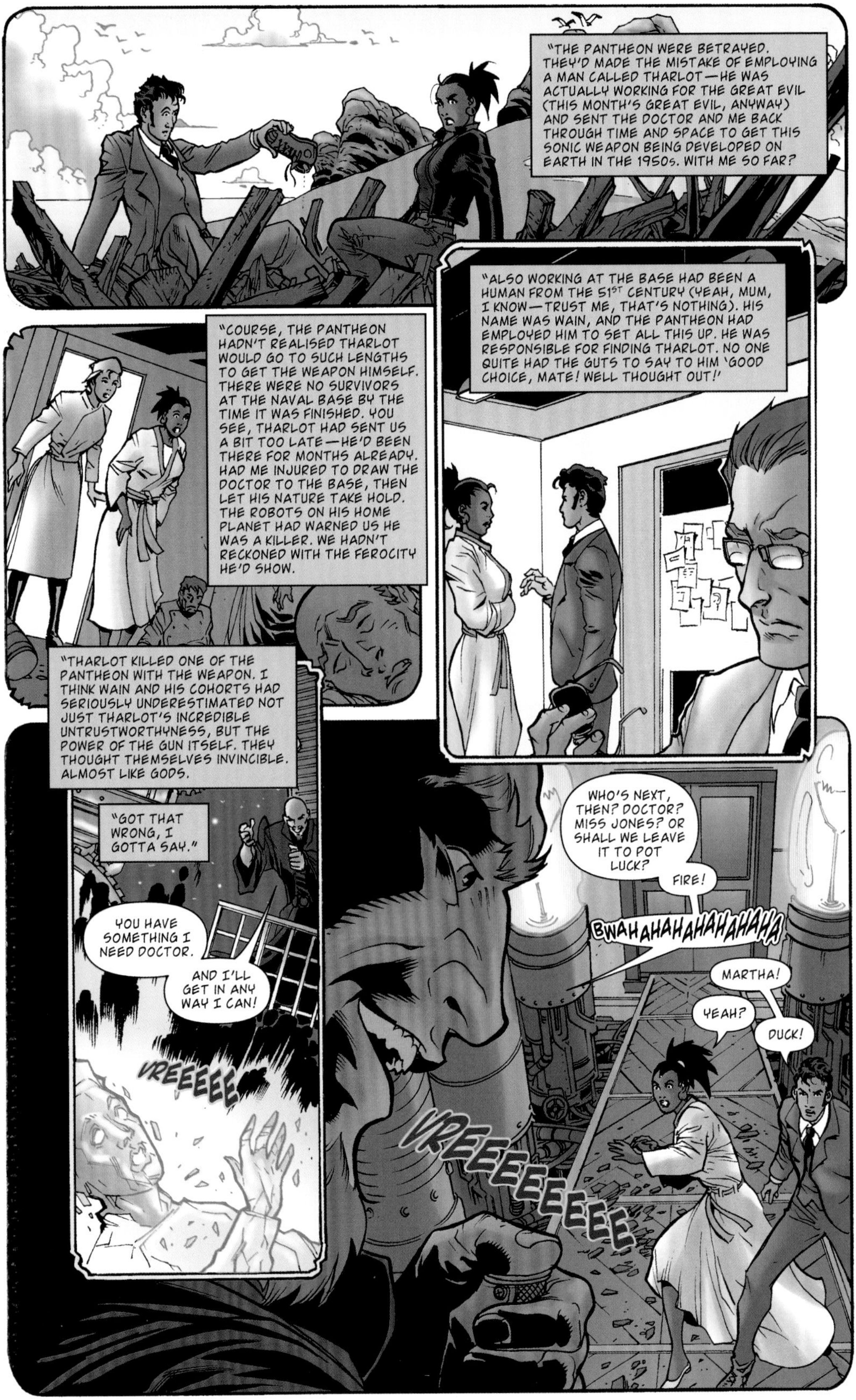
"THE PANTHEON WERE BETRAYED. THEY'D MADE THE MISTAKE OF EMPLOYING A MAN CALLED THARLOT—HE WAS ACTUALLY WORKING FOR THE GREAT EVIL (THIS MONTH'S GREAT EVIL, ANYWAY) AND SENT THE DOCTOR AND ME BACK THROUGH TIME AND SPACE TO GET THIS SONIC WEAPON BEING DEVELOPED ON EARTH IN THE 1950s. WITH ME SO FAR?
"COURSE, THE PANTHEON HADN'T REALISED THARLOT WOULD GO TO SUCH LENGTHS TO GET THE WEAPON HIMSELF. THERE WERE NO SURVIVORS AT THE NAVAL BASE BY THE TIME IT WAS FINISHED. YOU SEE, THARLOT HAD SENT US A BIT TOO LATE—HE'D BEEN THERE FOR MONTHS ALREADY. HAD ME INJURED TO DRAW THE DOCTOR TO THE BASE, THEN LET HIS NATURE TAKE HOLD. THE ROBOTS ON HIS HOME PLANET HAD WARNED US HE WAS A KILLER. WE HADN'T RECKONED WITH THE FEROCITY HE'D SHOW.
"ALSO WORKING AT THE BASE HAD BEEN A HUMAN FROM THE 51ST CENTURY (YEAH, MUM, I KNOW—TRUST ME, THAT'S NOTHING). HIS NAME WAS WAIN, AND THE PANTHEON HAD EMPLOYED HIM TO SET ALL THIS UP. HE WAS RESPONSIBLE FOR FINDING THARLOT. NO ONE QUITE HAD THE GUTS TO SAY TO HIM 'GOOD CHOICE, MATE! WELL THOUGHT OUT!'
"THARLOT KILLED ONE OF THE PANTHEON WITH THE WEAPON. I THINK WAIN AND HIS COHORTS HAD SERIOUSLY UNDERESTIMATED NOT JUST THARLOT'S INCREDIBLE UNTRUSTWORTHYNESS, BUT THE POWER OF THE GUN ITSELF. THEY THOUGHT THEMSELVES INVINCIBLE. ALMOST LIKE GODS.
"GOT THAT WRONG, I GOTTA SAY."
YOU HAVE SOMETHING I NEED DOCTOR.
AND I'LL GET IN ANY WAY I CAN!
VREEEEE
WHO'S NEXT, THEN? DOCTOR? MISS JONES? OR SHALL WE LEAVE IT TO POT LUCK?
FIRE!
BWAHAHAHAHAHAHAHA
MARTHA!
YEAH?
DUCK!
VREEEEEEEEEEEE

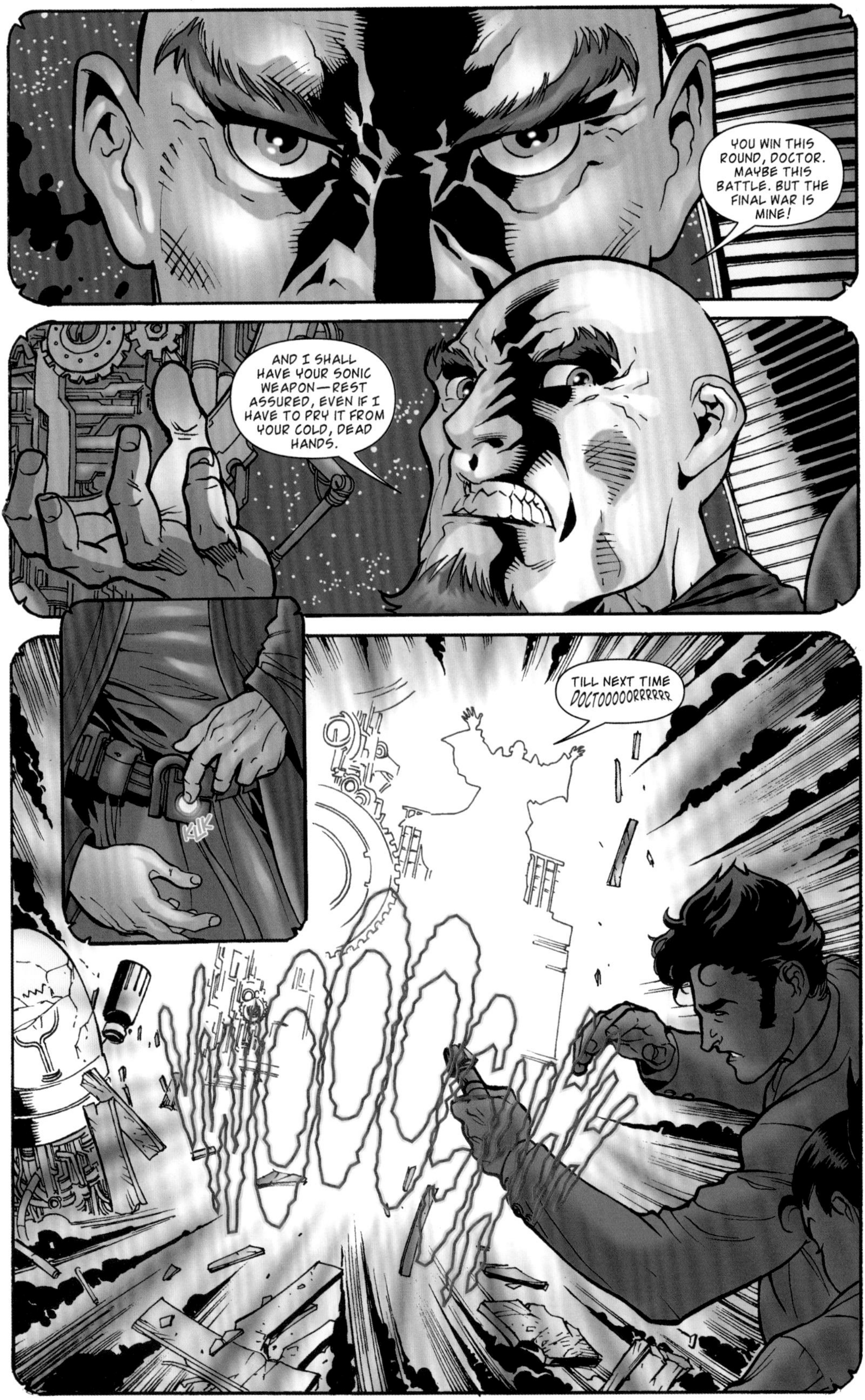
YOU WIN THIS ROUND, DOCTOR. MAYBE THIS BATTLE. BUT THE FINAL WAR IS MINE!
AND I SHALL HAVE YOUR SONIC WEAPON—REST ASSURED, EVEN IF I HAVE TO PRY IT FROM YOUR COLD, DEAD HANDS.
KLIK
TILL NEXT TIME DOCTOOOOORRRRRR

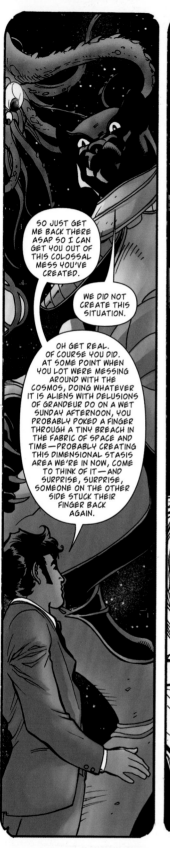

SO JUST GET ME BACK THERE ASAP SO I CAN GET YOU OUT OF THIS COLOSSAL MESS YOU'VE CREATED.

WE DID NOT CREATE THIS SITUATION.

OH GET REAL. OF COURSE YOU DID. AT SOME POINT WHEN YOU LOT WERE MESSING AROUND WITH THE COSMOS, DOING WHATEVER IT IS ALIENS WITH DELUSIONS OF GRANDEUR DO ON A WET SUNDAY AFTERNOON, YOU PROBABLY POKED A FINGER THROUGH A TINY BREACH IN THE FABRIC OF SPACE AND TIME — PROBABLY CREATING THIS DIMENSIONAL STASIS AREA WE'RE IN NOW, COME TO THINK OF IT — AND SURPRISE, SURPRISE, SOMEONE ON THE OTHER SIDE STUCK THEIR FINGER BACK AGAIN.

HOW DARE YOU! DO YOU NOT KNOW WHO YOU ARE CHASTISING? WE ARE THE PANTHEON, WE ARE THE—

OH DO BELT UP! THERE ARE BILLIONS OF PEOPLE OUT THERE, WHIPPED OFF THEIR HOME PLANETS, CONFUSED, SCARED, ANGRY (ESPECIALLY THE TAUREANS, THEY HAVE TEMPERS MILDLY SHORTER THAN MINE AT TIMES LIKE THIS) AND UNAWARE THEY'RE PART OF SOME UNIVERSAL WEAPON YOU'VE KNOCKED TOGETHER WITH THEIR PLANETARY ALIGNMENTS TO SEAL THAT BREACH.

AND NOW YOU'VE LET SOME DESPOT RUN OFF WITH THE ONLY VERY REAL WEAPON WE COULD USE TO CLOSE IT. COS YEAH, ALL THAT PSYCHIC ENERGY YOU WERE RELYING ON, THAT MIGHT STOP THE CREATURE, BUT IT WON'T BE ENOUGH TO SEAL THE BREACH. FOR THAT, YOU NEED TO REWRITE THE MOLECULES OF THE GASH ITSELF. AND SONICS ARE DEAD GOOD FOR THAT. AND, AS THARLOT KNEW, CHUCK MY SONIC SCREWDRIVER — MY LOVELY FULL OF GALLIFREYAN TIME LORD TECHNOLOGY SCREWDRIVER — INTO THE MIX AND BINGO, YOU HAVE WHAT YOU NEED.

BUT THARLOT BETRAYED YOU COS HE'S BEEN CONTACTED BY THE CREATURE THAT'S COMING THROUGH THE BREACH ALREADY. AND THARLOT'S MAD. AND A CONVICTED MASS MURDERER. YEAH, SOME GREAT ALL-POWERFUL BEINGS YOU ARE. ALL THAT POWER, ALL THAT REALITY-WARPING ENERGY, AND DIMENSIONAL DISPLACEMENT THEORY, AND ALL THAT SHAPE-CHANGING ABILITIES AND WHAT YOU REALLY NEED AT THE END OF THE DAY IS A TIME LORD, A FANTASTIC HUMAN FROM SOUTH LONDON AND A SONIC SCREWDRIVER.

JUST AS WELL THAT'S EXACTLY WHAT THEY'VE GOT THEN.

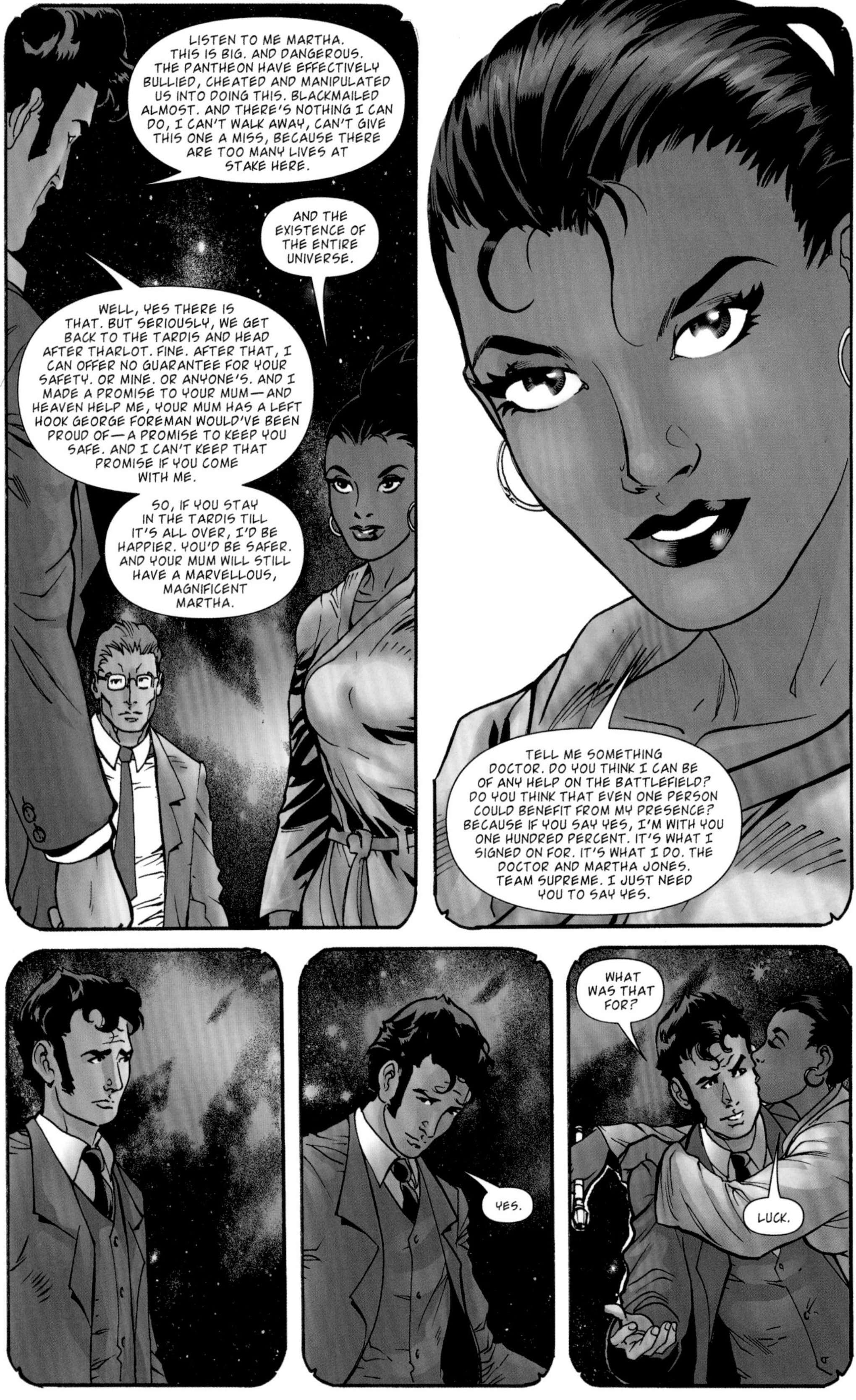
LISTEN TO ME MARTHA. THIS IS BIG. AND DANGEROUS. THE PANTHEON HAVE EFFECTIVELY BULLIED, CHEATED AND MANIPULATED US INTO DOING THIS. BLACKMAILED ALMOST. AND THERE'S NOTHING I CAN DO, I CAN'T WALK AWAY, CAN'T GIVE THIS ONE A MISS, BECAUSE THERE ARE TOO MANY LIVES AT STAKE HERE.
AND THE EXISTENCE OF THE ENTIRE UNIVERSE.
WELL, YES THERE IS THAT. BUT SERIOUSLY, WE GET BACK TO THE TARDIS AND HEAD AFTER THARLOT. FINE. AFTER THAT, I CAN OFFER NO GUARANTEE FOR YOUR SAFETY. OR MINE. OR ANYONE'S. AND I MADE A PROMISE TO YOUR MUM—AND HEAVEN HELP ME, YOUR MUM HAS A LEFT HOOK GEORGE FOREMAN WOULD'VE BEEN PROUD OF—A PROMISE TO KEEP YOU SAFE. AND I CAN'T KEEP THAT PROMISE IF YOU COME WITH ME.
SO, IF YOU STAY IN THE TARDIS TILL IT'S ALL OVER, I'D BE HAPPIER. YOU'D BE SAFER. AND YOUR MUM WILL STILL HAVE A MARVELLOUS, MAGNIFICENT MARTHA.
TELL ME SOMETHING DOCTOR. DO YOU THINK I CAN BE OF ANY HELP ON THE BATTLEFIELD? DO YOU THINK THAT EVEN ONE PERSON COULD BENEFIT FROM MY PRESENCE? BECAUSE IF YOU SAY YES, I'M WITH YOU ONE HUNDRED PERCENT. IT'S WHAT I SIGNED ON FOR. IT'S WHAT I DO. THE DOCTOR AND MARTHA JONES. TEAM SUPREME. I JUST NEED YOU TO SAY YES.
YES.
WHAT WAS THAT FOR?
LUCK.

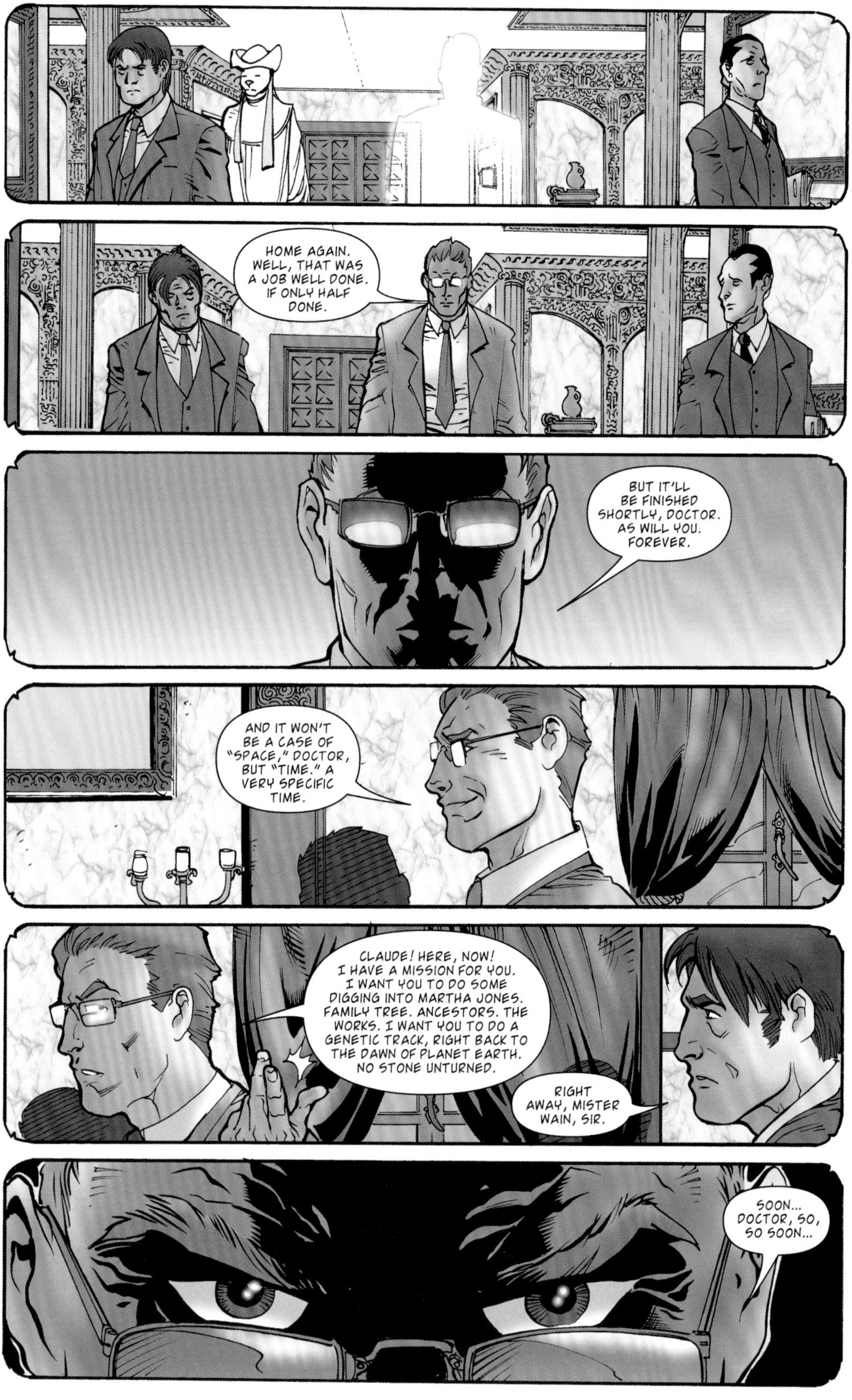
HOME AGAIN. WELL, THAT WAS A JOB WELL DONE. IF ONLY HALF DONE.
BUT IT'LL BE FINISHED SHORTLY, DOCTOR. AS WILL YOU. FOREVER.
AND IT WON'T BE A CASE OF "SPACE," DOCTOR, BUT "TIME." A VERY SPECIFIC TIME.
CLAUDE! HERE, NOW! I HAVE A MISSION FOR YOU. I WANT YOU TO DO SOME DIGGING INTO MARTHA JONES. FAMILY TREE. ANCESTORS. THE WORKS. I WANT YOU TO DO A GENETIC TRACK, RIGHT BACK TO THE DAWN OF PLANET EARTH. NO STONE UNTURNED.
RIGHT AWAY, MISTER WAIN, SIR.
SOON... DOCTOR, SO, SO SOON...

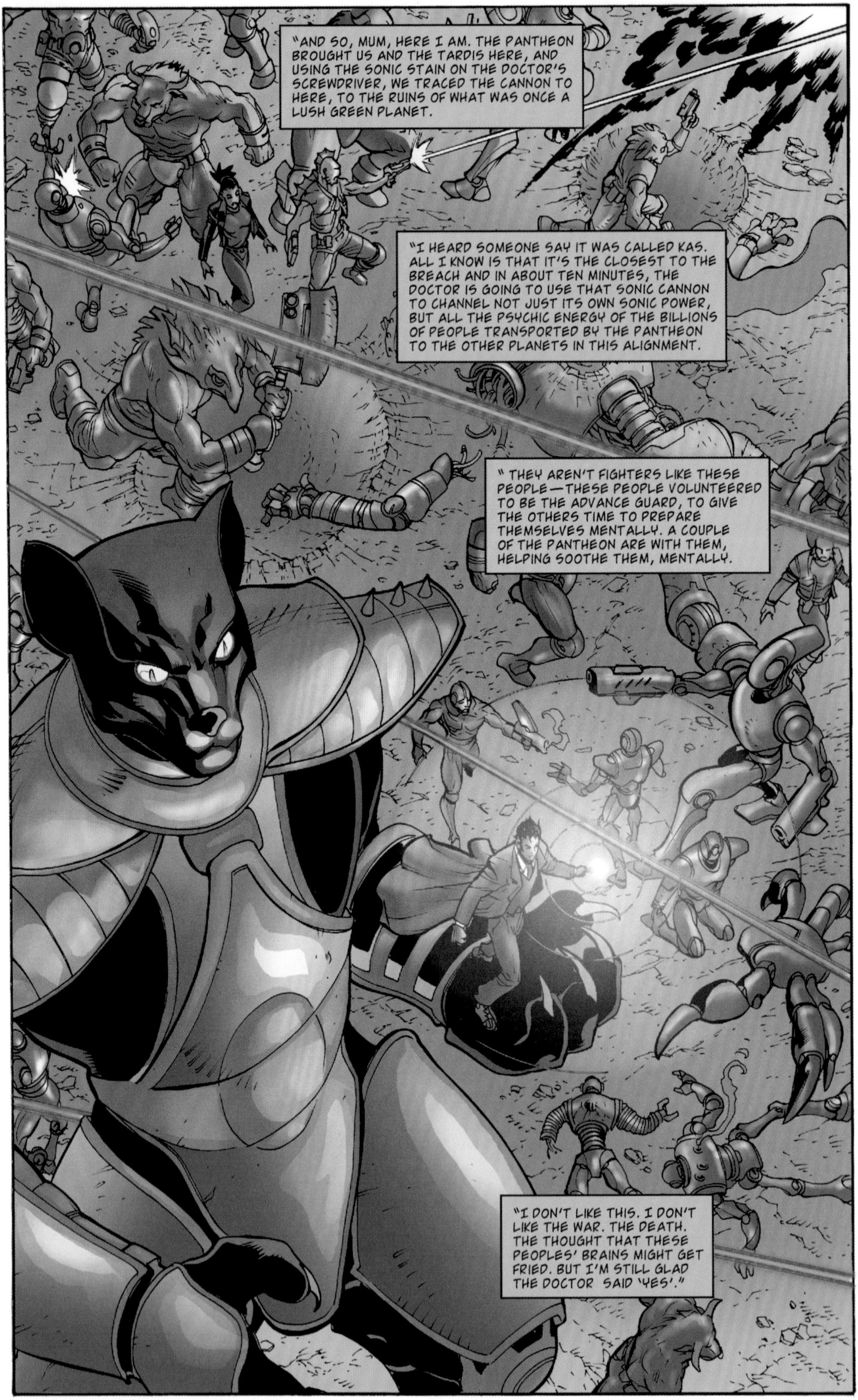
"AND SO, MUM, HERE I AM. THE PANTHEON BROUGHT US AND THE TARDIS HERE, AND USING THE SONIC STAIN ON THE DOCTOR'S SCREWDRIVER, WE TRACED THE CANNON TO HERE, TO THE RUINS OF WHAT WAS ONCE A LUSH GREEN PLANET.
"I HEARD SOMEONE SAY IT WAS CALLED KAS. ALL I KNOW IS THAT IT'S THE CLOSEST TO THE BREACH AND IN ABOUT TEN MINUTES, THE DOCTOR IS GOING TO USE THAT SONIC CANNON TO CHANNEL NOT JUST ITS OWN SONIC POWER, BUT ALL THE PSYCHIC ENERGY OF THE BILLIONS OF PEOPLE TRANSPORTED BY THE PANTHEON TO THE OTHER PLANETS IN THIS ALIGNMENT.
" THEY AREN'T FIGHTERS LIKE THESE PEOPLE—THESE PEOPLE VOLUNTEERED TO BE THE ADVANCE GUARD, TO GIVE THE OTHERS TIME TO PREPARE THEMSELVES MENTALLY. A COUPLE OF THE PANTHEON ARE WITH THEM, HELPING SOOTHE THEM, MENTALLY.
"I DON'T LIKE THIS. I DON'T LIKE THE WAR. THE DEATH. THE THOUGHT THAT THESE PEOPLES' BRAINS MIGHT GET FRIED. BUT I'M STILL GLAD THE DOCTOR SAID 'YES'."

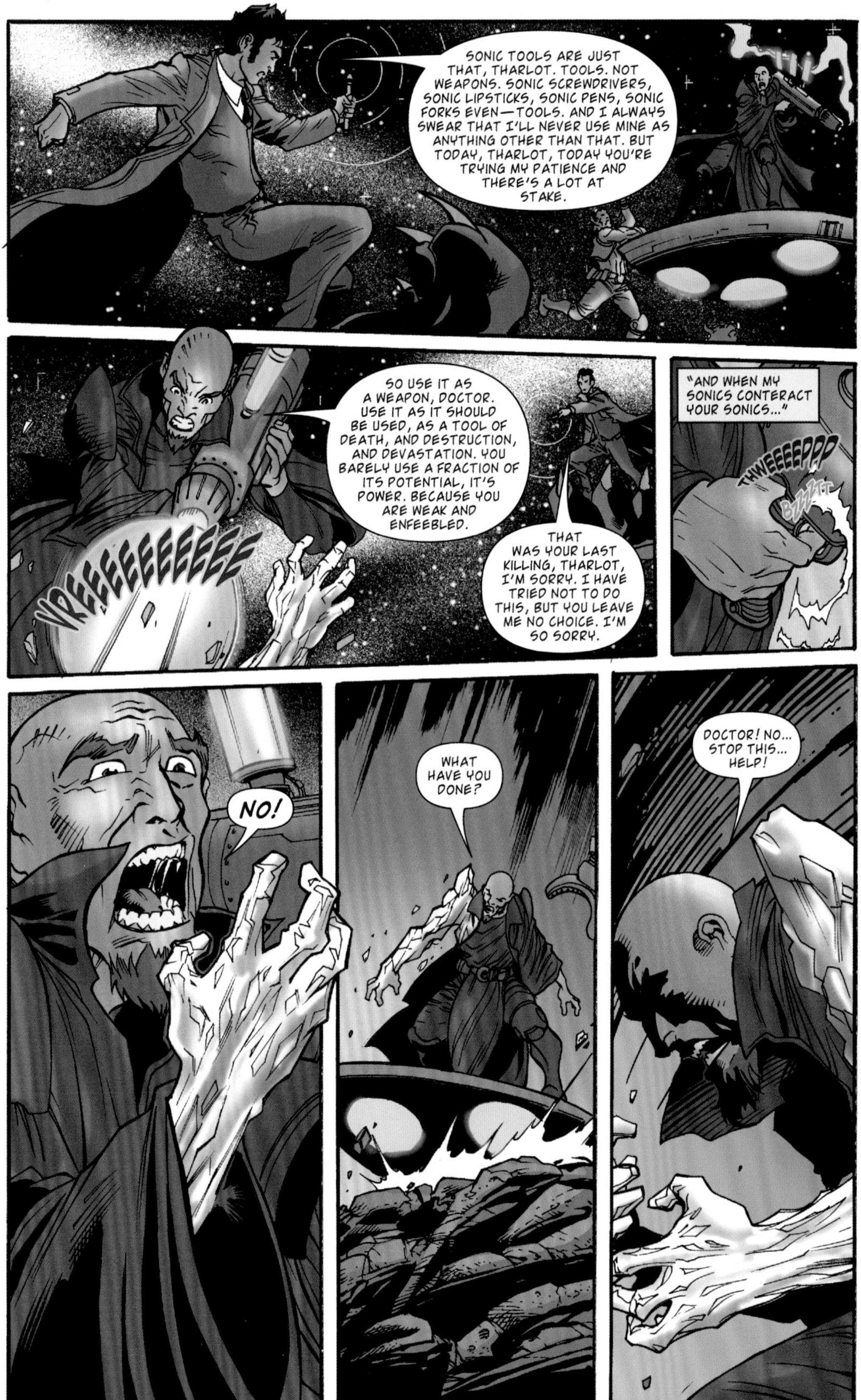
SONIC TOOLS ARE JUST THAT, THARLOT. TOOLS. NOT WEAPONS. SONIC SCREWDRIVERS, SONIC LIPSTICKS, SONIC PENS, SONIC FORKS EVEN—TOOLS. AND I ALWAYS SWEAR THAT I'LL NEVER USE MINE AS ANYTHING OTHER THAN THAT. BUT TODAY, THARLOT, TODAY YOU'RE TRYING MY PATIENCE AND THERE'S A LOT AT STAKE.
SO USE IT AS A WEAPON, DOCTOR. USE IT AS IT SHOULD BE USED, AS A TOOL OF DEATH, AND DESTRUCTION, AND DEVASTATION. YOU BARELY USE A FRACTION OF ITS POTENTIAL, IT'S POWER. BECAUSE YOU ARE WEAK AND ENFEEBLED.
VREEEEEEEEEE
THAT WAS YOUR LAST KILLING, THARLOT, I'M SORRY. I HAVE TRIED NOT TO DO THIS, BUT YOU LEAVE ME NO CHOICE. I'M SO SORRY.
"AND WHEN MY SONICS CONTERACT YOUR SONICS..."
THWEEEEPPP
BZZZTT
NO!
WHAT HAVE YOU DONE?
DOCTOR! NO... STOP THIS... HELP!

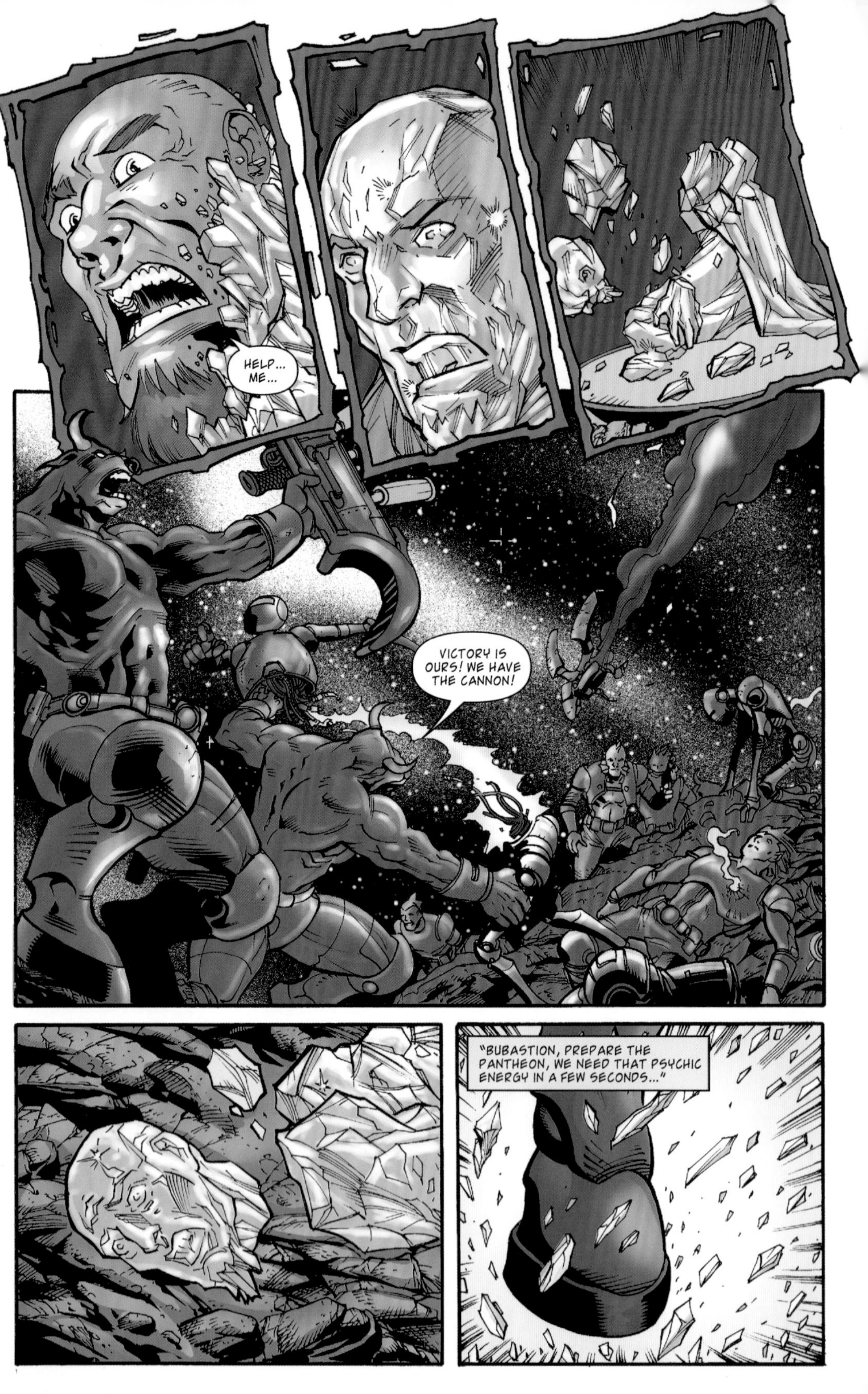
HELP... ME...
VICTORY IS OURS! WE HAVE THE CANNON!
"BUBASTION, PREPARE THE PANTHEON, WE NEED THAT PSYCHIC ENERGY IN A FEW SECONDS..."

"THEY ARE READY DOCTOR!"

THIS BETTER WORK, BUBASTION, OR IT'S THE SHORTEST, MOST PYRRHIC VICTORY IN HISTORY...

OH YES!

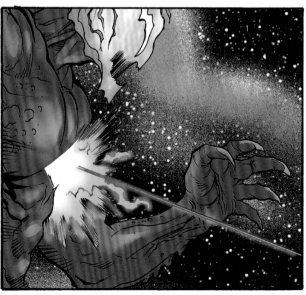

NOW, BUBASTION, WE NEED THE THOUGHTS OF A BILLION SOULS. NOW!

GOD, I HOPE THIS WORKS...

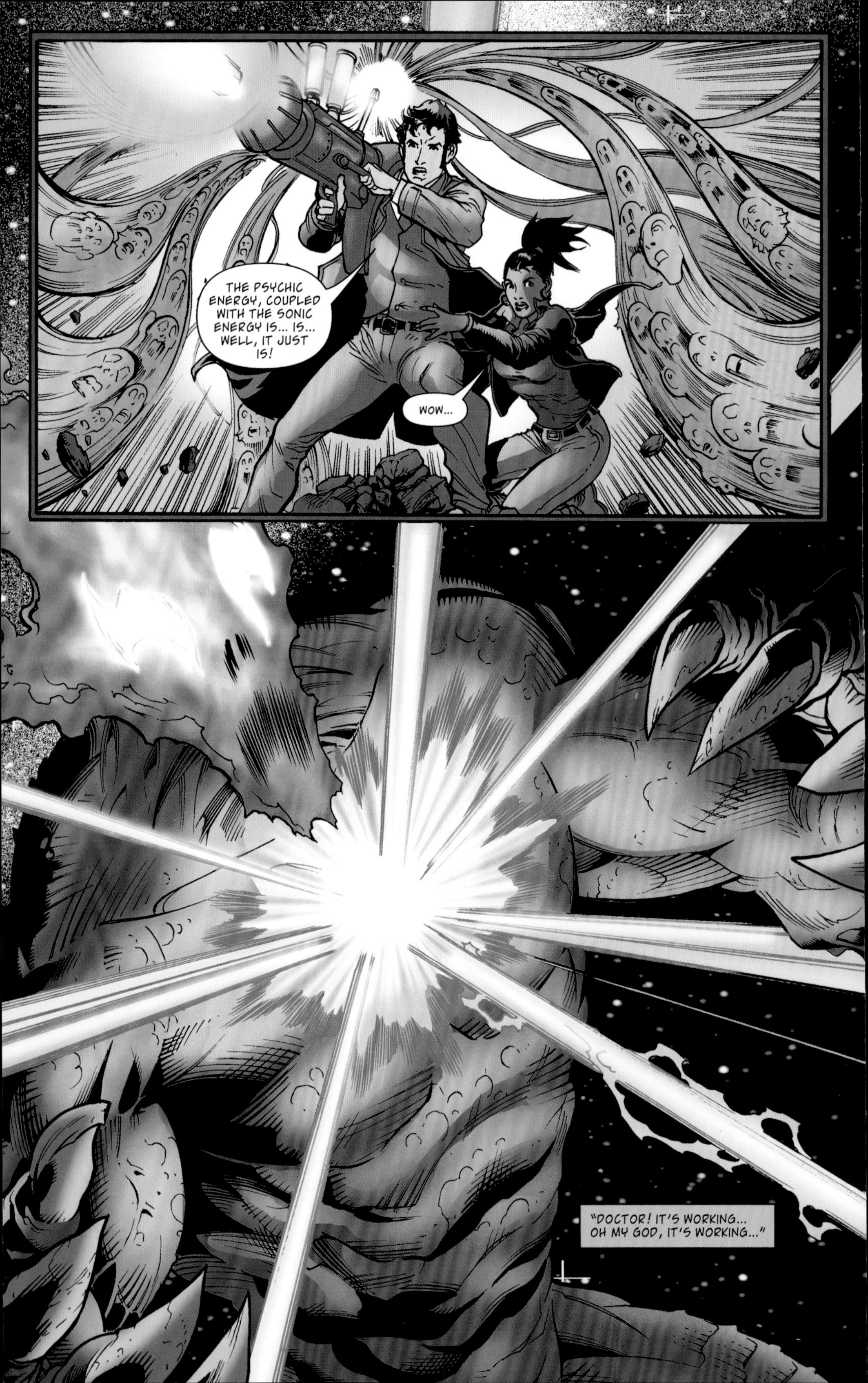
THE PSYCHIC ENERGY, COUPLED WITH THE SONIC ENERGY IS... IS... WELL, IT JUST IS!
WOW...
"DOCTOR! IT'S WORKING... OH MY GOD, IT'S WORKING..."

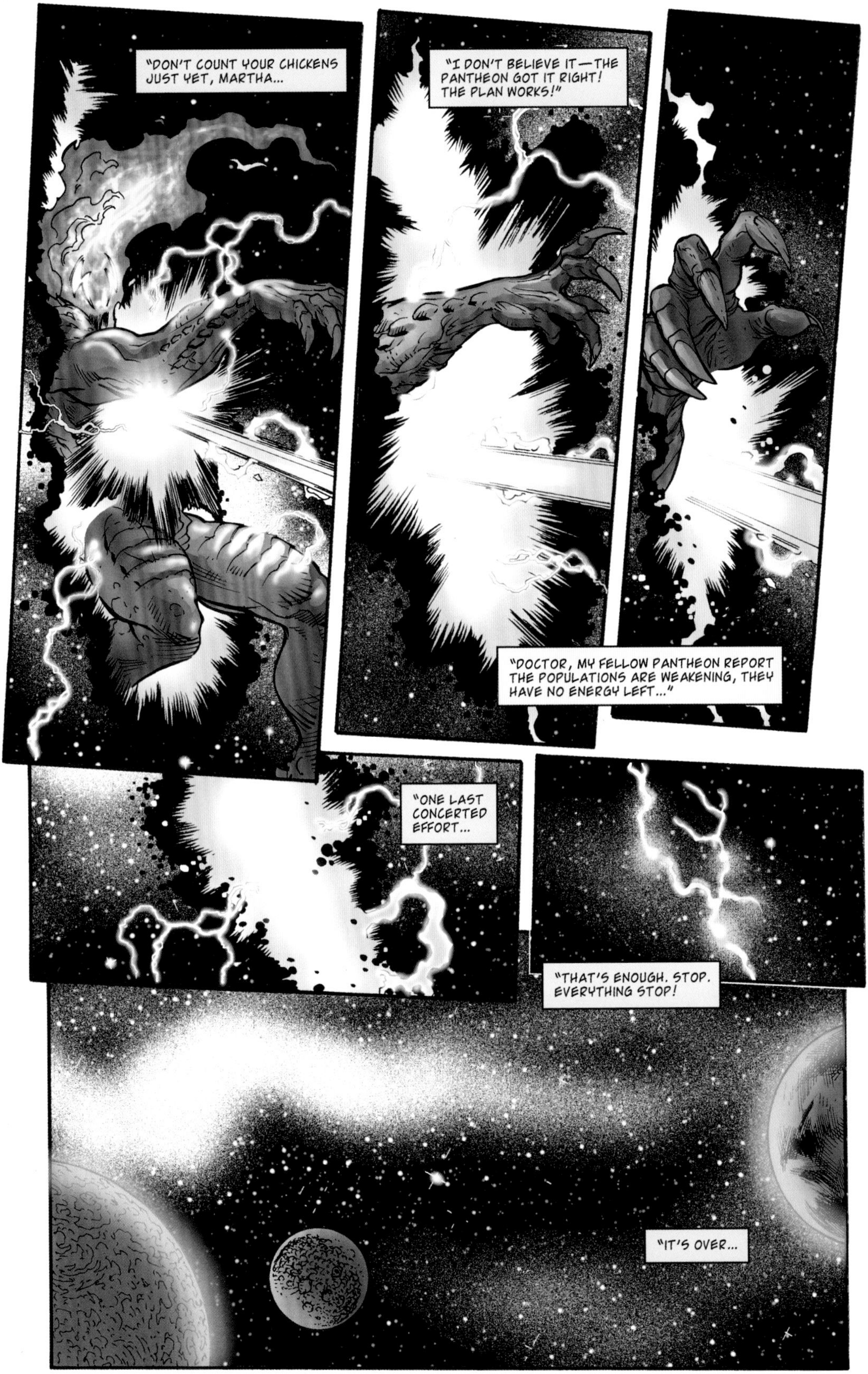
"DON'T COUNT YOUR CHICKENS JUST YET, MARTHA...
"I DON'T BELIEVE IT—THE PANTHEON GOT IT RIGHT! THE PLAN WORKS!"
"DOCTOR, MY FELLOW PANTHEON REPORT THE POPULATIONS ARE WEAKENING, THEY HAVE NO ENERGY LEFT..."
"ONE LAST CONCERTED EFFORT...
"THAT'S ENOUGH. STOP. EVERYTHING STOP!
"IT'S OVER...

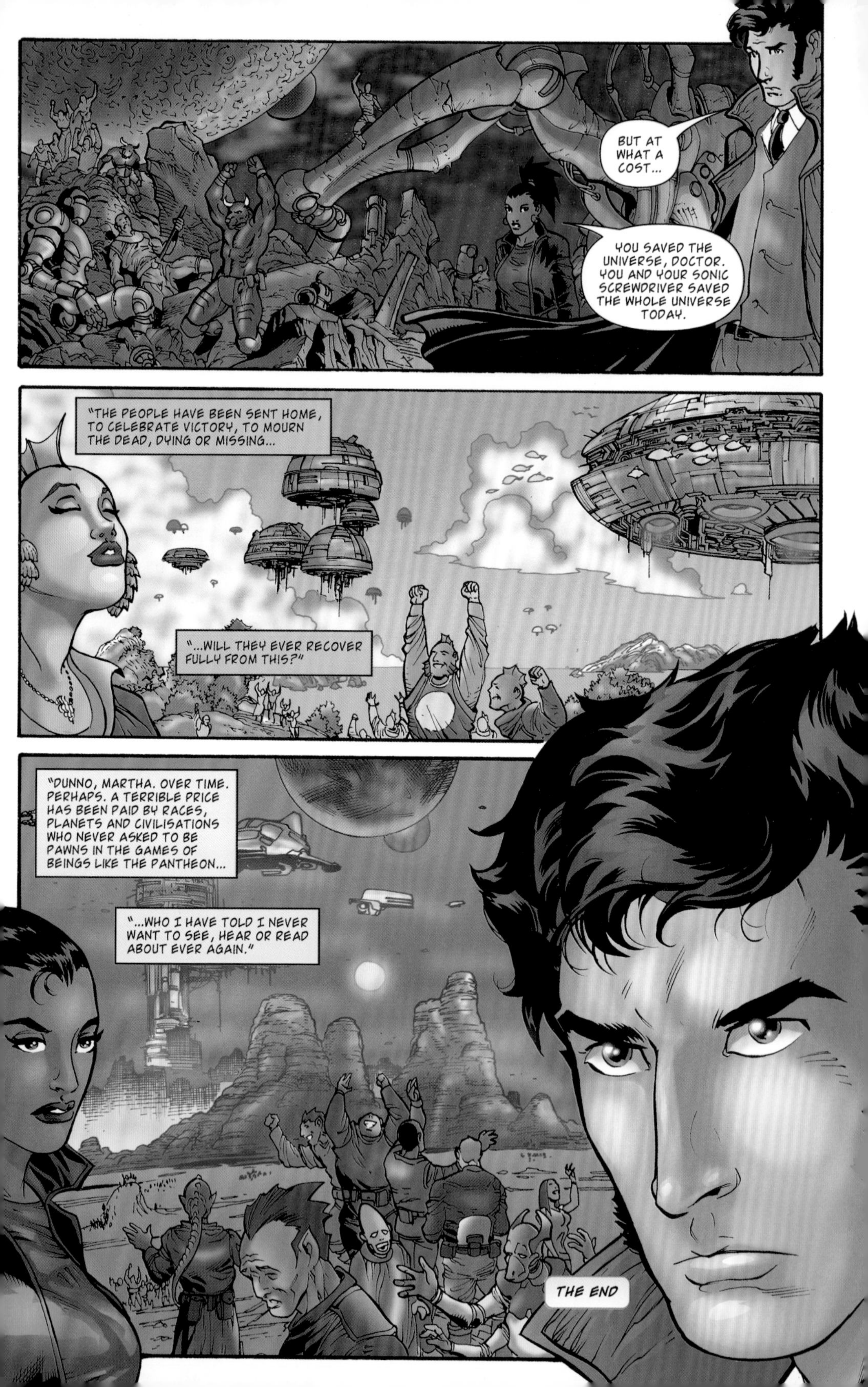
BUT AT WHAT A COST...
YOU SAVED THE UNIVERSE, DOCTOR. YOU AND YOUR SONIC SCREWDRIVER SAVED THE WHOLE UNIVERSE TODAY.
"THE PEOPLE HAVE BEEN SENT HOME, TO CELEBRATE VICTORY, TO MOURN THE DEAD, DYING OR MISSING...
"...WILL THEY EVER RECOVER FULLY FROM THIS?"
"DUNNO, MARTHA. OVER TIME. PERHAPS. A TERRIBLE PRICE HAS BEEN PAID BY RACES, PLANETS AND CIVILISATIONS WHO NEVER ASKED TO BE PAWNS IN THE GAMES OF BEINGS LIKE THE PANTHEON...
"...WHO I HAVE TOLD I NEVER WANT TO SEE, HEAR OR READ ABOUT EVER AGAIN."
THE END

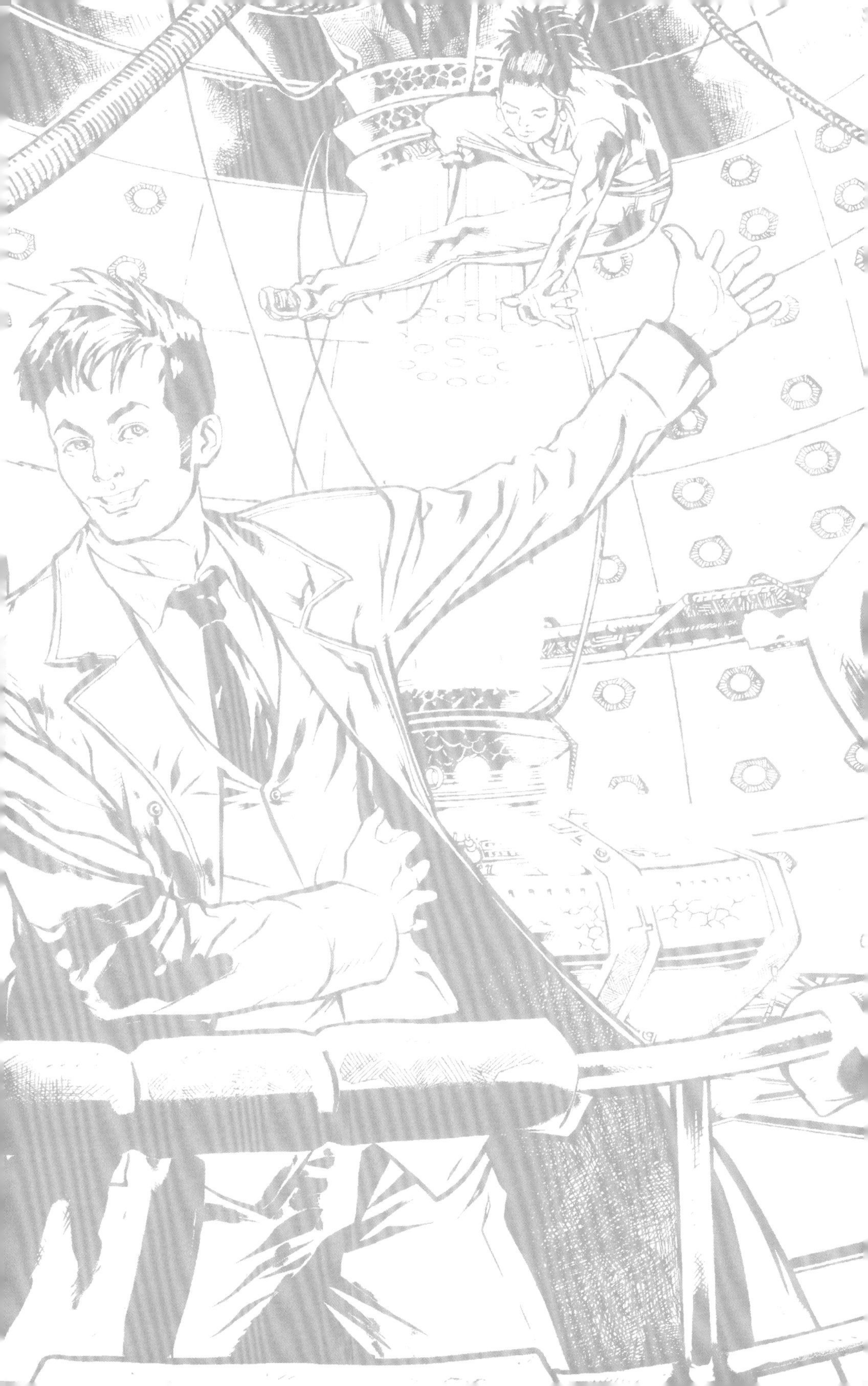

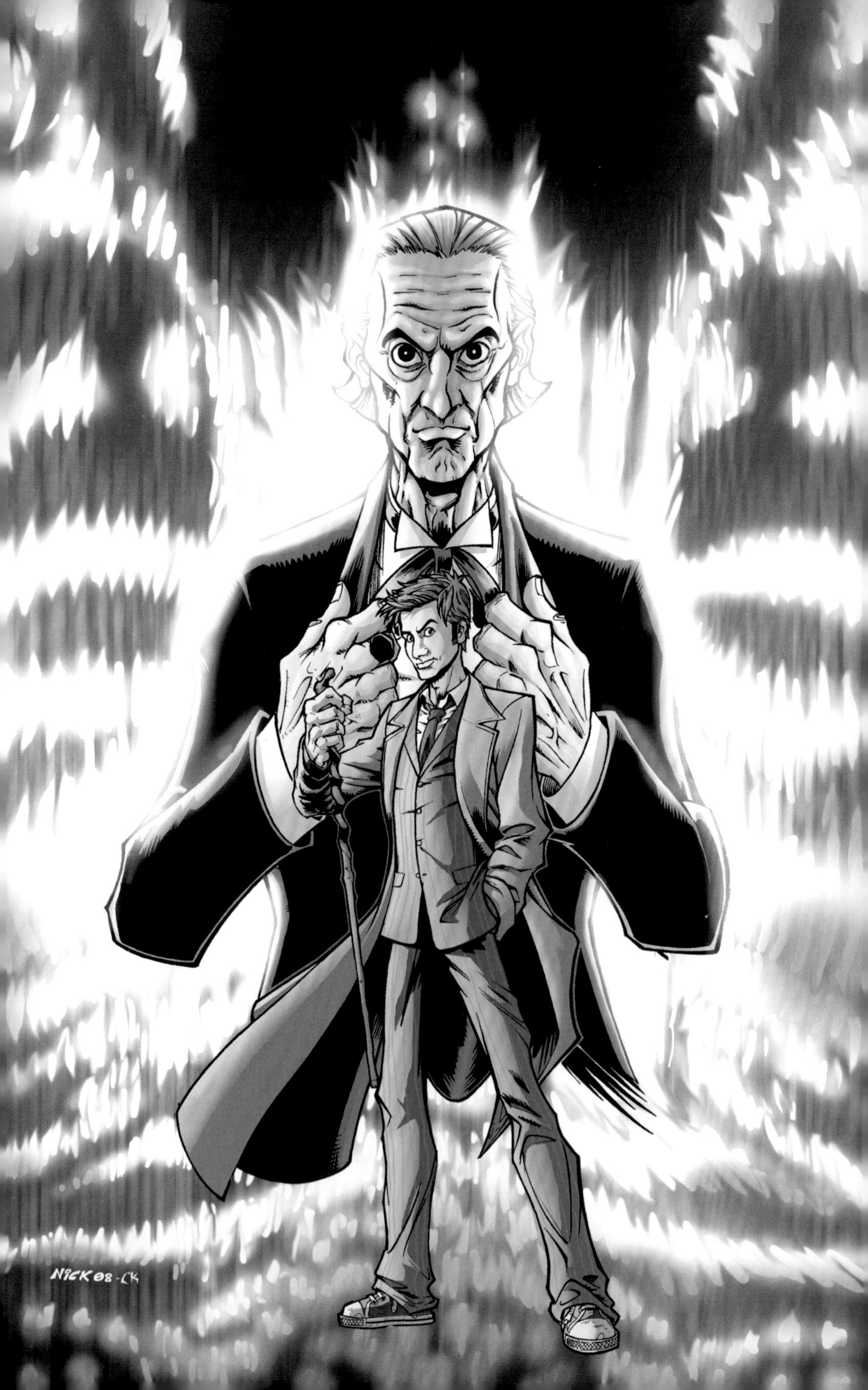
NiCK 08-CK

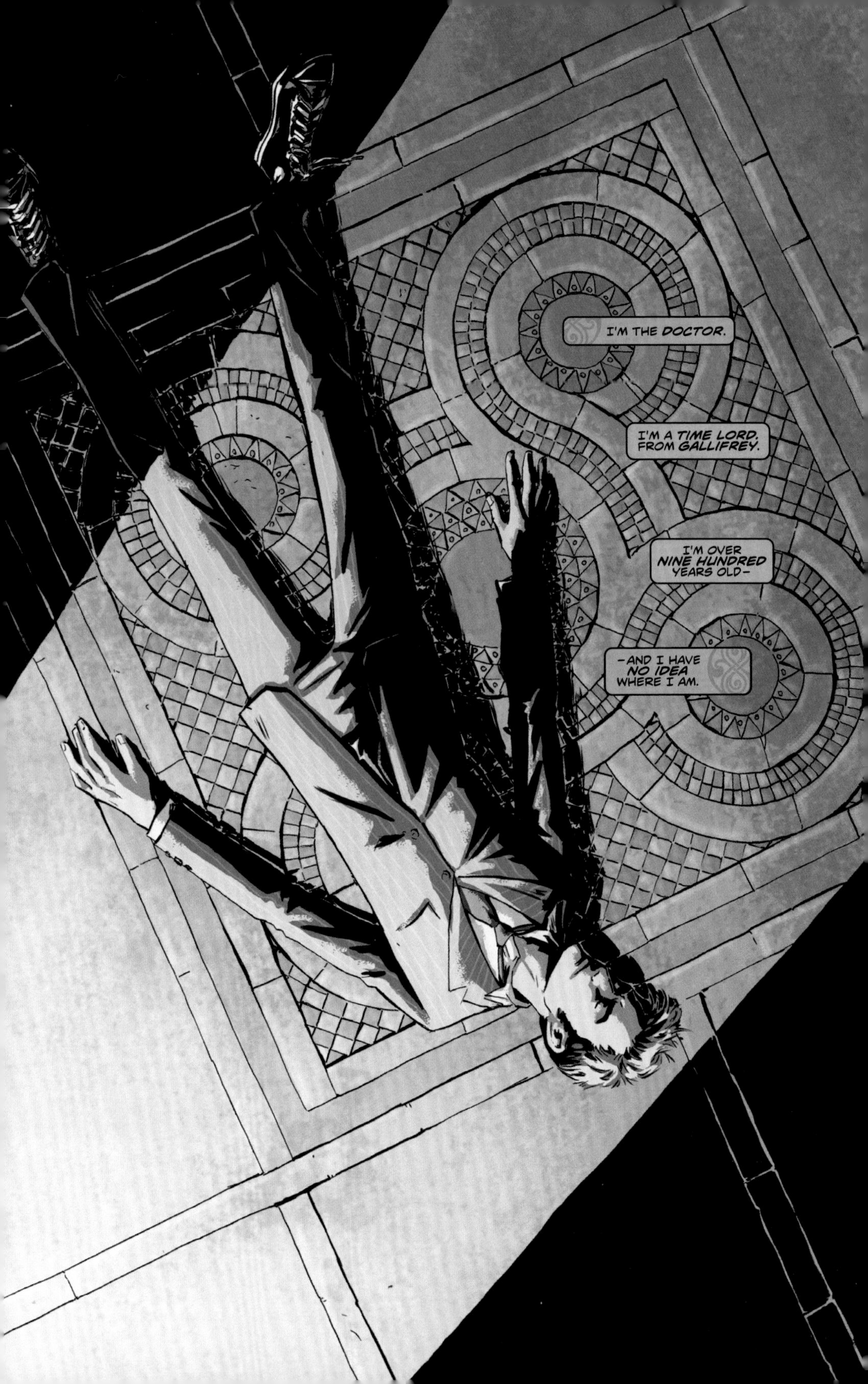
I'M THE DOCTOR.
I'M A TIME LORD, FROM GALLIFREY.
I'M OVER NINE HUNDRED YEARS OLD–
–AND I HAVE NO IDEA WHERE I AM.

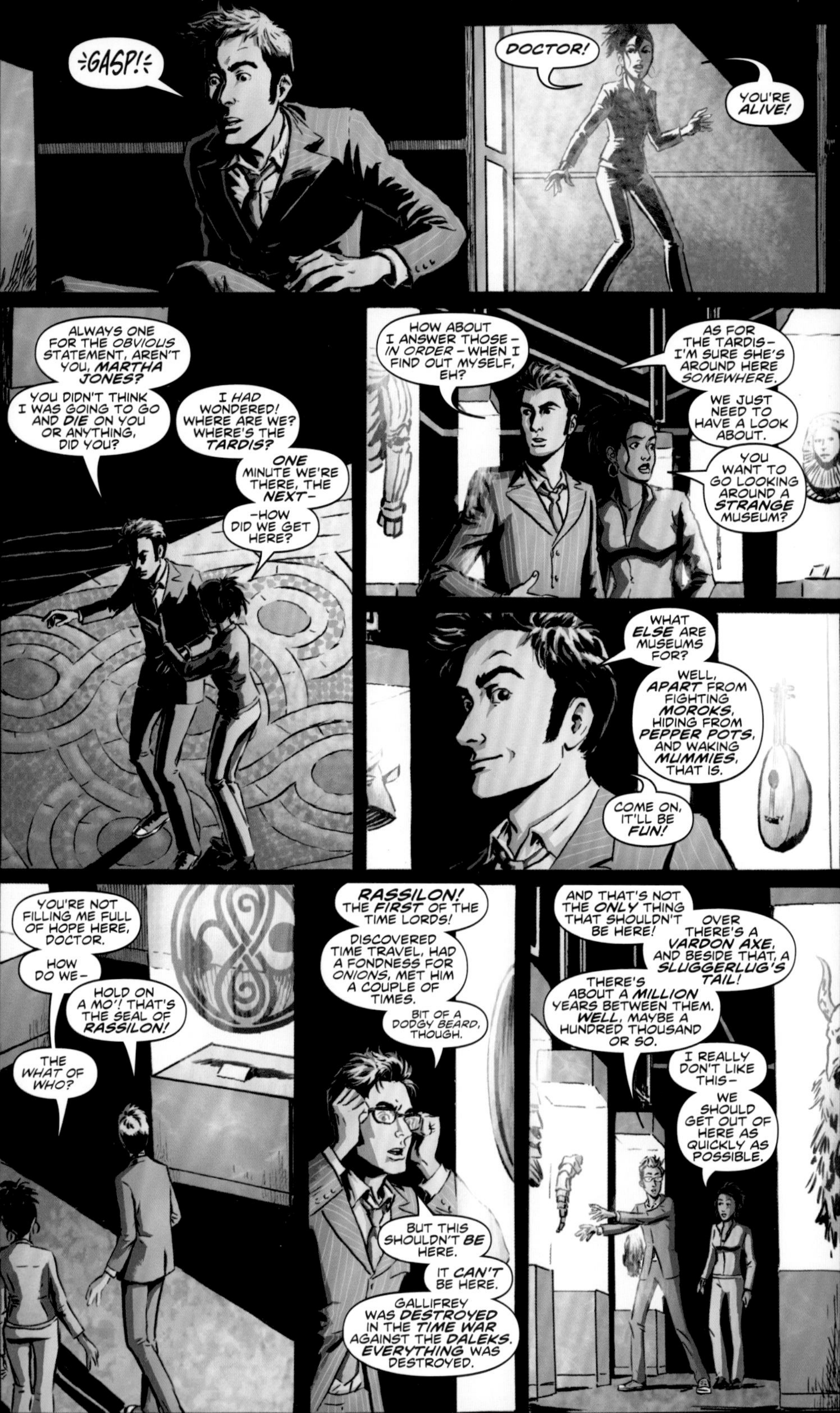

GASP!
DOCTOR!
YOU'RE ALIVE!
ALWAYS ONE FOR THE OBVIOUS STATEMENT, AREN'T YOU, MARTHA JONES?
YOU DIDN'T THINK I WAS GOING TO GO AND DIE ON YOU OR ANYTHING, DID YOU?
I HAD WONDERED! WHERE ARE WE? WHERE'S THE TARDIS?
ONE MINUTE WE'RE THERE, THE NEXT–
–HOW DID WE GET HERE?
HOW ABOUT I ANSWER THOSE – IN ORDER – WHEN I FIND OUT MYSELF, EH?
AS FOR THE TARDIS– I'M SURE SHE'S AROUND HERE SOMEWHERE.
WE JUST NEED TO HAVE A LOOK ABOUT.
YOU WANT TO GO LOOKING AROUND A STRANGE MUSEUM?
WHAT ELSE ARE MUSEUMS FOR?
WELL, APART FROM FIGHTING MOROKS, HIDING FROM PEPPER POTS, AND WAKING MUMMIES, THAT IS.
COME ON, IT'LL BE FUN!
YOU'RE NOT FILLING ME FULL OF HOPE HERE, DOCTOR.
HOW DO WE–
HOLD ON A MO'! THAT'S THE SEAL OF RASSILON!
THE WHAT OF WHO?
RASSILON! THE FIRST OF THE TIME LORDS!
DISCOVERED TIME TRAVEL, HAD A FONDNESS FOR ONIONS, MET HIM A COUPLE OF TIMES.
BIT OF A DODGY BEARD, THOUGH.
BUT THIS SHOULDN'T BE HERE.
IT CAN'T BE HERE.
GALLIFREY WAS DESTROYED IN THE TIME WAR AGAINST THE DALEKS. EVERYTHING WAS DESTROYED.
AND THAT'S NOT THE ONLY THING THAT SHOULDN'T BE HERE!
OVER THERE'S A VARDON AXE, AND BESIDE THAT, A SLUGGERLUG'S TAIL!
THERE'S ABOUT A MILLION YEARS BETWEEN THEM. WELL, MAYBE A HUNDRED THOUSAND OR SO.
I REALLY DON'T LIKE THIS–
WE SHOULD GET OUT OF HERE AS QUICKLY AS POSSIBLE.

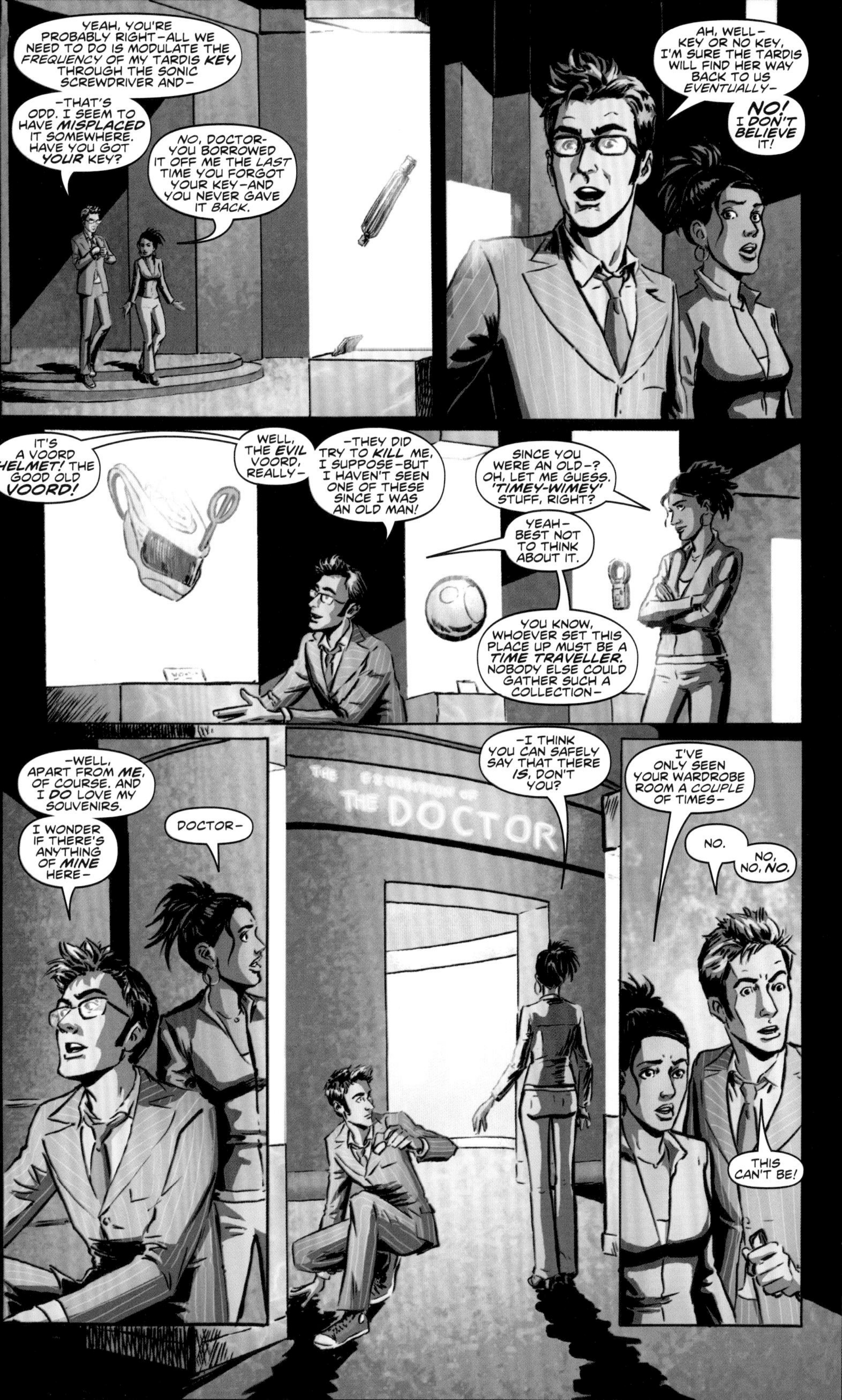

YEAH, YOU'RE PROBABLY RIGHT—ALL WE NEED TO DO IS MODULATE THE *FREQUENCY* OF MY TARDIS ***KEY*** THROUGH THE SONIC SCREWDRIVER AND—
—THAT'S ODD. I SEEM TO HAVE ***MISPLACED*** IT SOMEWHERE. HAVE YOU GOT ***YOUR*** KEY?
NO, DOCTOR- YOU BORROWED IT OFF ME THE *LAST* TIME YOU FORGOT YOUR KEY—AND YOU NEVER GAVE IT *BACK.*
AH, WELL— KEY OR NO KEY, I'M SURE THE TARDIS WILL FIND HER WAY BACK TO US *EVENTUALLY*—
NO! I ***DON'T BELIEVE*** IT!
IT'S A VOORD ***HELMET!*** THE GOOD OLD ***VOORD!***
WELL, THE ***EVIL*** VOORD, REALLY—
—THEY DID TRY TO ***KILL*** ME, I SUPPOSE—BUT I HAVEN'T SEEN ONE OF THESE SINCE I WAS AN OLD MAN!
SINCE YOU WERE AN OLD—? OH, LET ME GUESS. ***'TIMEY-WIMEY'*** STUFF, RIGHT?
YEAH— BEST NOT TO THINK ABOUT IT.
YOU KNOW, WHOEVER SET THIS PLACE UP MUST BE A ***TIME TRAVELLER.*** NOBODY ELSE COULD GATHER SUCH A COLLECTION—
—WELL, APART FROM ***ME,*** OF COURSE. AND I ***DO*** LOVE MY SOUVENIRS.
I WONDER IF THERE'S ANYTHING OF ***MINE*** HERE—
DOCTOR—
THE DOCTOR
—I THINK YOU CAN SAFELY SAY THAT THERE ***IS,*** DON'T YOU?
I'VE ONLY SEEN YOUR WARDROBE ROOM *A COUPLE* OF TIMES—
NO.
NO, NO, ***NO.***
THIS CAN'T BE!

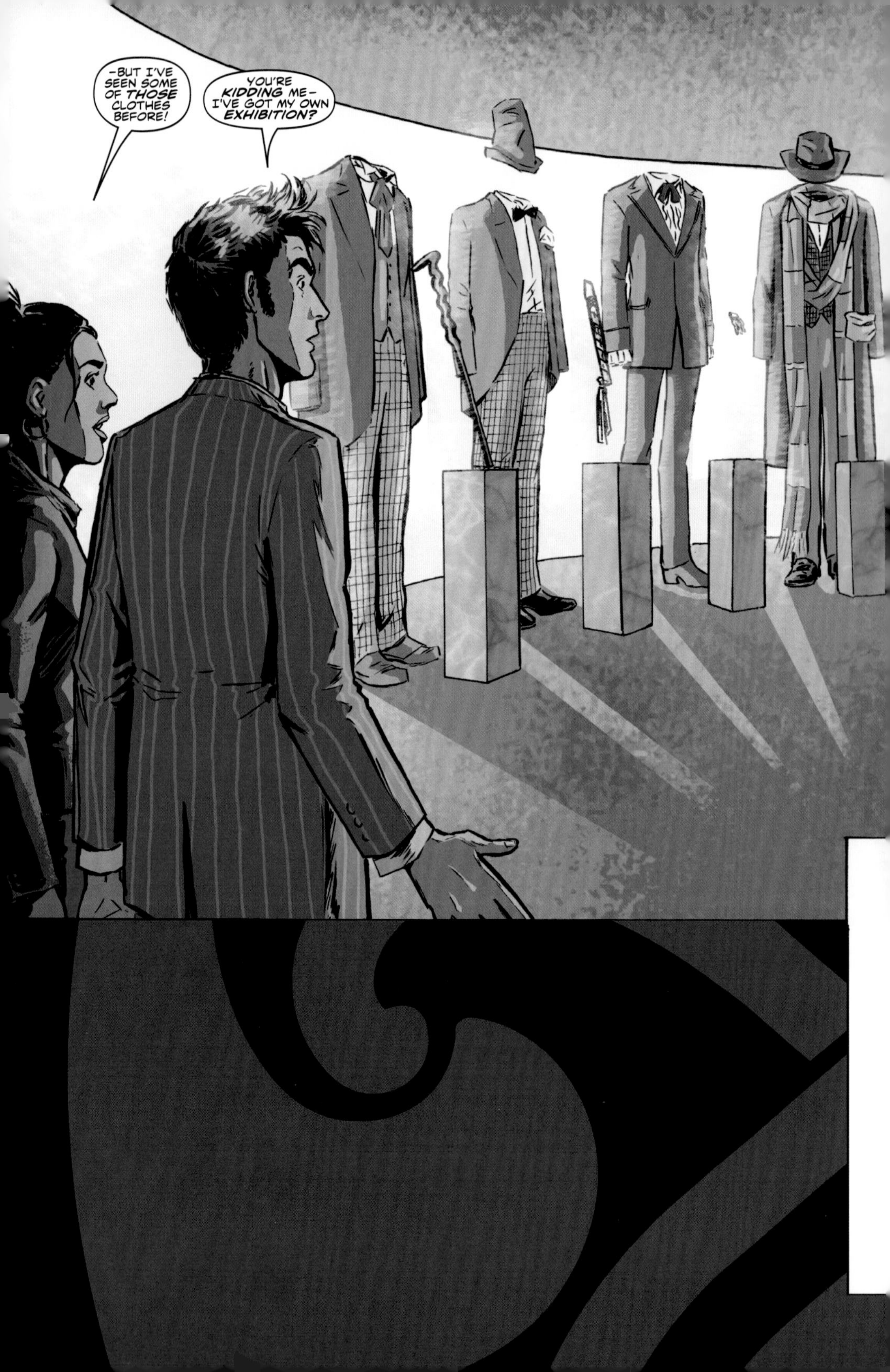
-BUT I'VE SEEN SOME OF THOSE CLOTHES BEFORE!
YOU'RE KIDDING ME- I'VE GOT MY OWN EXHIBITION?

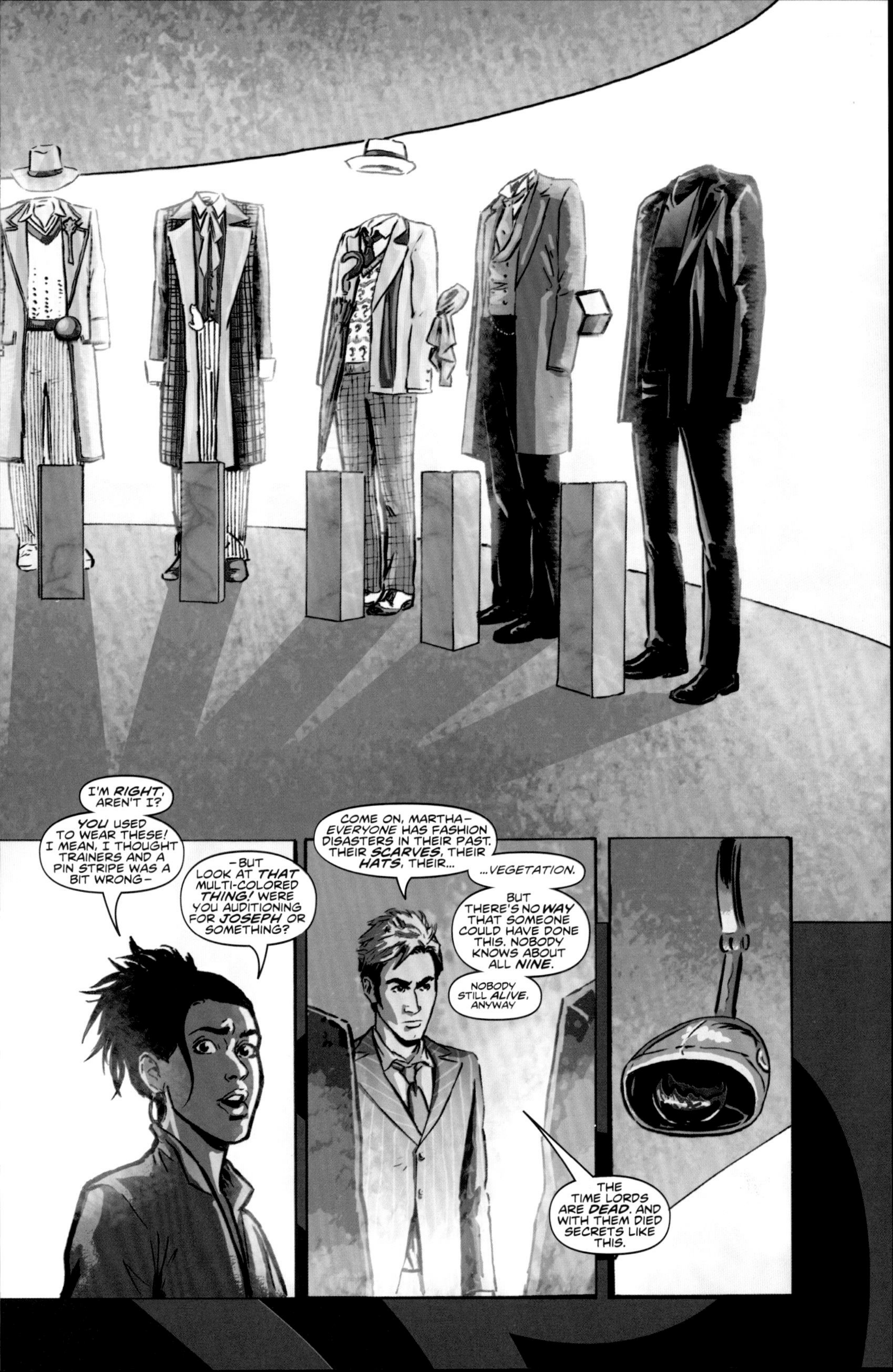

I'M RIGHT, AREN'T I?
YOU USED TO WEAR THESE! I MEAN, I THOUGHT TRAINERS AND A PIN STRIPE WAS A BIT WRONG–
–BUT LOOK AT THAT MULTI-COLORED THING! WERE YOU AUDITIONING FOR JOSEPH OR SOMETHING?
COME ON, MARTHA– EVERYONE HAS FASHION DISASTERS IN THEIR PAST. THEIR SCARVES, THEIR HATS, THEIR...
...VEGETATION.
BUT THERE'S NO WAY THAT SOMEONE COULD HAVE DONE THIS. NOBODY KNOWS ABOUT ALL NINE.
NOBODY STILL ALIVE, ANYWAY
THE TIME LORDS ARE DEAD. AND WITH THEM DIED SECRETS LIKE THIS.

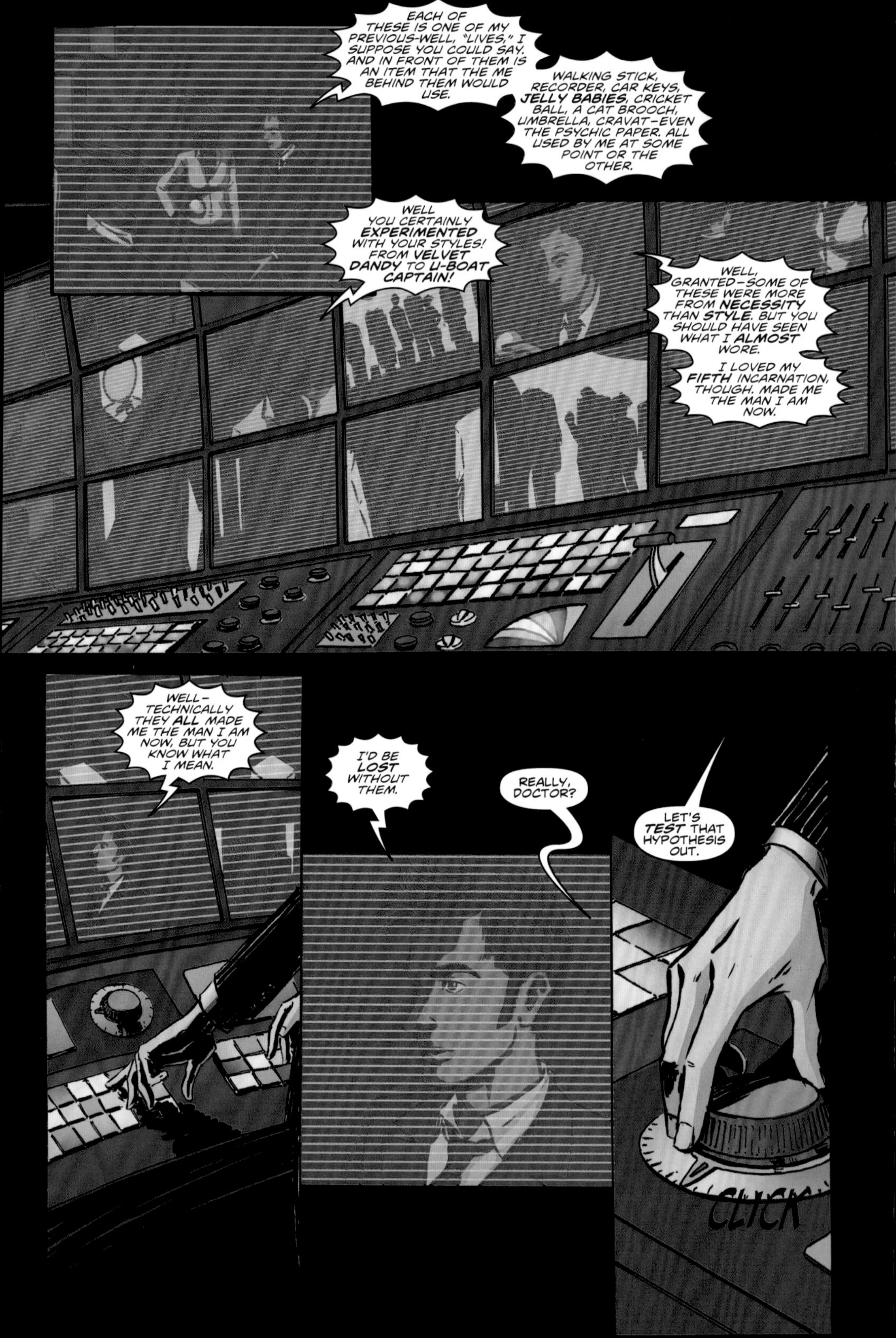
EACH OF THESE IS ONE OF MY PREVIOUS-WELL, "LIVES," I SUPPOSE YOU COULD SAY. AND IN FRONT OF THEM IS AN ITEM THAT THE ME BEHIND THEM WOULD USE.
WALKING STICK, RECORDER, CAR KEYS, JELLY BABIES, CRICKET BALL, A CAT BROOCH, UMBRELLA, CRAVAT–EVEN THE PSYCHIC PAPER. ALL USED BY ME AT SOME POINT OR THE OTHER.
WELL YOU CERTAINLY EXPERIMENTED WITH YOUR STYLES! FROM VELVET DANDY TO U-BOAT CAPTAIN!
WELL, GRANTED–SOME OF THESE WERE MORE FROM NECESSITY THAN STYLE. BUT YOU SHOULD HAVE SEEN WHAT I ALMOST WORE.
I LOVED MY FIFTH INCARNATION, THOUGH. MADE ME THE MAN I AM NOW.
WELL– TECHNICALLY THEY ALL MADE ME THE MAN I AM NOW, BUT YOU KNOW WHAT I MEAN.
I'D BE LOST WITHOUT THEM.
REALLY, DOCTOR?
LET'S TEST THAT HYPOTHESIS OUT.
CLICK

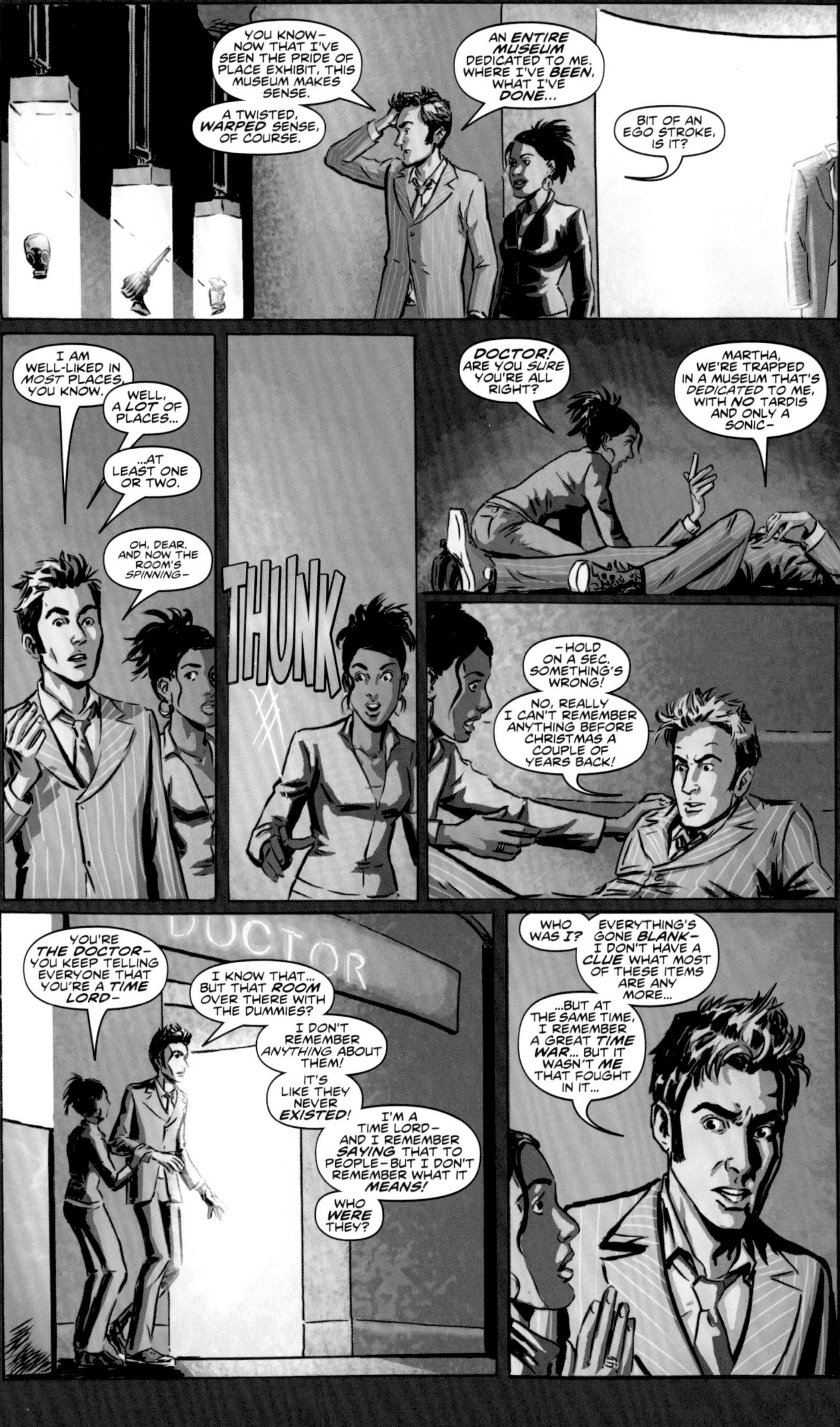
YOU KNOW– NOW THAT I'VE SEEN THE PRIDE OF PLACE EXHIBIT, THIS MUSEUM MAKES SENSE.
A TWISTED, WARPED SENSE, OF COURSE.
AN ENTIRE MUSEUM DEDICATED TO ME. WHERE I'VE BEEN, WHAT I'VE DONE...
BIT OF AN EGO STROKE, IS IT?
I AM WELL-LIKED IN MOST PLACES, YOU KNOW.
WELL, A LOT OF PLACES...
...AT LEAST ONE OR TWO.
OH, DEAR. AND NOW THE ROOM'S SPINNING–
THUNK
DOCTOR! ARE YOU SURE YOU'RE ALL RIGHT?
MARTHA, WE'RE TRAPPED IN A MUSEUM THAT'S DEDICATED TO ME, WITH NO TARDIS AND ONLY A SONIC–
–HOLD ON A SEC. SOMETHING'S WRONG!
NO, REALLY I CAN'T REMEMBER ANYTHING BEFORE CHRISTMAS A COUPLE OF YEARS BACK!
DOCTOR
YOU'RE THE DOCTOR– YOU KEEP TELLING EVERYONE THAT YOU'RE A TIME LORD–
I KNOW THAT... BUT THAT ROOM OVER THERE WITH THE DUMMIES?
I DON'T REMEMBER ANYTHING ABOUT THEM!
IT'S LIKE THEY NEVER EXISTED!
I'M A TIME LORD– AND I REMEMBER SAYING THAT TO PEOPLE–BUT I DON'T REMEMBER WHAT IT MEANS!
WHO WERE THEY?
WHO WAS I?
EVERYTHING'S GONE BLANK– I DON'T HAVE A CLUE WHAT MOST OF THESE ITEMS ARE ANY MORE...
...BUT AT THE SAME TIME, I REMEMBER A GREAT TIME WAR... BUT IT WASN'T ME THAT FOUGHT IN IT...

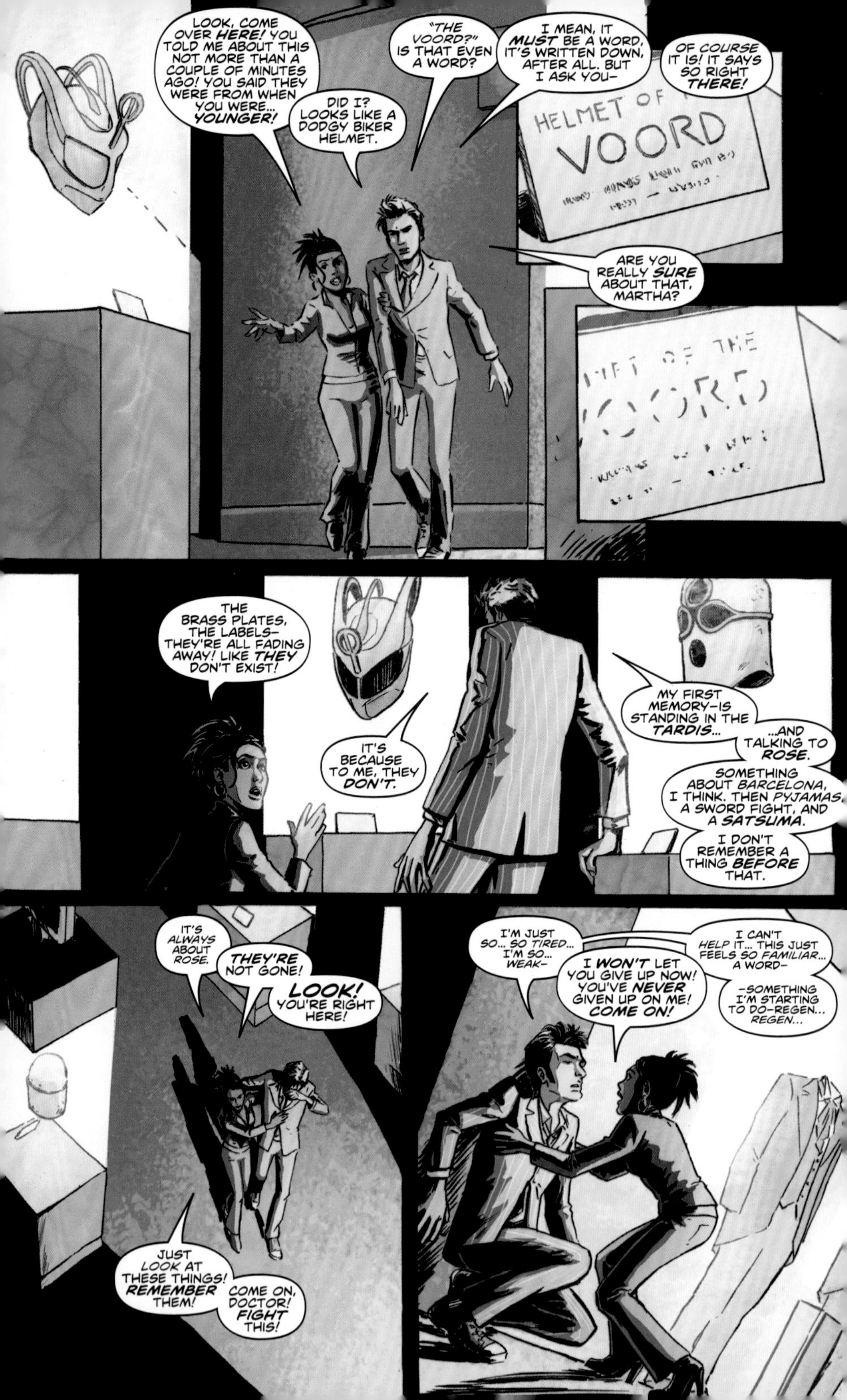

LOOK, COME OVER HERE! YOU TOLD ME ABOUT THIS NOT MORE THAN A COUPLE OF MINUTES AGO! YOU SAID THEY WERE FROM WHEN YOU WERE... YOUNGER!
DID I? LOOKS LIKE A DODGY BIKER HELMET.
"THE VOORD?" IS THAT EVEN A WORD?
I MEAN, IT MUST BE A WORD, IT'S WRITTEN DOWN, AFTER ALL. BUT I ASK YOU–
OF COURSE IT IS! IT SAYS SO RIGHT THERE!
HELMET OF T
VOORD
ARE YOU REALLY SURE ABOUT THAT, MARTHA?
THE BRASS PLATES, THE LABELS– THEY'RE ALL FADING AWAY! LIKE THEY DON'T EXIST!
IT'S BECAUSE TO ME, THEY DON'T.
MY FIRST MEMORY–IS STANDING IN THE TARDIS...
...AND TALKING TO ROSE.
SOMETHING ABOUT BARCELONA, I THINK. THEN PYJAMAS, A SWORD FIGHT, AND A SATSUMA.
I DON'T REMEMBER A THING BEFORE THAT.
IT'S ALWAYS ABOUT ROSE.
THEY'RE NOT GONE!
LOOK! YOU'RE RIGHT HERE!
JUST LOOK AT THESE THINGS! REMEMBER THEM!
COME ON, DOCTOR! FIGHT THIS!
I'M JUST SO... SO TIRED... I'M SO... WEAK–
I WON'T LET YOU GIVE UP NOW! YOU'VE NEVER GIVEN UP ON ME! COME ON!
I CAN'T HELP IT... THIS JUST FEELS SO FAMILIAR... A WORD–
–SOMETHING I'M STARTING TO DO–REGEN... REGEN...

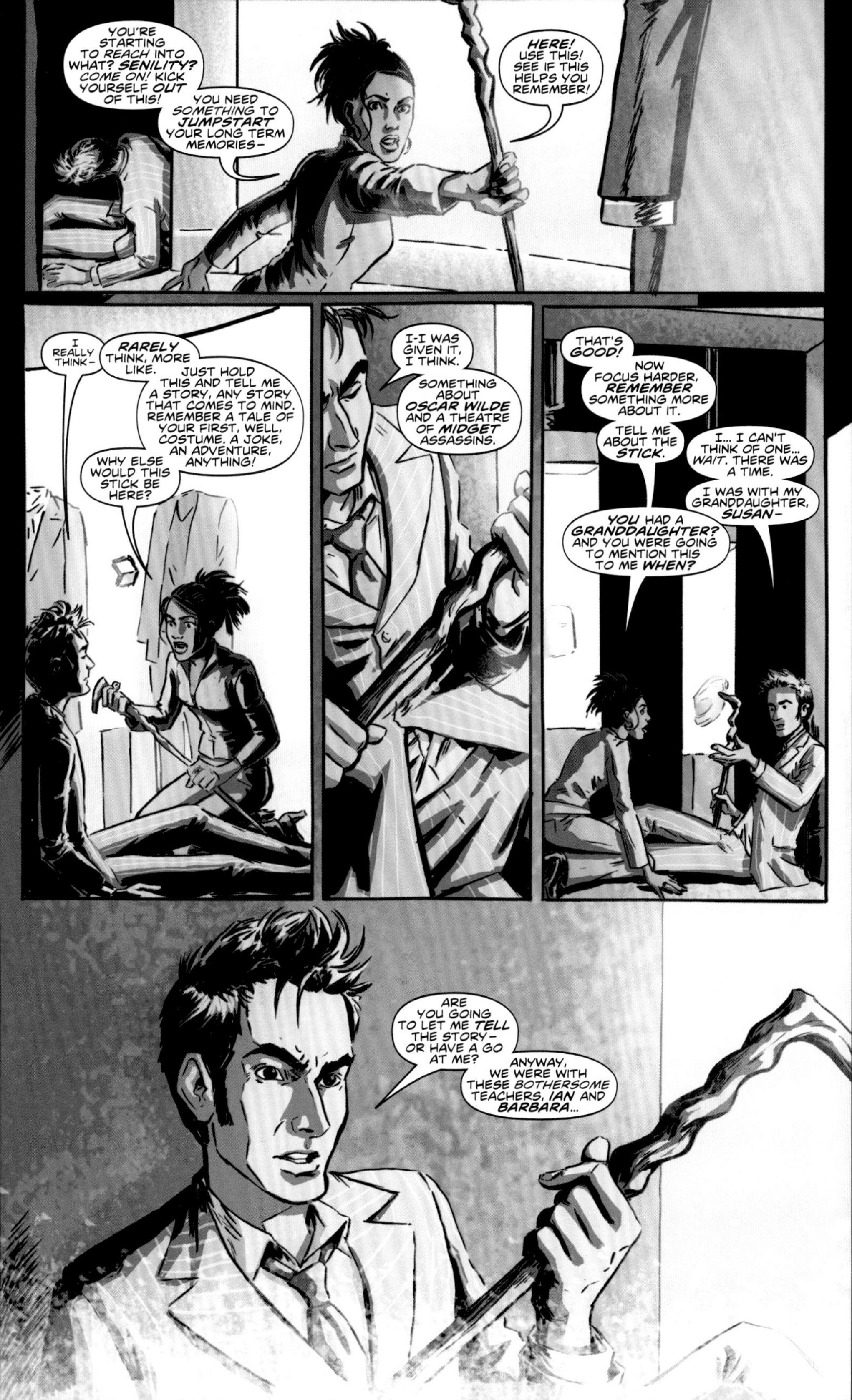
YOU'RE STARTING TO *REACH* INTO WHAT? **SENILITY?** *COME ON!* KICK YOURSELF **OUT** OF THIS!
YOU NEED SOMETHING TO **JUMPSTART** YOUR LONG TERM MEMORIES–
HERE! USE THIS! SEE IF THIS HELPS YOU REMEMBER!
I REALLY THINK–
RARELY THINK, MORE LIKE.
JUST HOLD THIS AND TELL ME A STORY, ANY STORY THAT COMES TO MIND. REMEMBER A TALE OF YOUR FIRST, WELL, COSTUME. A JOKE, AN ADVENTURE, ANYTHING!
WHY ELSE WOULD THIS STICK BE HERE?
I-I WAS GIVEN IT, I THINK.
SOMETHING ABOUT **OSCAR WILDE** AND A THEATRE OF **MIDGET** ASSASSINS.
THAT'S **GOOD!**
NOW FOCUS HARDER, **REMEMBER** SOMETHING MORE ABOUT IT.
TELL ME ABOUT THE **STICK**.
I... I CAN'T THINK OF ONE... *WAIT*. THERE WAS A TIME.
I WAS WITH MY GRANDDAUGHTER, **SUSAN**–
YOU HAD A **GRANDDAUGHTER?** AND YOU WERE GOING TO MENTION THIS TO ME **WHEN?**
ARE YOU GOING TO LET ME **TELL** THE STORY– OR HAVE A GO AT ME?
ANYWAY, WE WERE WITH THESE *BOTHERSOME* TEACHERS, **IAN** AND **BARBARA**...

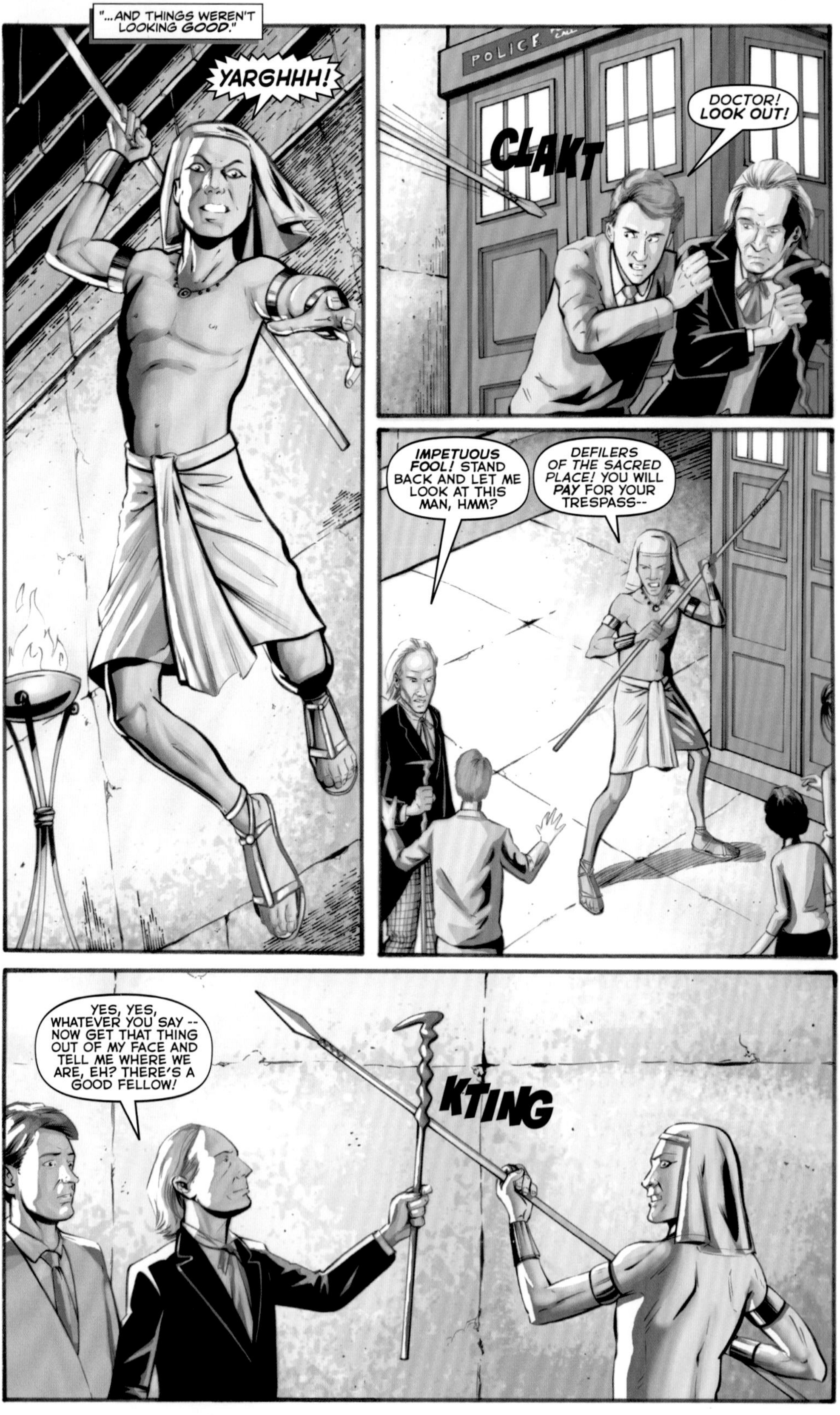
"...AND THINGS WEREN'T LOOKING GOOD."
YARGHHH!
POLICE
CLAKT
DOCTOR! LOOK OUT!
IMPETUOUS FOOL! STAND BACK AND LET ME LOOK AT THIS MAN, HMM?
DEFILERS OF THE SACRED PLACE! YOU WILL PAY FOR YOUR TRESPASS--
YES, YES, WHATEVER YOU SAY -- NOW GET THAT THING OUT OF MY FACE AND TELL ME WHERE WE ARE, EH? THERE'S A GOOD FELLOW!
KTING

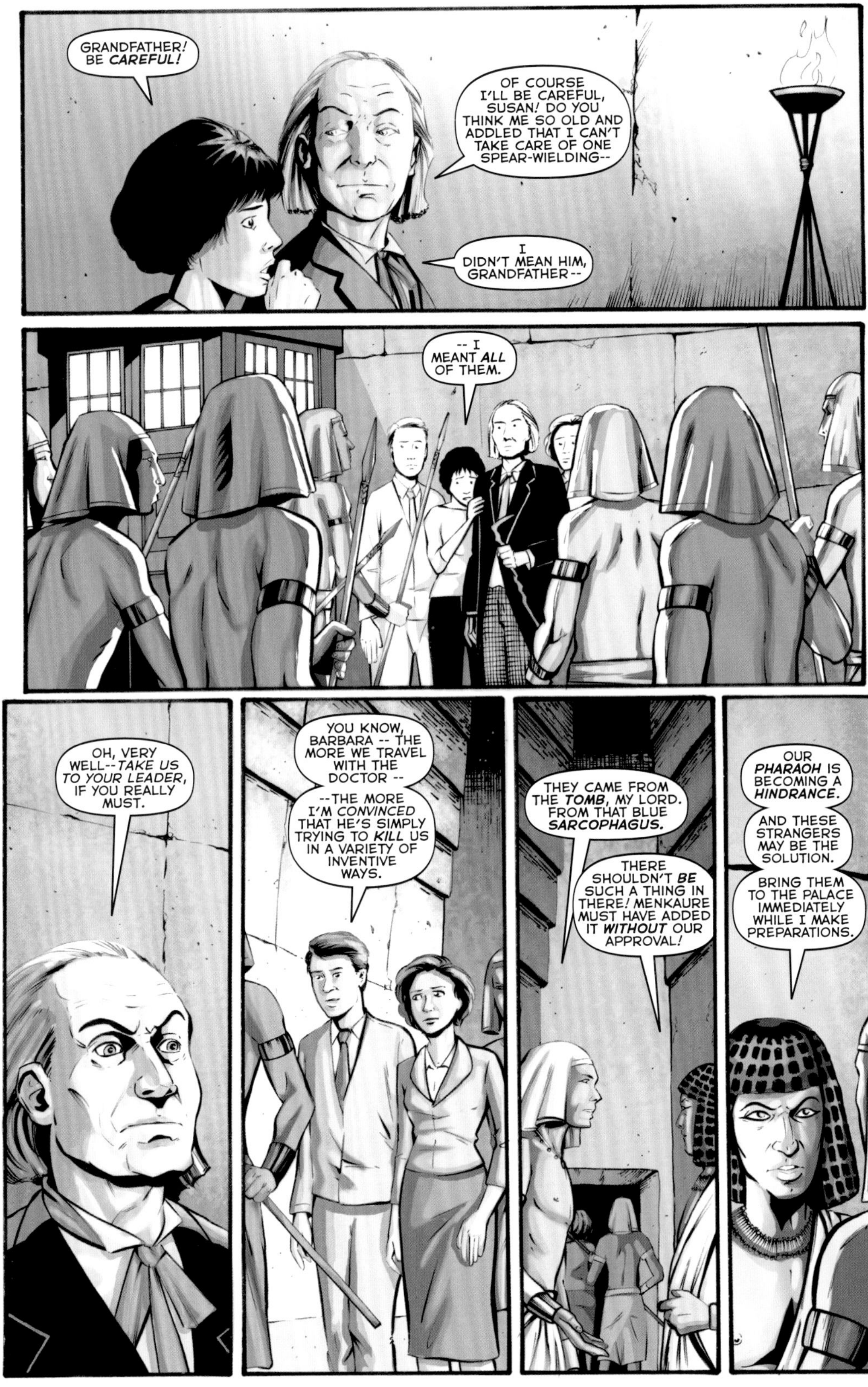
GRANDFATHER! BE *CAREFUL!*
OF COURSE I'LL BE CAREFUL, SUSAN! DO YOU THINK ME SO OLD AND ADDLED THAT I CAN'T TAKE CARE OF ONE SPEAR-WIELDING--
I DIDN'T MEAN HIM, GRANDFATHER--
-- I MEANT *ALL* OF THEM.
OH, VERY WELL--*TAKE US TO YOUR LEADER,* IF YOU REALLY MUST.
YOU KNOW, BARBARA -- THE MORE WE TRAVEL WITH THE DOCTOR --
--THE MORE I'M *CONVINCED* THAT HE'S SIMPLY TRYING TO *KILL* US IN A VARIETY OF INVENTIVE WAYS.
THEY CAME FROM THE *TOMB*, MY LORD. FROM THAT BLUE *SARCOPHAGUS.*
THERE SHOULDN'T *BE* SUCH A THING IN THERE! MENKAURE MUST HAVE ADDED IT *WITHOUT* OUR APPROVAL!
OUR *PHARAOH* IS BECOMING A *HINDRANCE.*
AND THESE STRANGERS MAY BE THE SOLUTION.
BRING THEM TO THE PALACE IMMEDIATELY WHILE I MAKE PREPARATIONS.

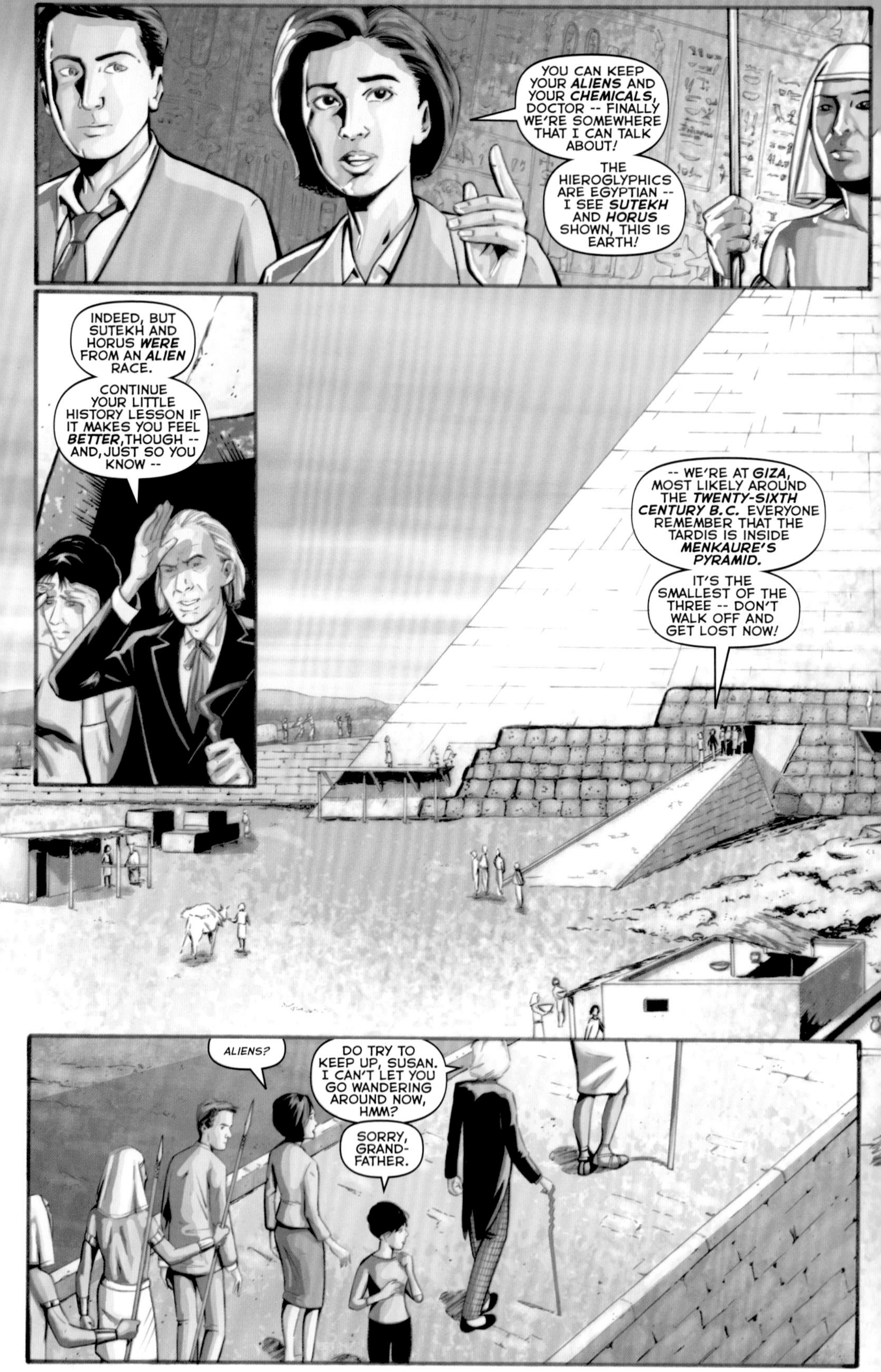

YOU CAN KEEP YOUR ALIENS AND YOUR CHEMICALS, DOCTOR -- FINALLY WE'RE SOMEWHERE THAT I CAN TALK ABOUT!
THE HIEROGLYPHICS ARE EGYPTIAN -- I SEE SUTEKH AND HORUS SHOWN, THIS IS EARTH!
INDEED, BUT SUTEKH AND HORUS WERE FROM AN ALIEN RACE.
CONTINUE YOUR LITTLE HISTORY LESSON IF IT MAKES YOU FEEL BETTER, THOUGH -- AND, JUST SO YOU KNOW --
-- WE'RE AT GIZA, MOST LIKELY AROUND THE TWENTY-SIXTH CENTURY B.C. EVERYONE REMEMBER THAT THE TARDIS IS INSIDE MENKAURE'S PYRAMID.
IT'S THE SMALLEST OF THE THREE -- DON'T WALK OFF AND GET LOST NOW!
ALIENS?
DO TRY TO KEEP UP, SUSAN. I CAN'T LET YOU GO WANDERING AROUND NOW, HMM?
SORRY, GRAND-FATHER.

GREETINGS, TRAVELERS! I AM *BUIKHU* AND I WELCOME YOU -- *VISITORS FROM THE STARS!*

"*FROM THE STARS?*" WHAT ON EARTH DOES HE MEAN BY --

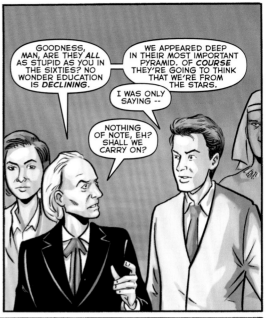

GOODNESS, MAN, ARE THEY *ALL* AS STUPID AS YOU IN THE SIXTIES? NO WONDER EDUCATION IS *DECLINING*.

WE APPEARED DEEP IN THEIR MOST IMPORTANT PYRAMID. OF *COURSE* THEY'RE GOING TO THINK THAT WE'RE FROM THE STARS.

I WAS ONLY SAYING --

NOTHING OF NOTE, EH? SHALL WE CARRY ON?

I REALLY HOPE THEY TURN *HIM* INTO A MUMMY.

WHY, SO HE'LL BE LESS SCARY?

NO -- SO THE *BANDAGES* COVER HIS *MOUTH.*

KEMNEBI -- I HAVE A *FAVOUR* TO ASK OF YOU. BRING YOUR BEST MAN TO THE PALACE WITH A BLOWPIPE AND DARTS.

WE HAVE AN OPPORTUNITY HERE TO *KILL* MENKAURE, AND BLAME THESE STRANGERS IN THE PROCESS.

AND HOW WOULD WE DO THAT, ITENNU?

POISON DARTS LEAVE NO VISIBLE WOUND. THE ONLY POSSIBLE ANSWER WILL BE THAT THESE "*VISITORS FROM THE STARS*" USED *MAGICS* TO KILL HIM.

AND ONCE WE CONVINCE THE POPULACE OF THIS, WE KILL *THEM.*

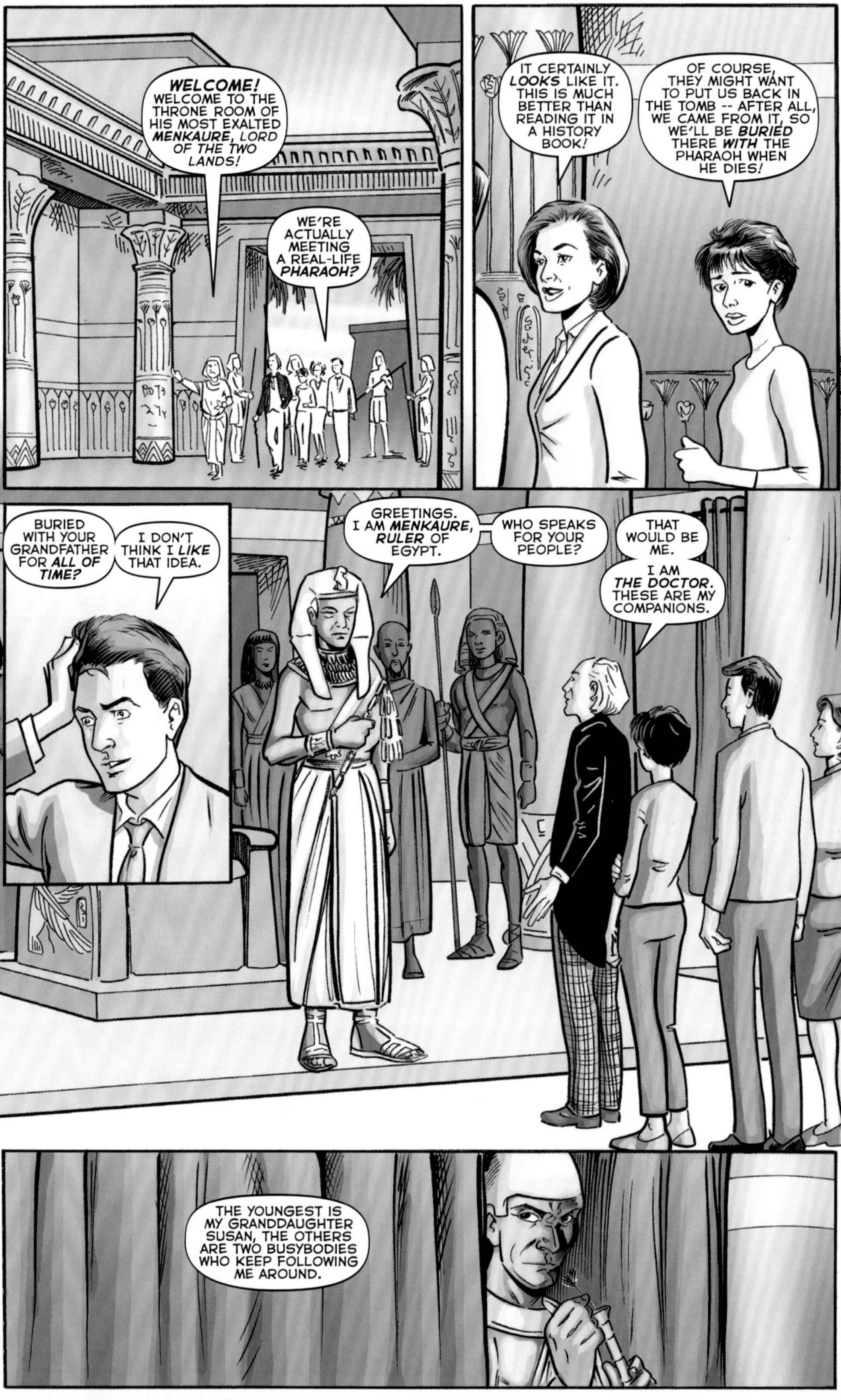

WELCOME! WELCOME TO THE THRONE ROOM OF HIS MOST EXALTED MENKAURE, LORD OF THE TWO LANDS!
WE'RE ACTUALLY MEETING A REAL-LIFE PHARAOH?
IT CERTAINLY LOOKS LIKE IT. THIS IS MUCH BETTER THAN READING IT IN A HISTORY BOOK!
OF COURSE, THEY MIGHT WANT TO PUT US BACK IN THE TOMB -- AFTER ALL, WE CAME FROM IT, SO WE'LL BE BURIED THERE WITH THE PHARAOH WHEN HE DIES!
BURIED WITH YOUR GRANDFATHER FOR ALL OF TIME?
I DON'T THINK I LIKE THAT IDEA.
GREETINGS. I AM MENKAURE, RULER OF EGYPT.
WHO SPEAKS FOR YOUR PEOPLE?
THAT WOULD BE ME.
I AM THE DOCTOR. THESE ARE MY COMPANIONS.
THE YOUNGEST IS MY GRANDDAUGHTER SUSAN, THE OTHERS ARE TWO BUSYBODIES WHO KEEP FOLLOWING ME AROUND.

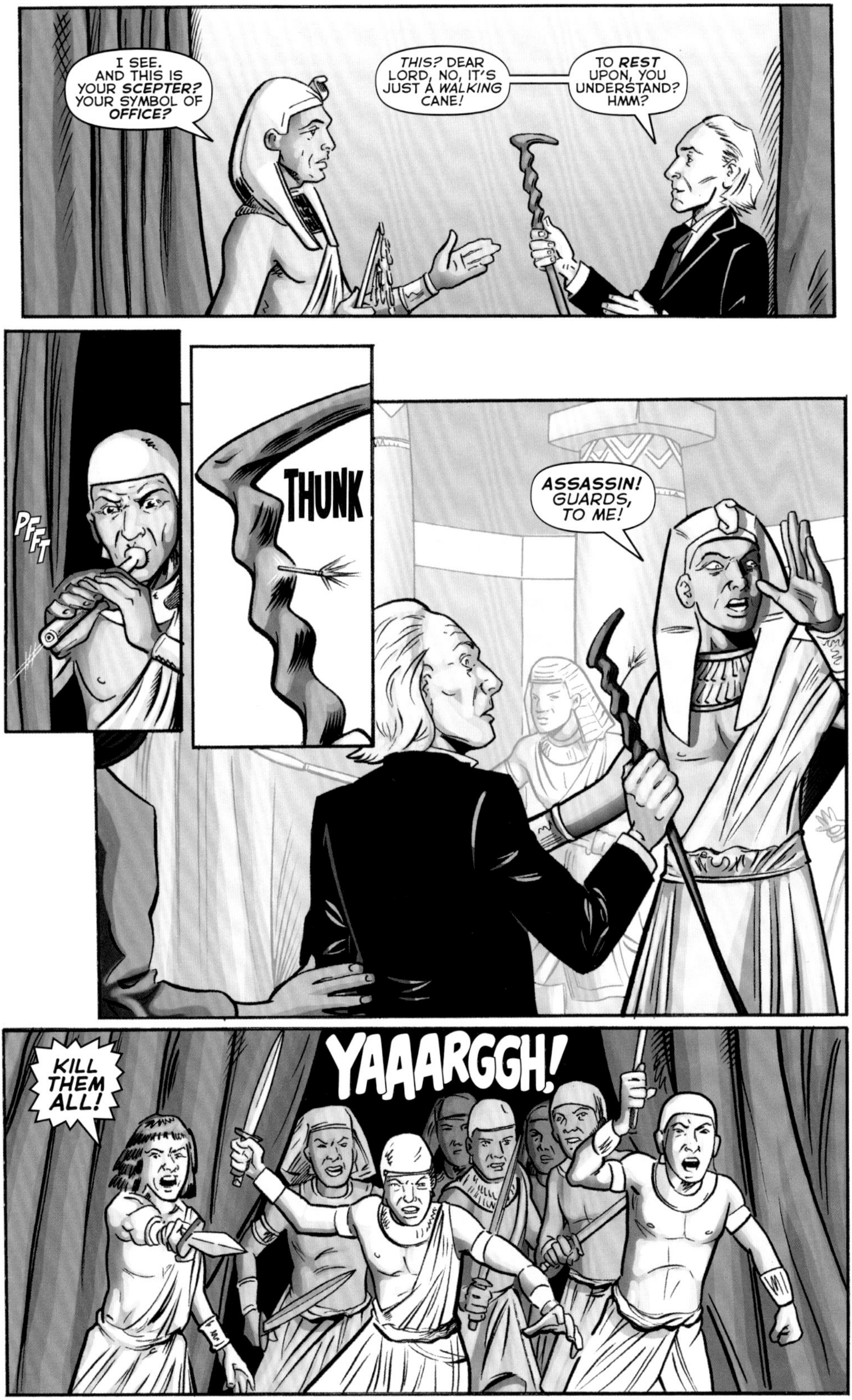
I SEE. AND THIS IS YOUR SCEPTER? YOUR SYMBOL OF OFFICE?
THIS? DEAR LORD, NO, IT'S JUST A WALKING CANE!
TO REST UPON, YOU UNDERSTAND? HMM?
PFFT
THUNK
ASSASSIN! GUARDS, TO ME!
KILL THEM ALL!
YAAARGGH!

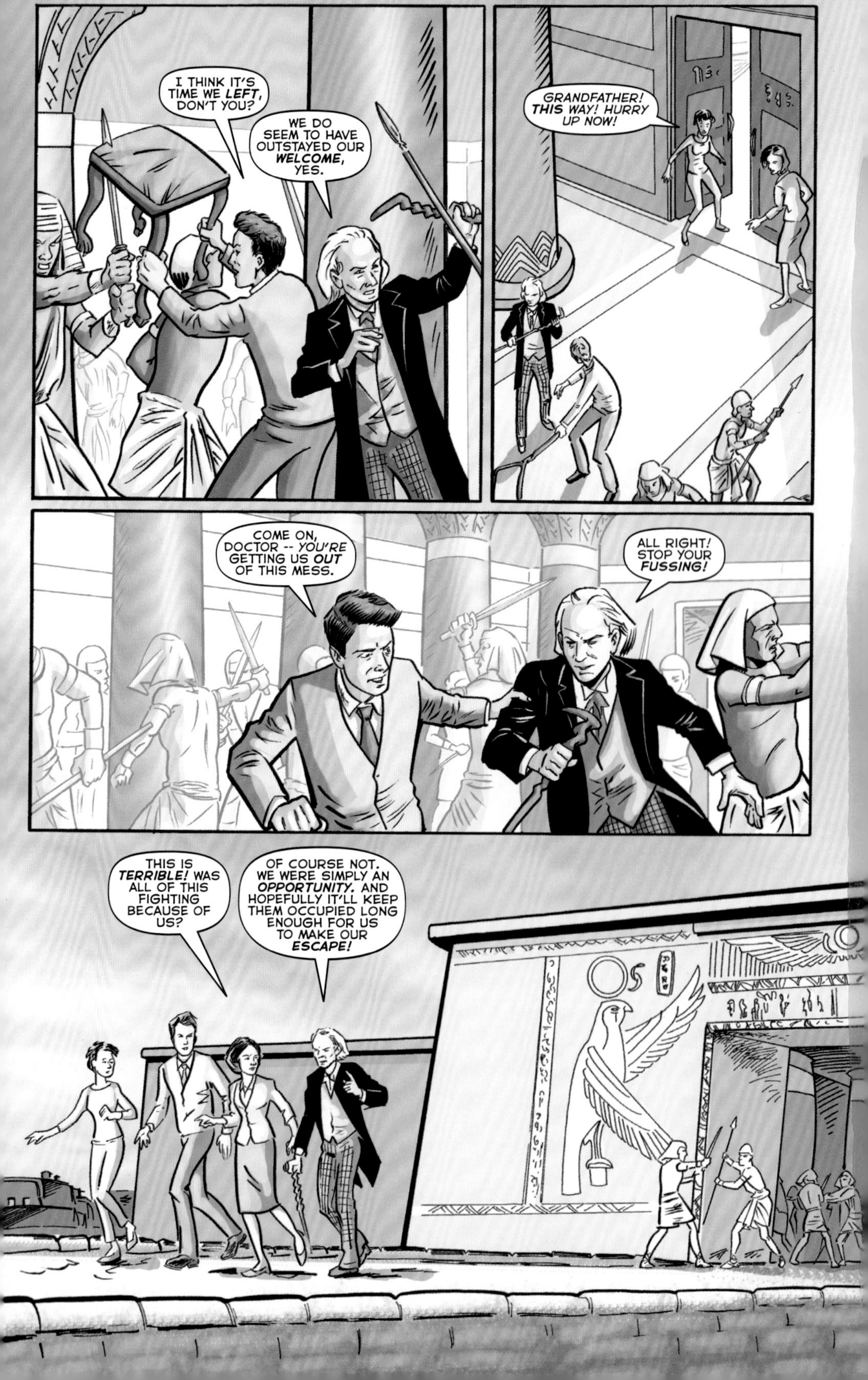
I THINK IT'S TIME WE **LEFT**, DON'T YOU?
WE DO SEEM TO HAVE OUTSTAYED OUR ***WELCOME***, YES.
*GRANDFATHER! **THIS** WAY! HURRY UP NOW!*
COME ON, DOCTOR -- *YOU'RE* GETTING US ***OUT*** OF THIS MESS.
ALL RIGHT! STOP YOUR ***FUSSING!***
THIS IS ***TERRIBLE!*** WAS ALL OF THIS FIGHTING BECAUSE OF US?
OF COURSE NOT. WE WERE SIMPLY AN ***OPPORTUNITY.*** AND HOPEFULLY IT'LL KEEP THEM OCCUPIED LONG ENOUGH FOR US TO MAKE OUR ***ESCAPE!***

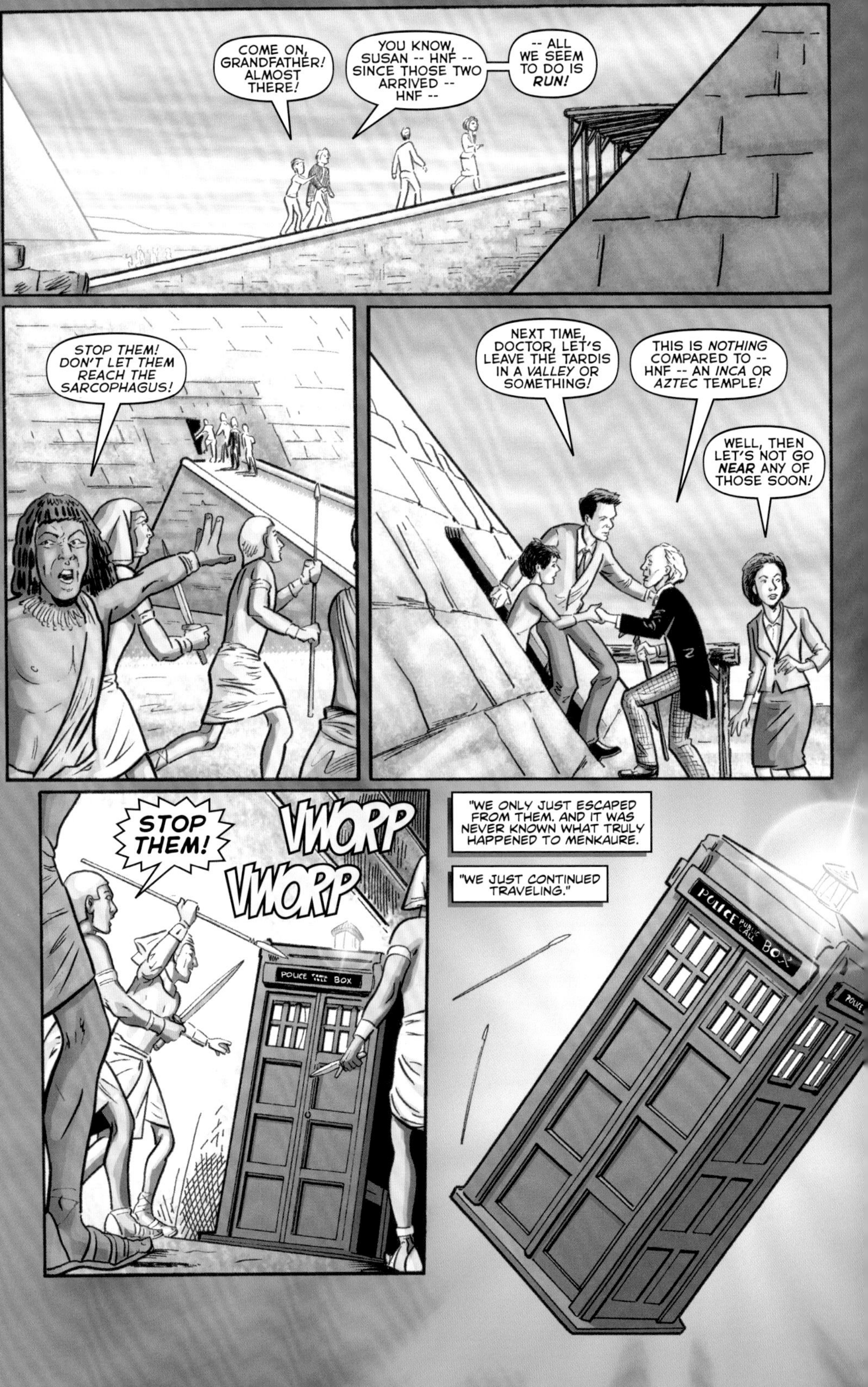
COME ON, GRANDFATHER! ALMOST THERE!
YOU KNOW, SUSAN -- HNF -- SINCE THOSE TWO ARRIVED -- HNF --
-- ALL WE SEEM TO DO IS *RUN!*
STOP THEM! DON'T LET THEM REACH THE SARCOPHAGUS!
NEXT TIME, DOCTOR, LET'S LEAVE THE TARDIS IN A *VALLEY* OR SOMETHING!
THIS IS *NOTHING* COMPARED TO -- HNF -- AN *INCA* OR *AZTEC* TEMPLE!
WELL, THEN LET'S NOT GO ***NEAR*** ANY OF THOSE SOON!
STOP THEM!
VWORP
VWORP
"WE ONLY JUST ESCAPED FROM THEM. AND IT WAS NEVER KNOWN WHAT TRULY HAPPENED TO MENKAURE.
"WE JUST CONTINUED TRAVELING."
POLICE PUBLIC CALL BOX

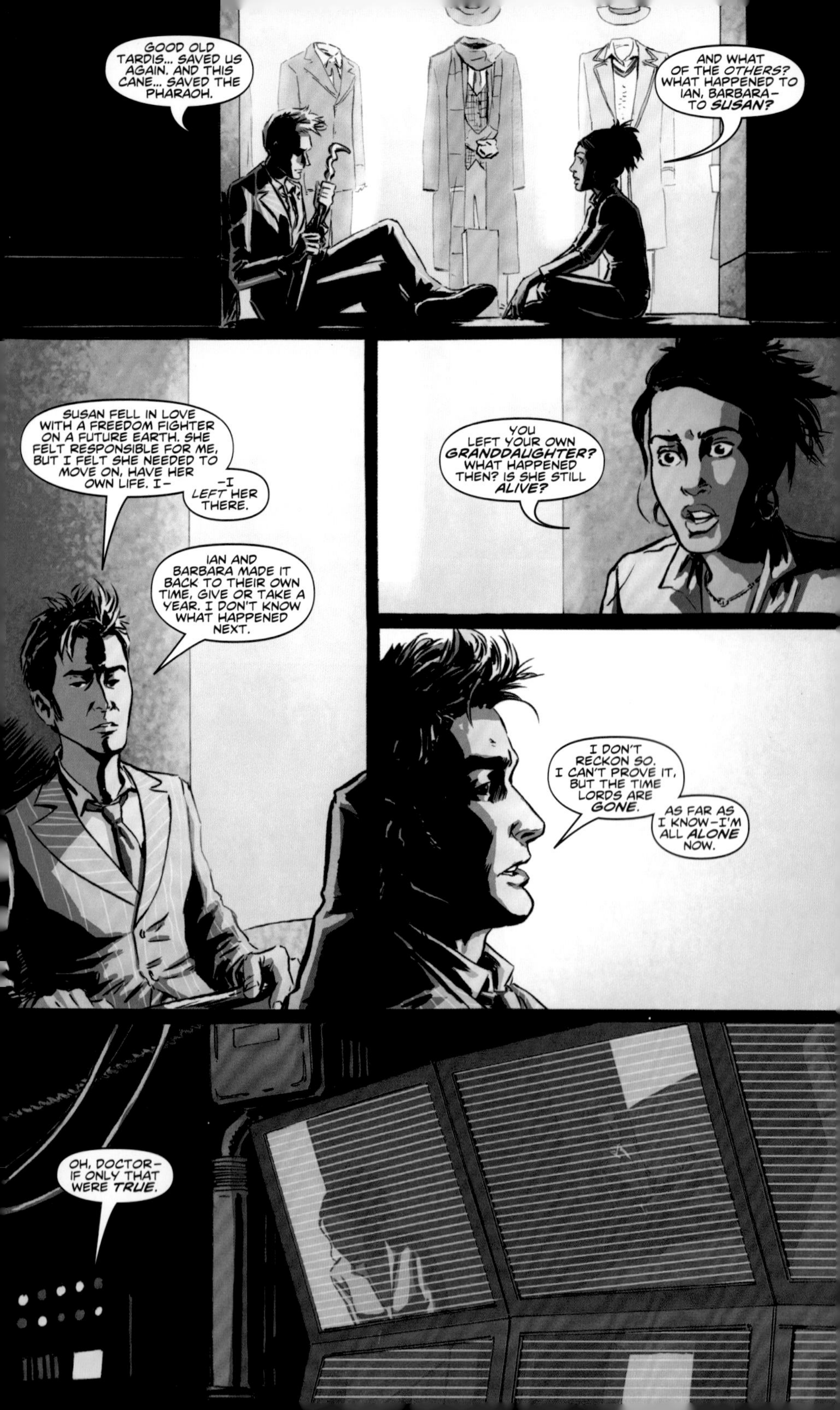
GOOD OLD TARDIS... SAVED US AGAIN. AND THIS CANE... SAVED THE PHARAOH.
AND WHAT OF THE OTHERS? WHAT HAPPENED TO IAN, BARBARA– TO SUSAN?
SUSAN FELL IN LOVE WITH A FREEDOM FIGHTER ON A FUTURE EARTH. SHE FELT RESPONSIBLE FOR ME, BUT I FELT SHE NEEDED TO MOVE ON, HAVE HER OWN LIFE. I–
–I LEFT HER THERE.
YOU LEFT YOUR OWN GRANDDAUGHTER? WHAT HAPPENED THEN? IS SHE STILL ALIVE?
IAN AND BARBARA MADE IT BACK TO THEIR OWN TIME, GIVE OR TAKE A YEAR. I DON'T KNOW WHAT HAPPENED NEXT.
I DON'T RECKON SO. I CAN'T PROVE IT, BUT THE TIME LORDS ARE GONE.
AS FAR AS I KNOW–I'M ALL ALONE NOW.
OH, DOCTOR– IF ONLY THAT WERE TRUE.

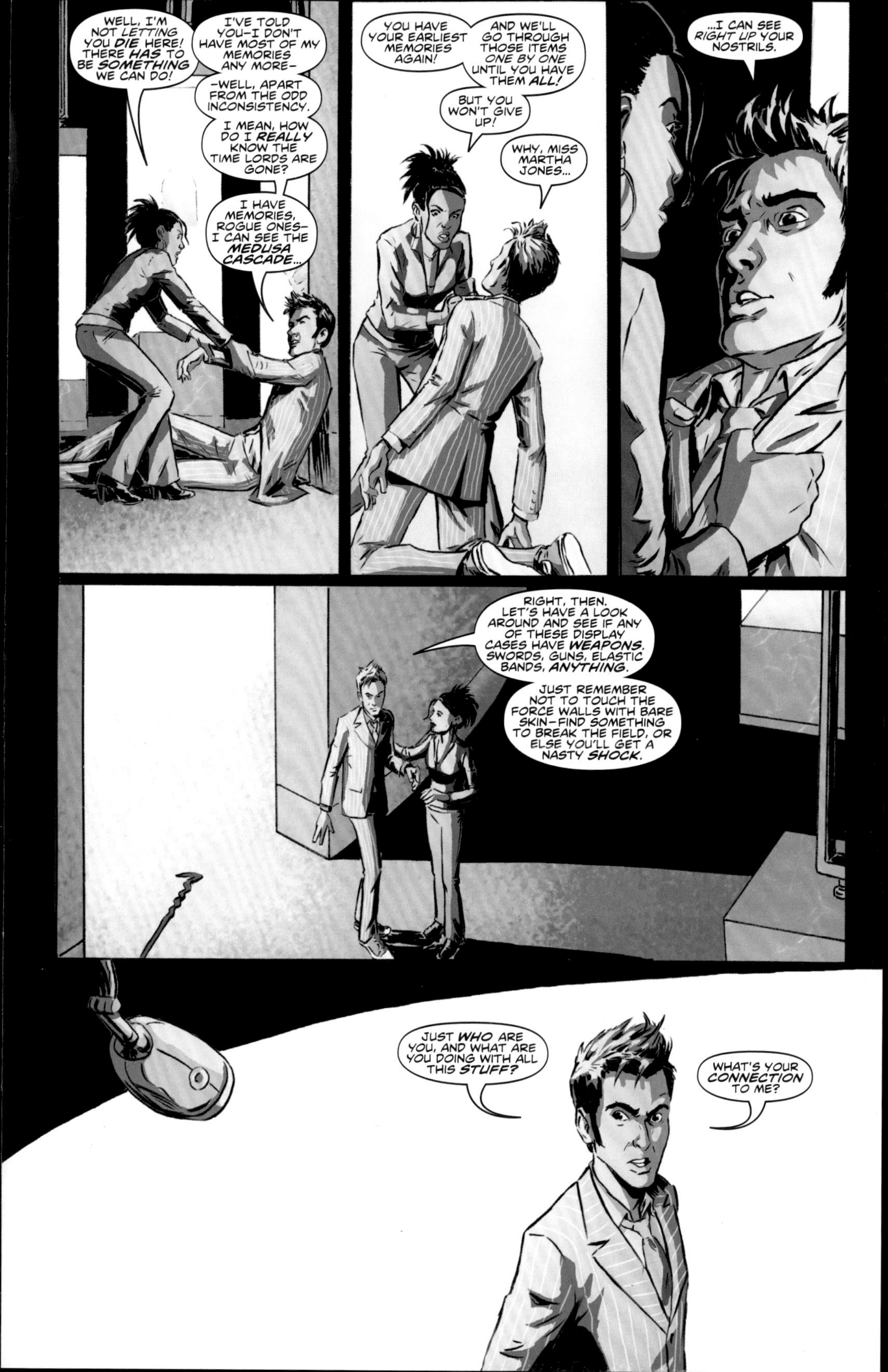
WELL, I'M NOT LETTING YOU DIE HERE! THERE HAS TO BE SOMETHING WE CAN DO!
I'VE TOLD YOU–I DON'T HAVE MOST OF MY MEMORIES ANY MORE–
–WELL, APART FROM THE ODD INCONSISTENCY.
I MEAN, HOW DO I REALLY KNOW THE TIME LORDS ARE GONE?
I HAVE MEMORIES, ROGUE ONES–I CAN SEE THE MEDUSA CASCADE...
YOU HAVE YOUR EARLIEST MEMORIES AGAIN!
AND WE'LL GO THROUGH THOSE ITEMS ONE BY ONE UNTIL YOU HAVE THEM ALL!
BUT YOU WON'T GIVE UP!
WHY, MISS MARTHA JONES...
...I CAN SEE RIGHT UP YOUR NOSTRILS.
RIGHT, THEN. LET'S HAVE A LOOK AROUND AND SEE IF ANY OF THESE DISPLAY CASES HAVE WEAPONS. SWORDS, GUNS, ELASTIC BANDS, ANYTHING.
JUST REMEMBER NOT TO TOUCH THE FORCE WALLS WITH BARE SKIN–FIND SOMETHING TO BREAK THE FIELD, OR ELSE YOU'LL GET A NASTY SHOCK.
JUST WHO ARE YOU, AND WHAT ARE YOU DOING WITH ALL THIS STUFF?
WHAT'S YOUR CONNECTION TO ME?

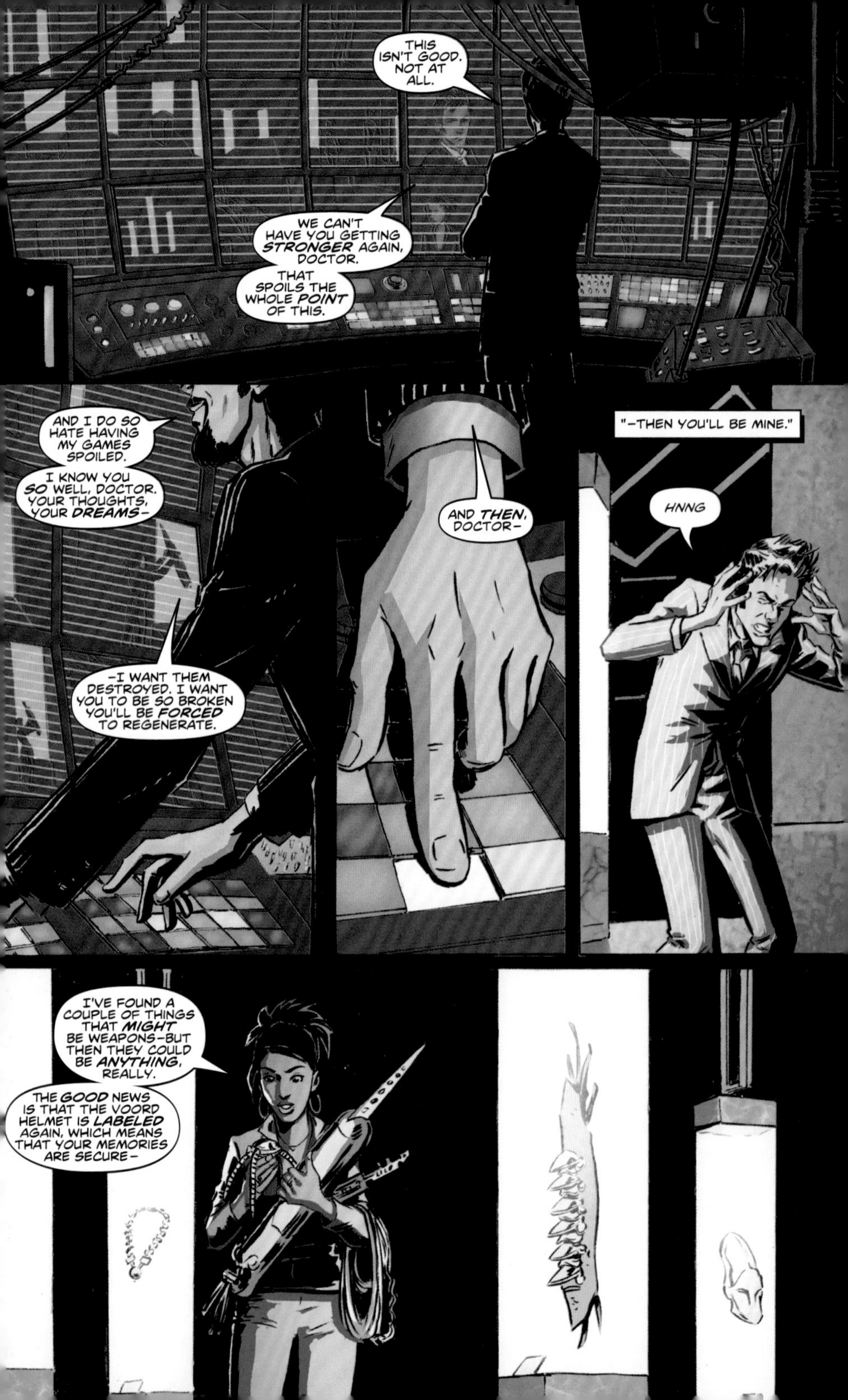
THIS ISN'T GOOD. NOT AT ALL.
WE CAN'T HAVE YOU GETTING STRONGER AGAIN, DOCTOR.
THAT SPOILS THE WHOLE POINT OF THIS.
AND I DO SO HATE HAVING MY GAMES SPOILED.
I KNOW YOU SO WELL, DOCTOR. YOUR THOUGHTS, YOUR DREAMS–
–I WANT THEM DESTROYED. I WANT YOU TO BE SO BROKEN YOU'LL BE FORCED TO REGENERATE.
AND THEN, DOCTOR–
"–THEN YOU'LL BE MINE."
HNNG
I'VE FOUND A COUPLE OF THINGS THAT MIGHT BE WEAPONS–BUT THEN THEY COULD BE ANYTHING, REALLY.
THE GOOD NEWS IS THAT THE VOORD HELMET IS LABELED AGAIN, WHICH MEANS THAT YOUR MEMORIES ARE SECURE–

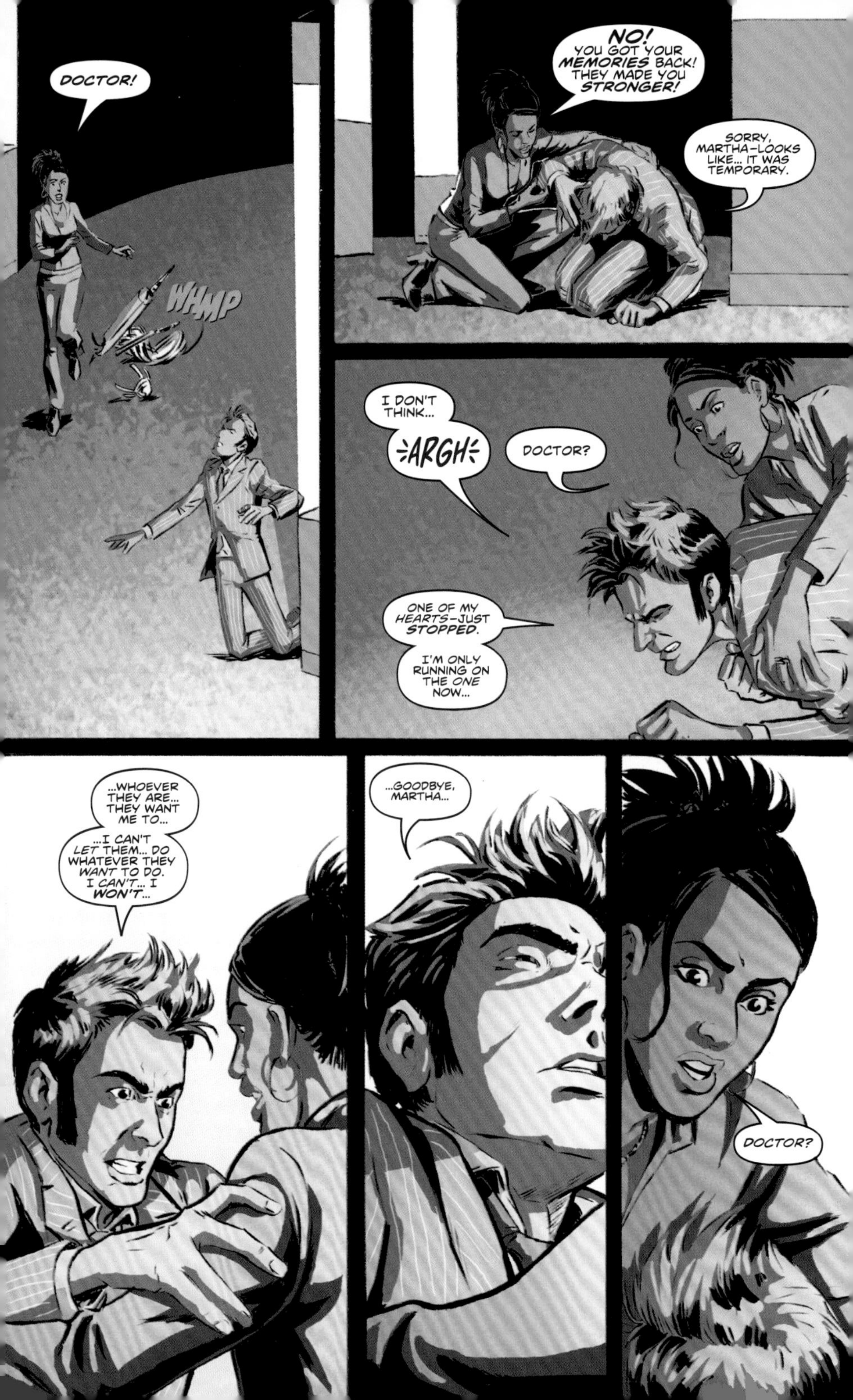
DOCTOR!
WHMP
NO! YOU GOT YOUR MEMORIES BACK! THEY MADE YOU STRONGER!
SORRY, MARTHA—LOOKS LIKE... IT WAS TEMPORARY.
I DON'T THINK...
ARGH
DOCTOR?
ONE OF MY HEARTS—JUST STOPPED.
I'M ONLY RUNNING ON THE ONE NOW...
...WHOEVER THEY ARE... THEY WANT ME TO...
...I CAN'T LET THEM... DO WHATEVER THEY WANT TO DO. I CAN'T... I WON'T...
...GOODBYE, MARTHA...
DOCTOR?

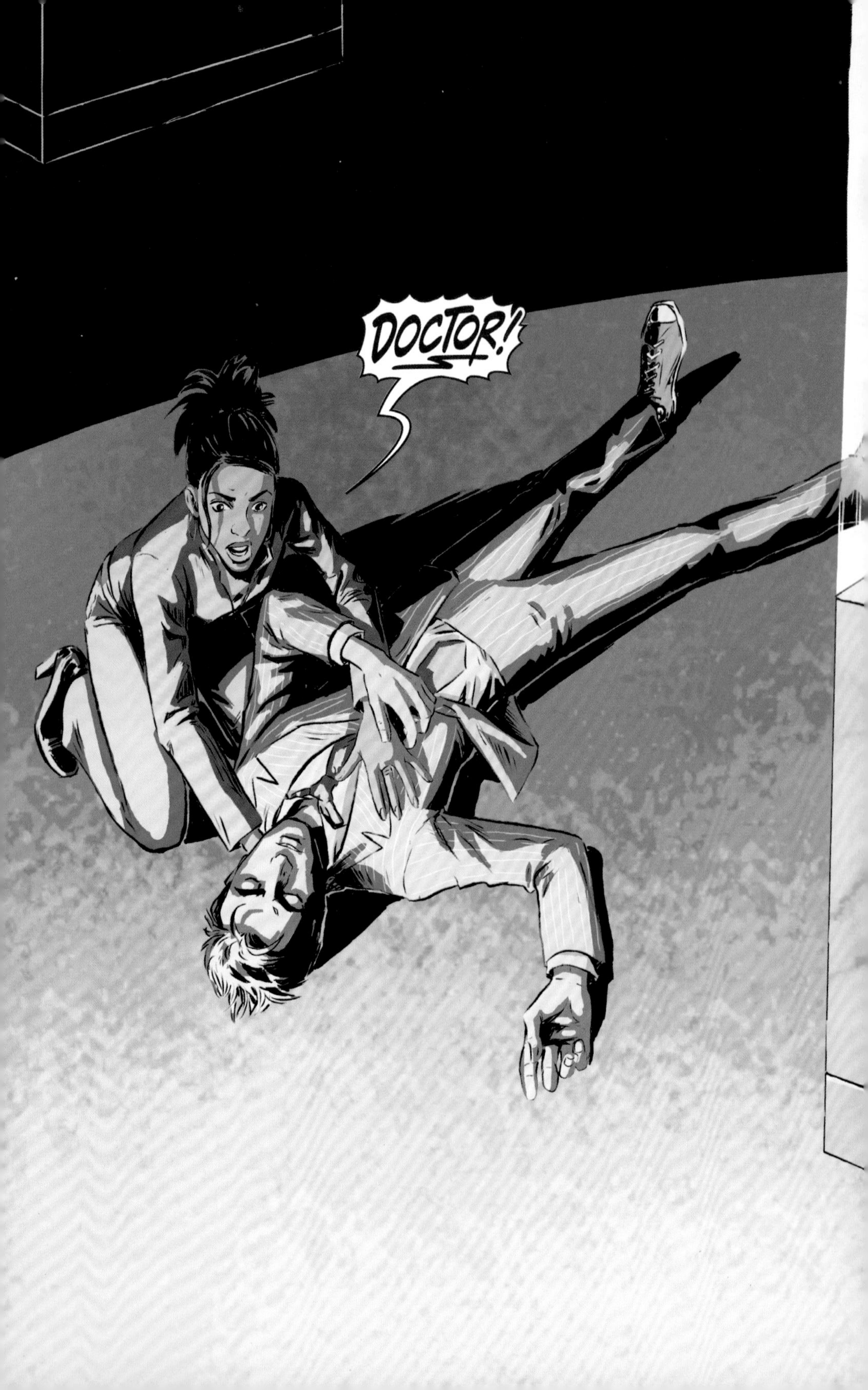
DOCTOR!

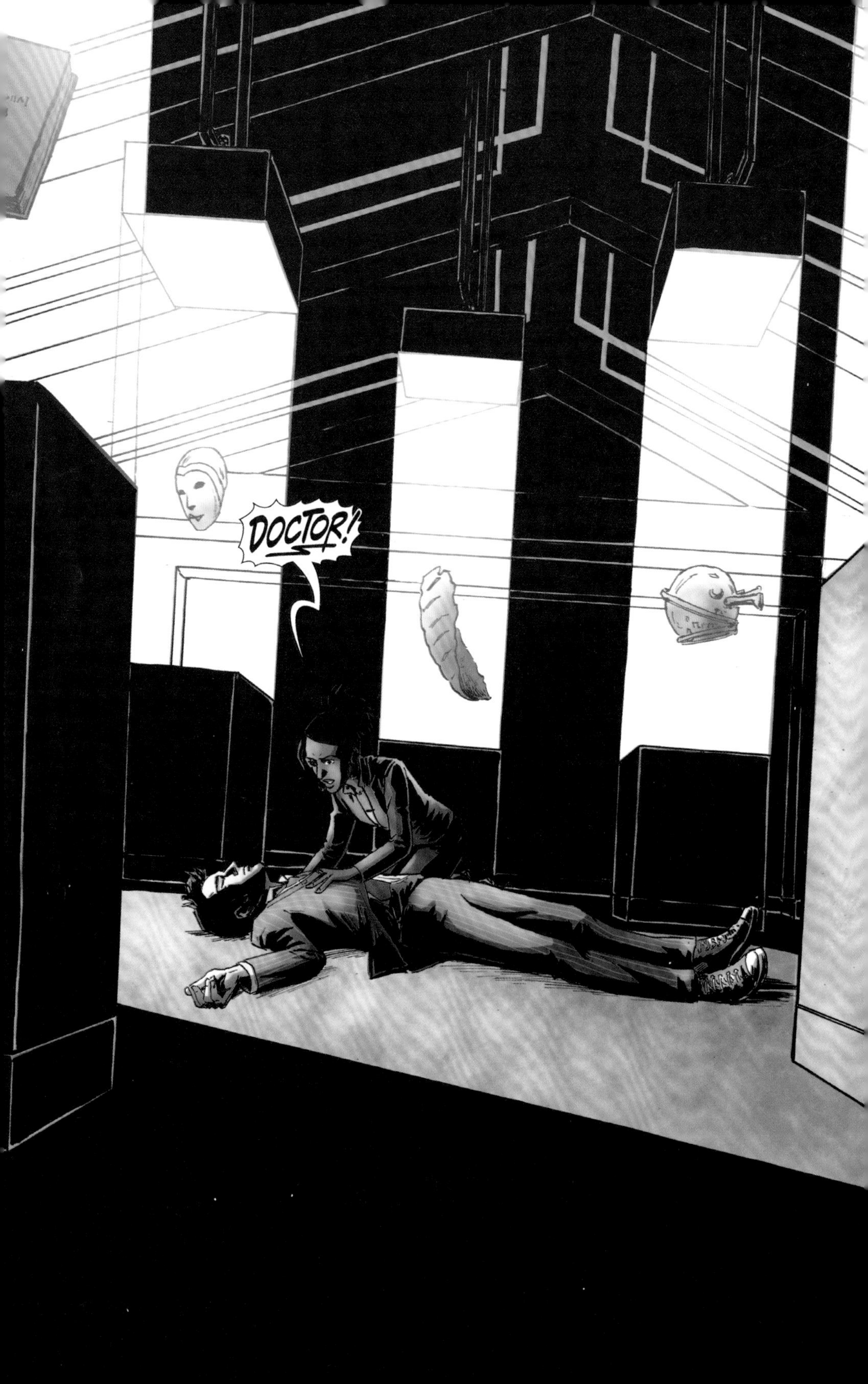
DOCTOR!

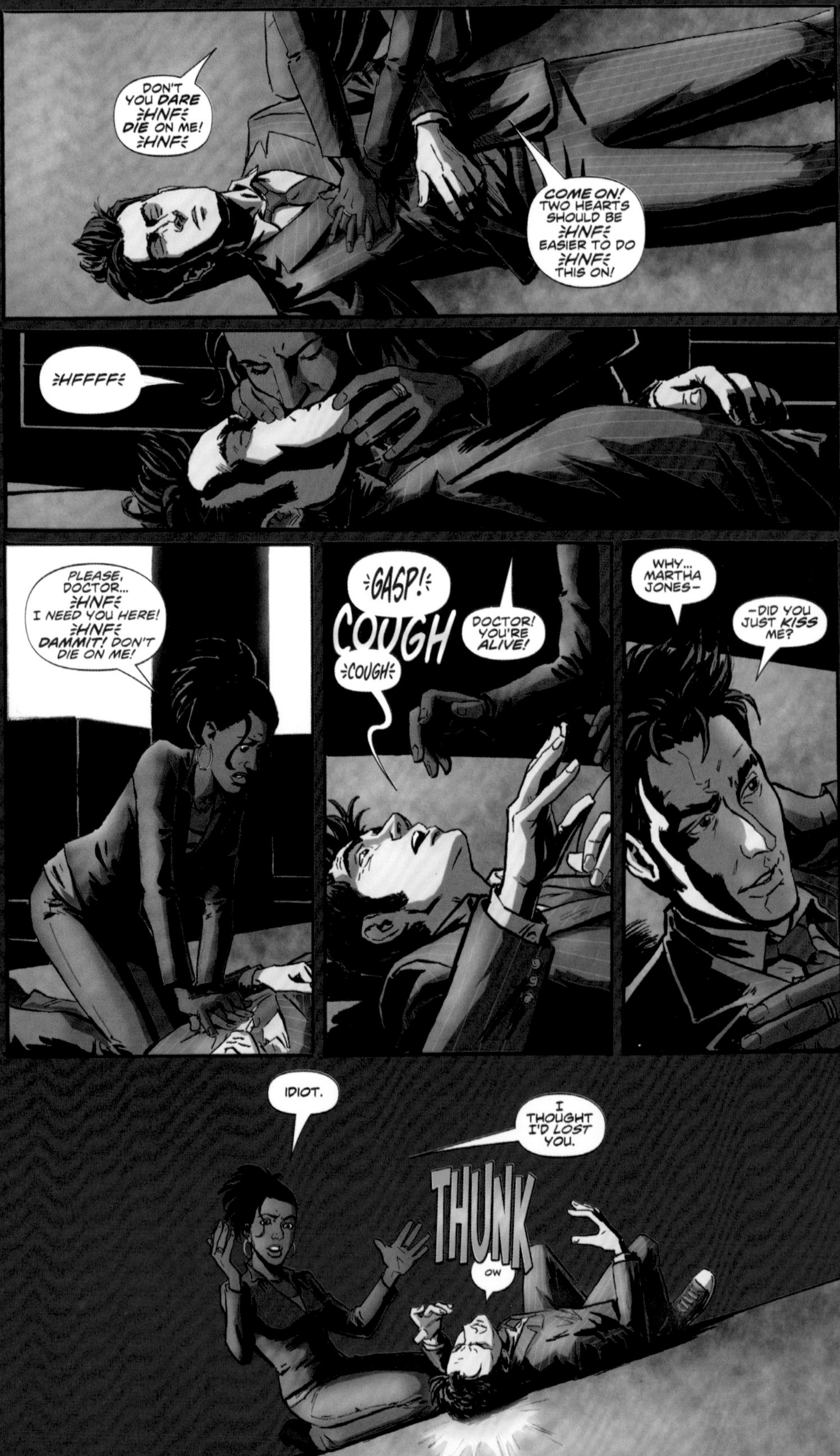

DON'T YOU DARE -HNF- DIE ON ME! -HNF-
COME ON! TWO HEARTS SHOULD BE -HNF- EASIER TO DO -HNF- THIS ON!
-HFFFF-
PLEASE, DOCTOR... -HNF- I NEED YOU HERE! -HNF- DAMMIT! DON'T DIE ON ME!
GASP!
COUGH
COUGH
DOCTOR! YOU'RE ALIVE!
WHY... MARTHA JONES—
—DID YOU JUST KISS ME?
IDIOT.
I THOUGHT I'D LOST YOU.
THUNK
OW

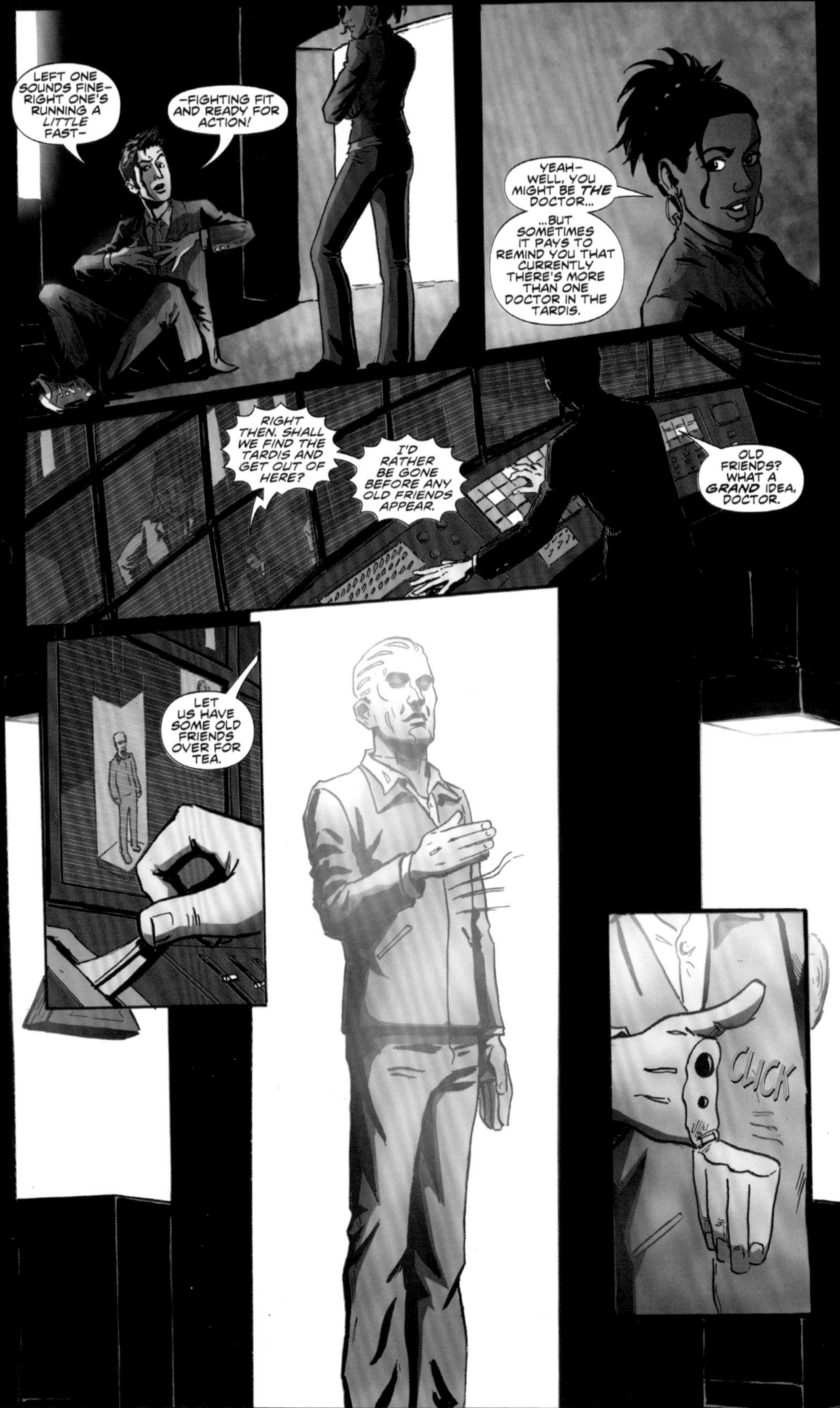

LEFT ONE SOUNDS FINE- RIGHT ONE'S RUNNING A *LITTLE* FAST-
-FIGHTING FIT AND READY FOR ACTION!
YEAH- WELL, YOU MIGHT BE ***THE*** DOCTOR...
...BUT SOMETIMES IT PAYS TO REMIND YOU THAT CURRENTLY THERE'S MORE THAN ONE DOCTOR IN THE TARDIS.
RIGHT THEN. SHALL WE FIND THE TARDIS AND GET OUT OF HERE?
I'D RATHER BE GONE BEFORE ANY OLD FRIENDS APPEAR.
OLD FRIENDS? WHAT A ***GRAND*** IDEA, DOCTOR.
LET US HAVE SOME OLD FRIENDS OVER FOR TEA.
CLICK

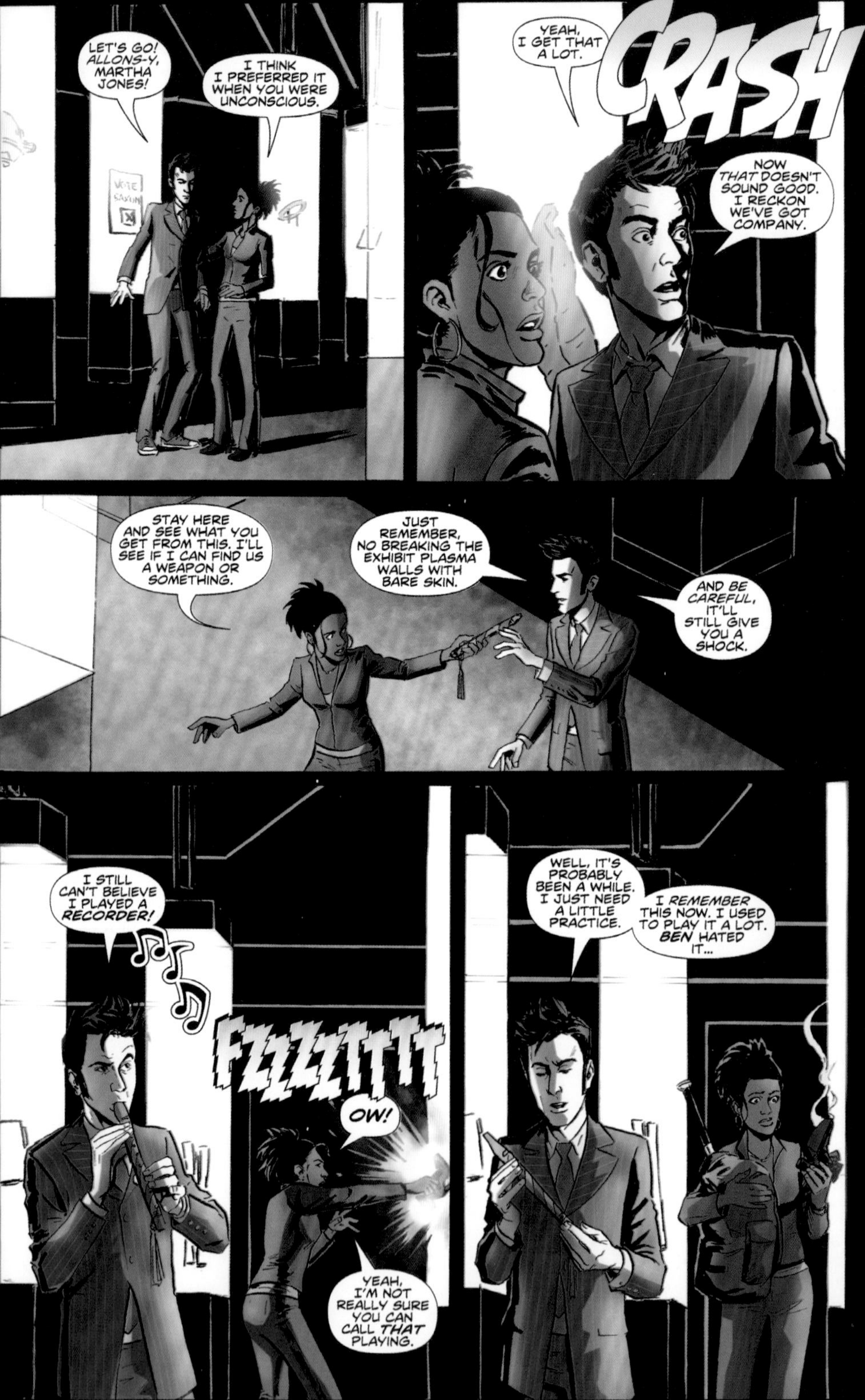
LET'S GO! ALLONS-Y, MARTHA JONES!
I THINK I PREFERRED IT WHEN YOU WERE UNCONSCIOUS.
VOTE SAXON
YEAH, I GET THAT A LOT.
CRASH
NOW THAT DOESN'T SOUND GOOD. I RECKON WE'VE GOT COMPANY.
STAY HERE AND SEE WHAT YOU GET FROM THIS. I'LL SEE IF I CAN FIND US A WEAPON OR SOMETHING.
JUST REMEMBER, NO BREAKING THE EXHIBIT PLASMA WALLS WITH BARE SKIN.
AND BE CAREFUL, IT'LL STILL GIVE YOU A SHOCK.
I STILL CAN'T BELIEVE I PLAYED A RECORDER!
FZZZZTTTT
OW!
YEAH, I'M NOT REALLY SURE YOU CAN CALL THAT PLAYING.
WELL, IT'S PROBABLY BEEN A WHILE. I JUST NEED A LITTLE PRACTICE.
I REMEMBER THIS NOW. I USED TO PLAY IT A LOT. BEN HATED IT...

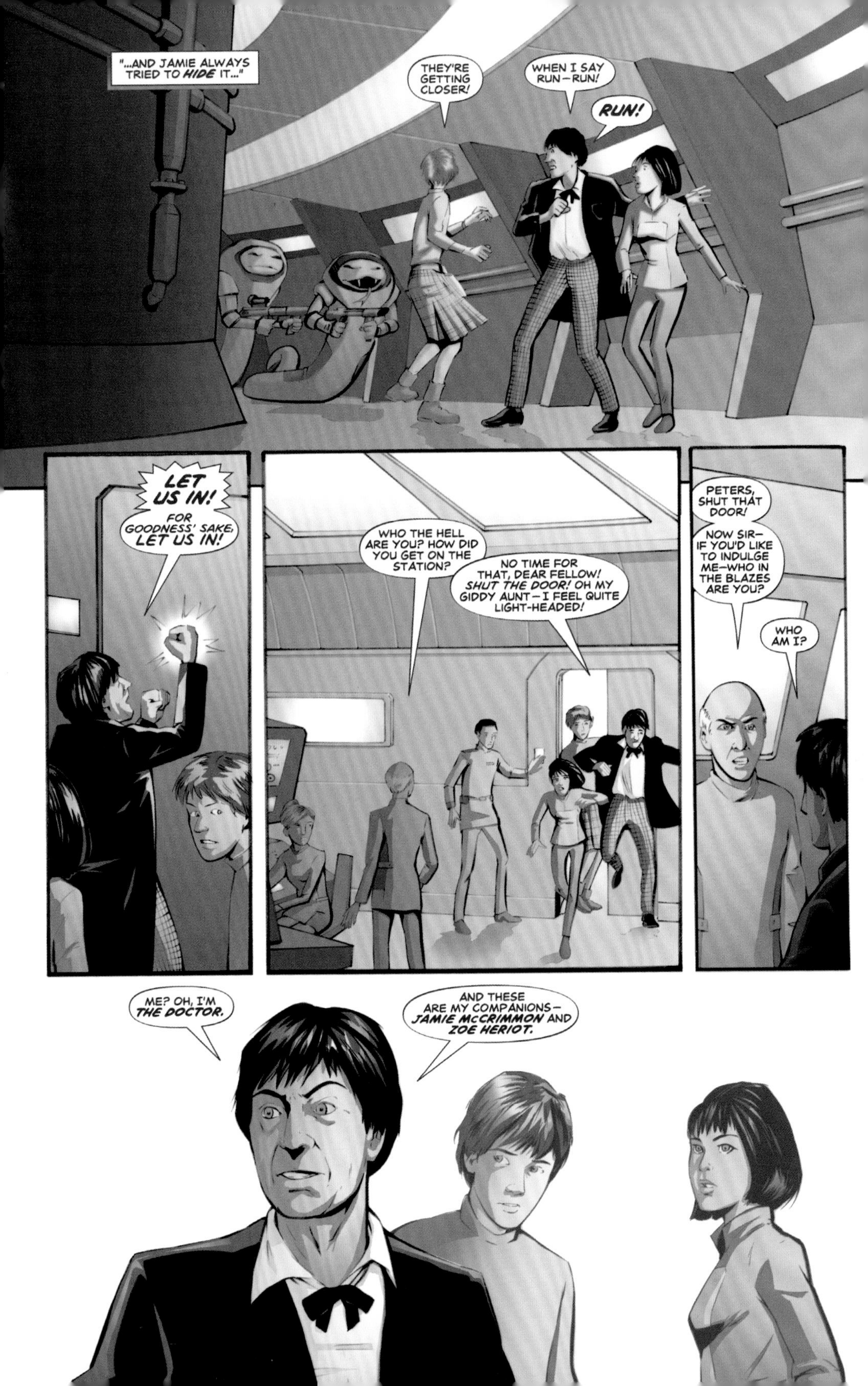

"...AND JAMIE ALWAYS TRIED TO *HIDE* IT..."
THEY'RE GETTING CLOSER!
WHEN I SAY RUN—RUN!
RUN!
LET US IN!
FOR GOODNESS' SAKE, LET US IN!
WHO THE HELL ARE YOU? HOW DID YOU GET ON THE STATION?
NO TIME FOR THAT, DEAR FELLOW! *SHUT THE DOOR!* OH MY GIDDY AUNT—I FEEL QUITE LIGHT-HEADED!
PETERS, SHUT THAT DOOR!
NOW SIR—IF YOU'D LIKE TO INDULGE ME—WHO IN THE BLAZES ARE YOU?
WHO AM I?
ME? OH, I'M *THE DOCTOR.*
AND THESE ARE MY COMPANIONS—*JAMIE McCRIMMON* AND *ZOE HERIOT.*

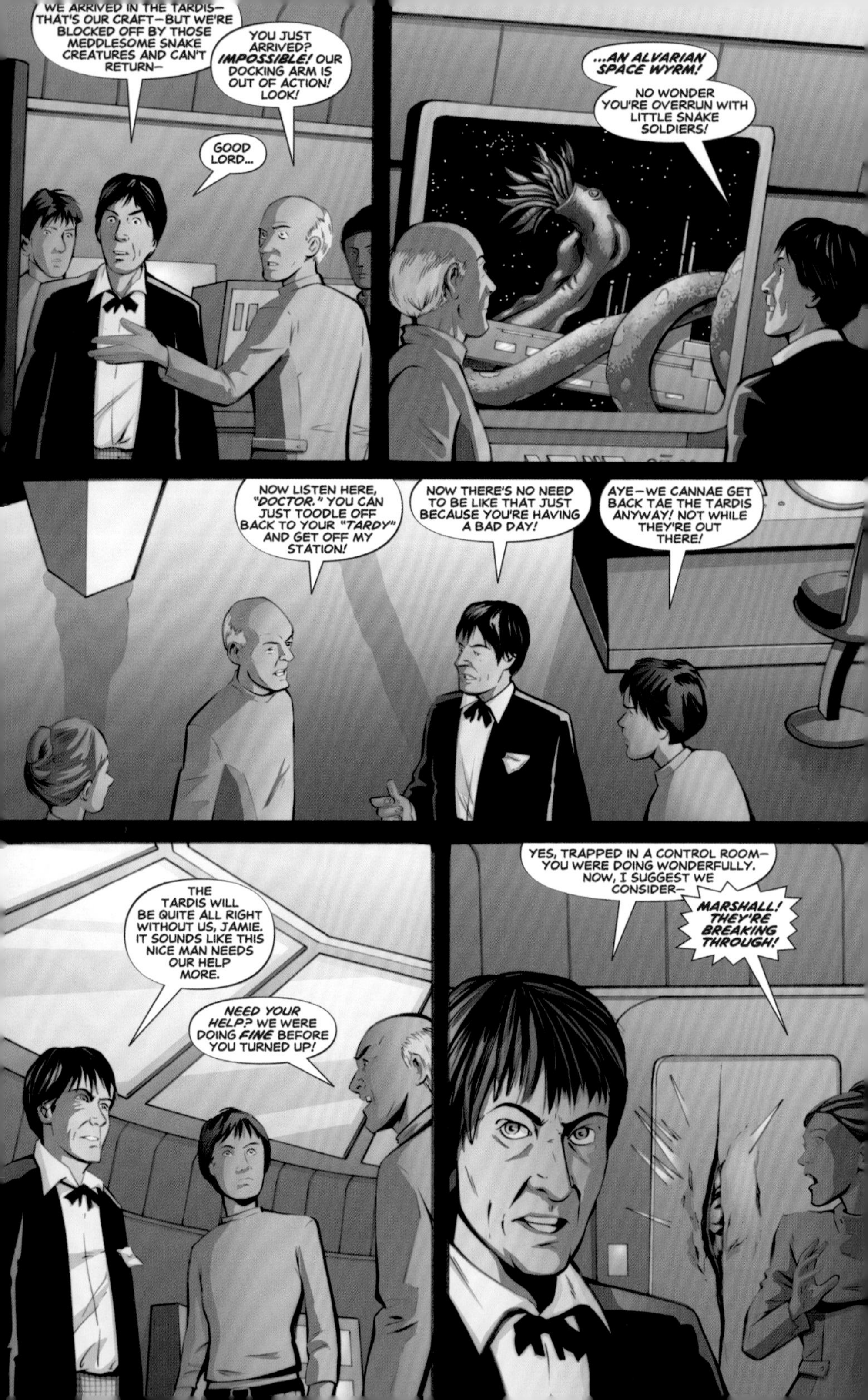
WE ARRIVED IN THE TARDIS—THAT'S OUR CRAFT—BUT WE'RE BLOCKED OFF BY THOSE MEDDLESOME SNAKE CREATURES AND CAN'T RETURN—
YOU JUST ARRIVED? IMPOSSIBLE! OUR DOCKING ARM IS OUT OF ACTION! LOOK!
GOOD LORD...
...AN ALVARIAN SPACE WYRM!
NO WONDER YOU'RE OVERRUN WITH LITTLE SNAKE SOLDIERS!
NOW LISTEN HERE, "DOCTOR," YOU CAN JUST TOODLE OFF BACK TO YOUR "TARDY" AND GET OFF MY STATION!
NOW THERE'S NO NEED TO BE LIKE THAT JUST BECAUSE YOU'RE HAVING A BAD DAY!
AYE—WE CANNAE GET BACK TAE THE TARDIS ANYWAY! NOT WHILE THEY'RE OUT THERE!
THE TARDIS WILL BE QUITE ALL RIGHT WITHOUT US, JAMIE. IT SOUNDS LIKE THIS NICE MAN NEEDS OUR HELP MORE.
NEED YOUR HELP? WE WERE DOING FINE BEFORE YOU TURNED UP!
YES, TRAPPED IN A CONTROL ROOM—YOU WERE DOING WONDERFULLY. NOW, I SUGGEST WE CONSIDER—
MARSHALL! THEY'RE BREAKING THROUGH!

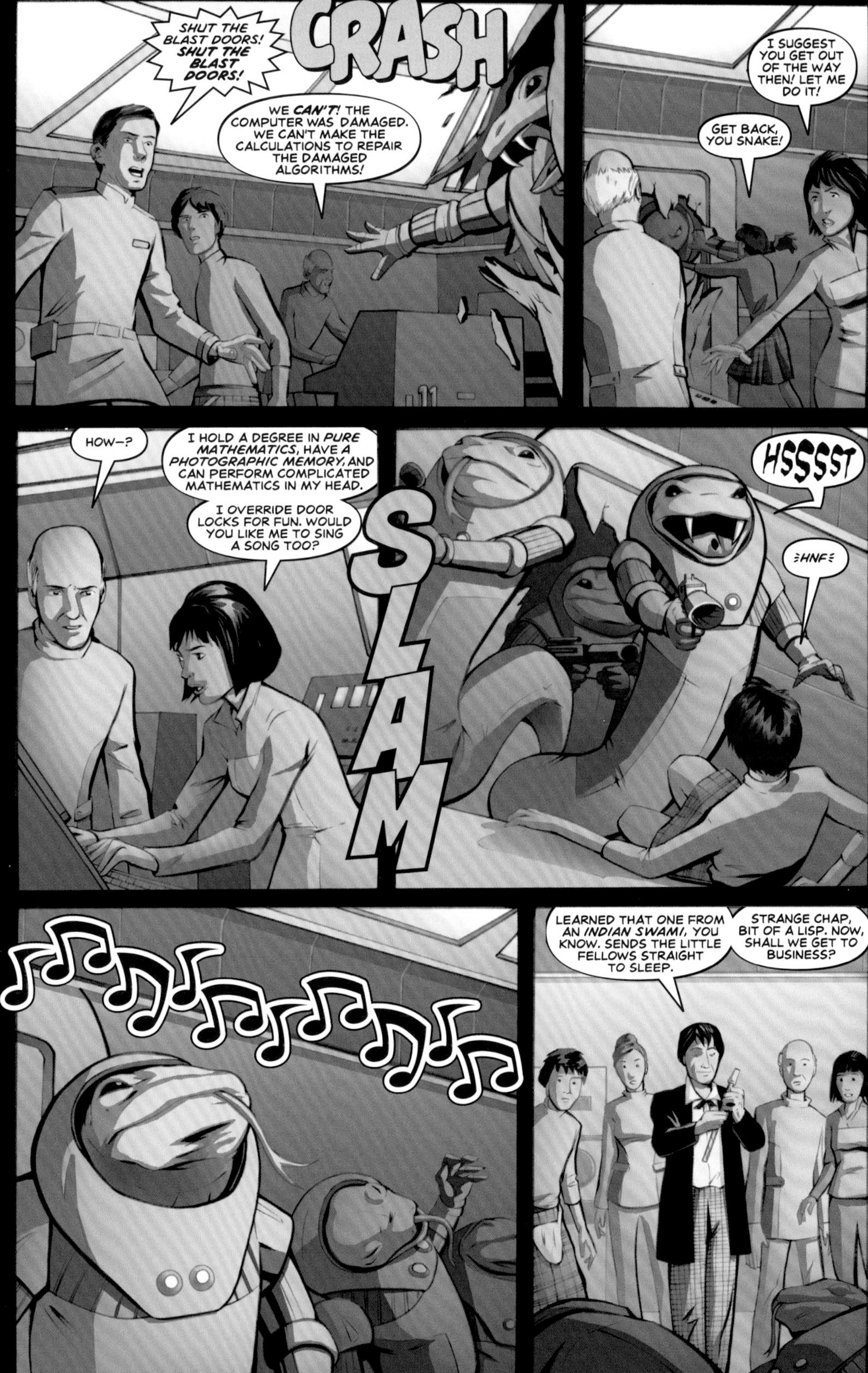

SHUT THE BLAST DOORS! SHUT THE BLAST DOORS!
CRASH
WE CAN'T! THE COMPUTER WAS DAMAGED. WE CAN'T MAKE THE CALCULATIONS TO REPAIR THE DAMAGED ALGORITHMS!
I SUGGEST YOU GET OUT OF THE WAY THEN! LET ME DO IT!
GET BACK, YOU SNAKE!
HOW—?
I HOLD A DEGREE IN PURE MATHEMATICS, HAVE A PHOTOGRAPHIC MEMORY, AND CAN PERFORM COMPLICATED MATHEMATICS IN MY HEAD.
I OVERRIDE DOOR LOCKS FOR FUN. WOULD YOU LIKE ME TO SING A SONG TOO?
SLAM
HSSSST
HNF
LEARNED THAT ONE FROM AN INDIAN SWAMI, YOU KNOW. SENDS THE LITTLE FELLOWS STRAIGHT TO SLEEP.
STRANGE CHAP, BIT OF A LISP. NOW, SHALL WE GET TO BUSINESS?

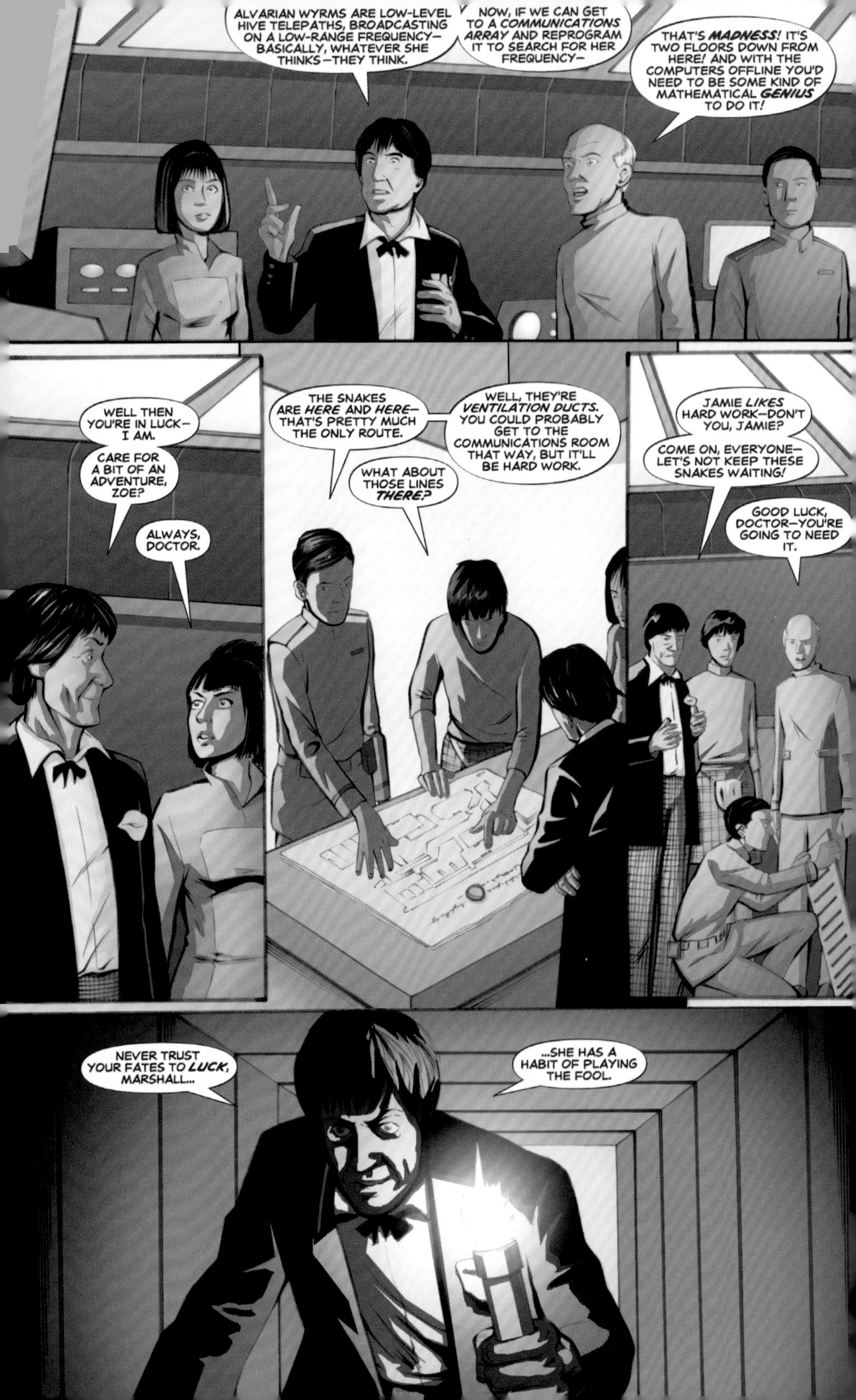
ALVARIAN WYRMS ARE LOW-LEVEL HIVE TELEPATHS, BROADCASTING ON A LOW-RANGE FREQUENCY—BASICALLY, WHATEVER SHE THINKS—THEY THINK.
NOW, IF WE CAN GET TO A *COMMUNICATIONS ARRAY* AND REPROGRAM IT TO SEARCH FOR HER FREQUENCY—
THAT'S ***MADNESS!*** IT'S TWO FLOORS DOWN FROM HERE! AND WITH THE COMPUTERS OFFLINE YOU'D NEED TO BE SOME KIND OF MATHEMATICAL ***GENIUS*** TO DO IT!
WELL THEN YOU'RE IN LUCK—I AM.
CARE FOR A BIT OF AN ADVENTURE, ZOE?
ALWAYS, DOCTOR.
THE SNAKES ARE *HERE* AND *HERE*—THAT'S PRETTY MUCH THE ONLY ROUTE.
WELL, THEY'RE *VENTILATION DUCTS.* YOU COULD PROBABLY GET TO THE COMMUNICATIONS ROOM THAT WAY, BUT IT'LL BE HARD WORK.
WHAT ABOUT THOSE LINES ***THERE?***
JAMIE *LIKES* HARD WORK—DON'T YOU, JAMIE?
COME ON, EVERYONE—LET'S NOT KEEP THESE SNAKES WAITING!
GOOD LUCK, DOCTOR—YOU'RE GOING TO NEED IT.
NEVER TRUST YOUR FATES TO *LUCK*, MARSHALL...
...SHE HAS A HABIT OF PLAYING THE FOOL.

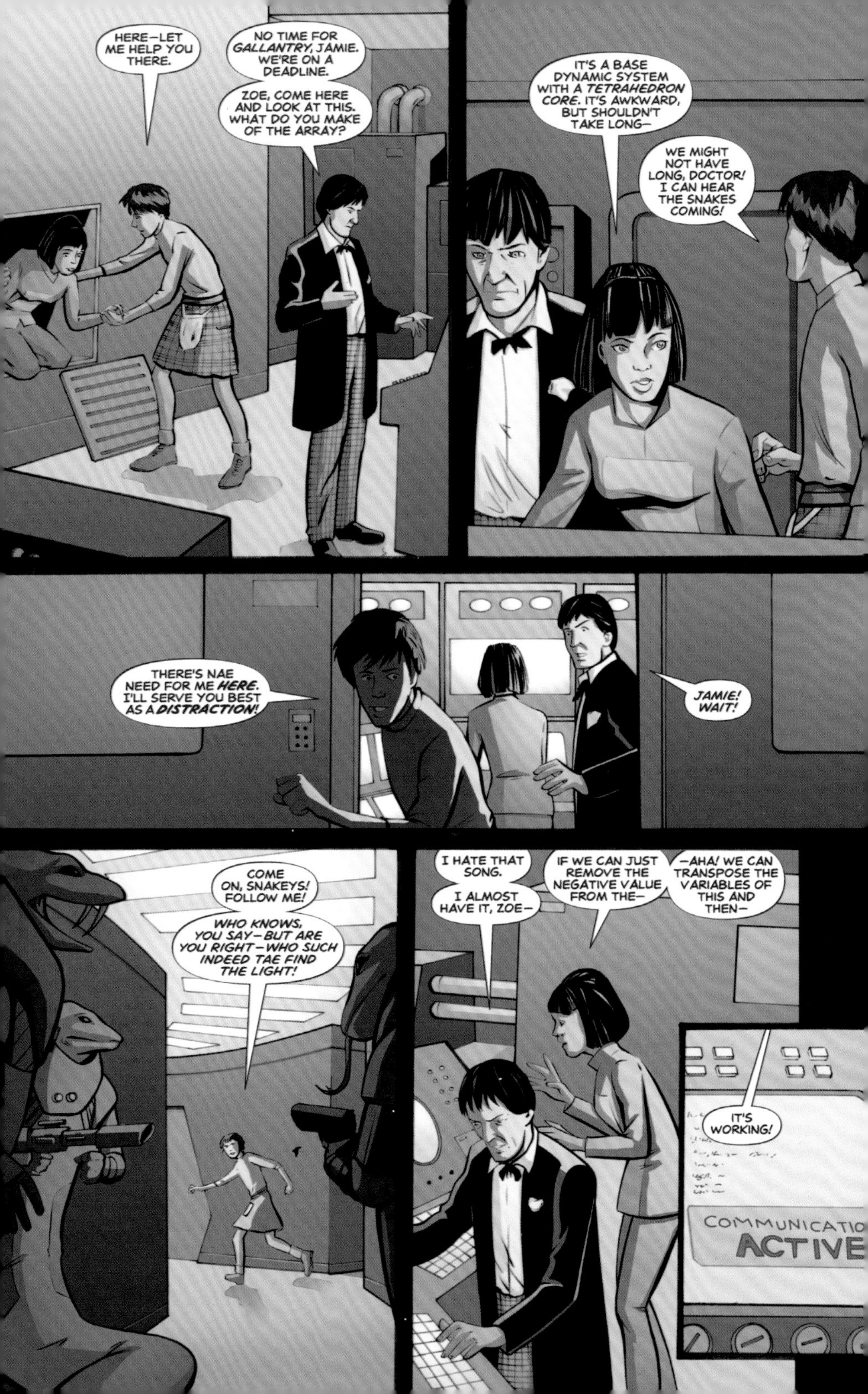
HERE—LET ME HELP YOU THERE.
NO TIME FOR GALLANTRY, JAMIE. WE'RE ON A DEADLINE.
ZOE, COME HERE AND LOOK AT THIS. WHAT DO YOU MAKE OF THE ARRAY?
IT'S A BASE DYNAMIC SYSTEM WITH A TETRAHEDRON CORE. IT'S AWKWARD, BUT SHOULDN'T TAKE LONG—
WE MIGHT NOT HAVE LONG, DOCTOR! I CAN HEAR THE SNAKES COMING!
THERE'S NAE NEED FOR ME HERE. I'LL SERVE YOU BEST AS A DISTRACTION!
JAMIE! WAIT!
COME ON, SNAKEYS! FOLLOW ME!
WHO KNOWS, YOU SAY—BUT ARE YOU RIGHT—WHO SUCH INDEED TAE FIND THE LIGHT!
I HATE THAT SONG.
I ALMOST HAVE IT, ZOE—
IF WE CAN JUST REMOVE THE NEGATIVE VALUE FROM THE—
—AHA! WE CAN TRANSPOSE THE VARIABLES OF THIS AND THEN—
IT'S WORKING!
COMMUNICATIO
ACTIVE

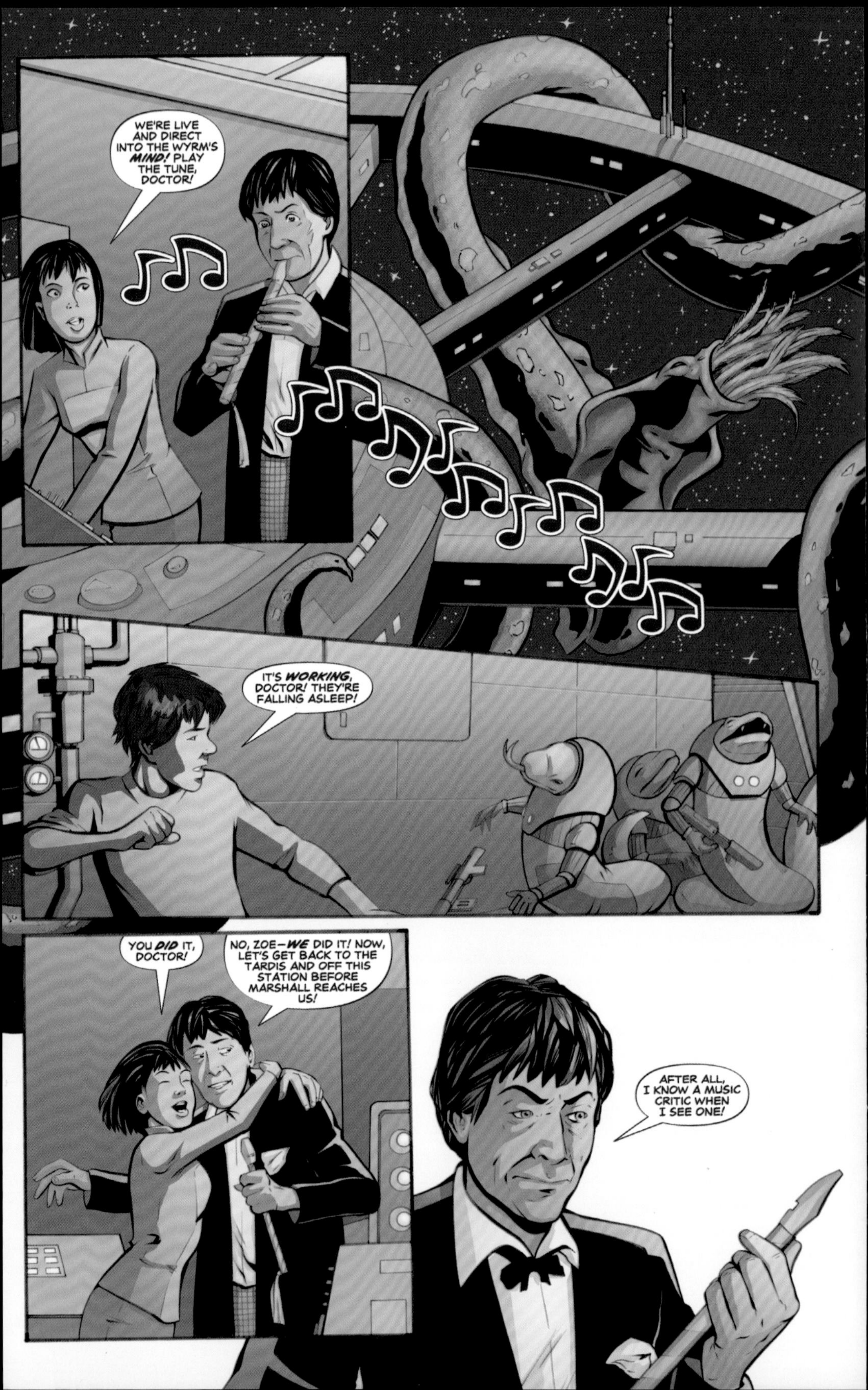
WE'RE LIVE AND DIRECT INTO THE WYRM'S MIND! PLAY THE TUNE, DOCTOR!
IT'S WORKING, DOCTOR! THEY'RE FALLING ASLEEP!
YOU DID IT, DOCTOR!
NO, ZOE—WE DID IT! NOW, LET'S GET BACK TO THE TARDIS AND OFF THIS STATION BEFORE MARSHALL REACHES US!
AFTER ALL, I KNOW A MUSIC CRITIC WHEN I SEE ONE!

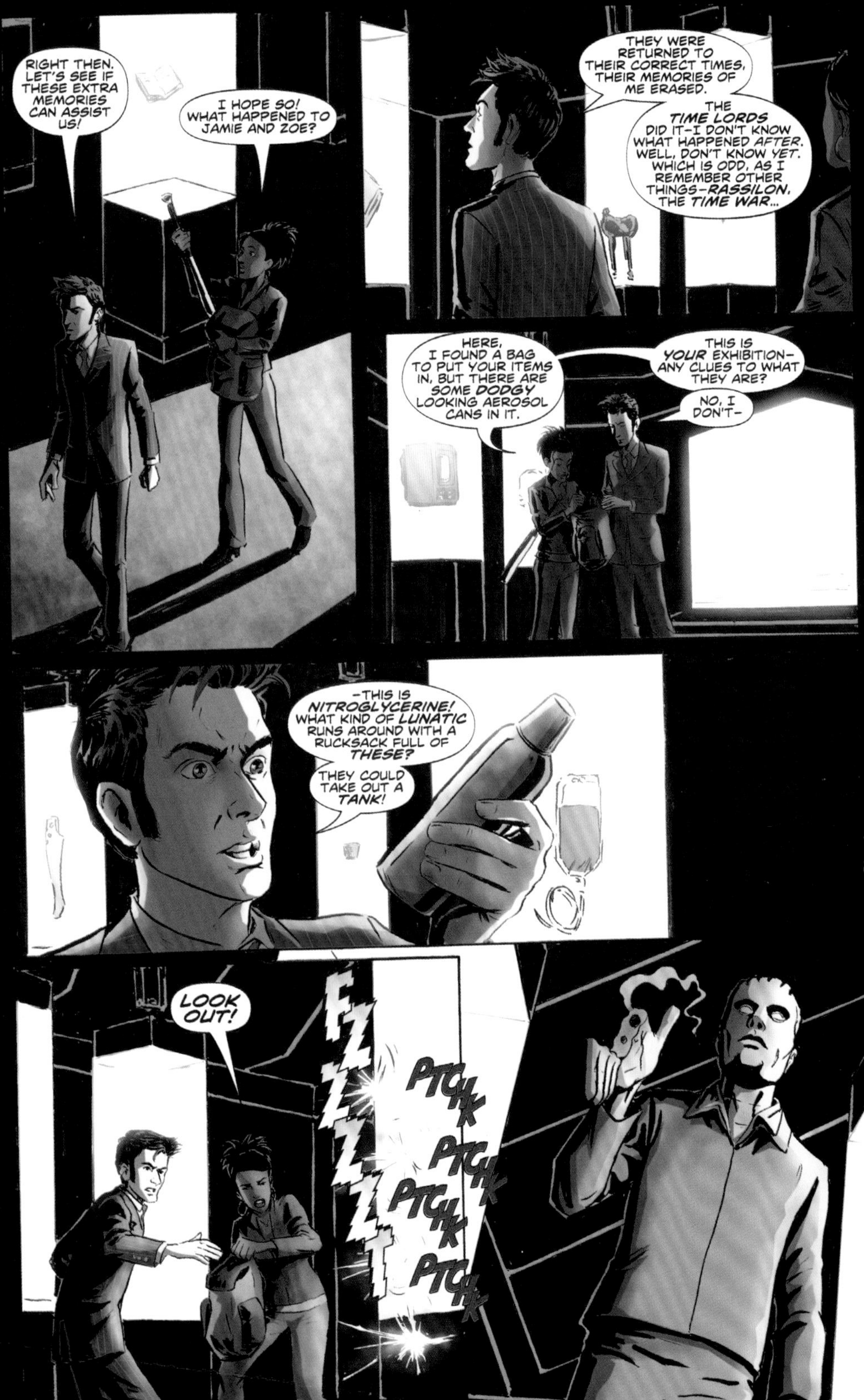

RIGHT THEN. LET'S SEE IF THESE EXTRA MEMORIES CAN ASSIST US!
I HOPE SO! WHAT HAPPENED TO JAMIE AND ZOE?
THEY WERE RETURNED TO THEIR CORRECT TIMES, THEIR MEMORIES OF ME ERASED.
THE TIME LORDS DID IT–I DON'T KNOW WHAT HAPPENED AFTER. WELL, DON'T KNOW YET. WHICH IS ODD, AS I REMEMBER OTHER THINGS–RASSILON, THE TIME WAR...
HERE, I FOUND A BAG TO PUT YOUR ITEMS IN, BUT THERE ARE SOME DODGY LOOKING AEROSOL CANS IN IT.
THIS IS YOUR EXHIBITION– ANY CLUES TO WHAT THEY ARE?
NO, I DON'T–
–THIS IS NITROGLYCERINE! WHAT KIND OF LUNATIC RUNS AROUND WITH A RUCKSACK FULL OF THESE?
THEY COULD TAKE OUT A TANK!
LOOK OUT!
FZZZZZZT
PTCHK
PTCHK
PTCHK
PTCHK

MARTHA! **RUN!**

DOCTOR, WHAT *IS* IT?

YEAH, I'LL GET BACK TO YOU ON THAT! NOT THE FOGGIEST!

BUT WHATEVER IT IS, IT'S FOLLOWING US!

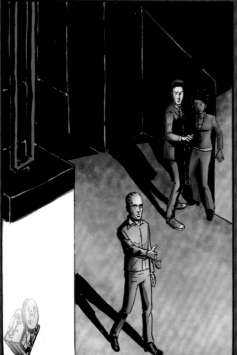

THEN AGAIN— PERHAPS IT *ISN'T.*

IT MUST BE FROM LATER IN YOUR LIFE. WE NEED TO GAIN MORE MEMORIES. HERE—

—WHAT DO THESE KEYS TELL YOU?

I... I REMEMBER A NAME.

BESSIE.

LET ME GUESS— ANOTHER COMPANION? YOU COLLECT THEM LIKE PEOPLE COLLECT TRADING CARDS!

OH, BESSIE WAS MORE THAN A COMPANION.

MUCH, MUCH MORE...

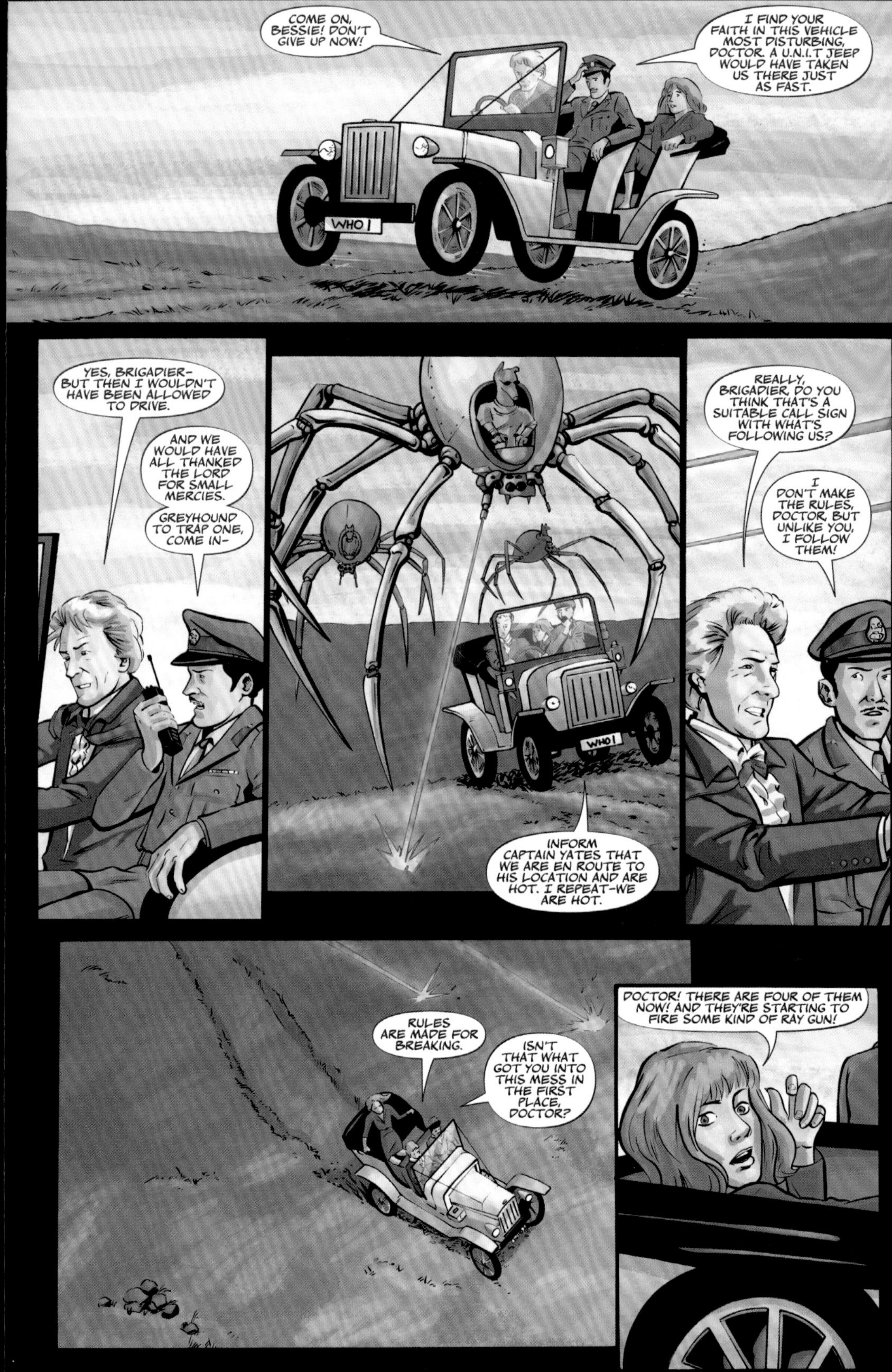
COME ON, BESSIE! DON'T GIVE UP NOW!
I FIND YOUR FAITH IN THIS VEHICLE MOST DISTURBING, DOCTOR. A U.N.I.T JEEP WOULD HAVE TAKEN US THERE JUST AS FAST.
WHO 1
YES, BRIGADIER- BUT THEN I WOULDN'T HAVE BEEN ALLOWED TO DRIVE.
AND WE WOULD HAVE ALL THANKED THE LORD FOR SMALL MERCIES.
GREYHOUND TO TRAP ONE, COME IN-
WHO 1
INFORM CAPTAIN YATES THAT WE ARE EN ROUTE TO HIS LOCATION AND ARE HOT. I REPEAT-WE ARE HOT.
REALLY, BRIGADIER, DO YOU THINK THAT'S A SUITABLE CALL SIGN WITH WHAT'S FOLLOWING US?
I DON'T MAKE THE RULES, DOCTOR, BUT UNLIKE YOU, I FOLLOW THEM!
RULES ARE MADE FOR BREAKING.
ISN'T THAT WHAT GOT YOU INTO THIS MESS IN THE FIRST PLACE, DOCTOR?
DOCTOR! THERE ARE FOUR OF THEM NOW! AND THEY'RE STARTING TO FIRE SOME KIND OF RAY GUN!

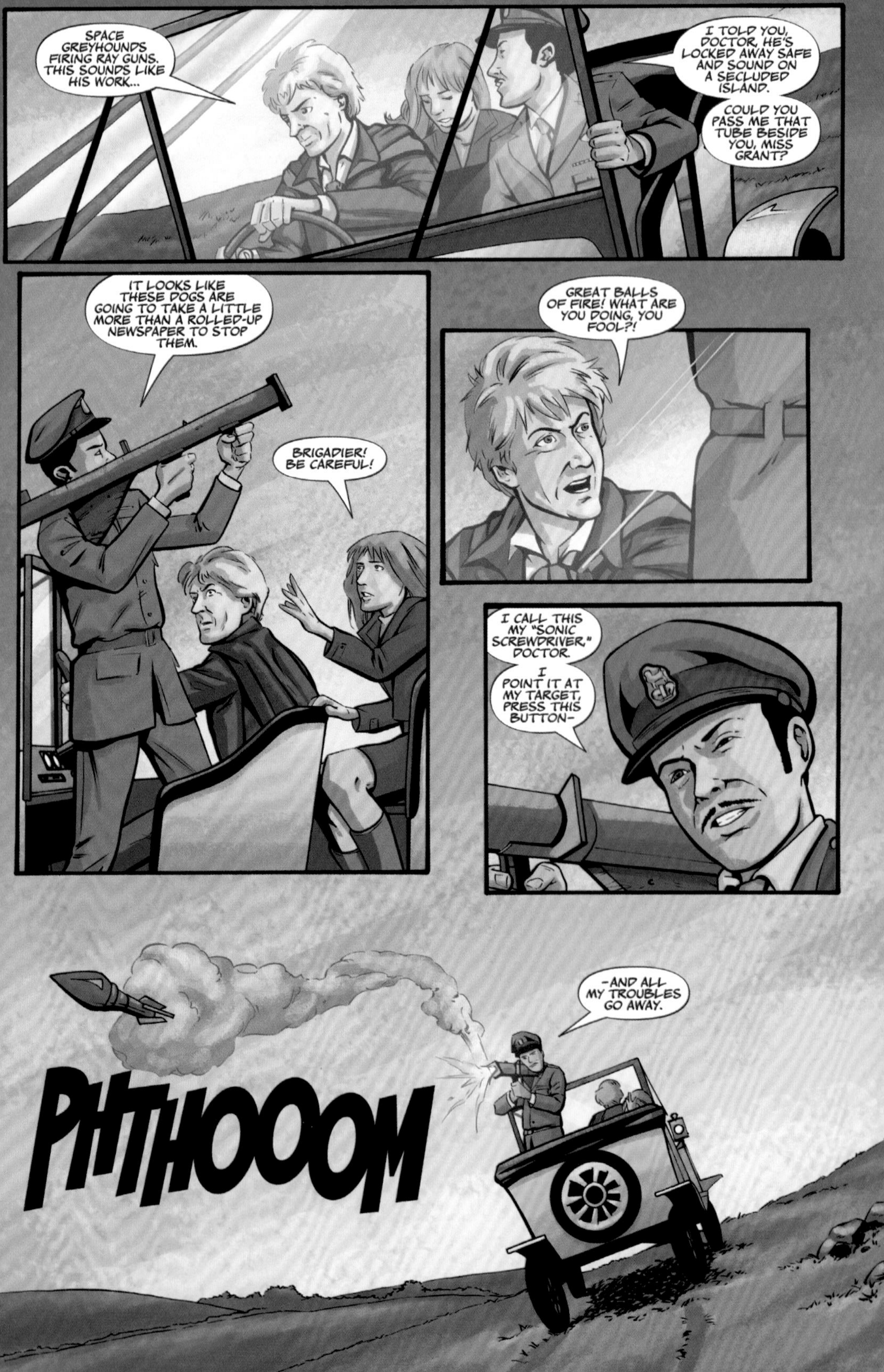
SPACE GREYHOUNDS FIRING RAY GUNS. THIS SOUNDS LIKE HIS WORK...
I TOLD YOU, DOCTOR, HE'S LOCKED AWAY SAFE AND SOUND ON A SECLUDED ISLAND.
COULD YOU PASS ME THAT TUBE BESIDE YOU, MISS GRANT?
IT LOOKS LIKE THESE DOGS ARE GOING TO TAKE A LITTLE MORE THAN A ROLLED-UP NEWSPAPER TO STOP THEM.
BRIGADIER! BE CAREFUL!
GREAT BALLS OF FIRE! WHAT ARE YOU DOING, YOU FOOL?!
I CALL THIS MY "SONIC SCREWDRIVER," DOCTOR.
I POINT IT AT MY TARGET, PRESS THIS BUTTON-
-AND ALL MY TROUBLES GO AWAY.
PHTHOOOM

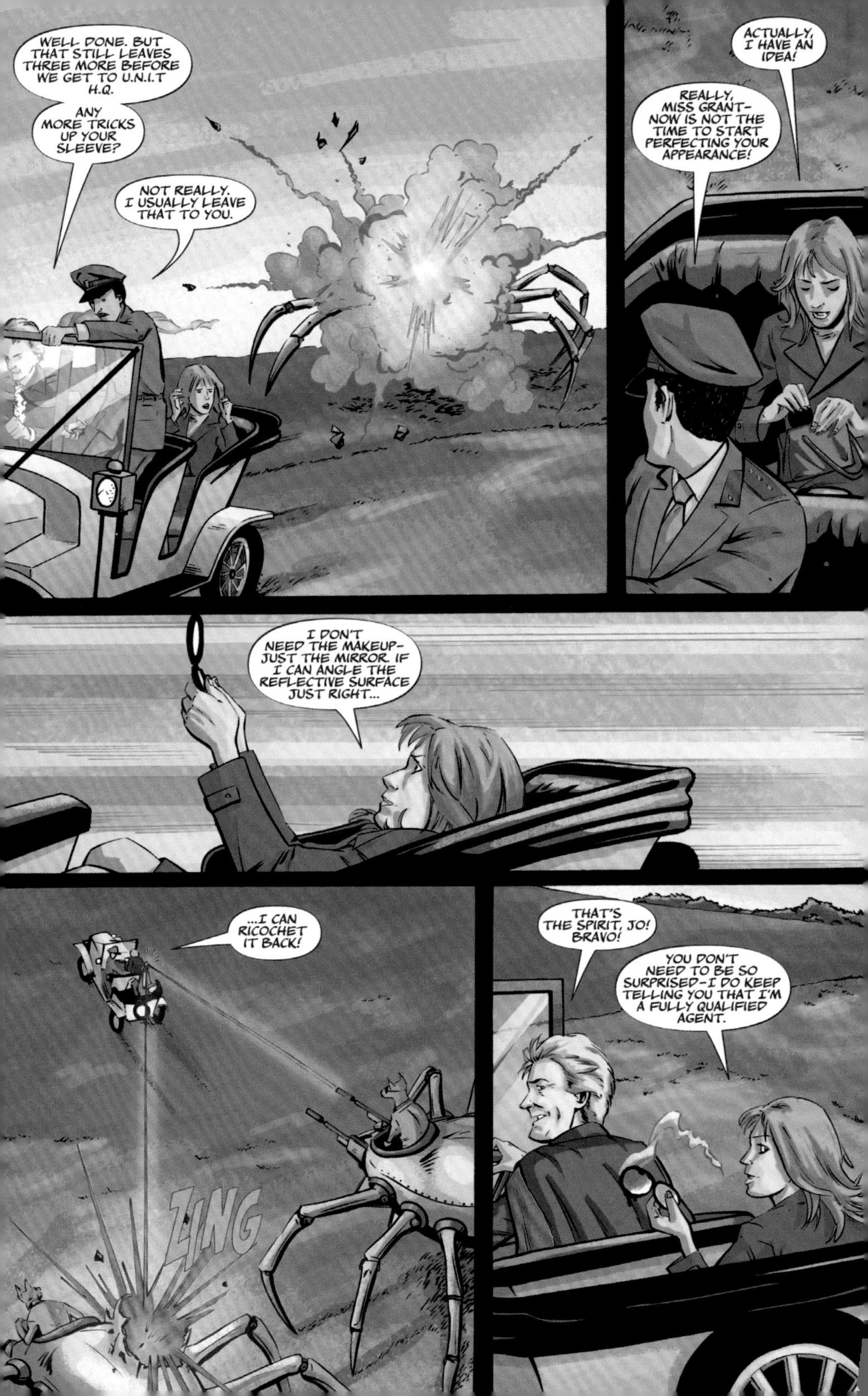
WELL DONE. BUT THAT STILL LEAVES THREE MORE BEFORE WE GET TO U.N.I.T H.Q.
ANY MORE TRICKS UP YOUR SLEEVE?
NOT REALLY. I USUALLY LEAVE THAT TO YOU.
ACTUALLY, I HAVE AN IDEA!
REALLY, MISS GRANT- NOW IS NOT THE TIME TO START PERFECTING YOUR APPEARANCE!
I DON'T NEED THE MAKEUP- JUST THE MIRROR. IF I CAN ANGLE THE REFLECTIVE SURFACE JUST RIGHT...
...I CAN RICOCHET IT BACK!
ZING
THAT'S THE SPIRIT, JO! BRAVO!
YOU DON'T NEED TO BE SO SURPRISED-I DO KEEP TELLING YOU THAT I'M A FULLY QUALIFIED AGENT.

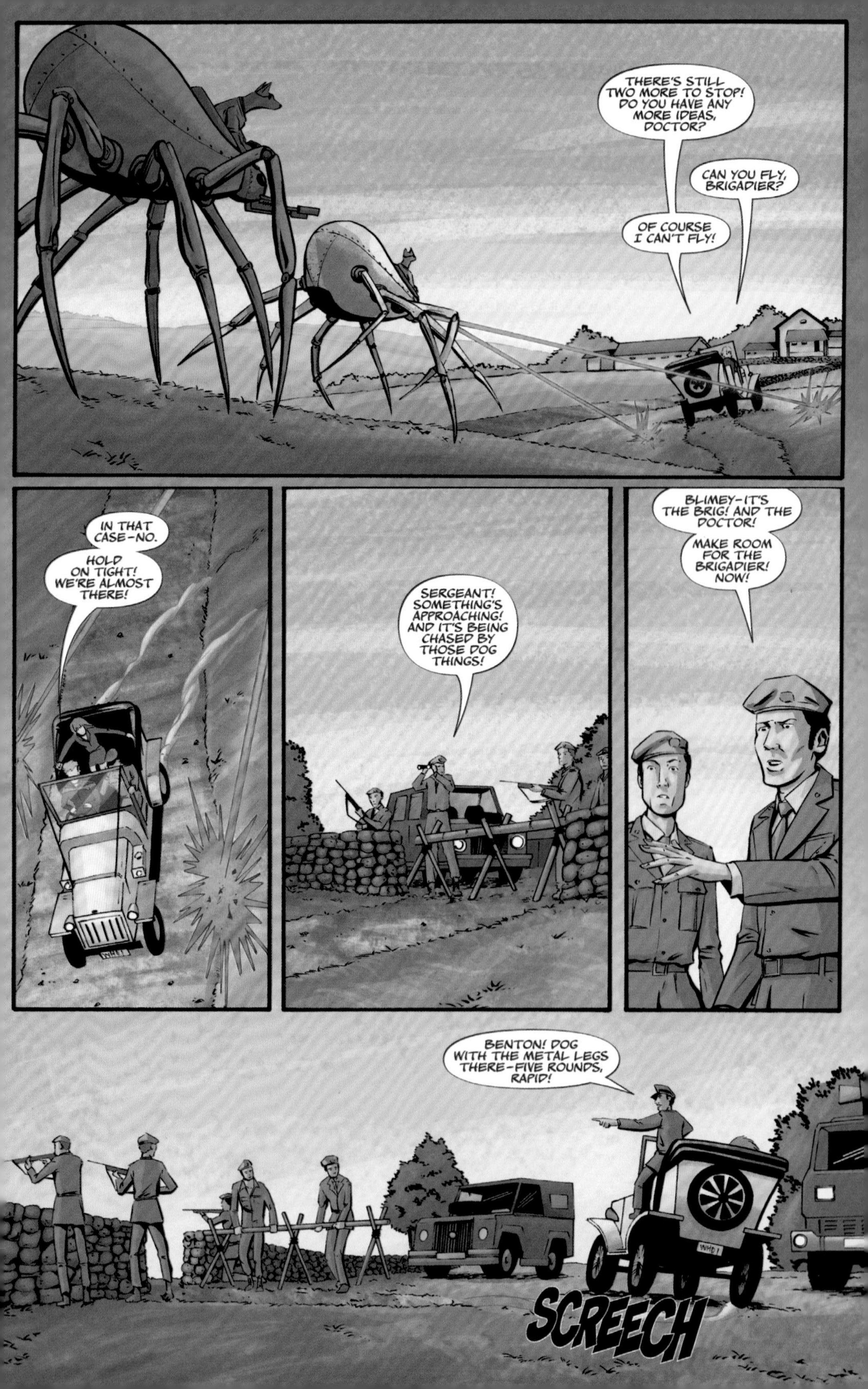
THERE'S STILL TWO MORE TO STOP! DO YOU HAVE ANY MORE IDEAS, DOCTOR?
CAN YOU FLY, BRIGADIER?
OF COURSE I CAN'T FLY!
IN THAT CASE–NO.
HOLD ON TIGHT! WE'RE ALMOST THERE!
SERGEANT! SOMETHING'S APPROACHING! AND IT'S BEING CHASED BY THOSE DOG THINGS!
BLIMEY–IT'S THE BRIG! AND THE DOCTOR!
MAKE ROOM FOR THE BRIGADIER! NOW!
BENTON! DOG WITH THE METAL LEGS THERE–FIVE ROUNDS, RAPID!
SCREECH

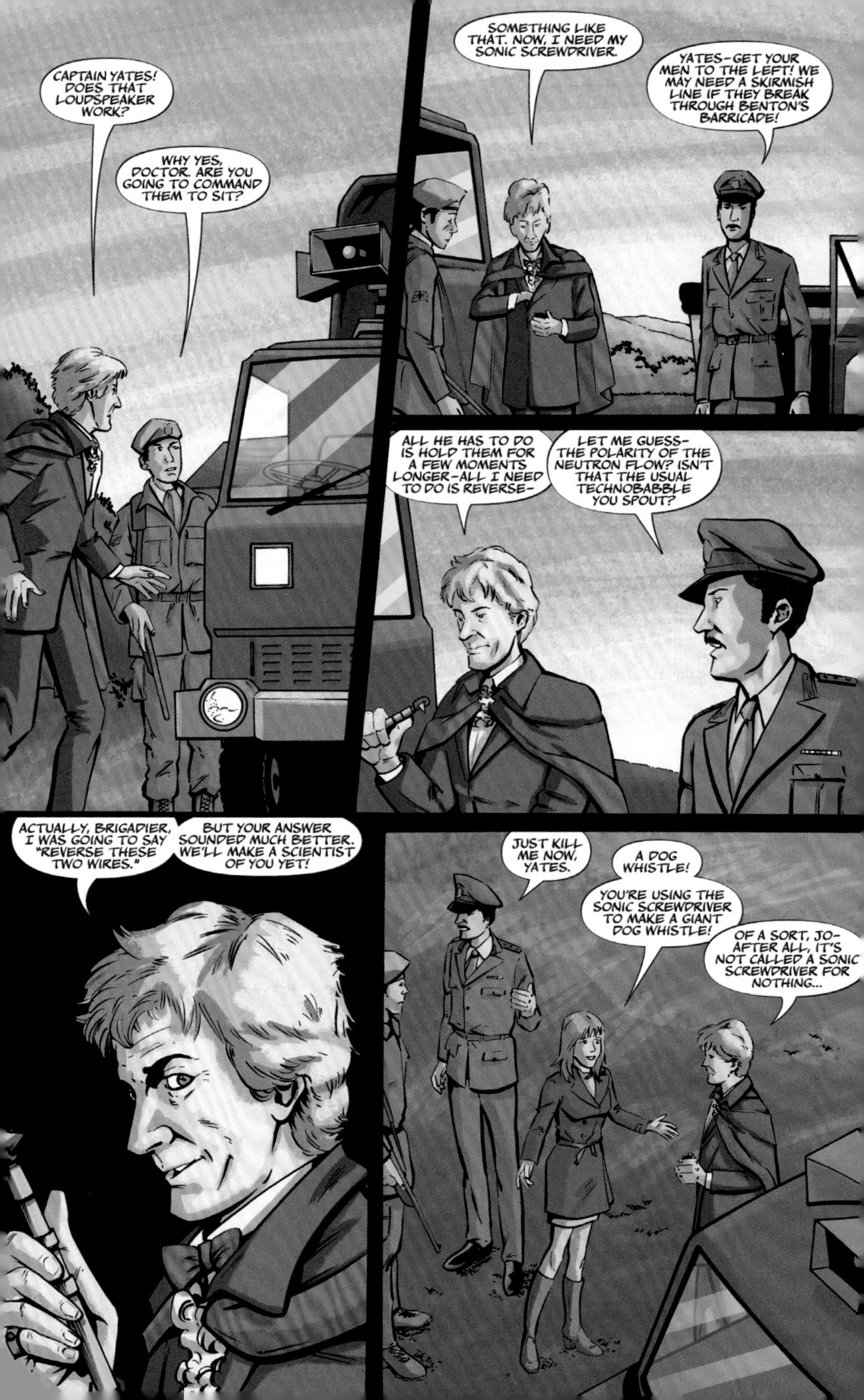
CAPTAIN YATES! DOES THAT LOUDSPEAKER WORK?
WHY YES, DOCTOR. ARE YOU GOING TO COMMAND THEM TO SIT?
SOMETHING LIKE THAT. NOW, I NEED MY SONIC SCREWDRIVER.
YATES–GET YOUR MEN TO THE LEFT! WE MAY NEED A SKIRMISH LINE IF THEY BREAK THROUGH BENTON'S BARRICADE!
ALL HE HAS TO DO IS HOLD THEM FOR A FEW MOMENTS LONGER–ALL I NEED TO DO IS REVERSE–
LET ME GUESS–THE POLARITY OF THE NEUTRON FLOW? ISN'T THAT THE USUAL TECHNOBABBLE YOU SPOUT?
ACTUALLY, BRIGADIER, I WAS GOING TO SAY "REVERSE THESE TWO WIRES."
BUT YOUR ANSWER SOUNDED MUCH BETTER. WE'LL MAKE A SCIENTIST OF YOU YET!
JUST KILL ME NOW, YATES.
A DOG WHISTLE!
YOU'RE USING THE SONIC SCREWDRIVER TO MAKE A GIANT DOG WHISTLE!
OF A SORT, JO–AFTER ALL, IT'S NOT CALLED A SONIC SCREWDRIVER FOR NOTHING...

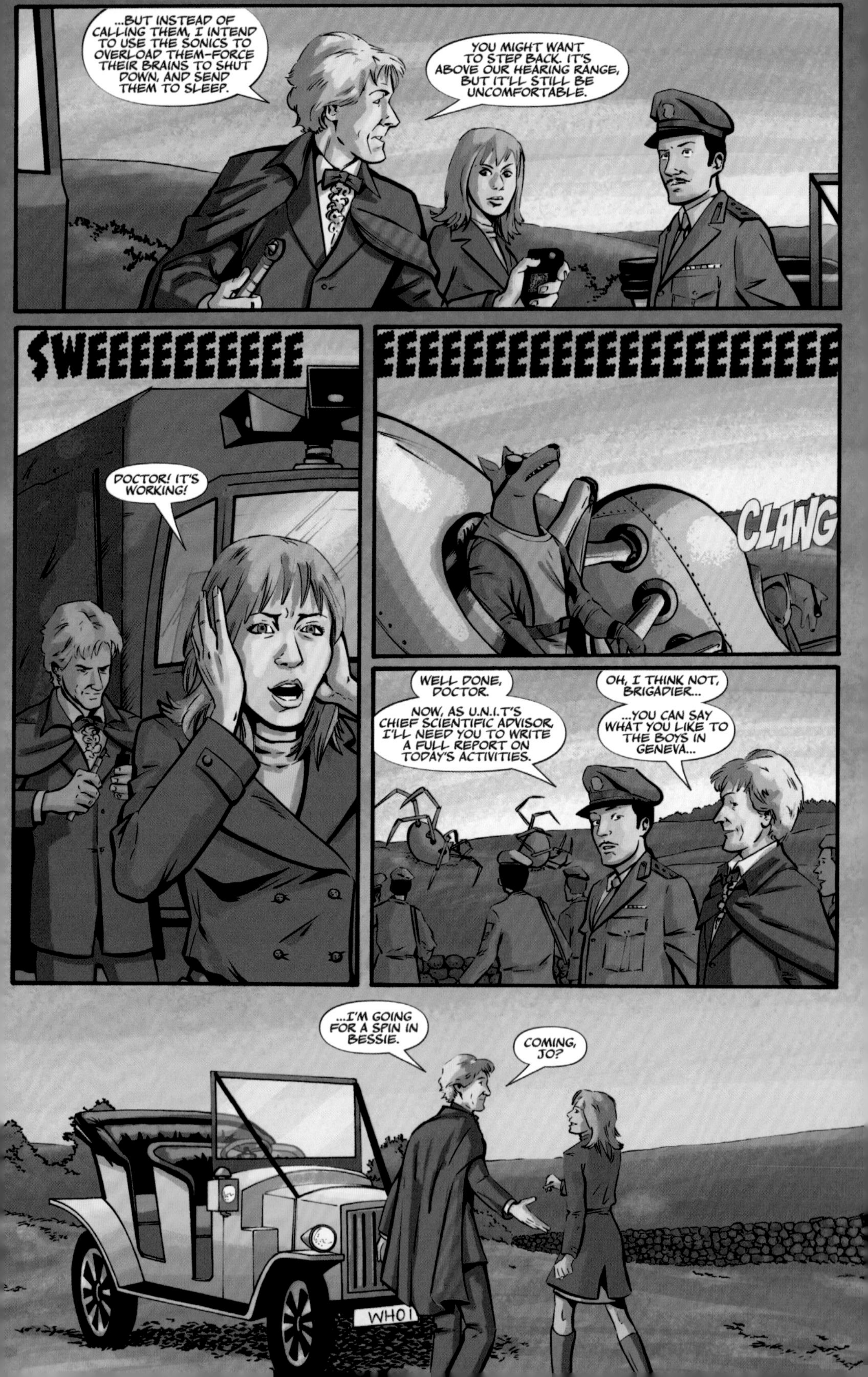
...BUT INSTEAD OF CALLING THEM, I INTEND TO USE THE SONICS TO OVERLOAD THEM-FORCE THEIR BRAINS TO SHUT DOWN, AND SEND THEM TO SLEEP.
YOU MIGHT WANT TO STEP BACK. IT'S ABOVE OUR HEARING RANGE, BUT IT'LL STILL BE UNCOMFORTABLE.
SWEEEEEEEEEE
DOCTOR! IT'S WORKING!
EEEEEEEEEEEEEEEEEEEEEEE
CLANG
WELL DONE, DOCTOR.
NOW, AS U.N.I.T'S CHIEF SCIENTIFIC ADVISOR, I'LL NEED YOU TO WRITE A FULL REPORT ON TODAY'S ACTIVITIES.
OH, I THINK NOT, BRIGADIER...
...YOU CAN SAY WHAT YOU LIKE TO THE BOYS IN GENEVA...
...I'M GOING FOR A SPIN IN BESSIE.
COMING, JO?
WHO 1

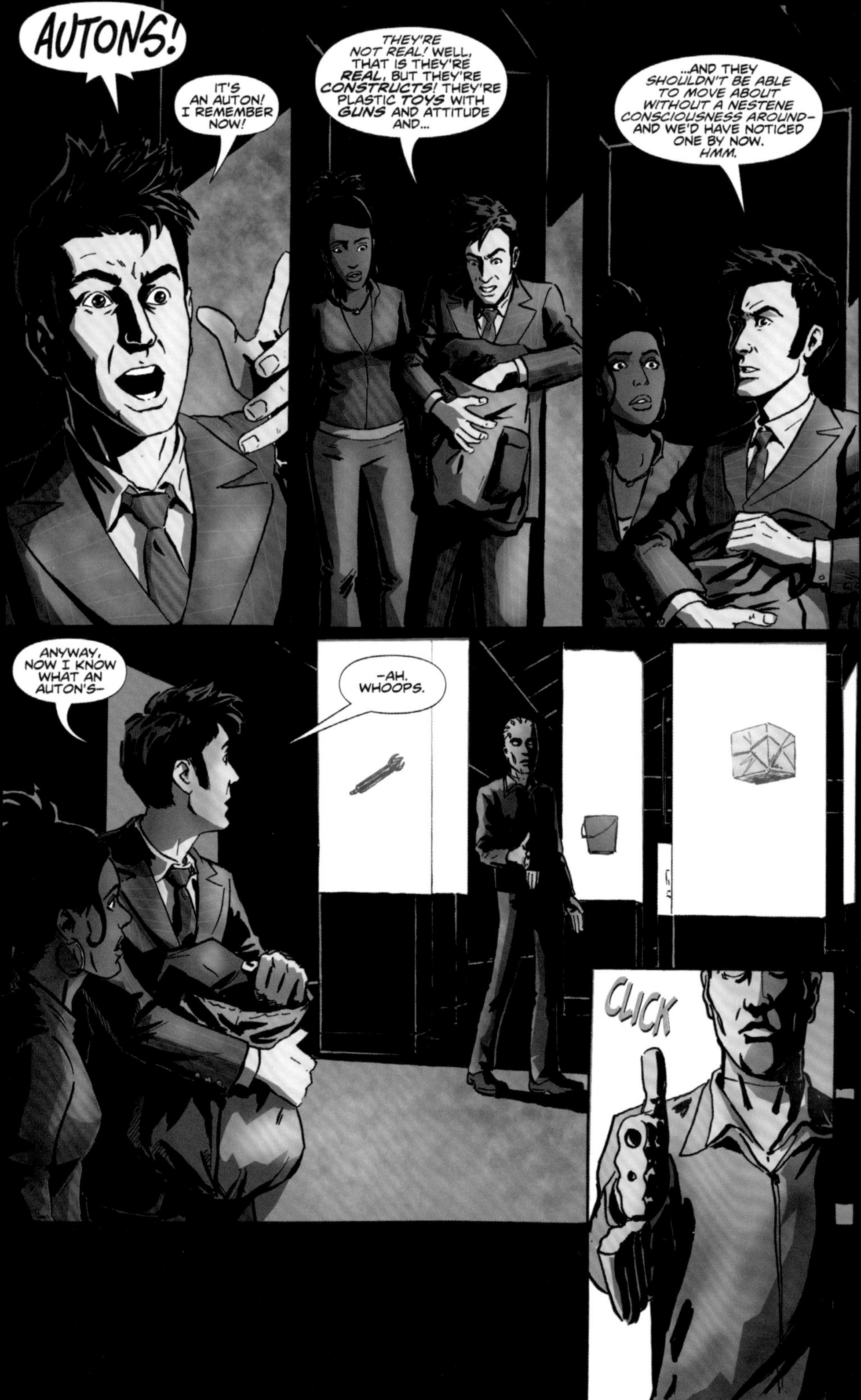
AUTONS!
IT'S AN AUTON! I REMEMBER NOW!
THEY'RE NOT REAL! WELL, THAT IS THEY'RE REAL, BUT THEY'RE CONSTRUCTS! THEY'RE PLASTIC TOYS WITH GUNS AND ATTITUDE AND...
...AND THEY SHOULDN'T BE ABLE TO MOVE ABOUT WITHOUT A NESTENE CONSCIOUSNESS AROUND– AND WE'D HAVE NOTICED ONE BY NOW. HMM.
ANYWAY, NOW I KNOW WHAT AN AUTON'S–
–AH. WHOOPS.
CLICK

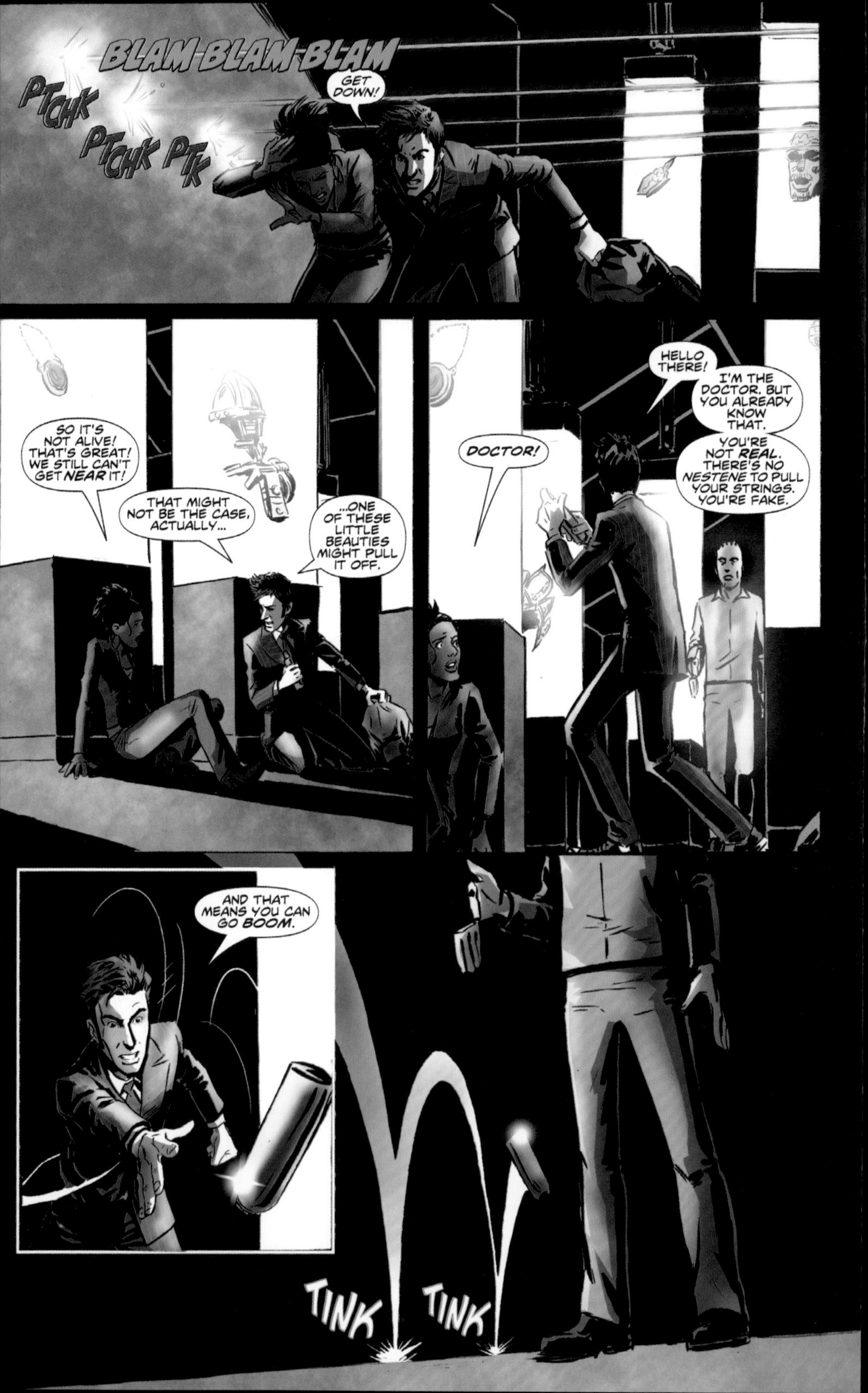
BLAM BLAM BLAM
PTCHK PTCHK PTK
GET DOWN!
SO IT'S NOT ALIVE! THAT'S GREAT! WE STILL CAN'T GET NEAR IT!
THAT MIGHT NOT BE THE CASE, ACTUALLY...
...ONE OF THESE LITTLE BEAUTIES MIGHT PULL IT OFF.
DOCTOR!
HELLO THERE!
I'M THE DOCTOR. BUT YOU ALREADY KNOW THAT.
YOU'RE NOT REAL. THERE'S NO NESTENE TO PULL YOUR STRINGS. YOU'RE FAKE.
AND THAT MEANS YOU CAN GO BOOM.
TINK TINK

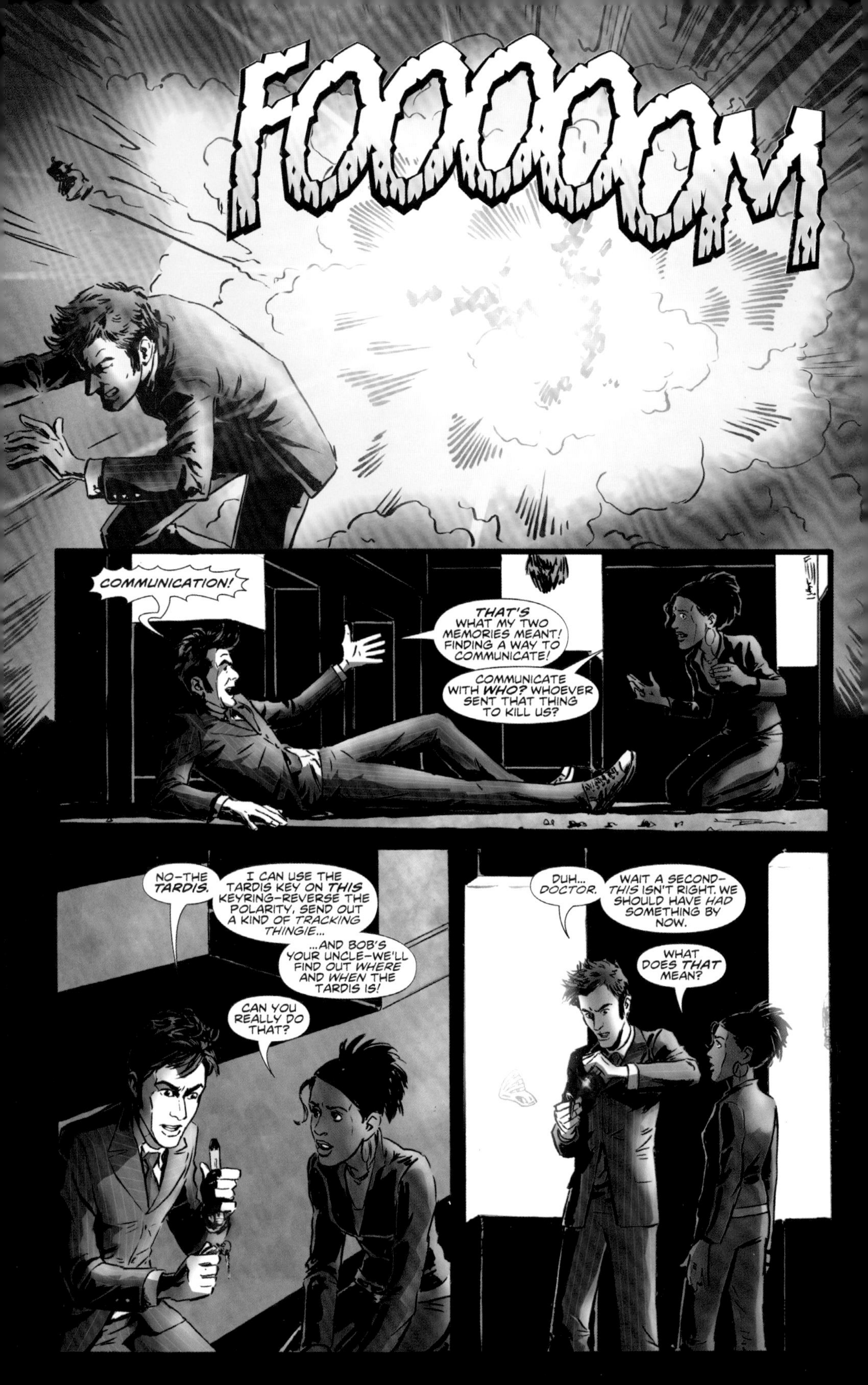
FOOOOOM
COMMUNICATION!
THAT'S WHAT MY TWO MEMORIES MEANT! FINDING A WAY TO COMMUNICATE!
COMMUNICATE WITH WHO? WHOEVER SENT THAT THING TO KILL US?
NO—THE TARDIS.
I CAN USE THE TARDIS KEY ON THIS KEYRING—REVERSE THE POLARITY, SEND OUT A KIND OF TRACKING THINGIE...
...AND BOB'S YOUR UNCLE—WE'LL FIND OUT WHERE AND WHEN THE TARDIS IS!
CAN YOU REALLY DO THAT?
DUH... DOCTOR.
WAIT A SECOND—THIS ISN'T RIGHT. WE SHOULD HAVE HAD SOMETHING BY NOW.
WHAT DOES THAT MEAN?

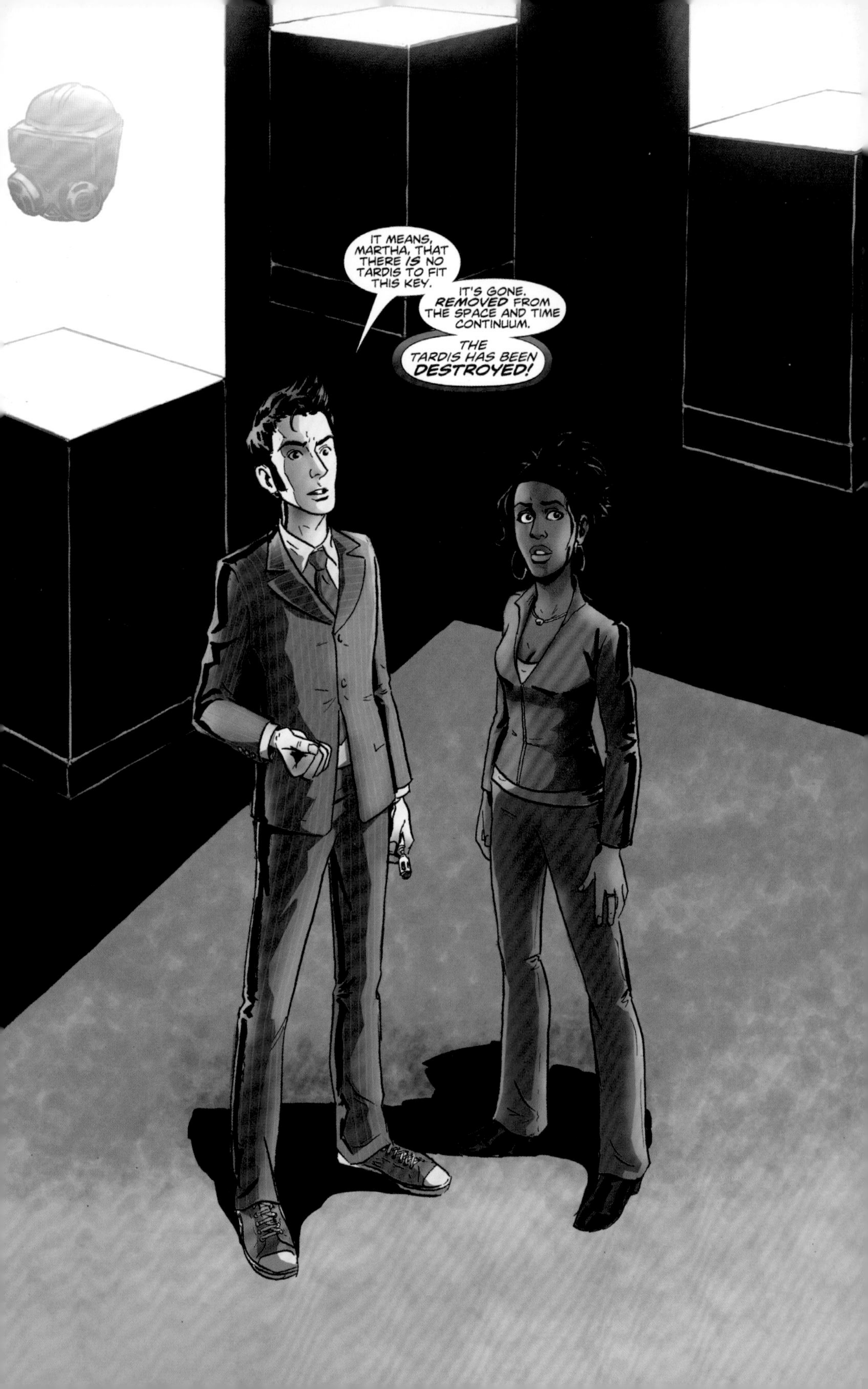
IT MEANS, MARTHA, THAT THERE *IS* NO TARDIS TO FIT THIS KEY.
IT'S GONE. **REMOVED** FROM THE SPACE AND TIME CONTINUUM.
THE TARDIS HAS BEEN ***DESTROYED!***

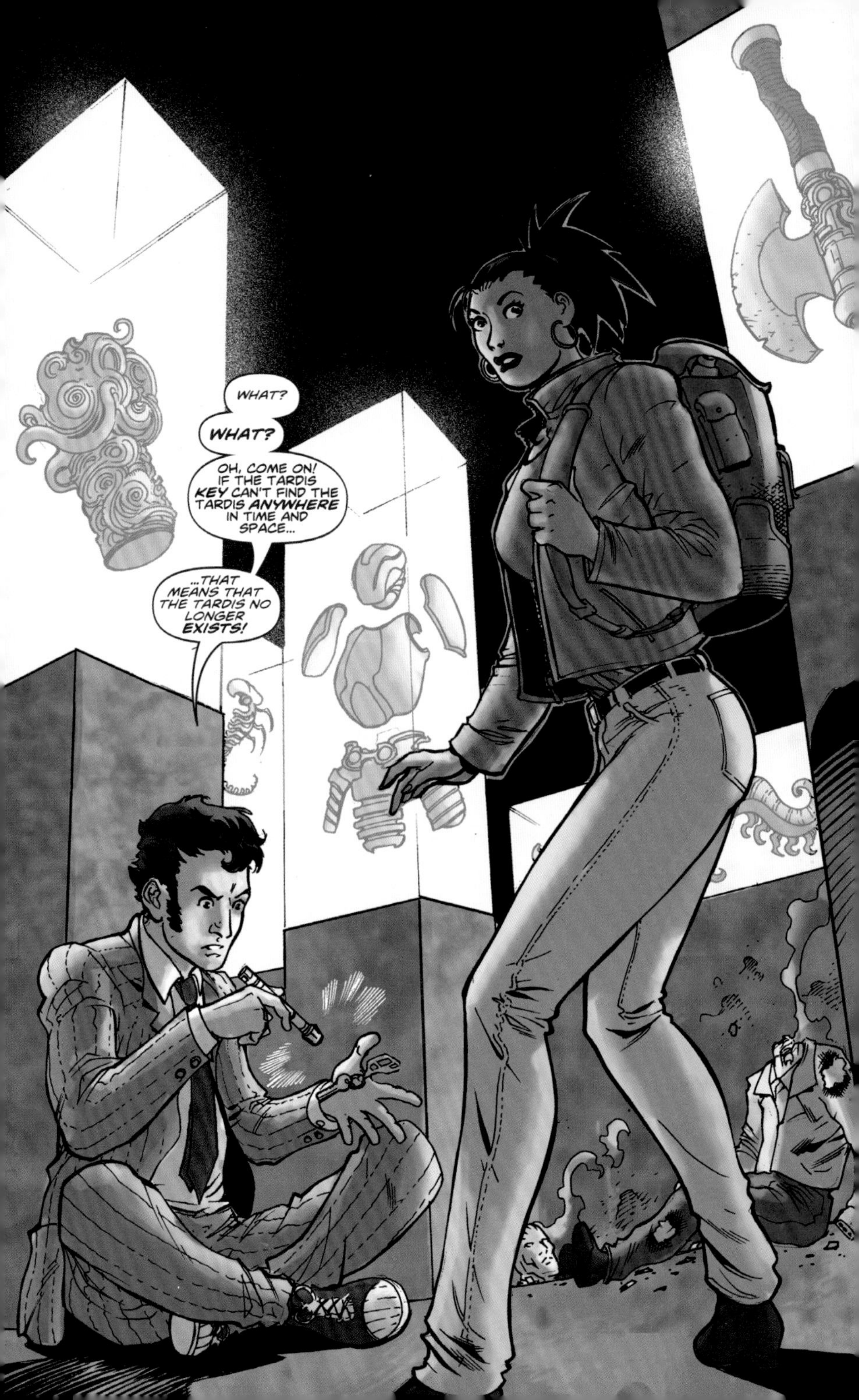
WHAT?
WHAT?
OH, COME ON! IF THE TARDIS KEY CAN'T FIND THE TARDIS ANYWHERE IN TIME AND SPACE...
...THAT MEANS THAT THE TARDIS NO LONGER EXISTS!

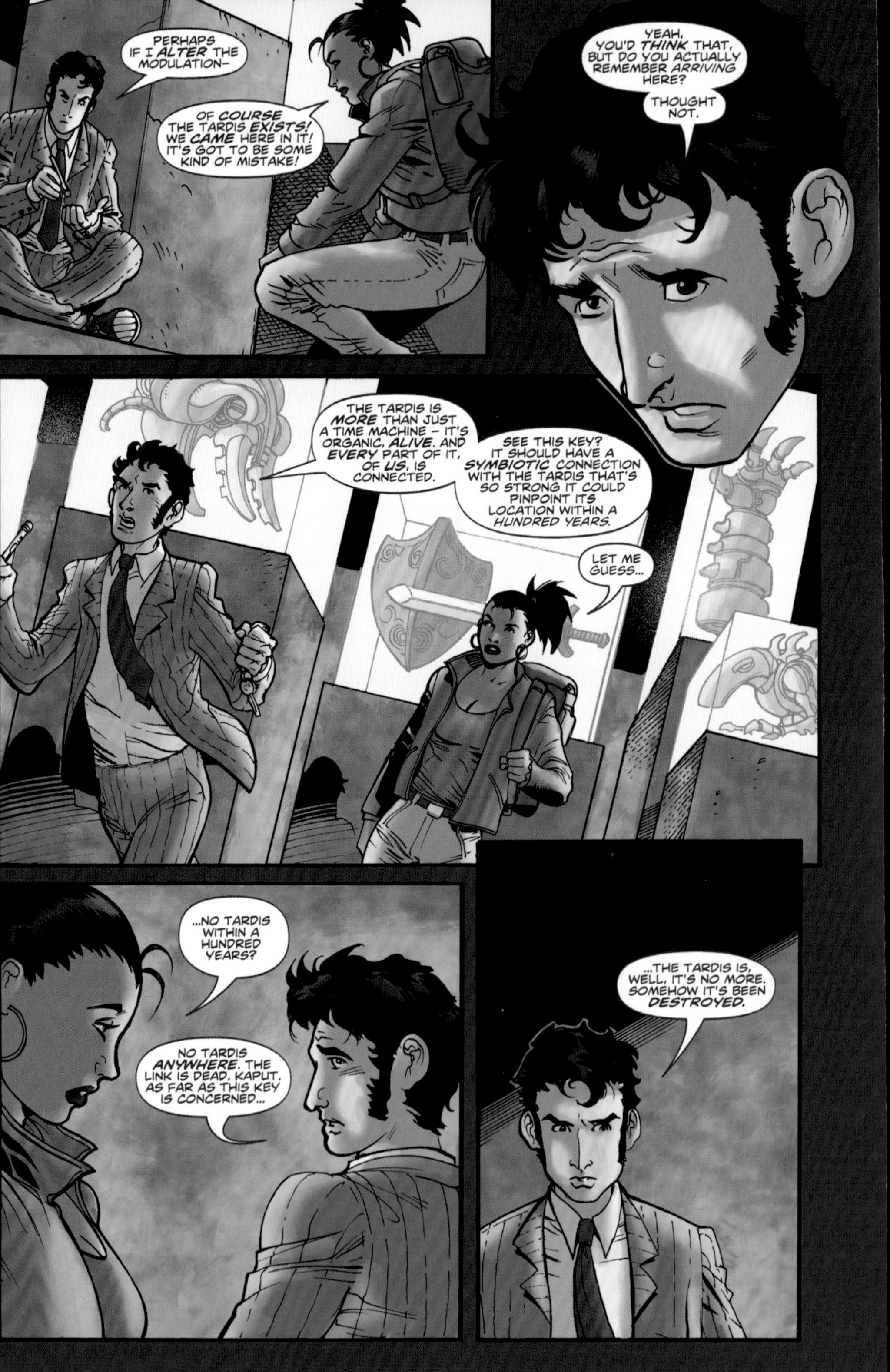
PERHAPS IF I ALTER THE MODULATION–
OF COURSE THE TARDIS EXISTS! WE CAME HERE IN IT! IT'S GOT TO BE SOME KIND OF MISTAKE!
YEAH, YOU'D THINK THAT, BUT DO YOU ACTUALLY REMEMBER ARRIVING HERE?
THOUGHT NOT.
THE TARDIS IS MORE THAN JUST A TIME MACHINE – IT'S ORGANIC, ALIVE. AND EVERY PART OF IT, OF US, IS CONNECTED.
SEE THIS KEY? IT SHOULD HAVE A SYMBIOTIC CONNECTION WITH THE TARDIS THAT'S SO STRONG IT COULD PINPOINT ITS LOCATION WITHIN A HUNDRED YEARS.
LET ME GUESS...
...NO TARDIS WITHIN A HUNDRED YEARS?
NO TARDIS ANYWHERE. THE LINK IS DEAD. KAPUT. AS FAR AS THIS KEY IS CONCERNED...
...THE TARDIS IS, WELL, IT'S NO MORE. SOMEHOW IT'S BEEN DESTROYED.

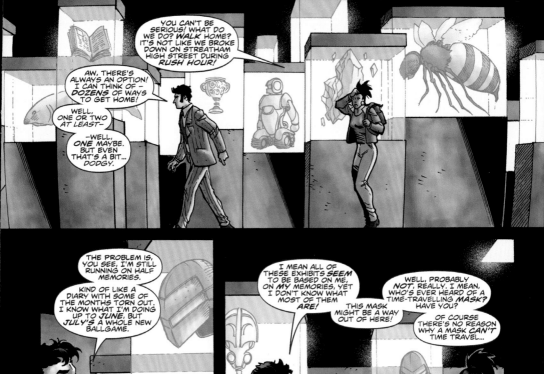

YOU CAN'T BE SERIOUS! WHAT DO WE DO? *WALK HOME?* IT'S NOT LIKE WE BROKE DOWN ON STREATHAM HIGH STREET DURING *RUSH HOUR!*

AW, THERE'S ALWAYS AN OPTION! I CAN THINK OF – *DOZENS* OF WAYS TO GET HOME!

WELL, ONE OR TWO AT LEAST–

–WELL, *ONE* MAYBE. BUT EVEN... THAT'S A BIT... DODGY.

THE PROBLEM IS, YOU SEE, I'M STILL RUNNING ON HALF MEMORIES.

KIND OF LIKE A DIARY WITH SOME OF THE MONTHS TORN OUT. I KNOW WHAT I'M DOING UP TO *JUNE*, BUT *JULY'S* A WHOLE NEW BALLGAME.

I MEAN ALL OF THESE EXHIBITS *SEEM* TO BE BASED ON ME, ON *MY* MEMORIES, YET I DON'T KNOW WHAT MOST OF THEM *ARE!*

THIS MASK MIGHT BE A WAY OUT OF HERE!

WELL, PROBABLY *NOT*, REALLY. I MEAN, WHO'S EVER HEARD OF A TIME-TRAVELLING *MASK?* HAVE YOU?

OF COURSE THERE'S NO REASON WHY A MASK *CAN'T* TIME TRAVEL...

WELL, IN *THAT* CASE, DOCTOR, HOW ABOUT I GO AND LOOK AROUND WHILE YOU TRY TO REMEMBER SOME MORE ABOUT YOUR PAST?

JELLY BABIES? THAT DOESN'T SEEM VERY *ME*, DOES IT?

I MEAN, I *LIKE* JELLY BABIES AND ALL THAT–

WILL YOU *STOP* TALKING AND START REMEMBERING?

LOOK FOR A SIGN MARKED "*EXIT*." IT IS *MY* MUSEUM, AFTER ALL. NOBODY ELSE SEEMS TO BE VISITING. FUNNY THAT – – YOU'D *THINK* THAT A MEMORIAL TO THE LAST TIME LORD WOULD HAVE PULLED IN AT LEAST A *COUPLE* OF VISITORS.

I MEAN...

I'LL TAKE A LOOK ABOUT WHILE YOU'RE SITTING THERE AND SEE IF I CAN FIND A WAY OUT.

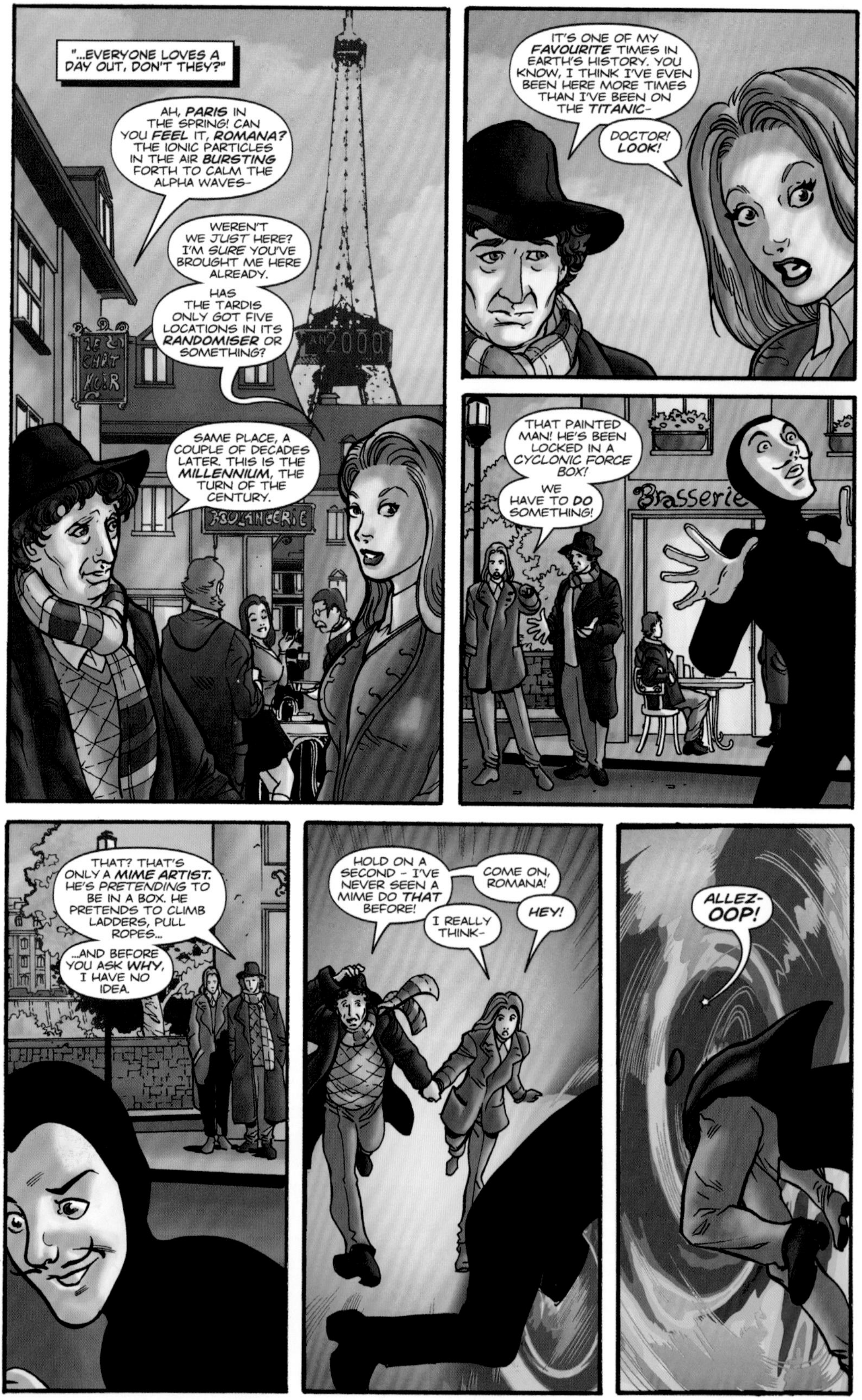
"...EVERYONE LOVES A DAY OUT, DON'T THEY?"
AH, PARIS IN THE SPRING! CAN YOU FEEL IT, ROMANA? THE IONIC PARTICLES IN THE AIR BURSTING FORTH TO CALM THE ALPHA WAVES-
WEREN'T WE JUST HERE? I'M SURE YOU'VE BROUGHT ME HERE ALREADY.
HAS THE TARDIS ONLY GOT FIVE LOCATIONS IN ITS RANDOMISER OR SOMETHING?
LE CHAT NOIR
AN 2000
SAME PLACE, A COUPLE OF DECADES LATER. THIS IS THE MILLENNIUM, THE TURN OF THE CENTURY.
BOULANGERIE
IT'S ONE OF MY FAVOURITE TIMES IN EARTH'S HISTORY. YOU KNOW, I THINK I'VE EVEN BEEN HERE MORE TIMES THAN I'VE BEEN ON THE TITANIC-
DOCTOR! LOOK!
THAT PAINTED MAN! HE'S BEEN LOCKED IN A CYCLONIC FORCE BOX!
WE HAVE TO DO SOMETHING!
Brasserie
THAT? THAT'S ONLY A MIME ARTIST. HE'S PRETENDING TO BE IN A BOX. HE PRETENDS TO CLIMB LADDERS, PULL ROPES...
...AND BEFORE YOU ASK WHY, I HAVE NO IDEA.
HOLD ON A SECOND - I'VE NEVER SEEN A MIME DO THAT BEFORE!
COME ON, ROMANA!
I REALLY THINK-
HEY!
ALLEZ-OOP!

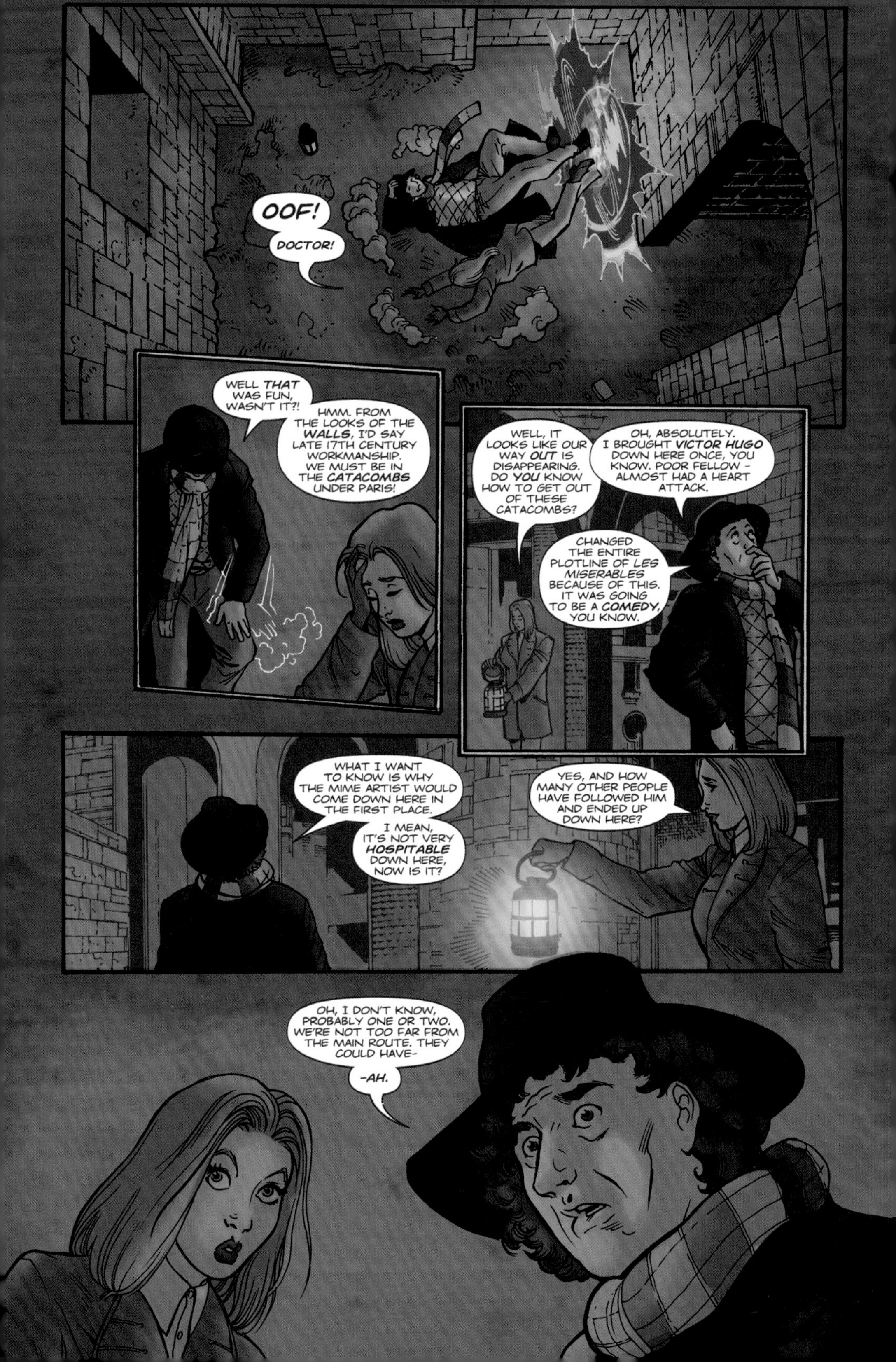
OOF!
DOCTOR!
WELL THAT WAS FUN, WASN'T IT?!
HMM. FROM THE LOOKS OF THE WALLS, I'D SAY LATE 17TH CENTURY WORKMANSHIP. WE MUST BE IN THE CATACOMBS UNDER PARIS!
WELL, IT LOOKS LIKE OUR WAY OUT IS DISAPPEARING. DO YOU KNOW HOW TO GET OUT OF THESE CATACOMBS?
OH, ABSOLUTELY. I BROUGHT VICTOR HUGO DOWN HERE ONCE, YOU KNOW. POOR FELLOW - ALMOST HAD A HEART ATTACK.
CHANGED THE ENTIRE PLOTLINE OF LES MISERABLES BECAUSE OF THIS. IT WAS GOING TO BE A COMEDY, YOU KNOW.
WHAT I WANT TO KNOW IS WHY THE MIME ARTIST WOULD COME DOWN HERE IN THE FIRST PLACE.
I MEAN, IT'S NOT VERY HOSPITABLE DOWN HERE, NOW IS IT?
YES, AND HOW MANY OTHER PEOPLE HAVE FOLLOWED HIM AND ENDED UP DOWN HERE?
OH, I DON'T KNOW, PROBABLY ONE OR TWO. WE'RE NOT TOO FAR FROM THE MAIN ROUTE. THEY COULD HAVE-
-AH.

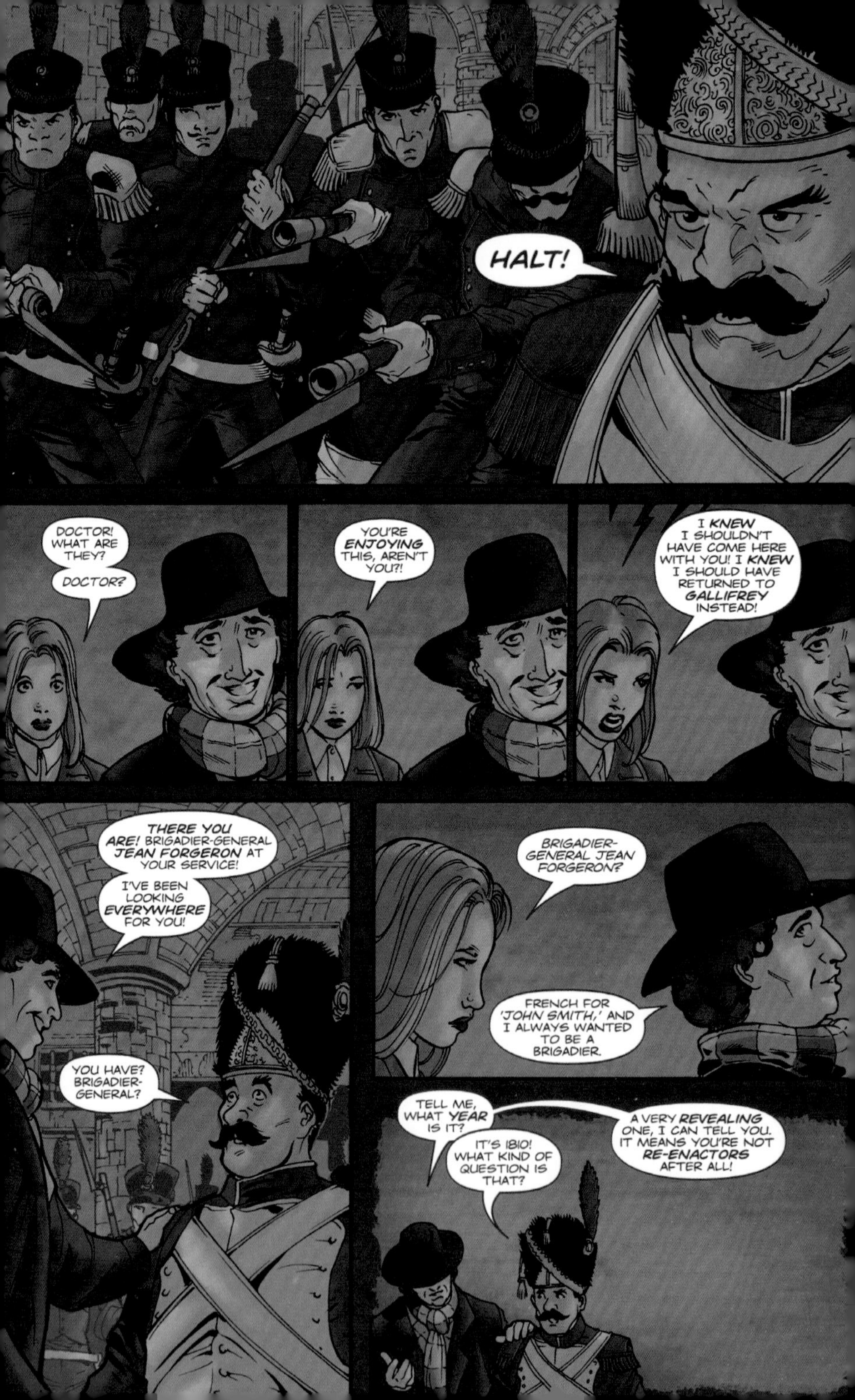
HALT!
DOCTOR! WHAT ARE THEY?
DOCTOR?
YOU'RE ENJOYING THIS, AREN'T YOU?!
I KNEW I SHOULDN'T HAVE COME HERE WITH YOU! I KNEW I SHOULD HAVE RETURNED TO GALLIFREY INSTEAD!
THERE YOU ARE! BRIGADIER-GENERAL JEAN FORGERON AT YOUR SERVICE!
I'VE BEEN LOOKING EVERYWHERE FOR YOU!
YOU HAVE? BRIGADIER-GENERAL?
BRIGADIER-GENERAL JEAN FORGERON?
FRENCH FOR 'JOHN SMITH,' AND I ALWAYS WANTED TO BE A BRIGADIER.
TELL ME, WHAT YEAR IS IT?
IT'S 1810! WHAT KIND OF QUESTION IS THAT?
A VERY REVEALING ONE, I CAN TELL YOU. IT MEANS YOU'RE NOT RE-ENACTORS AFTER ALL!

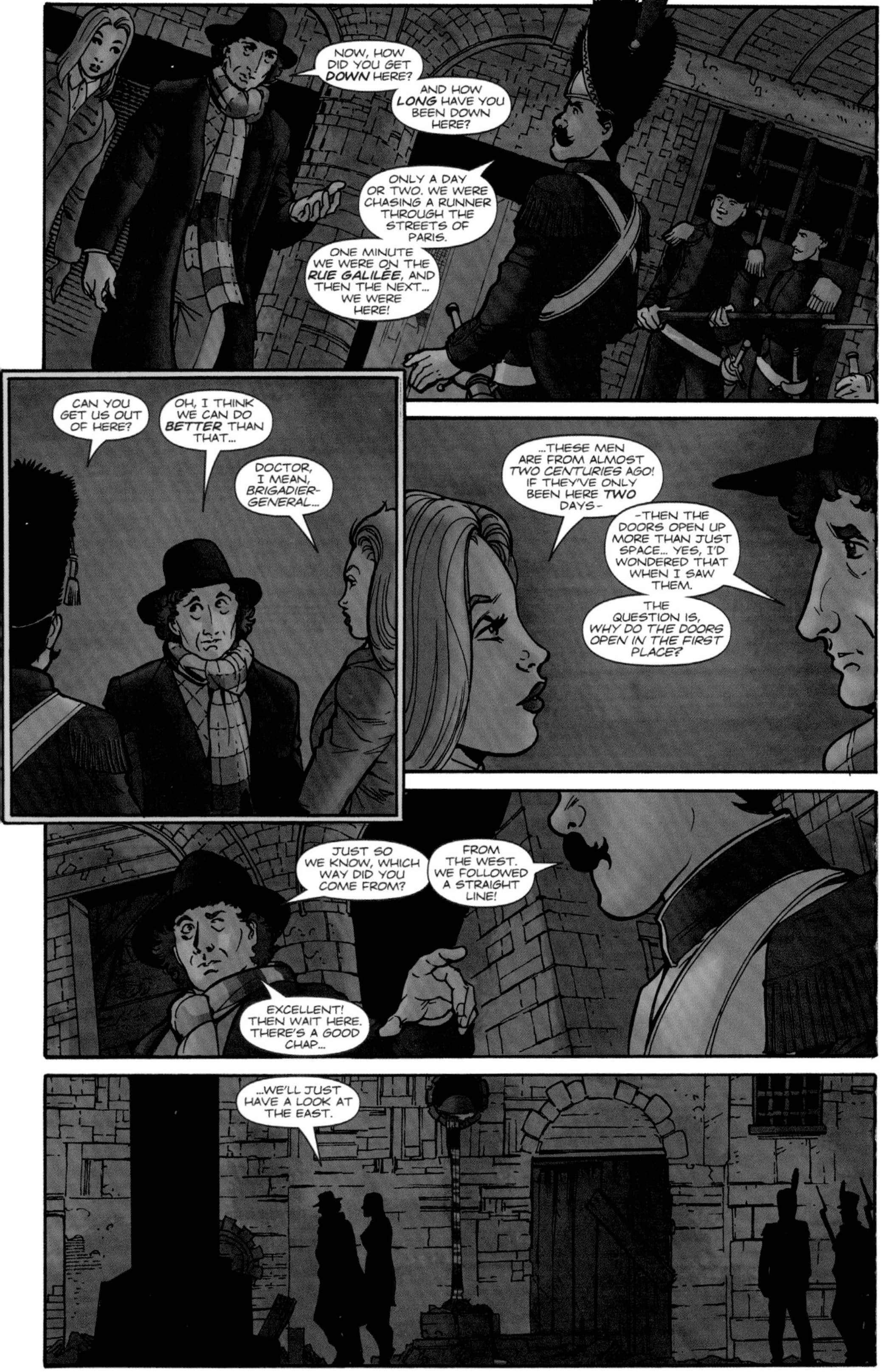
NOW, HOW DID YOU GET DOWN HERE?
AND HOW LONG HAVE YOU BEEN DOWN HERE?
ONLY A DAY OR TWO. WE WERE CHASING A RUNNER THROUGH THE STREETS OF PARIS.
ONE MINUTE WE WERE ON THE RUE GALILÉE, AND THEN THE NEXT... WE WERE HERE!
CAN YOU GET US OUT OF HERE?
OH, I THINK WE CAN DO BETTER THAN THAT...
DOCTOR, I MEAN, BRIGADIER-GENERAL...
...THESE MEN ARE FROM ALMOST TWO CENTURIES AGO! IF THEY'VE ONLY BEEN HERE TWO DAYS-
-THEN THE DOORS OPEN UP MORE THAN JUST SPACE... YES, I'D WONDERED THAT WHEN I SAW THEM.
THE QUESTION IS, WHY DO THE DOORS OPEN IN THE FIRST PLACE?
JUST SO WE KNOW, WHICH WAY DID YOU COME FROM?
FROM THE WEST. WE FOLLOWED A STRAIGHT LINE!
EXCELLENT! THEN WAIT HERE. THERE'S A GOOD CHAP...
...WE'LL JUST HAVE A LOOK AT THE EAST.

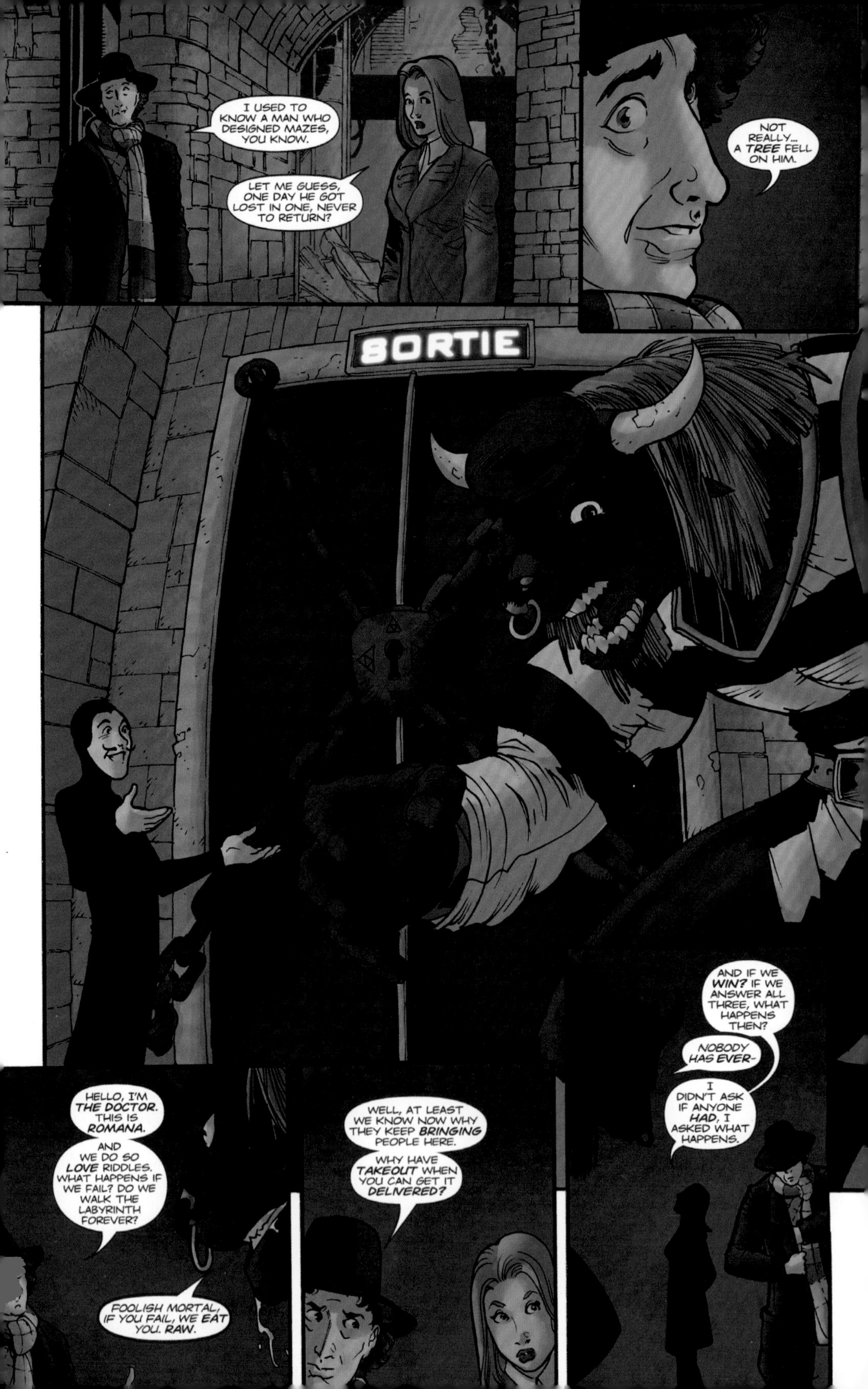
I USED TO KNOW A MAN WHO DESIGNED MAZES, YOU KNOW.
LET ME GUESS, ONE DAY HE GOT LOST IN ONE, NEVER TO RETURN?
NOT REALLY... A TREE FELL ON HIM.
SORTIE
HELLO, I'M THE DOCTOR. THIS IS ROMANA.
AND WE DO SO LOVE RIDDLES. WHAT HAPPENS IF WE FAIL? DO WE WALK THE LABYRINTH FOREVER?
FOOLISH MORTAL, IF YOU FAIL, WE EAT YOU. RAW.
WELL, AT LEAST WE KNOW NOW WHY THEY KEEP BRINGING PEOPLE HERE.
WHY HAVE TAKEOUT WHEN YOU CAN GET IT DELIVERED?
AND IF WE WIN? IF WE ANSWER ALL THREE, WHAT HAPPENS THEN?
NOBODY HAS EVER-
I DIDN'T ASK IF ANYONE HAD, I ASKED WHAT HAPPENS.

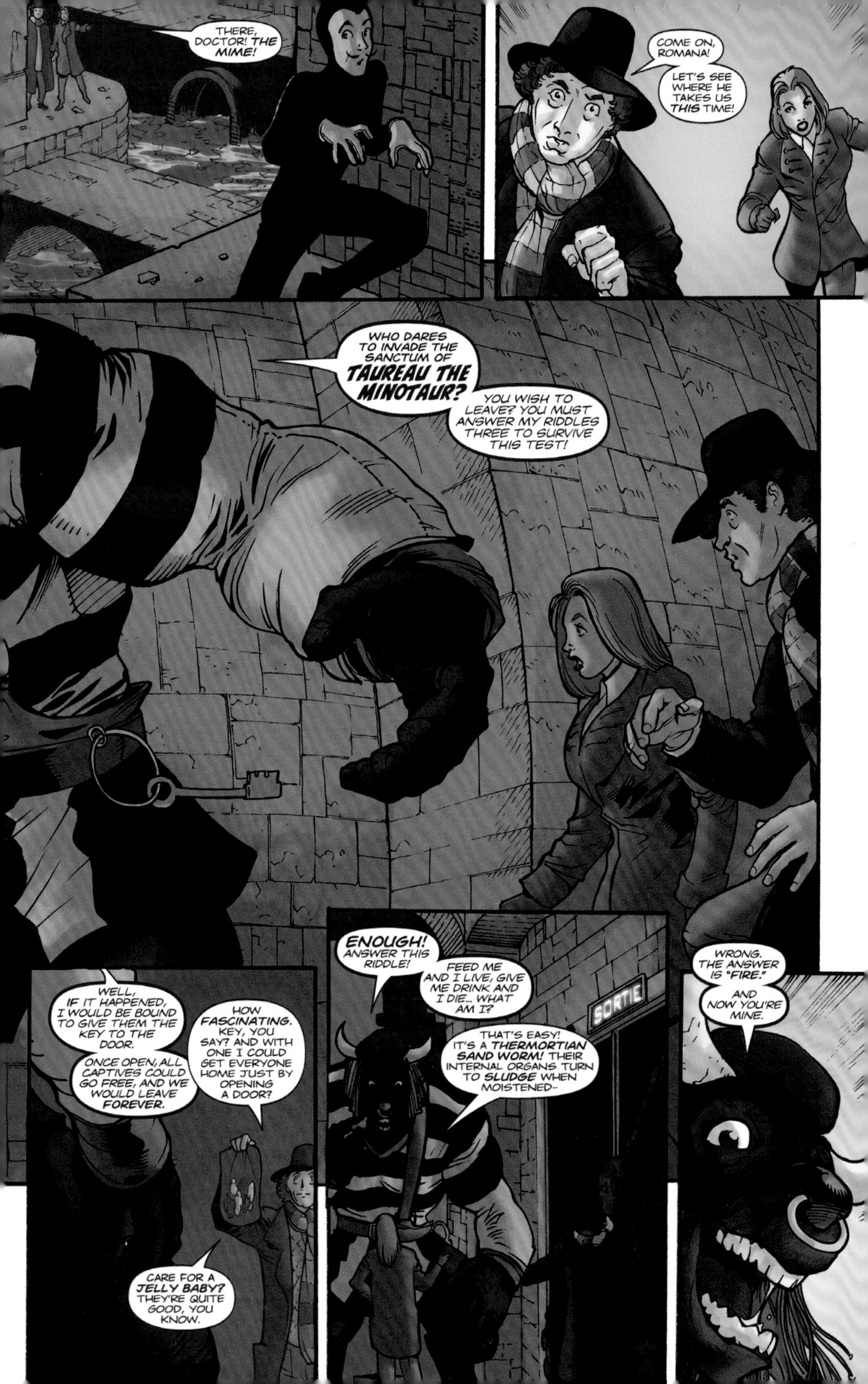

THERE, DOCTOR! THE MIME!
COME ON, ROMANA!
LET'S SEE WHERE HE TAKES US THIS TIME!
WHO DARES TO INVADE THE SANCTUM OF TAUREAU THE MINOTAUR?
YOU WISH TO LEAVE? YOU MUST ANSWER MY RIDDLES THREE TO SURVIVE THIS TEST!
WELL, IF IT HAPPENED, I WOULD BE BOUND TO GIVE THEM THE KEY TO THE DOOR.
ONCE OPEN, ALL CAPTIVES COULD GO FREE, AND WE WOULD LEAVE FOREVER.
HOW FASCINATING. KEY, YOU SAY? AND WITH ONE I COULD GET EVERYONE HOME JUST BY OPENING A DOOR?
CARE FOR A JELLY BABY? THEY'RE QUITE GOOD, YOU KNOW.
ENOUGH! ANSWER THIS RIDDLE!
FEED ME AND I LIVE, GIVE ME DRINK AND I DIE... WHAT AM I?
SORTIE
THAT'S EASY! IT'S A THERMORTIAN SAND WORM! THEIR INTERNAL ORGANS TURN TO SLUDGE WHEN MOISTENED-
WRONG. THE ANSWER IS "FIRE."
AND NOW YOU'RE MINE.

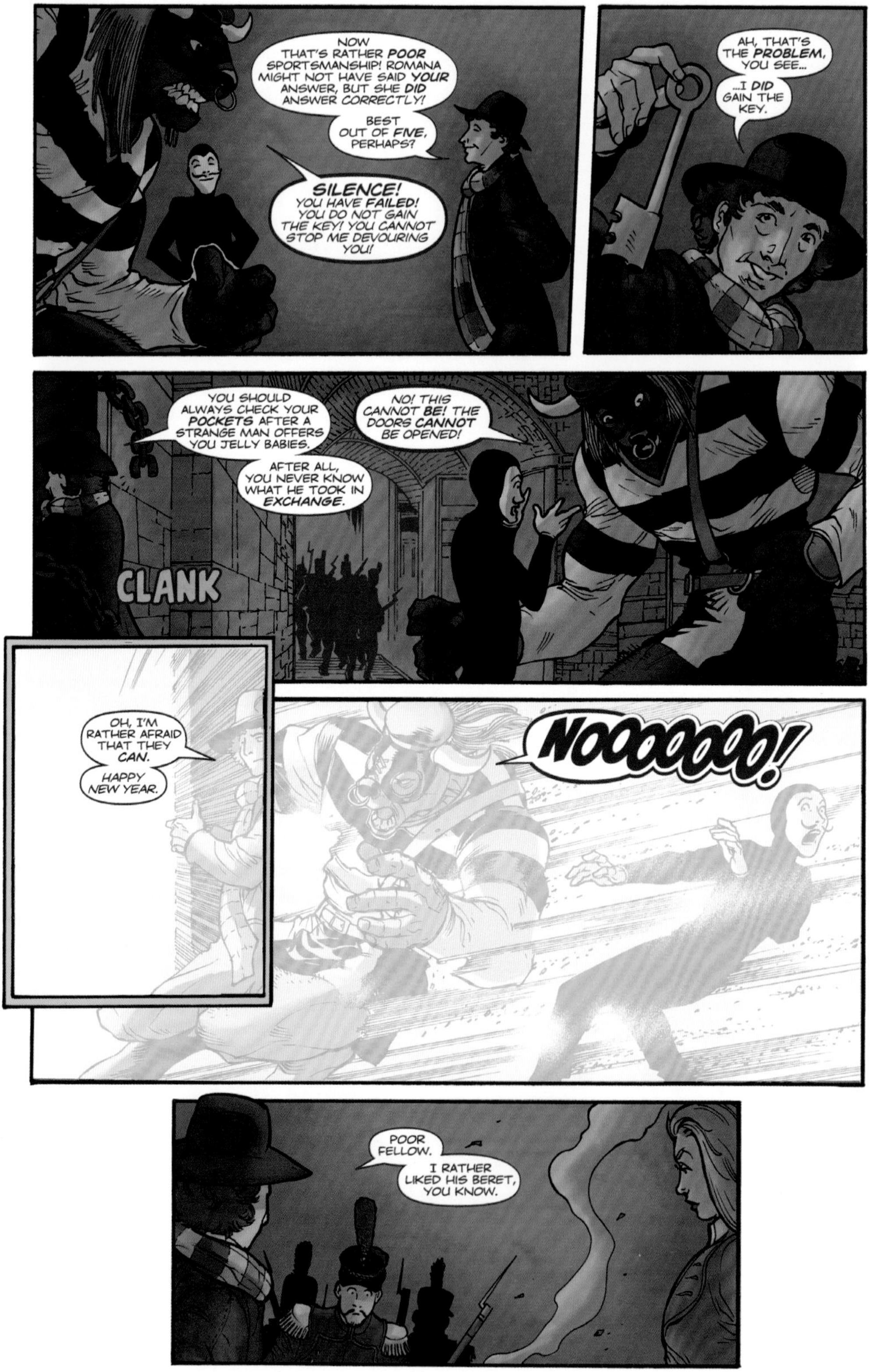
NOW THAT'S RATHER POOR SPORTSMANSHIP! ROMANA MIGHT NOT HAVE SAID YOUR ANSWER, BUT SHE DID ANSWER CORRECTLY!
BEST OUT OF FIVE, PERHAPS?
SILENCE! YOU HAVE FAILED! YOU DO NOT GAIN THE KEY! YOU CANNOT STOP ME DEVOURING YOU!
AH, THAT'S THE PROBLEM, YOU SEE...
...I DID GAIN THE KEY.
YOU SHOULD ALWAYS CHECK YOUR POCKETS AFTER A STRANGE MAN OFFERS YOU JELLY BABIES.
AFTER ALL, YOU NEVER KNOW WHAT HE TOOK IN EXCHANGE.
NO! THIS CANNOT BE! THE DOORS CANNOT BE OPENED!
CLANK
OH, I'M RATHER AFRAID THAT THEY CAN.
HAPPY NEW YEAR.
NOOOOOOO!
POOR FELLOW.
I RATHER LIKED HIS BERET, YOU KNOW.

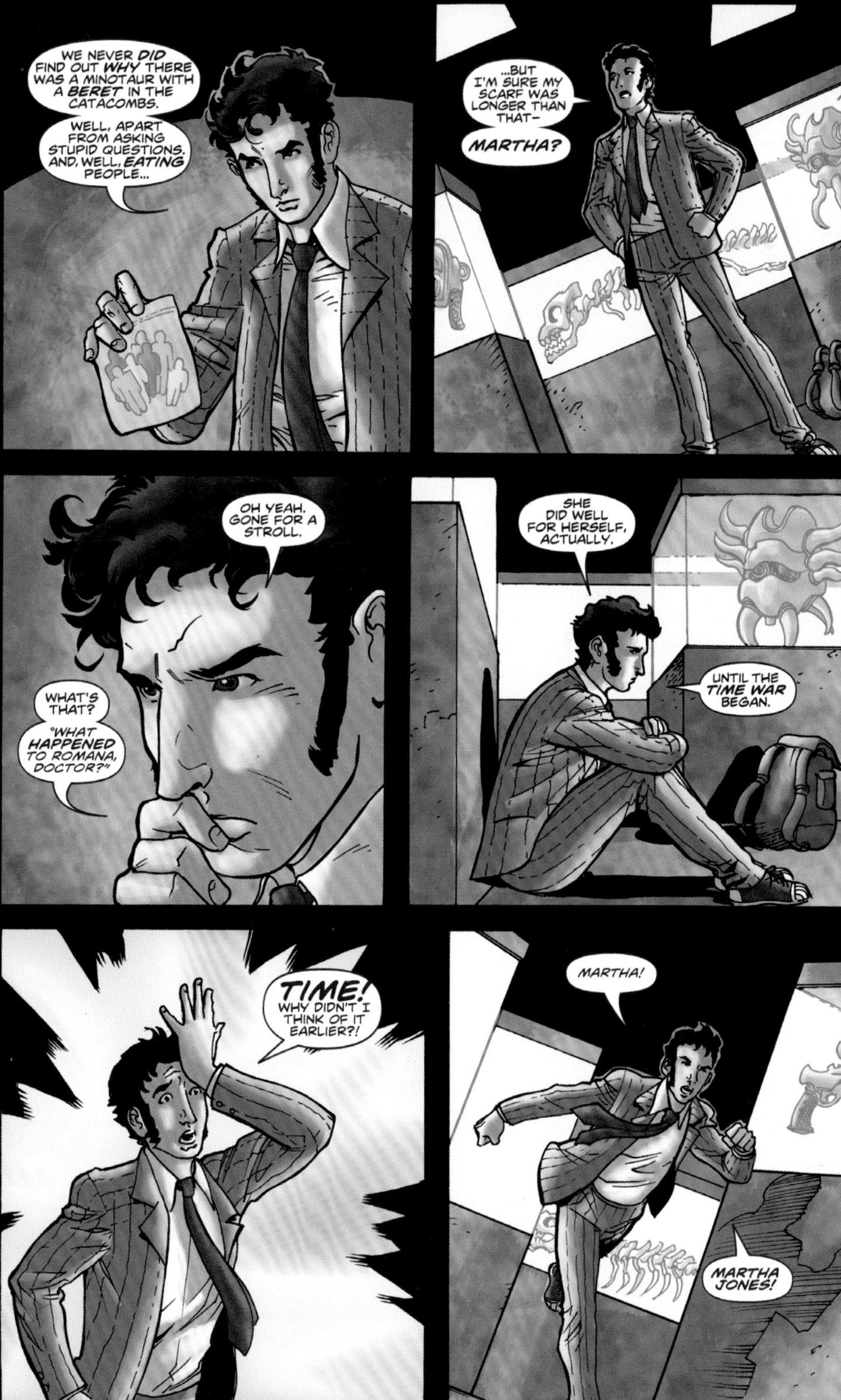
WE NEVER DID FIND OUT WHY THERE WAS A MINOTAUR WITH A BERET IN THE CATACOMBS.
WELL, APART FROM ASKING STUPID QUESTIONS. AND, WELL, EATING PEOPLE...
...BUT I'M SURE MY SCARF WAS LONGER THAN THAT–
MARTHA?
OH YEAH. GONE FOR A STROLL.
WHAT'S THAT? "WHAT HAPPENED TO ROMANA, DOCTOR?"
SHE DID WELL FOR HERSELF, ACTUALLY.
UNTIL THE TIME WAR BEGAN.
TIME! WHY DIDN'T I THINK OF IT EARLIER?!
MARTHA!
MARTHA JONES!

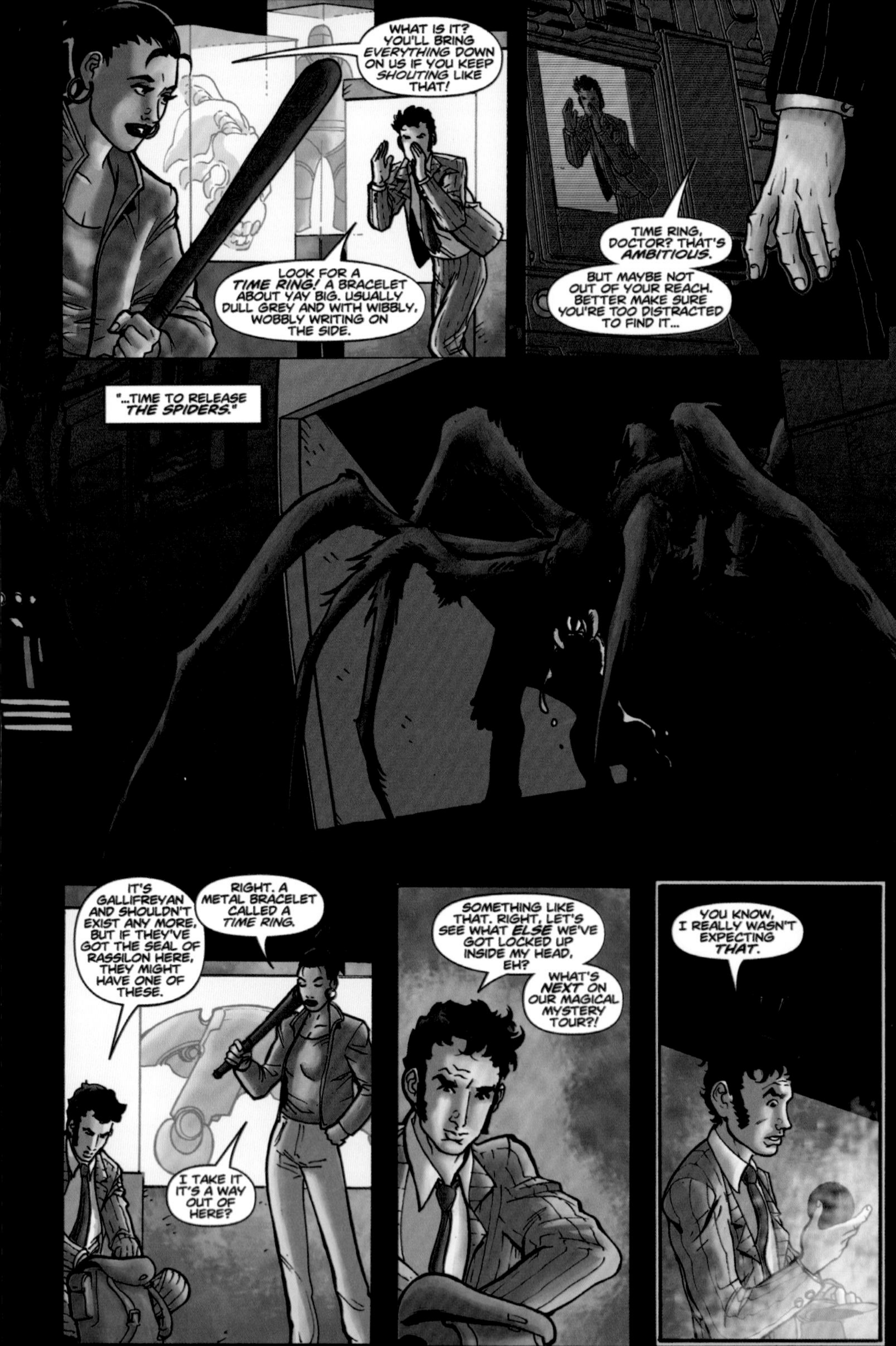
WHAT IS IT? YOU'LL BRING EVERYTHING DOWN ON US IF YOU KEEP SHOUTING LIKE THAT!
LOOK FOR A TIME RING! A BRACELET ABOUT YAY BIG. USUALLY DULL GREY AND WITH WIBBLY, WOBBLY WRITING ON THE SIDE.
TIME RING, DOCTOR? THAT'S AMBITIOUS.
BUT MAYBE NOT OUT OF YOUR REACH. BETTER MAKE SURE YOU'RE TOO DISTRACTED TO FIND IT...
"...TIME TO RELEASE THE SPIDERS."
RIGHT. A METAL BRACELET CALLED A TIME RING.
IT'S GALLIFREYAN AND SHOULDN'T EXIST ANY MORE, BUT IF THEY'VE GOT THE SEAL OF RASSILON HERE, THEY MIGHT HAVE ONE OF THESE.
I TAKE IT IT'S A WAY OUT OF HERE?
SOMETHING LIKE THAT. RIGHT, LET'S SEE WHAT ELSE WE'VE GOT LOCKED UP INSIDE MY HEAD, EH?
WHAT'S NEXT ON OUR MAGICAL MYSTERY TOUR?!
YOU KNOW, I REALLY WASN'T EXPECTING THAT.

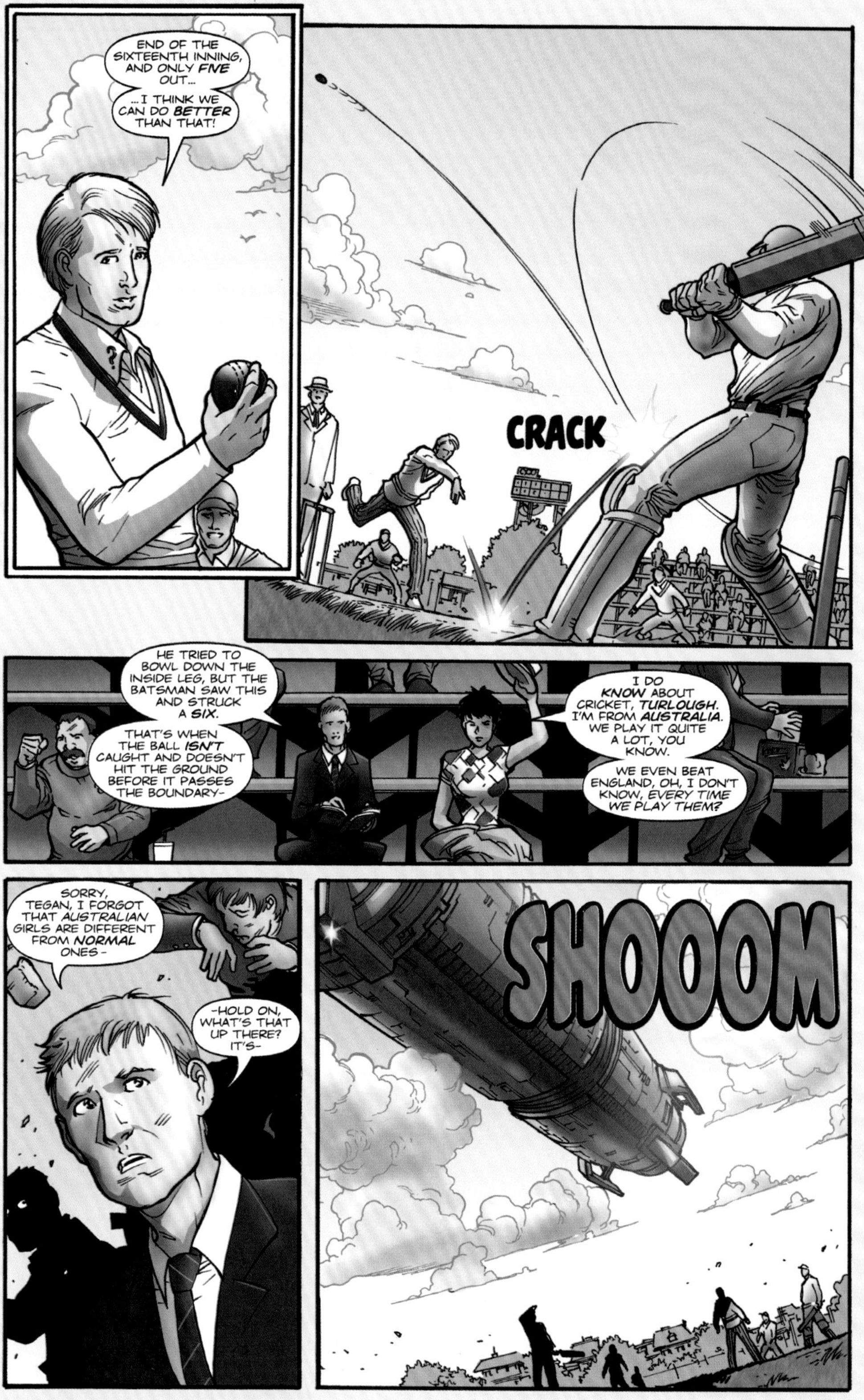
END OF THE SIXTEENTH INNING, AND ONLY FIVE OUT...
...I THINK WE CAN DO BETTER THAN THAT!
CRACK
HE TRIED TO BOWL DOWN THE INSIDE LEG, BUT THE BATSMAN SAW THIS AND STRUCK A SIX.
THAT'S WHEN THE BALL ISN'T CAUGHT AND DOESN'T HIT THE GROUND BEFORE IT PASSES THE BOUNDARY-
I DO KNOW ABOUT CRICKET, TURLOUGH. I'M FROM AUSTRALIA. WE PLAY IT QUITE A LOT, YOU KNOW.
WE EVEN BEAT ENGLAND, OH, I DON'T KNOW, EVERY TIME WE PLAY THEM?
SORRY, TEGAN, I FORGOT THAT AUSTRALIAN GIRLS ARE DIFFERENT FROM NORMAL ONES-
-HOLD ON, WHAT'S THAT UP THERE? IT'S-
SHOOOM

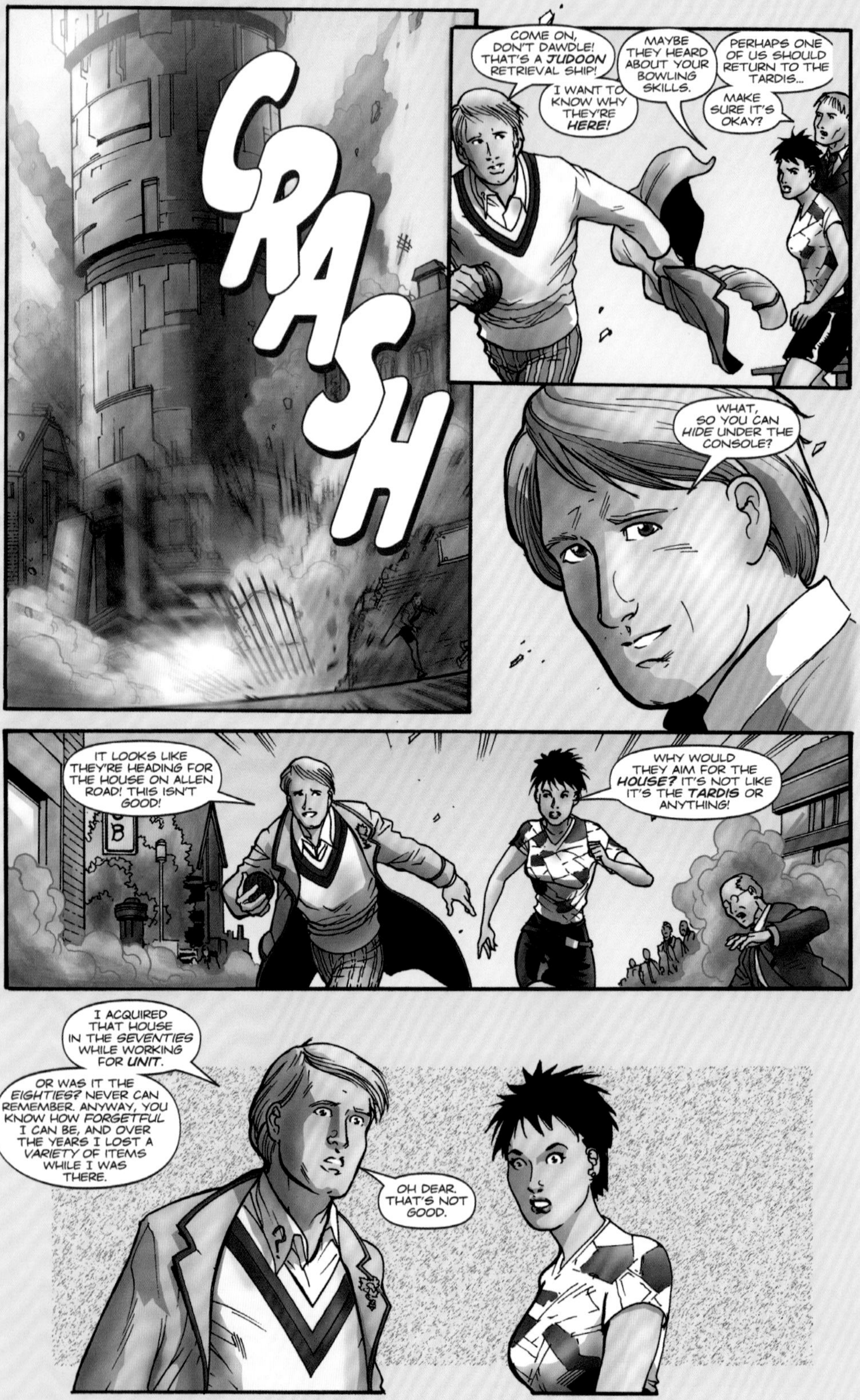
CRASH
COME ON, DON'T DAWDLE! THAT'S A JUDOON RETRIEVAL SHIP!
I WANT TO KNOW WHY THEY'RE HERE!
MAYBE THEY HEARD ABOUT YOUR BOWLING SKILLS.
PERHAPS ONE OF US SHOULD RETURN TO THE TARDIS...
MAKE SURE IT'S OKAY?
WHAT, SO YOU CAN HIDE UNDER THE CONSOLE?
IT LOOKS LIKE THEY'RE HEADING FOR THE HOUSE ON ALLEN ROAD! THIS ISN'T GOOD!
WHY WOULD THEY AIM FOR THE HOUSE? IT'S NOT LIKE IT'S THE TARDIS OR ANYTHING!
I ACQUIRED THAT HOUSE IN THE SEVENTIES WHILE WORKING FOR UNIT.
OR WAS IT THE EIGHTIES? NEVER CAN REMEMBER. ANYWAY, YOU KNOW HOW FORGETFUL I CAN BE, AND OVER THE YEARS I LOST A VARIETY OF ITEMS WHILE I WAS THERE.
OH DEAR. THAT'S NOT GOOD.

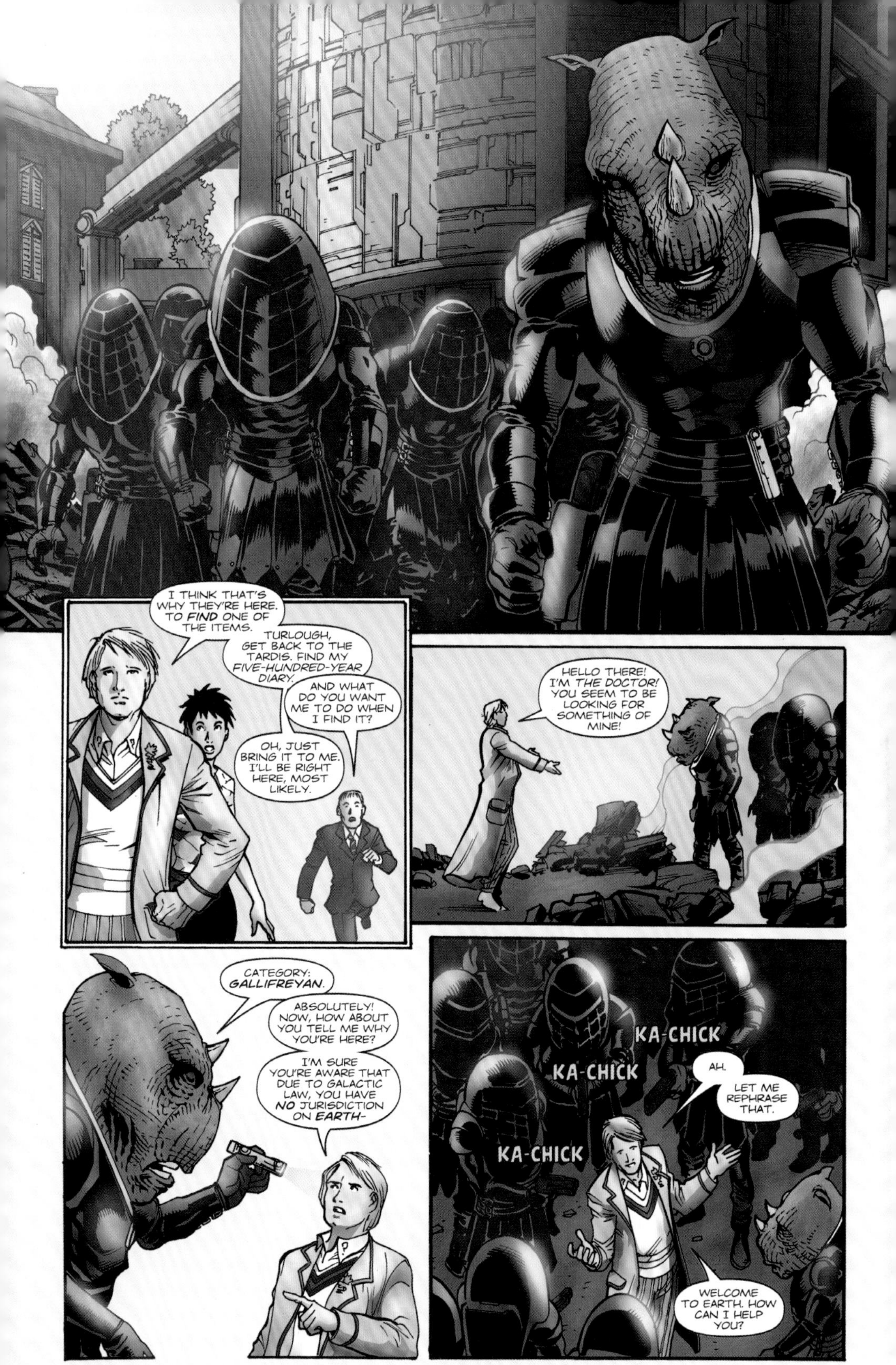
I THINK THAT'S WHY THEY'RE HERE. TO FIND ONE OF THE ITEMS.
TURLOUGH, GET BACK TO THE TARDIS. FIND MY FIVE-HUNDRED-YEAR DIARY.
AND WHAT DO YOU WANT ME TO DO WHEN I FIND IT?
OH, JUST BRING IT TO ME. I'LL BE RIGHT HERE, MOST LIKELY.
HELLO THERE! I'M THE DOCTOR! YOU SEEM TO BE LOOKING FOR SOMETHING OF MINE!
CATEGORY: GALLIFREYAN.
ABSOLUTELY! NOW, HOW ABOUT YOU TELL ME WHY YOU'RE HERE?
I'M SURE YOU'RE AWARE THAT DUE TO GALACTIC LAW, YOU HAVE NO JURISDICTION ON EARTH-
KA-CHICK
KA-CHICK
KA-CHICK
AH.
LET ME REPHRASE THAT.
WELCOME TO EARTH. HOW CAN I HELP YOU?

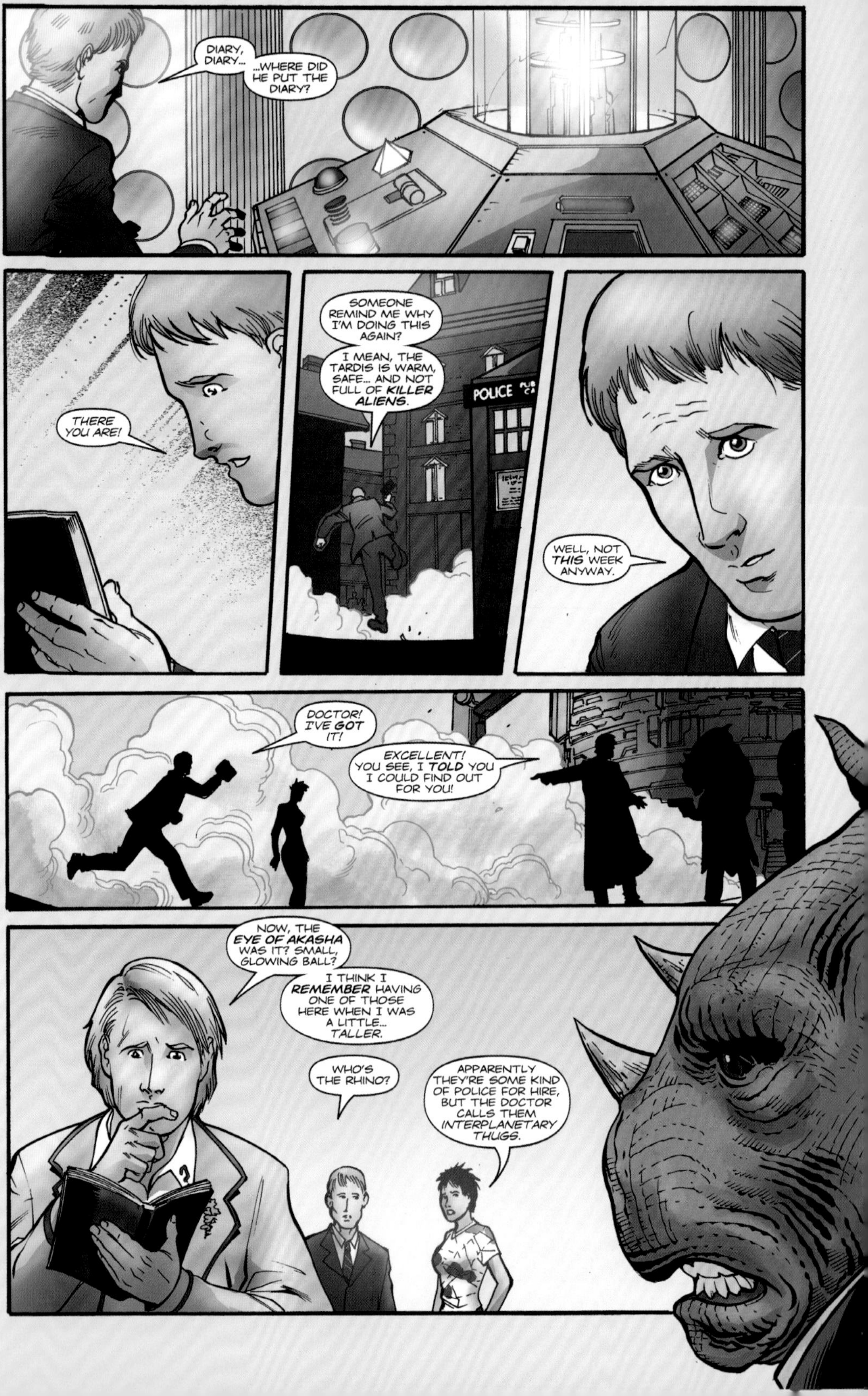
DIARY, DIARY...
...WHERE DID HE PUT THE DIARY?
THERE YOU ARE!
SOMEONE REMIND ME WHY I'M DOING THIS AGAIN?
I MEAN, THE TARDIS IS WARM, SAFE... AND NOT FULL OF KILLER ALIENS.
POLICE
WELL, NOT THIS WEEK ANYWAY.
DOCTOR! I'VE GOT IT!
EXCELLENT! YOU SEE, I TOLD YOU I COULD FIND OUT FOR YOU!
NOW, THE EYE OF AKASHA WAS IT? SMALL, GLOWING BALL?
I THINK I REMEMBER HAVING ONE OF THOSE HERE WHEN I WAS A LITTLE... TALLER.
WHO'S THE RHINO?
APPARENTLY THEY'RE SOME KIND OF POLICE FOR HIRE, BUT THE DOCTOR CALLS THEM INTERPLANETARY THUGS.

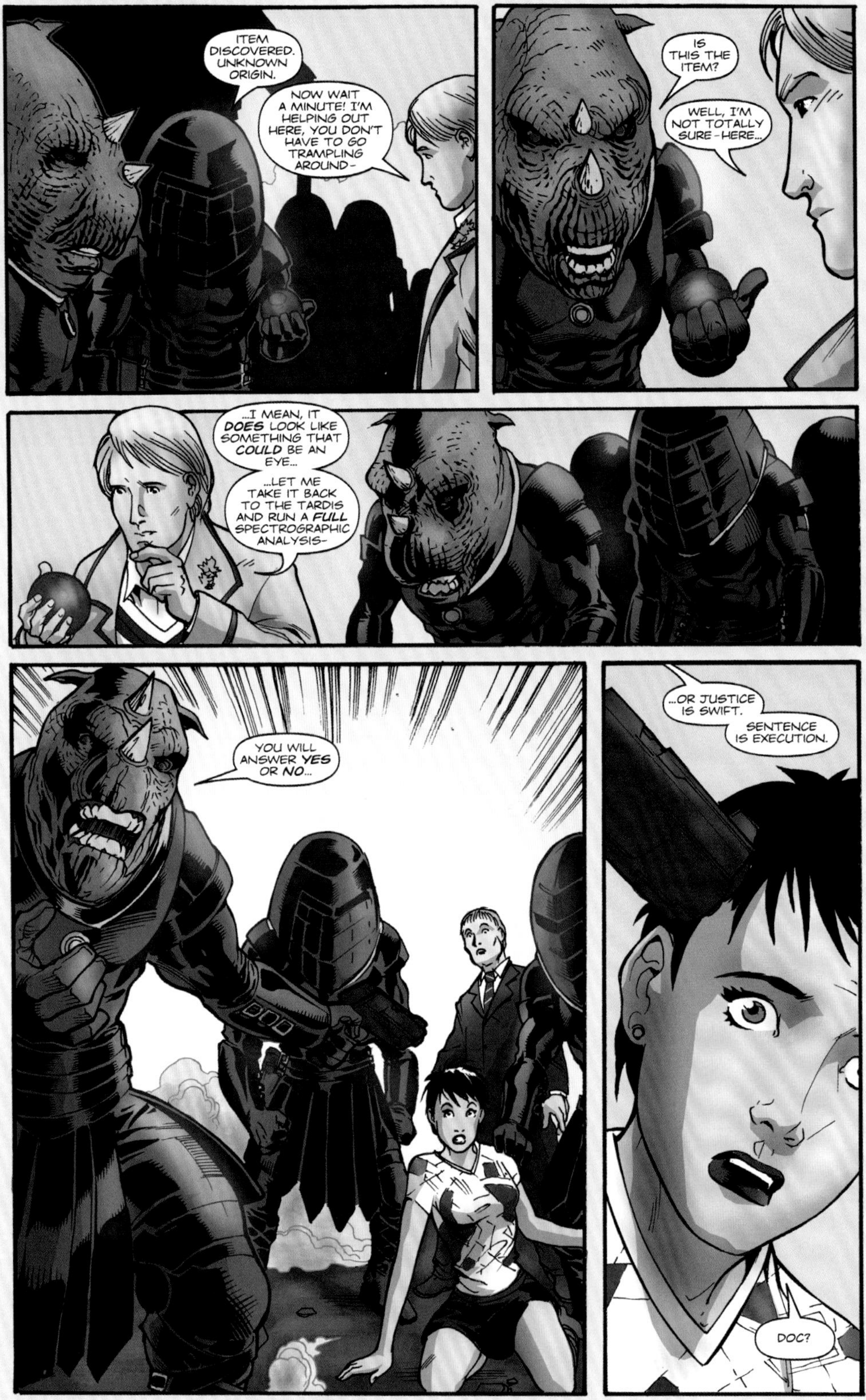
ITEM DISCOVERED. UNKNOWN ORIGIN.
NOW WAIT A MINUTE! I'M HELPING OUT HERE, YOU DON'T HAVE TO GO TRAMPLING AROUND-
IS THIS THE ITEM?
WELL, I'M NOT TOTALLY SURE-HERE...
...I MEAN, IT DOES LOOK LIKE SOMETHING THAT COULD BE AN EYE...
...LET ME TAKE IT BACK TO THE TARDIS AND RUN A FULL SPECTROGRAPHIC ANALYSIS-
YOU WILL ANSWER YES OR NO...
...OR JUSTICE IS SWIFT.
SENTENCE IS EXECUTION.
DOC?

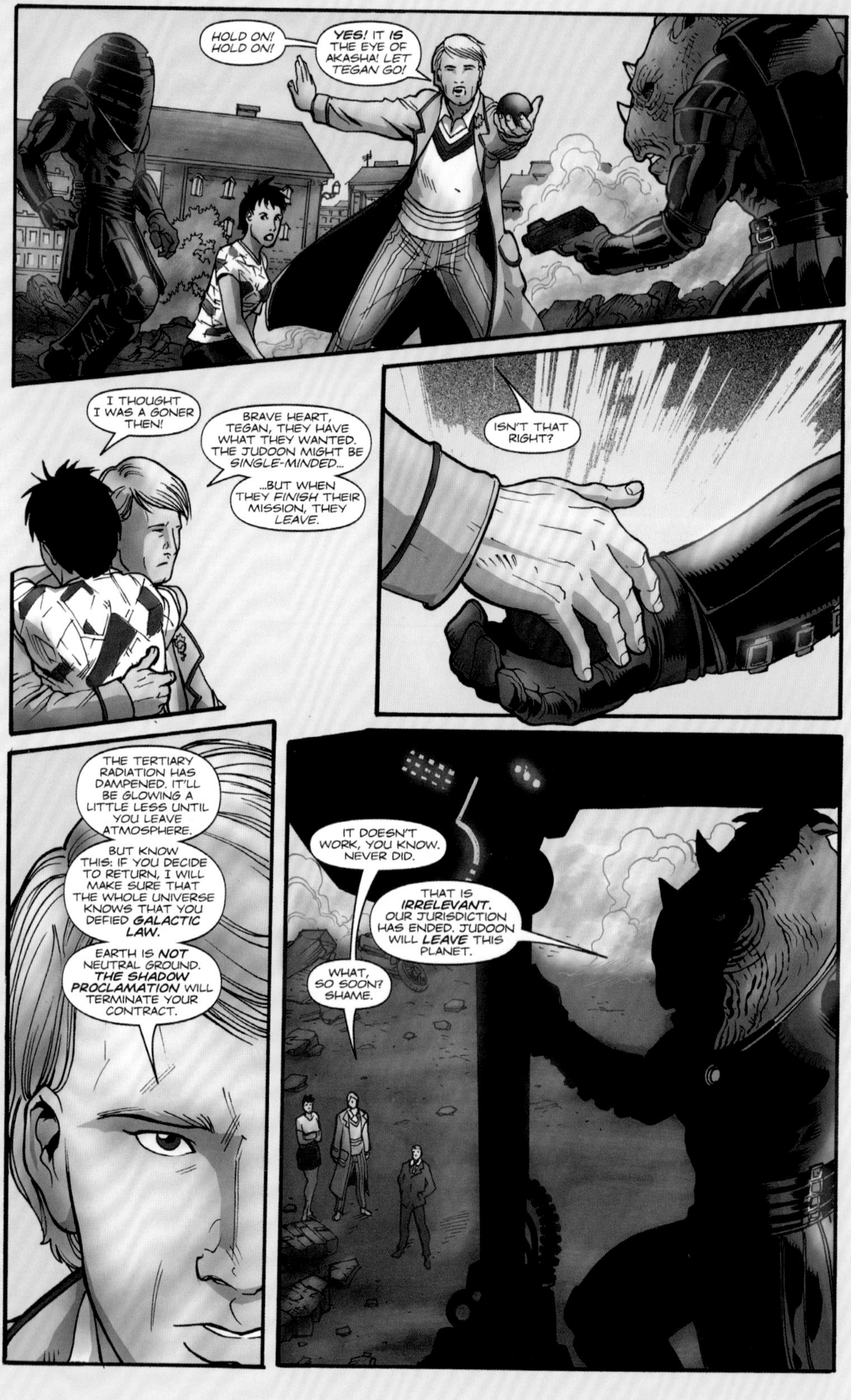
HOLD ON! HOLD ON!
YES! IT IS THE EYE OF AKASHA! LET TEGAN GO!
I THOUGHT I WAS A GONER THEN!
BRAVE HEART, TEGAN, THEY HAVE WHAT THEY WANTED. THE JUDOON MIGHT BE SINGLE-MINDED...
...BUT WHEN THEY FINISH THEIR MISSION, THEY LEAVE.
ISN'T THAT RIGHT?
THE TERTIARY RADIATION HAS DAMPENED. IT'LL BE GLOWING A LITTLE LESS UNTIL YOU LEAVE ATMOSPHERE.
BUT KNOW THIS: IF YOU DECIDE TO RETURN, I WILL MAKE SURE THAT THE WHOLE UNIVERSE KNOWS THAT YOU DEFIED GALACTIC LAW.
EARTH IS NOT NEUTRAL GROUND. THE SHADOW PROCLAMATION WILL TERMINATE YOUR CONTRACT.
IT DOESN'T WORK, YOU KNOW. NEVER DID.
THAT IS IRRELEVANT. OUR JURISDICTION HAS ENDED. JUDOON WILL LEAVE THIS PLANET.
WHAT, SO SOON? SHAME.

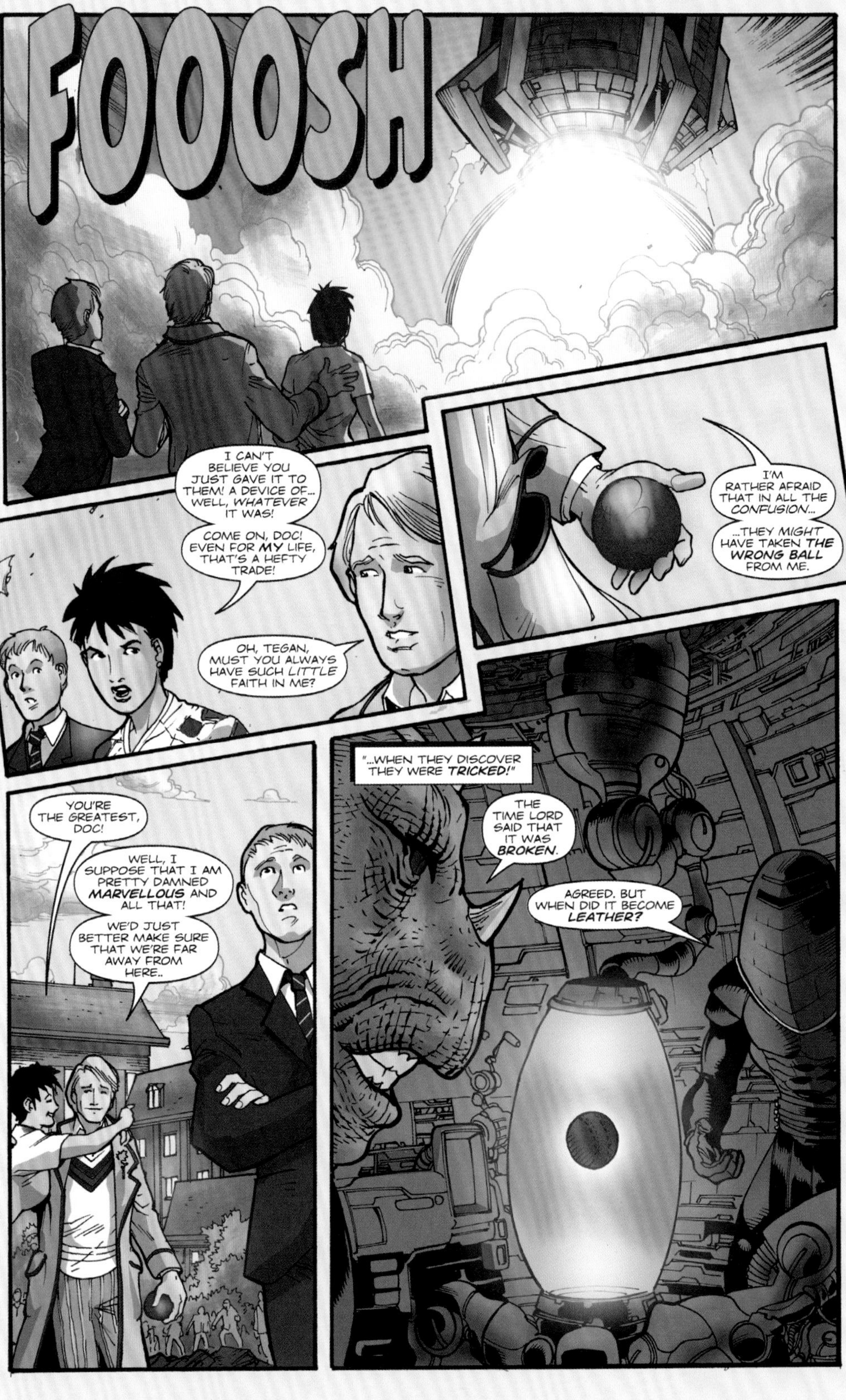
FOOOSH
I CAN'T BELIEVE YOU JUST GAVE IT TO THEM! A DEVICE OF... WELL, WHATEVER IT WAS!
COME ON, DOC! EVEN FOR MY LIFE, THAT'S A HEFTY TRADE!
OH, TEGAN, MUST YOU ALWAYS HAVE SUCH LITTLE FAITH IN ME?
I'M RATHER AFRAID THAT IN ALL THE CONFUSION...
...THEY MIGHT HAVE TAKEN THE WRONG BALL FROM ME.
YOU'RE THE GREATEST, DOC!
WELL, I SUPPOSE THAT I AM PRETTY DAMNED MARVELLOUS AND ALL THAT!
WE'D JUST BETTER MAKE SURE THAT WE'RE FAR AWAY FROM HERE..
"...WHEN THEY DISCOVER THEY WERE TRICKED!"
THE TIME LORD SAID THAT IT WAS BROKEN.
AGREED. BUT WHEN DID IT BECOME LEATHER?

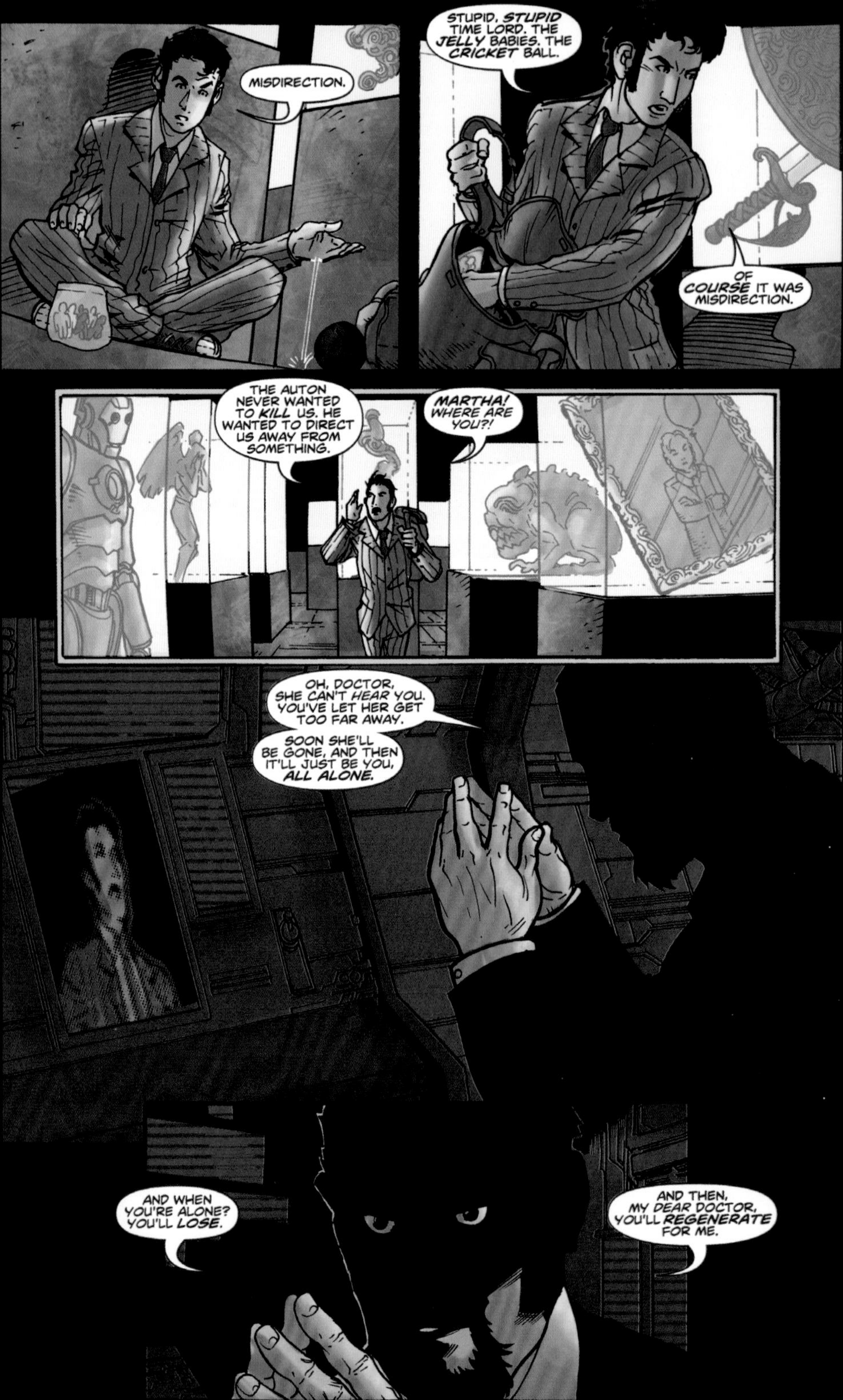
MISDIRECTION.
STUPID, STUPID TIME LORD. THE JELLY BABIES. THE CRICKET BALL.
OF COURSE IT WAS MISDIRECTION.
THE AUTON NEVER WANTED TO KILL US. HE WANTED TO DIRECT US AWAY FROM SOMETHING.
MARTHA! WHERE ARE YOU?!
OH, DOCTOR, SHE CAN'T HEAR YOU. YOU'VE LET HER GET TOO FAR AWAY.
SOON SHE'LL BE GONE, AND THEN IT'LL JUST BE YOU, ALL ALONE.
AND WHEN YOU'RE ALONE? YOU'LL LOSE.
AND THEN, MY DEAR DOCTOR, YOU'LL REGENERATE FOR ME.

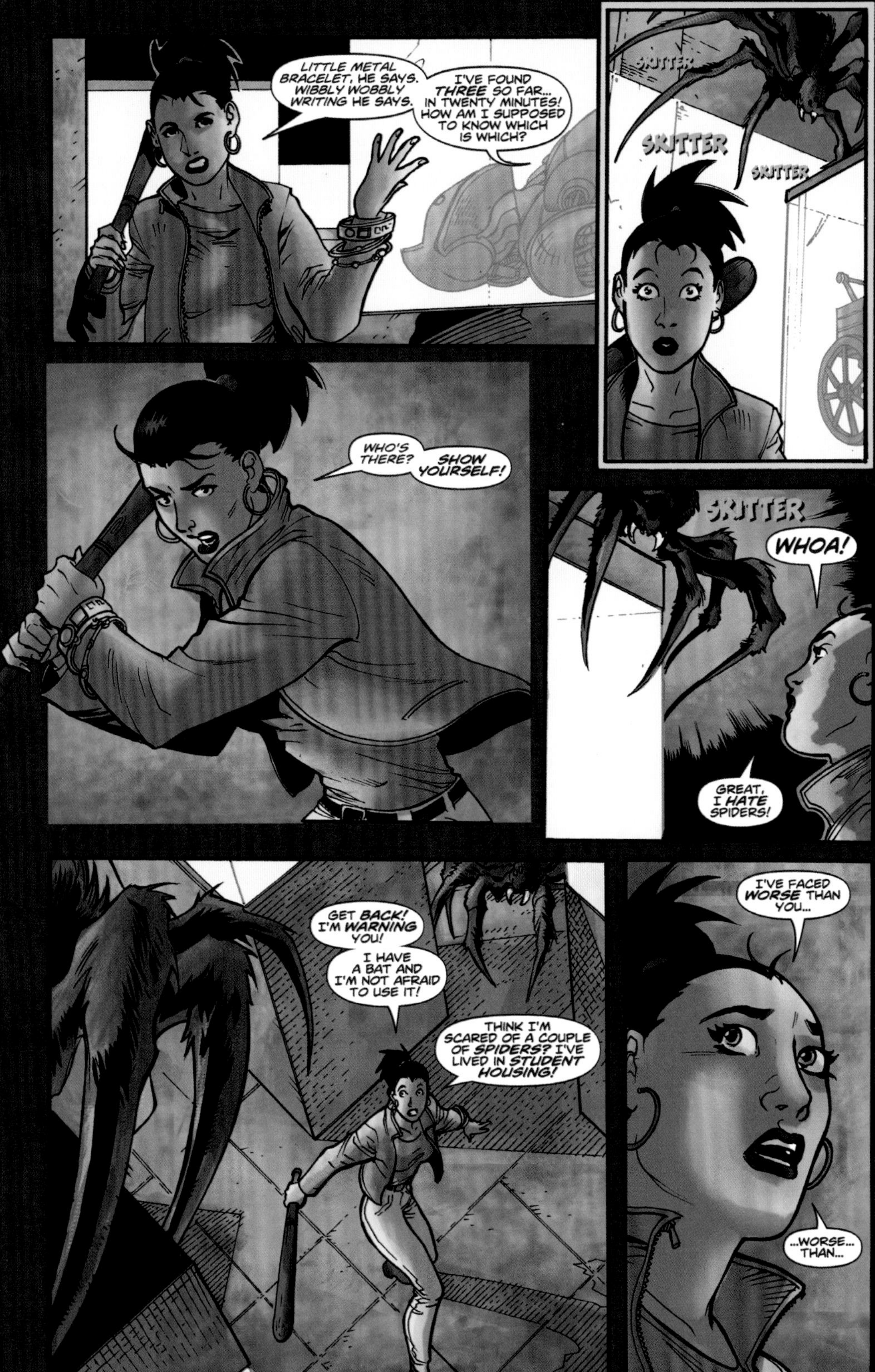
LITTLE METAL BRACELET, HE SAYS. WIBBLY WOBBLY WRITING HE SAYS.
I'VE FOUND THREE SO FAR... IN TWENTY MINUTES! HOW AM I SUPPOSED TO KNOW WHICH IS WHICH?
SKITTER
SKITTER
SKITTER
WHO'S THERE? SHOW YOURSELF!
SKITTER
WHOA!
GREAT, I HATE SPIDERS!
GET BACK! I'M WARNING YOU!
I HAVE A BAT AND I'M NOT AFRAID TO USE IT!
THINK I'M SCARED OF A COUPLE OF SPIDERS? I'VE LIVED IN STUDENT HOUSING!
I'VE FACED WORSE THAN YOU...
...WORSE... THAN...

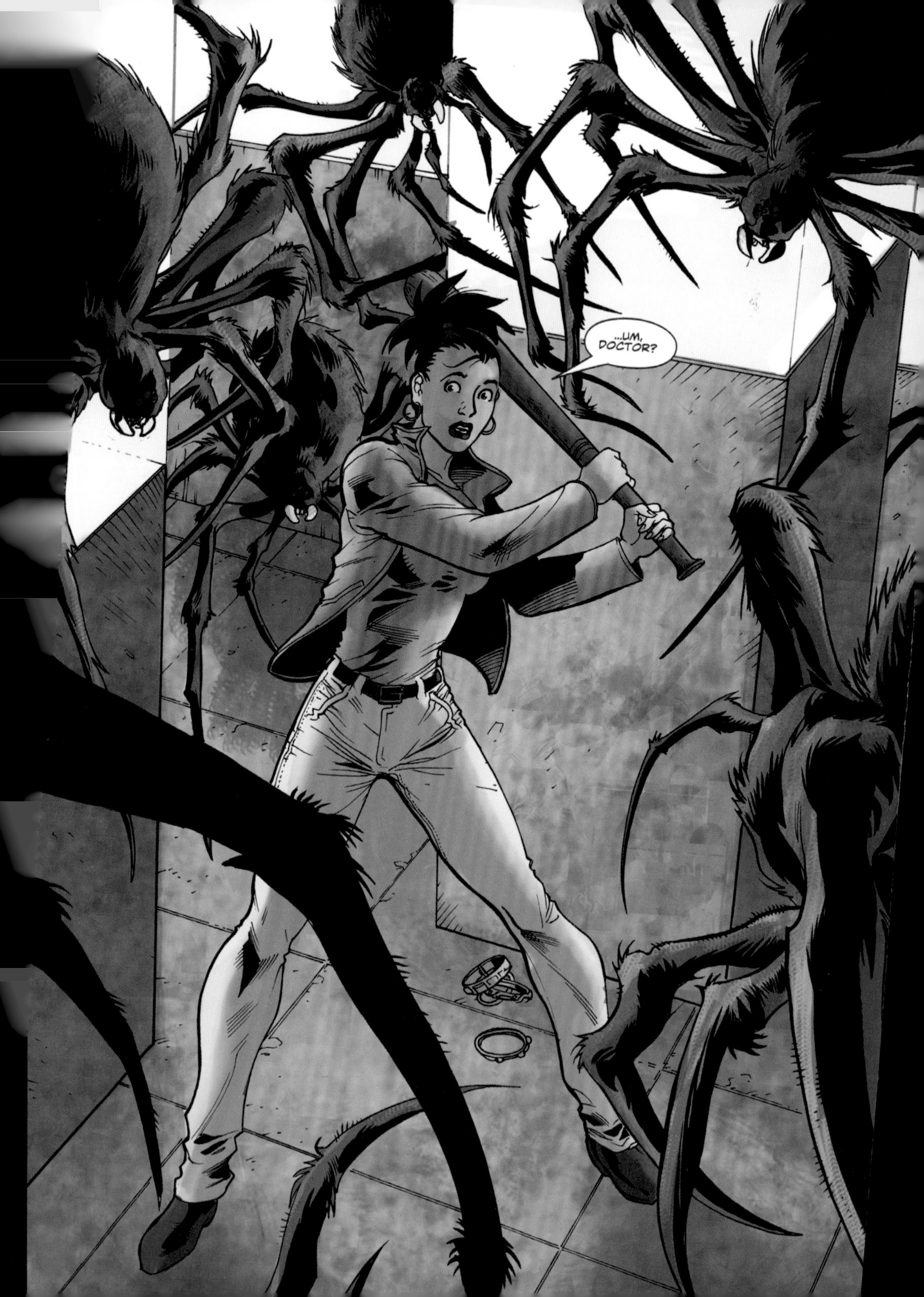
...UM, DOCTOR?

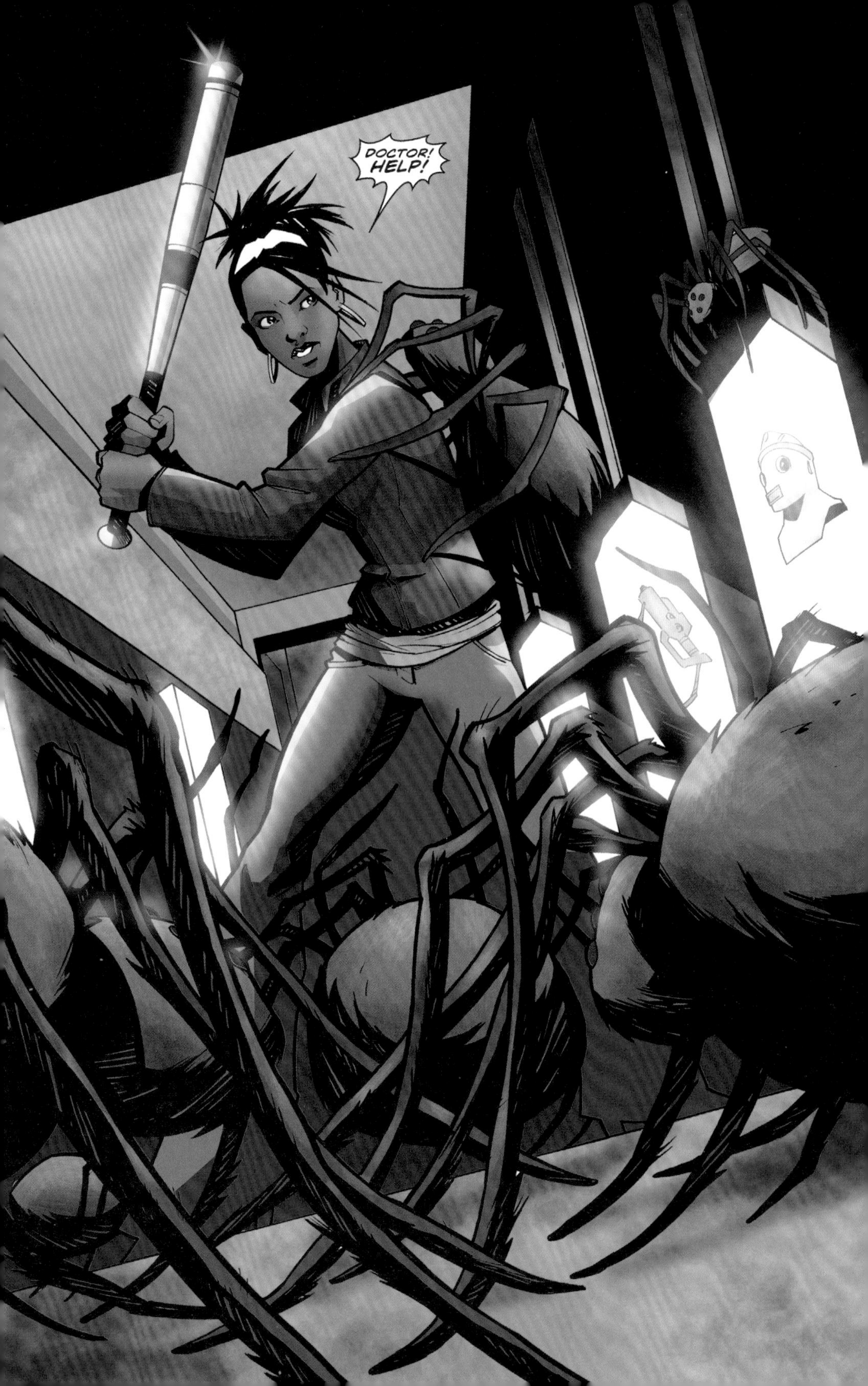
DOCTOR! HELP!

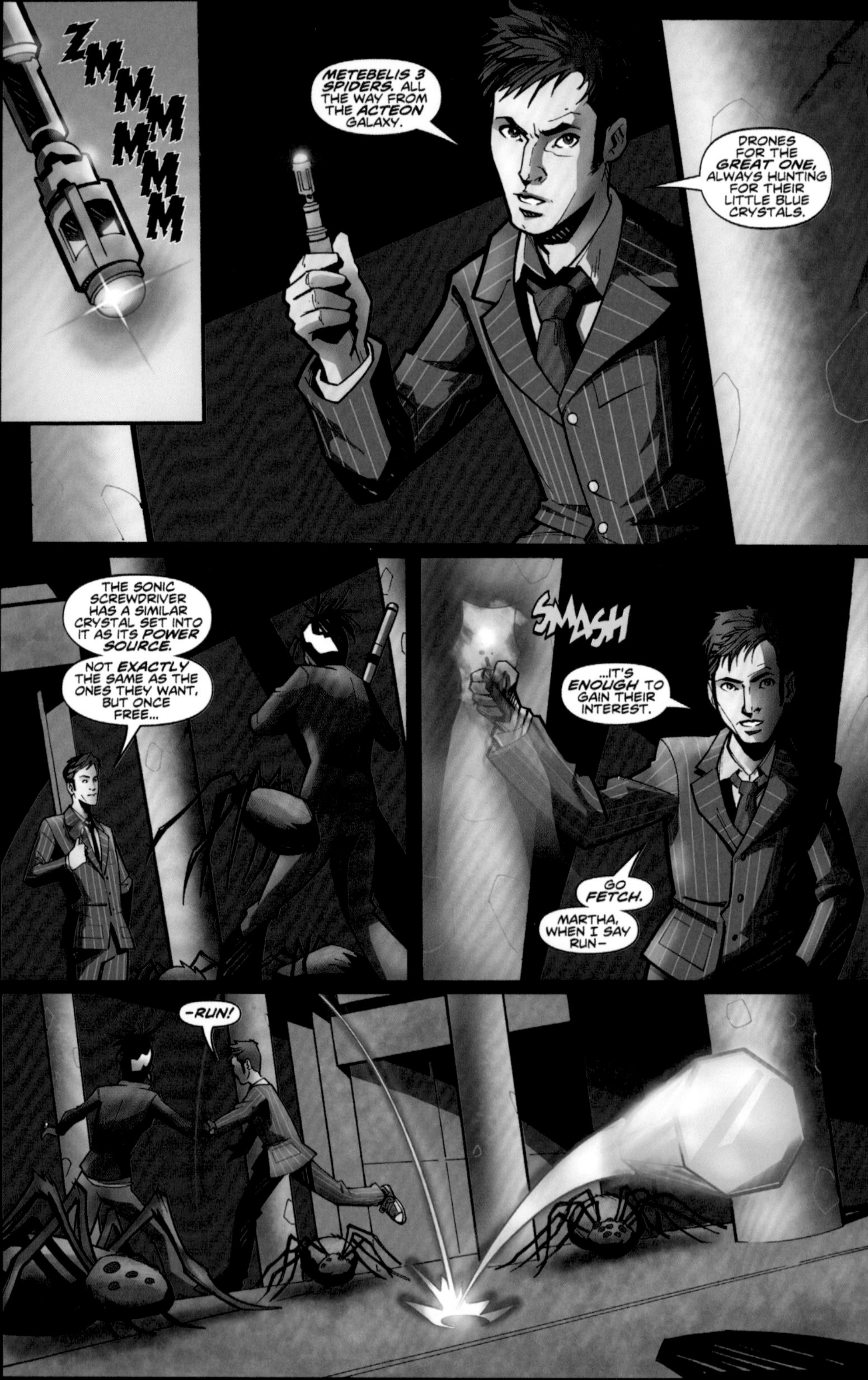
ZMMMMMMMM
METEBELIS 3 SPIDERS. ALL THE WAY FROM THE ACTEON GALAXY.
DRONES FOR THE GREAT ONE, ALWAYS HUNTING FOR THEIR LITTLE BLUE CRYSTALS.
THE SONIC SCREWDRIVER HAS A SIMILAR CRYSTAL SET INTO IT AS ITS POWER SOURCE.
NOT EXACTLY THE SAME AS THE ONES THEY WANT, BUT ONCE FREE...
SMASH
...IT'S ENOUGH TO GAIN THEIR INTEREST.
GO FETCH.
MARTHA, WHEN I SAY RUN–
–RUN!

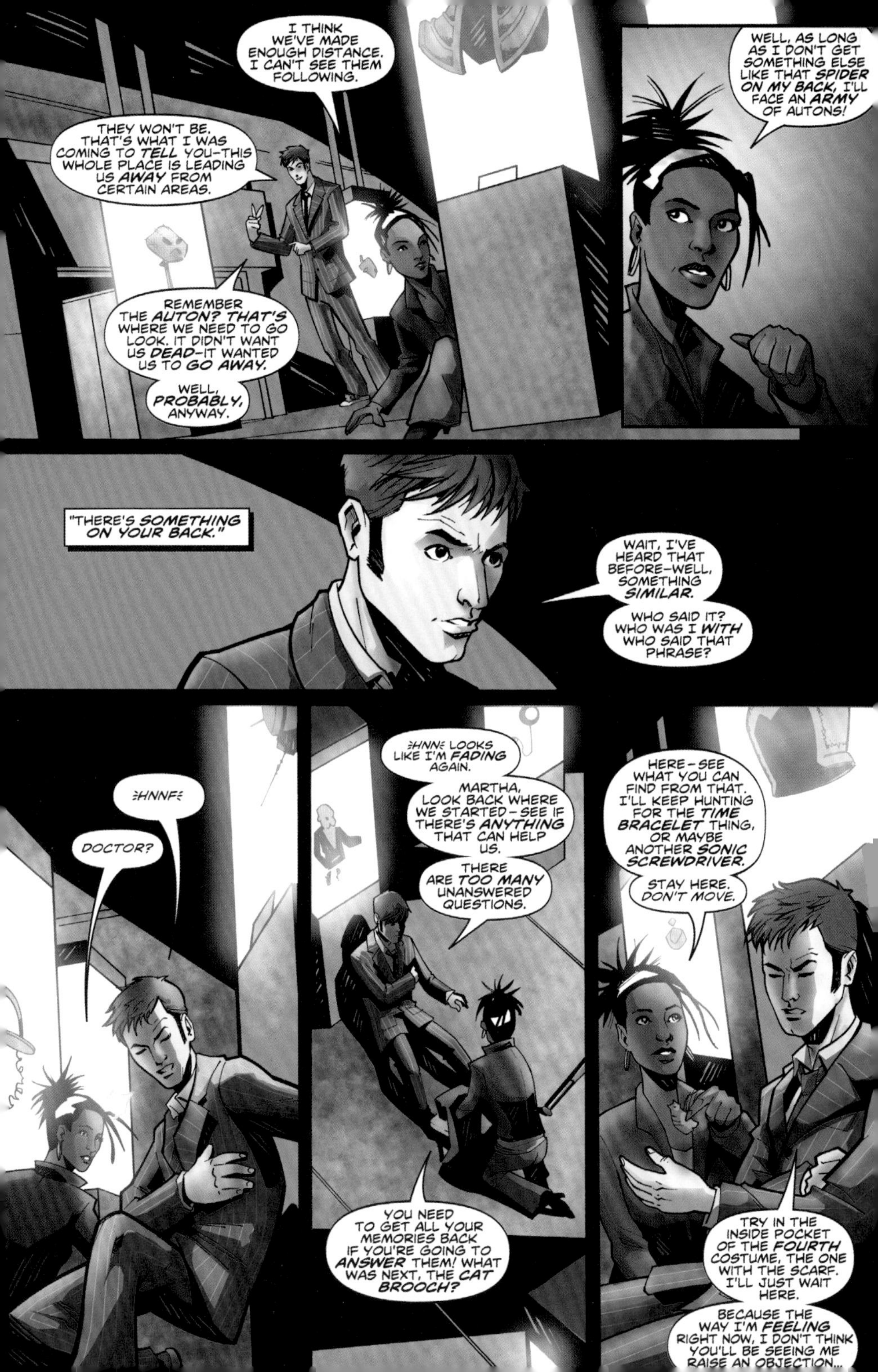
I THINK WE'VE MADE ENOUGH DISTANCE. I CAN'T SEE THEM FOLLOWING.
THEY WON'T BE. THAT'S WHAT I WAS COMING TO TELL YOU–THIS WHOLE PLACE IS LEADING US AWAY FROM CERTAIN AREAS.
REMEMBER THE AUTON? THAT'S WHERE WE NEED TO GO LOOK. IT DIDN'T WANT US DEAD–IT WANTED US TO GO AWAY.
WELL, PROBABLY, ANYWAY.
WELL, AS LONG AS I DON'T GET SOMETHING ELSE LIKE THAT SPIDER ON MY BACK, I'LL FACE AN ARMY OF AUTONS!
"THERE'S SOMETHING ON YOUR BACK."
WAIT, I'VE HEARD THAT BEFORE–WELL, SOMETHING SIMILAR.
WHO SAID IT? WHO WAS I WITH WHO SAID THAT PHRASE?
HNNF
DOCTOR?
HNN LOOKS LIKE I'M FADING AGAIN.
MARTHA, LOOK BACK WHERE WE STARTED–SEE IF THERE'S ANYTHING THAT CAN HELP US.
THERE ARE TOO MANY UNANSWERED QUESTIONS.
YOU NEED TO GET ALL YOUR MEMORIES BACK IF YOU'RE GOING TO ANSWER THEM! WHAT WAS NEXT, THE CAT BROOCH?
HERE–SEE WHAT YOU CAN FIND FROM THAT. I'LL KEEP HUNTING FOR THE TIME BRACELET THING, OR MAYBE ANOTHER SONIC SCREWDRIVER.
STAY HERE. DON'T MOVE.
TRY IN THE INSIDE POCKET OF THE FOURTH COSTUME, THE ONE WITH THE SCARF. I'LL JUST WAIT HERE.
BECAUSE THE WAY I'M FEELING RIGHT NOW, I DON'T THINK YOU'LL BE SEEING ME RAISE AN OBJECTION...

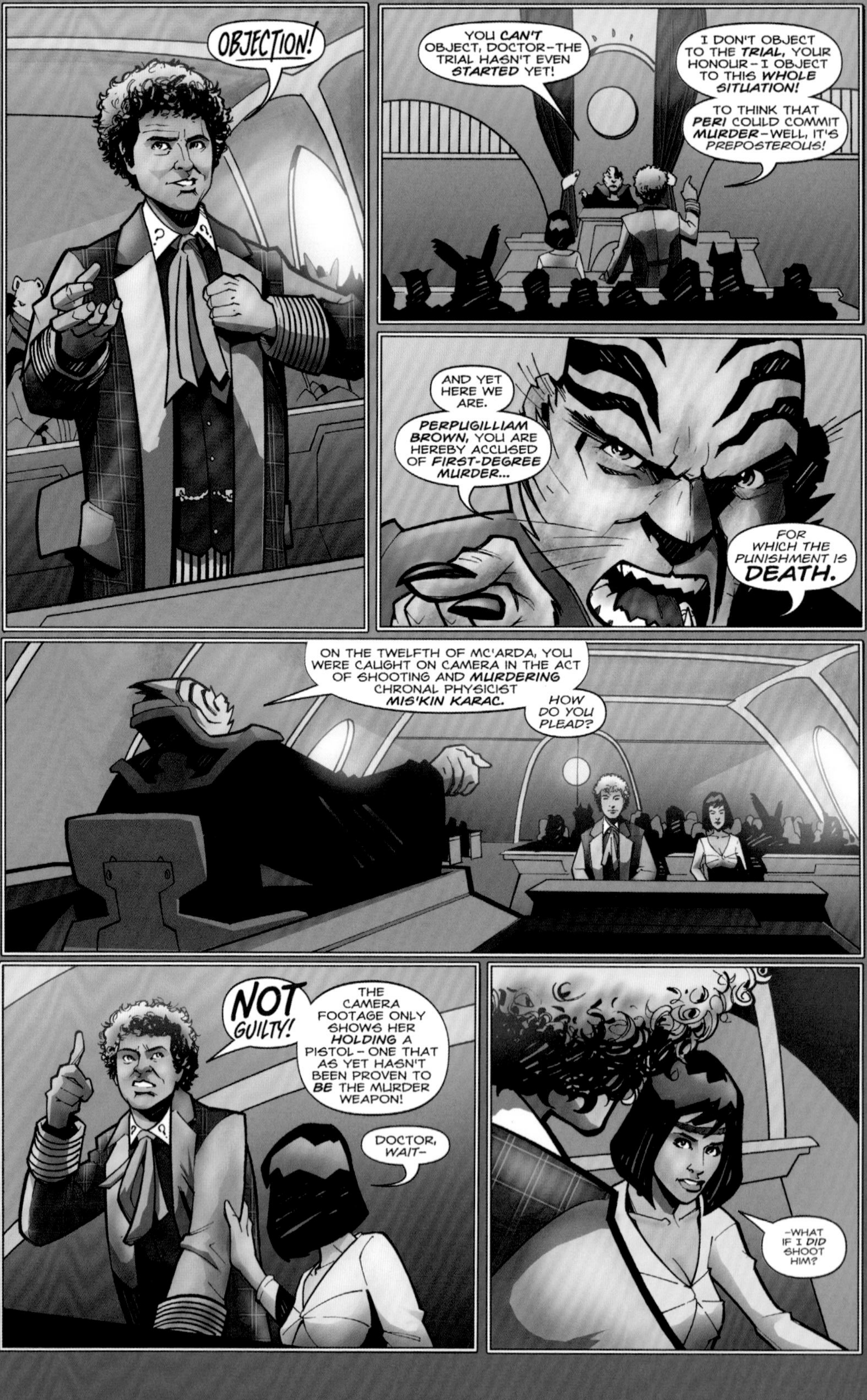
OBJECTION!
YOU CAN'T OBJECT, DOCTOR–THE TRIAL HASN'T EVEN STARTED YET!
I DON'T OBJECT TO THE TRIAL, YOUR HONOUR–I OBJECT TO THIS WHOLE SITUATION!
TO THINK THAT PERI COULD COMMIT MURDER–WELL, IT'S PREPOSTEROUS!
AND YET HERE WE ARE.
PERPUGILLIAM BROWN, YOU ARE HEREBY ACCUSED OF FIRST-DEGREE MURDER...
FOR WHICH THE PUNISHMENT IS DEATH.
ON THE TWELFTH OF MC'ARDA, YOU WERE CAUGHT ON CAMERA IN THE ACT OF SHOOTING AND MURDERING CHRONAL PHYSICIST MIS'KIN KARAC.
HOW DO YOU PLEAD?
NOT GUILTY!
THE CAMERA FOOTAGE ONLY SHOWS HER HOLDING A PISTOL – ONE THAT AS YET HASN'T BEEN PROVEN TO BE THE MURDER WEAPON!
DOCTOR, WAIT–
–WHAT IF I DID SHOOT HIM?

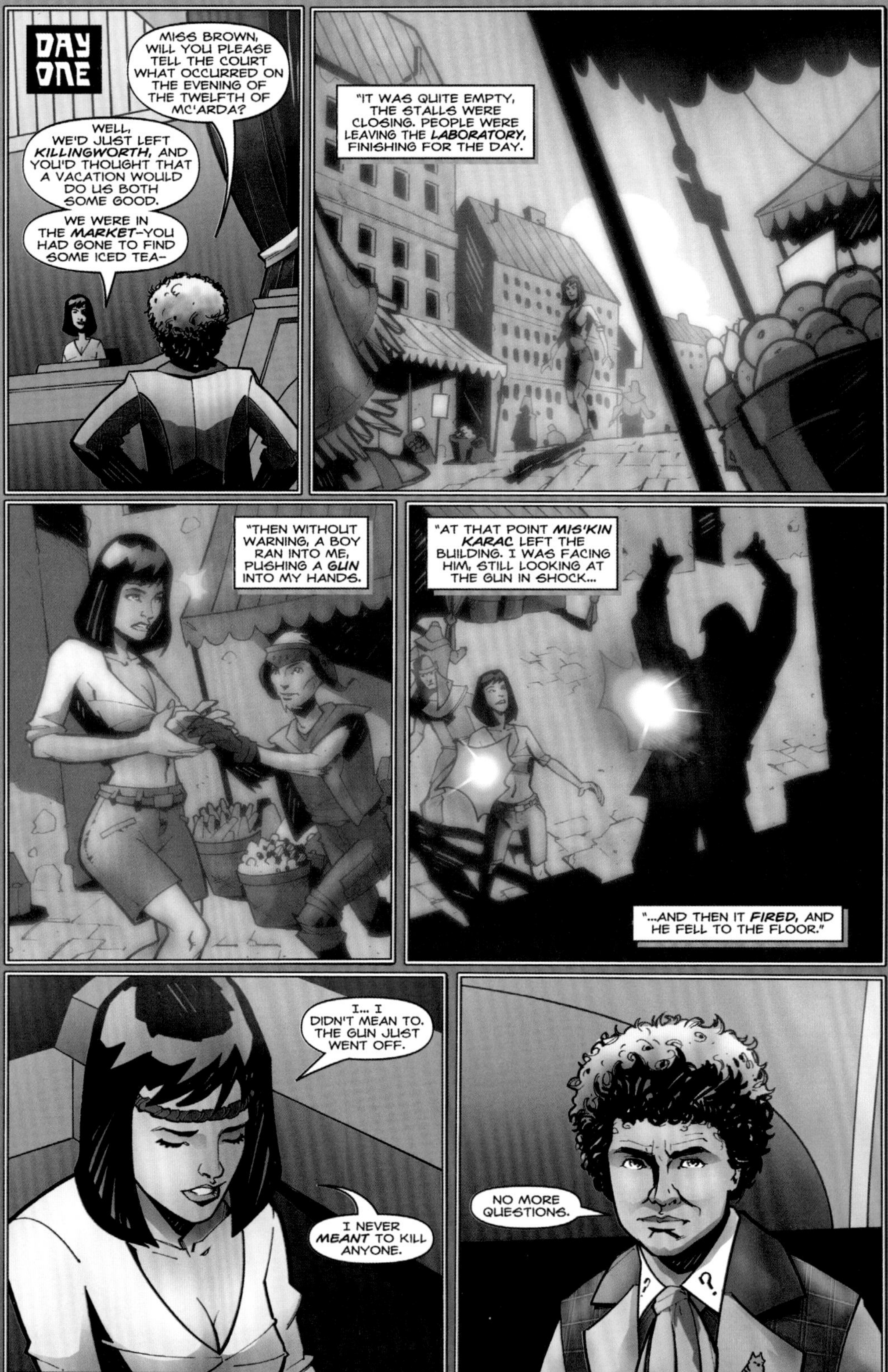

DAY ONE
MISS BROWN, WILL YOU PLEASE TELL THE COURT WHAT OCCURRED ON THE EVENING OF THE TWELFTH OF MC'ARDA?
WELL, WE'D JUST LEFT KILLINGWORTH, AND YOU'D THOUGHT THAT A VACATION WOULD DO US BOTH SOME GOOD.
WE WERE IN THE MARKET–YOU HAD GONE TO FIND SOME ICED TEA–
"IT WAS QUITE EMPTY, THE STALLS WERE CLOSING. PEOPLE WERE LEAVING THE LABORATORY, FINISHING FOR THE DAY.
"THEN WITHOUT WARNING, A BOY RAN INTO ME, PUSHING A GUN INTO MY HANDS.
"AT THAT POINT MIS'KIN KARAC LEFT THE BUILDING. I WAS FACING HIM, STILL LOOKING AT THE GUN IN SHOCK...
"...AND THEN IT FIRED, AND HE FELL TO THE FLOOR."
I... I DIDN'T MEAN TO. THE GUN JUST WENT OFF.
I NEVER MEANT TO KILL ANYONE.
NO MORE QUESTIONS.

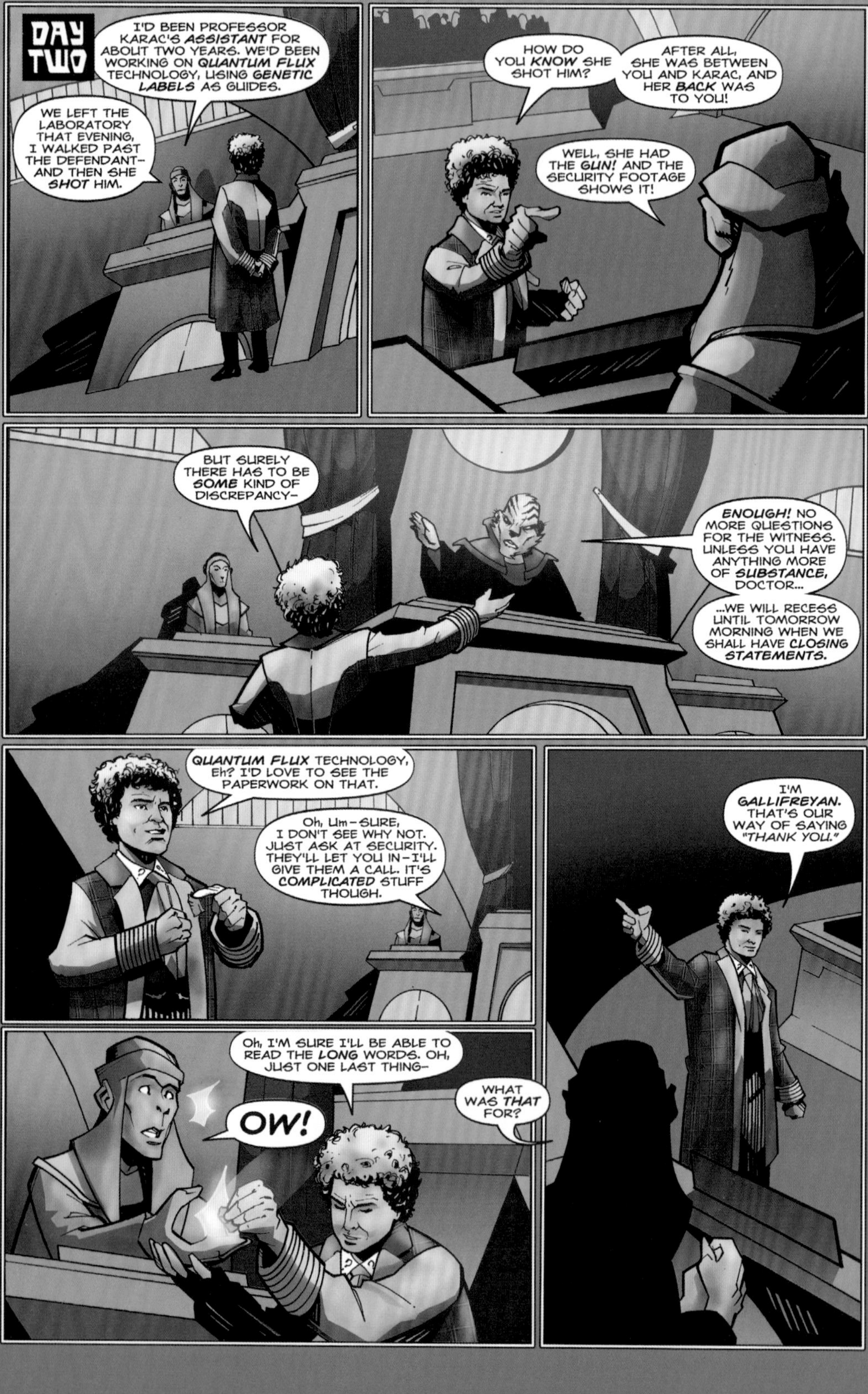
DAY TWO
I'D BEEN PROFESSOR KARAC'S ASSISTANT FOR ABOUT TWO YEARS. WE'D BEEN WORKING ON QUANTUM FLUX TECHNOLOGY, USING GENETIC LABELS AS GUIDES.
WE LEFT THE LABORATORY THAT EVENING, I WALKED PAST THE DEFENDANT– AND THEN SHE SHOT HIM.
HOW DO YOU KNOW SHE SHOT HIM?
AFTER ALL, SHE WAS BETWEEN YOU AND KARAC, AND HER BACK WAS TO YOU!
WELL, SHE HAD THE GUN! AND THE SECURITY FOOTAGE SHOWS IT!
BUT SURELY THERE HAS TO BE SOME KIND OF DISCREPANCY–
ENOUGH! NO MORE QUESTIONS FOR THE WITNESS. UNLESS YOU HAVE ANYTHING MORE OF SUBSTANCE, DOCTOR...
...WE WILL RECESS UNTIL TOMORROW MORNING WHEN WE SHALL HAVE CLOSING STATEMENTS.
QUANTUM FLUX TECHNOLOGY, EH? I'D LOVE TO SEE THE PAPERWORK ON THAT.
OH, UM–SURE, I DON'T SEE WHY NOT. JUST ASK AT SECURITY. THEY'LL LET YOU IN–I'LL GIVE THEM A CALL. IT'S COMPLICATED STUFF THOUGH.
OH, I'M SURE I'LL BE ABLE TO READ THE LONG WORDS. OH, JUST ONE LAST THING–
OW!
WHAT WAS THAT FOR?
I'M GALLIFREYAN. THAT'S OUR WAY OF SAYING "THANK YOU."

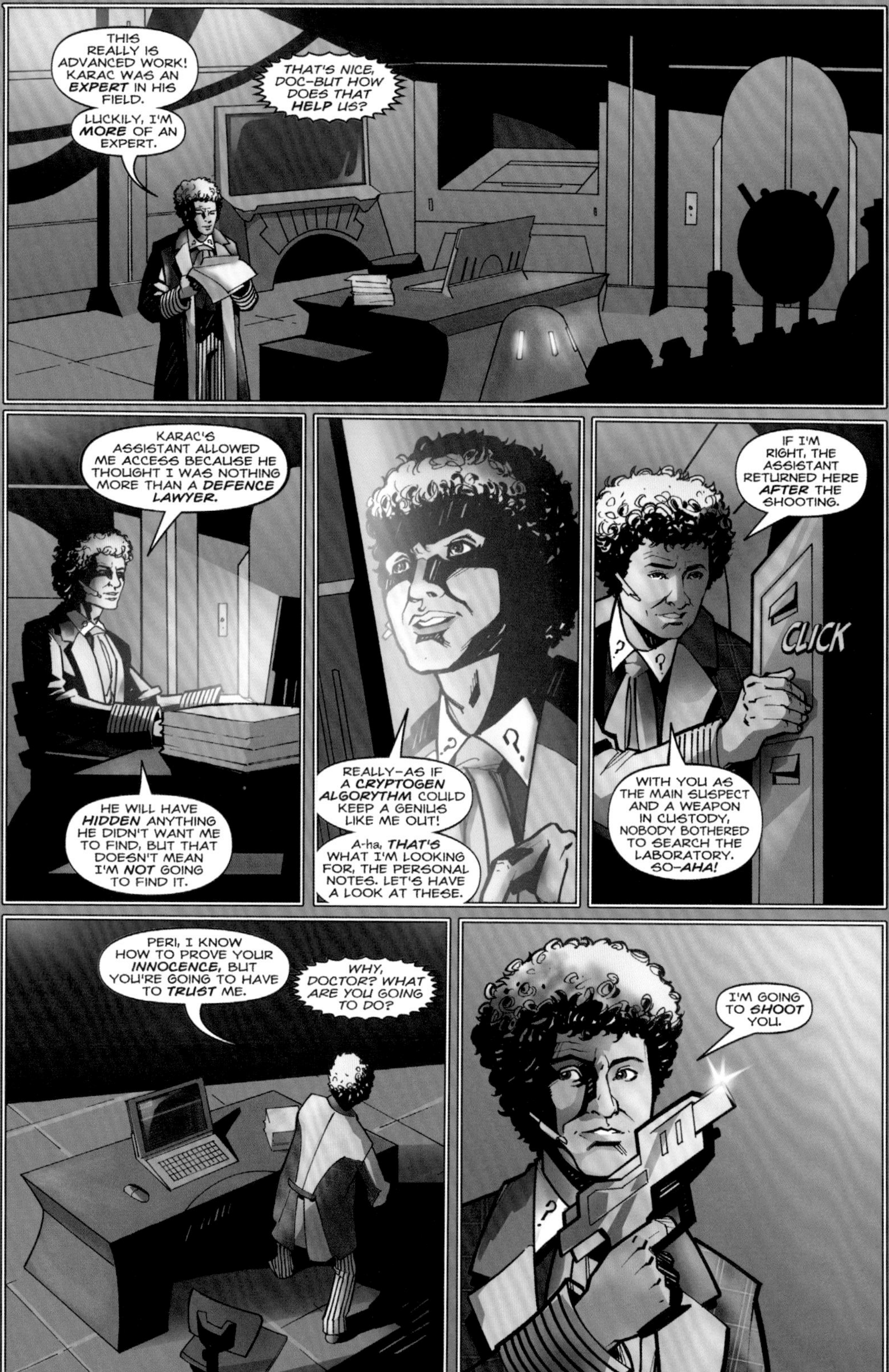
THIS REALLY IS ADVANCED WORK! KARAC WAS AN EXPERT IN HIS FIELD.
LUCKILY, I'M MORE OF AN EXPERT.
THAT'S NICE, DOC—BUT HOW DOES THAT HELP US?
KARAC'S ASSISTANT ALLOWED ME ACCESS BECAUSE HE THOUGHT I WAS NOTHING MORE THAN A DEFENCE LAWYER.
HE WILL HAVE HIDDEN ANYTHING HE DIDN'T WANT ME TO FIND, BUT THAT DOESN'T MEAN I'M NOT GOING TO FIND IT.
REALLY—AS IF A CRYPTOGEN ALGORYTHM COULD KEEP A GENIUS LIKE ME OUT!
A-ha, THAT'S WHAT I'M LOOKING FOR, THE PERSONAL NOTES. LET'S HAVE A LOOK AT THESE.
IF I'M RIGHT, THE ASSISTANT RETURNED HERE AFTER THE SHOOTING.
CLICK
WITH YOU AS THE MAIN SUSPECT AND A WEAPON IN CUSTODY, NOBODY BOTHERED TO SEARCH THE LABORATORY. SO—AHA!
PERI, I KNOW HOW TO PROVE YOUR INNOCENCE, BUT YOU'RE GOING TO HAVE TO TRUST ME.
WHY, DOCTOR? WHAT ARE YOU GOING TO DO?
I'M GOING TO SHOOT YOU.

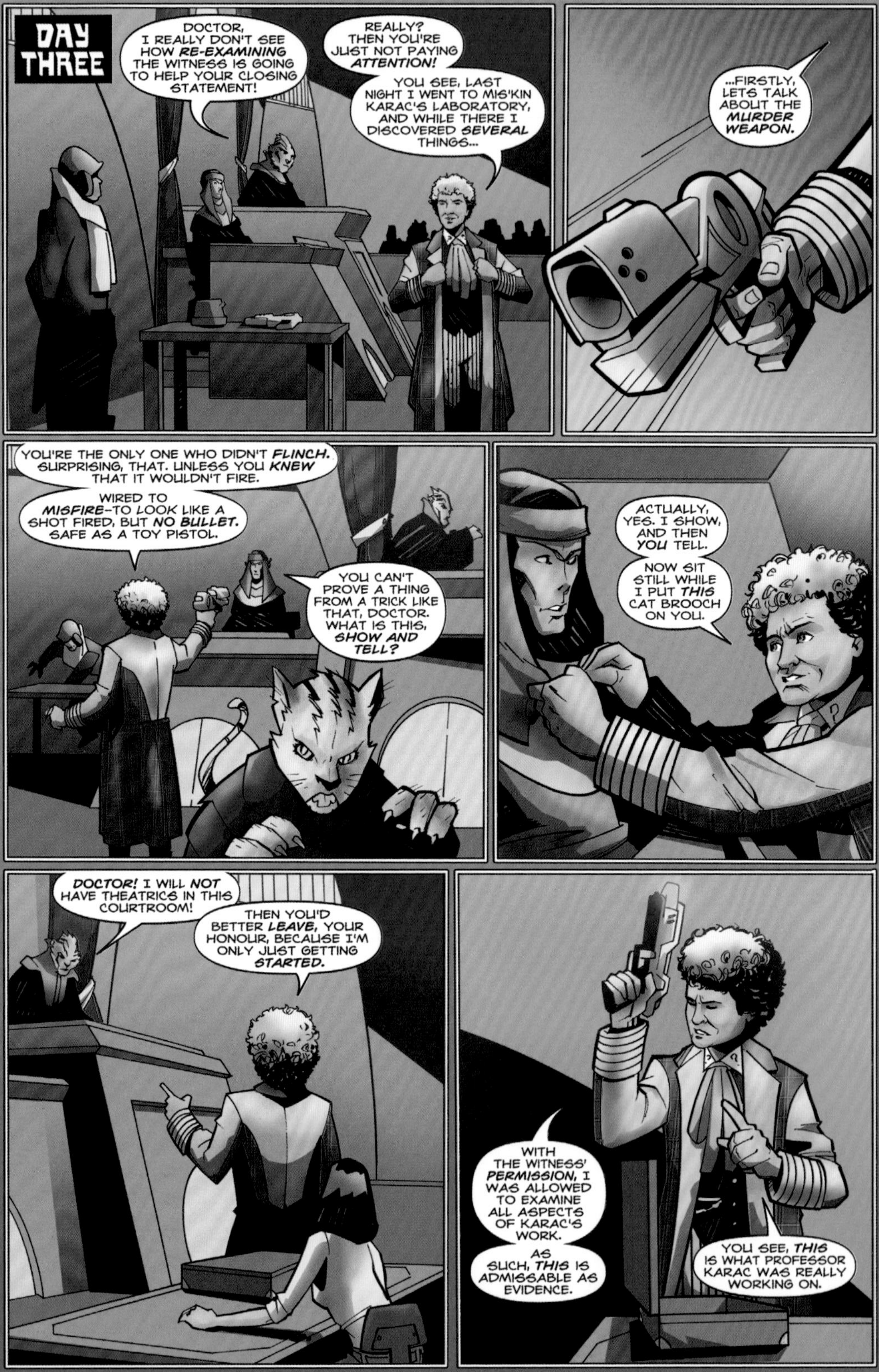
DAY THREE
DOCTOR, I REALLY DON'T SEE HOW RE-EXAMINING THE WITNESS IS GOING TO HELP YOUR CLOSING STATEMENT!
REALLY? THEN YOU'RE JUST NOT PAYING ATTENTION!
YOU SEE, LAST NIGHT I WENT TO MIS'KIN KARAC'S LABORATORY, AND WHILE THERE I DISCOVERED SEVERAL THINGS...
...FIRSTLY, LETS TALK ABOUT THE MURDER WEAPON.
YOU'RE THE ONLY ONE WHO DIDN'T FLINCH. SURPRISING, THAT. UNLESS YOU KNEW THAT IT WOULDN'T FIRE.
WIRED TO MISFIRE–TO LOOK LIKE A SHOT FIRED, BUT NO BULLET. SAFE AS A TOY PISTOL.
YOU CAN'T PROVE A THING FROM A TRICK LIKE THAT, DOCTOR. WHAT IS THIS, SHOW AND TELL?
ACTUALLY, YES. I SHOW, AND THEN YOU TELL.
NOW SIT STILL WHILE I PUT THIS CAT BROOCH ON YOU.
DOCTOR! I WILL NOT HAVE THEATRICS IN THIS COURTROOM!
THEN YOU'D BETTER LEAVE, YOUR HONOUR, BECAUSE I'M ONLY JUST GETTING STARTED.
WITH THE WITNESS' PERMISSION, I WAS ALLOWED TO EXAMINE ALL ASPECTS OF KARAC'S WORK.
AS SUCH, THIS IS ADMISSABLE AS EVIDENCE.
YOU SEE, THIS IS WHAT PROFESSOR KARAC WAS REALLY WORKING ON.

QUANTUM FLUX TECHNOLOGY IS THE ABILITY TO MAKE SOMETHING *INTANGIBLE* UNTIL IT'S NEEDED.

THIS GUN IS SATURATED IN *CHRONAL ENERGY.* SO WAS PROFESSOR KARAC'S *I.D. PASS,* WHICH THE BULLET HIT, DEAD CENTER.

Um, DOCTOR?

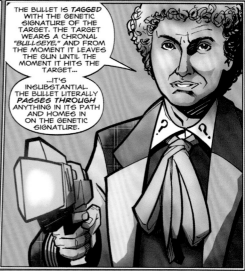

THE BULLET IS *TAGGED* WITH THE GENETIC SIGNATURE OF THE TARGET. THE TARGET WEARS A CHRONAL *"BULLSEYE,"* AND FROM THE MOMENT IT LEAVES THE GUN UNTIL THE MOMENT IT HITS THE TARGET...

...IT'S *INSUBSTANTIAL.* THE BULLET LITERALLY *PASSES THROUGH* ANYTHING IN ITS PATH AND HOMES IN ON THE GENETIC SIGNATURE.

THAT IS WHY YOU WERE *DIRECTLY BEHIND* PERI. YOU DIDN'T NEED A *CLEAR* VIEW—AND THE PATHOLOGISTS WOULD BELIEVE THAT THE ANGLE OF THE SHOT MATCHED HER GUN...

...A GUN THAT *YOU* GAVE HER.

THIS IS *INSANE!* WHAT YOU SUGGEST IS IN THE WORLD OF FANTASY! *NOBODY* CAN DO SUCH A THING!

IF YOU FIRE THAT GUN, ALL YOU DO IS *KILL YOUR FRIEND!*

REALLY? LET'S TEST THAT. YOU SEE THAT *CAT BROOCH* YOU WEAR? *DRENCHED* IN CHRONAL ENERGY, YOU KNOW.

AND ON IT? A DROP OF *BLOOD* THAT I TOOK FROM YOU YESTERDAY WHEN I PRICKED YOU. THE SAME GENETIC TAG THAT THIS BULLET HAS BEEN PRIMED TO *SEARCH* FOR.

BUT WHY WOULD YOU *CARE?* THIS ISN'T GOING TO WORK. I'LL JUST KILL *PERI,* AND THE COURT WAS GOING TO DO THAT ANYWAY.

SO... THREE, TWO—

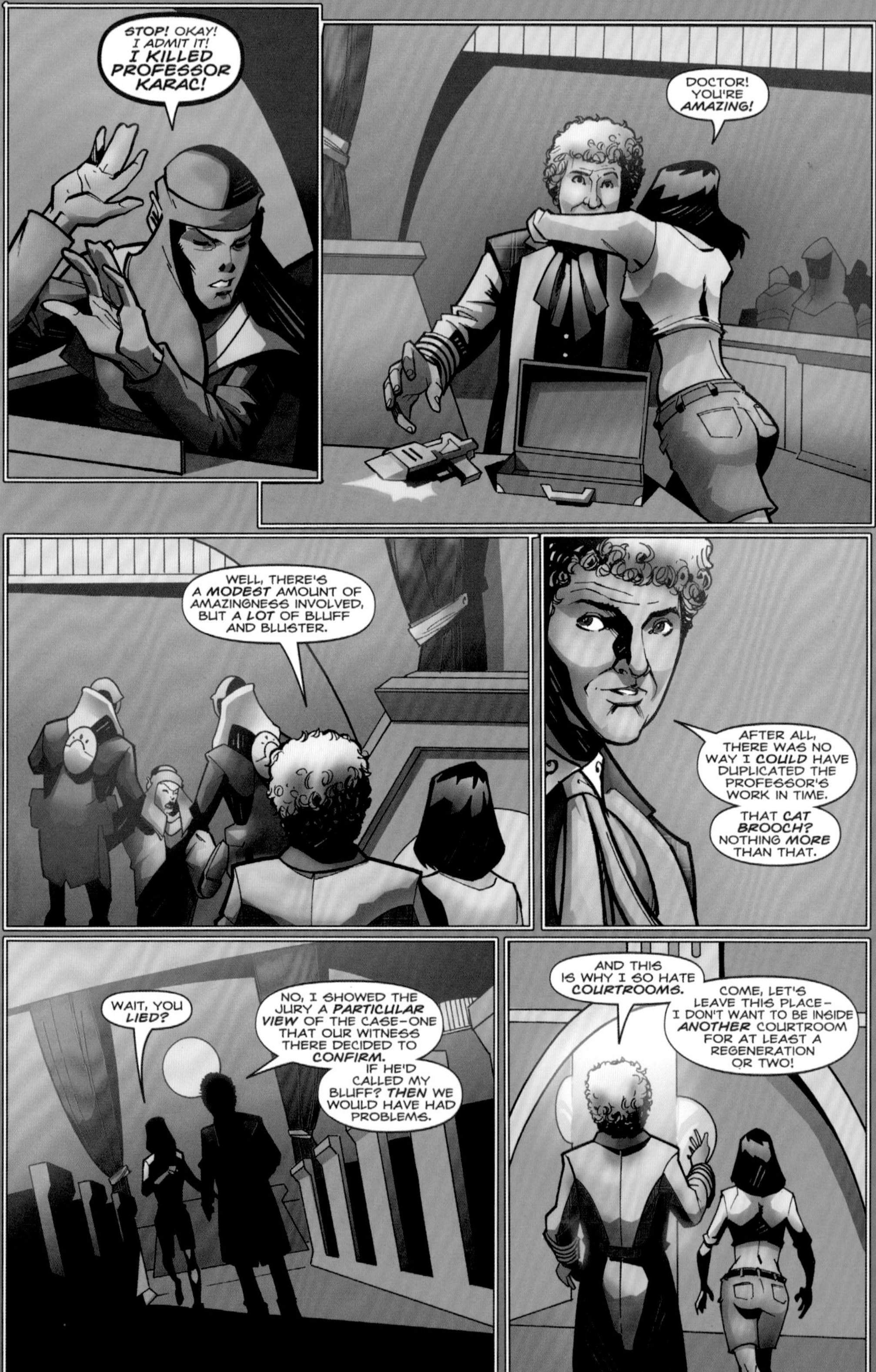
STOP! OKAY! I ADMIT IT! I KILLED PROFESSOR KARAC!
DOCTOR! YOU'RE AMAZING!
WELL, THERE'S A MODEST AMOUNT OF AMAZINGNESS INVOLVED, BUT A LOT OF BLUFF AND BLUSTER.
AFTER ALL, THERE WAS NO WAY I COULD HAVE DUPLICATED THE PROFESSOR'S WORK IN TIME.
THAT CAT BROOCH? NOTHING MORE THAN THAT.
WAIT, YOU LIED?
NO, I SHOWED THE JURY A PARTICULAR VIEW OF THE CASE–ONE THAT OUR WITNESS THERE DECIDED TO CONFIRM.
IF HE'D CALLED MY BLUFF? THEN WE WOULD HAVE HAD PROBLEMS.
AND THIS IS WHY I SO HATE COURTROOMS.
COME, LET'S LEAVE THIS PLACE– I DON'T WANT TO BE INSIDE ANOTHER COURTROOM FOR AT LEAST A REGENERATION OR TWO!

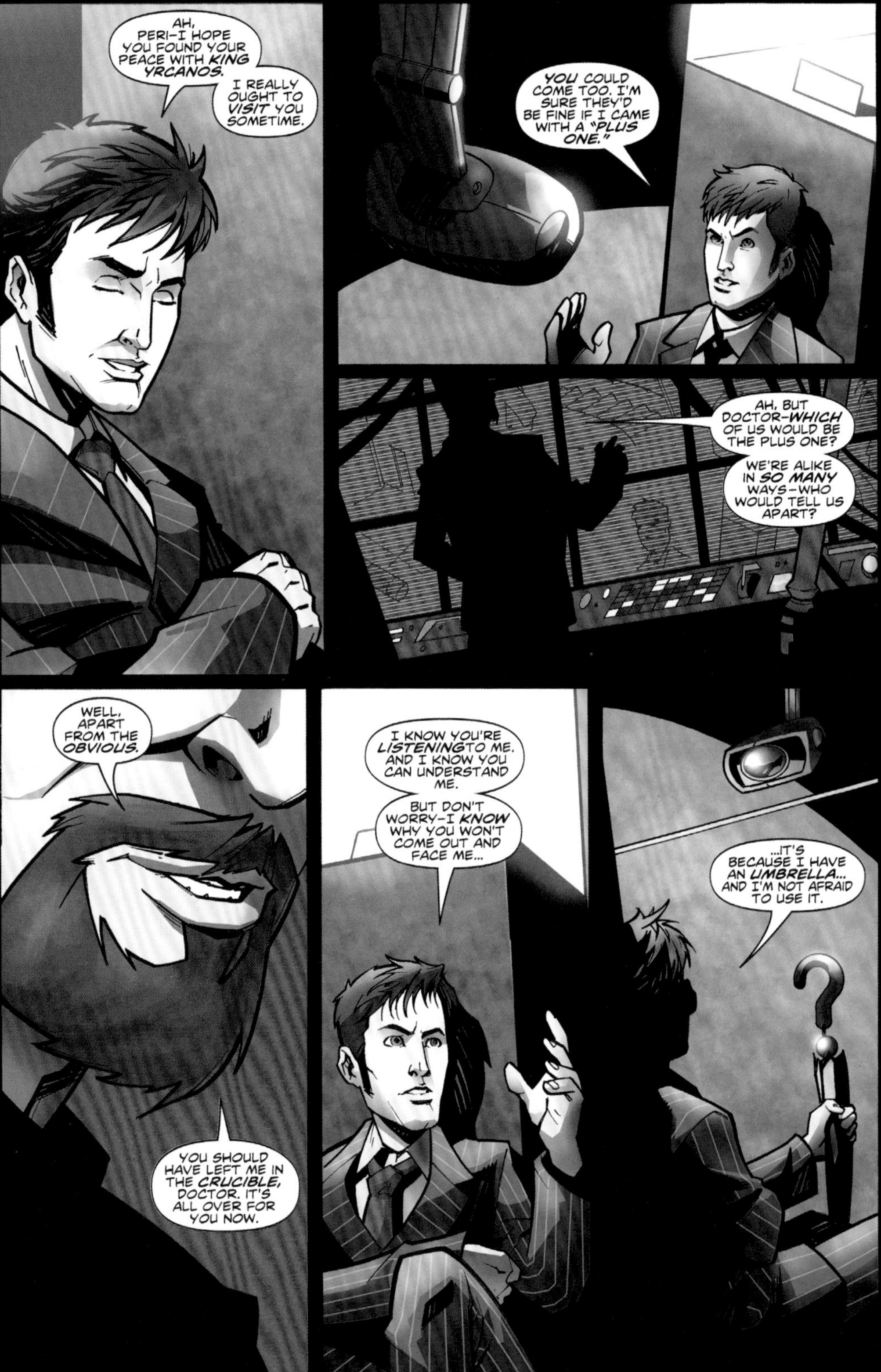
AH, PERI–I HOPE YOU FOUND YOUR PEACE WITH KING YRCANOS.
I REALLY OUGHT TO VISIT YOU SOMETIME.
YOU COULD COME TOO. I'M SURE THEY'D BE FINE IF I CAME WITH A "PLUS ONE."
AH, BUT DOCTOR–WHICH OF US WOULD BE THE PLUS ONE?
WE'RE ALIKE IN SO MANY WAYS–WHO WOULD TELL US APART?
WELL, APART FROM THE OBVIOUS.
YOU SHOULD HAVE LEFT ME IN THE CRUCIBLE, DOCTOR. IT'S ALL OVER FOR YOU NOW.
I KNOW YOU'RE LISTENING TO ME. AND I KNOW YOU CAN UNDERSTAND ME.
BUT DON'T WORRY–I KNOW WHY YOU WON'T COME OUT AND FACE ME...
...IT'S BECAUSE I HAVE AN UMBRELLA... AND I'M NOT AFRAID TO USE IT.

COME ON, ACE—*HURRY!*

I'M RUNNING AS FAST AS I CAN, *PROFESSOR!* THIS BACKPACK IS HEAVY!

WELL, I *DID* TELL YOU TO TRAVEL LIGHT.

AT LEAST YOU DON'T HAVE THAT AWFUL *TAPE PLAYER.*

HEY! THAT'S *CUTTING-EDGE* TECHNOLOGY!

ANYWAY, I THOUGHT IT MIGHT *STAND* OUT A LITTLE.

LOOK, ARE YOU *SURE* THAT WE COULDN'T HAVE LANDED THE TARDIS A LITTLE *CLOSER?*

THE WAR OF *AGROVAN SEVEN* HAS LASTED FOR *FIFTEEN HUNDRED* YEARS. THE TIME LORDS HAVE DECREED IT A NON-INTERVENTION SITE.

WHICH *OBVIOUSLY* MEANS THAT YOU'RE GOING TO *IGNORE* THEM.

THE *DOCTOR,* AT YOUR SERVICE. ANYWAY, IF I'D LANDED *CLOSER,* THEY'D HAVE SEEN IT.

I MAY KEEP TELLING THEM I'M *PRESIDENT-ELECT,* BUT THAT ISN'T A *"GET OUT OF JAIL FREE"* CARD.

THE PROBLEM WITH NON-INTERVENTION IS THAT SOMEONE *ALWAYS* IGNORES IT.

THE *STRYKES* AND THE *MARATS* HAVE BEEN EQUALLY MATCHED FOR GENERATIONS. THEIR ENTIRE STRUCTURE IS *BUILT* ON THIS.

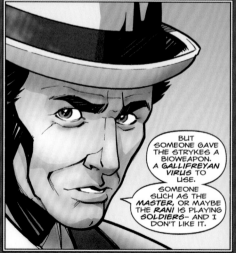

BUT SOMEONE GAVE THE STRYKES A BIOWEAPON. A GALLIFREYAN *VIRUS* TO USE.

SOMEONE SUCH AS THE *MASTER,* OR MAYBE THE *RANI* IS PLAYING *SOLDIERS*— AND I DON'T LIKE IT.

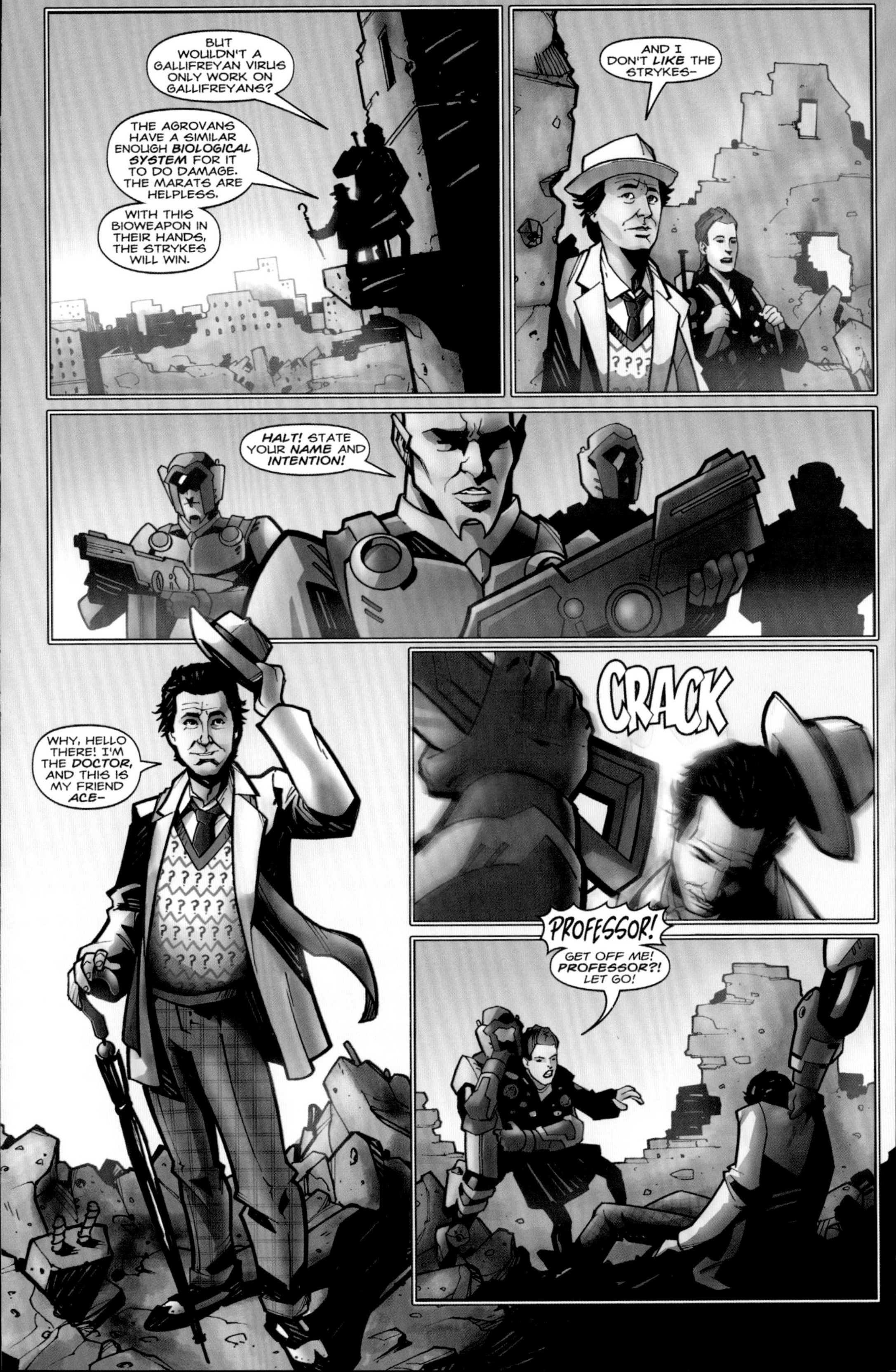

BUT WOULDN'T A GALLIFREYAN VIRUS ONLY WORK ON GALLIFREYANS?
THE AGROVANS HAVE A SIMILAR ENOUGH BIOLOGICAL SYSTEM FOR IT TO DO DAMAGE. THE MARATS ARE HELPLESS.
WITH THIS BIOWEAPON IN THEIR HANDS, THE STRYKES WILL WIN.
AND I DON'T LIKE THE STRYKES–
HALT! STATE YOUR NAME AND INTENTION!
WHY, HELLO THERE! I'M THE DOCTOR, AND THIS IS MY FRIEND ACE–
CRACK
PROFESSOR!
GET OFF ME! PROFESSOR?! LET GO!

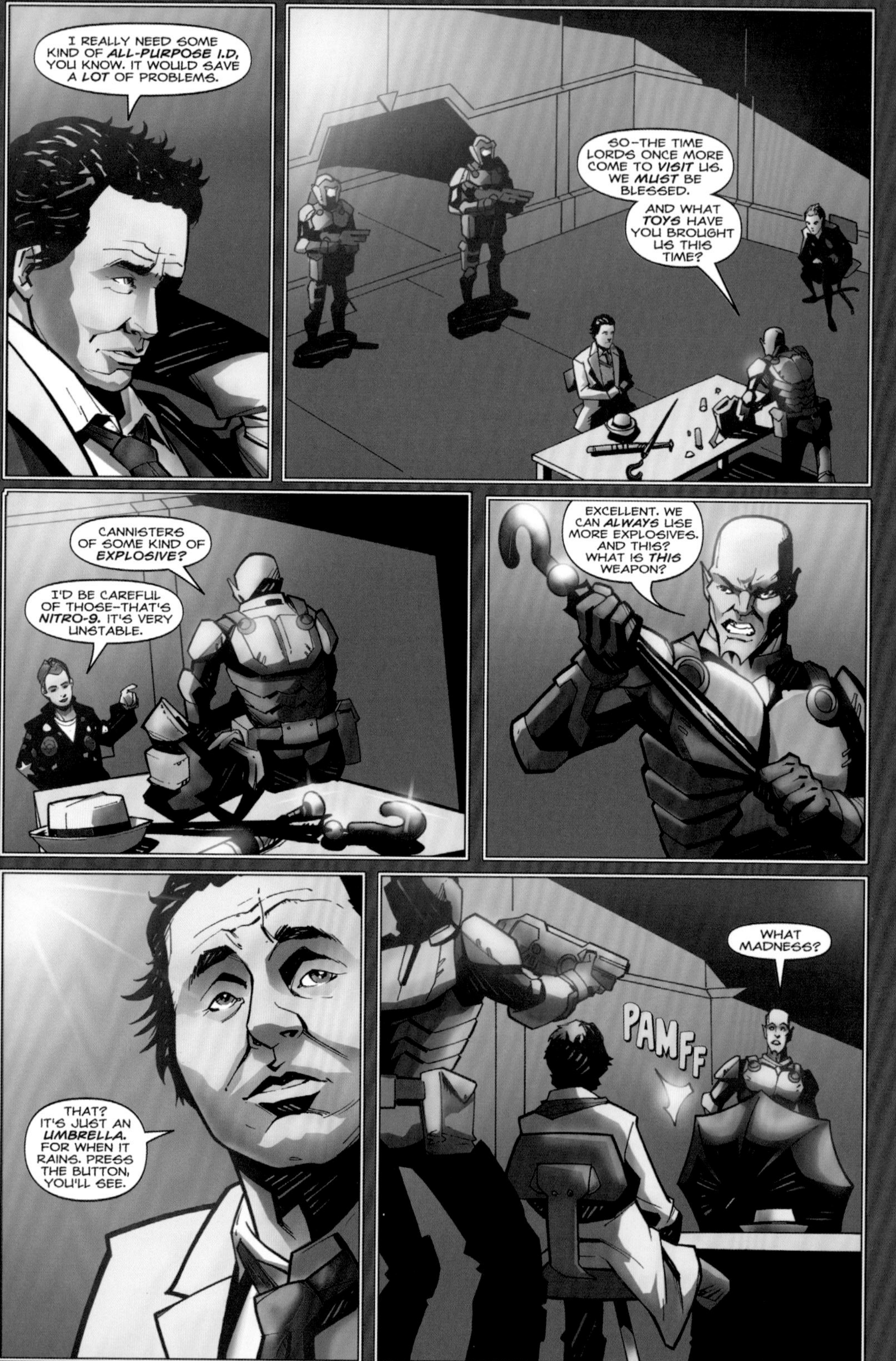
I REALLY NEED SOME KIND OF ALL-PURPOSE I.D, YOU KNOW. IT WOULD SAVE A LOT OF PROBLEMS.
SO—THE TIME LORDS ONCE MORE COME TO VISIT US. WE MUST BE BLESSED.
AND WHAT TOYS HAVE YOU BROUGHT US THIS TIME?
CANNISTERS OF SOME KIND OF EXPLOSIVE?
I'D BE CAREFUL OF THOSE—THAT'S NITRO-9. IT'S VERY UNSTABLE.
EXCELLENT. WE CAN ALWAYS USE MORE EXPLOSIVES. AND THIS? WHAT IS THIS WEAPON?
THAT? IT'S JUST AN UMBRELLA. FOR WHEN IT RAINS. PRESS THE BUTTON, YOU'LL SEE.
WHAT MADNESS?
PAMFF

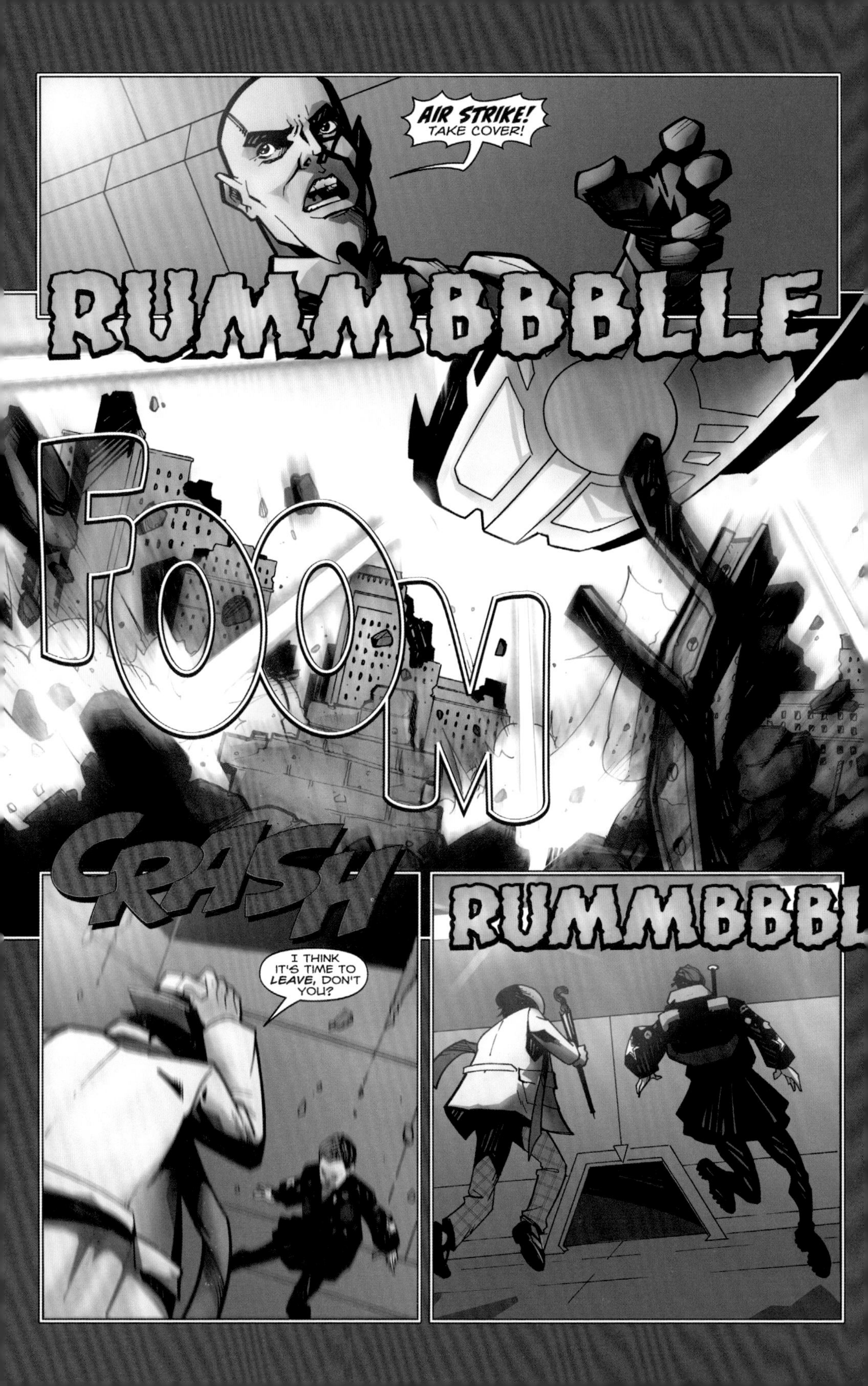
AIR STRIKE! TAKE COVER!
RUMMBBBLLE
FOOOM
CRASH
I THINK IT'S TIME TO LEAVE, DON'T YOU?
RUMMBBBL

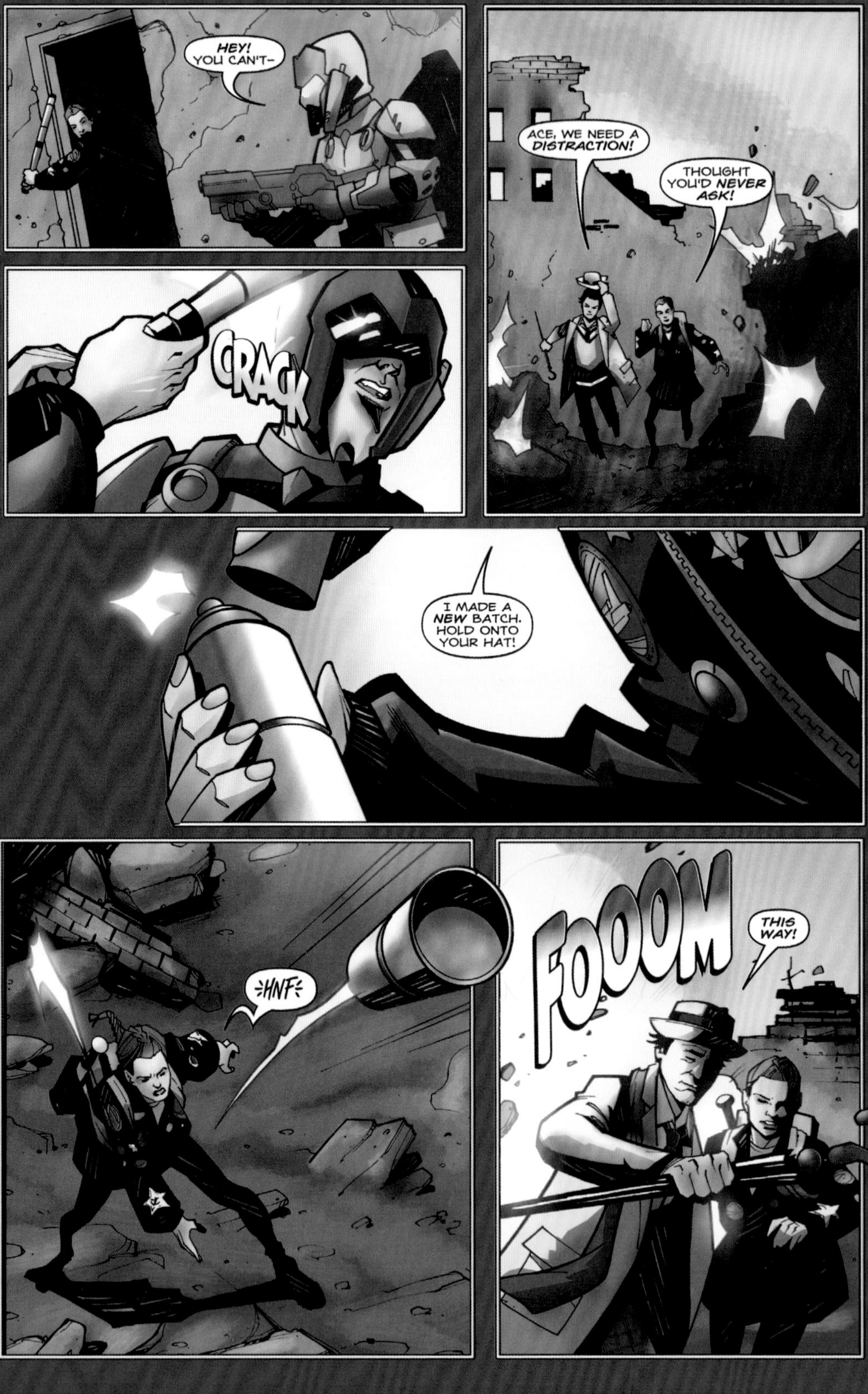
HEY! YOU CAN'T-
ACE, WE NEED A DISTRACTION!
THOUGHT YOU'D NEVER ASK!
CRACK
I MADE A NEW BATCH. HOLD ONTO YOUR HAT!
HNF
FOOOM
THIS WAY!

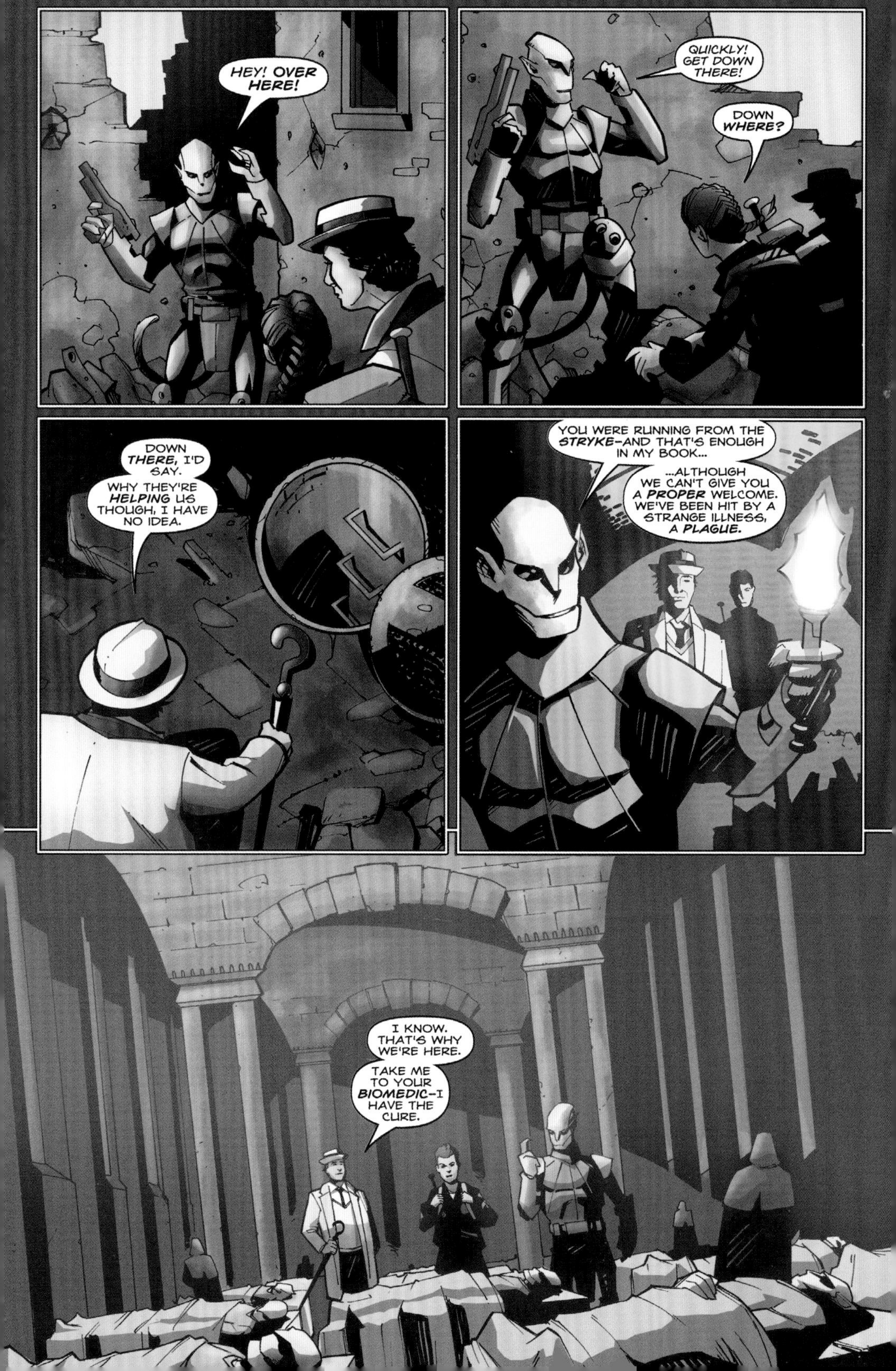
HEY! OVER HERE!
QUICKLY! GET DOWN THERE!
DOWN WHERE?
DOWN THERE, I'D SAY.
WHY THEY'RE HELPING US THOUGH, I HAVE NO IDEA.
YOU WERE RUNNING FROM THE STRYKE–AND THAT'S ENOUGH IN MY BOOK...
...ALTHOUGH WE CAN'T GIVE YOU A PROPER WELCOME. WE'VE BEEN HIT BY A STRANGE ILLNESS, A PLAGUE.
I KNOW. THAT'S WHY WE'RE HERE.
TAKE ME TO YOUR BIOMEDIC–I HAVE THE CURE.

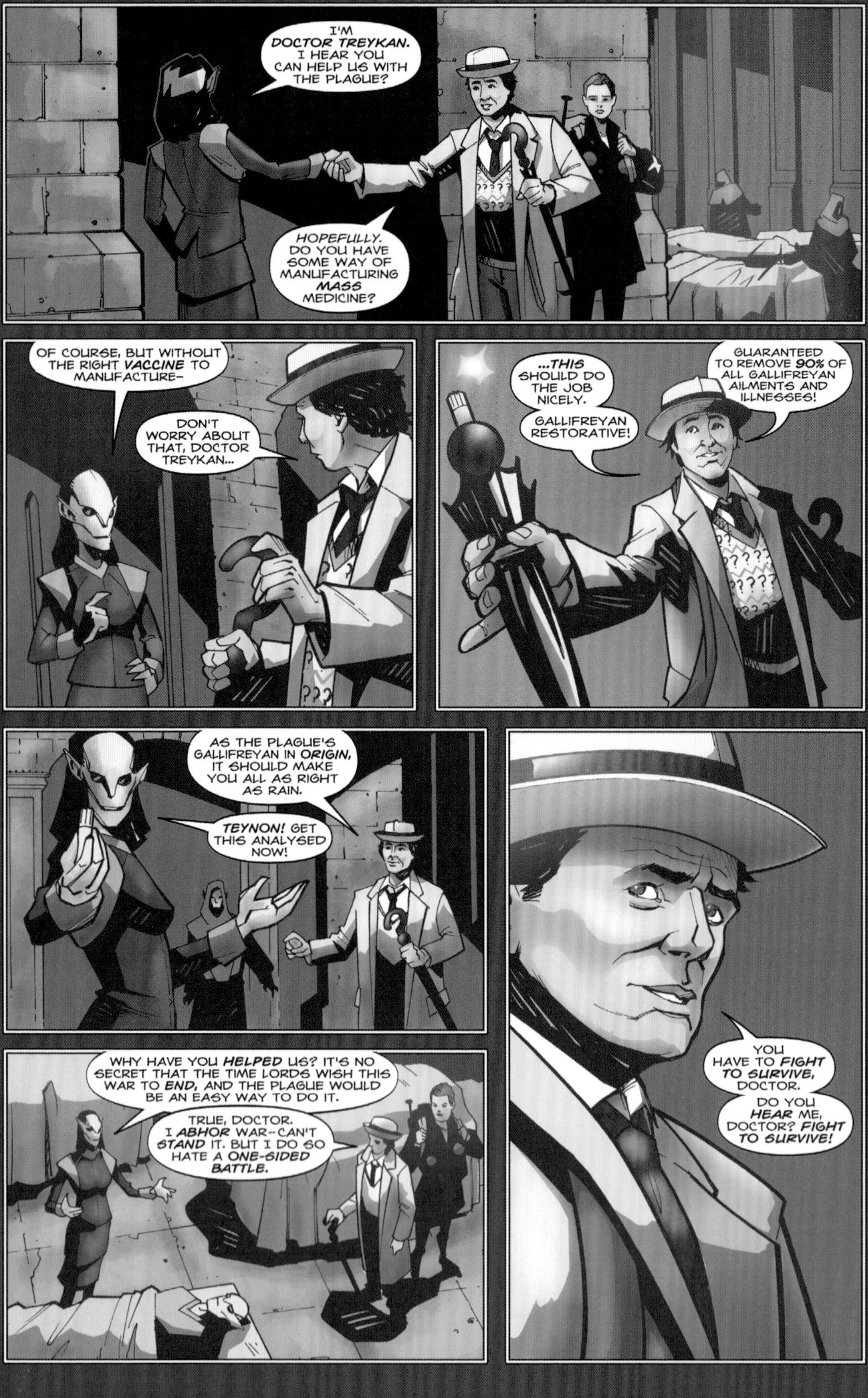
I'M DOCTOR TREYKAN. I HEAR YOU CAN HELP US WITH THE PLAGUE?
HOPEFULLY. DO YOU HAVE SOME WAY OF MANUFACTURING MASS MEDICINE?
OF COURSE, BUT WITHOUT THE RIGHT VACCINE TO MANUFACTURE–
DON'T WORRY ABOUT THAT, DOCTOR TREYKAN...
...THIS SHOULD DO THE JOB NICELY.
GALLIFREYAN RESTORATIVE!
GUARANTEED TO REMOVE 90% OF ALL GALLIFREYAN AILMENTS AND ILLNESSES!
AS THE PLAGUE'S GALLIFREYAN IN ORIGIN, IT SHOULD MAKE YOU ALL AS RIGHT AS RAIN.
TEYNON! GET THIS ANALYSED NOW!
WHY HAVE YOU HELPED US? IT'S NO SECRET THAT THE TIME LORDS WISH THIS WAR TO END, AND THE PLAGUE WOULD BE AN EASY WAY TO DO IT.
TRUE, DOCTOR. I ABHOR WAR–CAN'T STAND IT. BUT I DO SO HATE A ONE-SIDED BATTLE.
YOU HAVE TO FIGHT TO SURVIVE, DOCTOR.
DO YOU HEAR ME, DOCTOR? FIGHT TO SURVIVE!

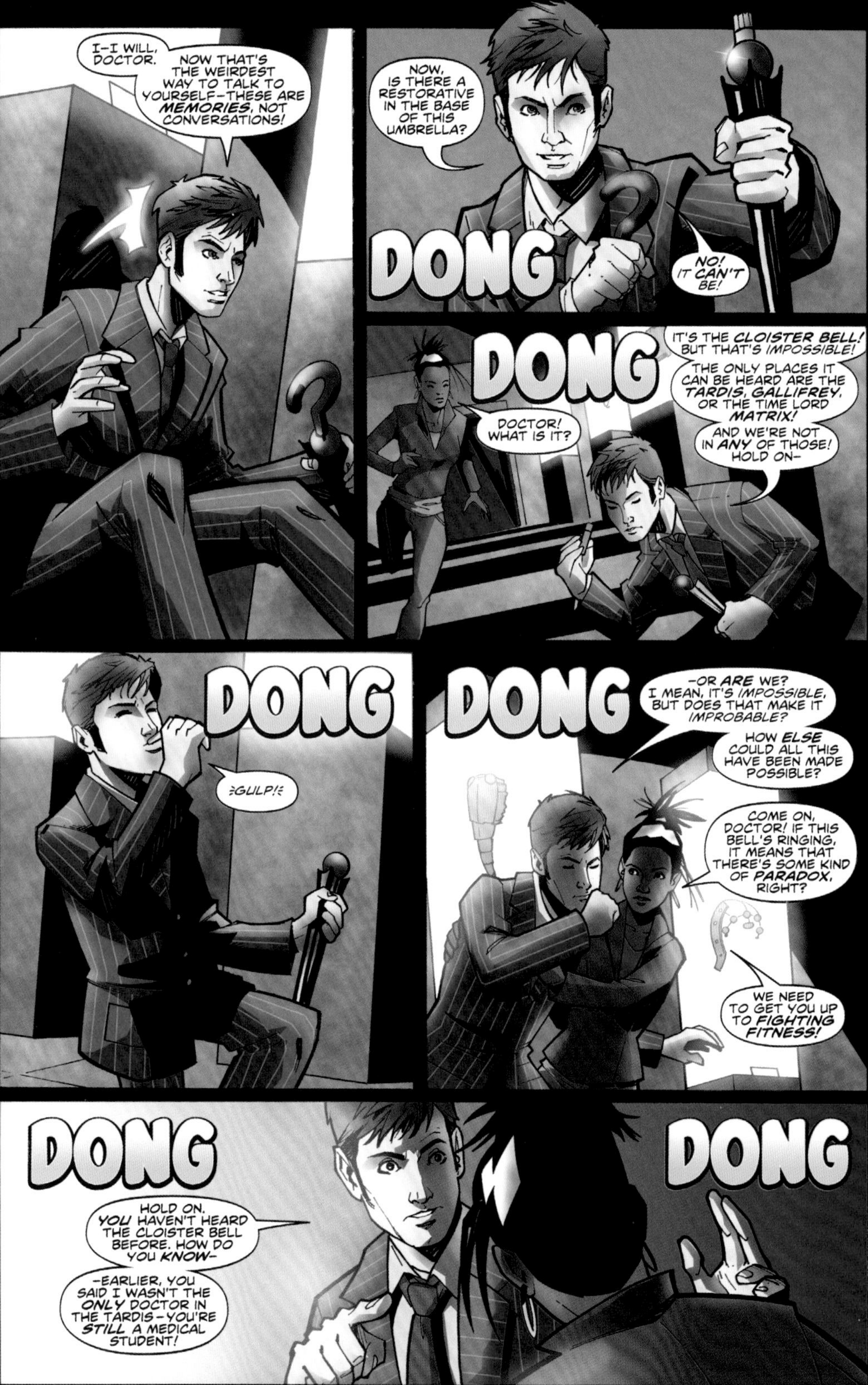
I–I WILL, DOCTOR.
NOW THAT'S THE WEIRDEST WAY TO TALK TO YOURSELF–THESE ARE MEMORIES, NOT CONVERSATIONS!
NOW, IS THERE A RESTORATIVE IN THE BASE OF THIS UMBRELLA?
DONG
NO! IT CAN'T BE!
DONG
DOCTOR! WHAT IS IT?
IT'S THE CLOISTER BELL! BUT THAT'S IMPOSSIBLE!
THE ONLY PLACES IT CAN BE HEARD ARE THE TARDIS, GALLIFREY, OR THE TIME LORD MATRIX!
AND WE'RE NOT IN ANY OF THOSE! HOLD ON–
DONG
GULP!
DONG
–OR ARE WE? I MEAN, IT'S IMPOSSIBLE, BUT DOES THAT MAKE IT IMPROBABLE?
HOW ELSE COULD ALL THIS HAVE BEEN MADE POSSIBLE?
COME ON, DOCTOR! IF THIS BELL'S RINGING, IT MEANS THAT THERE'S SOME KIND OF PARADOX, RIGHT?
WE NEED TO GET YOU UP TO FIGHTING FITNESS!
DONG
DONG
HOLD ON. YOU HAVEN'T HEARD THE CLOISTER BELL BEFORE. HOW DO YOU KNOW–
–EARLIER, YOU SAID I WASN'T THE ONLY DOCTOR IN THE TARDIS–YOU'RE STILL A MEDICAL STUDENT!

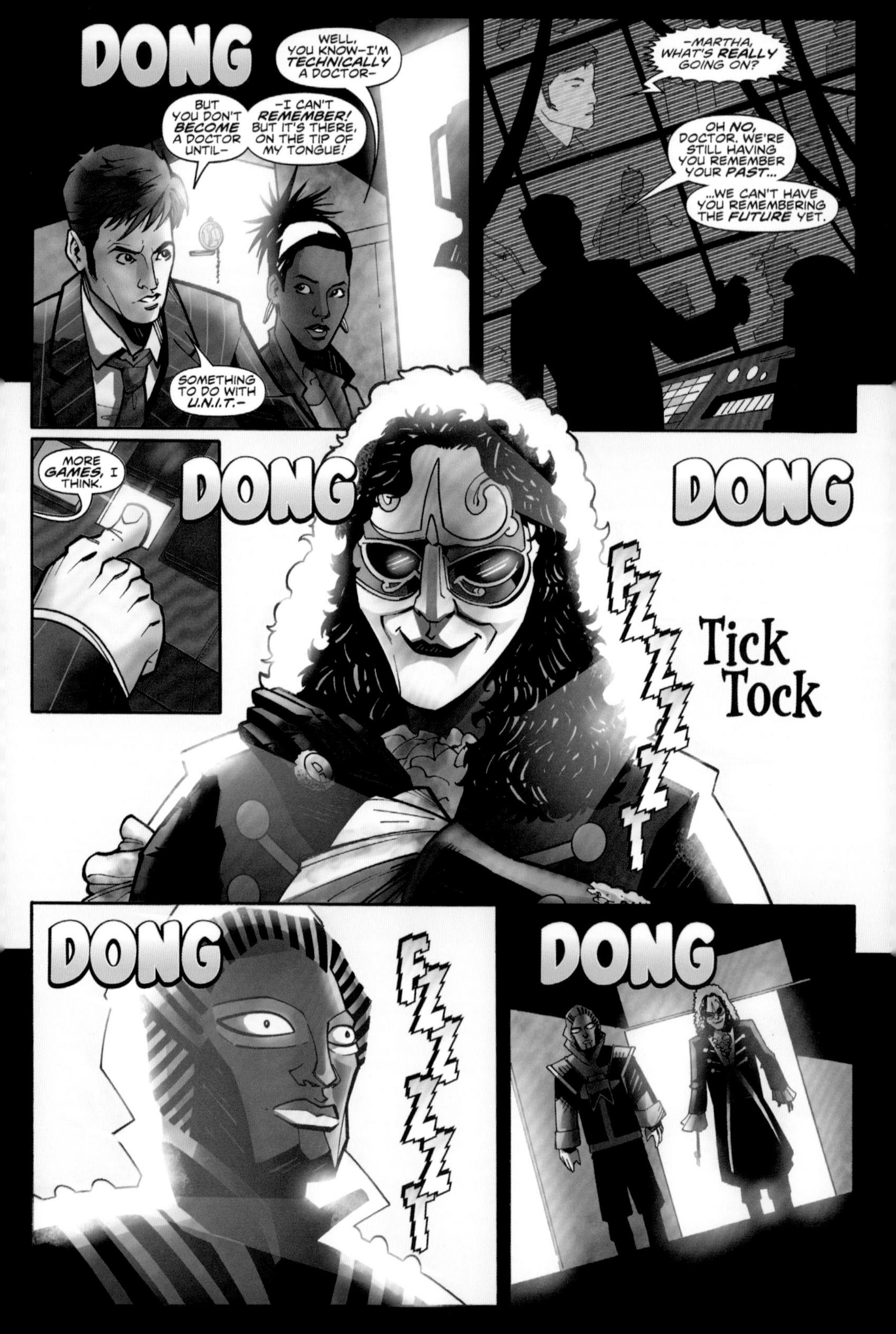
DONG
WELL, YOU KNOW—I'M TECHNICALLY A DOCTOR—
BUT YOU DON'T BECOME A DOCTOR UNTIL—
—I CAN'T REMEMBER! BUT IT'S THERE, ON THE TIP OF MY TONGUE!
SOMETHING TO DO WITH U.N.I.T.—
—MARTHA, WHAT'S REALLY GOING ON?
OH NO, DOCTOR, WE'RE STILL HAVING YOU REMEMBER YOUR PAST...
...WE CAN'T HAVE YOU REMEMBERING THE FUTURE YET.
MORE GAMES, I THINK.
DONG
DONG
FZZZZZT
Tick Tock
DONG
FZZZZZT
DONG

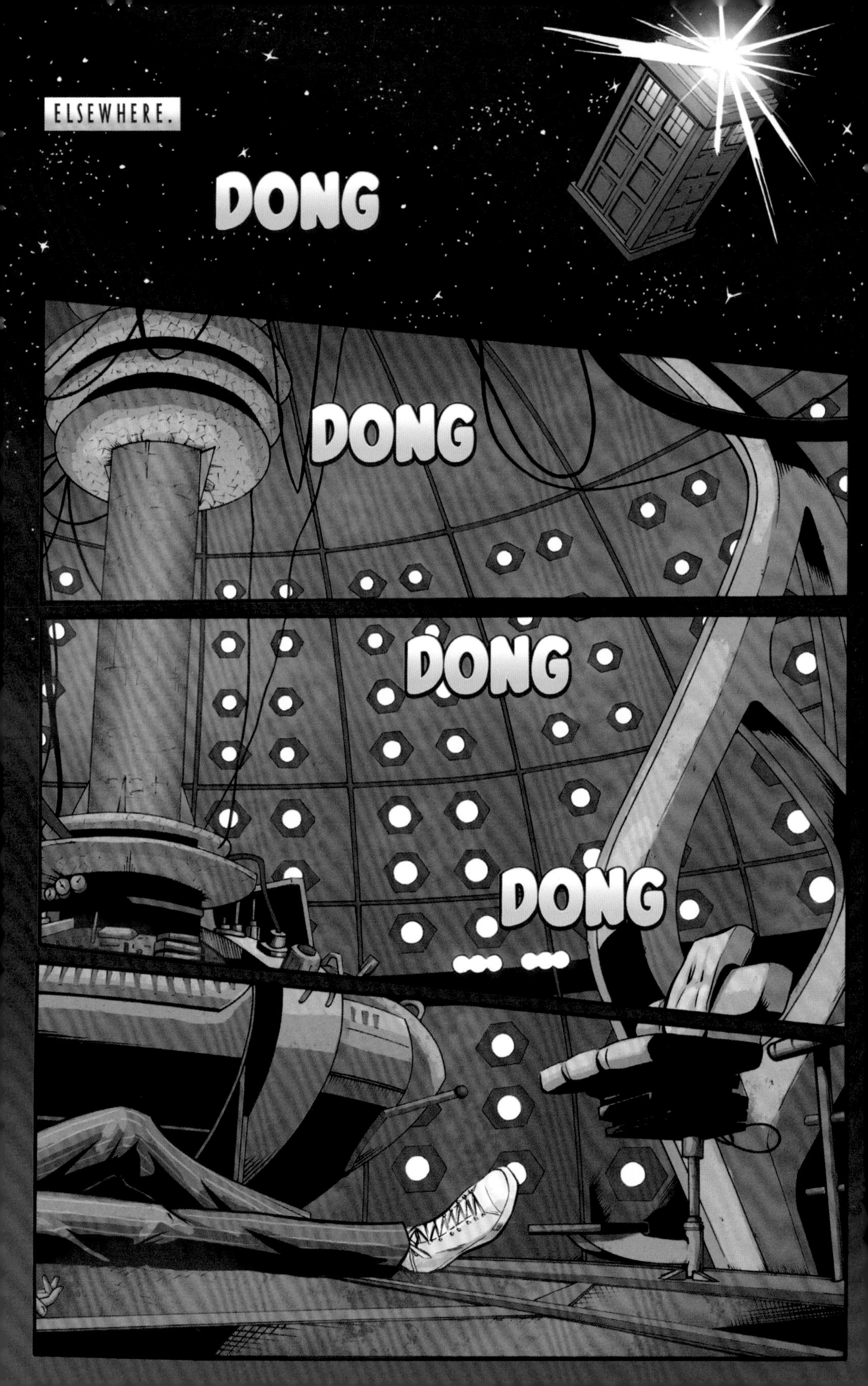
ELSEWHERE.
DONG
DONG
DONG
DONG

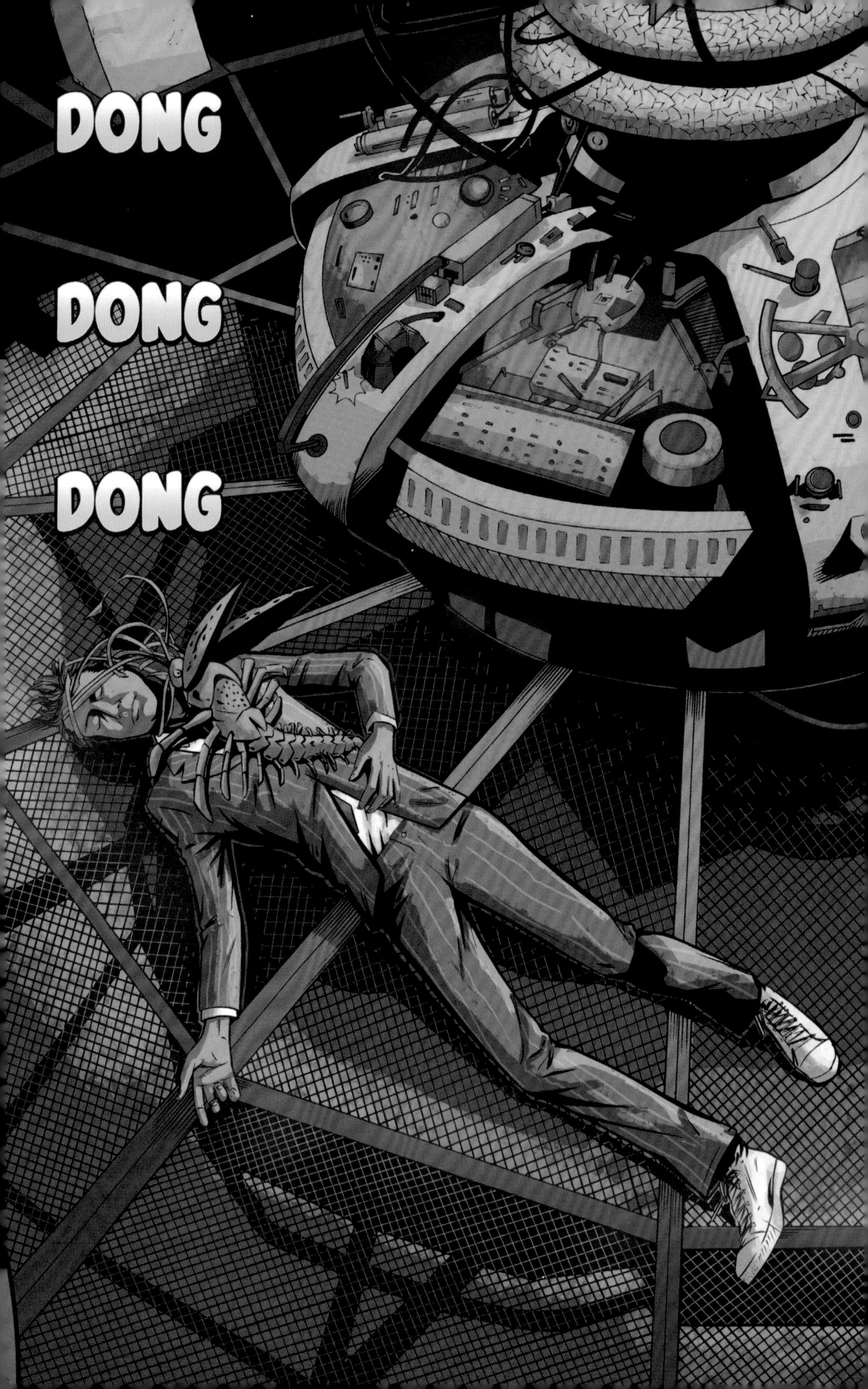
DONG
DONG
DONG

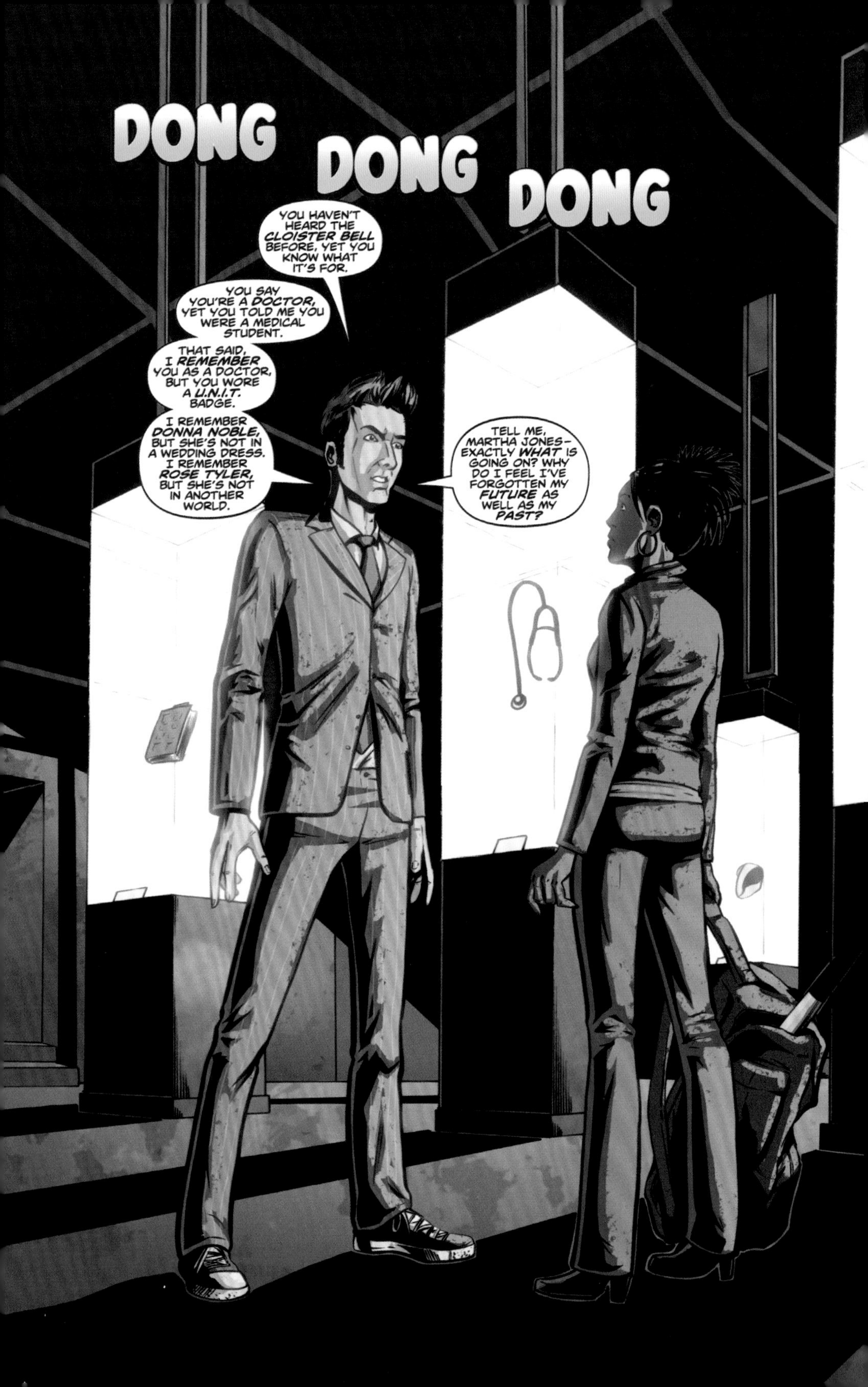
DONG DONG DONG
YOU HAVEN'T HEARD THE CLOISTER BELL BEFORE, YET YOU KNOW WHAT IT'S FOR.
YOU SAY YOU'RE A DOCTOR, YET YOU TOLD ME YOU WERE A MEDICAL STUDENT.
THAT SAID, I REMEMBER YOU AS A DOCTOR, BUT YOU WORE A U.N.I.T. BADGE.
I REMEMBER DONNA NOBLE, BUT SHE'S NOT IN A WEDDING DRESS. I REMEMBER ROSE TYLER, BUT SHE'S NOT IN ANOTHER WORLD.
TELL ME, MARTHA JONES– EXACTLY WHAT IS GOING ON? WHY DO I FEEL I'VE FORGOTTEN MY FUTURE AS WELL AS MY PAST?

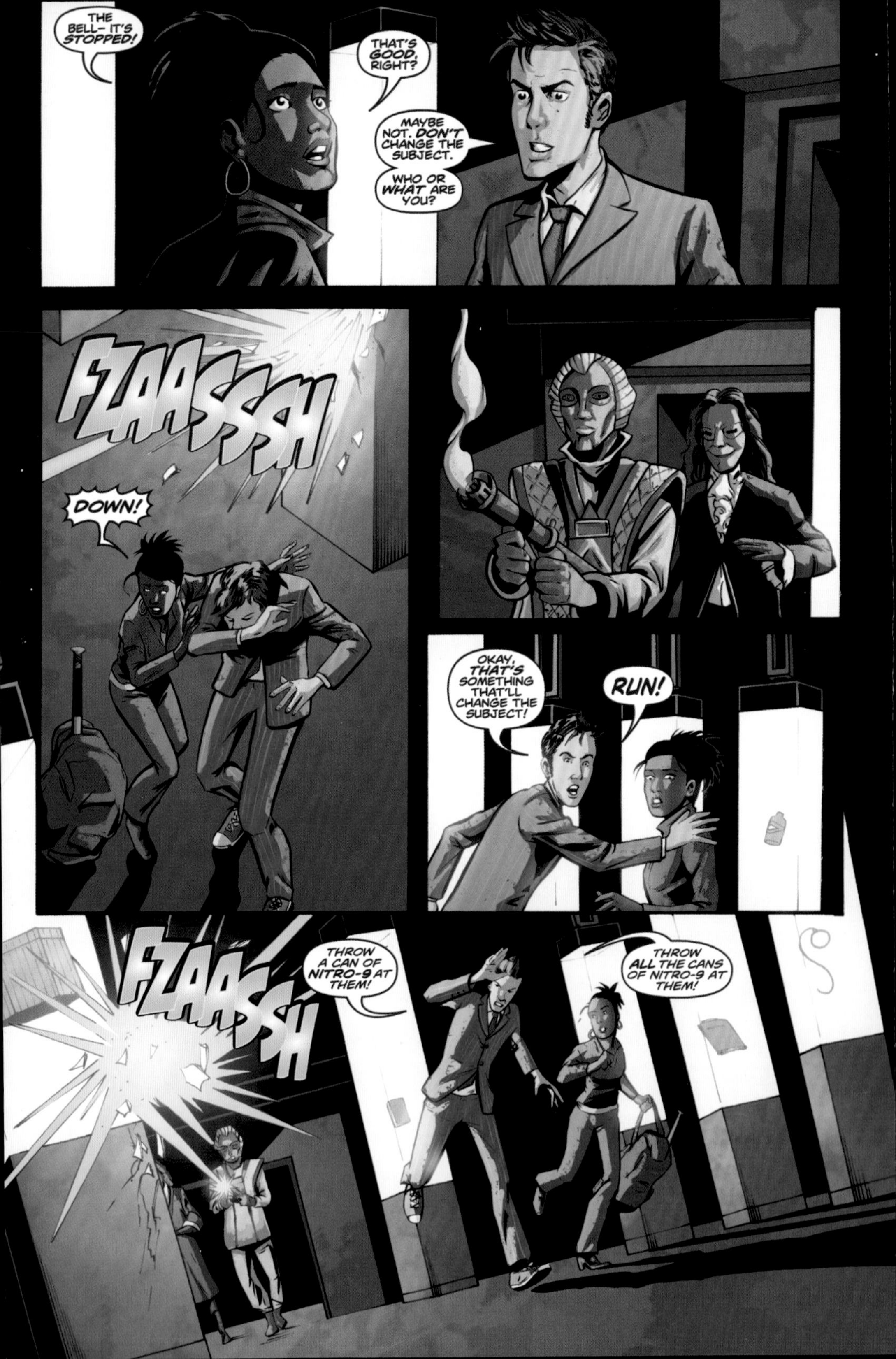

THE BELL– IT'S STOPPED!
THAT'S GOOD, RIGHT?
MAYBE NOT. DON'T CHANGE THE SUBJECT.
WHO OR WHAT ARE YOU?
FZAASSSH
DOWN!
OKAY, THAT'S SOMETHING THAT'LL CHANGE THE SUBJECT!
RUN!
FZAASSH
THROW A CAN OF NITRO-9 AT THEM!
THROW ALL THE CANS OF NITRO-9 AT THEM!

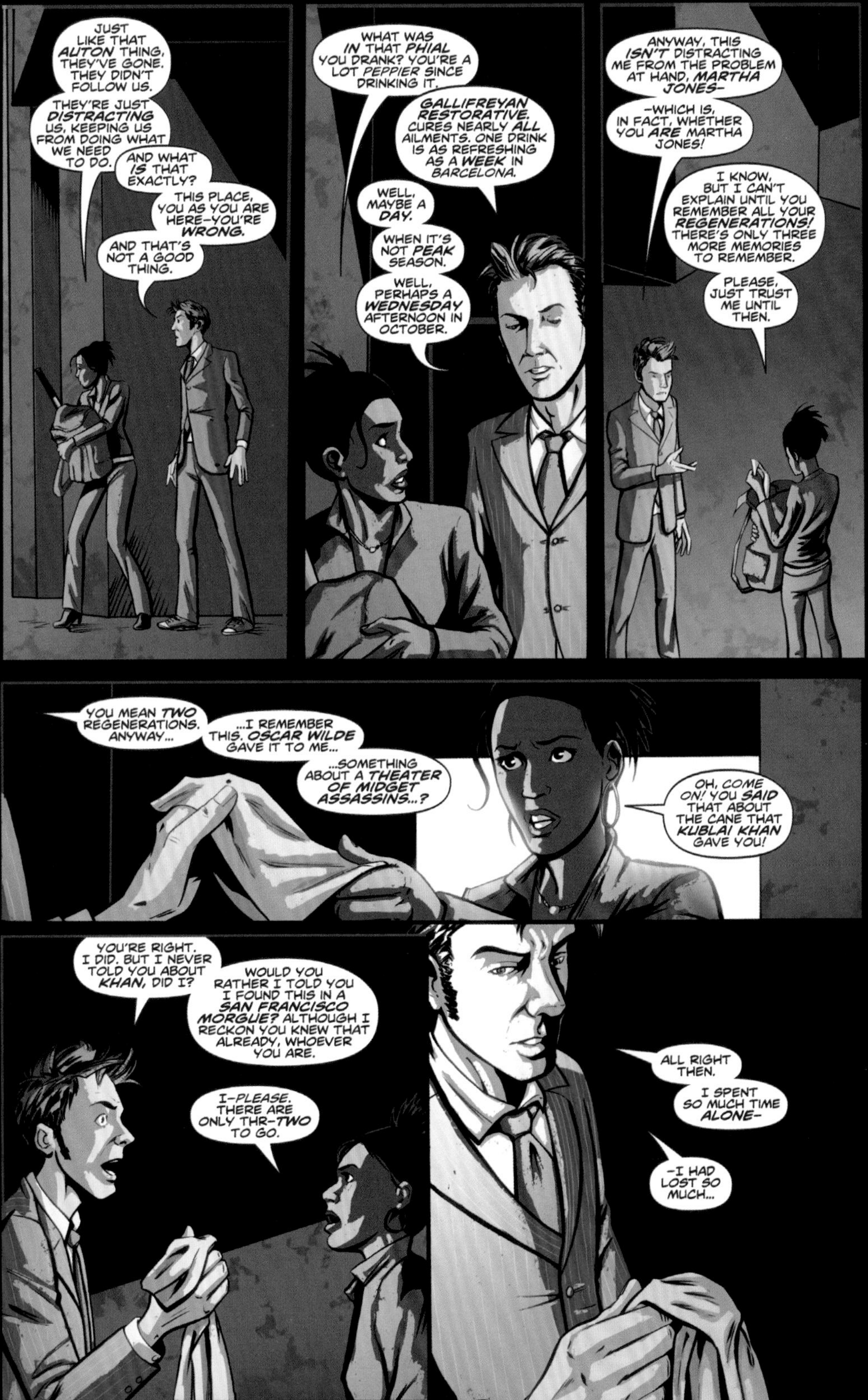
JUST LIKE THAT AUTON THING, THEY'VE GONE. THEY DIDN'T FOLLOW US.
THEY'RE JUST DISTRACTING US, KEEPING US FROM DOING WHAT WE NEED TO DO.
AND WHAT IS THAT EXACTLY?
THIS PLACE, YOU AS YOU ARE HERE–YOU'RE WRONG.
AND THAT'S NOT A GOOD THING.
WHAT WAS IN THAT PHIAL YOU DRANK? YOU'RE A LOT PEPPIER SINCE DRINKING IT.
GALLIFREYAN RESTORATIVE. CURES NEARLY ALL AILMENTS. ONE DRINK IS AS REFRESHING AS A WEEK IN BARCELONA.
WELL, MAYBE A DAY.
WHEN IT'S NOT PEAK SEASON.
WELL, PERHAPS A WEDNESDAY AFTERNOON IN OCTOBER.
ANYWAY, THIS ISN'T DISTRACTING ME FROM THE PROBLEM AT HAND, MARTHA JONES–
–WHICH IS, IN FACT, WHETHER YOU ARE MARTHA JONES!
I KNOW, BUT I CAN'T EXPLAIN UNTIL YOU REMEMBER ALL YOUR REGENERATIONS! THERE'S ONLY THREE MORE MEMORIES TO REMEMBER.
PLEASE, JUST TRUST ME UNTIL THEN.
YOU MEAN TWO REGENERATIONS. ANYWAY...
...I REMEMBER THIS. OSCAR WILDE GAVE IT TO ME...
...SOMETHING ABOUT A THEATER OF MIDGET ASSASSINS...?
OH, COME ON! YOU SAID THAT ABOUT THE CANE THAT KUBLAI KHAN GAVE YOU!
YOU'RE RIGHT. I DID. BUT I NEVER TOLD YOU ABOUT KHAN, DID I?
WOULD YOU RATHER I TOLD YOU I FOUND THIS IN A SAN FRANCISCO MORGUE? ALTHOUGH I RECKON YOU KNEW THAT ALREADY, WHOEVER YOU ARE.
I–PLEASE. THERE ARE ONLY THR–TWO TO GO.
ALL RIGHT THEN.
I SPENT SO MUCH TIME ALONE–
–I HAD LOST SO MUCH...

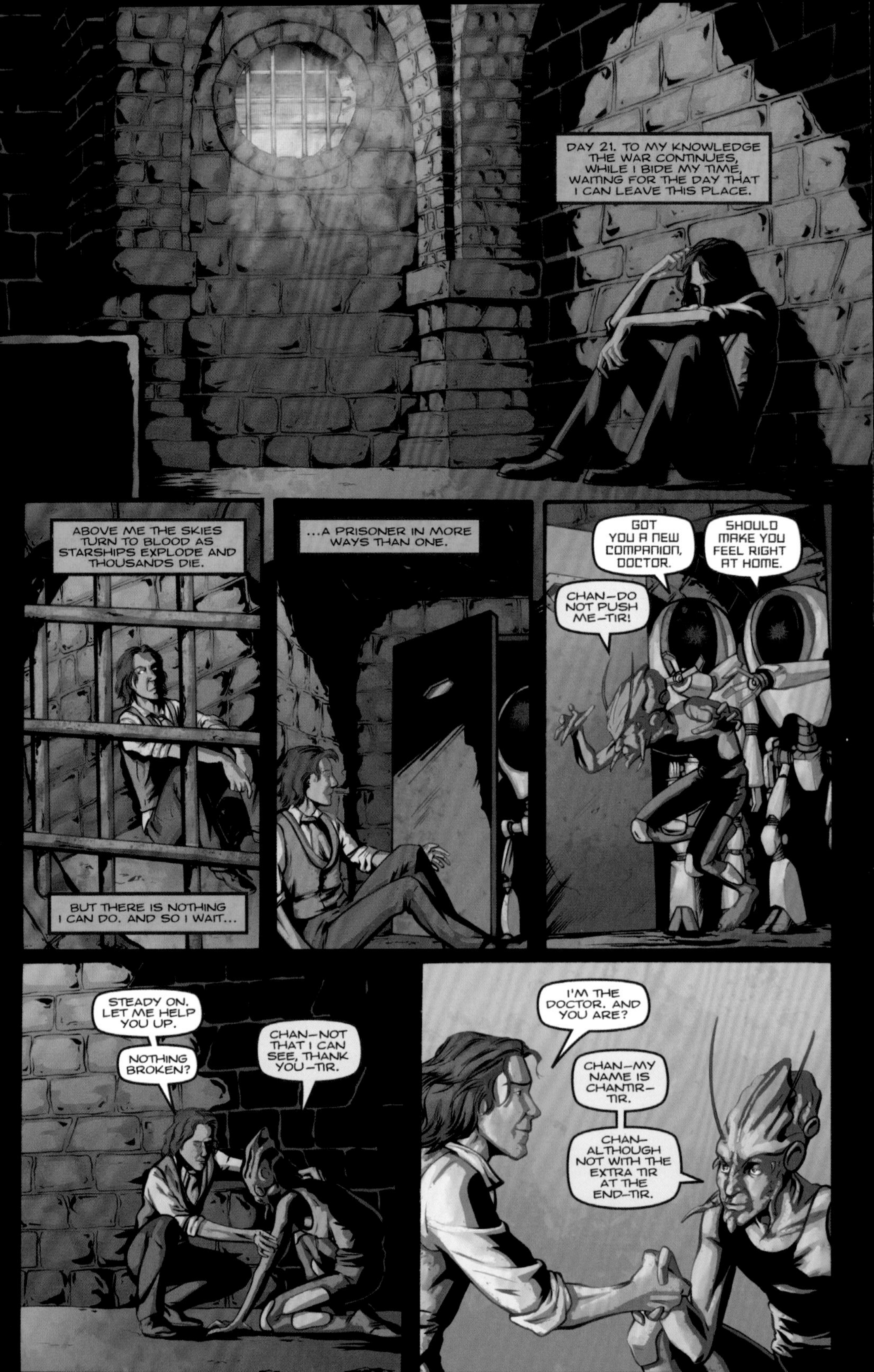
DAY 21. TO MY KNOWLEDGE THE WAR CONTINUES, WHILE I BIDE MY TIME, WAITING FOR THE DAY THAT I CAN LEAVE THIS PLACE.
ABOVE ME THE SKIES TURN TO BLOOD AS STARSHIPS EXPLODE AND THOUSANDS DIE.
BUT THERE IS NOTHING I CAN DO. AND SO I WAIT...
...A PRISONER IN MORE WAYS THAN ONE.
GOT YOU A NEW COMPANION, DOCTOR.
SHOULD MAKE YOU FEEL RIGHT AT HOME.
CHAN—DO NOT PUSH ME—TIR!
STEADY ON. LET ME HELP YOU UP.
NOTHING BROKEN?
CHAN—NOT THAT I CAN SEE, THANK YOU—TIR.
I'M THE DOCTOR. AND YOU ARE?
CHAN—MY NAME IS CHANTIR—TIR.
CHAN—ALTHOUGH NOT WITH THE EXTRA TIR AT THE END—TIR.

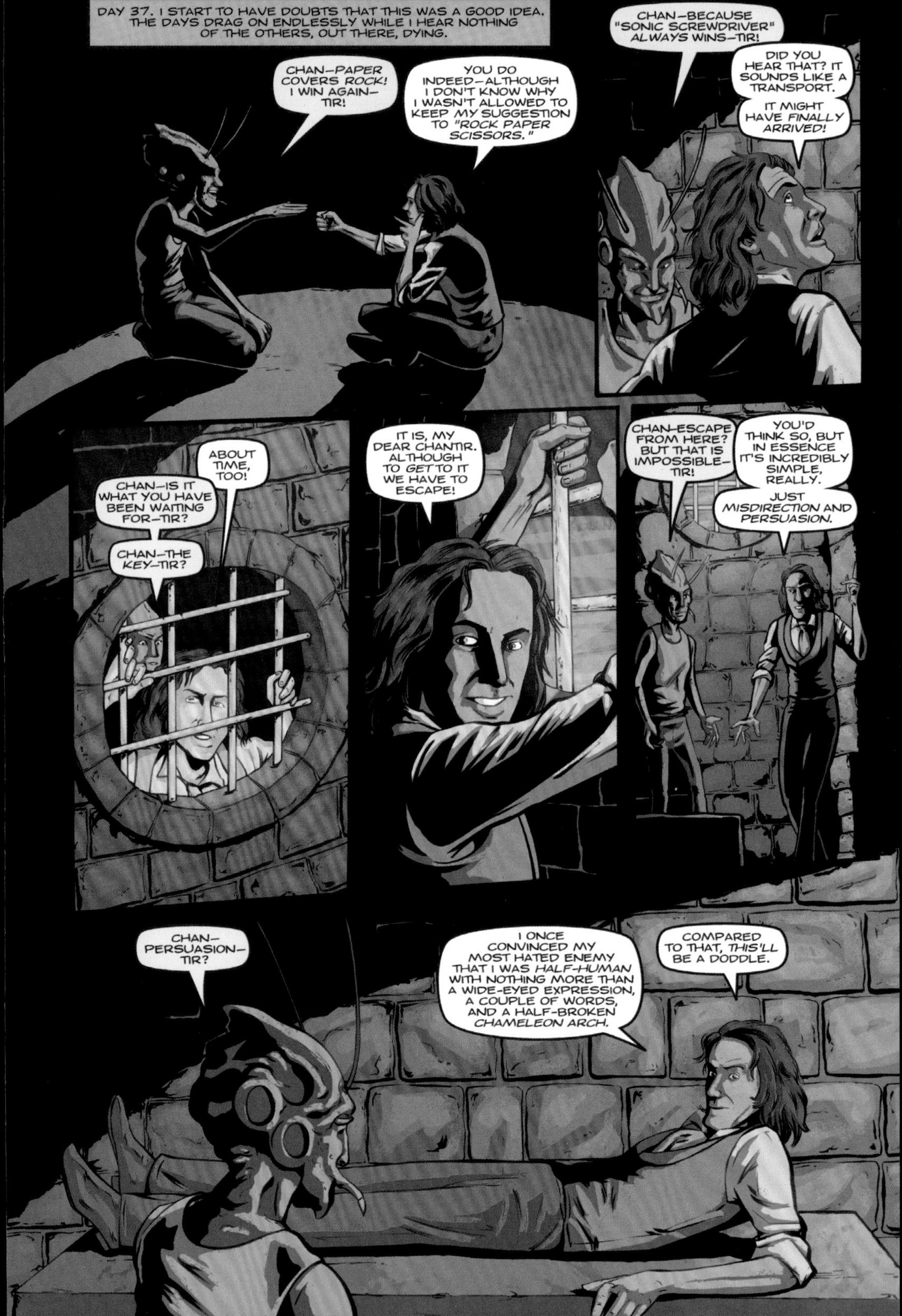

DAY 37. I START TO HAVE DOUBTS THAT THIS WAS A GOOD IDEA. THE DAYS DRAG ON ENDLESSLY WHILE I HEAR NOTHING OF THE OTHERS, OUT THERE, DYING.
CHAN—PAPER COVERS *ROCK!* I WIN AGAIN—TIR!
YOU DO INDEED—ALTHOUGH I DON'T KNOW WHY I WASN'T ALLOWED TO KEEP MY SUGGESTION TO *"ROCK PAPER SCISSORS."*
CHAN—BECAUSE "SONIC SCREWDRIVER" *ALWAYS* WINS—TIR!
DID YOU HEAR THAT? IT SOUNDS LIKE A TRANSPORT.
IT MIGHT HAVE *FINALLY* ARRIVED!
CHAN—IS IT WHAT YOU HAVE BEEN WAITING FOR—TIR?
ABOUT TIME, TOO!
CHAN—THE KEY—TIR?
IT IS, MY DEAR CHANTIR. ALTHOUGH TO *GET* TO IT WE HAVE TO ESCAPE!
CHAN—ESCAPE FROM HERE? BUT THAT IS IMPOSSIBLE—TIR!
YOU'D THINK SO, BUT IN ESSENCE IT'S INCREDIBLY SIMPLE, REALLY.
JUST *MISDIRECTION* AND *PERSUASION.*
CHAN—PERSUASION—TIR?
I ONCE CONVINCED MY MOST HATED ENEMY THAT I WAS *HALF-HUMAN* WITH NOTHING MORE THAN A WIDE-EYED EXPRESSION, A COUPLE OF WORDS, AND A HALF-BROKEN *CHAMELEON ARCH.*
COMPARED TO THAT, *THIS'LL* BE A DODDLE.

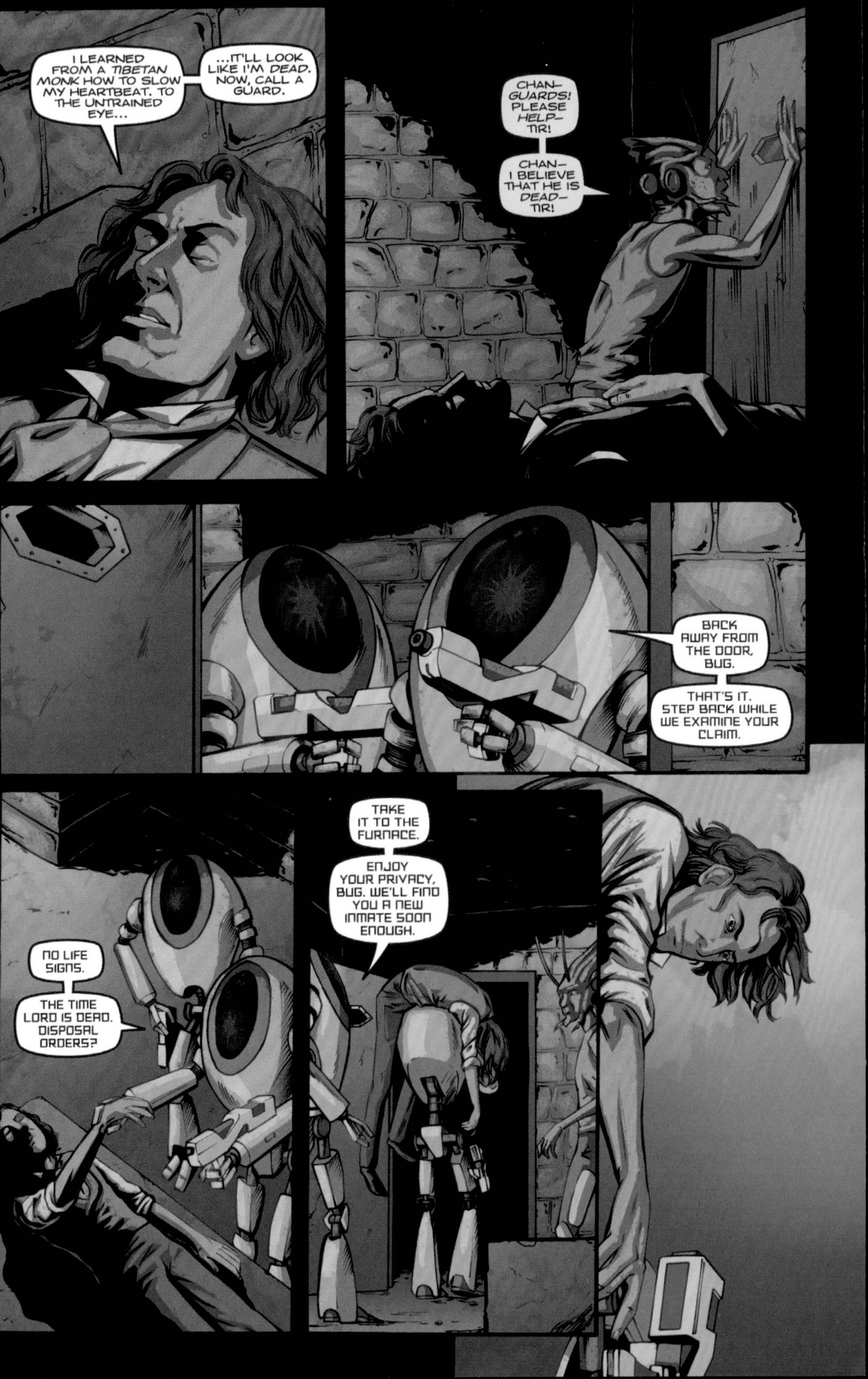
I LEARNED FROM A TIBETAN MONK HOW TO SLOW MY HEARTBEAT. TO THE UNTRAINED EYE...
...IT'LL LOOK LIKE I'M DEAD. NOW, CALL A GUARD.
CHAN-GUARDS! PLEASE HELP-TIR!
CHAN-I BELIEVE THAT HE IS DEAD-TIR!
BACK AWAY FROM THE DOOR, BUG.
THAT'S IT. STEP BACK WHILE WE EXAMINE YOUR CLAIM.
NO LIFE SIGNS.
THE TIME LORD IS DEAD. DISPOSAL ORDERS?
TAKE IT TO THE FURNACE.
ENJOY YOUR PRIVACY, BUG. WE'LL FIND YOU A NEW INMATE SOON ENOUGH.

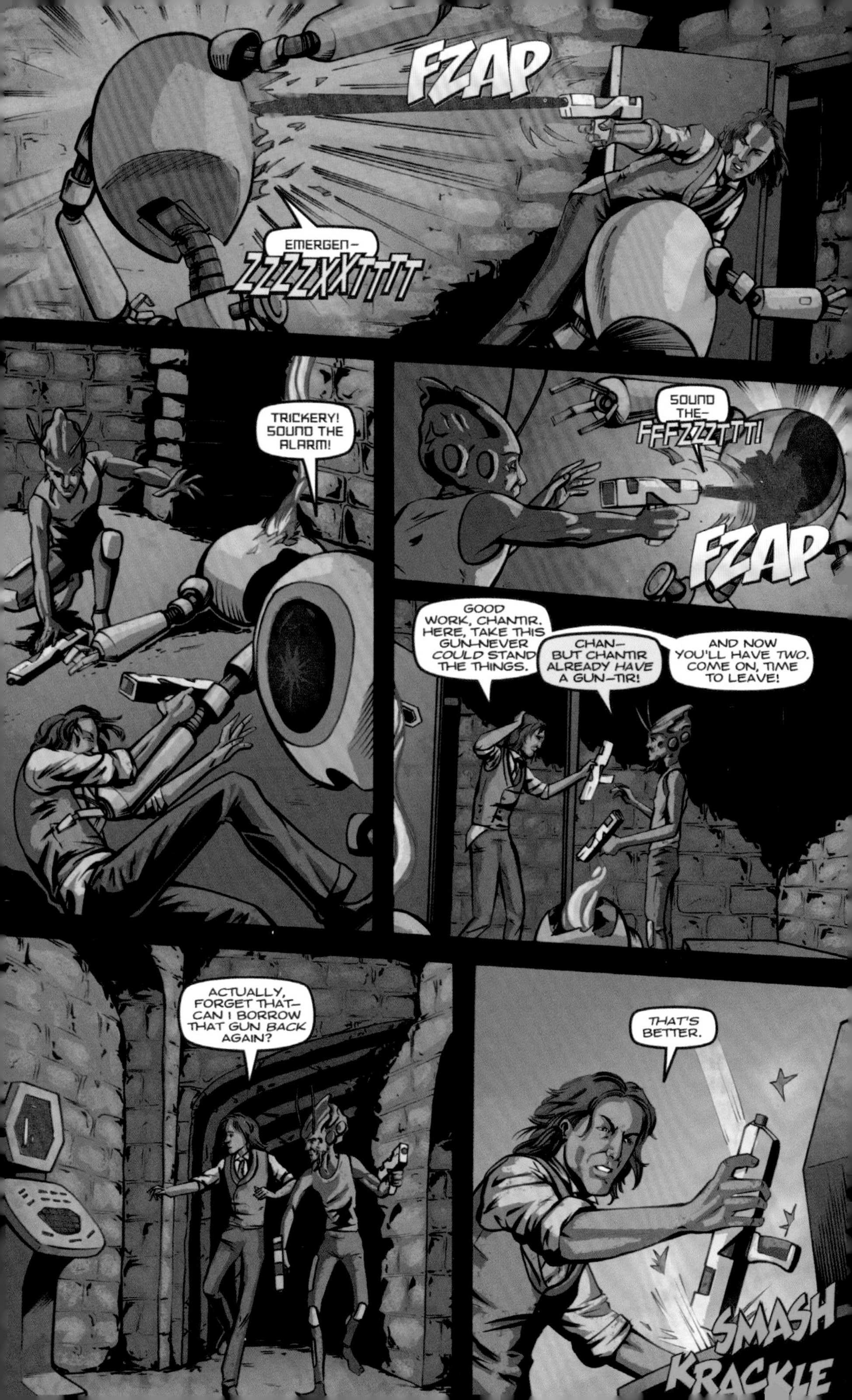
FZAP
EMERGEN—
ZZZZXXTTTT
TRICKERY! SOUND THE ALARM!
SOUND THE—
FFFZZZTTT!
FZAP
GOOD WORK, CHANTIR. HERE, TAKE THIS GUN—NEVER COULD STAND THE THINGS.
CHAN— BUT CHANTIR ALREADY HAVE A GUN—TIR!
AND NOW YOU'LL HAVE TWO. COME ON, TIME TO LEAVE!
ACTUALLY, FORGET THAT— CAN I BORROW THAT GUN BACK AGAIN?
THAT'S BETTER.
SMASH
KRACKLE

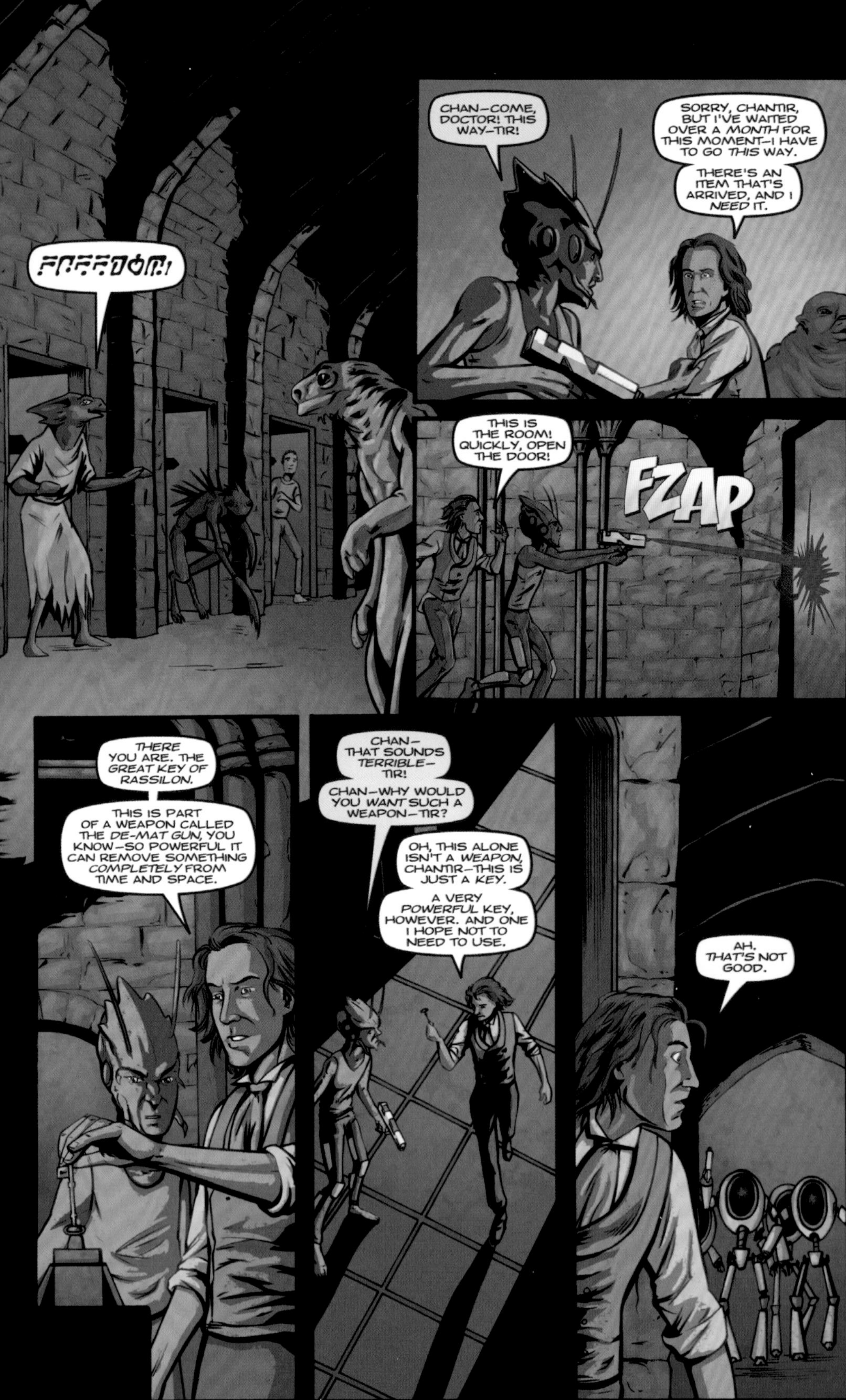
FREEDOM!
CHAN—COME, DOCTOR! THIS WAY—TIR!
SORRY, CHANTIR, BUT I'VE WAITED OVER A MONTH FOR THIS MOMENT—I HAVE TO GO THIS WAY.
THERE'S AN ITEM THAT'S ARRIVED, AND I NEED IT.
THIS IS THE ROOM! QUICKLY, OPEN THE DOOR!
FZAP
THERE YOU ARE. THE GREAT KEY OF RASSILON.
THIS IS PART OF A WEAPON CALLED THE DE-MAT GUN, YOU KNOW—SO POWERFUL IT CAN REMOVE SOMETHING COMPLETELY FROM TIME AND SPACE.
CHAN—THAT SOUNDS TERRIBLE—TIR!
CHAN—WHY WOULD YOU WANT SUCH A WEAPON—TIR?
OH, THIS ALONE ISN'T A WEAPON, CHANTIR—THIS IS JUST A KEY.
A VERY POWERFUL KEY, HOWEVER. AND ONE I HOPE NOT TO NEED TO USE.
AH. THAT'S NOT GOOD.

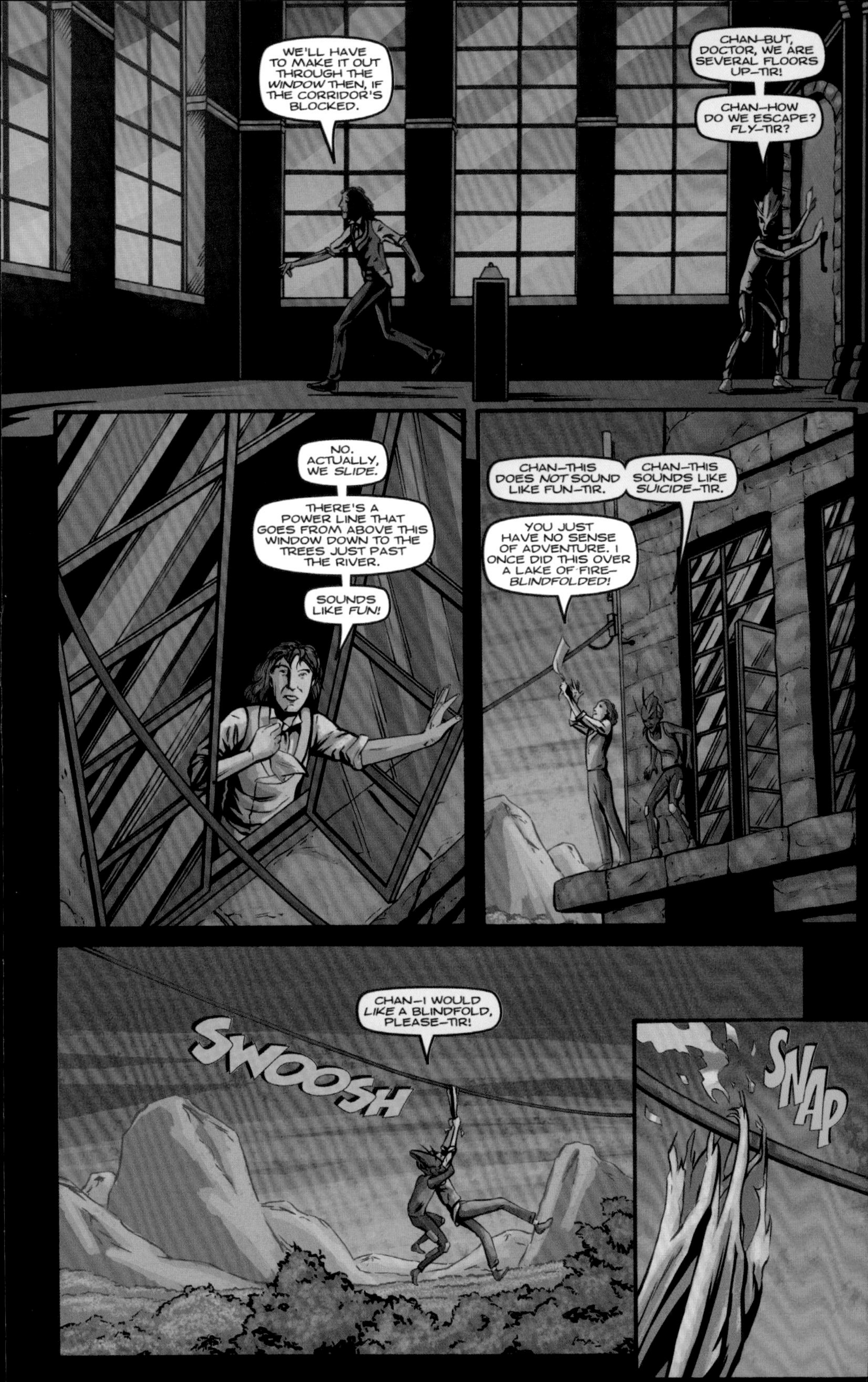
WE'LL HAVE TO MAKE IT OUT THROUGH THE *WINDOW* THEN, IF THE CORRIDOR'S BLOCKED.
CHAN—BUT, DOCTOR, WE ARE SEVERAL FLOORS UP—TIR!
CHAN—HOW DO WE ESCAPE? *FLY*—TIR?
NO. ACTUALLY, WE *SLIDE*.
THERE'S A POWER LINE THAT GOES FROM ABOVE THIS WINDOW DOWN TO THE TREES JUST PAST THE RIVER.
SOUNDS LIKE *FUN!*
CHAN—THIS DOES *NOT* SOUND LIKE FUN—TIR.
CHAN—THIS SOUNDS LIKE *SUICIDE*—TIR.
YOU JUST HAVE NO SENSE OF ADVENTURE. I ONCE DID THIS OVER A LAKE OF FIRE—*BLINDFOLDED!*
SWOOSH
CHAN—I WOULD LIKE A BLINDFOLD, PLEASE—TIR!
SNAP

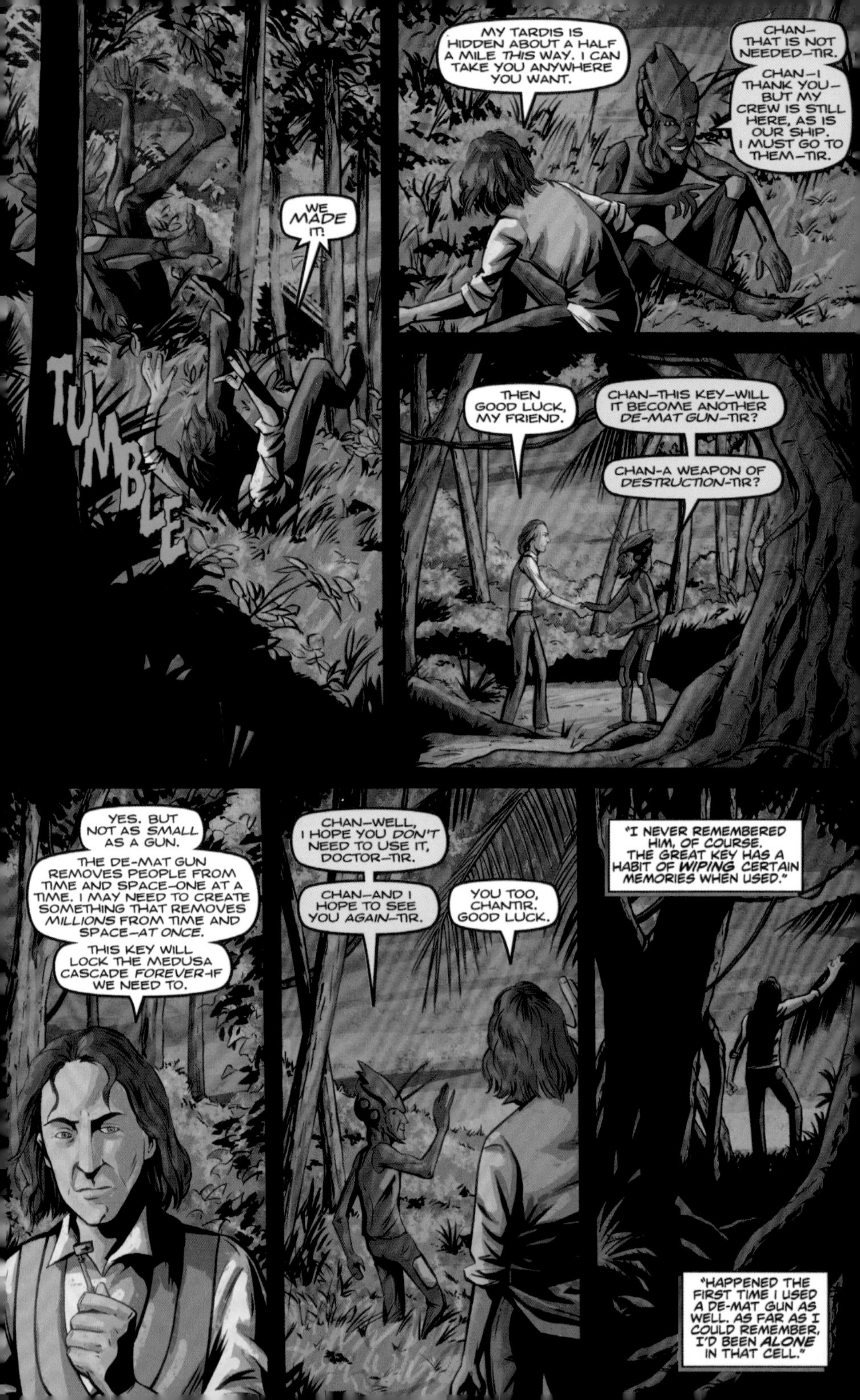

WE MADE IT!
TUMBLE
MY TARDIS IS HIDDEN ABOUT A HALF A MILE THIS WAY. I CAN TAKE YOU ANYWHERE YOU WANT.
CHAN—THAT IS NOT NEEDED—TIR.
CHAN—I THANK YOU—BUT MY CREW IS STILL HERE, AS IS OUR SHIP. I MUST GO TO THEM—TIR.
THEN GOOD LUCK, MY FRIEND.
CHAN—THIS KEY—WILL IT BECOME ANOTHER DE-MAT GUN—TIR?
CHAN—A WEAPON OF DESTRUCTION—TIR?
YES. BUT NOT AS SMALL AS A GUN.
THE DE-MAT GUN REMOVES PEOPLE FROM TIME AND SPACE—ONE AT A TIME. I MAY NEED TO CREATE SOMETHING THAT REMOVES MILLIONS FROM TIME AND SPACE—AT ONCE.
THIS KEY WILL LOCK THE MEDUSA CASCADE FOREVER—IF WE NEED TO.
CHAN—WELL, I HOPE YOU DON'T NEED TO USE IT, DOCTOR—TIR.
CHAN—AND I HOPE TO SEE YOU AGAIN—TIR.
YOU TOO, CHANTIR. GOOD LUCK.
"I NEVER REMEMBERED HIM, OF COURSE. THE GREAT KEY HAS A HABIT OF WIPING CERTAIN MEMORIES WHEN USED."
"HAPPENED THE FIRST TIME I USED A DE-MAT GUN AS WELL. AS FAR AS I COULD REMEMBER, I'D BEEN ALONE IN THAT CELL."

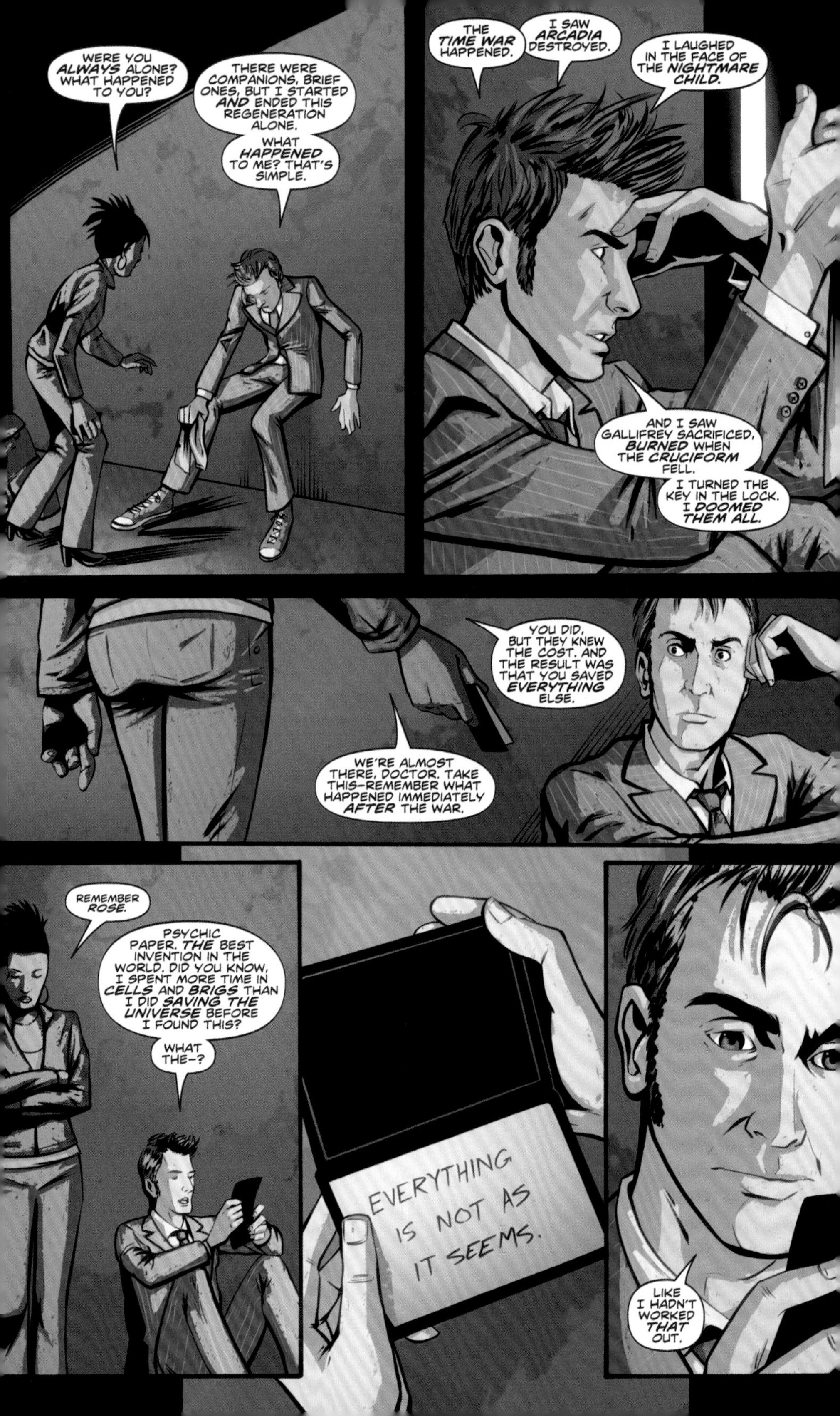

WERE YOU ALWAYS ALONE? WHAT HAPPENED TO YOU?
THERE WERE COMPANIONS, BRIEF ONES, BUT I STARTED AND ENDED THIS REGENERATION ALONE.
WHAT HAPPENED TO ME? THAT'S SIMPLE.
THE TIME WAR HAPPENED.
I SAW ARCADIA DESTROYED.
I LAUGHED IN THE FACE OF THE NIGHTMARE CHILD.
AND I SAW GALLIFREY SACRIFICED, BURNED WHEN THE CRUCIFORM FELL.
I TURNED THE KEY IN THE LOCK. I DOOMED THEM ALL.
YOU DID, BUT THEY KNEW THE COST. AND THE RESULT WAS THAT YOU SAVED EVERYTHING ELSE.
WE'RE ALMOST THERE, DOCTOR. TAKE THIS–REMEMBER WHAT HAPPENED IMMEDIATELY AFTER THE WAR.
REMEMBER ROSE.
PSYCHIC PAPER. THE BEST INVENTION IN THE WORLD. DID YOU KNOW, I SPENT MORE TIME IN CELLS AND BRIGS THAN I DID SAVING THE UNIVERSE BEFORE I FOUND THIS?
WHAT THE–?
EVERYTHING IS NOT AS IT SEEMS.
LIKE I HADN'T WORKED THAT OUT.

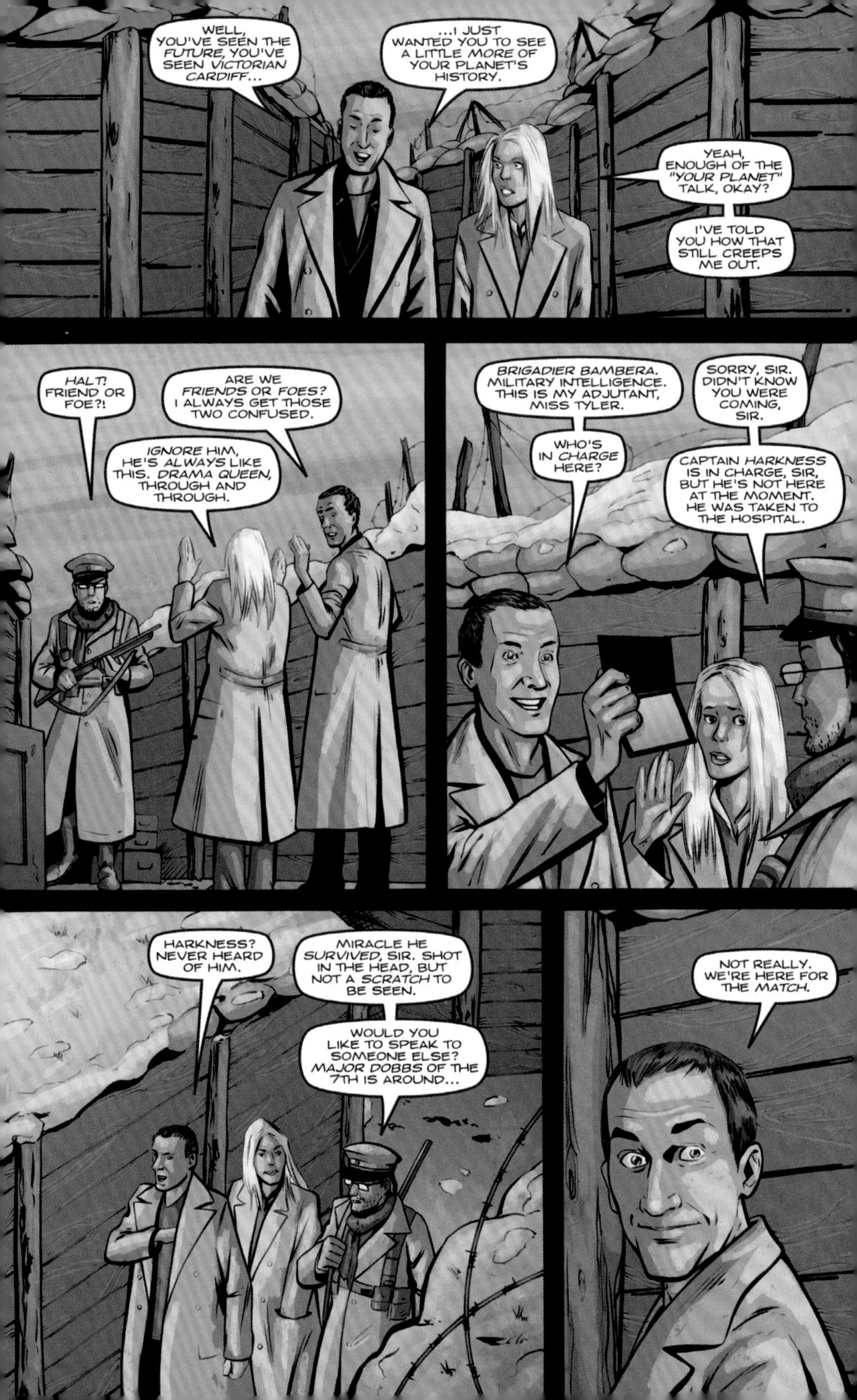

WELL, YOU'VE SEEN THE *FUTURE*, YOU'VE SEEN *VICTORIAN CARDIFF*...
...I JUST WANTED YOU TO SEE A LITTLE *MORE* OF YOUR PLANET'S HISTORY.
YEAH, ENOUGH OF THE *"YOUR PLANET"* TALK, OKAY?
I'VE TOLD YOU HOW THAT STILL CREEPS ME OUT.
HALT! FRIEND OR FOE?!
ARE WE *FRIENDS* OR *FOES*? I ALWAYS GET THOSE TWO CONFUSED.
IGNORE HIM, HE'S *ALWAYS* LIKE THIS. *DRAMA QUEEN*, THROUGH AND THROUGH.
BRIGADIER BAMBERA. MILITARY INTELLIGENCE. THIS IS MY ADJUTANT, MISS TYLER.
WHO'S IN *CHARGE* HERE?
SORRY, SIR. DIDN'T KNOW YOU WERE COMING, SIR.
CAPTAIN *HARKNESS* IS IN CHARGE, SIR, BUT HE'S NOT HERE AT THE MOMENT. HE WAS TAKEN TO THE HOSPITAL.
HARKNESS? NEVER HEARD OF HIM.
MIRACLE HE *SURVIVED*, SIR. SHOT IN THE HEAD, BUT NOT A *SCRATCH* TO BE SEEN.
WOULD YOU LIKE TO SPEAK TO SOMEONE ELSE? *MAJOR DOBBS* OF THE 7TH IS AROUND...
NOT REALLY. WE'RE HERE FOR THE *MATCH*.

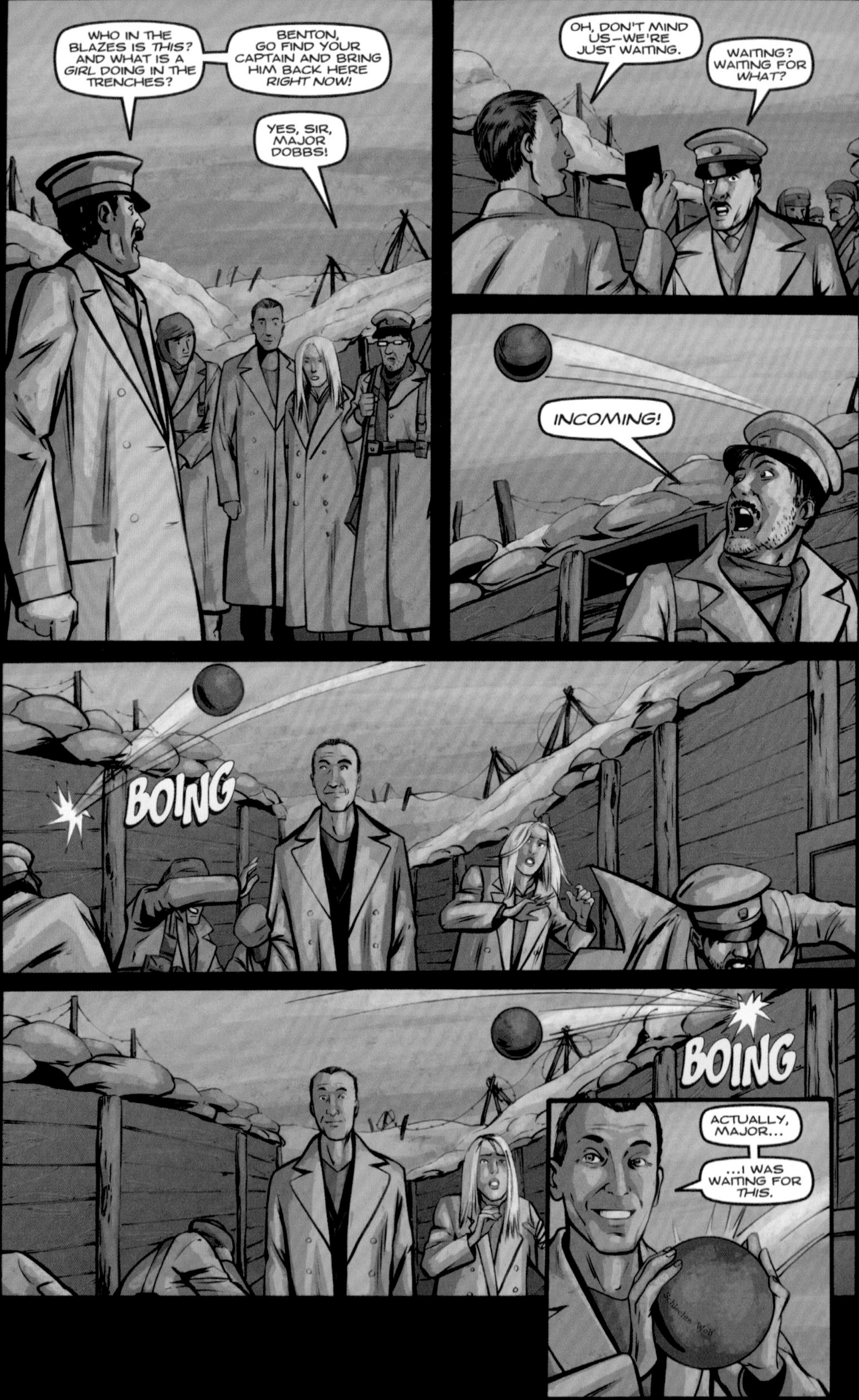
WHO IN THE BLAZES IS THIS? AND WHAT IS A GIRL DOING IN THE TRENCHES?
BENTON, GO FIND YOUR CAPTAIN AND BRING HIM BACK HERE RIGHT NOW!
YES, SIR, MAJOR DOBBS!
OH, DON'T MIND US—WE'RE JUST WAITING.
WAITING? WAITING FOR WHAT?
INCOMING!
BOING
BOING
ACTUALLY, MAJOR...
...I WAS WAITING FOR THIS.

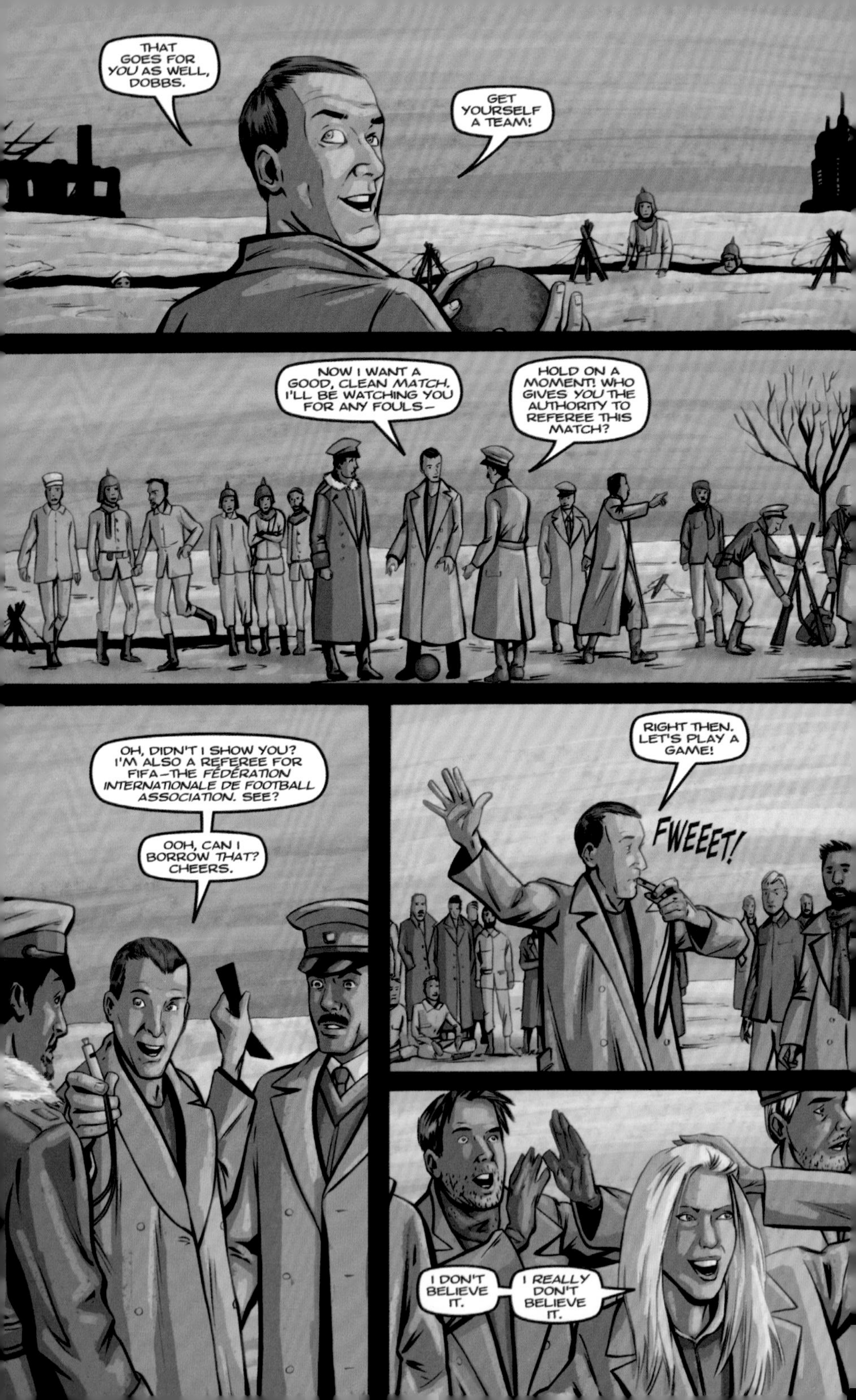

THAT GOES FOR YOU AS WELL, DOBBS.
GET YOURSELF A TEAM!
NOW I WANT A GOOD, CLEAN MATCH. I'LL BE WATCHING YOU FOR ANY FOULS—
HOLD ON A MOMENT! WHO GIVES YOU THE AUTHORITY TO REFEREE THIS MATCH?
OH, DIDN'T I SHOW YOU? I'M ALSO A REFEREE FOR FIFA—THE FÉDÉRATION INTERNATIONALE DE FOOTBALL ASSOCIATION. SEE?
OOH, CAN I BORROW THAT? CHEERS.
RIGHT THEN. LET'S PLAY A GAME!
FWEEET!
I DON'T BELIEVE IT.
I REALLY DON'T BELIEVE IT.

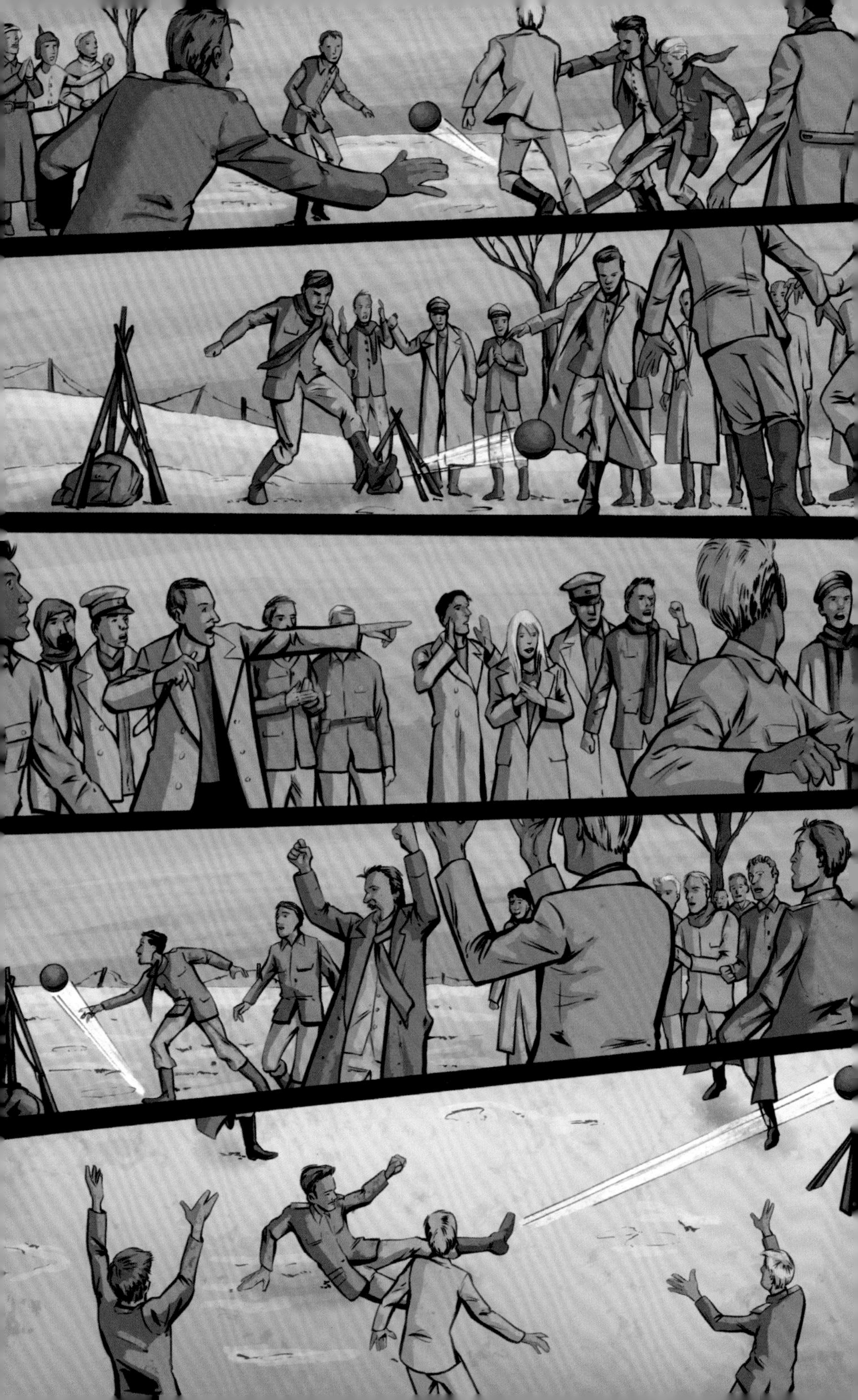

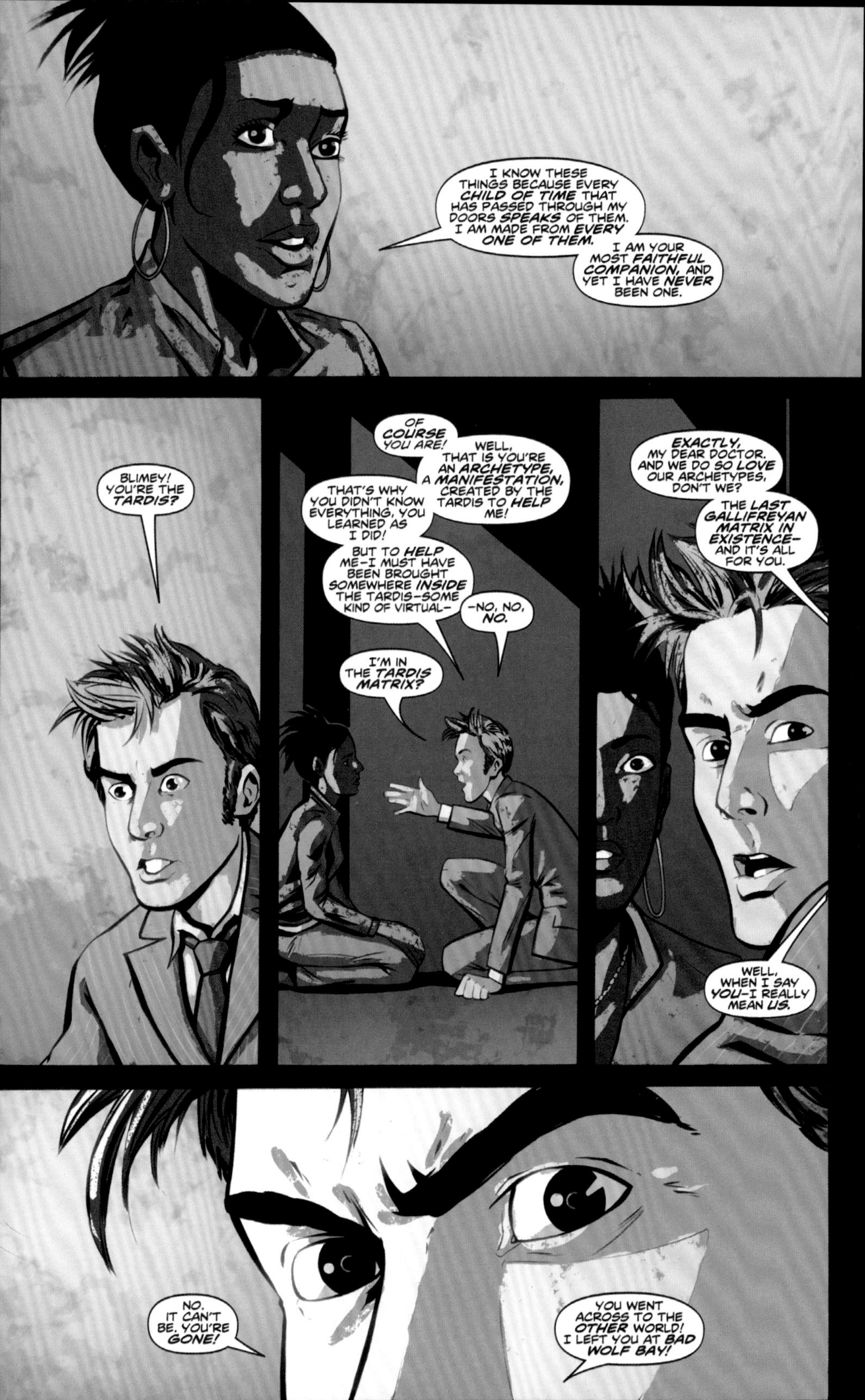
I KNOW THESE THINGS BECAUSE EVERY CHILD OF TIME THAT HAS PASSED THROUGH MY DOORS SPEAKS OF THEM. I AM MADE FROM EVERY ONE OF THEM.
I AM YOUR MOST FAITHFUL COMPANION, AND YET I HAVE NEVER BEEN ONE.
BLIMEY! YOU'RE THE TARDIS?
OF COURSE YOU ARE!
WELL, THAT IS YOU'RE AN ARCHETYPE, A MANIFESTATION, CREATED BY THE TARDIS TO HELP ME!
THAT'S WHY YOU DIDN'T KNOW EVERYTHING, YOU LEARNED AS I DID!
BUT TO HELP ME–I MUST HAVE BEEN BROUGHT SOMEWHERE INSIDE THE TARDIS–SOME KIND OF VIRTUAL–
–NO, NO, NO.
I'M IN THE TARDIS MATRIX?
EXACTLY, MY DEAR DOCTOR. AND WE DO SO LOVE OUR ARCHETYPES, DON'T WE?
THE LAST GALLIFREYAN MATRIX IN EXISTENCE– AND IT'S ALL FOR YOU.
WELL, WHEN I SAY YOU–I REALLY MEAN US.
NO. IT CAN'T BE. YOU'RE GONE!
YOU WENT ACROSS TO THE OTHER WORLD! I LEFT YOU AT BAD WOLF BAY!

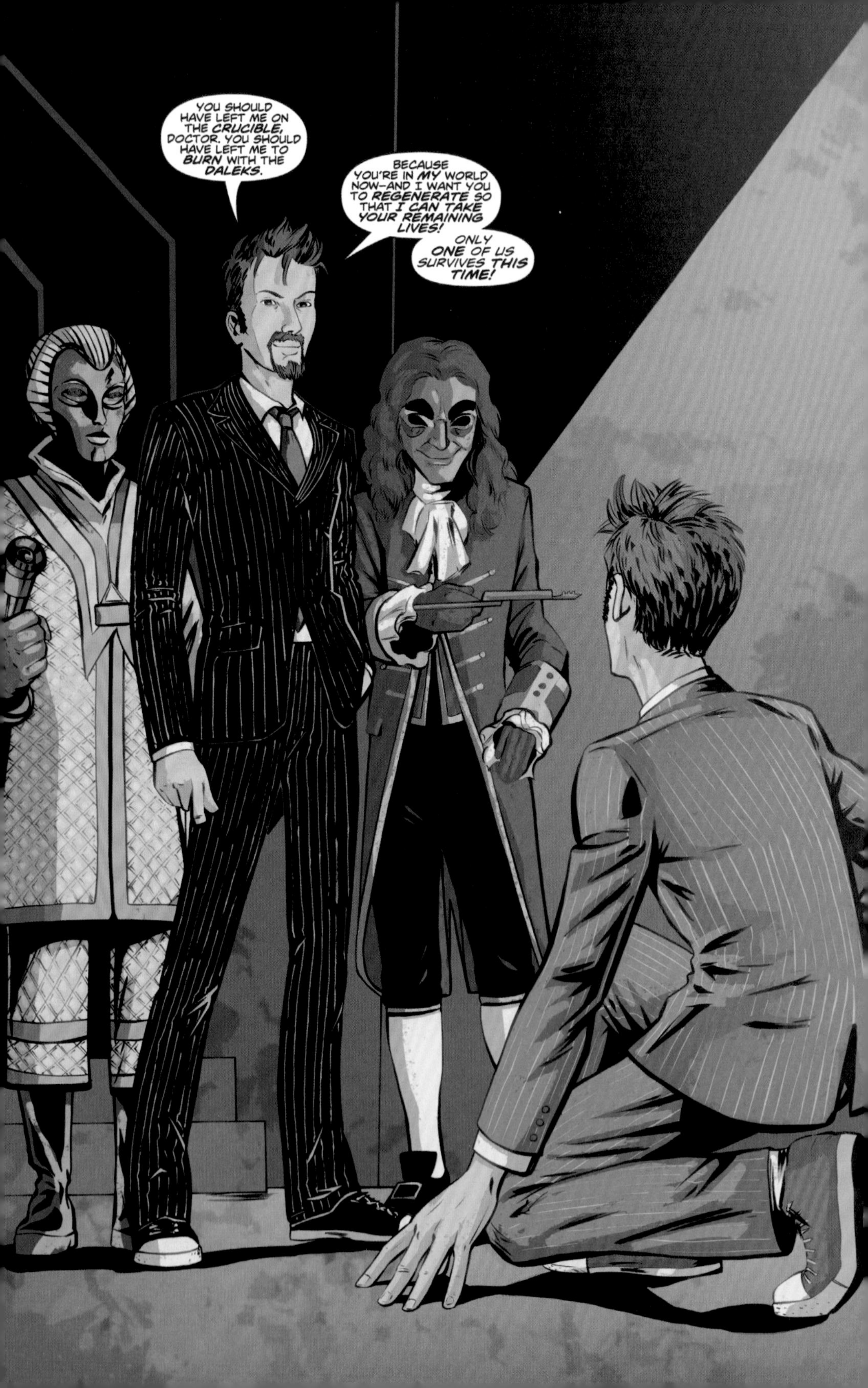
YOU SHOULD HAVE LEFT ME ON THE CRUCIBLE, DOCTOR. YOU SHOULD HAVE LEFT ME TO BURN WITH THE DALEKS.
BECAUSE YOU'RE IN MY WORLD NOW—AND I WANT YOU TO REGENERATE SO THAT I CAN TAKE YOUR REMAINING LIVES!
ONLY ONE OF US SURVIVES THIS TIME!

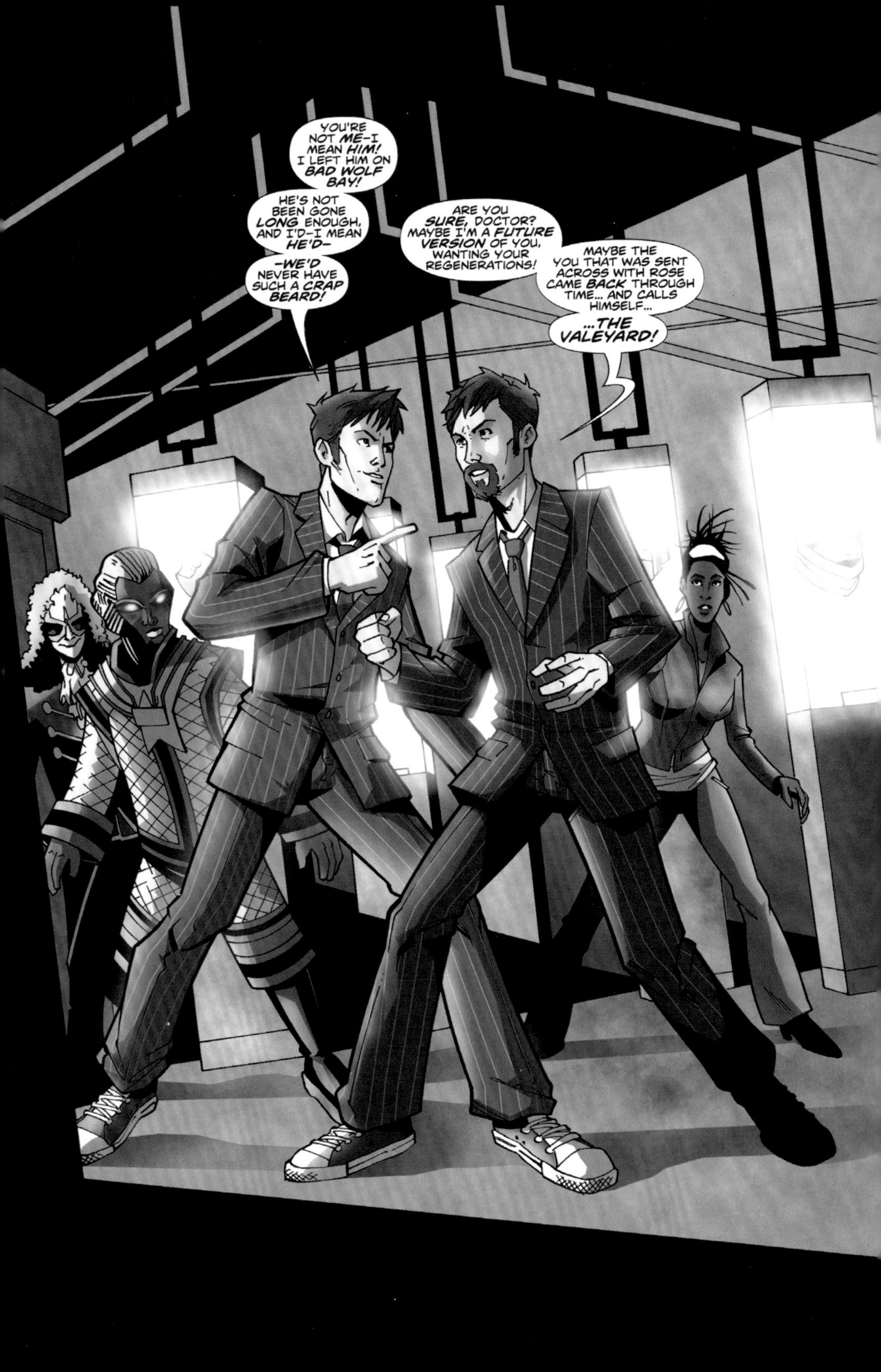
YOU'RE NOT ME–I MEAN HIM! I LEFT HIM ON BAD WOLF BAY!
HE'S NOT BEEN GONE LONG ENOUGH, AND I'D–I MEAN HE'D–
–WE'D NEVER HAVE SUCH A CRAP BEARD!
ARE YOU SURE, DOCTOR? MAYBE I'M A FUTURE VERSION OF YOU, WANTING YOUR REGENERATIONS!
MAYBE THE YOU THAT WAS SENT ACROSS WITH ROSE CAME BACK THROUGH TIME... AND CALLS HIMSELF...
...THE VALEYARD!

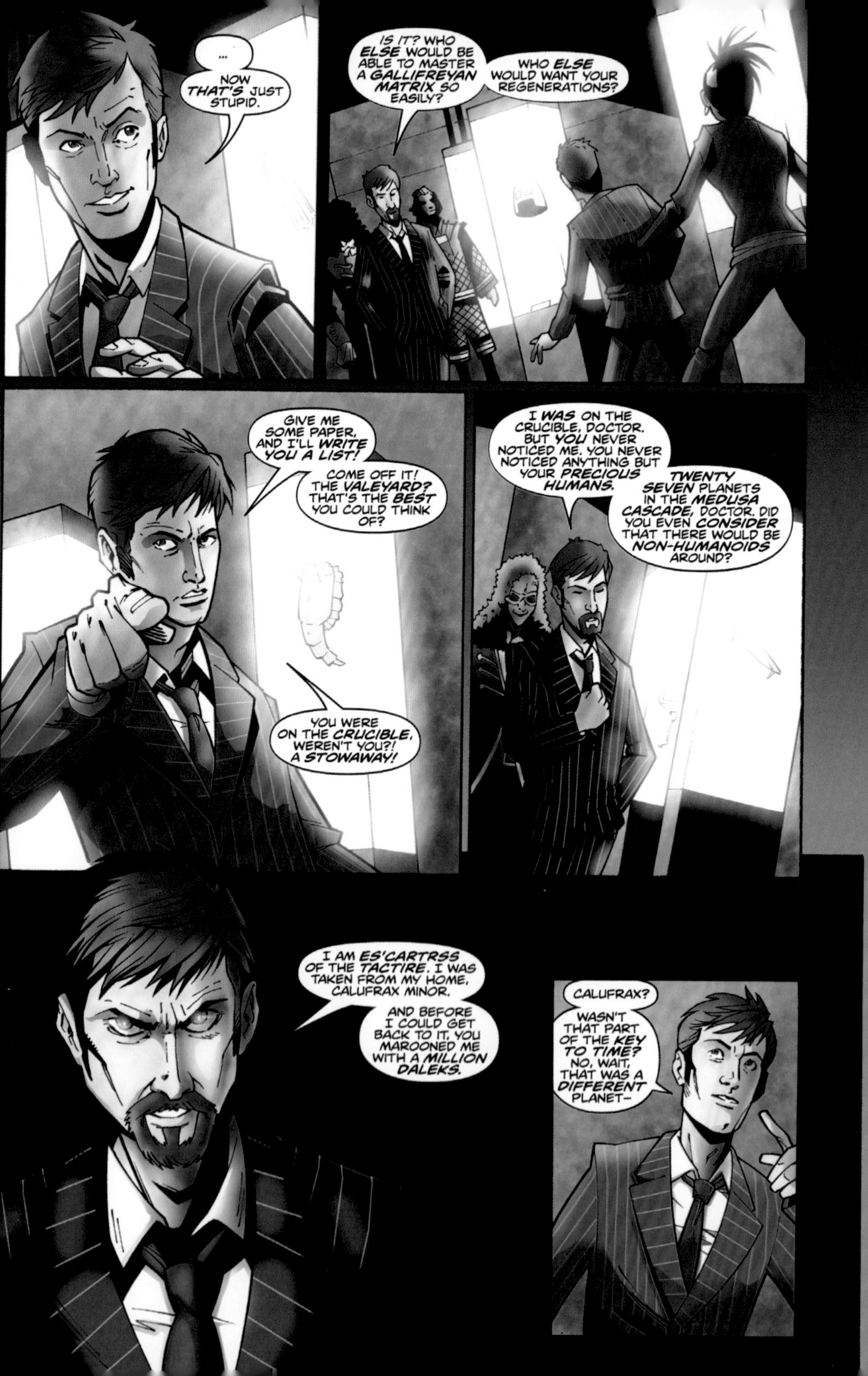
...
NOW THAT'S JUST STUPID.
IS IT? WHO ELSE WOULD BE ABLE TO MASTER A GALLIFREYAN MATRIX SO EASILY?
WHO ELSE WOULD WANT YOUR REGENERATIONS?
GIVE ME SOME PAPER, AND I'LL WRITE YOU A LIST!
COME OFF IT! THE VALEYARD? THAT'S THE BEST YOU COULD THINK OF?
YOU WERE ON THE CRUCIBLE, WEREN'T YOU?! A STOWAWAY!
I WAS ON THE CRUCIBLE, DOCTOR. BUT YOU NEVER NOTICED ME. YOU NEVER NOTICED ANYTHING BUT YOUR PRECIOUS HUMANS.
TWENTY SEVEN PLANETS IN THE MEDUSA CASCADE, DOCTOR. DID YOU EVEN CONSIDER THAT THERE WOULD BE NON-HUMANOIDS AROUND?
I AM ES'CARTRSS OF THE TACTIRE. I WAS TAKEN FROM MY HOME, CALUFRAX MINOR.
AND BEFORE I COULD GET BACK TO IT, YOU MAROONED ME WITH A MILLION DALEKS.
CALUFRAX?
WASN'T THAT PART OF THE KEY TO TIME? NO, WAIT, THAT WAS A DIFFERENT PLANET-

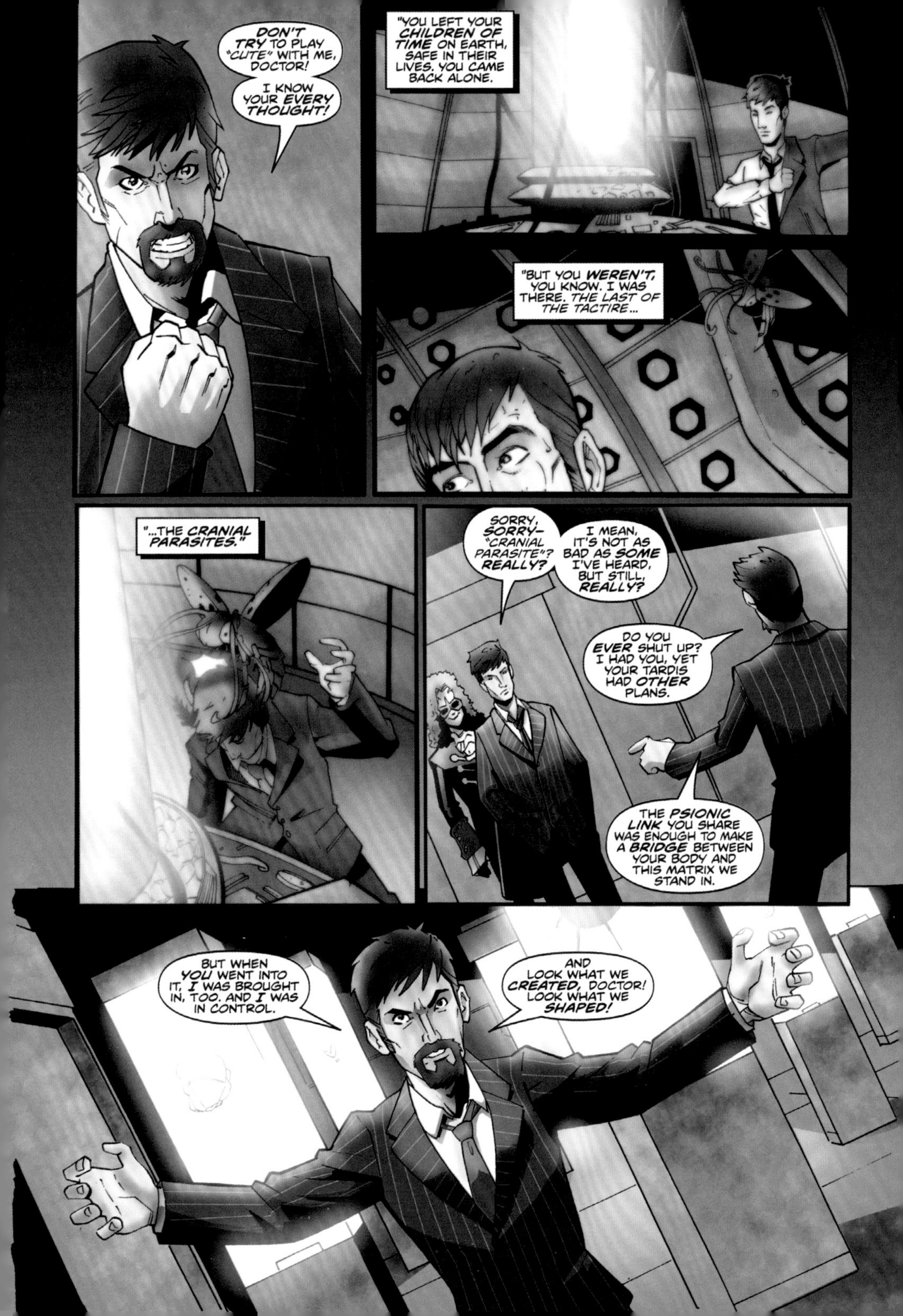

DON'T TRY TO PLAY "CUTE" WITH ME, DOCTOR!
I KNOW YOUR EVERY THOUGHT!
"YOU LEFT YOUR CHILDREN OF TIME ON EARTH, SAFE IN THEIR LIVES. YOU CAME BACK ALONE.
"BUT YOU WEREN'T, YOU KNOW. I WAS THERE. THE LAST OF THE TACTIRE...
"...THE CRANIAL PARASITES."
SORRY, SORRY— "CRANIAL PARASITE"? REALLY?
I MEAN, IT'S NOT AS BAD AS SOME I'VE HEARD, BUT STILL, REALLY?
DO YOU EVER SHUT UP? I HAD YOU, YET YOUR TARDIS HAD OTHER PLANS.
THE PSIONIC LINK YOU SHARE WAS ENOUGH TO MAKE A BRIDGE BETWEEN YOUR BODY AND THIS MATRIX WE STAND IN.
BUT WHEN YOU WENT INTO IT, I WAS BROUGHT IN, TOO. AND I WAS IN CONTROL.
AND LOOK WHAT WE CREATED, DOCTOR! LOOK WHAT WE SHAPED!

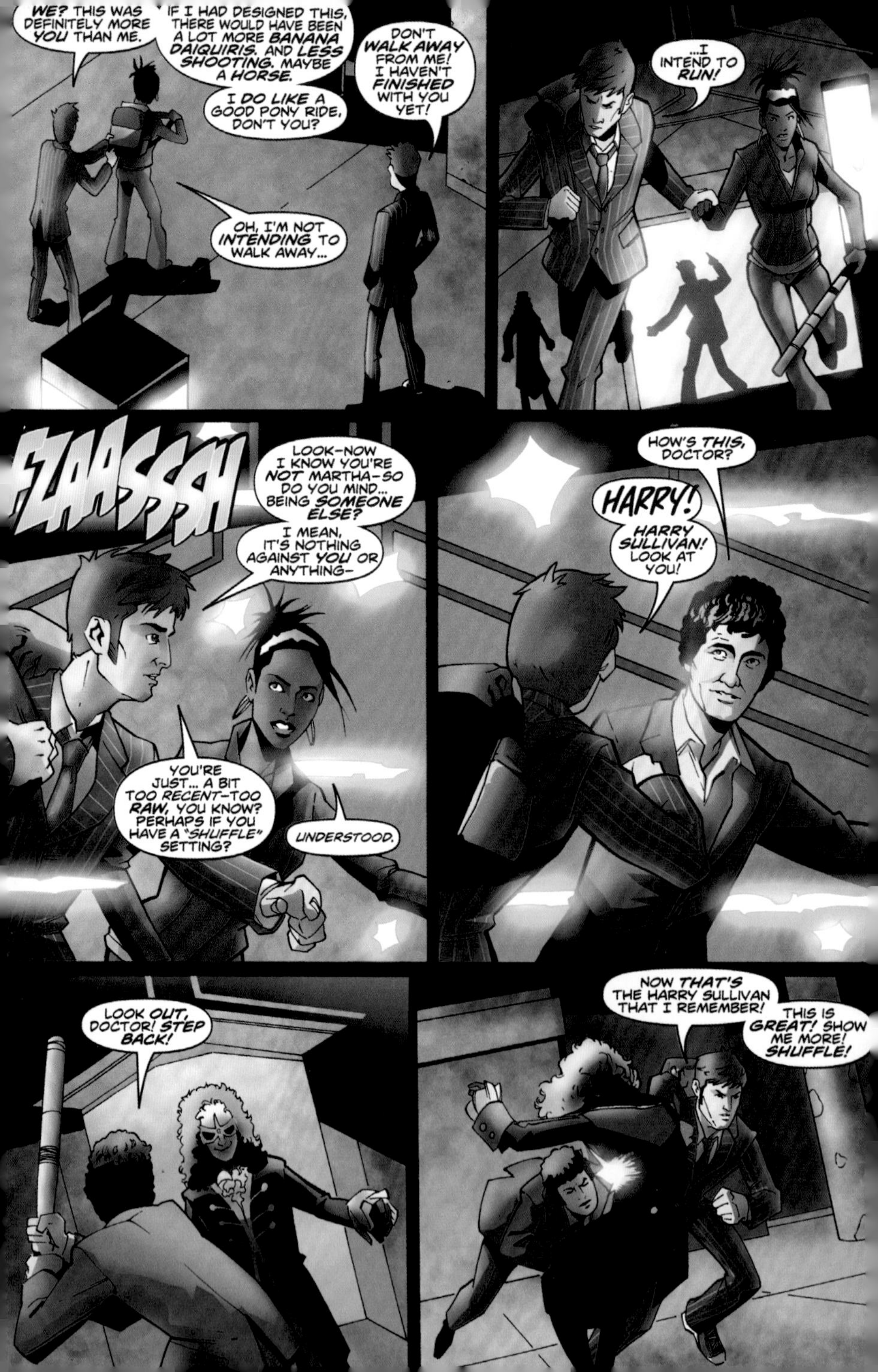
WE? THIS WAS DEFINITELY MORE YOU THAN ME.
IF I HAD DESIGNED THIS, THERE WOULD HAVE BEEN A LOT MORE BANANA DAIQUIRIS, AND LESS SHOOTING. MAYBE A HORSE.
I DO LIKE A GOOD PONY RIDE, DON'T YOU?
DON'T WALK AWAY FROM ME! I HAVEN'T FINISHED WITH YOU YET!
OH, I'M NOT INTENDING TO WALK AWAY...
...I INTEND TO RUN!
FZAASSSH
LOOK—NOW I KNOW YOU'RE NOT MARTHA—SO DO YOU MIND... BEING SOMEONE ELSE?
I MEAN, IT'S NOTHING AGAINST YOU OR ANYTHING—
YOU'RE JUST... A BIT TOO RECENT—TOO RAW, YOU KNOW? PERHAPS IF YOU HAVE A "SHUFFLE" SETTING?
UNDERSTOOD.
HOW'S THIS, DOCTOR?
HARRY! HARRY SULLIVAN! LOOK AT YOU!
LOOK OUT, DOCTOR! STEP BACK!
NOW THAT'S THE HARRY SULLIVAN THAT I REMEMBER!
THIS IS GREAT! SHOW ME MORE! SHUFFLE!

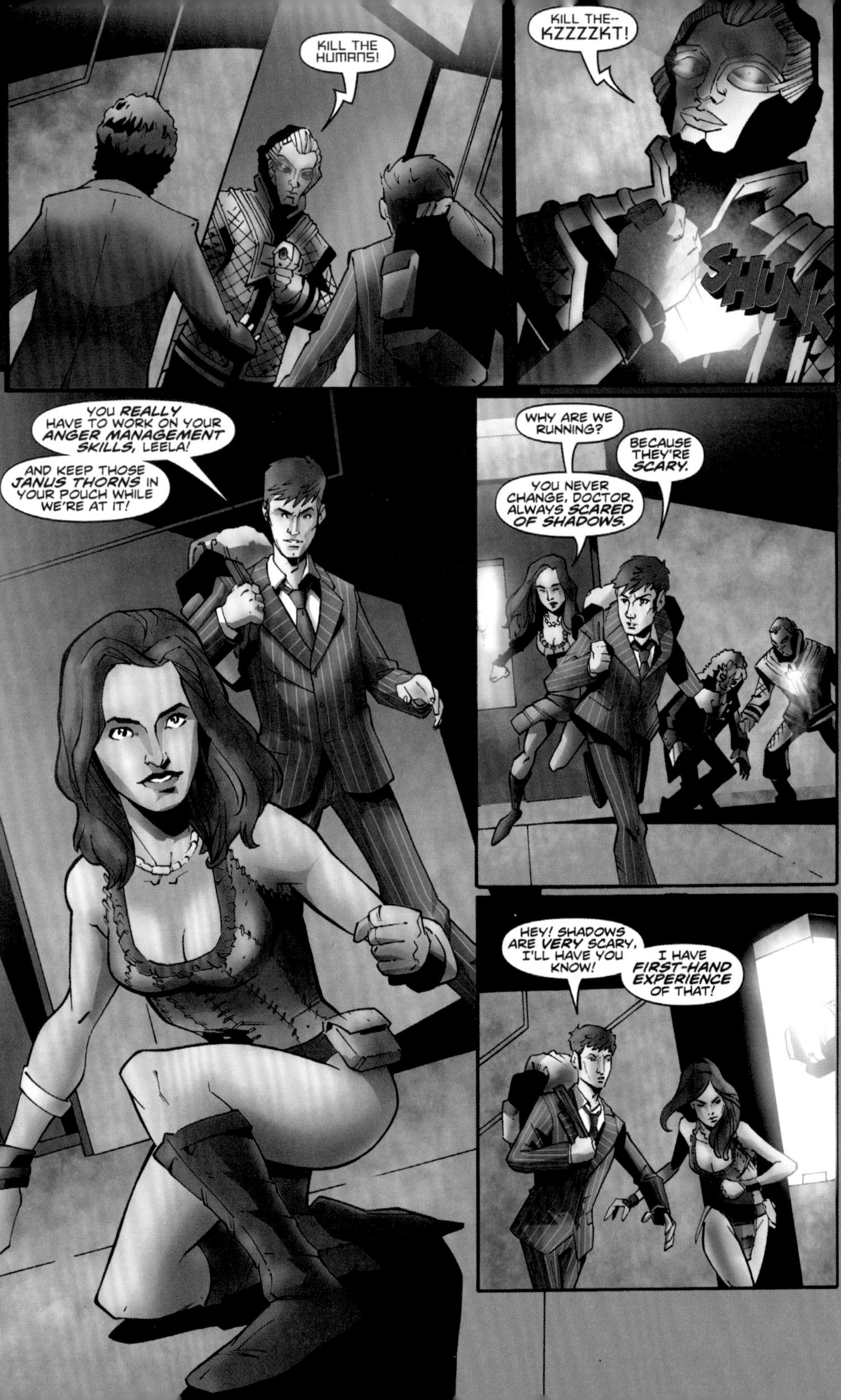
KILL THE HUMANS!
KILL THE-- KZZZZKT!
SHUNK
YOU REALLY HAVE TO WORK ON YOUR ANGER MANAGEMENT SKILLS, LEELA!
AND KEEP THOSE JANUS THORNS IN YOUR POUCH WHILE WE'RE AT IT!
WHY ARE WE RUNNING?
BECAUSE THEY'RE SCARY.
YOU NEVER CHANGE, DOCTOR. ALWAYS SCARED OF SHADOWS.
HEY! SHADOWS ARE VERY SCARY, I'LL HAVE YOU KNOW!
I HAVE FIRST-HAND EXPERIENCE OF THAT!

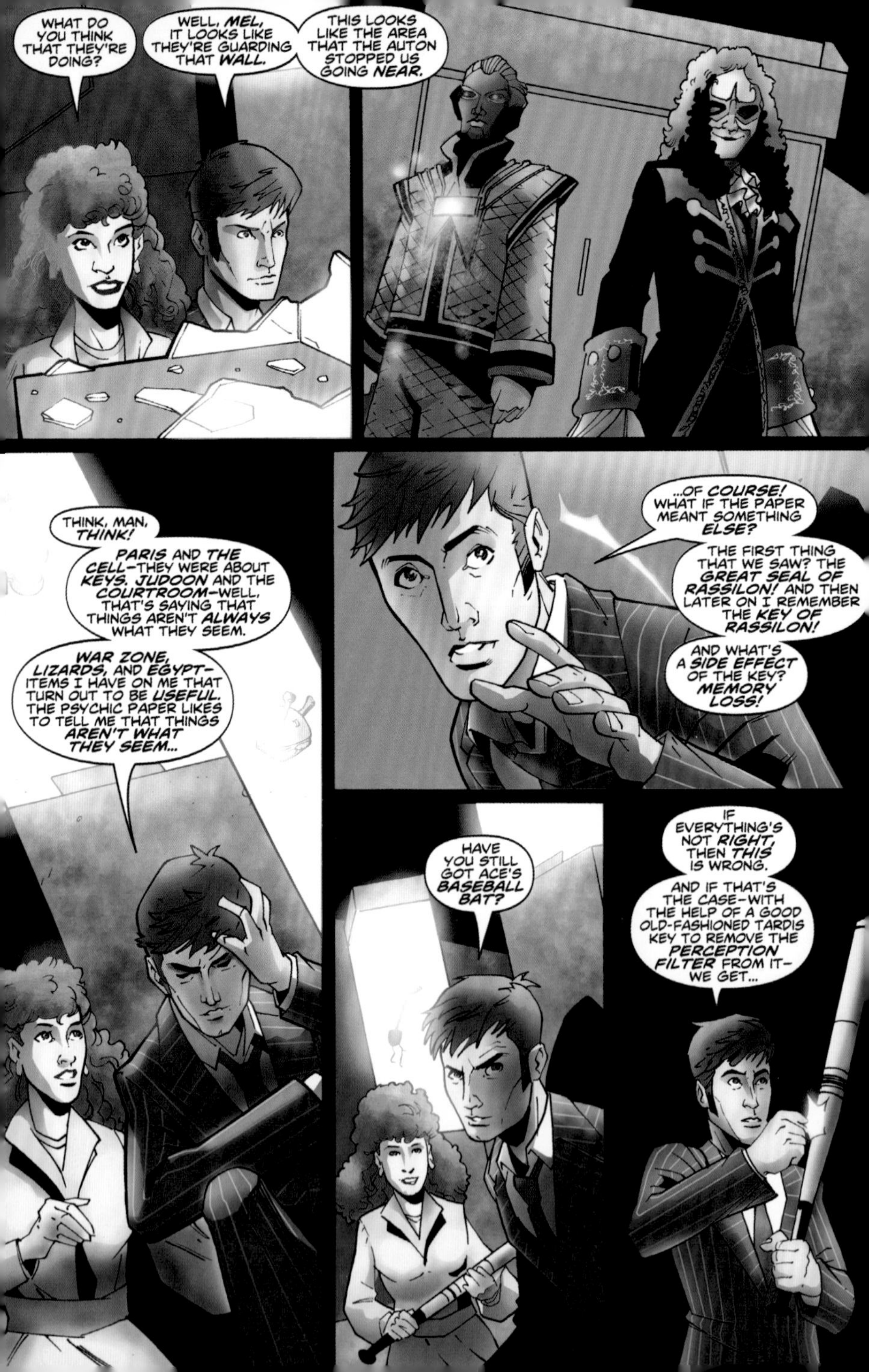
WHAT DO YOU THINK THAT THEY'RE DOING?
WELL, MEL, IT LOOKS LIKE THEY'RE GUARDING THAT WALL.
THIS LOOKS LIKE THE AREA THAT THE AUTON STOPPED US GOING NEAR.
THINK, MAN, THINK!
PARIS AND THE CELL–THEY WERE ABOUT KEYS. JUDOON AND THE COURTROOM–WELL, THAT'S SAYING THAT THINGS AREN'T ALWAYS WHAT THEY SEEM.
WAR ZONE, LIZARDS, AND EGYPT–ITEMS I HAVE ON ME THAT TURN OUT TO BE USEFUL. THE PSYCHIC PAPER LIKES TO TELL ME THAT THINGS AREN'T WHAT THEY SEEM...
...OF COURSE! WHAT IF THE PAPER MEANT SOMETHING ELSE?
THE FIRST THING THAT WE SAW? THE GREAT SEAL OF RASSILON! AND THEN LATER ON I REMEMBER THE KEY OF RASSILON!
AND WHAT'S A SIDE EFFECT OF THE KEY? MEMORY LOSS!
HAVE YOU STILL GOT ACE'S BASEBALL BAT?
IF EVERYTHING'S NOT RIGHT, THEN THIS IS WRONG.
AND IF THAT'S THE CASE–WITH THE HELP OF A GOOD OLD-FASHIONED TARDIS KEY TO REMOVE THE PERCEPTION FILTER FROM IT–WE GET...

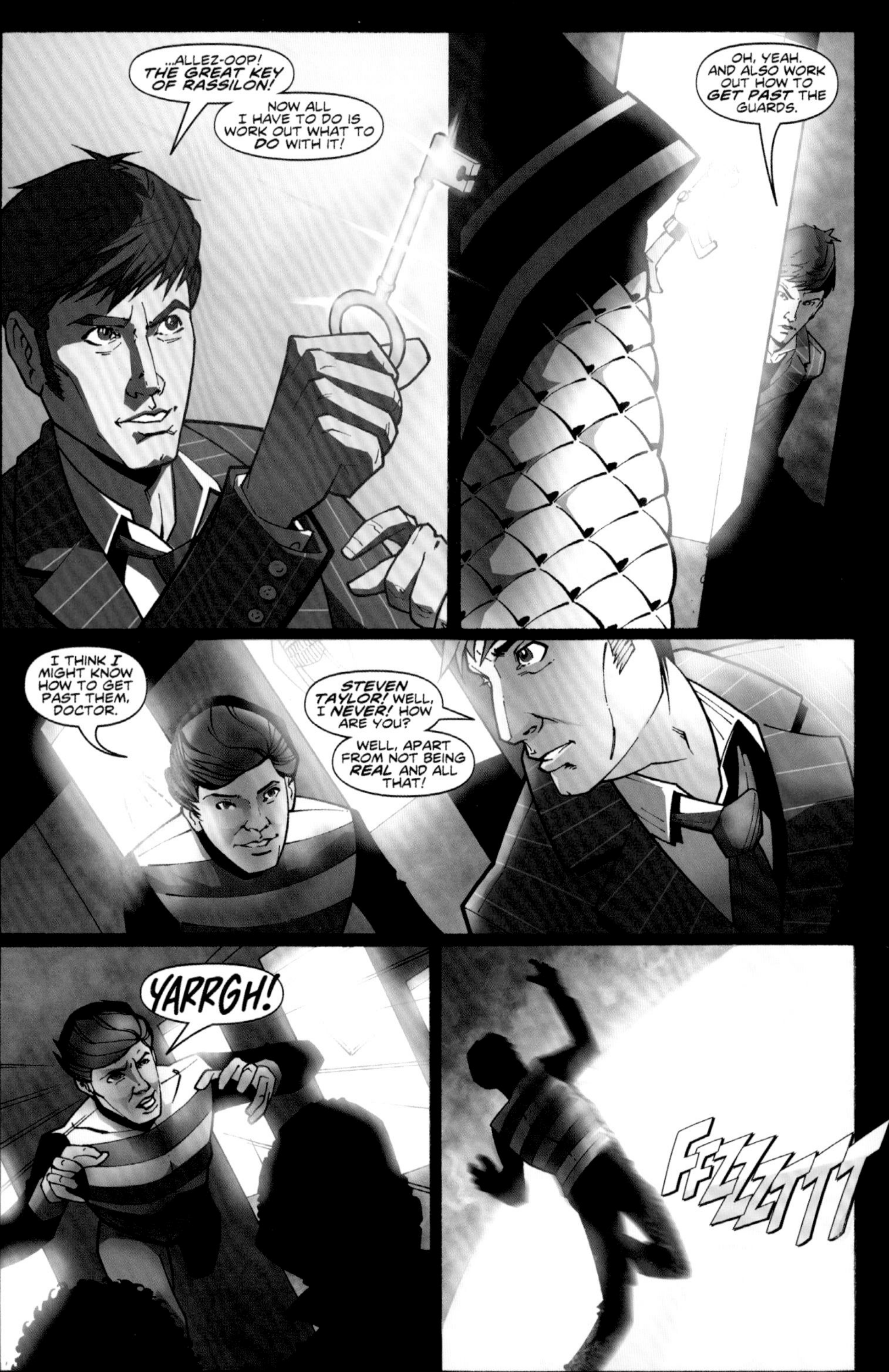
...ALLEZ-OOP! THE GREAT KEY OF RASSILON!
NOW ALL I HAVE TO DO IS WORK OUT WHAT TO DO WITH IT!
OH, YEAH. AND ALSO WORK OUT HOW TO GET PAST THE GUARDS.
I THINK I MIGHT KNOW HOW TO GET PAST THEM, DOCTOR.
STEVEN TAYLOR! WELL, I NEVER! HOW ARE YOU?
WELL, APART FROM NOT BEING REAL AND ALL THAT!
YARRGH!
FFZZZTTT

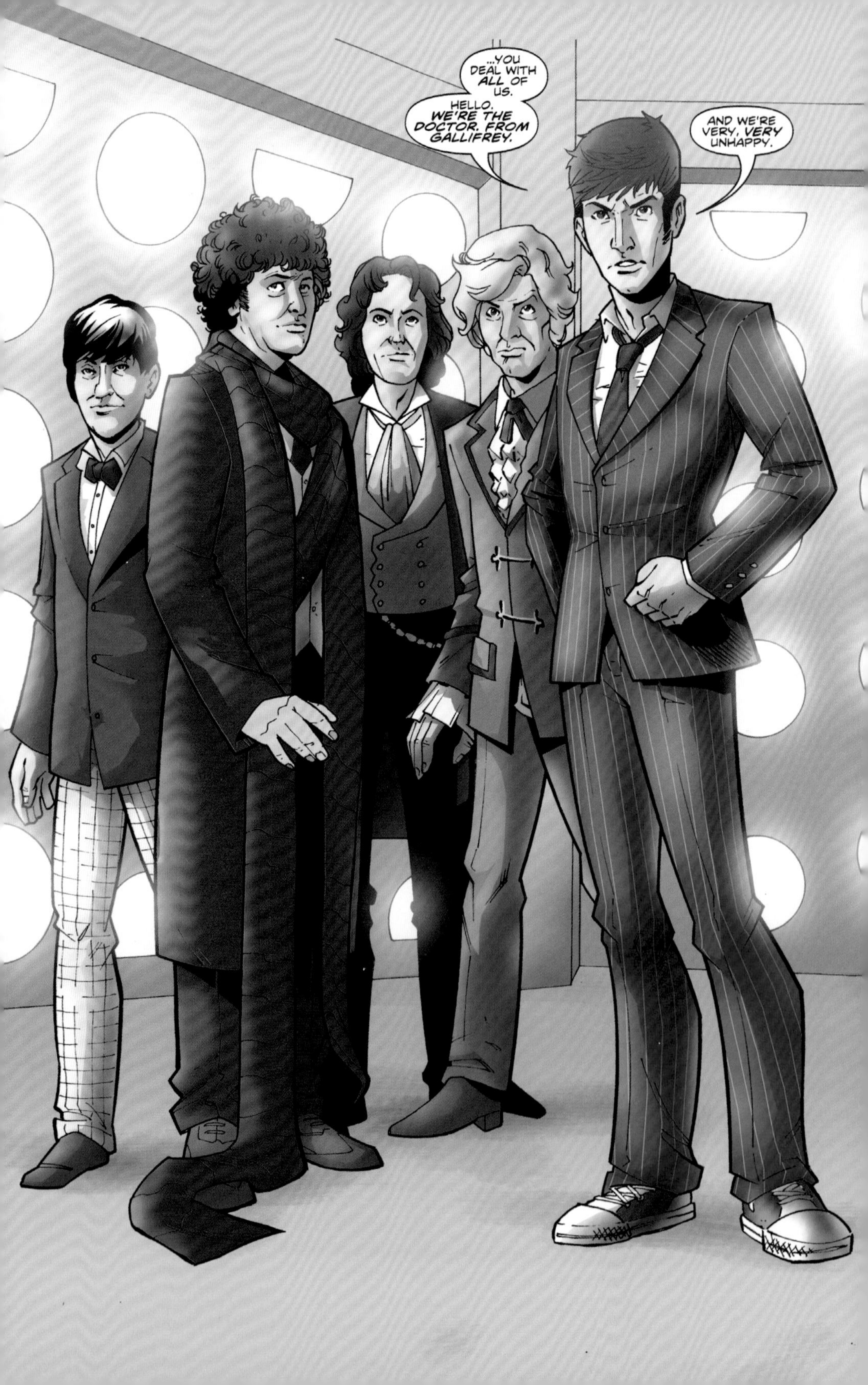
...YOU DEAL WITH ALL OF US.
HELLO. WE'RE THE DOCTOR. FROM GALLIFREY.
AND WE'RE VERY, VERY UNHAPPY.

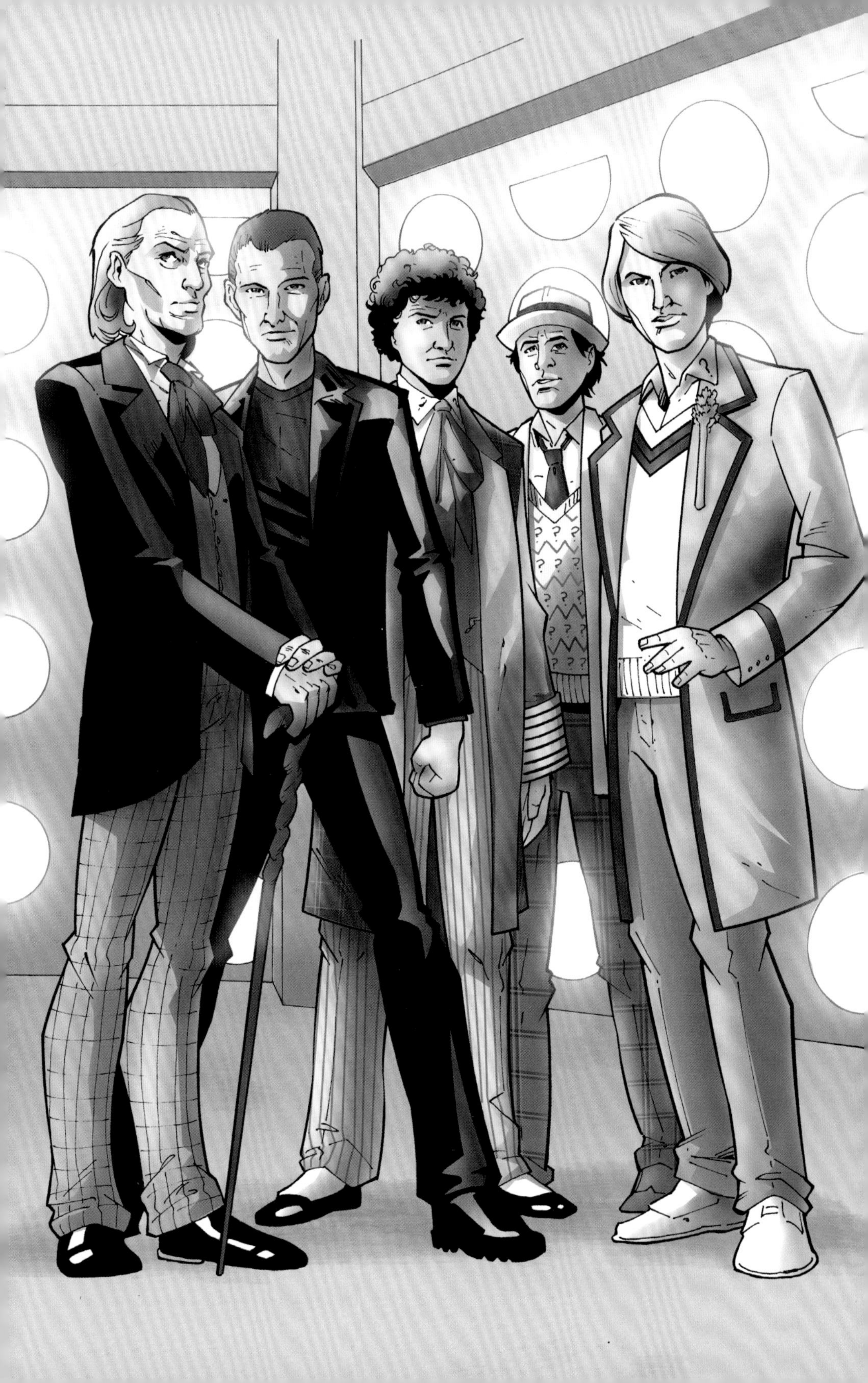

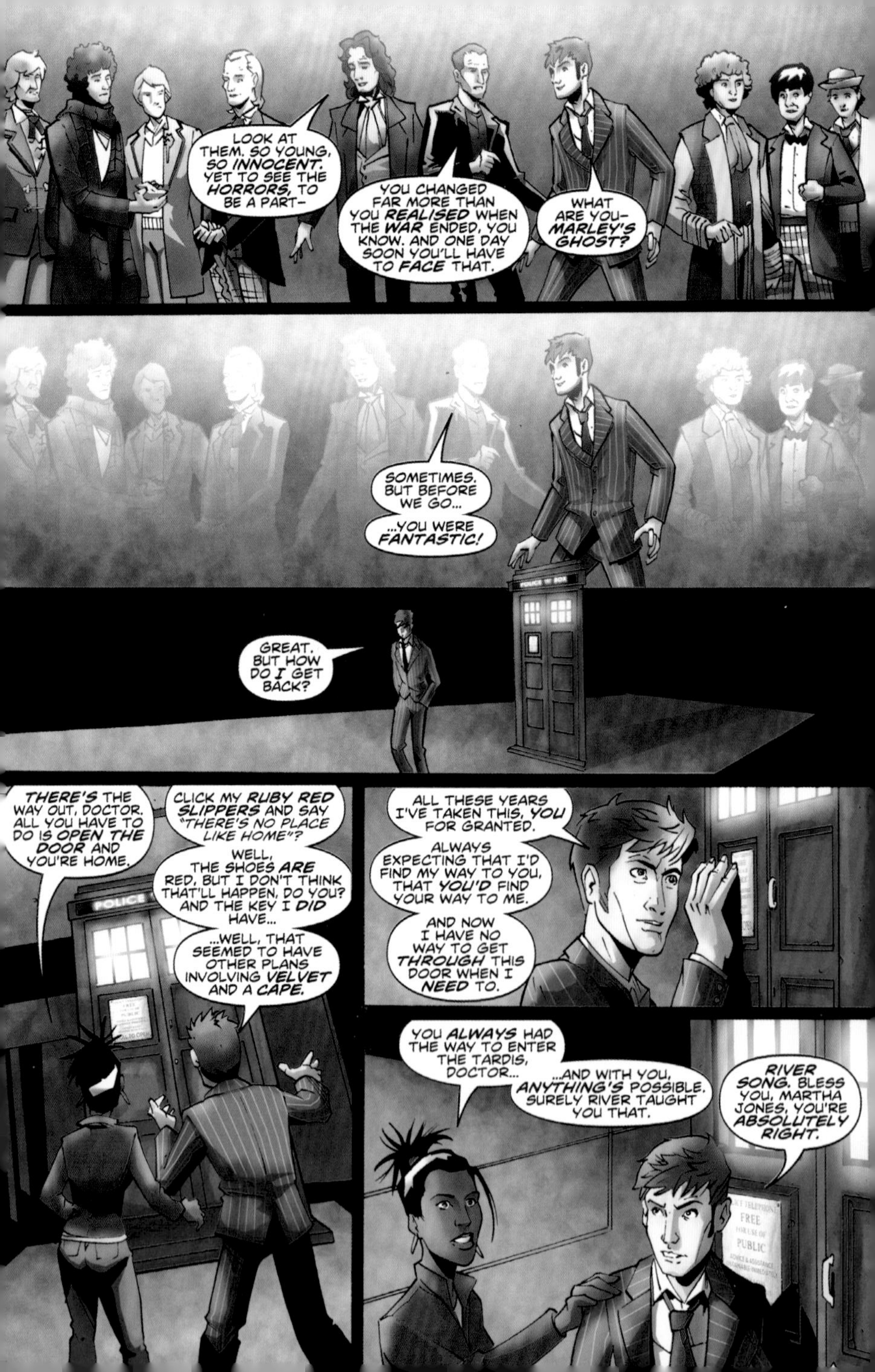
LOOK AT THEM. SO YOUNG, SO INNOCENT. YET TO SEE THE HORRORS, TO BE A PART–
YOU CHANGED FAR MORE THAN YOU REALISED WHEN THE WAR ENDED, YOU KNOW. AND ONE DAY SOON YOU'LL HAVE TO FACE THAT.
WHAT ARE YOU– MARLEY'S GHOST?
SOMETIMES. BUT BEFORE WE GO...
...YOU WERE FANTASTIC!
GREAT. BUT HOW DO I GET BACK?
THERE'S THE WAY OUT, DOCTOR. ALL YOU HAVE TO DO IS OPEN THE DOOR AND YOU'RE HOME.
CLICK MY RUBY RED SLIPPERS AND SAY "THERE'S NO PLACE LIKE HOME"?
WELL, THE SHOES ARE RED, BUT I DON'T THINK THAT'LL HAPPEN, DO YOU? AND THE KEY I DID HAVE...
...WELL, THAT SEEMED TO HAVE OTHER PLANS INVOLVING VELVET AND A CAPE.
ALL THESE YEARS I'VE TAKEN THIS, YOU FOR GRANTED.
ALWAYS EXPECTING THAT I'D FIND MY WAY TO YOU, THAT YOU'D FIND YOUR WAY TO ME.
AND NOW I HAVE NO WAY TO GET THROUGH THIS DOOR WHEN I NEED TO.
YOU ALWAYS HAD THE WAY TO ENTER THE TARDIS, DOCTOR...
...AND WITH YOU, ANYTHING'S POSSIBLE. SURELY RIVER TAUGHT YOU THAT.
RIVER SONG. BLESS YOU, MARTHA JONES, YOU'RE ABSOLUTELY RIGHT.

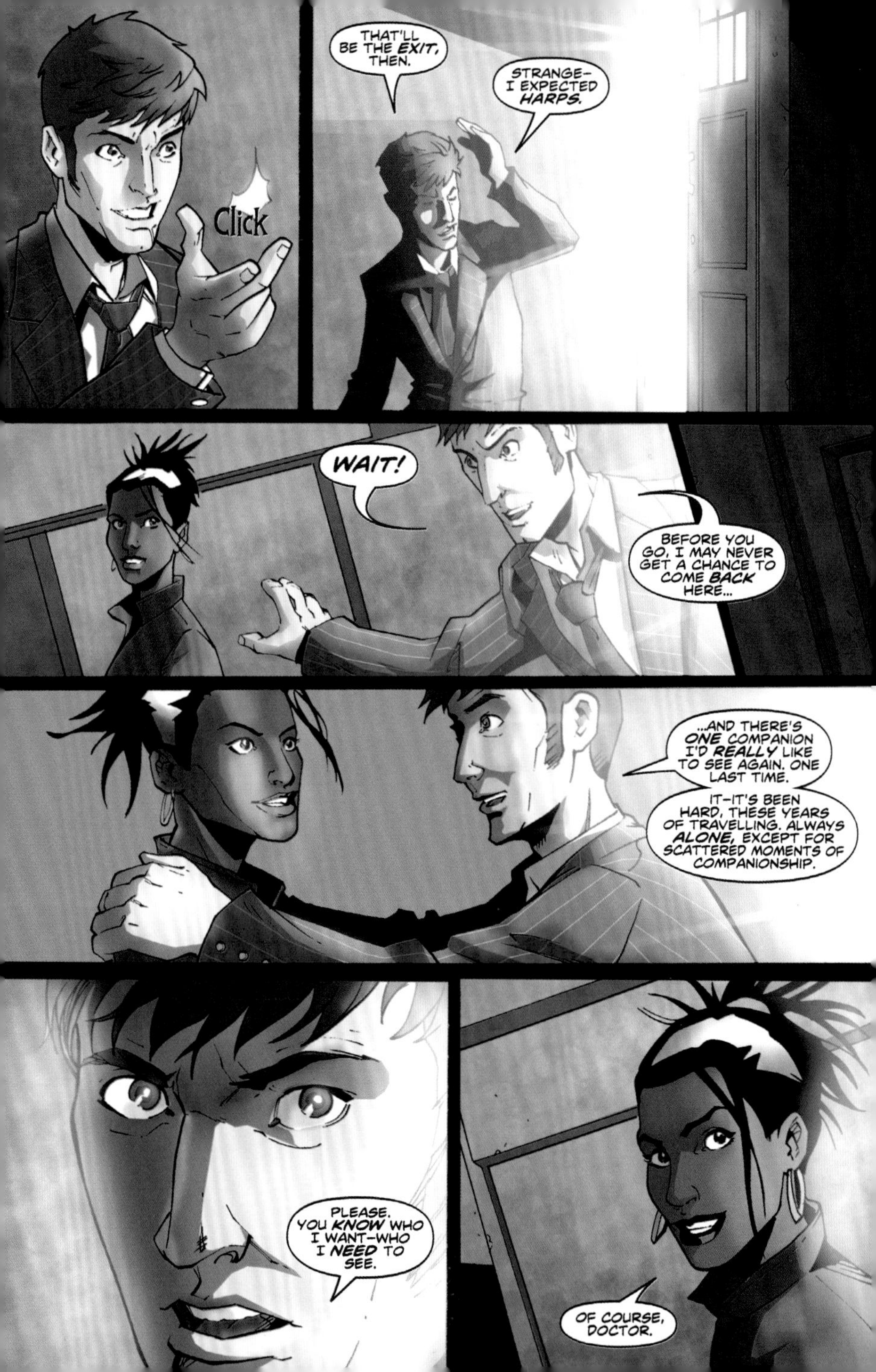
Click
THAT'LL BE THE EXIT, THEN.
STRANGE– I EXPECTED HARPS.
WAIT!
BEFORE YOU GO, I MAY NEVER GET A CHANCE TO COME BACK HERE...
...AND THERE'S ONE COMPANION I'D REALLY LIKE TO SEE AGAIN. ONE LAST TIME.
IT–IT'S BEEN HARD, THESE YEARS OF TRAVELLING. ALWAYS ALONE, EXCEPT FOR SCATTERED MOMENTS OF COMPANIONSHIP.
PLEASE. YOU KNOW WHO I WANT–WHO I NEED TO SEE.
OF COURSE, DOCTOR.

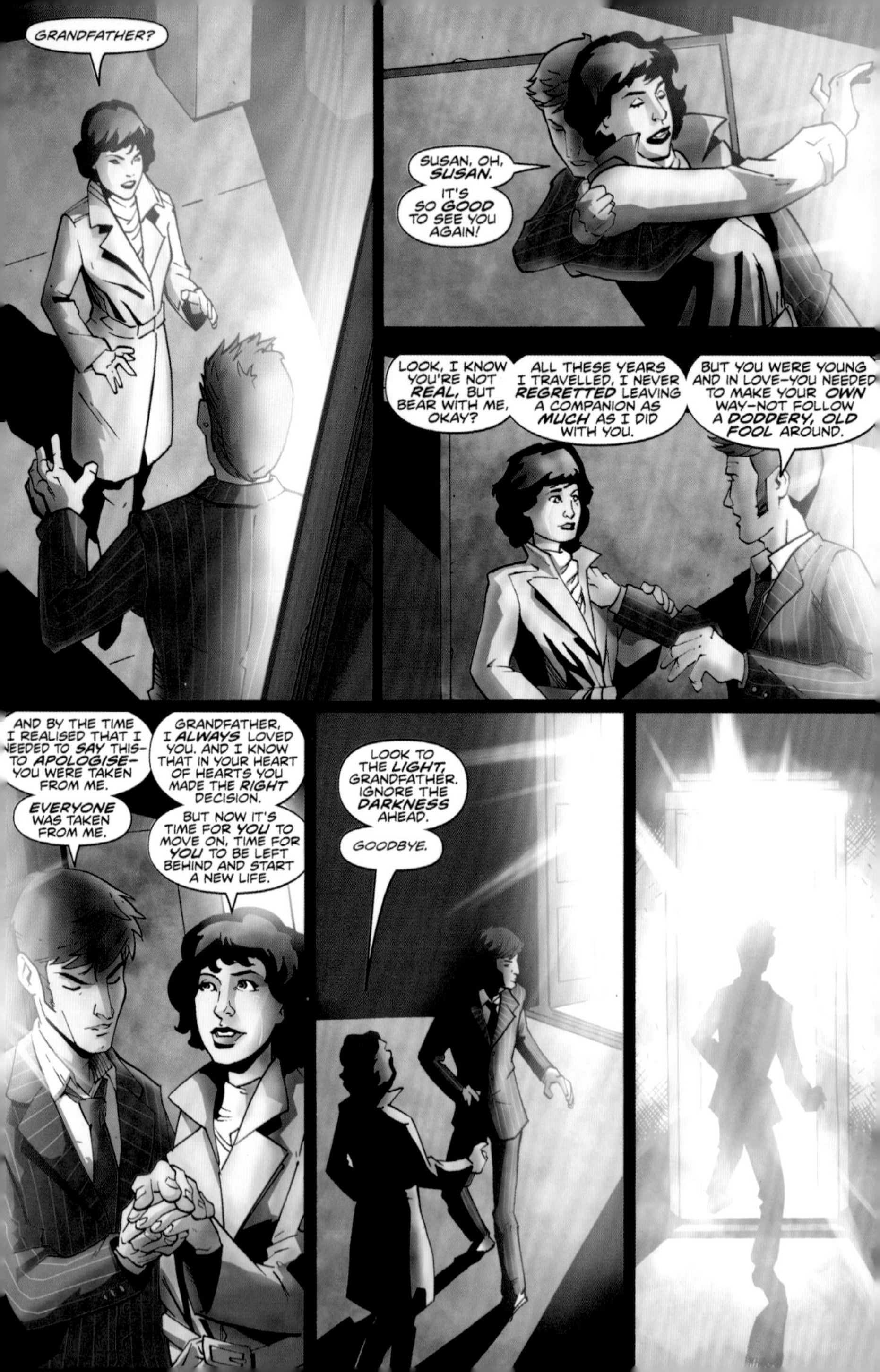
GRANDFATHER?
SUSAN, OH, SUSAN.
IT'S SO GOOD TO SEE YOU AGAIN!
LOOK, I KNOW YOU'RE NOT REAL, BUT BEAR WITH ME, OKAY?
ALL THESE YEARS I TRAVELLED, I NEVER REGRETTED LEAVING A COMPANION AS MUCH AS I DID WITH YOU.
BUT YOU WERE YOUNG AND IN LOVE–YOU NEEDED TO MAKE YOUR OWN WAY–NOT FOLLOW A DODDERY, OLD FOOL AROUND.
AND BY THE TIME I REALISED THAT I NEEDED TO SAY THIS–TO APOLOGISE–YOU WERE TAKEN FROM ME.
EVERYONE WAS TAKEN FROM ME.
GRANDFATHER, I ALWAYS LOVED YOU. AND I KNOW THAT IN YOUR HEART OF HEARTS YOU MADE THE RIGHT DECISION.
BUT NOW IT'S TIME FOR YOU TO MOVE ON, TIME FOR YOU TO BE LEFT BEHIND AND START A NEW LIFE.
LOOK TO THE LIGHT, GRANDFATHER. IGNORE THE DARKNESS AHEAD.
GOODBYE.

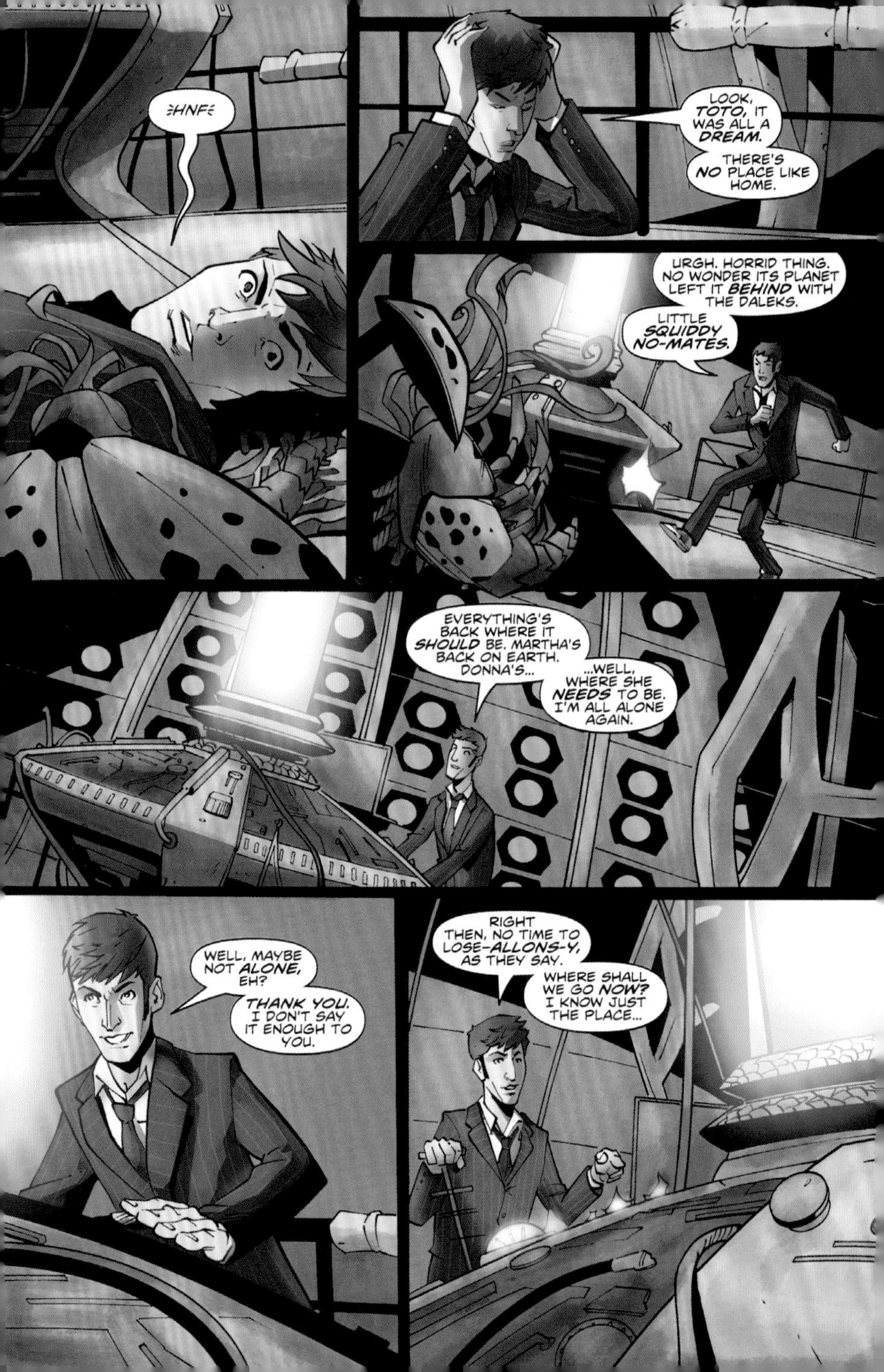
HNF
LOOK, TOTO, IT WAS ALL A DREAM.
THERE'S NO PLACE LIKE HOME.
URGH. HORRID THING. NO WONDER ITS PLANET LEFT IT BEHIND WITH THE DALEKS.
LITTLE SQUIDDY NO-MATES.
EVERYTHING'S BACK WHERE IT SHOULD BE. MARTHA'S BACK ON EARTH. DONNA'S...
...WELL, WHERE SHE NEEDS TO BE. I'M ALL ALONE AGAIN.
WELL, MAYBE NOT ALONE, EH?
THANK YOU. I DON'T SAY IT ENOUGH TO YOU.
RIGHT THEN, NO TIME TO LOSE–ALLONS-Y, AS THEY SAY.
WHERE SHALL WE GO NOW? I KNOW JUST THE PLACE...

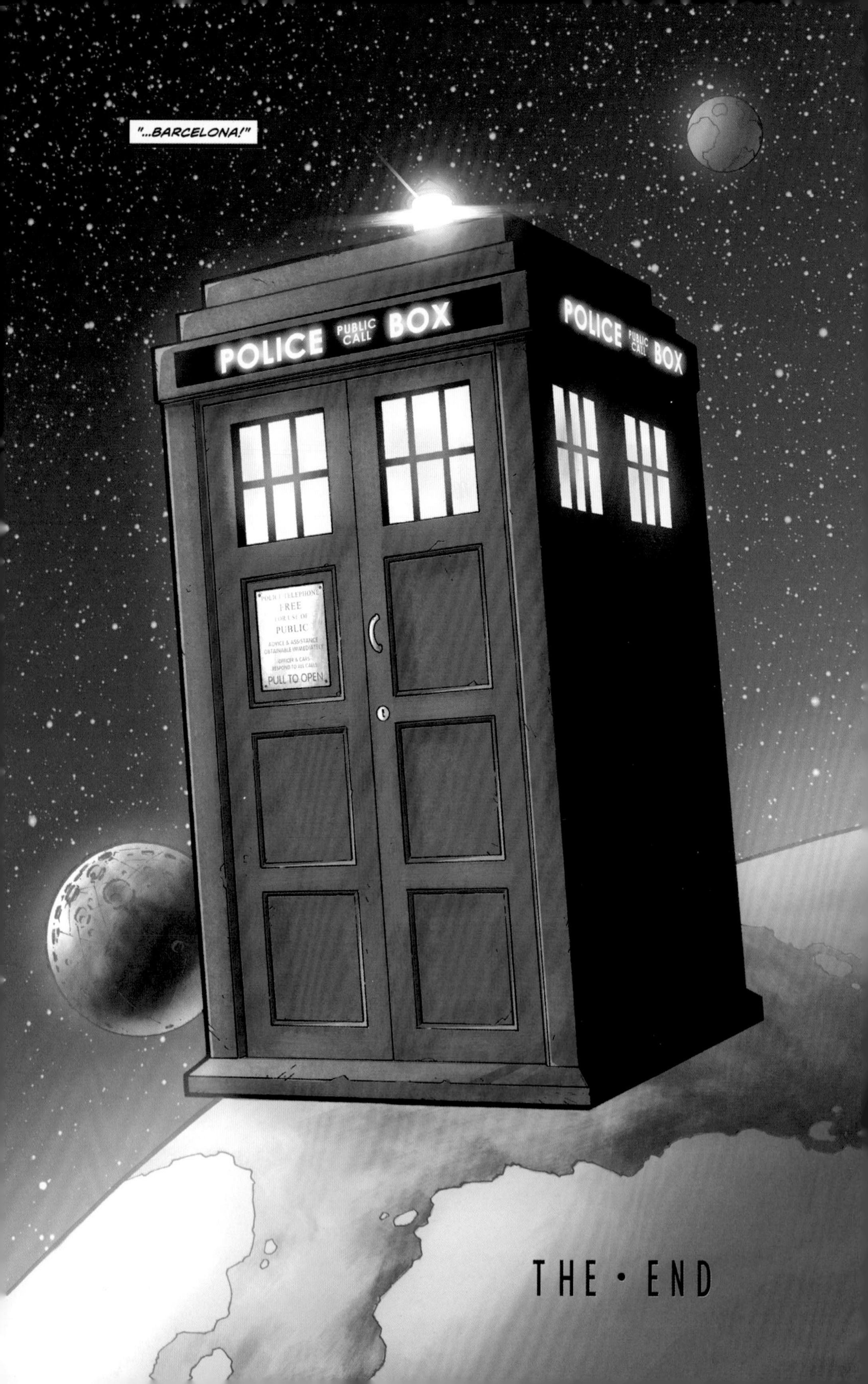
"...BARCELONA!"
POLICE PUBLIC CALL BOX
POLICE TELEPHONE
FREE
FOR USE OF
PUBLIC
PULL TO OPEN
THE • END

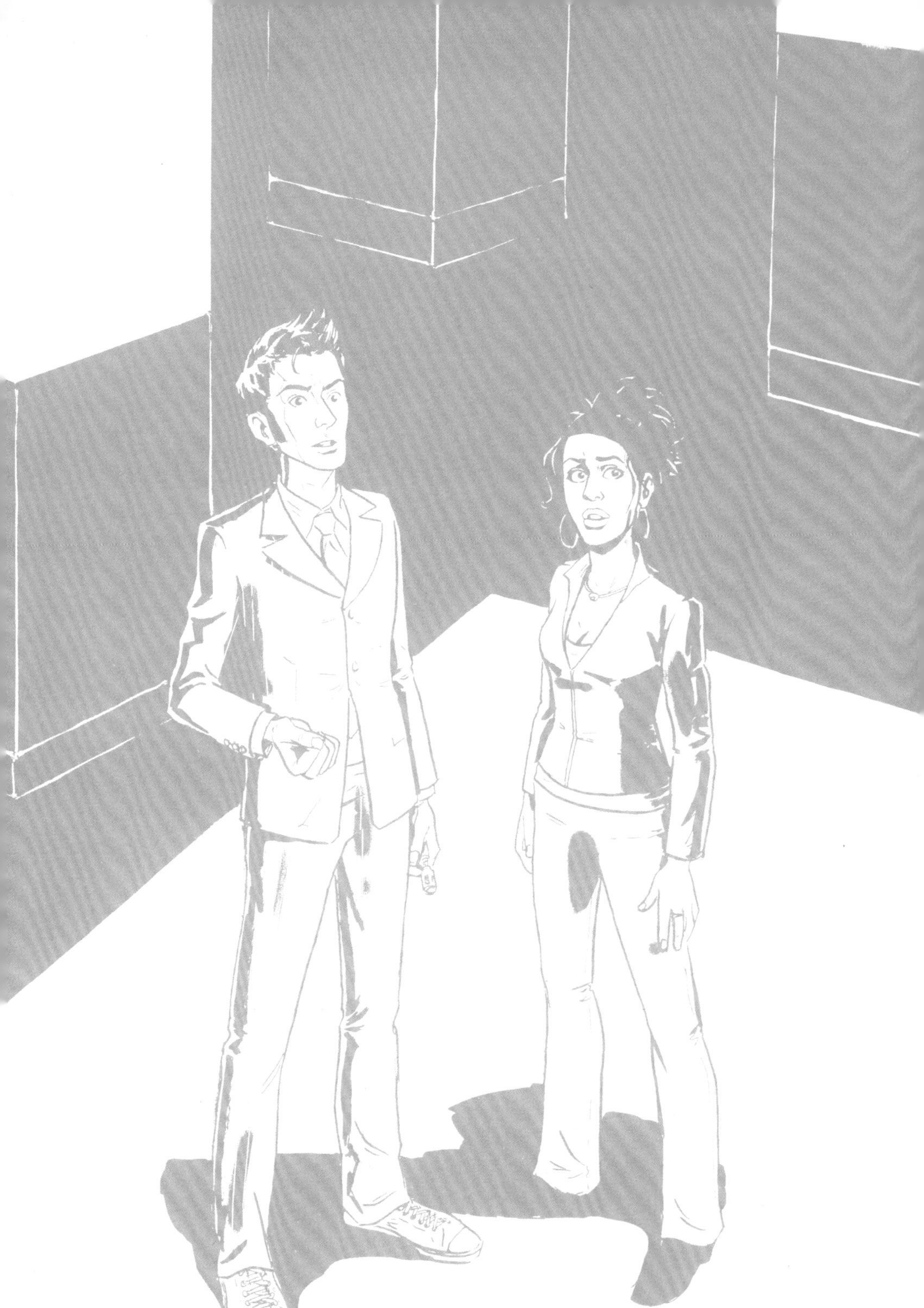

AGENT PROVOCATEUR

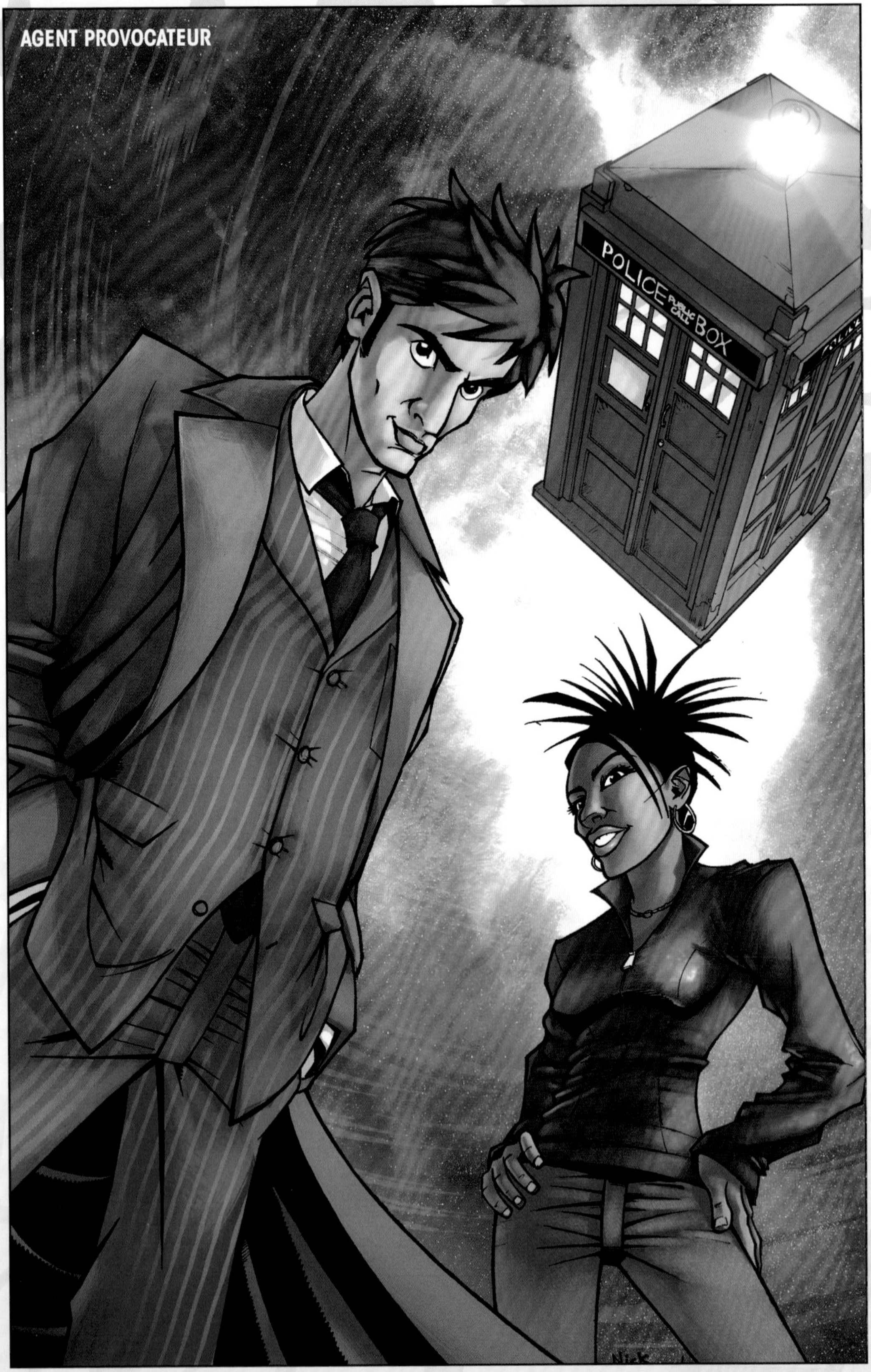
POLICE PUBLIC CALL BOX

AGENT PROVOCATEUR

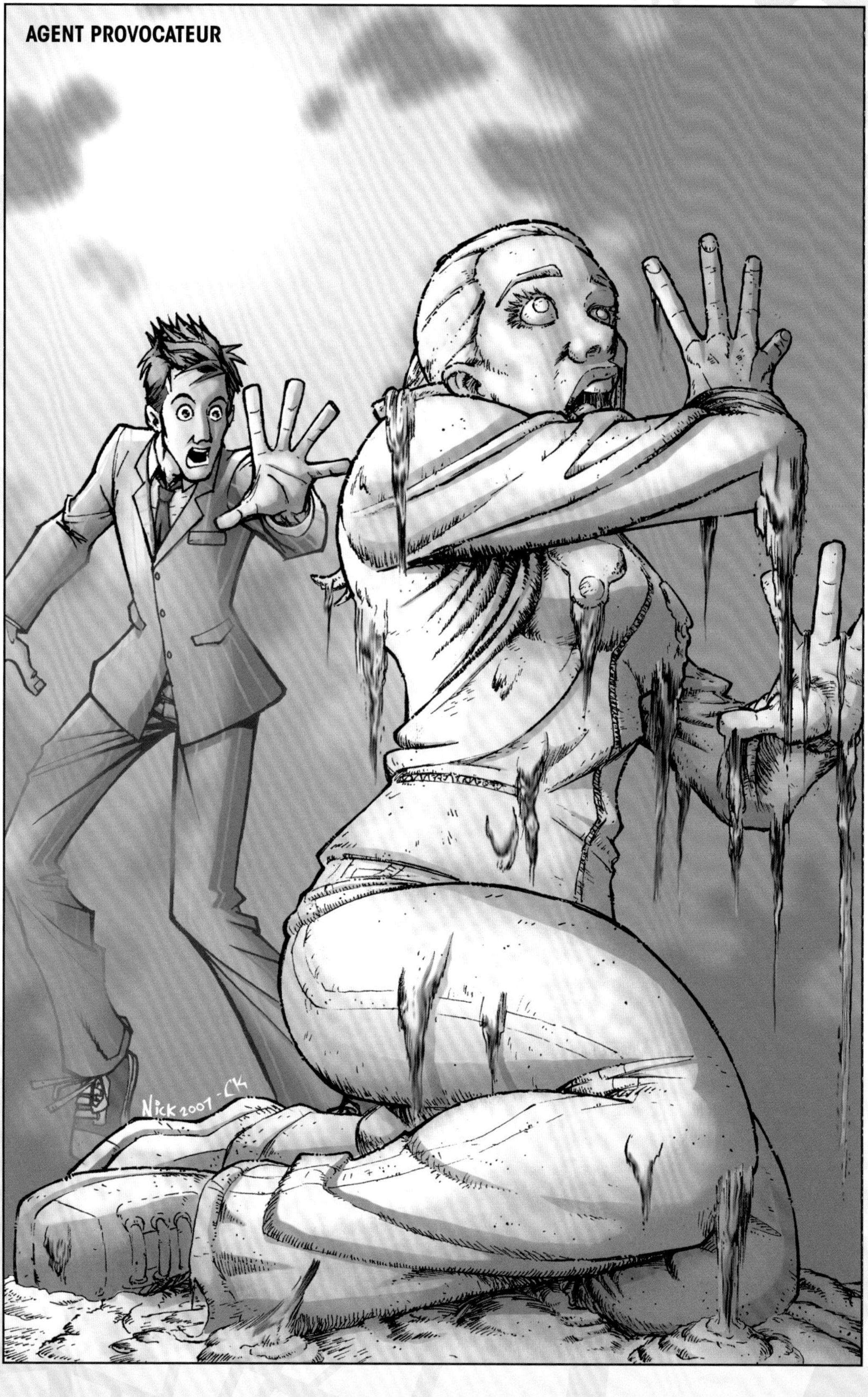
Nick 2007 - CK

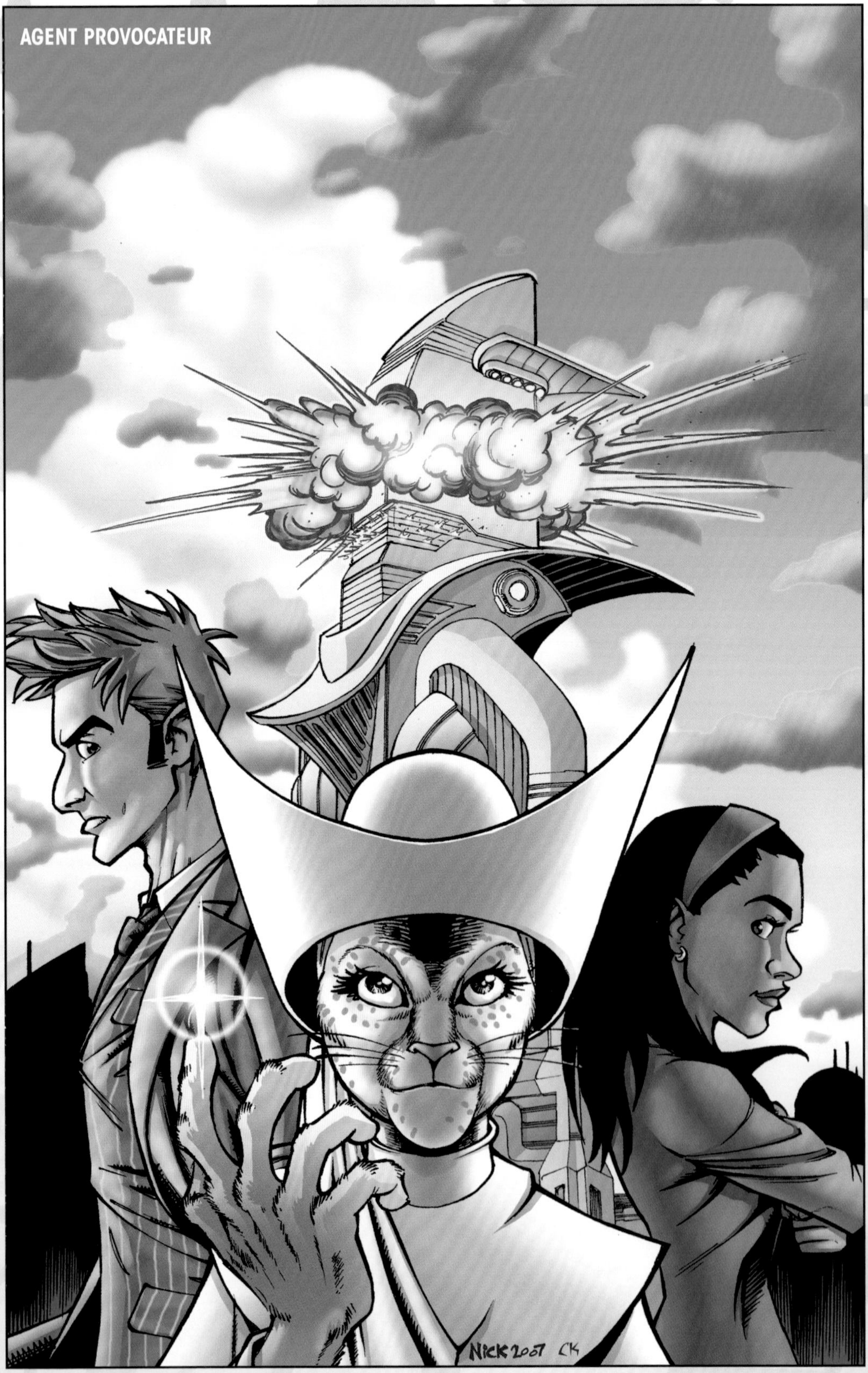
AGENT PROVOCATEUR
NICK 2007 CK

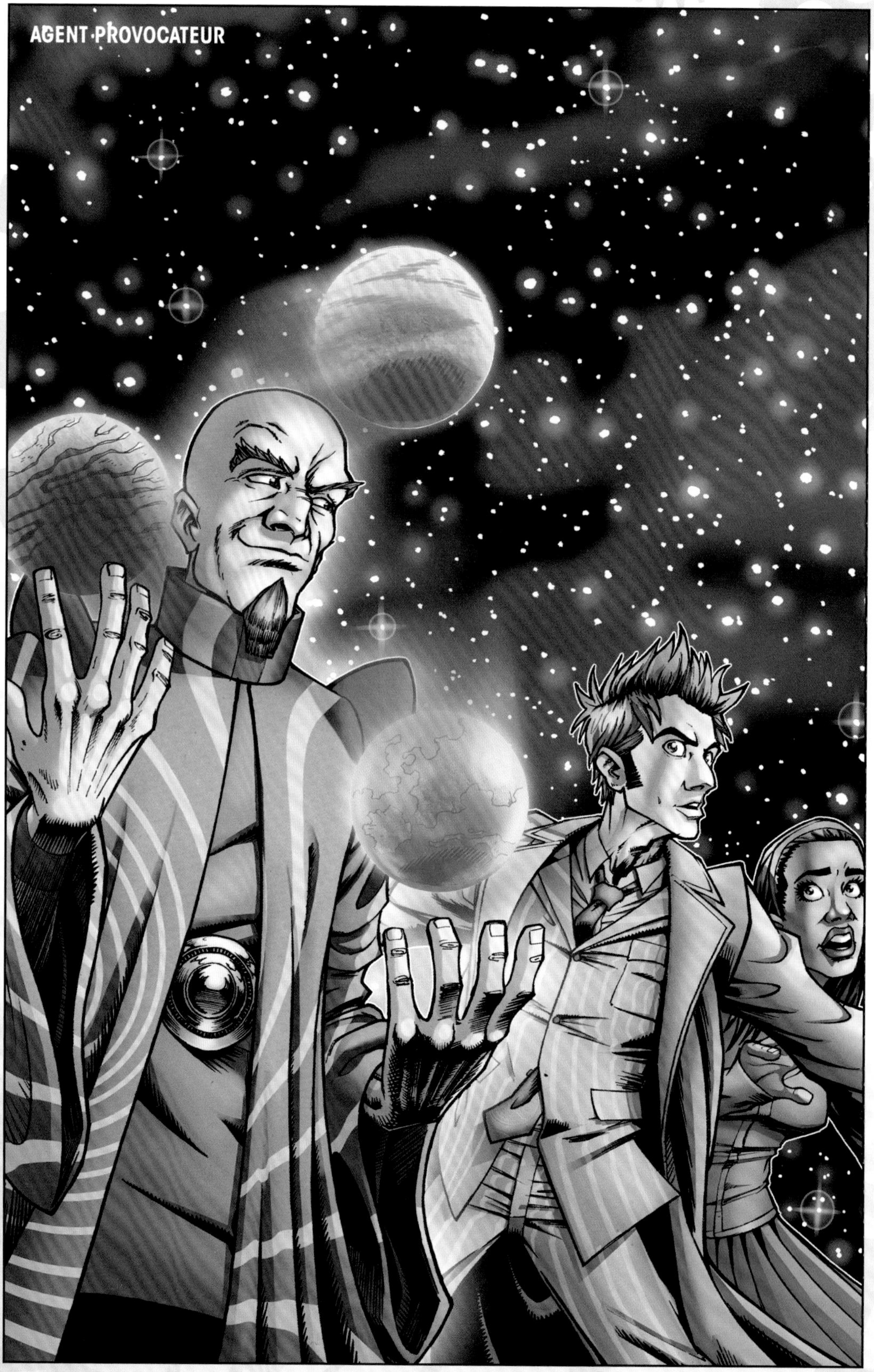
AGENT PROVOCATEUR

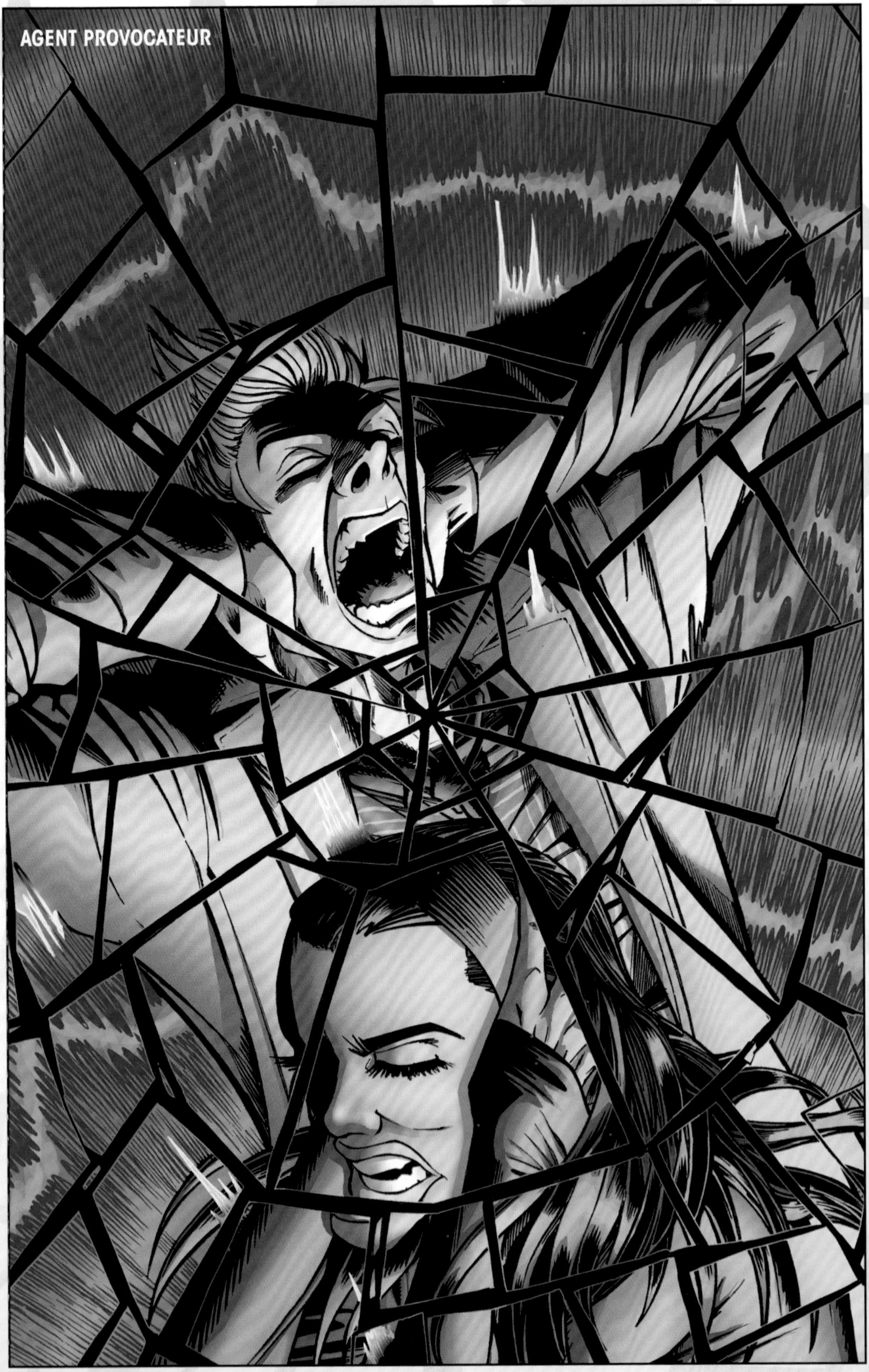

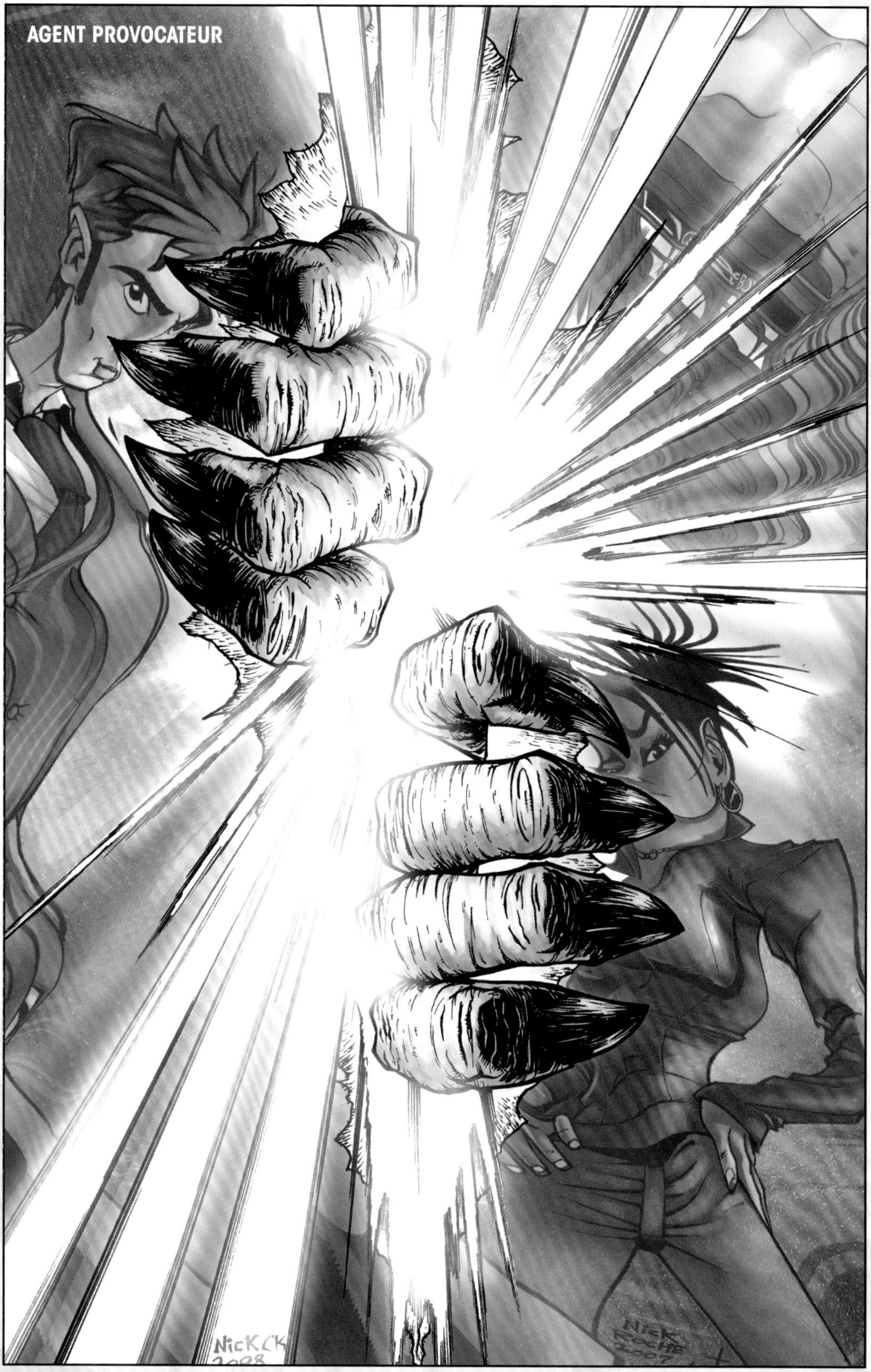
AGENT PROVOCATEUR
Nick Roche 2007

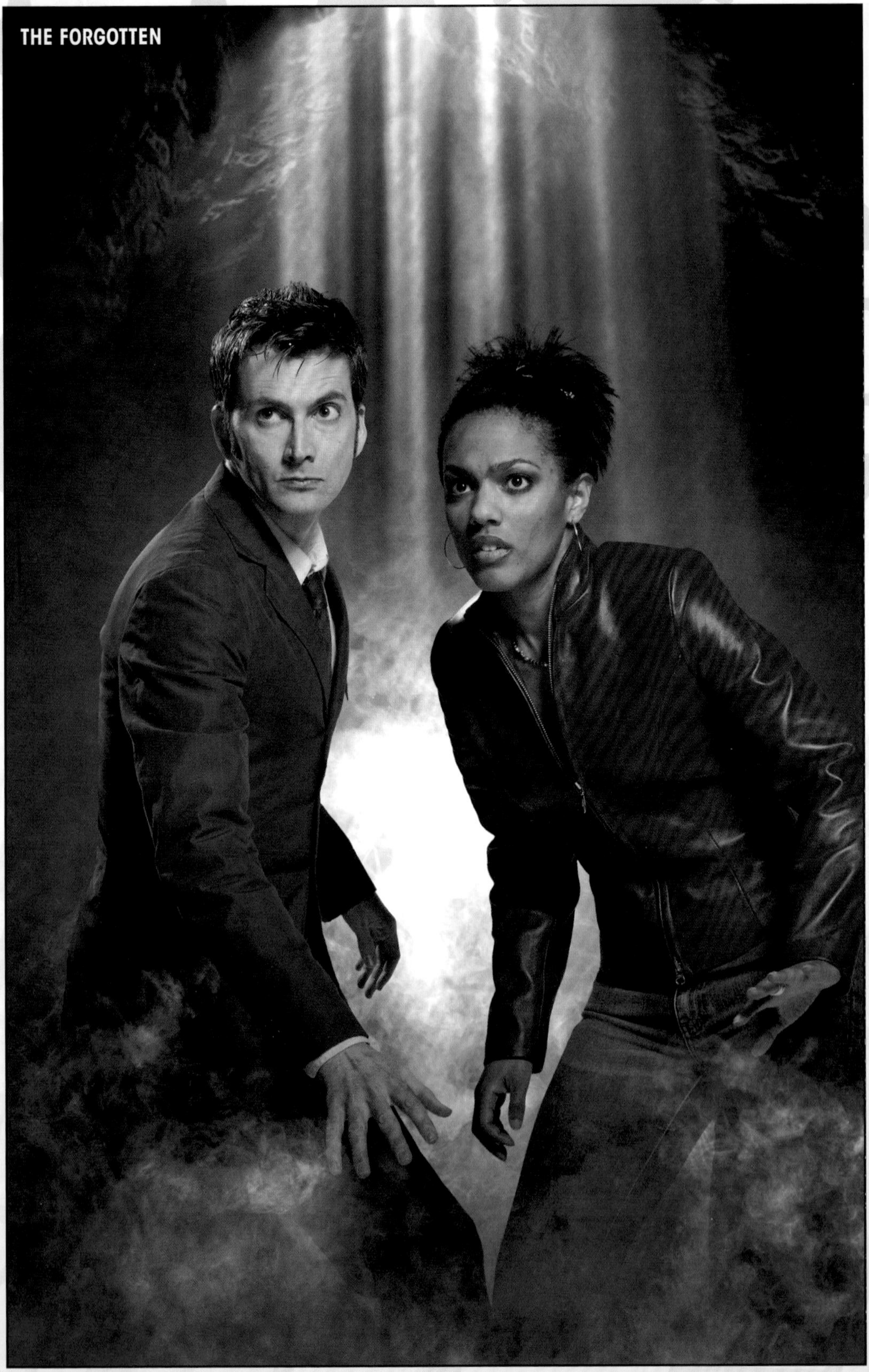
THE FORGOTTEN

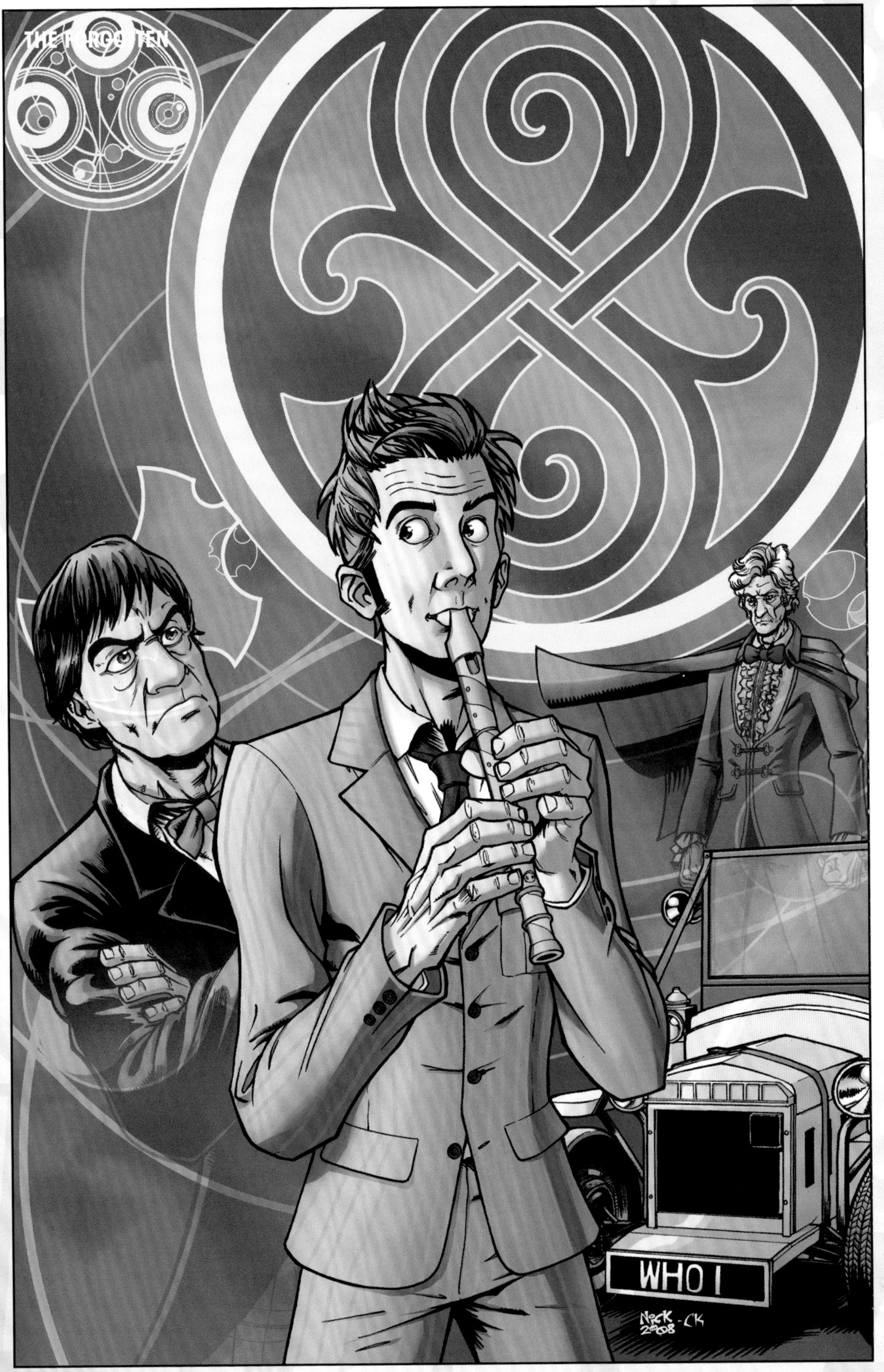
THE FORGOTTEN
WHO I
NICK 2008 - CK

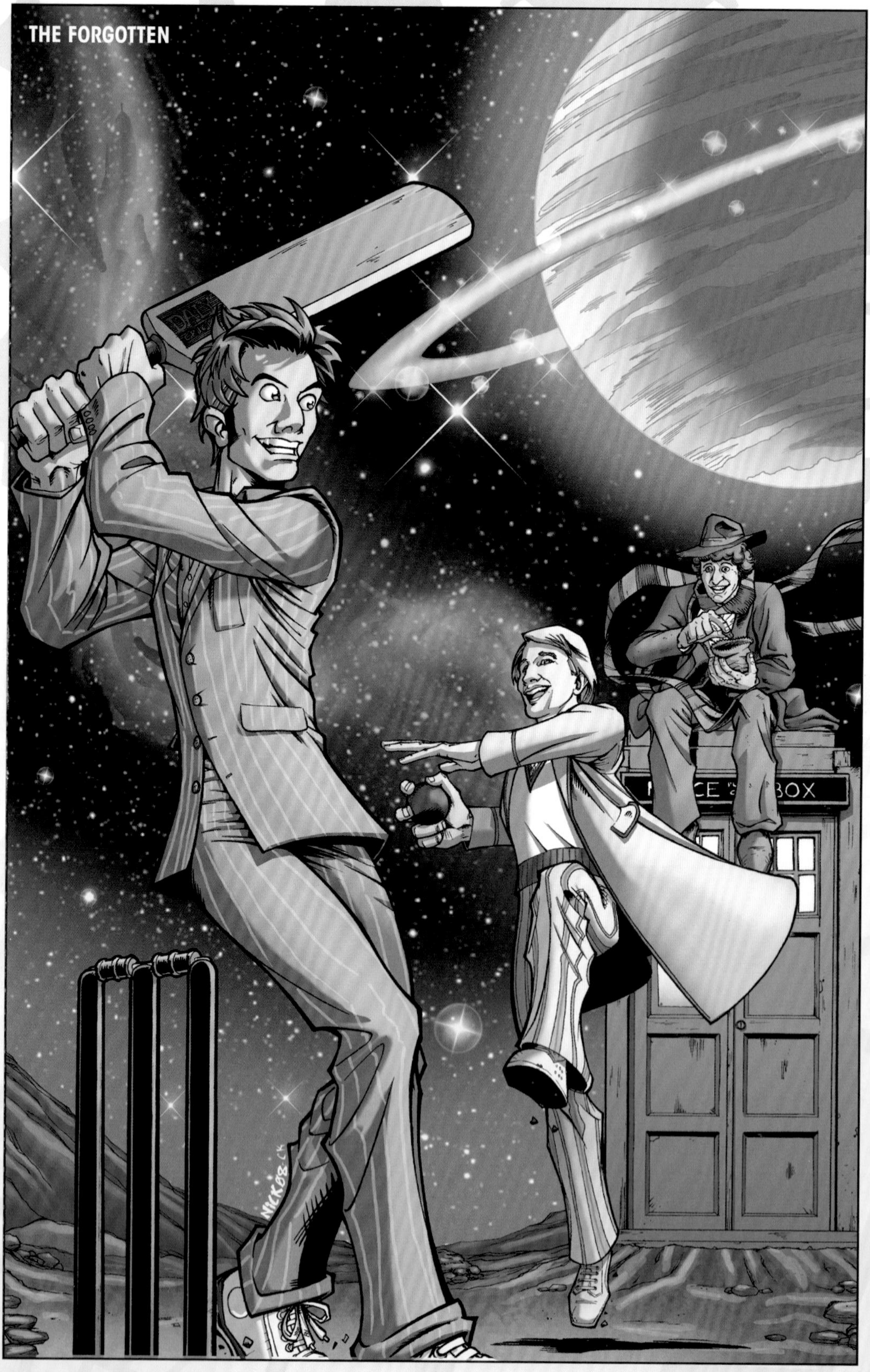
THE FORGOTTEN

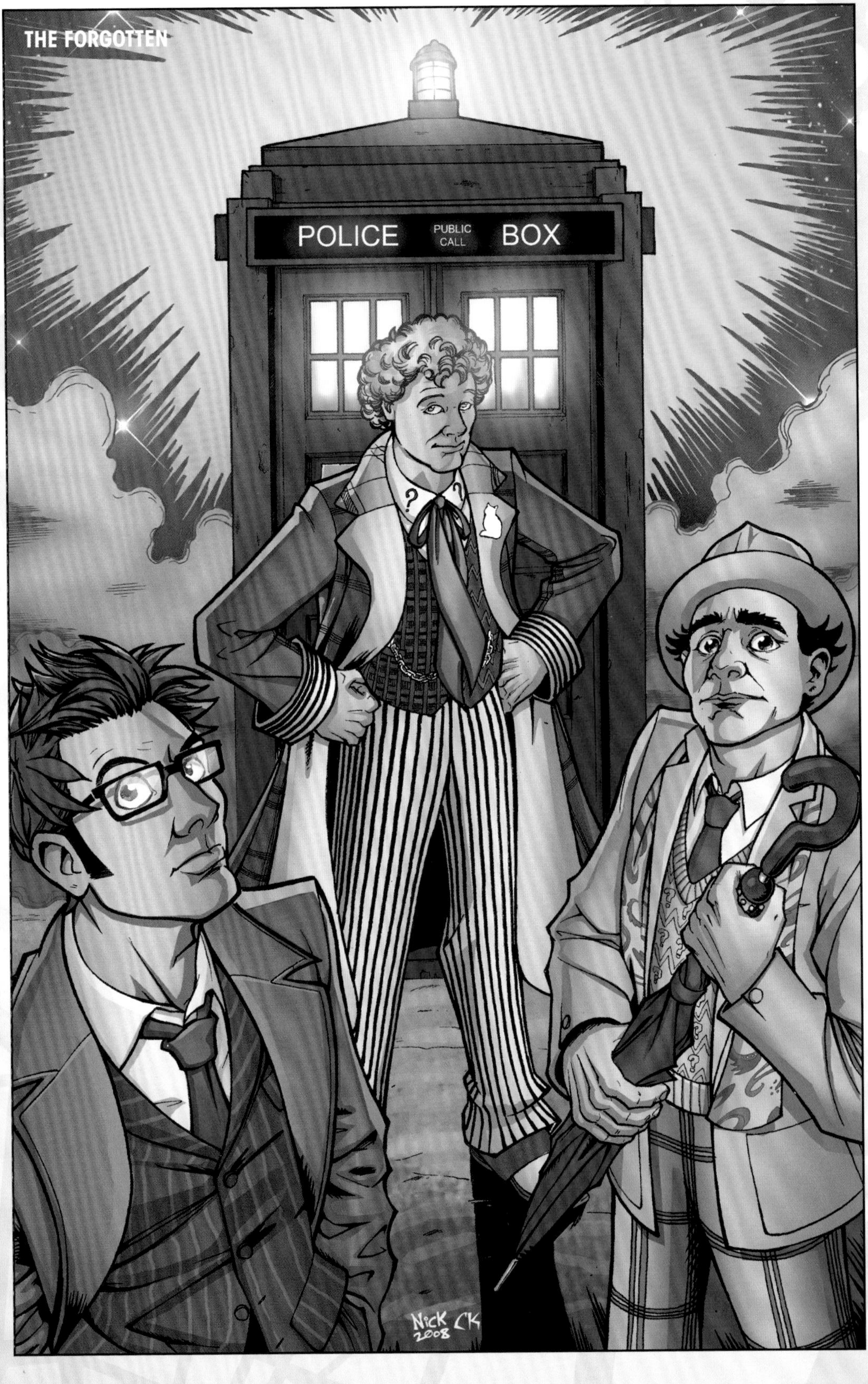
POLICE
PUBLIC CALL
BOX
Nick CK 2008

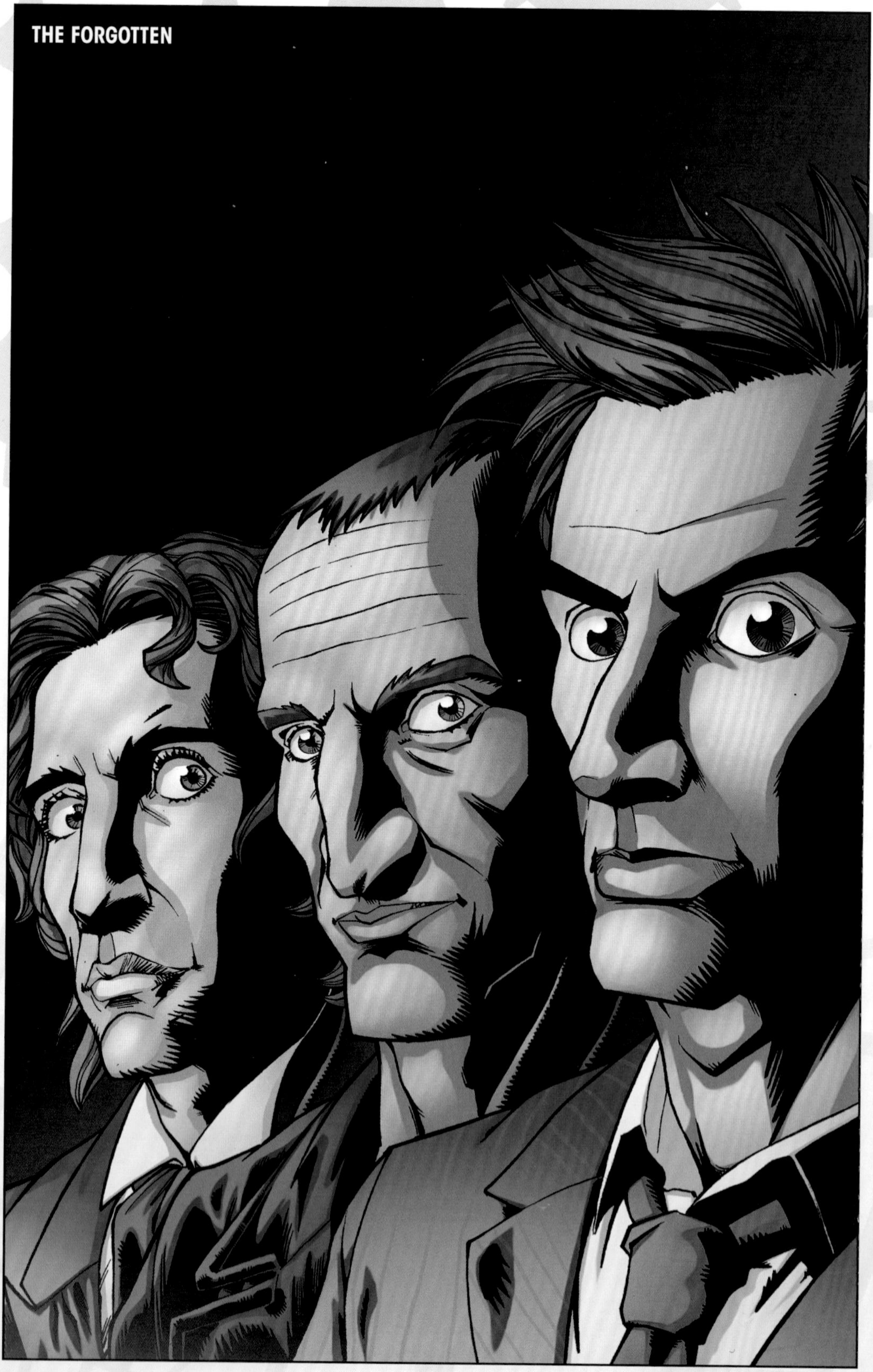
THE FORGOTTEN

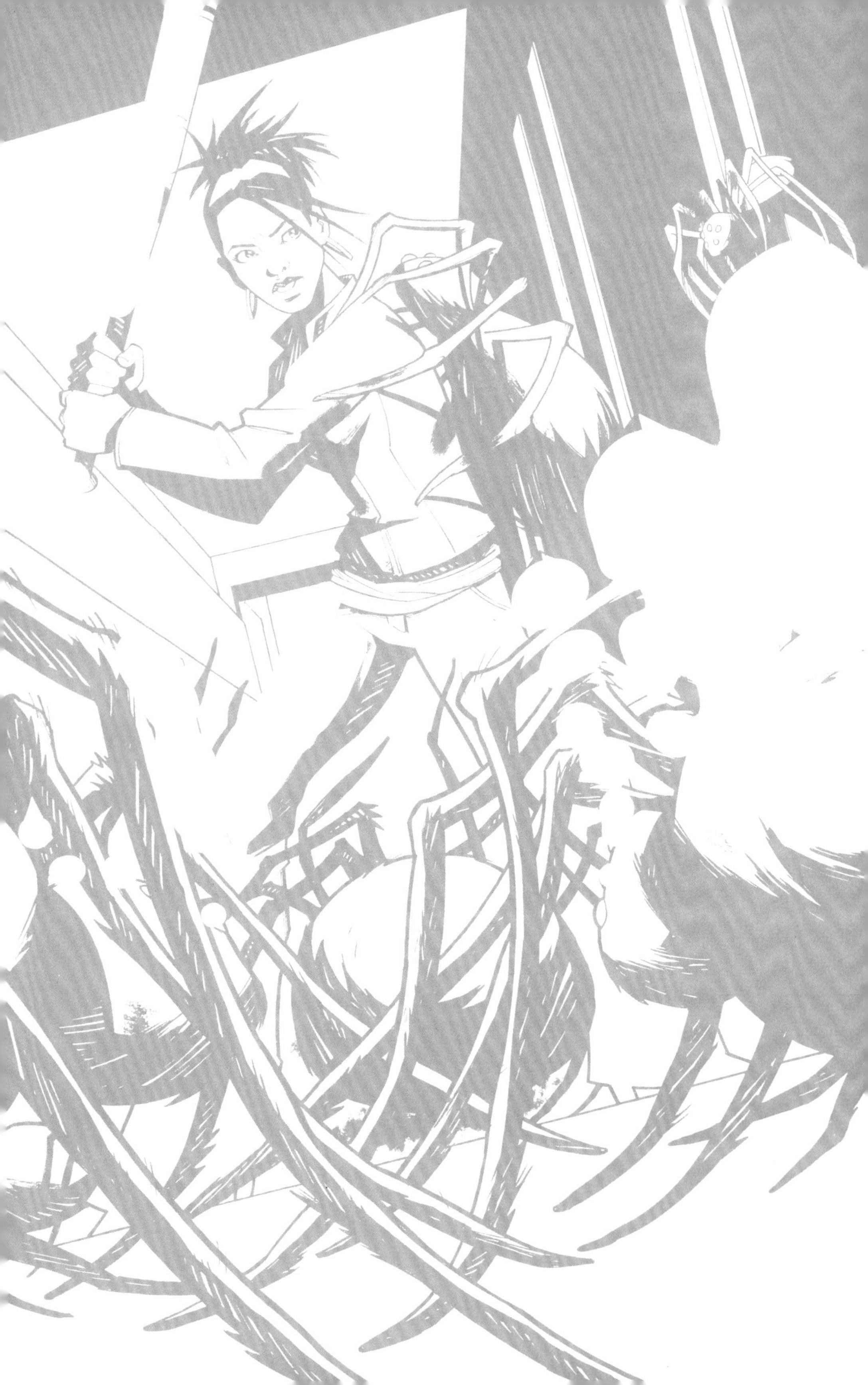

FOLLOW YOUR FAVORITE INCARNATIONS ACROSS THESE FANTASTIC COLLECTIONS!

DOCTOR WHO: THE TWELFTH DOCTOR VOL. 1: TERRORFORMER

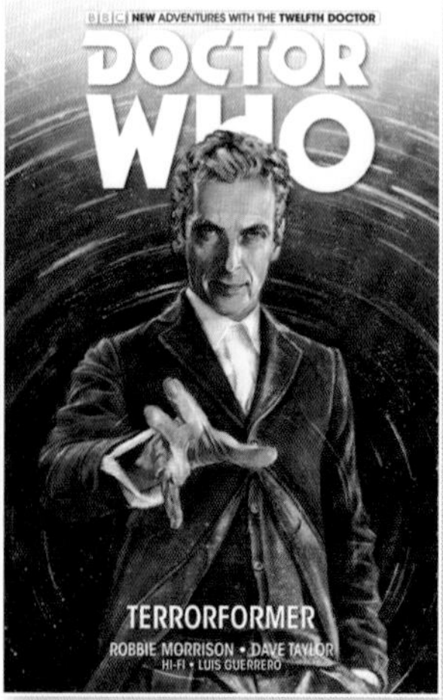
BBC NEW ADVENTURES WITH THE TWELFTH DOCTOR
DOCTOR WHO
TERRORFORMER
ROBBIE MORRISON • DAVE TAYLOR
HI-FI • LUIS GUERRERO

ON SALE NOW ISBN: 9781782761778
$19.99 / $22.95 CAN / £10.99
(UK EDITION ISBN: 9781782763864)

DOCTOR WHO: THE TWELFTH DOCTOR VOL. 2: FRACTURES

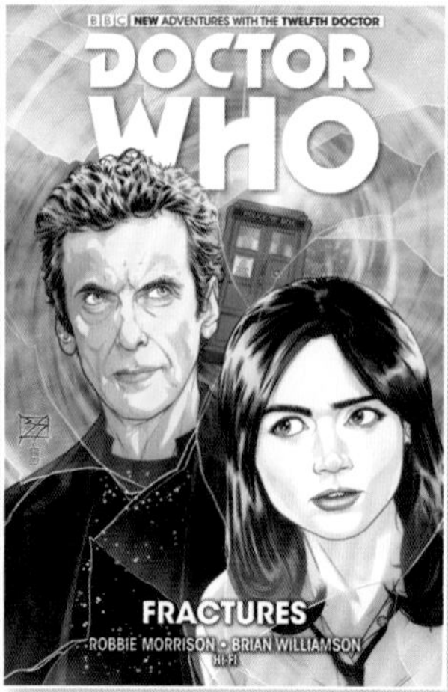
BBC NEW ADVENTURES WITH THE TWELFTH DOCTOR
DOCTOR WHO
FRACTURES
ROBBIE MORRISON • BRIAN WILLIAMSON
HI-FI

ON SALE NOW ISBN: 9781782763017
$19.99 / $25.99 CAN / £10.99
(UK EDITION ISBN: 9781782766599)

DOCTOR WHO: THE TWELFTH DOCTOR VOL. 3: HYPERION

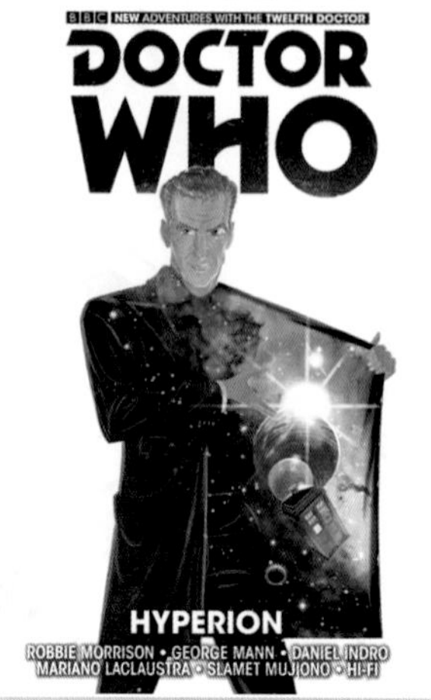
BBC NEW ADVENTURES WITH THE TWELFTH DOCTOR
DOCTOR WHO
HYPERION
ROBBIE MORRISON • GEORGE MANN • DANIEL INDRO
MARIANO LACLAUSTRA • SLAMET MUJIONO • HI-FI

COMING SOON ISBN: 9781782767473
$19.99 / $25.99 CAN / £10.99
(UK EDITION ISBN: 97817827674442)

DOCTOR WHO: THE TENTH DOCTOR VOL. 1: REVOLUTIONS OF TERROR

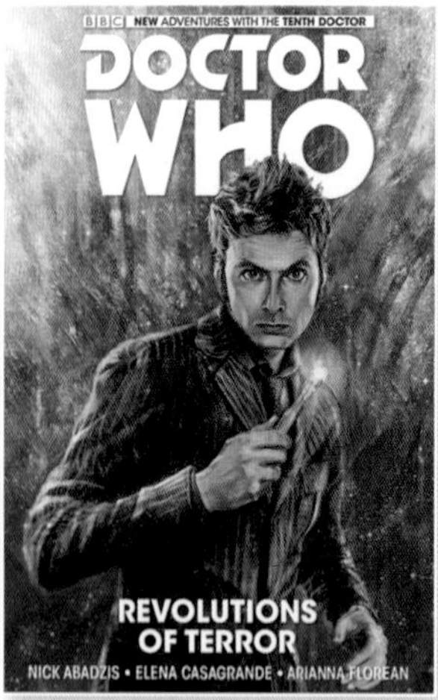
BBC NEW ADVENTURES WITH THE TENTH DOCTOR
DOCTOR WHO
REVOLUTIONS OF TERROR
NICK ABADZIS • ELENA CASAGRANDE • ARIANNA FLOREAN

ON SALE NOW ISBN: 9781782761730
$19.99 / $22.95 CAN / £10.99
(UK EDITION ISBN: 9781782763840)

DOCTOR WHO: THE TENTH DOCTOR VOL. 2: THE WEEPING ANGELS OF MONS

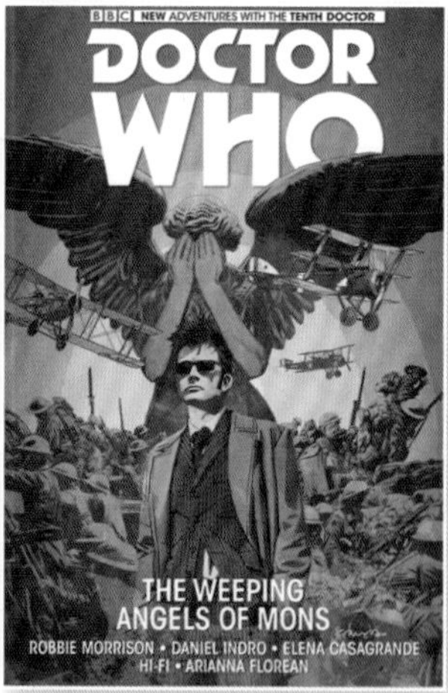
BBC NEW ADVENTURES WITH THE TENTH DOCTOR
DOCTOR WHO
THE WEEPING ANGELS OF MONS
ROBBIE MORRISON • DANIEL INDRO • ELENA CASAGRANDE
HI-FI • ARIANNA FLOREAN

ON SALE NOW ISBN: 9781782761754
$19.99 / $25.99 CAN / £10.99
(UK EDITION ISBN: 9781782766575)

DOCTOR WHO: THE TENTH DOCTOR VOL. 3: THE FOUNTAINS OF FOREVER

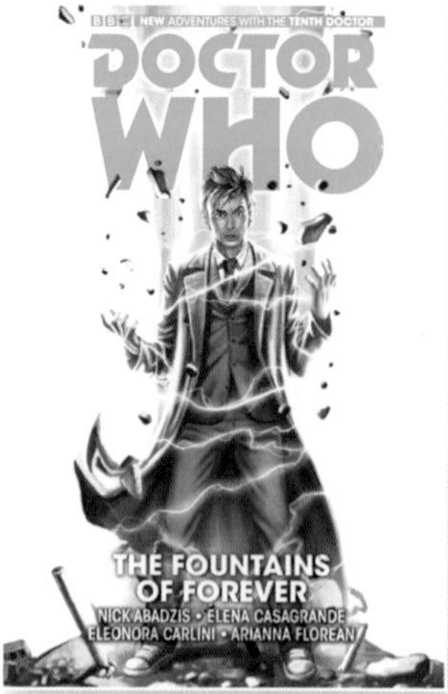
BBC NEW ADVENTURES WITH THE TENTH DOCTOR
DOCTOR WHO
THE FOUNTAINS OF FOREVER
NICK ABADZIS • ELENA CASAGRANDE
ELEONORA CARLINI • ARIANNA FLOREAN

ON SALE NOW ISBN: 9781782763024
$19.99 / $25.99 CAN/ £10.99
(UK EDITION ISBN: 9781782767404)

TITAN COMICS

For information on how to subscribe to our great Doctor Who titles, or to purchase them digitally for your favorite device, visit:

WWW.TITAN-COMICS.COM

JOIN THE ELEVENTH DOCTOR
FOR ALL-NEW ADVENTURES – AND
COMPLETE YOUR ARCHIVES!

DOCTOR WHO: THE ELEVENTH DOCTOR VOL. 1: AFTER LIFE

ON SALE NOW ISBN: 9781782761747
$19.99 / $22.95 CAN / £10.99
(UK EDITION ISBN: 9781782763857)

DOCTOR WHO: THE ELEVENTH DOCTOR VOL. 2: SERVE YOU

ON SALE NOW ISBN: 9781782761754
$19.99 / $25.99 CAN / £10.99
(UK EDITION ISBN: 9781782766582)

DOCTOR WHO: THE ELEVENTH DOCTOR VOL. 3: CONVERSION

ON SALE NOW ISBN: 9781782763024
$19.99 / $25.99 CAN / £10.99
(UK EDITION ISBN: 9781782767435)

DOCTOR WHO: THE ELEVENTH DOCTOR ARCHIVES VOL. 1

ON SALE NOW ISBN: 9781782767688
$24.99 / $32.99 CAN / £18.99

DOCTOR WHO: THE ELEVENTH DOCTOR ARCHIVES VOL. 2

ON SALE NOW ISBN: 9781782767695
$24.99 / $32.99 CAN / £18.99

DOCTOR WHO: PRISONERS OF TIME ARCHIVES

COMING SOON ISBN: 9781782767749
$24.99 / $32.99 CAN / £18.99

AVAILABLE IN ALL GOOD COMIC STORES,
BOOK STORES, AND DIGITAL PROVIDERS!

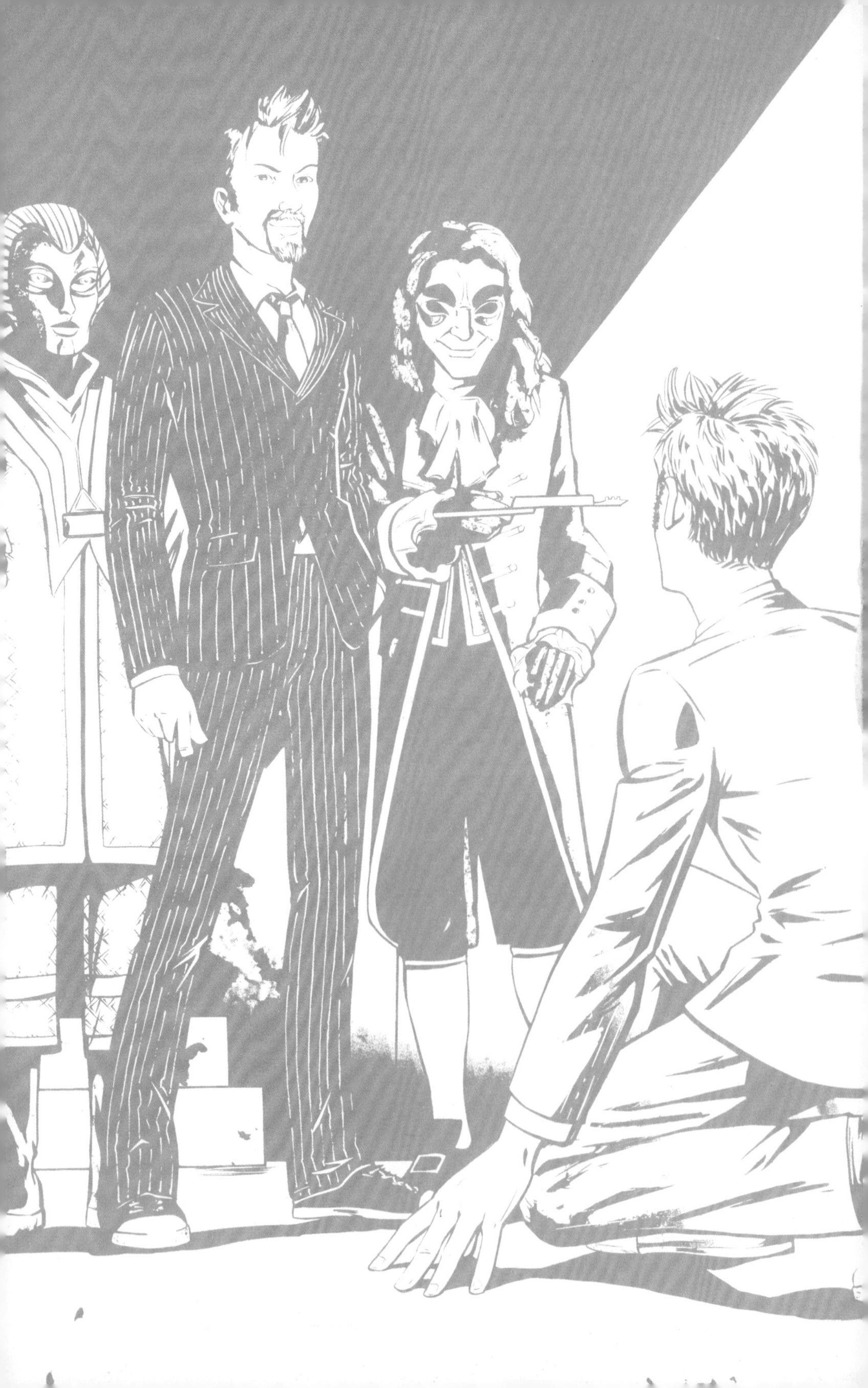